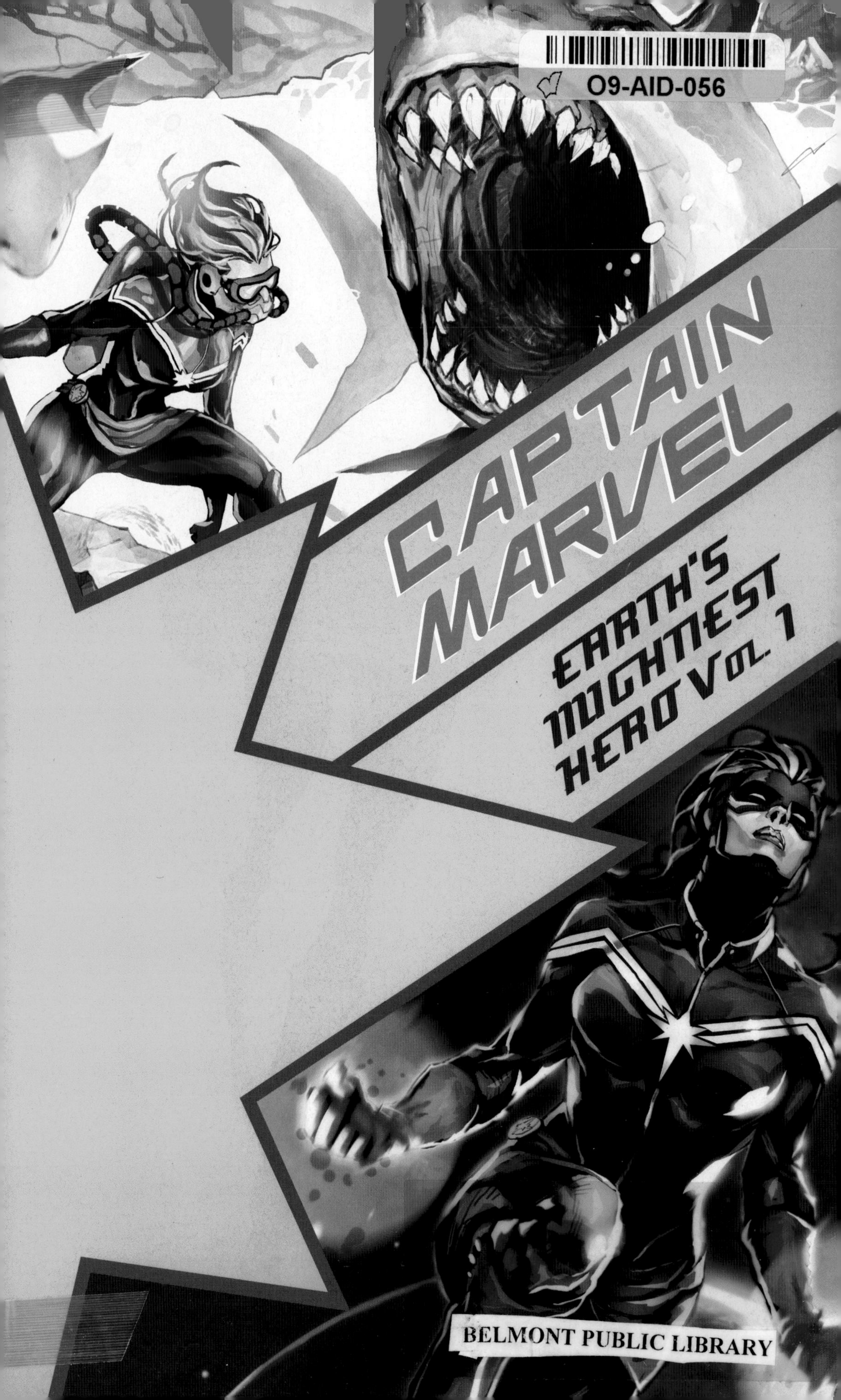
CAPTAIN MARVEL
EARTH'S MIGHTIEST HERO VOL. 1

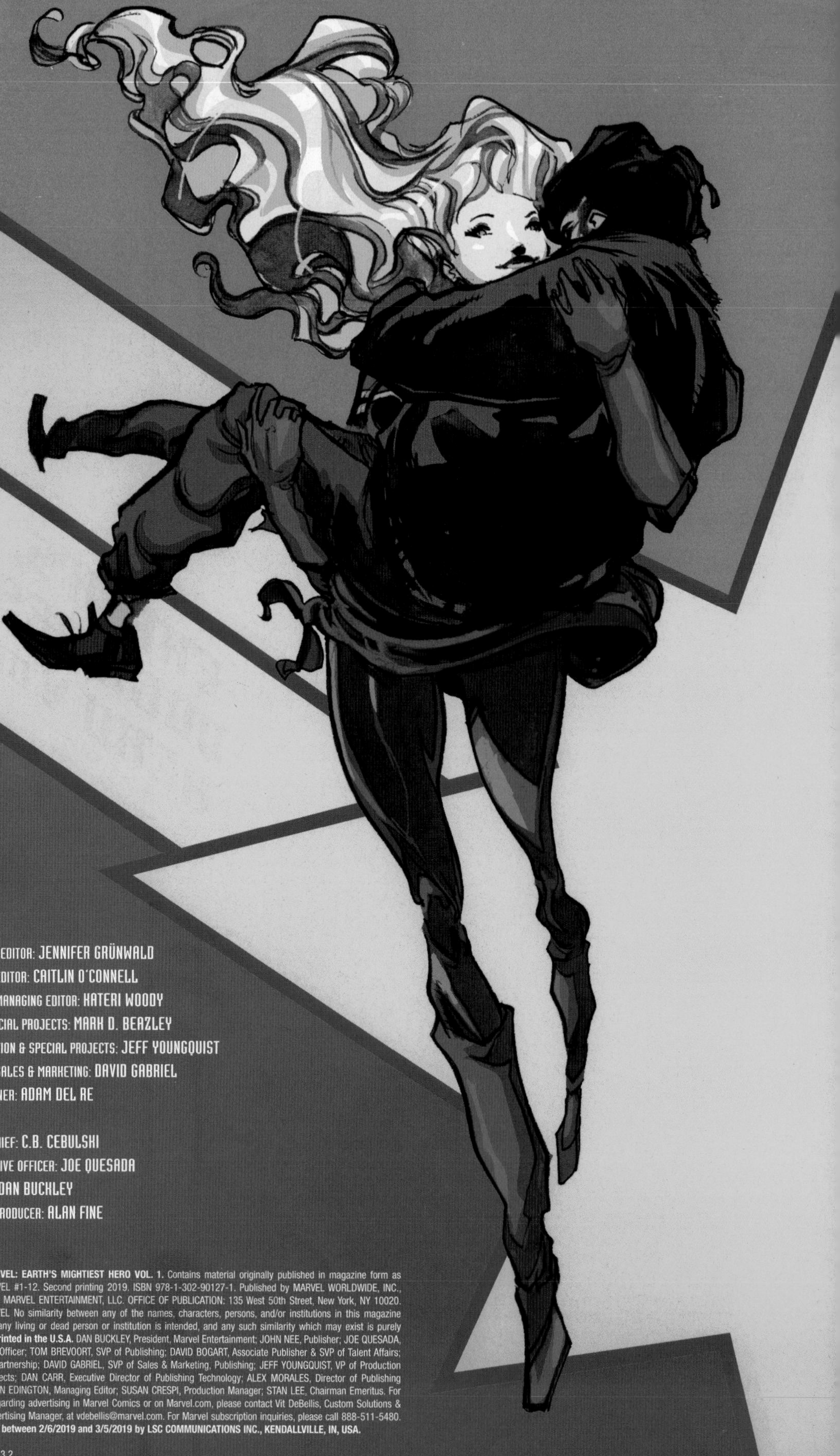

COLLECTION EDITOR: JENNIFER GRÜNWALD
ASSISTANT EDITOR: CAITLIN O'CONNELL
ASSOCIATE MANAGING EDITOR: KATERI WOODY
EDITOR, SPECIAL PROJECTS: MARK D. BEAZLEY
VP, PRODUCTION & SPECIAL PROJECTS: JEFF YOUNGQUIST
SVP PRINT, SALES & MARKETING: DAVID GABRIEL
BOOK DESIGNER: ADAM DEL RE

EDITOR IN CHIEF: C.B. CEBULSKI
CHIEF CREATIVE OFFICER: JOE QUESADA
PRESIDENT: DAN BUCKLEY
EXECUTIVE PRODUCER: ALAN FINE

CAPTAIN MARVEL: EARTH'S MIGHTIEST HERO VOL. 1. Contains material originally published in magazine form as CAPTAIN MARVEL #1-12. Second printing 2019. ISBN 978-1-302-90127-1. Published by MARVEL WORLDWIDE, INC., a subsidiary of MARVEL ENTERTAINMENT, LLC. OFFICE OF PUBLICATION: 135 West 50th Street, New York, NY 10020.

Printed in the U.S.A. DAN BUCKLEY, President, Marvel Entertainment; JOHN NEE, Publisher; JOE QUESADA, Chief Creative Officer; TOM BREVOORT, SVP of Publishing; DAVID BOGART, Associate Publisher & SVP of Talent Affairs; Publishing & Partnership; DAVID GABRIEL, SVP of Sales & Marketing, Publishing; JEFF YOUNGQUIST, VP of Production & Special Projects; DAN CARR, Executive Director of Publishing Technology; ALEX MORALES, Director of Publishing Operations; DAN EDINGTON, Managing Editor; SUSAN CRESPI, Production Manager; STAN LEE, Chairman Emeritus. For information regarding advertising in Marvel Comics or on Marvel.com, please contact Vit DeBellis, Custom Solutions & Integrated Advertising Manager, at vdebellis@marvel.com. For Marvel subscription inquiries, please call 888-511-5480. **Manufactured between 2/6/2019 and 3/5/2019 by LSC COMMUNICATIONS INC., KENDALLVILLE, IN, USA.**

10 9 8 7 6 5 4 3 2

WRITERS: **KELLY SUE DeCONNICH** WITH **CHRISTOPHER SEBELA** [#7-8 & #10-12]

ISSUES #1-4, #7
ARTISTS: **DEXTER SOY** WITH **RICHARD ELSON** & **WIL QUINTANA** [#3, PP. 17-18], **KARL KESEL** & **JAVIER RODRÍGUEZ** [#3, P. 19] AND
AL BARRIONUEVO & **WIL QUINTANA** [#4, PP. 16-20]
COVER ART: **ED McGUINNESS, DEXTER VINES** & **JAVIER RODRÍGUEZ** [#1-4] AND **JAMIE McELVIE** & **JORDIE BELLAIRE** [#7]

ISSUES #5-6
ARTISTS: **EMMA RÍOS** WITH **ÁLVARO LÓPEZ** [INKER, #6]
COLOR ARTIST: **JORDIE BELLAIRE**
COVER ART: **TERRY DODSON** & **RACHEL DODSON**

ISSUE #8
ARTIST: **DEXTER SOY**
COLOR ARTIST: **VERONICA GANDINI**
COVER ART: **DEXTER SOY**

ISSUES #9-12
ARTIST: **FILIPE ANDRADE**
COVER ART: **JAMIE McELVIE** & **JORDIE BELLAIRE** [#9] AND
JOE QUINONES [#10-12]

Y
GRAPHIC
CAP
v.1

CAPTAIN MARVEL

EARTH'S MIGHTIEST HERO Vol. 1

LETTERER: **VC's JOE CARAMAGNA**

ASSISTANT EDITOR: **ELLIE PYLE**
EDITOR: **SANA AMANAT**
SENIOR EDITOR: **STEPHEN WACKER**

CAPTAIN MARVEL COSTUME DESIGNED BY **JAMIE McELVIE**

SPECIAL THANKS TO **MAHI YAMANE** & **SIGRID ELLIS**

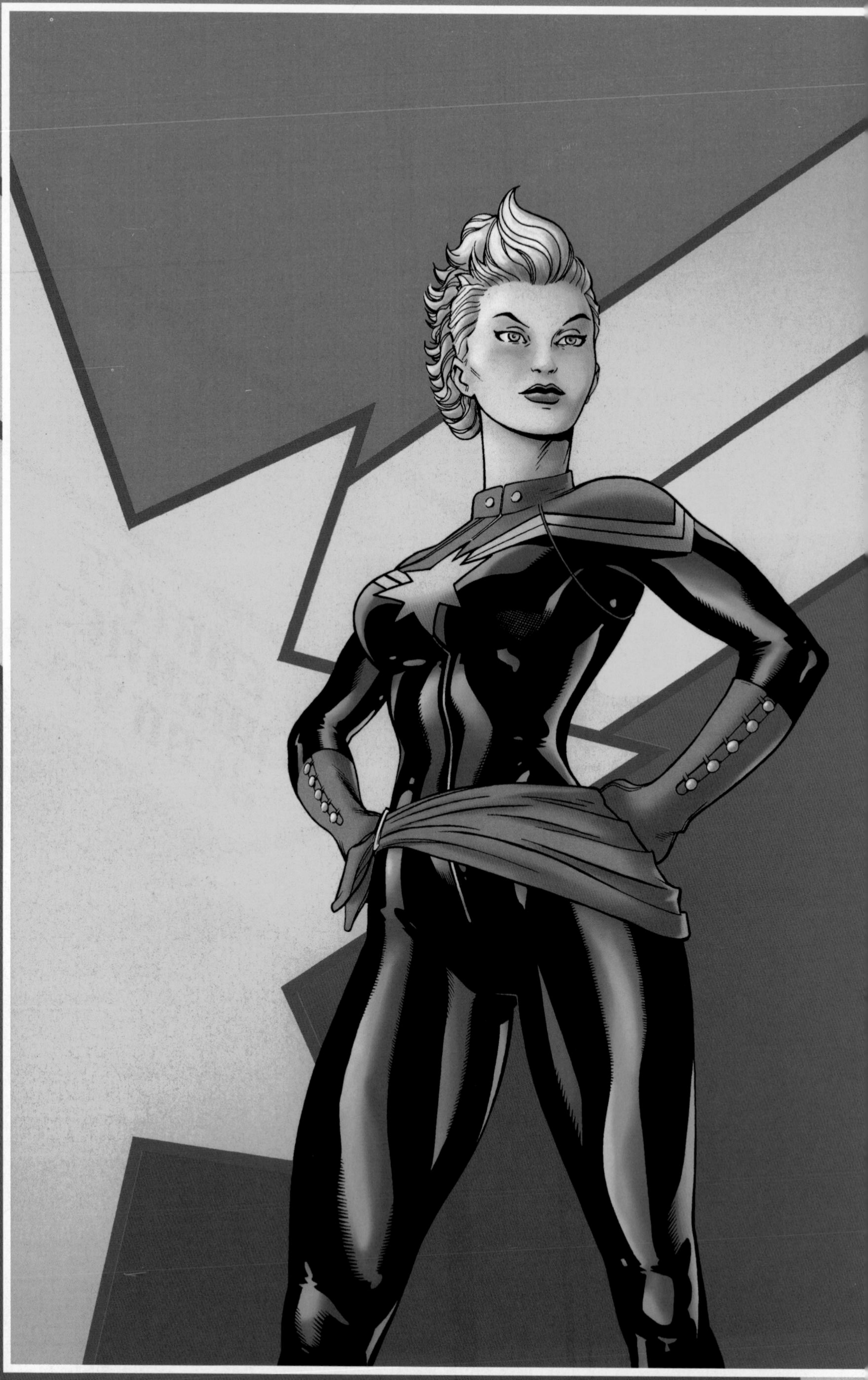

ONE

FINAL ☆☆☆☆

DAILY BUGLE®

SINCE 1897 ☆☆☆☆
$1.00 (in NYC)
$1.50 (outside city)

SPECIAL COMMEMORATIVE ISSUE!

INSIDE: BLONDE BOMBSHELL BRAVES BOSTON! DAREDEVIL SPOTTINGS CONFIRMED IN LATVERIA! LIZARDS LOOSE IN MANHATTAN! MORE...

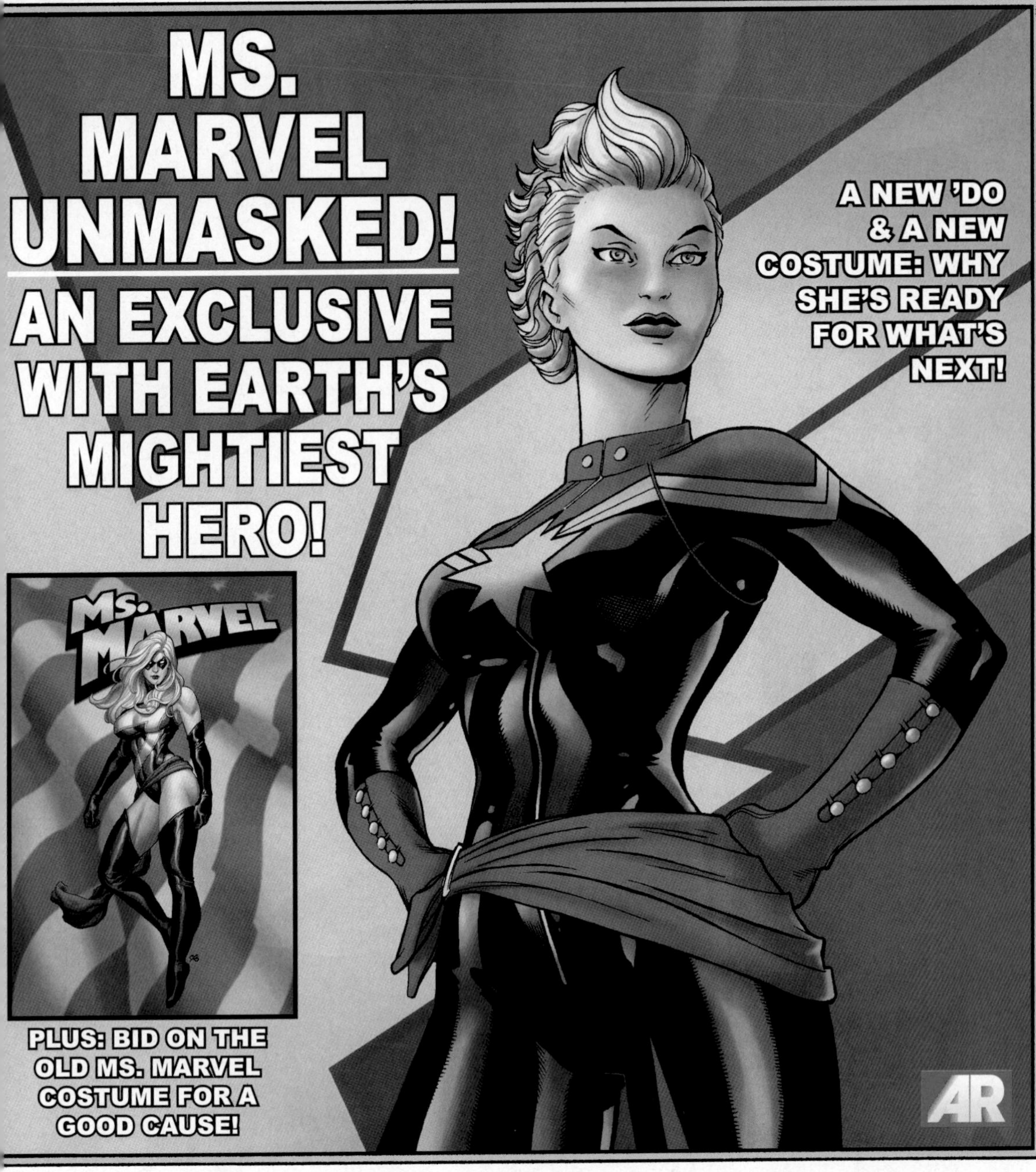
MS. MARVEL UNMASKED!
AN EXCLUSIVE WITH EARTH'S MIGHTIEST HERO!
A NEW 'DO & A NEW COSTUME: WHY SHE'S READY FOR WHAT'S NEXT!
MS. MARVEL
PLUS: BID ON THE OLD MS. MARVEL COSTUME FOR A GOOD CAUSE!
AR

When you see this: AR, open up the MARVEL AR APP (available on applicable Apple ® iOS or Android TM devices) and use your camera-enabled device to unlock extra-special exclusive features!

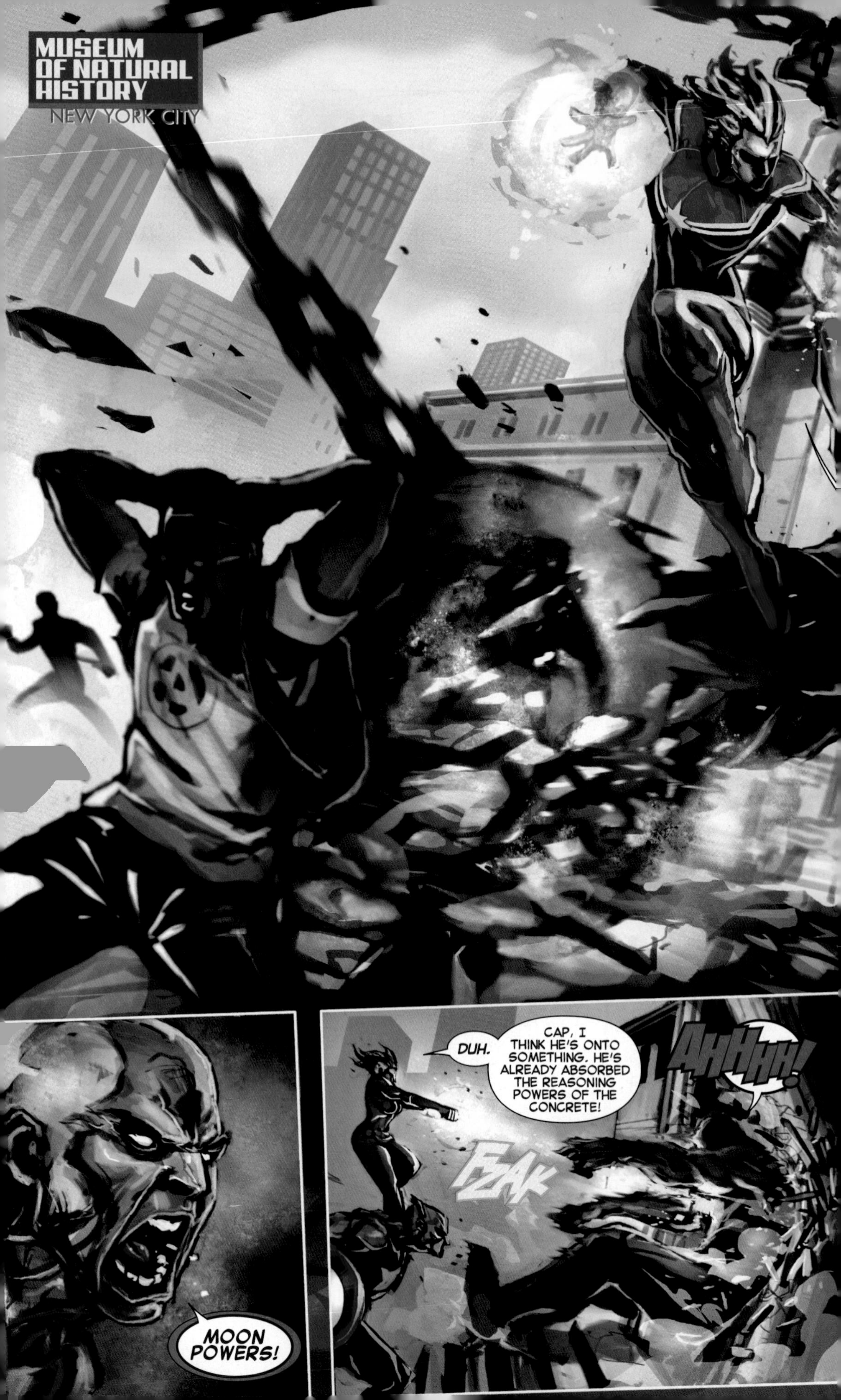
MUSEUM OF NATURAL HISTORY
NEW YORK CITY
MOON POWERS!
DUH.
CAP, I THINK HE'S ONTO SOMETHING. HE'S ALREADY ABSORBED THE REASONING POWERS OF THE CONCRETE!
AHHHH!
FZAK

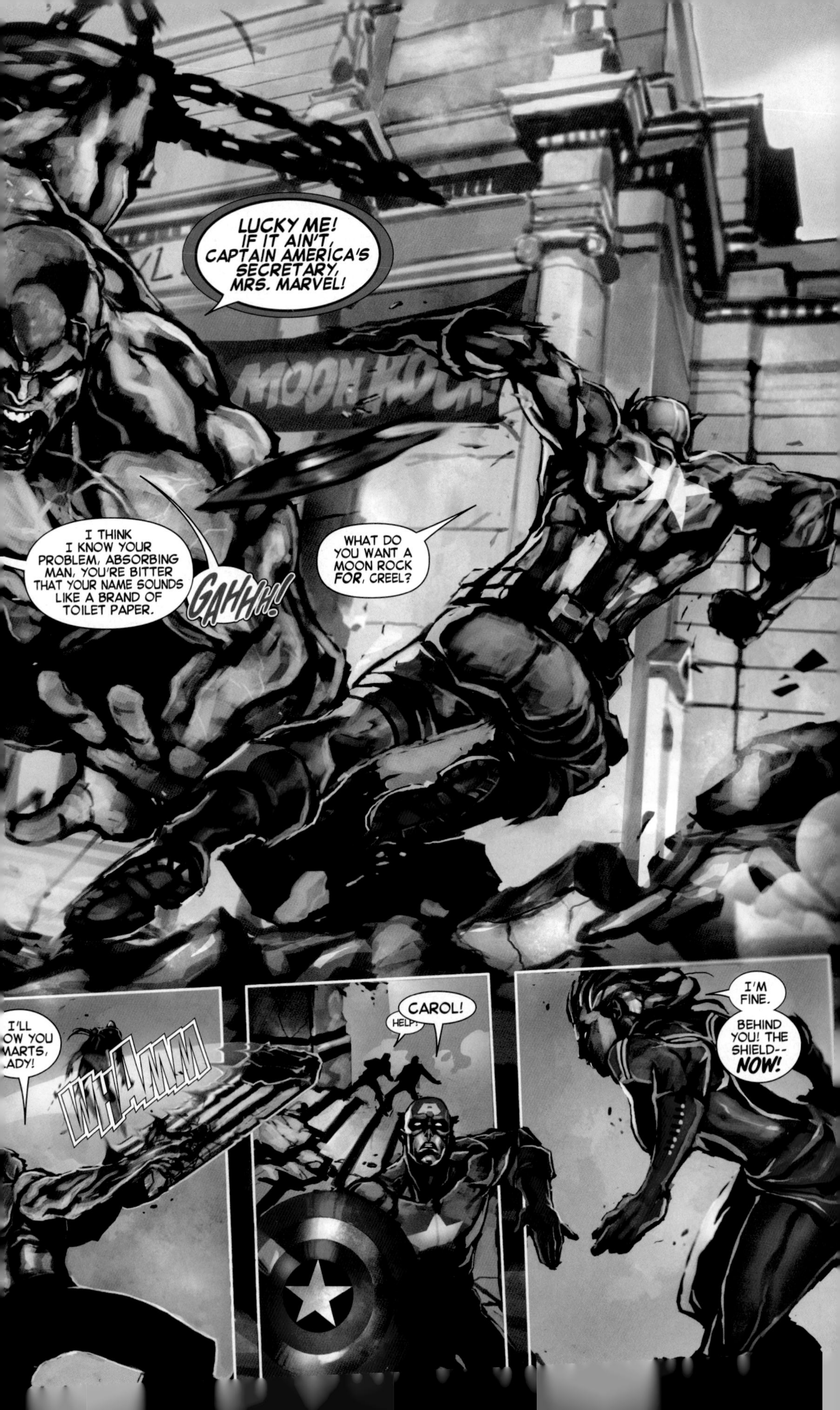
LUCKY ME! IF IT AIN'T, CAPTAIN AMERICA'S SECRETARY, MRS. MARVEL!
MOON ROCK
I THINK I KNOW YOUR PROBLEM, ABSORBING MAN, YOU'RE BITTER THAT YOUR NAME SOUNDS LIKE A BRAND OF TOILET PAPER.
GAHHH!
WHAT DO YOU WANT A MOON ROCK FOR, CREEL?
I'LL OW YOU MARTS, ADY!
WHAMM
HELP!
CAROL!
I'M FINE.
BEHIND YOU! THE SHIELD-- NOW!

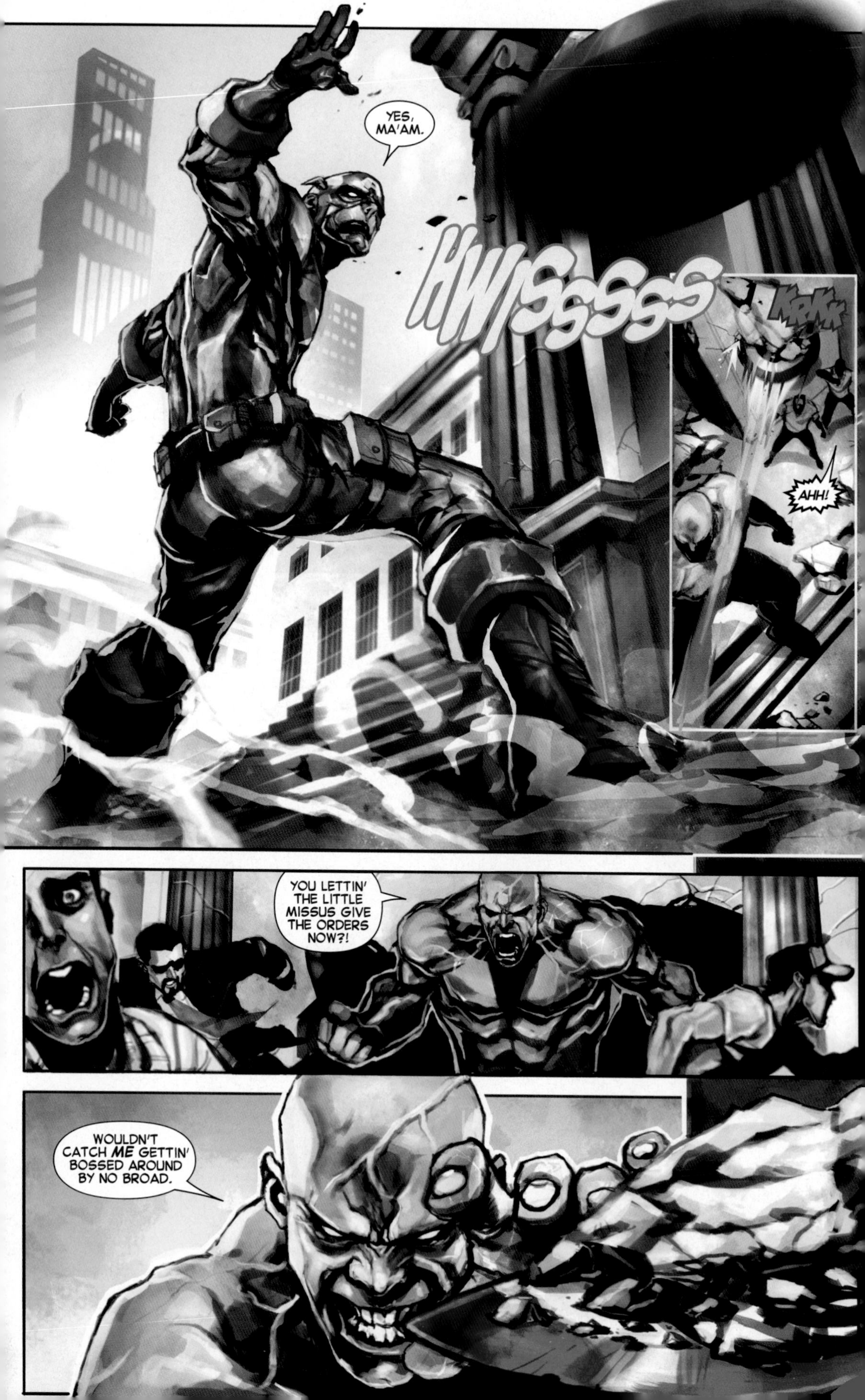
YES, MA'AM.
HWISSSSS
KRAKK
AHH!
YOU LETTIN' THE LITTLE MISSUS GIVE THE ORDERS NOW?!
WOULDN'T CATCH ME GETTIN' BOSSED AROUND BY NO BROAD.

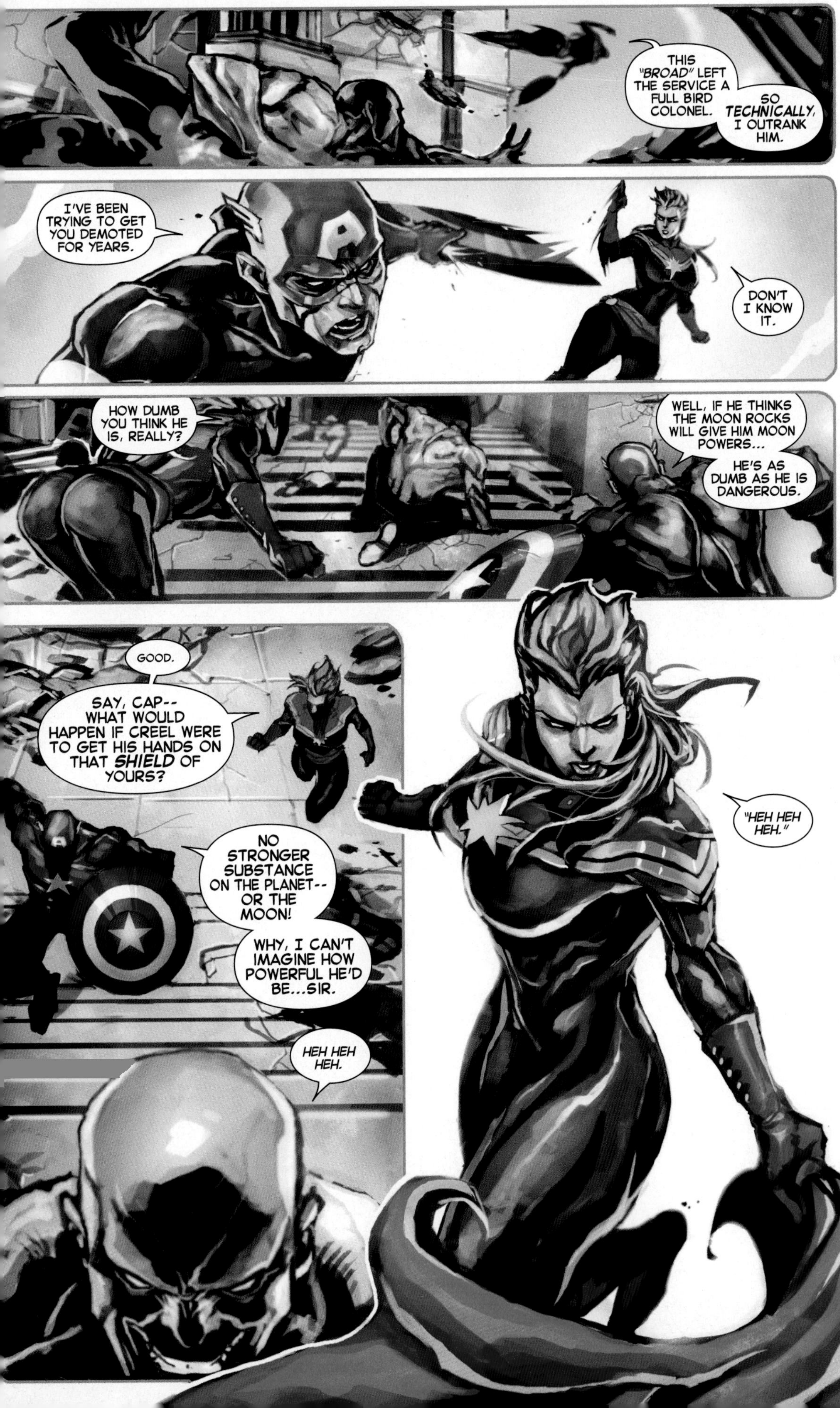
THIS "BROAD" LEFT THE SERVICE A FULL BIRD COLONEL.
SO TECHNICALLY, I OUTRANK HIM.
I'VE BEEN TRYING TO GET YOU DEMOTED FOR YEARS.
DON'T I KNOW IT.
HOW DUMB YOU THINK HE IS, REALLY?
WELL, IF HE THINKS THE MOON ROCKS WILL GIVE HIM MOON POWERS...
HE'S AS DUMB AS HE IS DANGEROUS.
GOOD.
SAY, CAP--WHAT WOULD HAPPEN IF CREEL WERE TO GET HIS HANDS ON THAT SHIELD OF YOURS?
NO STRONGER SUBSTANCE ON THE PLANET--OR THE MOON!
WHY, I CAN'T IMAGINE HOW POWERFUL HE'D BE...SIR.
HEH HEH HEH.
"HEH HEH HEH."

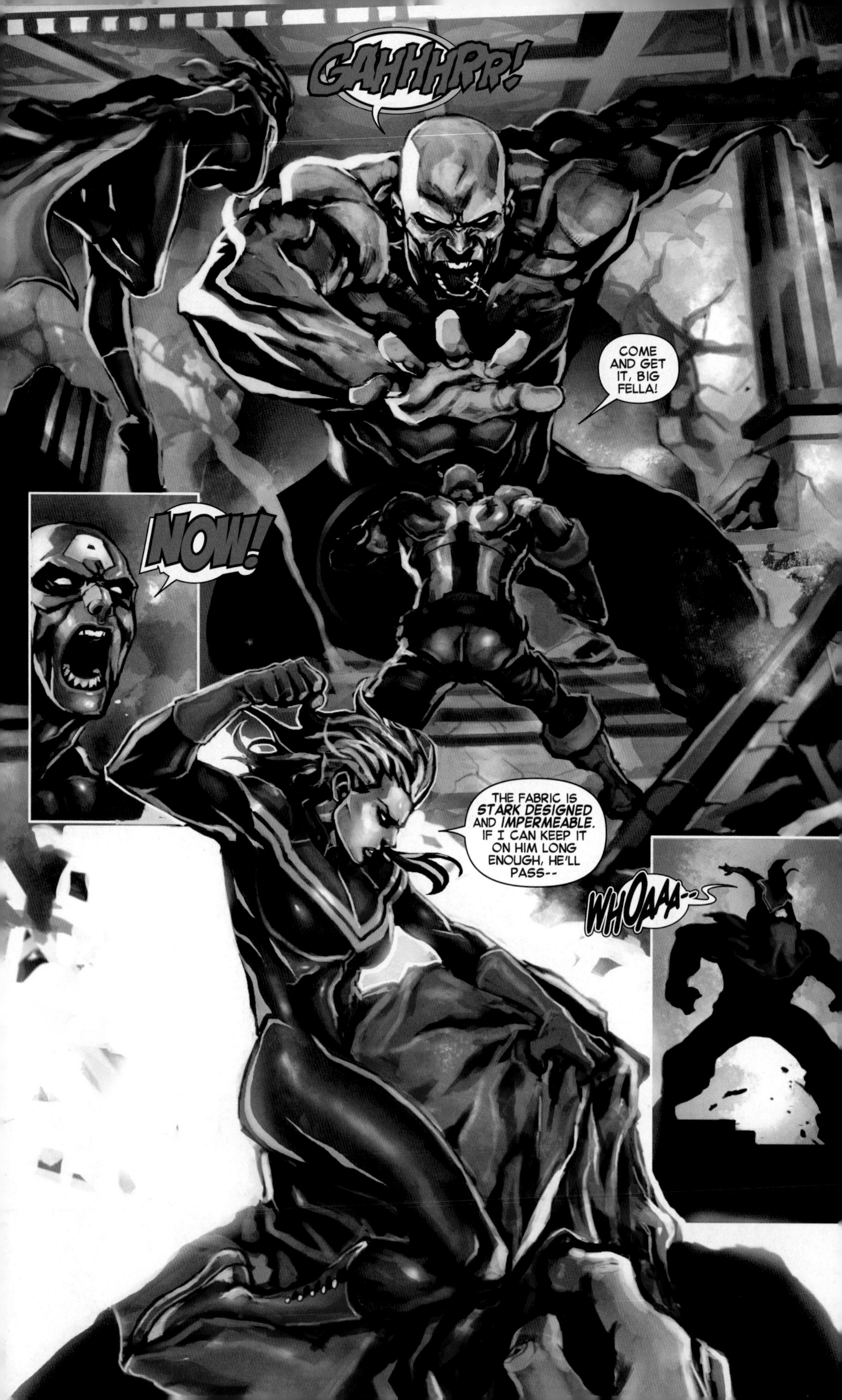
GAHHHRR!
COME AND GET IT, BIG FELLA!
NOW!
THE FABRIC IS STARK DESIGNED AND IMPERMEABLE. IF I CAN KEEP IT ON HIM LONG ENOUGH, HE'LL PASS--
WHOAAA--

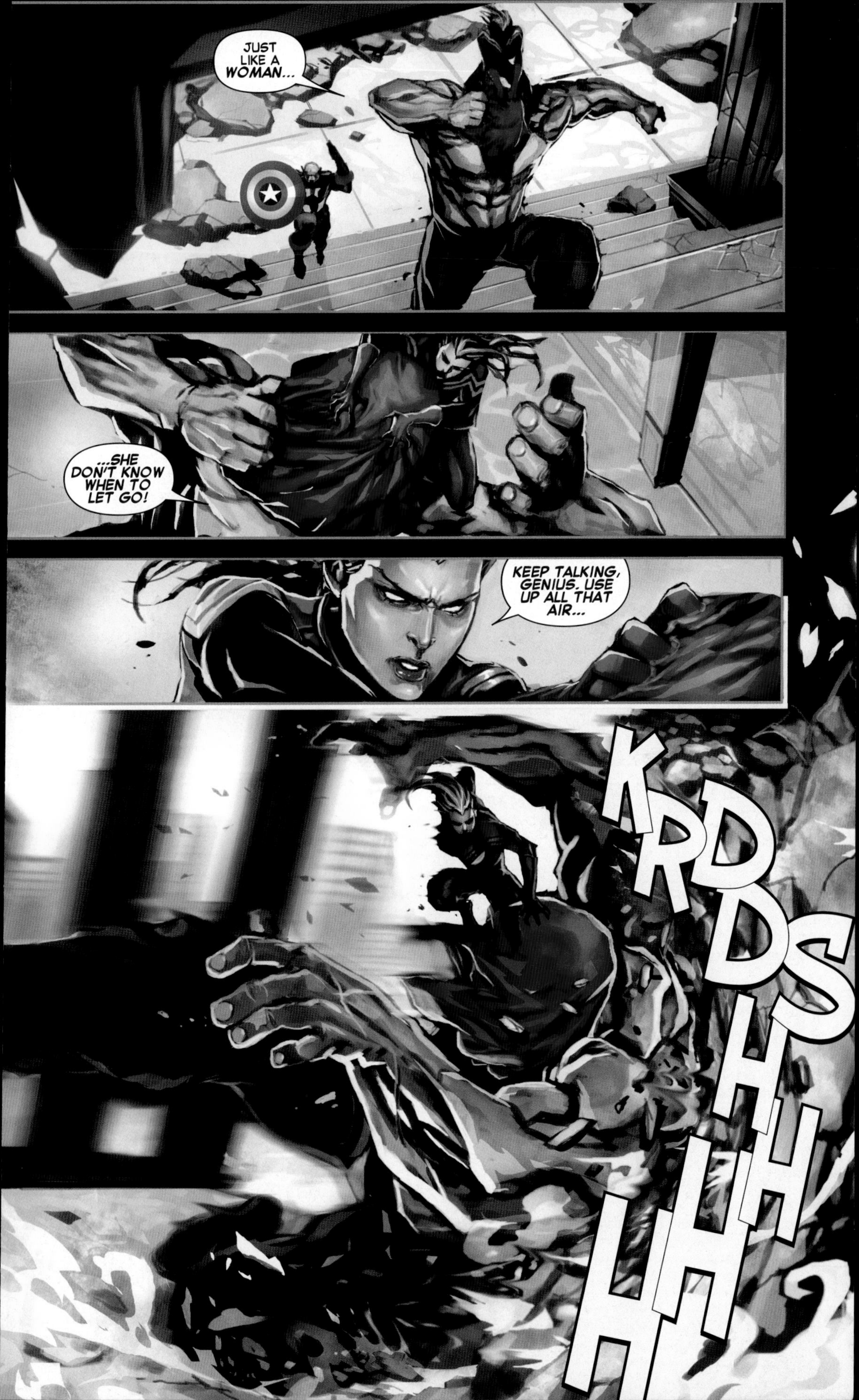
JUST LIKE A WOMAN...
...SHE DON'T KNOW WHEN TO LET GO!
KEEP TALKING, GENIUS. USE UP ALL THAT AIR...
KRDSHHHHHH

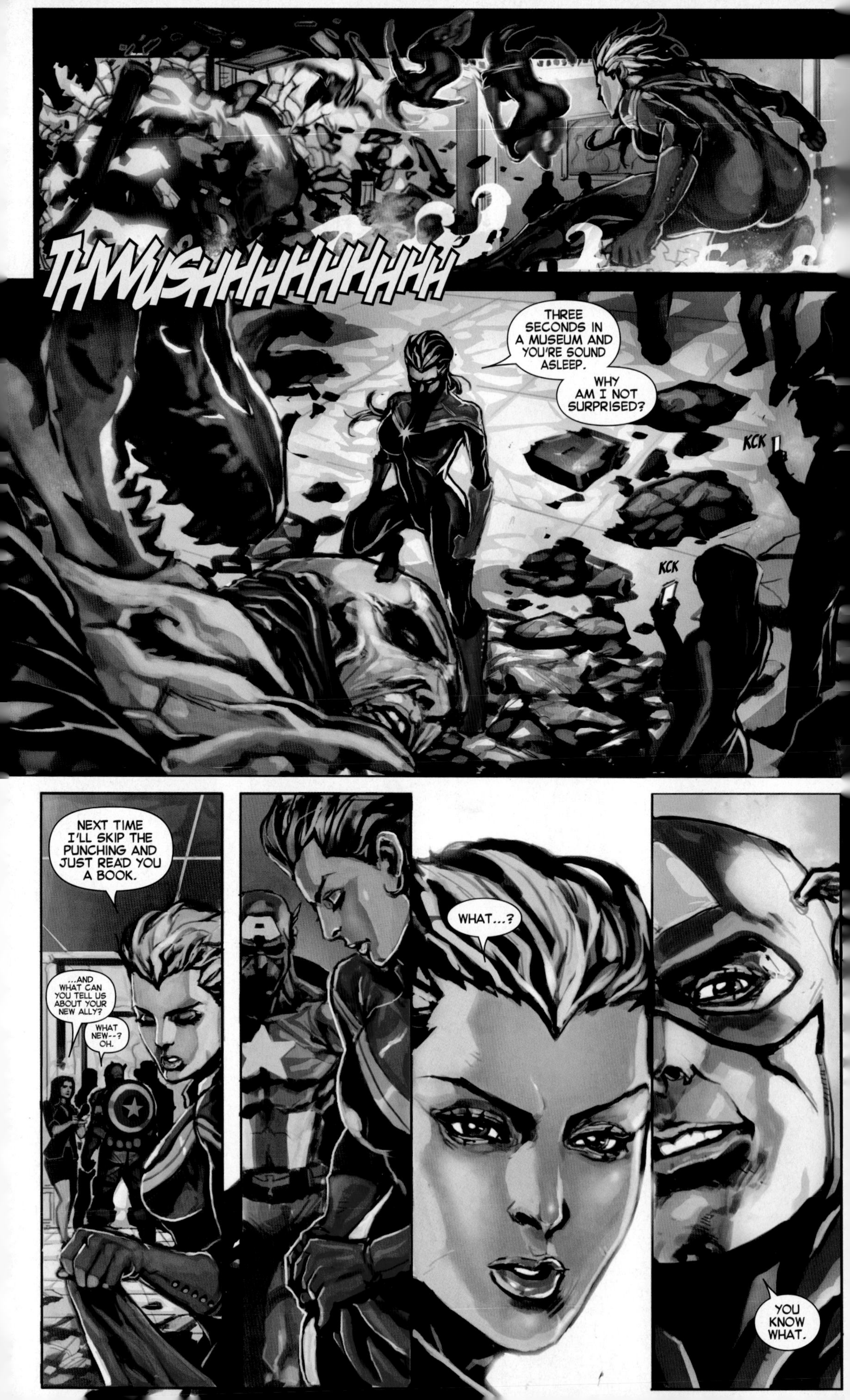
THWUSHHHHHHHHH
THREE SECONDS IN A MUSEUM AND YOU'RE SOUND ASLEEP.
WHY AM I NOT SURPRISED?
KCK
KCK
NEXT TIME I'LL SKIP THE PUNCHING AND JUST READ YOU A BOOK.
...AND WHAT CAN YOU TELL US ABOUT YOUR NEW ALLY?
WHAT NEW--? OH.
WHAT...?
YOU KNOW WHAT.

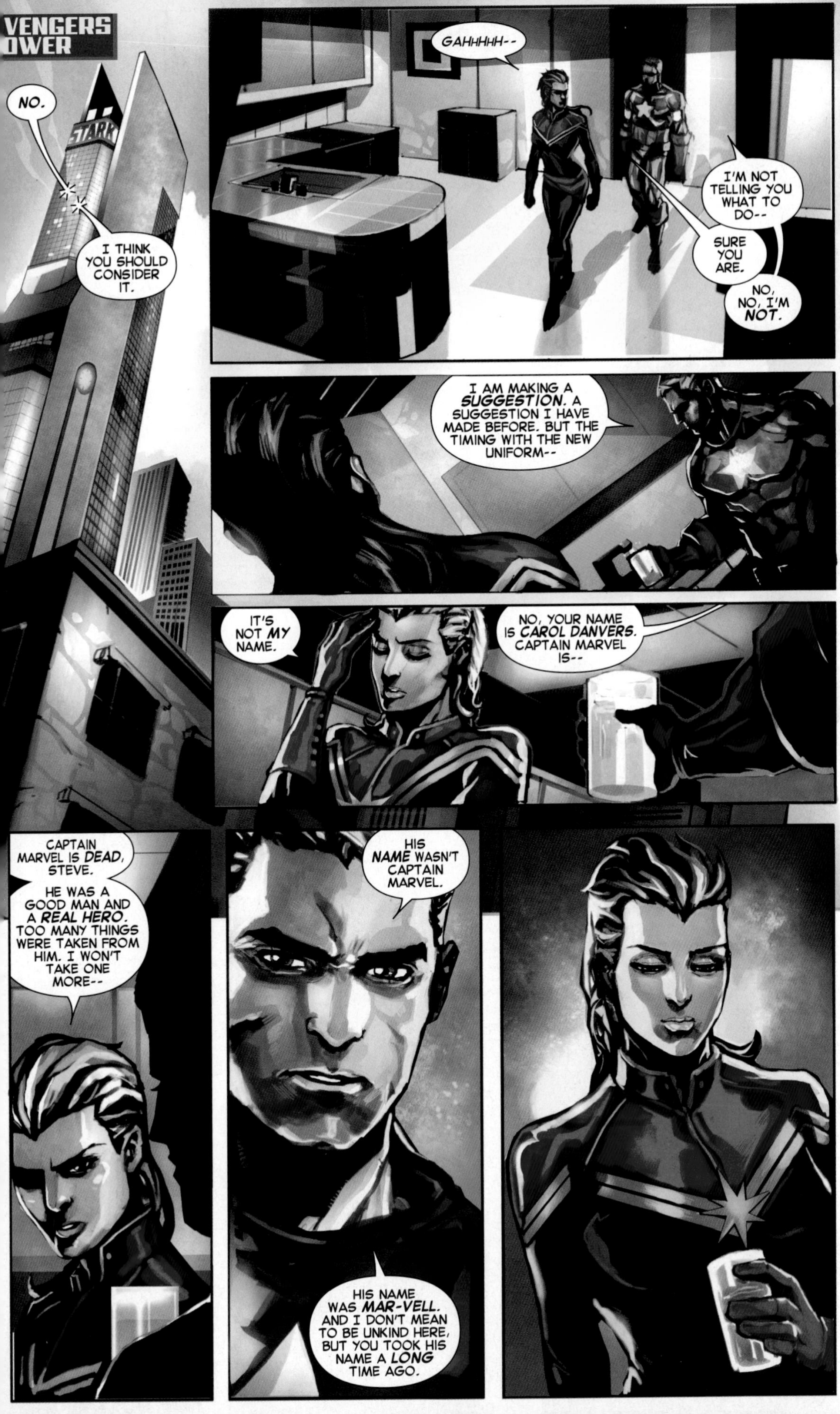
VENGERS
OWER
NO.
I THINK YOU SHOULD CONSIDER IT.
GAHHHHH--
I'M NOT TELLING YOU WHAT TO DO--
SURE YOU ARE.
NO, NO, I'M NOT.
I AM MAKING A SUGGESTION. A SUGGESTION I HAVE MADE BEFORE. BUT THE TIMING WITH THE NEW UNIFORM--
IT'S NOT MY NAME.
NO, YOUR NAME IS CAROL DANVERS. CAPTAIN MARVEL IS--
CAPTAIN MARVEL IS DEAD, STEVE.
HE WAS A GOOD MAN AND A REAL HERO. TOO MANY THINGS WERE TAKEN FROM HIM. I WON'T TAKE ONE MORE--
HIS NAME WASN'T CAPTAIN MARVEL.
HIS NAME WAS MAR-VELL. AND I DON'T MEAN TO BE UNKIND HERE, BUT YOU TOOK HIS NAME A LONG TIME AGO.

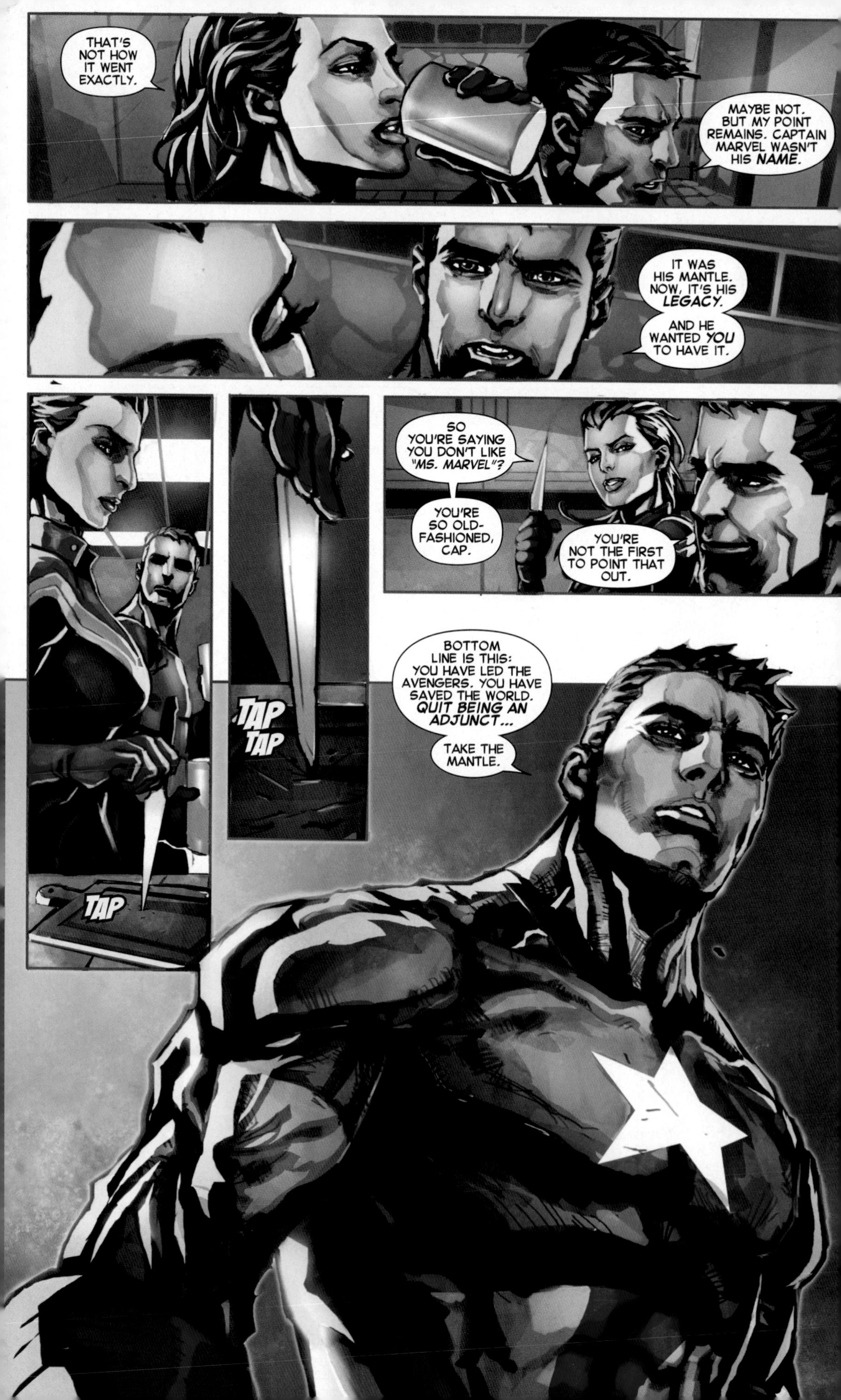
THAT'S NOT HOW IT WENT EXACTLY.
MAYBE NOT. BUT MY POINT REMAINS. CAPTAIN MARVEL WASN'T HIS NAME.
IT WAS HIS MANTLE. NOW, IT'S HIS LEGACY.
AND HE WANTED YOU TO HAVE IT.
TAP
TAP TAP
SO YOU'RE SAYING YOU DON'T LIKE "MS. MARVEL"?
YOU'RE SO OLD-FASHIONED, CAP.
YOU'RE NOT THE FIRST TO POINT THAT OUT.
BOTTOM LINE IS THIS: YOU HAVE LED THE AVENGERS. YOU HAVE SAVED THE WORLD. QUIT BEING AN ADJUNCT...
TAKE THE MANTLE.

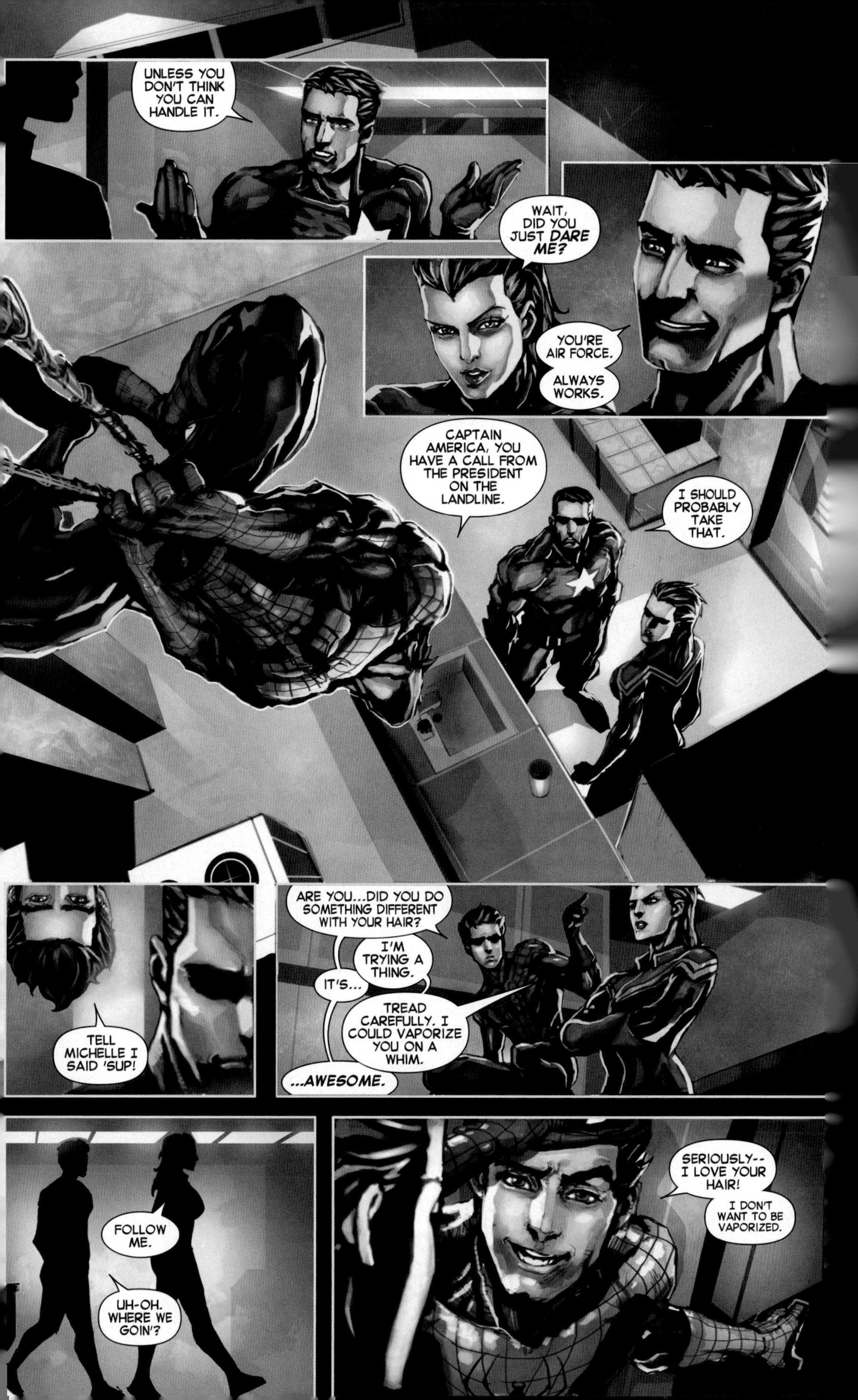
UNLESS YOU DON'T THINK YOU CAN HANDLE IT.
WAIT, DID YOU JUST DARE ME?
YOU'RE AIR FORCE.
ALWAYS WORKS.
CAPTAIN AMERICA, YOU HAVE A CALL FROM THE PRESIDENT ON THE LANDLINE.
I SHOULD PROBABLY TAKE THAT.
TELL MICHELLE I SAID 'SUP!
ARE YOU...DID YOU DO SOMETHING DIFFERENT WITH YOUR HAIR?
I'M TRYING A THING.
IT'S...
TREAD CAREFULLY. I COULD VAPORIZE YOU ON A WHIM.
...AWESOME.
FOLLOW ME.
UH-OH. WHERE WE GOIN'?
SERIOUSLY-- I LOVE YOUR HAIR!
I DON'T WANT TO BE VAPORIZED.

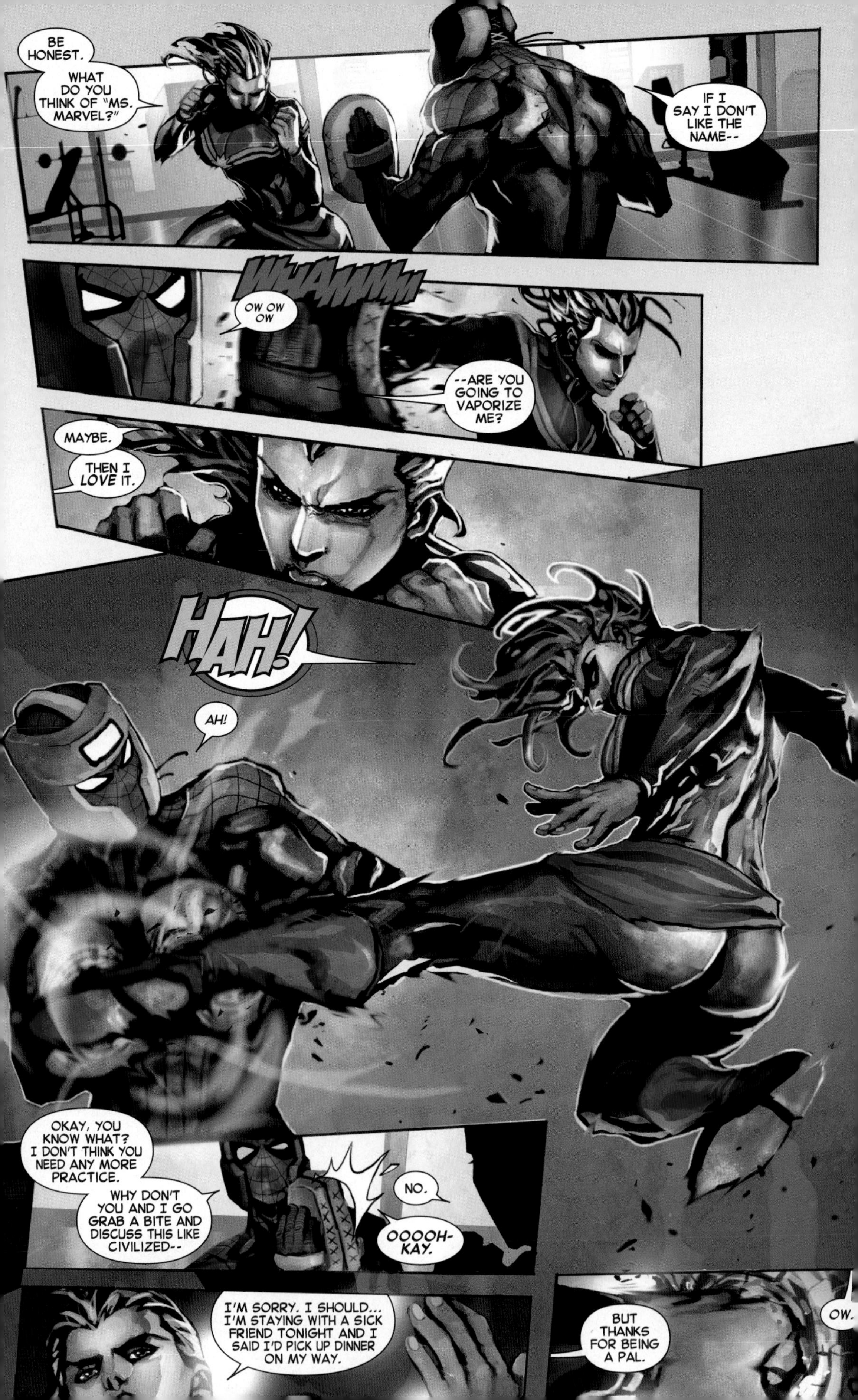
BE HONEST.
WHAT DO YOU THINK OF "MS. MARVEL?"
IF I SAY I DON'T LIKE THE NAME--
WHAAMMM
OW OW OW
--ARE YOU GOING TO VAPORIZE ME?
MAYBE.
THEN I *LOVE* IT.
HAH!
AH!
OKAY, YOU KNOW WHAT? I DON'T THINK YOU NEED ANY MORE PRACTICE.
WHY DON'T YOU AND I GO GRAB A BITE AND DISCUSS THIS LIKE CIVILIZED--
NO.
OOOOH-KAY.
I'M SORRY. I SHOULD... I'M STAYING WITH A SICK FRIEND TONIGHT AND I SAID I'D PICK UP DINNER ON MY WAY.
BUT THANKS FOR BEING A PAL.
OW.

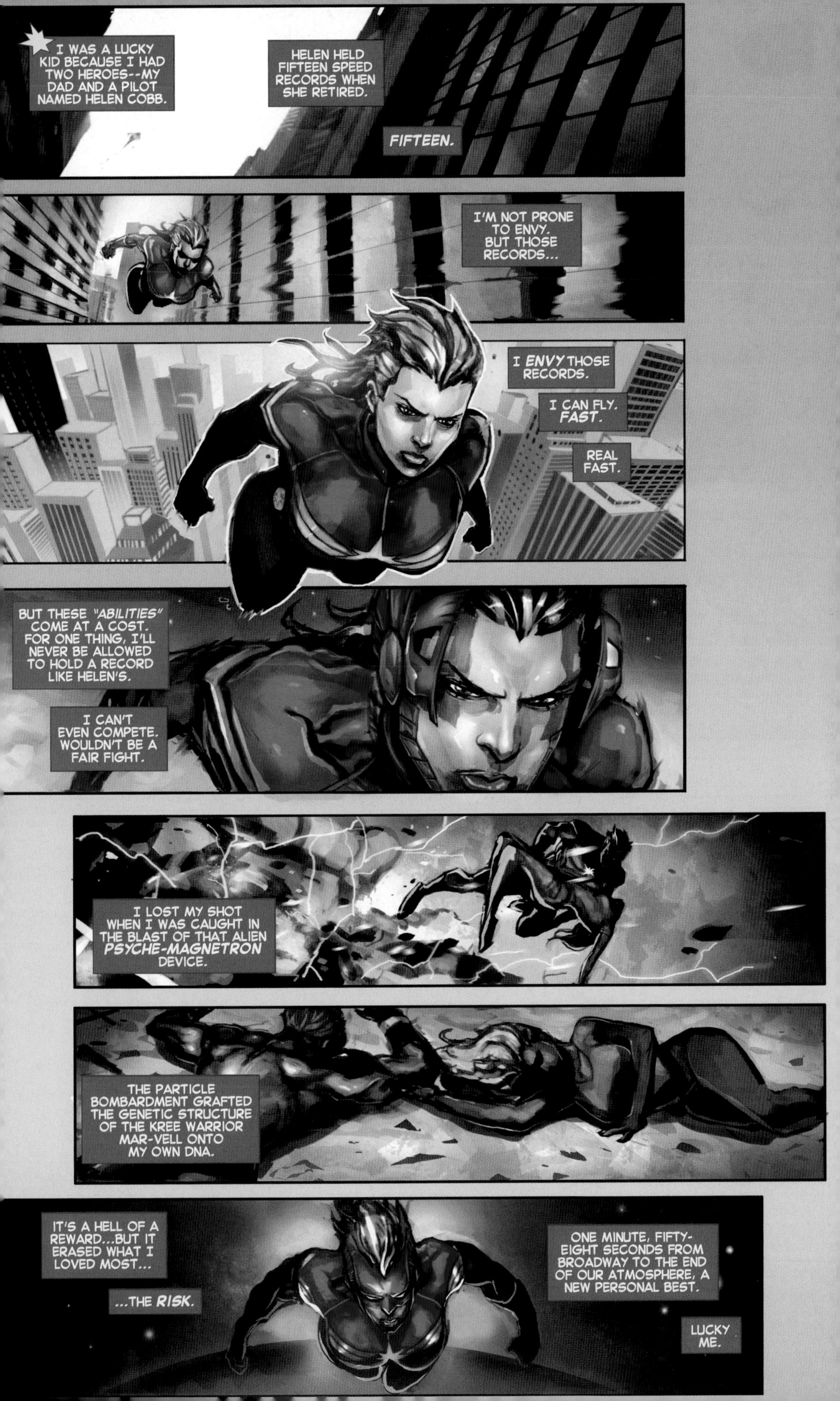

I WAS A LUCKY KID BECAUSE I HAD TWO HEROES--MY DAD AND A PILOT NAMED HELEN COBB.
HELEN HELD FIFTEEN SPEED RECORDS WHEN SHE RETIRED.
FIFTEEN.
I'M NOT PRONE TO ENVY. BUT THOSE RECORDS...
I ENVY THOSE RECORDS.
I CAN FLY. FAST.
REAL FAST.
BUT THESE "ABILITIES" COME AT A COST. FOR ONE THING, I'LL NEVER BE ALLOWED TO HOLD A RECORD LIKE HELEN'S.
I CAN'T EVEN COMPETE. WOULDN'T BE A FAIR FIGHT.
I LOST MY SHOT WHEN I WAS CAUGHT IN THE BLAST OF THAT ALIEN PSYCHE-MAGNETRON DEVICE.
THE PARTICLE BOMBARDMENT GRAFTED THE GENETIC STRUCTURE OF THE KREE WARRIOR MAR-VELL ONTO MY OWN DNA.
IT'S A HELL OF A REWARD...BUT IT ERASED WHAT I LOVED MOST...
...THE RISK.
ONE MINUTE, FIFTY-EIGHT SECONDS FROM BROADWAY TO THE END OF OUR ATMOSPHERE, A NEW PERSONAL BEST.
LUCKY ME.

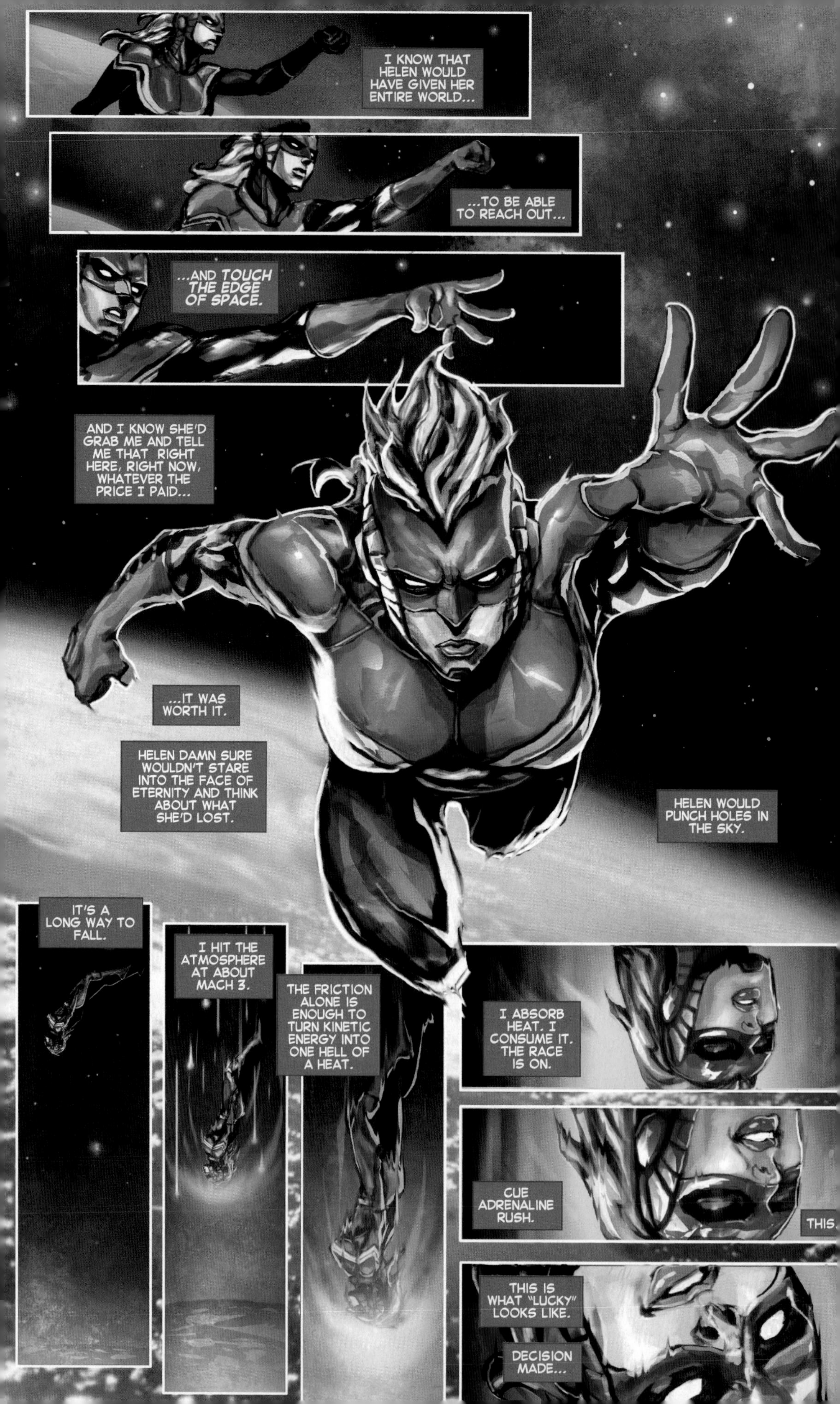
I KNOW THAT HELEN WOULD HAVE GIVEN HER ENTIRE WORLD...
...TO BE ABLE TO REACH OUT...
...AND TOUCH THE EDGE OF SPACE.
AND I KNOW SHE'D GRAB ME AND TELL ME THAT RIGHT HERE, RIGHT NOW, WHATEVER THE PRICE I PAID...
...IT WAS WORTH IT.
HELEN DAMN SURE WOULDN'T STARE INTO THE FACE OF ETERNITY AND THINK ABOUT WHAT SHE'D LOST.
HELEN WOULD PUNCH HOLES IN THE SKY.
IT'S A LONG WAY TO FALL.
I HIT THE ATMOSPHERE AT ABOUT MACH 3.
THE FRICTION ALONE IS ENOUGH TO TURN KINETIC ENERGY INTO ONE HELL OF A HEAT.
I ABSORB HEAT. I CONSUME IT. THE RACE IS ON.
CUE ADRENALINE RUSH.
THIS.
THIS IS WHAT "LUCKY" LOOKS LIKE.
DECISION MADE...

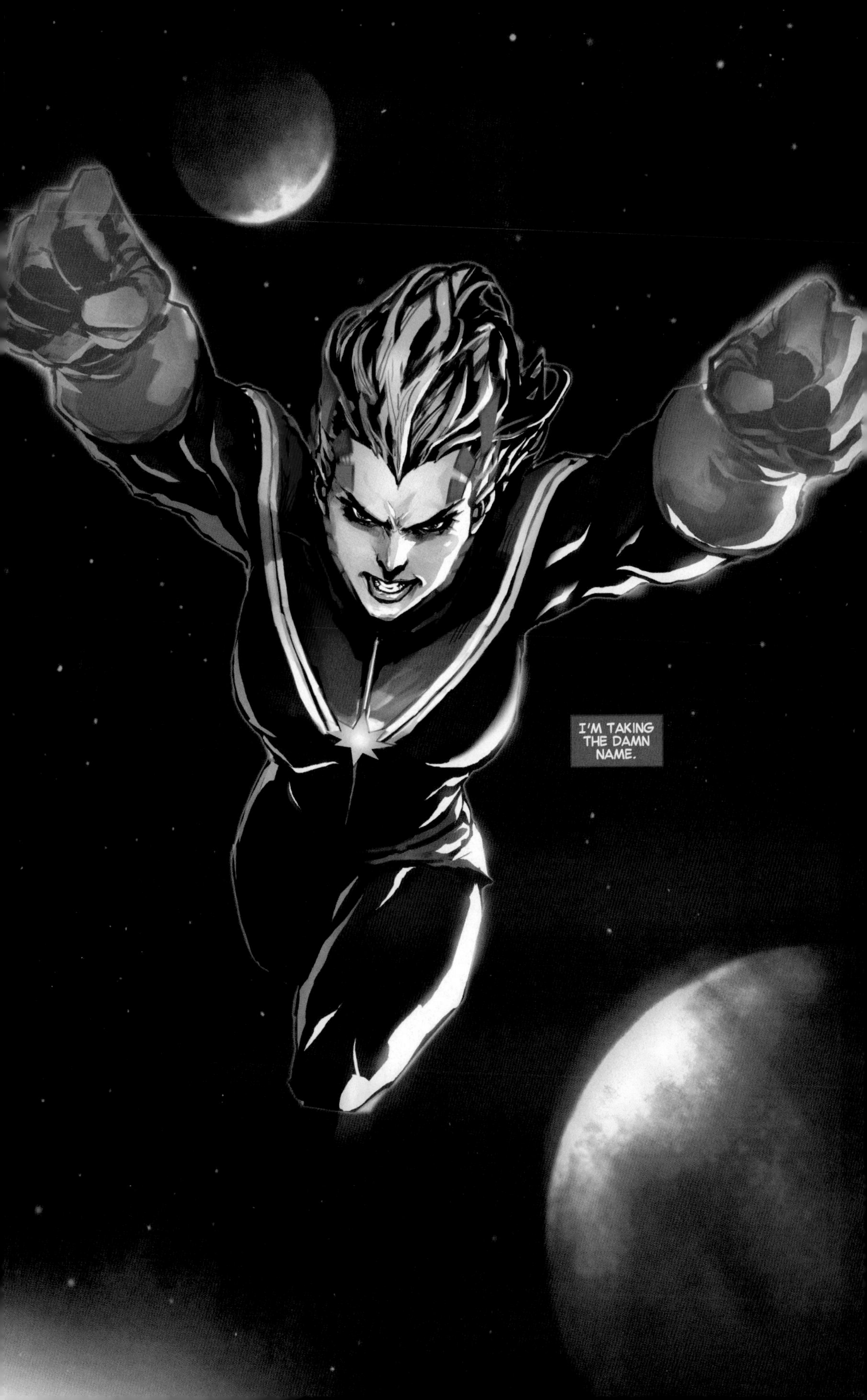
I'M TAKING THE DAMN NAME.

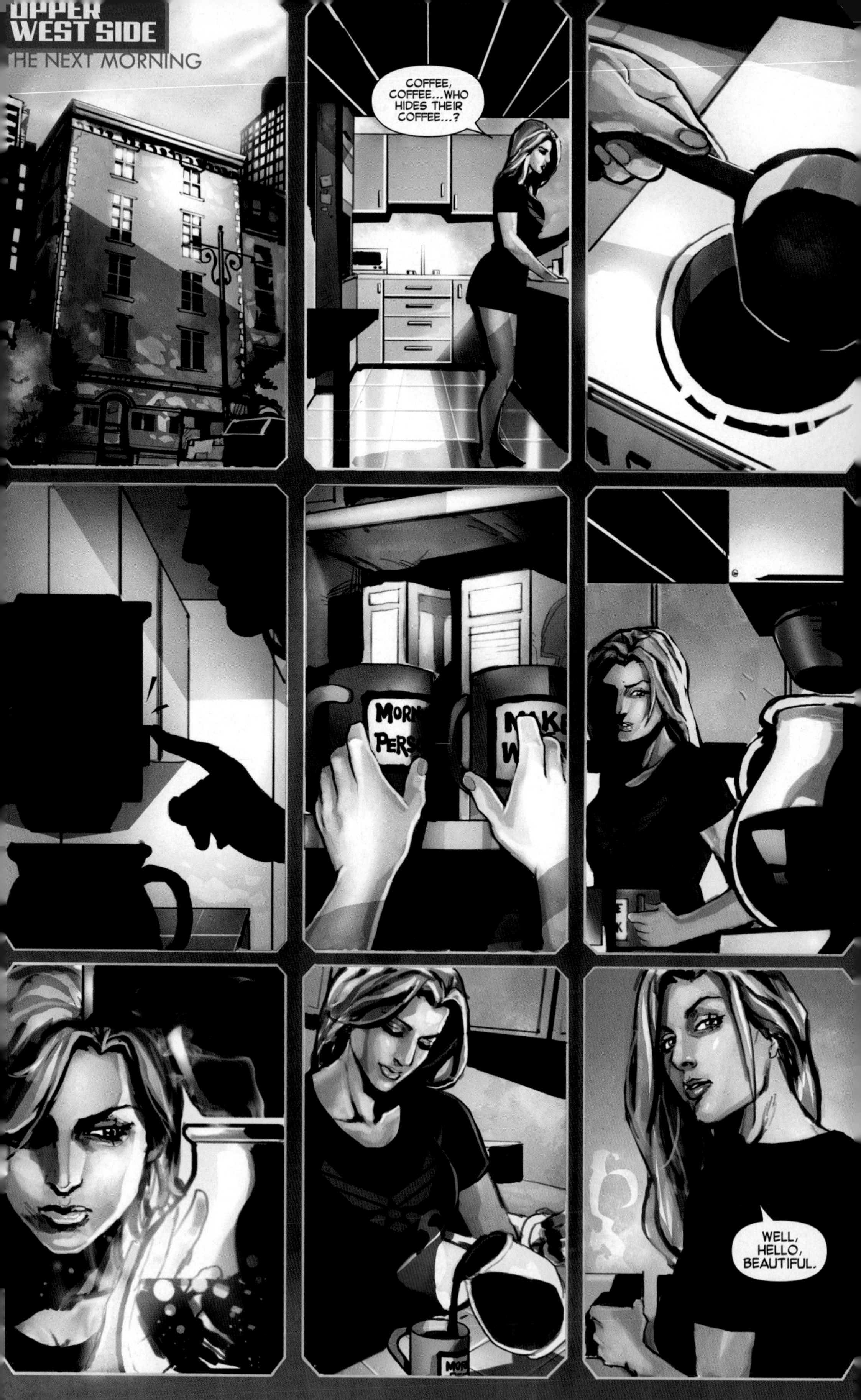
UPPER WEST SIDE
THE NEXT MORNING
COFFEE, COFFEE...WHO HIDES THEIR COFFEE...?
WELL, HELLO, BEAUTIFUL.

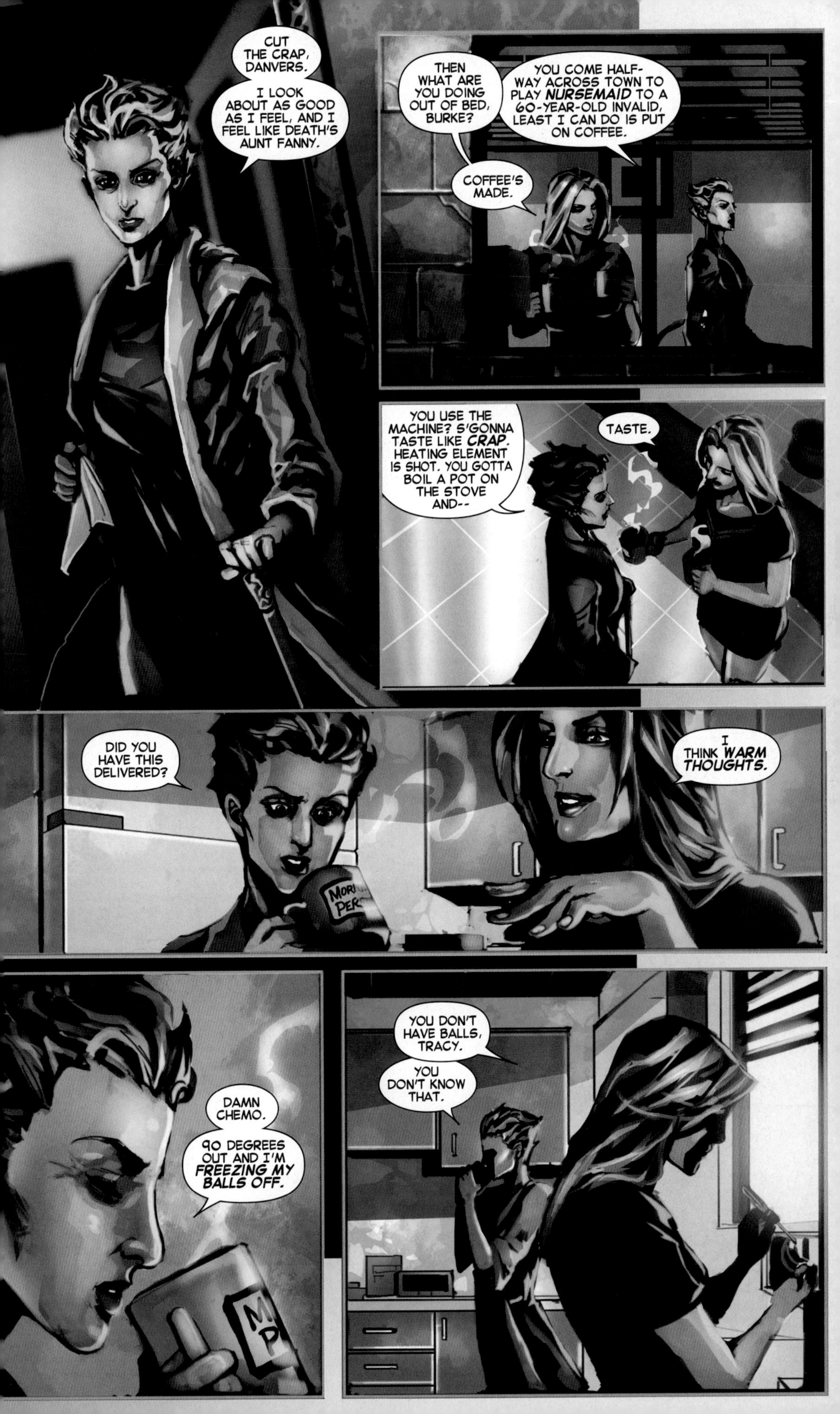
CUT THE CRAP, DANVERS.
I LOOK ABOUT AS GOOD AS I FEEL, AND I FEEL LIKE DEATH'S AUNT FANNY.
THEN WHAT ARE YOU DOING OUT OF BED, BURKE?
YOU COME HALF-WAY ACROSS TOWN TO PLAY NURSEMAID TO A 60-YEAR-OLD INVALID, LEAST I CAN DO IS PUT ON COFFEE.
COFFEE'S MADE.
YOU USE THE MACHINE? S'GONNA TASTE LIKE CRAP. HEATING ELEMENT IS SHOT. YOU GOTTA BOIL A POT ON THE STOVE AND--
TASTE.
DID YOU HAVE THIS DELIVERED?
I THINK WARM THOUGHTS.
DAMN CHEMO.
90 DEGREES OUT AND I'M FREEZING MY BALLS OFF.
YOU DON'T HAVE BALLS, TRACY.
YOU DON'T KNOW THAT.

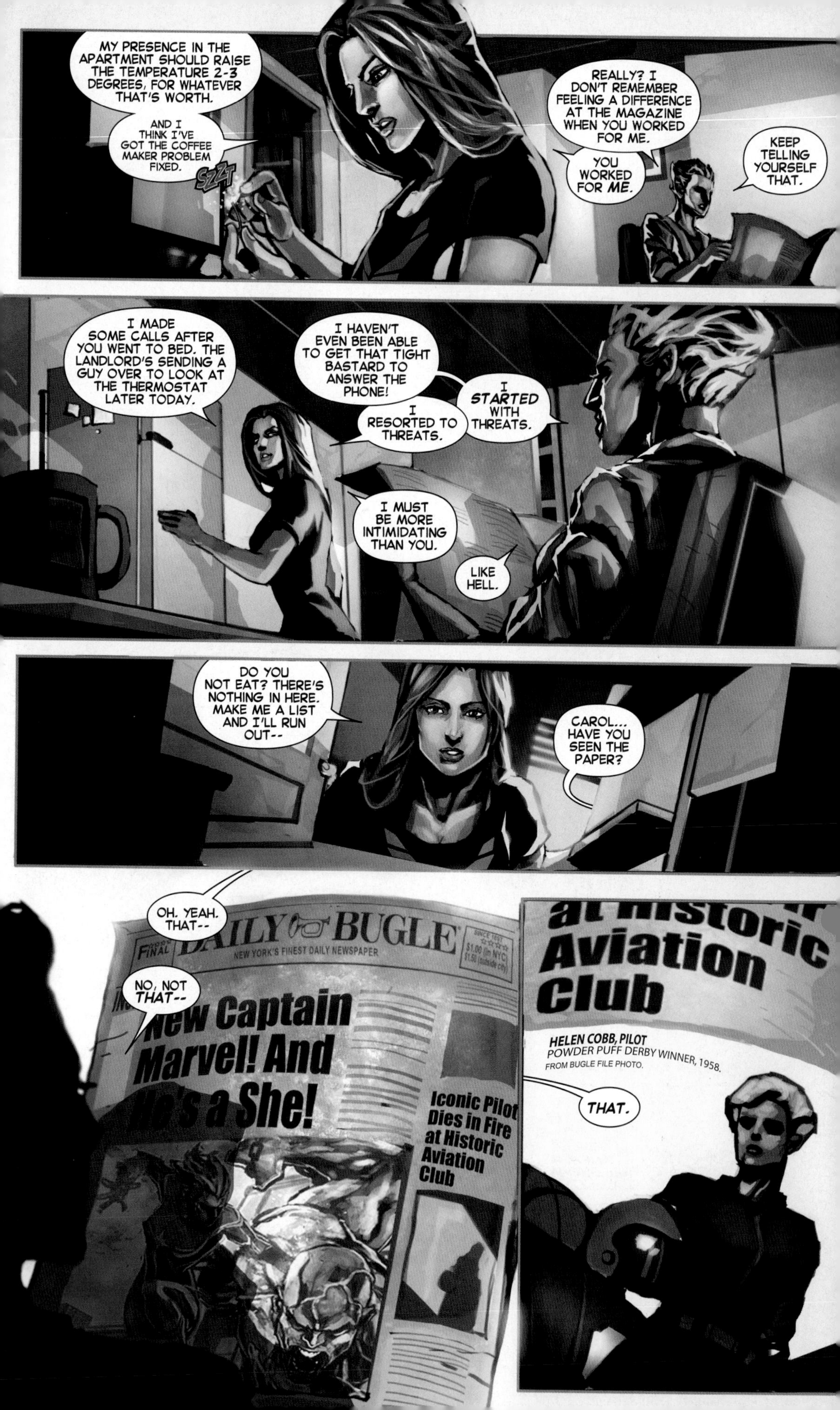
MY PRESENCE IN THE APARTMENT SHOULD RAISE THE TEMPERATURE 2-3 DEGREES, FOR WHATEVER THAT'S WORTH.
AND I THINK I'VE GOT THE COFFEE MAKER PROBLEM FIXED.
SZZT
REALLY? I DON'T REMEMBER FEELING A DIFFERENCE AT THE MAGAZINE WHEN YOU WORKED FOR ME.
YOU WORKED FOR ME.
KEEP TELLING YOURSELF THAT.
I MADE SOME CALLS AFTER YOU WENT TO BED. THE LANDLORD'S SENDING A GUY OVER TO LOOK AT THE THERMOSTAT LATER TODAY.
I HAVEN'T EVEN BEEN ABLE TO GET THAT TIGHT BASTARD TO ANSWER THE PHONE!
I STARTED WITH THREATS.
I RESORTED TO THREATS.
I MUST BE MORE INTIMIDATING THAN YOU.
LIKE HELL.
DO YOU NOT EAT? THERE'S NOTHING IN HERE. MAKE ME A LIST AND I'LL RUN OUT--
CAROL... HAVE YOU SEEN THE PAPER?
OH. YEAH. THAT--
NO, NOT THAT--
DAILY BUGLE
FINAL
NEW YORK'S FINEST DAILY NEWSPAPER
$1.00 (in NYC)
New Captain Marvel! And He's a She!
Iconic Pilot Dies in Fire at Historic Aviation Club
at Historic Aviation Club
HELEN COBB, PILOT
POWDER PUFF DERBY WINNER, 1958.
FROM BUGLE FILE PHOTO.
THAT.

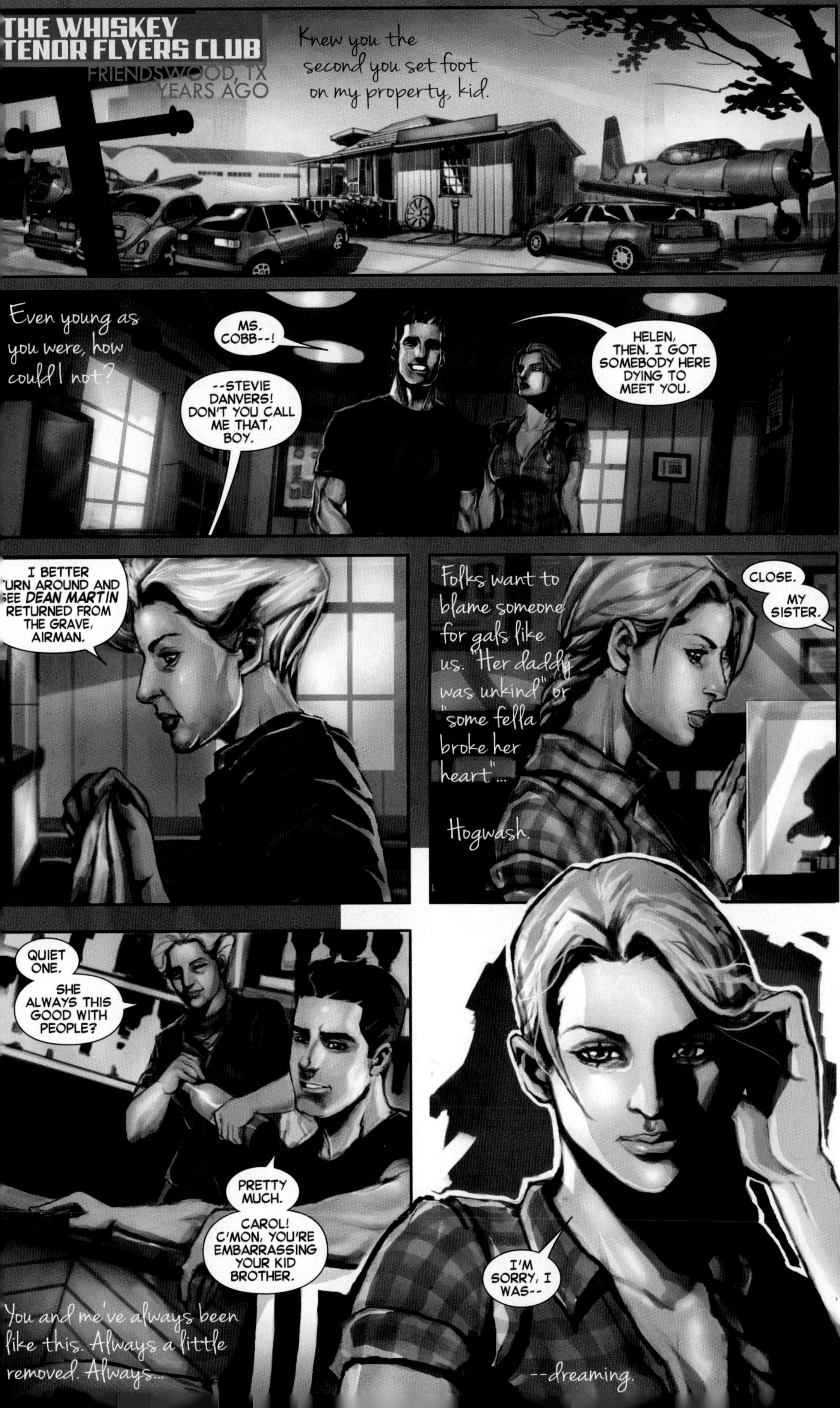
THE WHISKEY TENOR FLYERS CLUB
FRIENDSWOOD, TX
YEARS AGO
Knew you the second you set foot on my property, kid.
Even young as you were, how could I not?
MS. COBB--!
--STEVIE DANVERS! DON'T YOU CALL ME THAT, BOY.
HELEN, THEN. I GOT SOMEBODY HERE DYING TO MEET YOU.
I BETTER TURN AROUND AND SEE DEAN MARTIN RETURNED FROM THE GRAVE, AIRMAN.
Folks want to blame someone for gals like us. "Her daddy was unkind" or "some fella broke her heart"...
Hogwash.
CLOSE.
MY SISTER.
QUIET ONE.
SHE ALWAYS THIS GOOD WITH PEOPLE?
PRETTY MUCH.
CAROL! C'MON, YOU'RE EMBARRASSING YOUR KID BROTHER.
I'M SORRY, I WAS--
You and me've always been like this. Always a little removed. Always...
--dreaming.

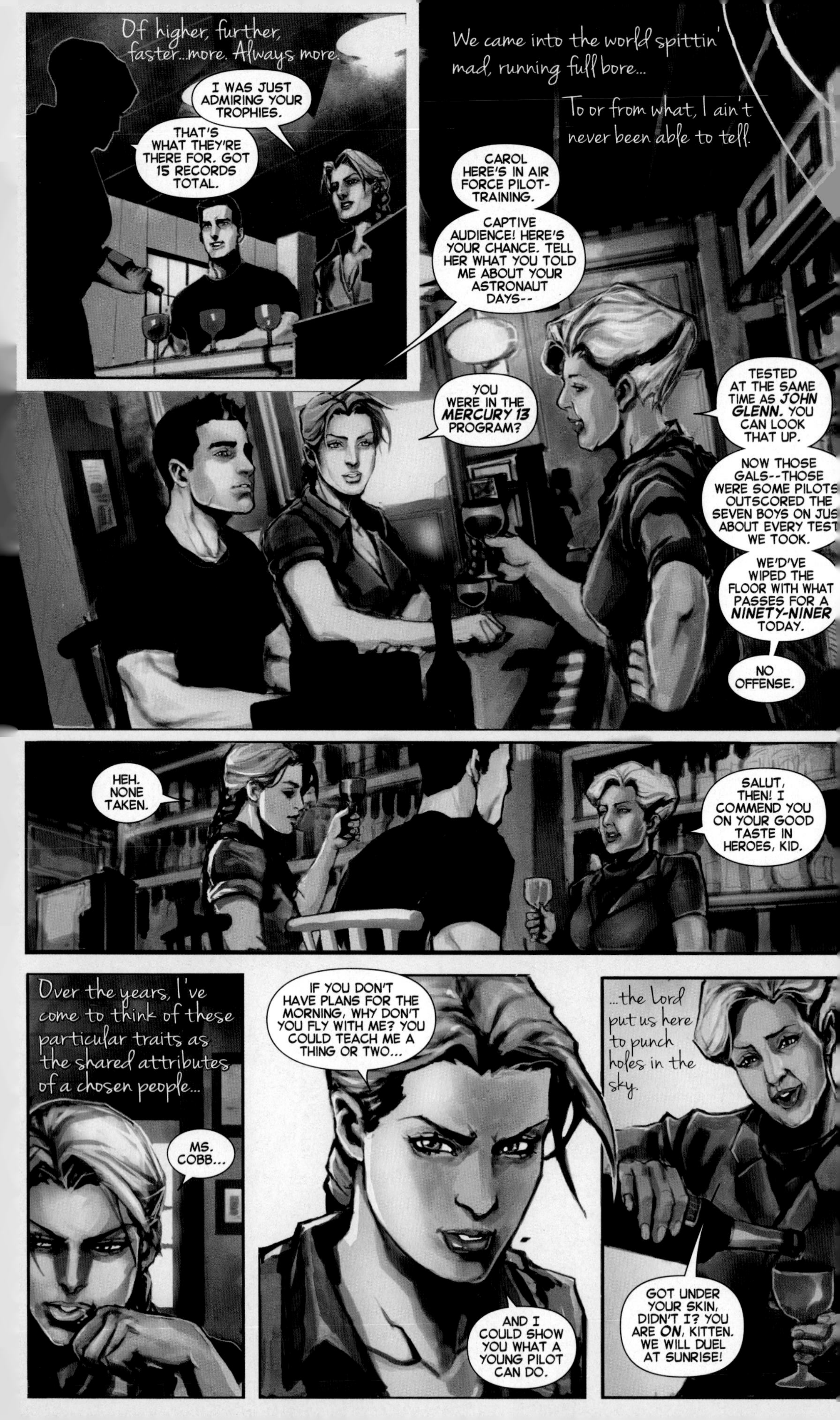

Of higher, further, faster...more. Always more.
I WAS JUST ADMIRING YOUR TROPHIES.
THAT'S WHAT THEY'RE THERE FOR. GOT 15 RECORDS TOTAL.
We came into the world spittin' mad, running full bore...
To or from what, I ain't never been able to tell.
CAROL HERE'S IN AIR FORCE PILOT-TRAINING.
CAPTIVE AUDIENCE! HERE'S YOUR CHANCE. TELL HER WHAT YOU TOLD ME ABOUT YOUR ASTRONAUT DAYS--
YOU WERE IN THE MERCURY 13 PROGRAM?
TESTED AT THE SAME TIME AS JOHN GLENN. YOU CAN LOOK THAT UP.
NOW THOSE GALS--THOSE WERE SOME PILOTS. OUTSCORED THE SEVEN BOYS ON JUS ABOUT EVERY TEST WE TOOK.
WE'D'VE WIPED THE FLOOR WITH WHAT PASSES FOR A NINETY-NINER TODAY.
NO OFFENSE.
HEH. NONE TAKEN.
SALUT, THEN! I COMMEND YOU ON YOUR GOOD TASTE IN HEROES, KID.
Over the years, I've come to think of these particular traits as the shared attributes of a chosen people...
MS. COBB...
IF YOU DON'T HAVE PLANS FOR THE MORNING, WHY DON'T YOU FLY WITH ME? YOU COULD TEACH ME A THING OR TWO...
AND I COULD SHOW YOU WHAT A YOUNG PILOT CAN DO.
...the Lord put us here to punch holes in the sky.
GOT UNDER YOUR SKIN, DIDN'T I? YOU ARE ON, KITTEN. WE WILL DUEL AT SUNRISE!

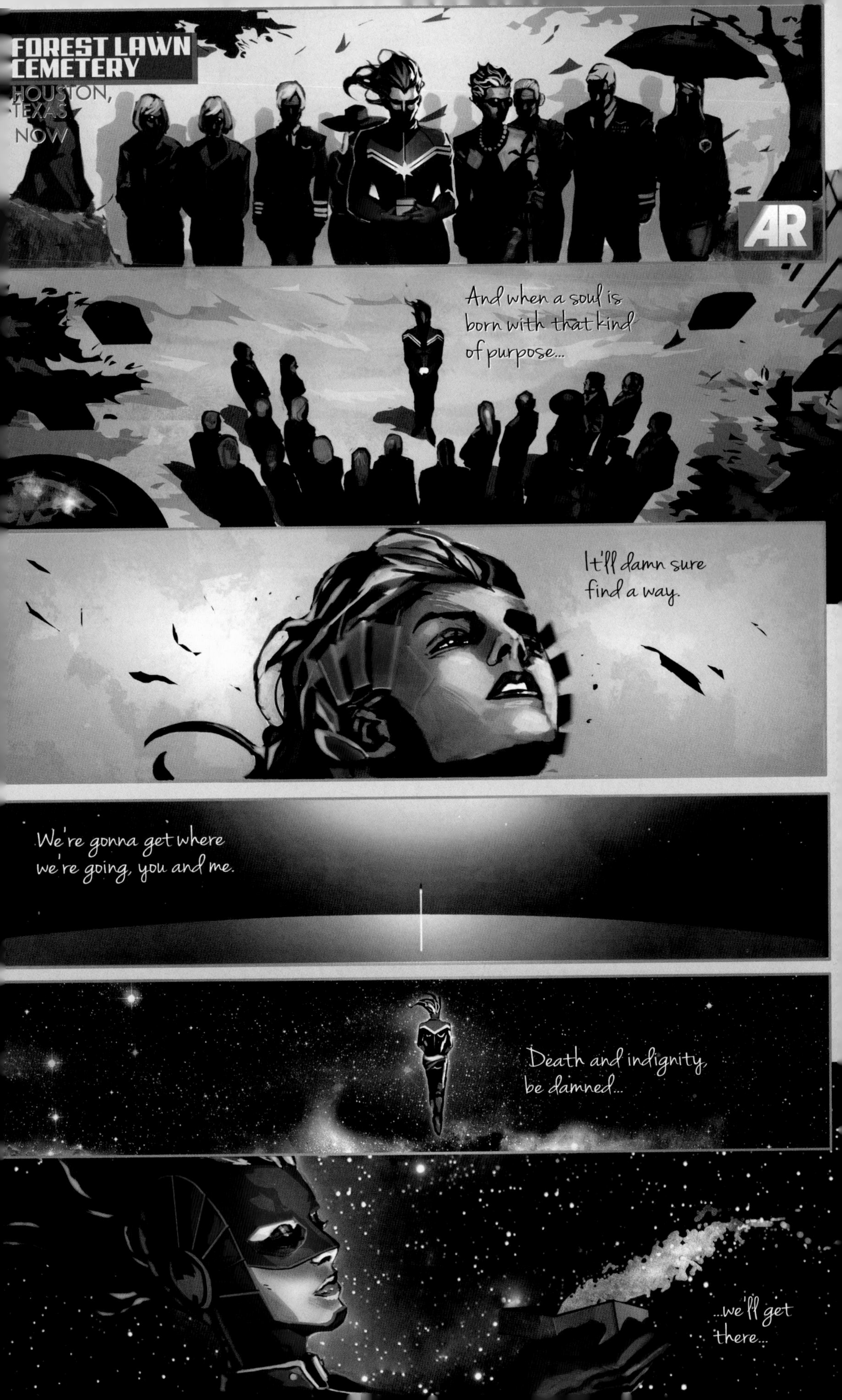

FOREST LAWN CEMETERY
HOUSTON, TEXAS NOW
And when a soul is born with that kind of purpose...
It'll damn sure find a way.
We're gonna get where we're going, you and me.
Death and indignity, be damned...
...we'll get there...

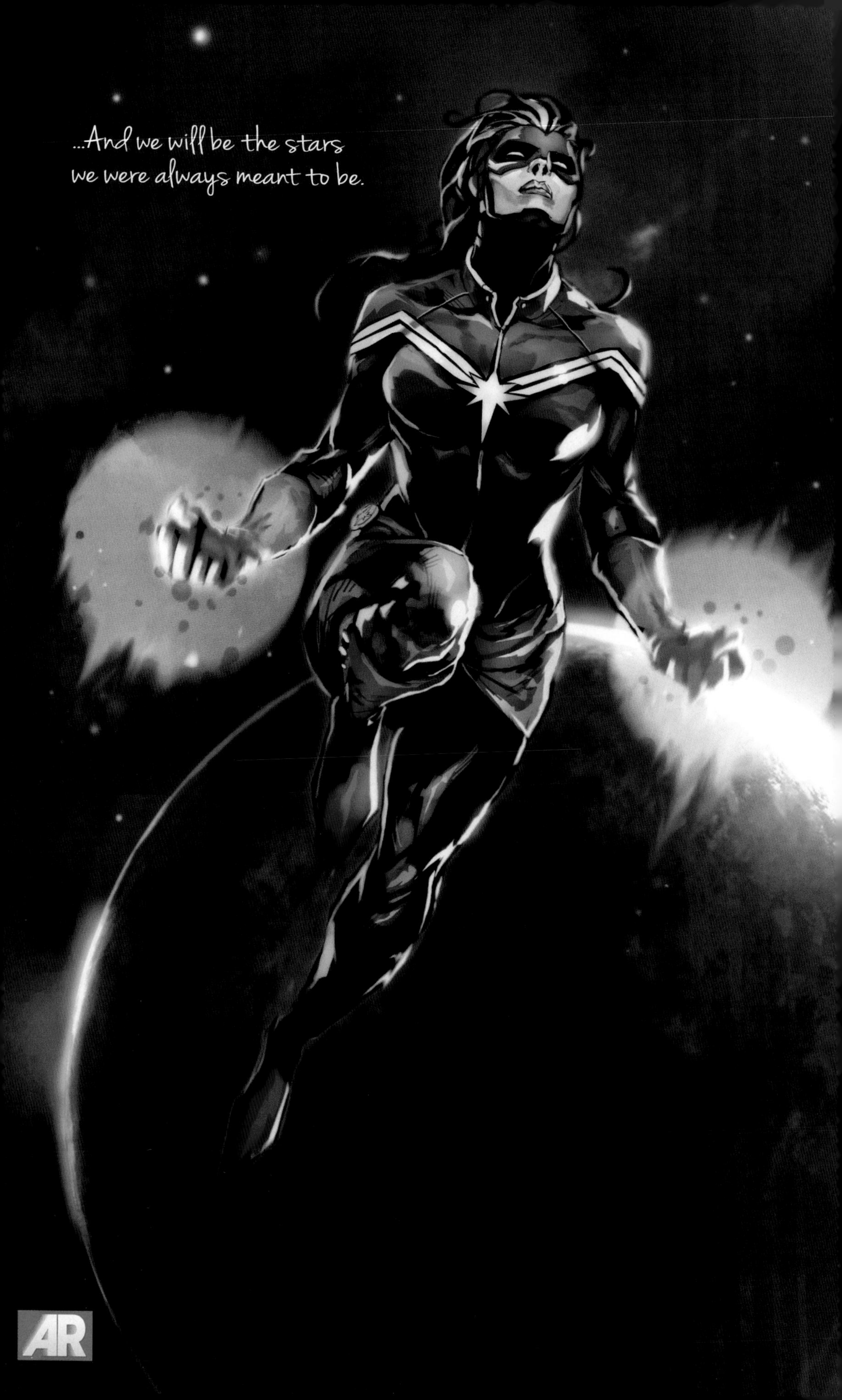
...And we will be the stars
we were always meant to be.

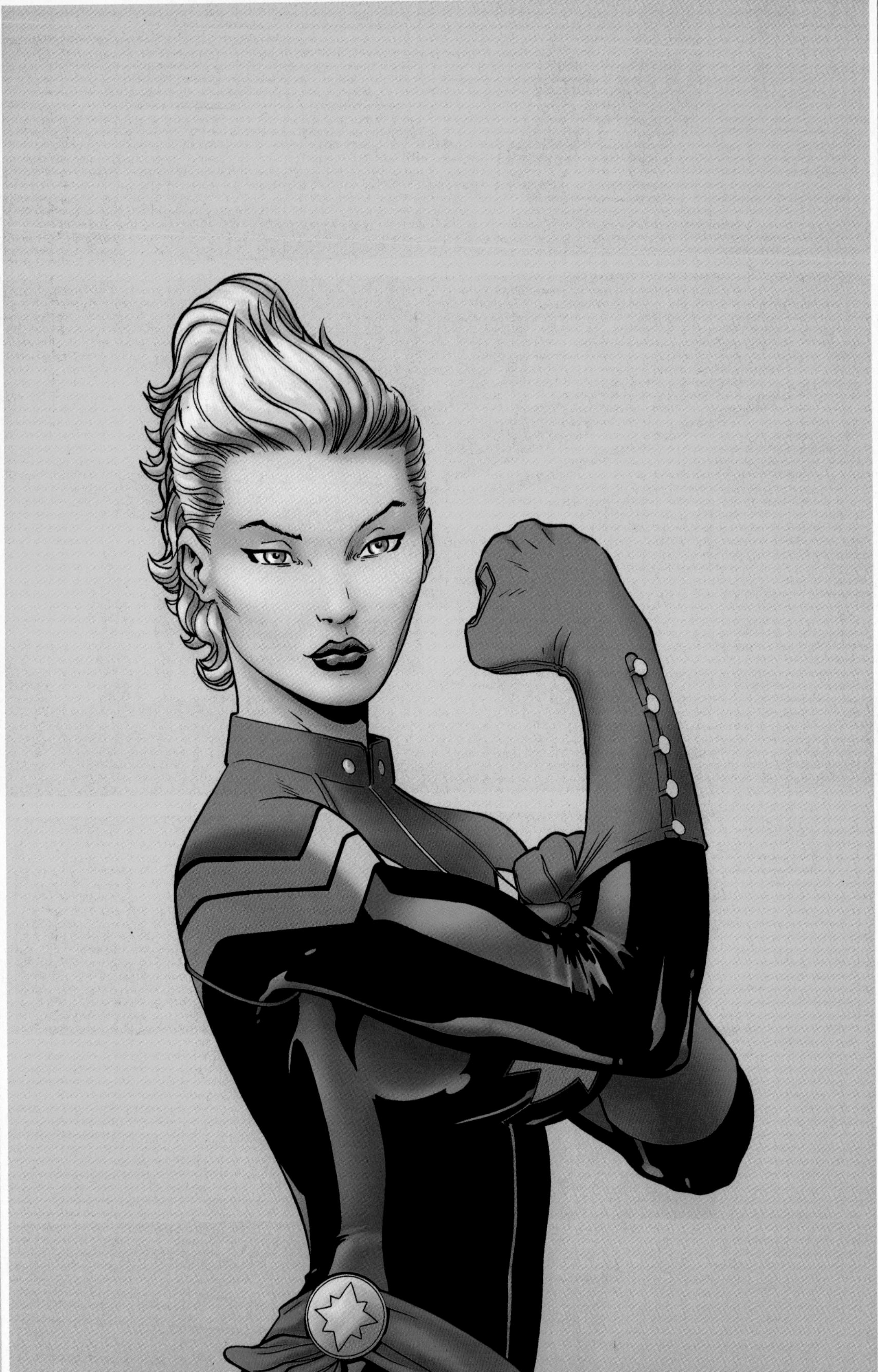

TWO

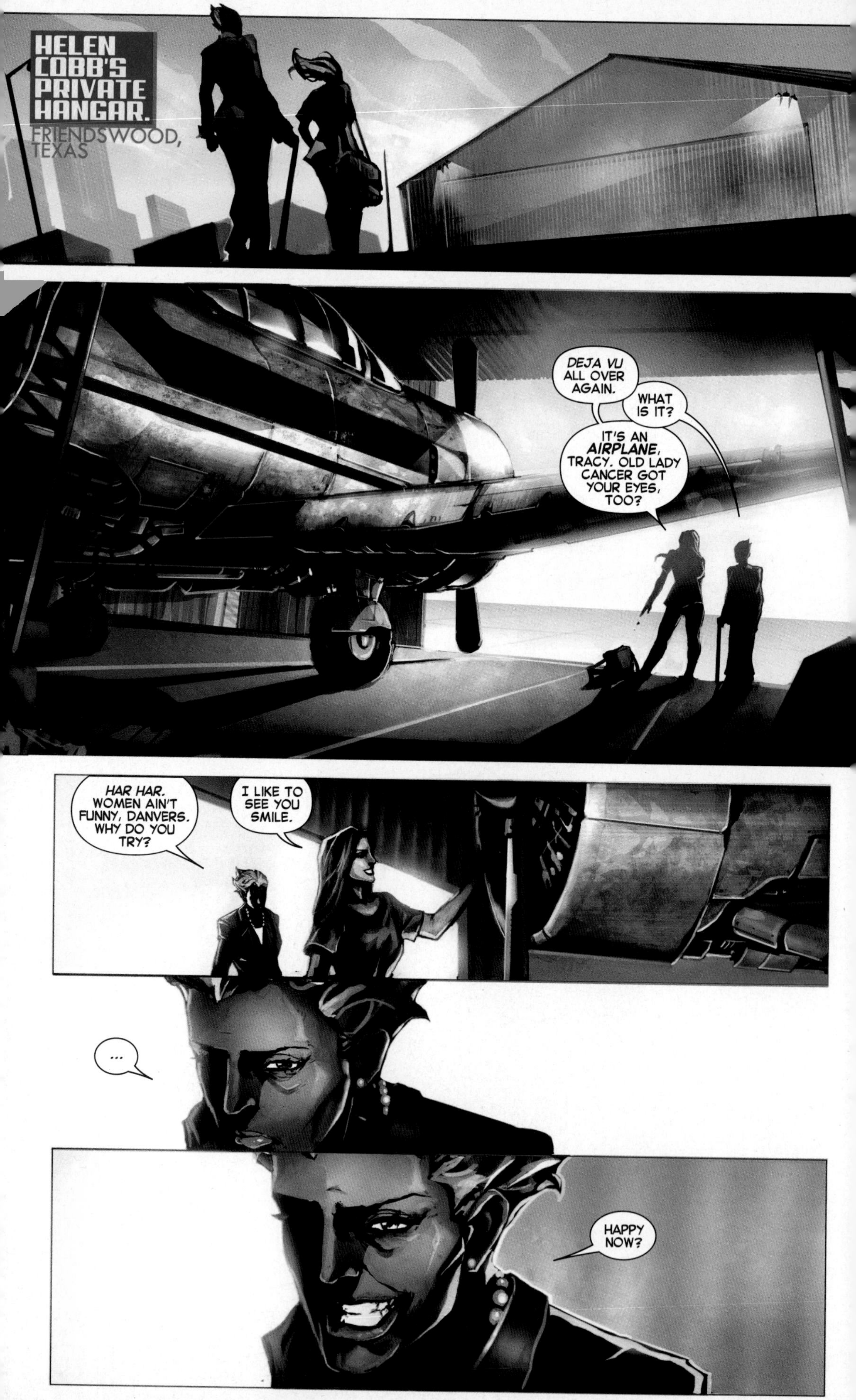
HELEN COBB'S PRIVATE HANGAR.
FRIENDSWOOD, TEXAS
DEJA VU ALL OVER AGAIN.
WHAT IS IT?
IT'S AN AIRPLANE, TRACY. OLD LADY CANCER GOT YOUR EYES, TOO?
HAR HAR. WOMEN AIN'T FUNNY, DANVERS. WHY DO YOU TRY?
I LIKE TO SEE YOU SMILE.
...
HAPPY NOW?

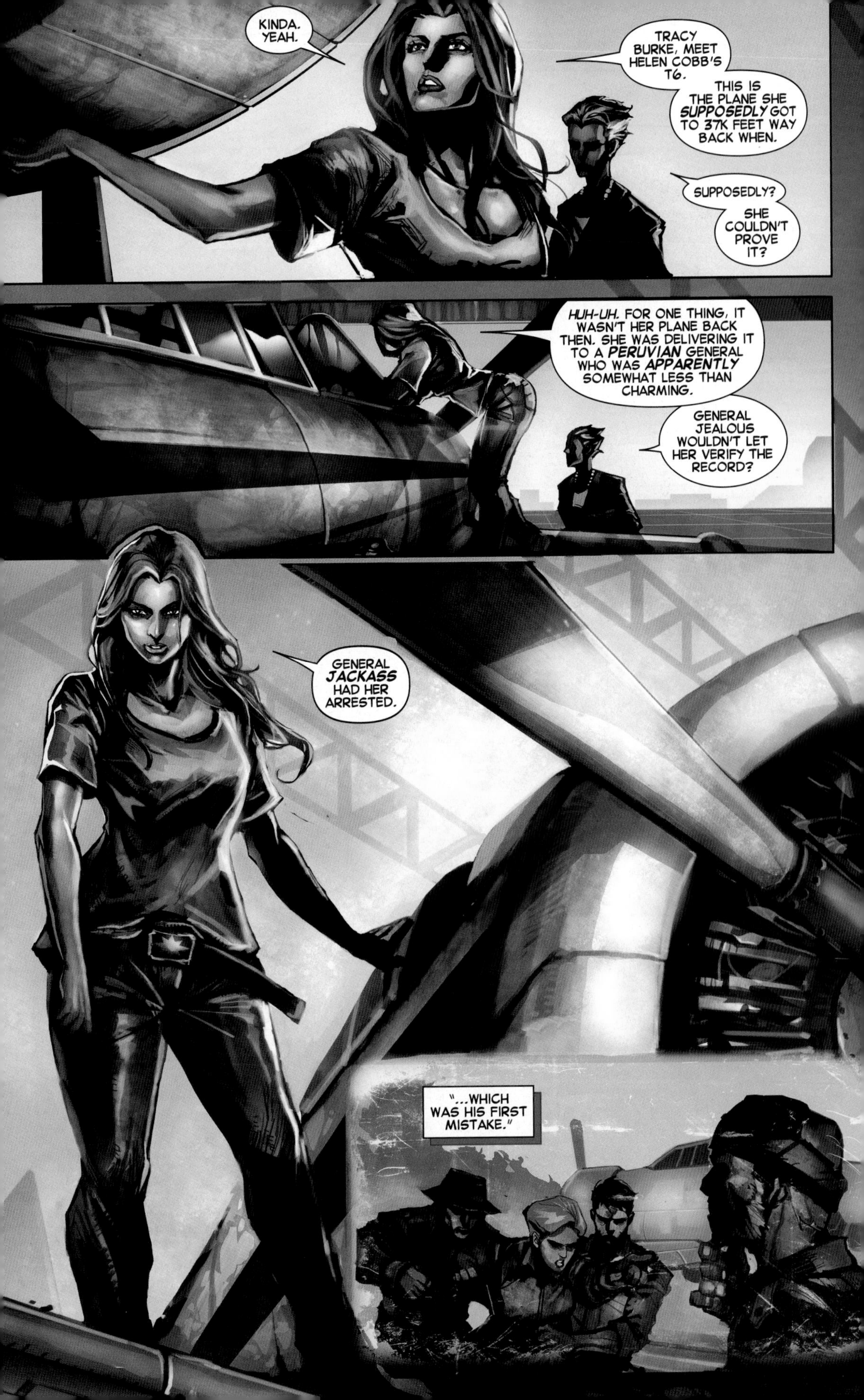
KINDA. YEAH.
TRACY BURKE, MEET HELEN COBB'S T6.
THIS IS THE PLANE SHE SUPPOSEDLY GOT TO 37K FEET WAY BACK WHEN.
SUPPOSEDLY?
SHE COULDN'T PROVE IT?
HUH-UH. FOR ONE THING, IT WASN'T HER PLANE BACK THEN. SHE WAS DELIVERING IT TO A PERUVIAN GENERAL WHO WAS APPARENTLY SOMEWHAT LESS THAN CHARMING.
GENERAL JEALOUS WOULDN'T LET HER VERIFY THE RECORD?
GENERAL JACKASS HAD HER ARRESTED.
"...WHICH WAS HIS FIRST MISTAKE."

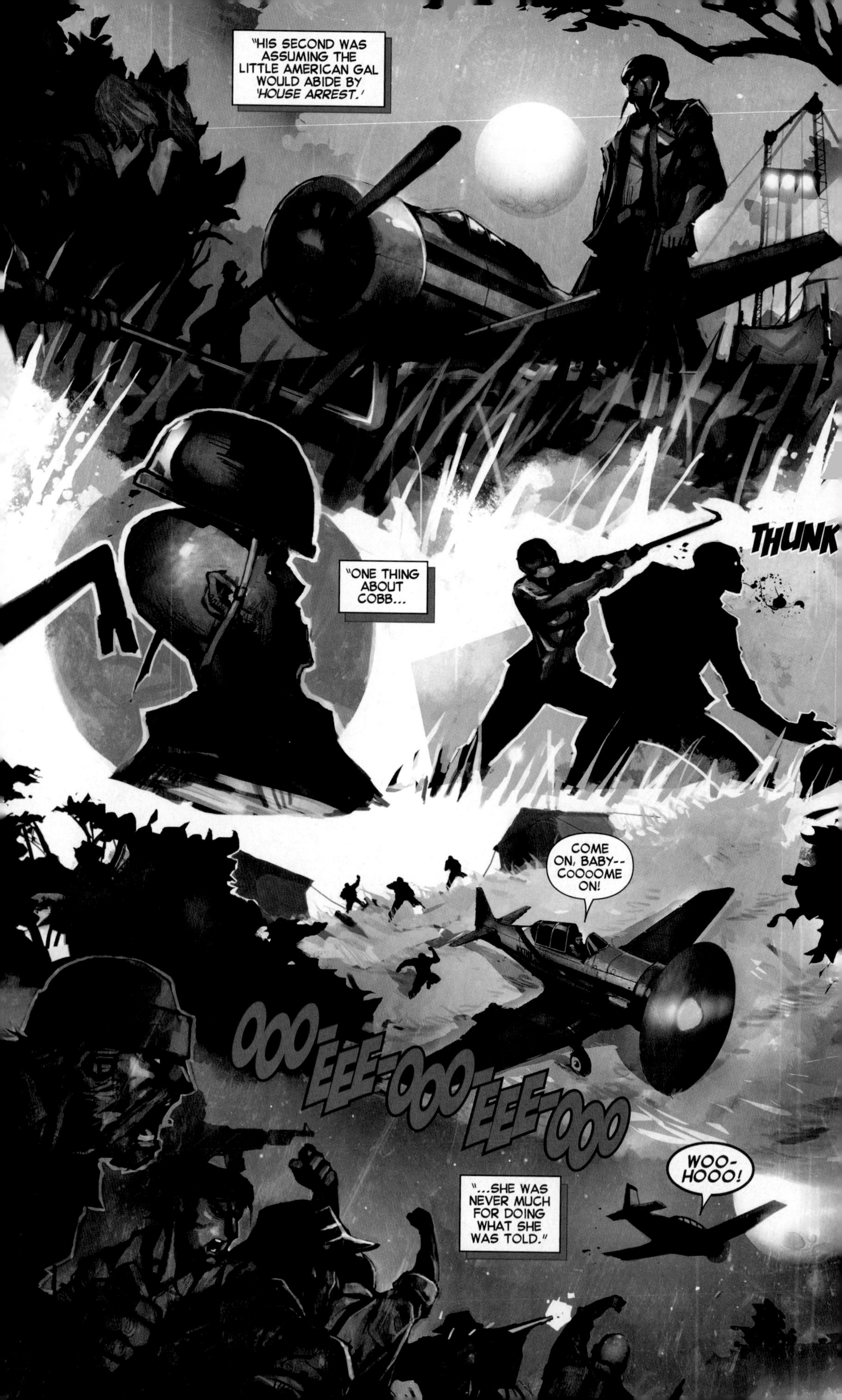
"HIS SECOND WAS ASSUMING THE LITTLE AMERICAN GAL WOULD ABIDE BY 'HOUSE ARREST.'
"ONE THING ABOUT COBB...
THUNK
COME ON, BABY-- COOOOME ON!
OOO-EEE-OOO-EEE-OOO
WOO-HOOO!
"...SHE WAS NEVER MUCH FOR DOING WHAT SHE WAS TOLD."

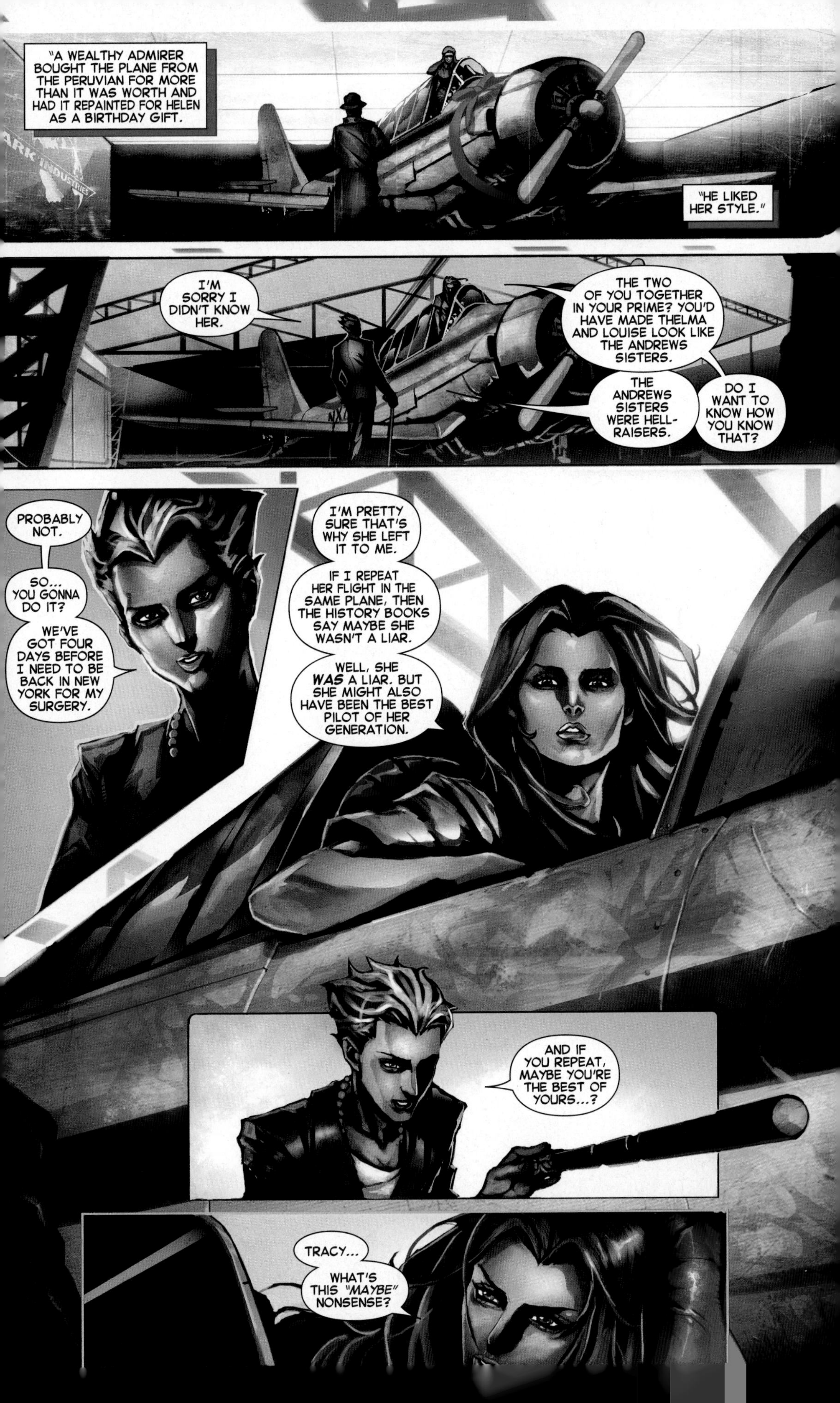
"A WEALTHY ADMIRER BOUGHT THE PLANE FROM THE PERUVIAN FOR MORE THAN IT WAS WORTH AND HAD IT REPAINTED FOR HELEN AS A BIRTHDAY GIFT.
"HE LIKED HER STYLE."
I'M SORRY I DIDN'T KNOW HER.
THE TWO OF YOU TOGETHER IN YOUR PRIME? YOU'D HAVE MADE THELMA AND LOUISE LOOK LIKE THE ANDREWS SISTERS.
THE ANDREWS SISTERS WERE HELL-RAISERS.
DO I WANT TO KNOW HOW YOU KNOW THAT?
PROBABLY NOT.
SO... YOU GONNA DO IT?
WE'VE GOT FOUR DAYS BEFORE I NEED TO BE BACK IN NEW YORK FOR MY SURGERY.
I'M PRETTY SURE THAT'S WHY SHE LEFT IT TO ME.
IF I REPEAT HER FLIGHT IN THE SAME PLANE, THEN THE HISTORY BOOKS SAY MAYBE SHE WASN'T A LIAR.
WELL, SHE *WAS* A LIAR. BUT SHE MIGHT ALSO HAVE BEEN THE BEST PILOT OF HER GENERATION.
AND IF YOU REPEAT, MAYBE YOU'RE THE BEST OF YOURS...?
TRACY...
WHAT'S THIS "*MAYBE*" NONSENSE?

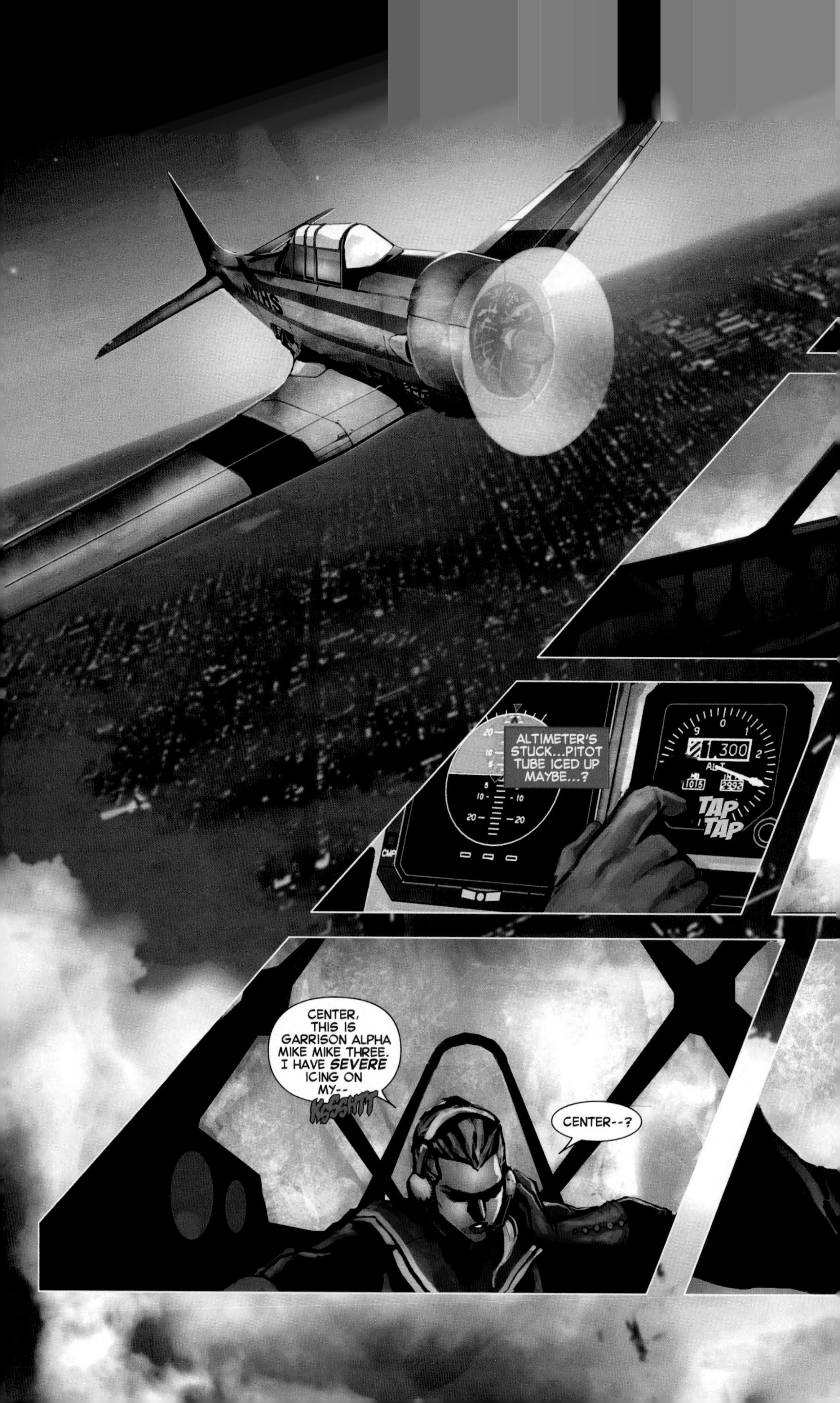
ALTIMETER'S STUCK...PITOT TUBE ICED UP MAYBE...?
TAP TAP
CENTER, THIS IS GARRISON ALPHA MIKE MIKE THREE. I HAVE SEVERE ICING ON MY--
CENTER--?

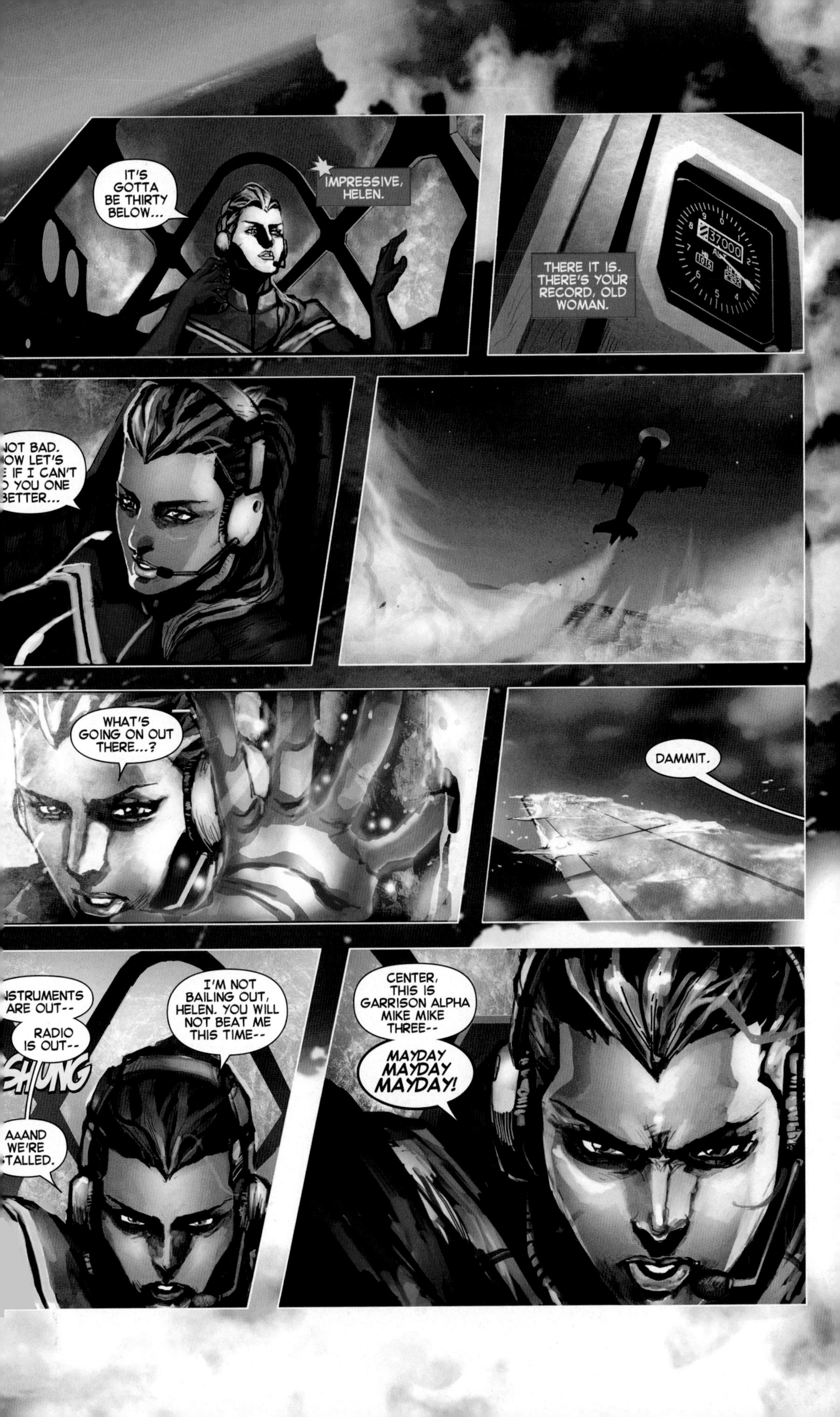
IT'S GOTTA BE THIRTY BELOW...
IMPRESSIVE, HELEN.
THERE IT IS. THERE'S YOUR RECORD, OLD WOMAN.
37000
NOT BAD. OW LET'S E IF I CAN'T O YOU ONE BETTER...
WHAT'S GOING ON OUT THERE...?
DAMMIT.
NSTRUMENTS ARE OUT--
RADIO IS OUT--
SHUNG
AAAND WE'RE TALLED.
I'M NOT BAILING OUT, HELEN. YOU WILL NOT BEAT ME THIS TIME--
CENTER, THIS IS GARRISON ALPHA MIKE MIKE THREE--
MAYDAY MAYDAY MAYDAY!

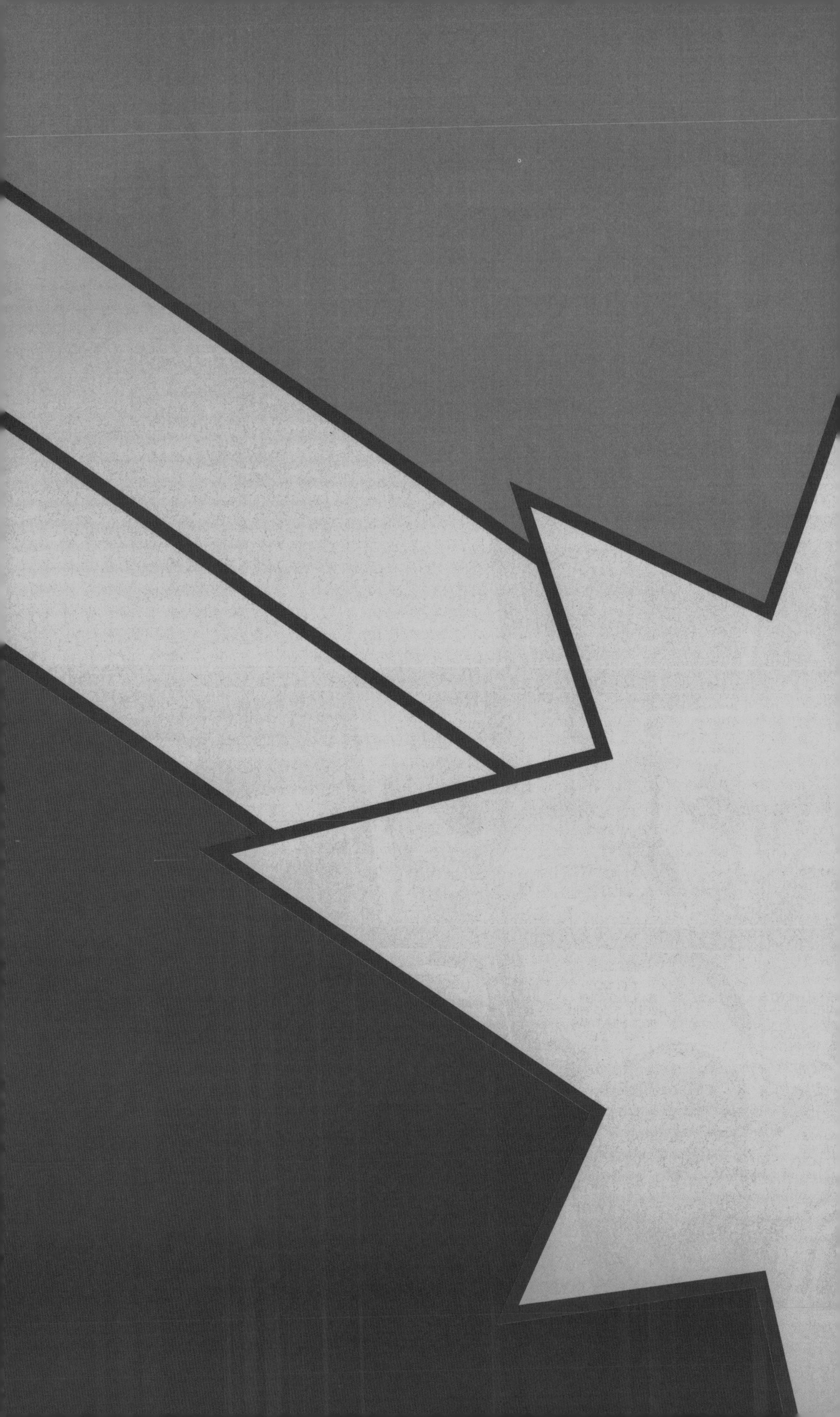

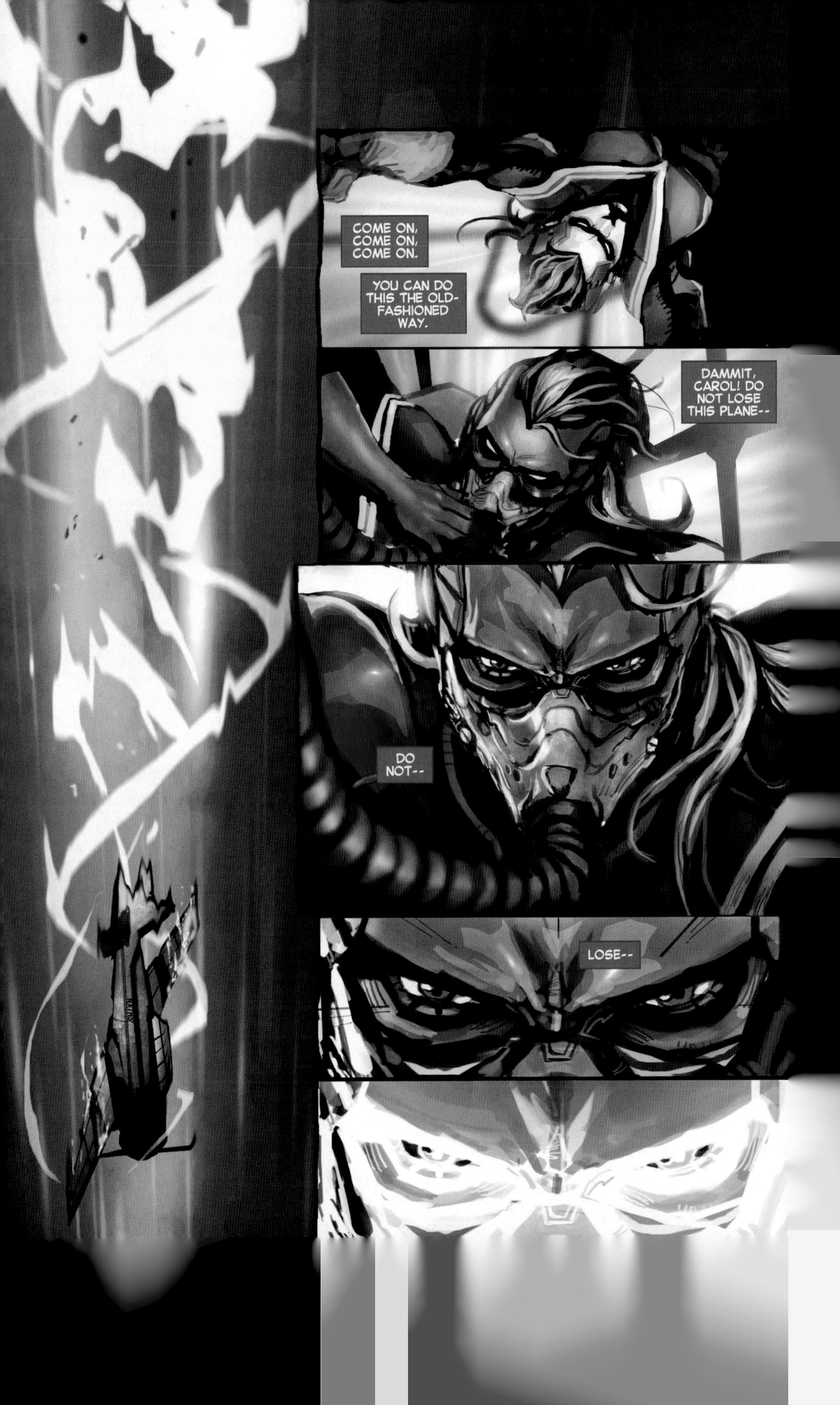

COME ON, COME ON, COME ON.
YOU CAN DO THIS THE OLD-FASHIONED WAY.
DAMMIT, CAROL! DO NOT LOSE THIS PLANE--
DO NOT--
LOSE--

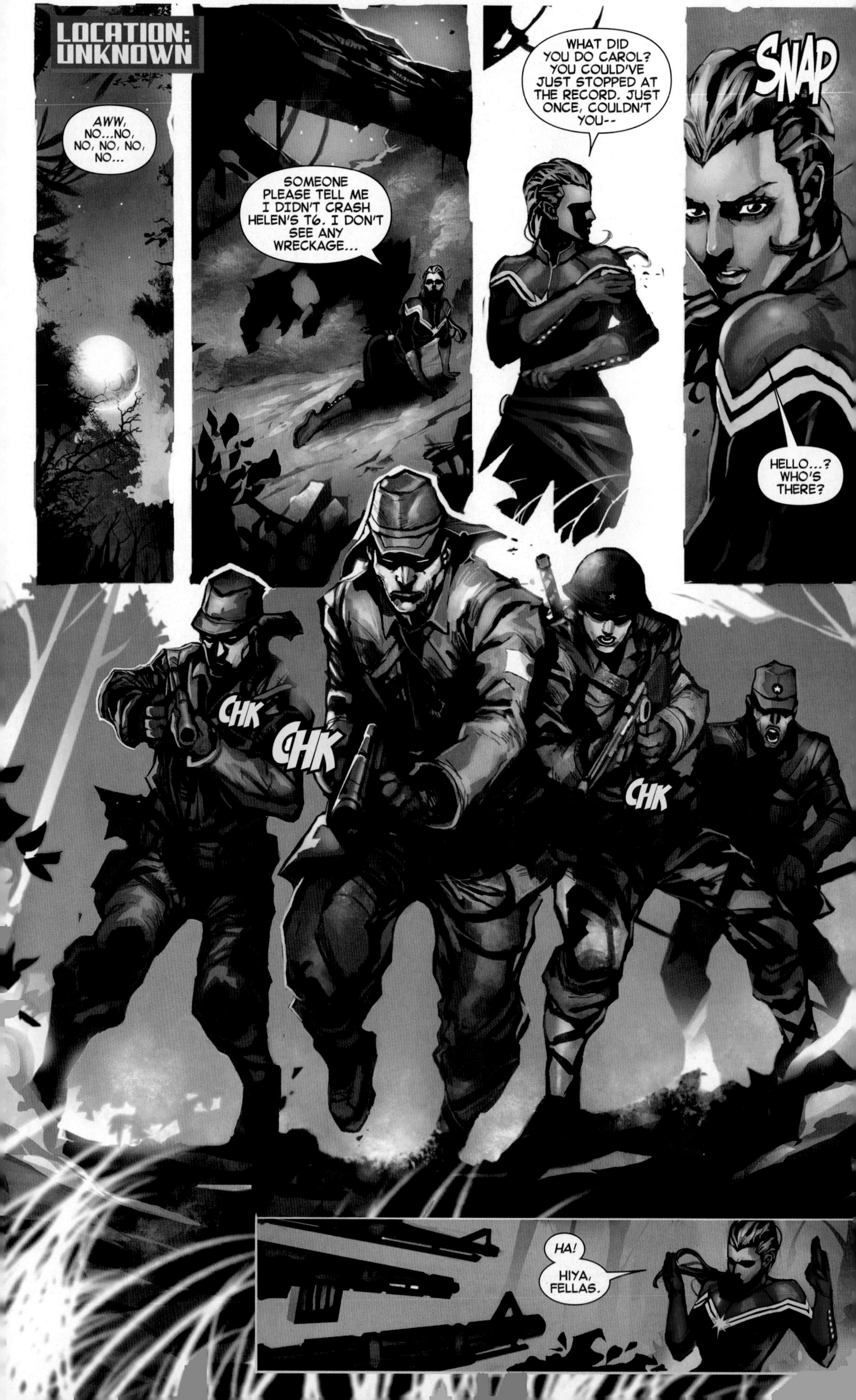
LOCATION: UNKNOWN
AWW, NO...NO, NO, NO, NO, NO...
SOMEONE PLEASE TELL ME I DIDN'T CRASH HELEN'S T6. I DON'T SEE ANY WRECKAGE...
WHAT DID YOU DO CAROL? YOU COULD'VE JUST STOPPED AT THE RECORD. JUST ONCE, COULDN'T YOU--
SNAP
HELLO...? WHO'S THERE?
CHK
CHK
CHK
HA!
HIYA, FELLAS.

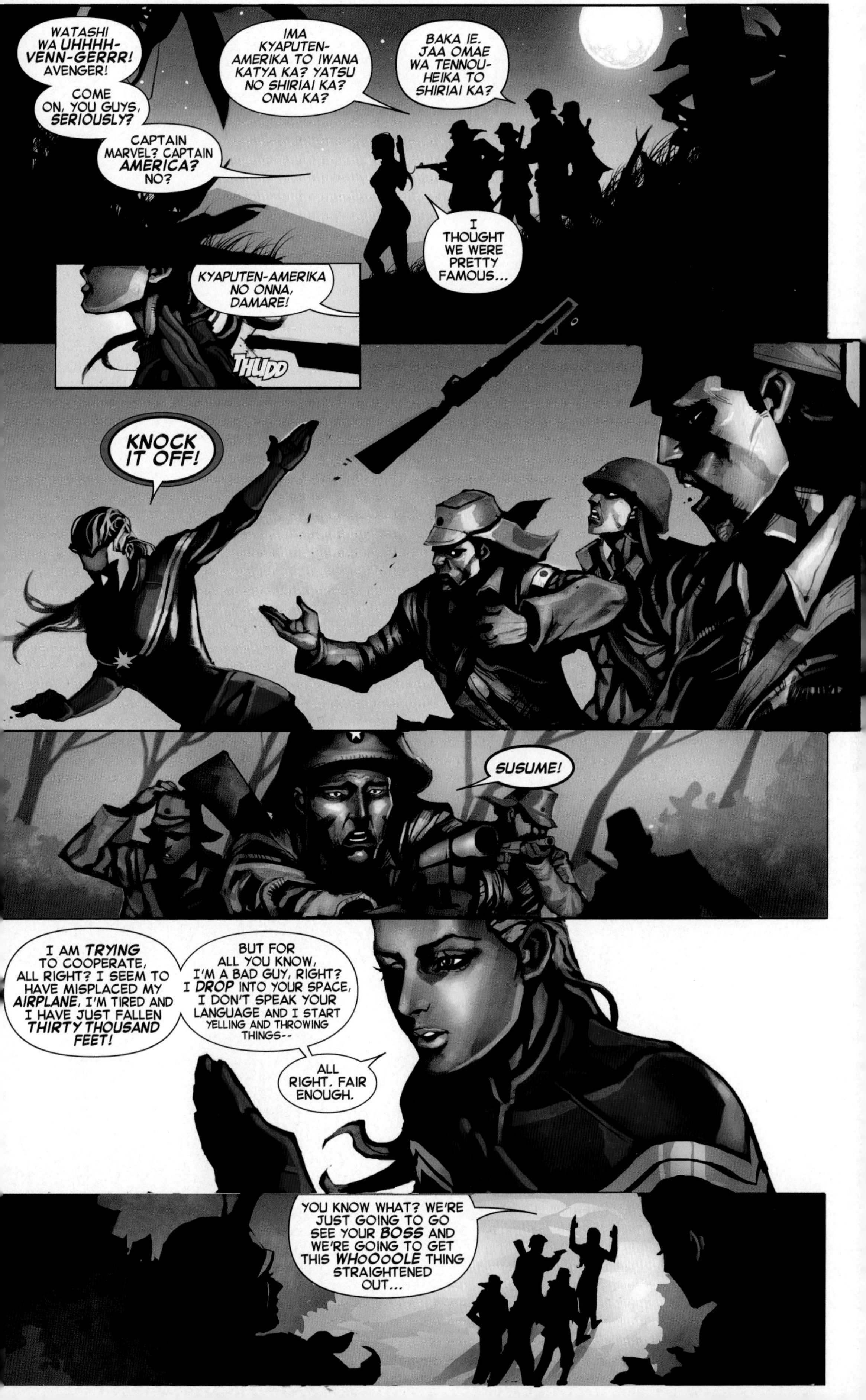
WATASHI WA UHHHH-VENN-GERRR! AVENGER!
COME ON, YOU GUYS, SERIOUSLY?
CAPTAIN MARVEL? CAPTAIN AMERICA? NO?
IMA KYAPUTEN-AMERIKA TO IWANA KATYA KA? YATSU NO SHIRIAI KA? ONNA KA?
BAKA IE. JAA OMAE WA TENNOU-HEIKA TO SHIRIAI KA?
I THOUGHT WE WERE PRETTY FAMOUS...
KYAPUTEN-AMERIKA NO ONNA, DAMARE!
THUDD
KNOCK IT OFF!
SUSUME!
I AM TRYING TO COOPERATE, ALL RIGHT? I SEEM TO HAVE MISPLACED MY AIRPLANE, I'M TIRED AND I HAVE JUST FALLEN THIRTY THOUSAND FEET!
BUT FOR ALL YOU KNOW, I'M A BAD GUY, RIGHT? I DROP INTO YOUR SPACE, I DON'T SPEAK YOUR LANGUAGE AND I START YELLING AND THROWING THINGS--
ALL RIGHT. FAIR ENOUGH.
YOU KNOW WHAT? WE'RE JUST GOING TO GO SEE YOUR BOSS AND WE'RE GOING TO GET THIS WHOOOOLE THING STRAIGHTENED OUT...

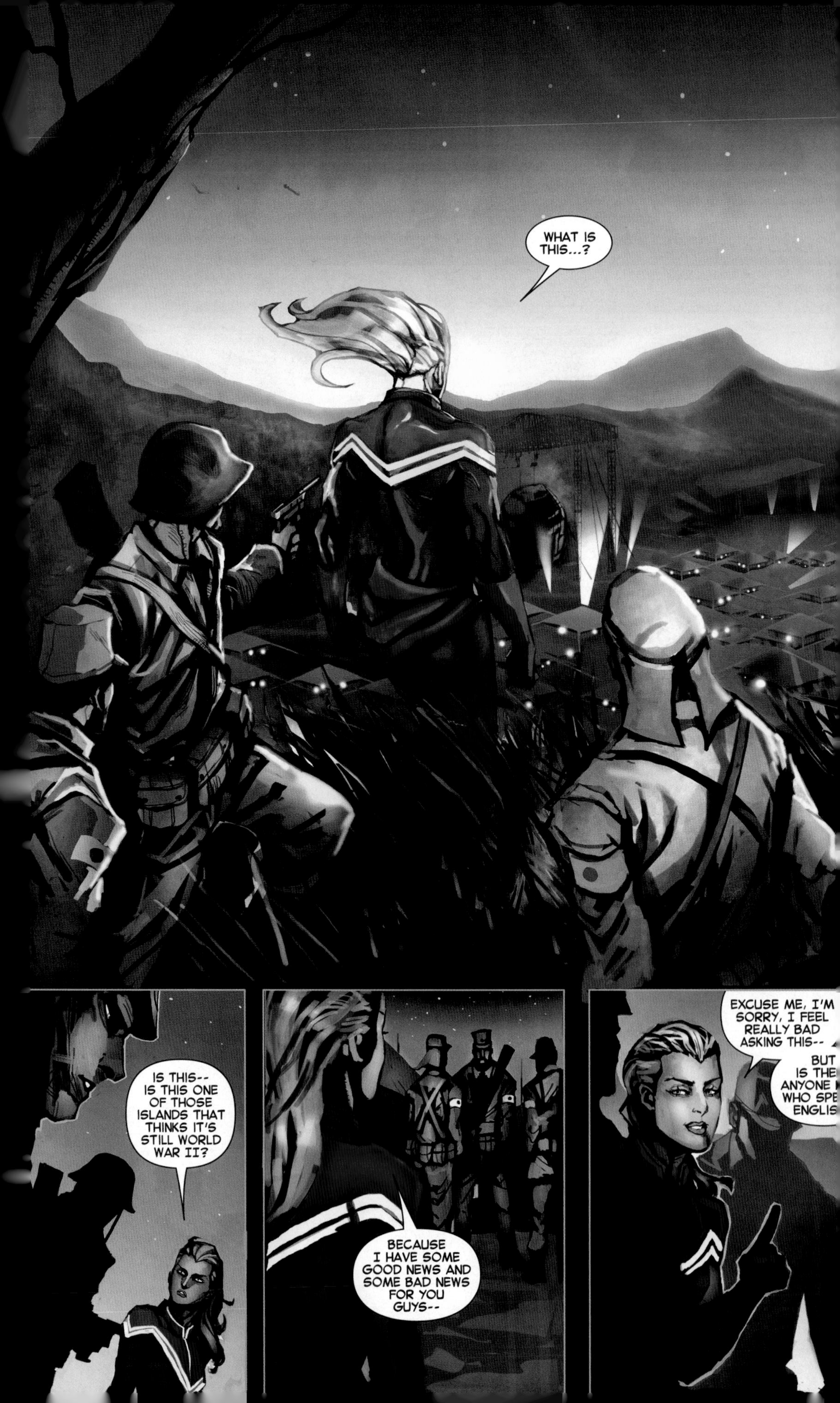
WHAT IS THIS...?
IS THIS-- IS THIS ONE OF THOSE ISLANDS THAT THINKS IT'S STILL WORLD WAR II?
BECAUSE I HAVE SOME GOOD NEWS AND SOME BAD NEWS FOR YOU GUYS--
EXCUSE ME, I'M SORRY, I FEEL REALLY BAD ASKING THIS--
BUT IS THE ANYONE WHO SPE ENGLIS

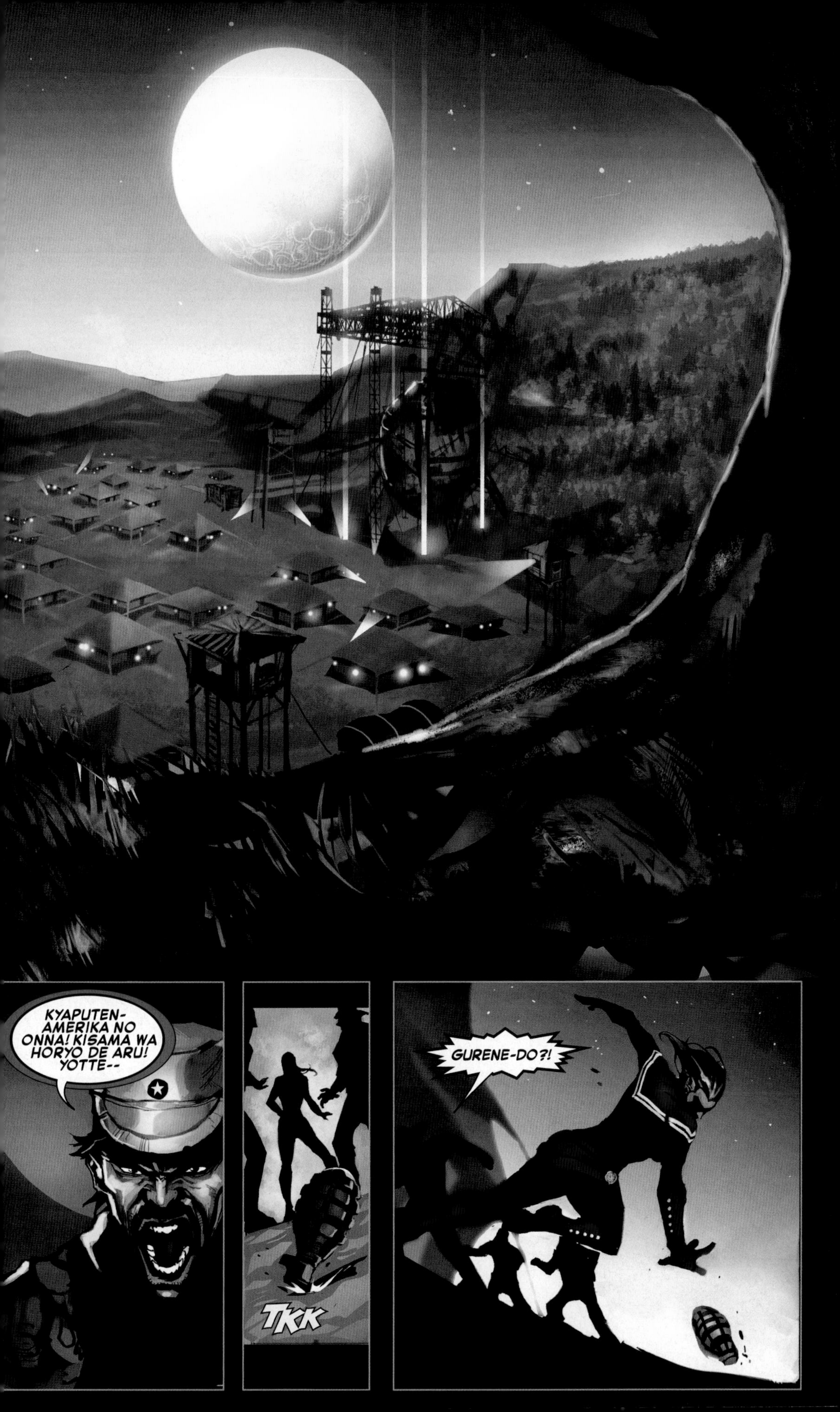
KYAPUTEN-AMERIKA NO ONNA! KISAMA WA HORYO DE ARU! YOTTE--
TKK
GURENE-DO?!

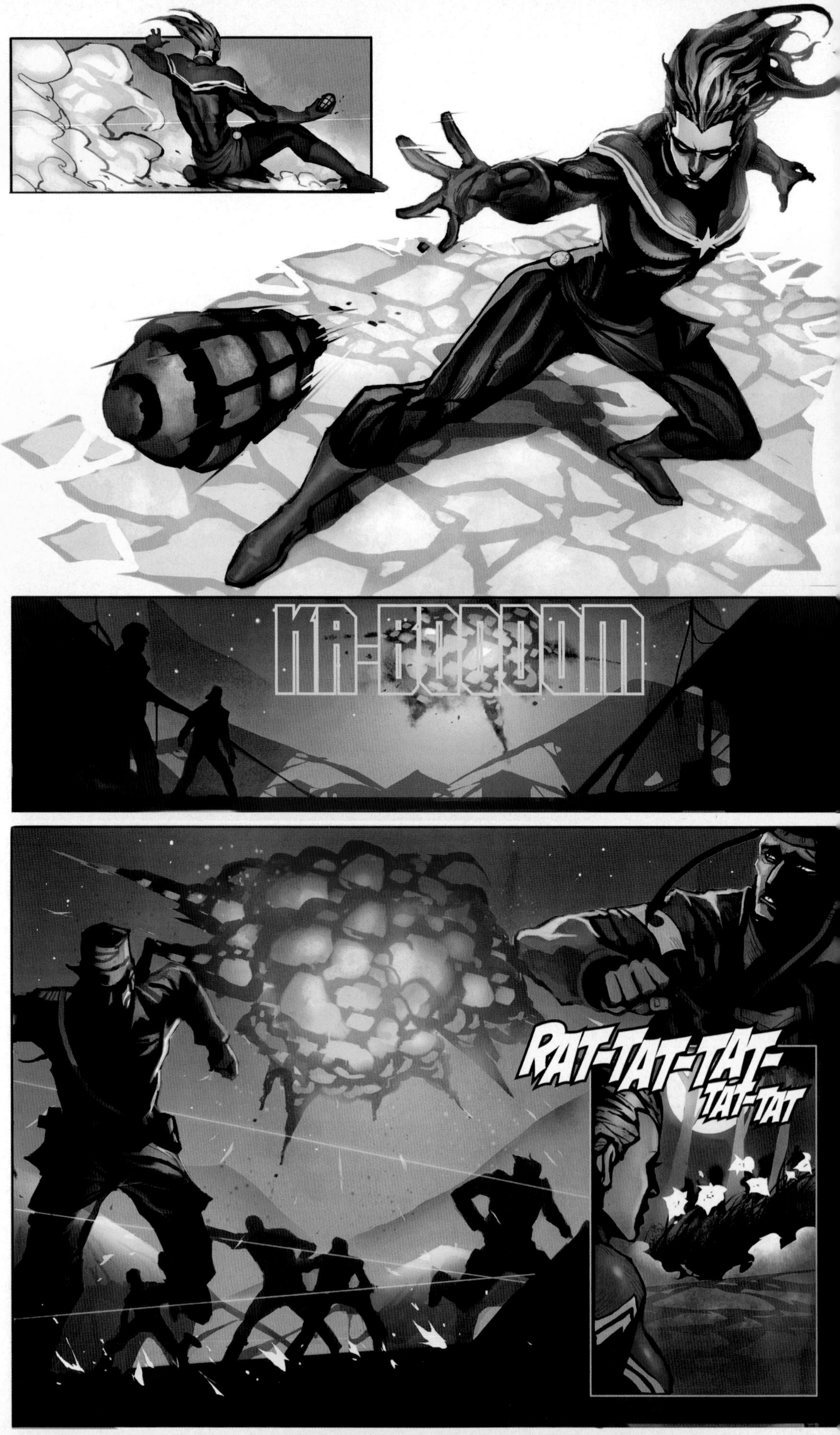
KA-BOOOOM
RAT-TAT-TAT-
TAT-TAT

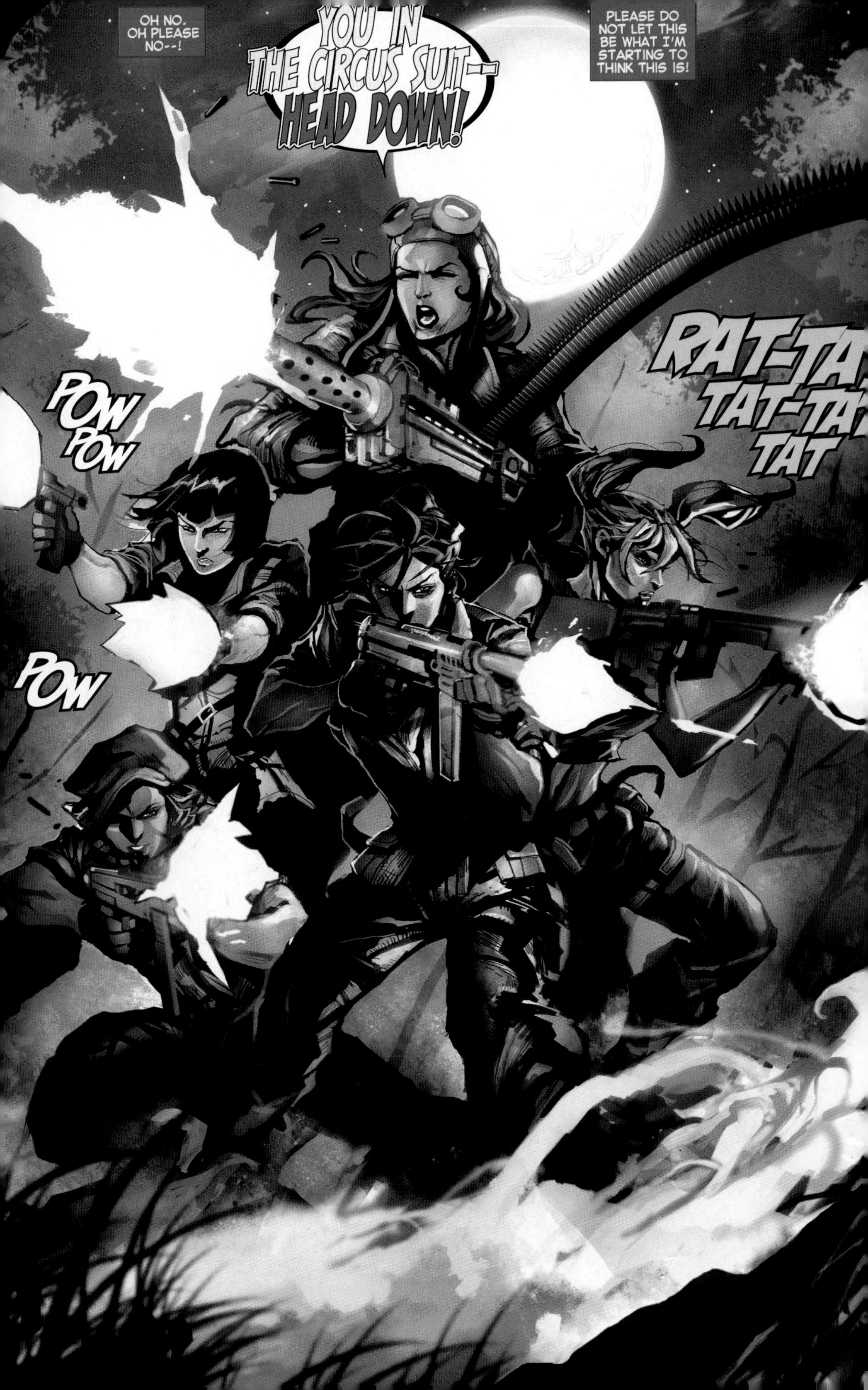
OH NO. OH PLEASE NO--!
YOU IN THE CIRCUS SUIT-- HEAD DOWN!
PLEASE DO NOT LET THIS BE WHAT I'M STARTING TO THINK THIS IS!
RAT-TA TAT-TA TAT
POW POW
POW

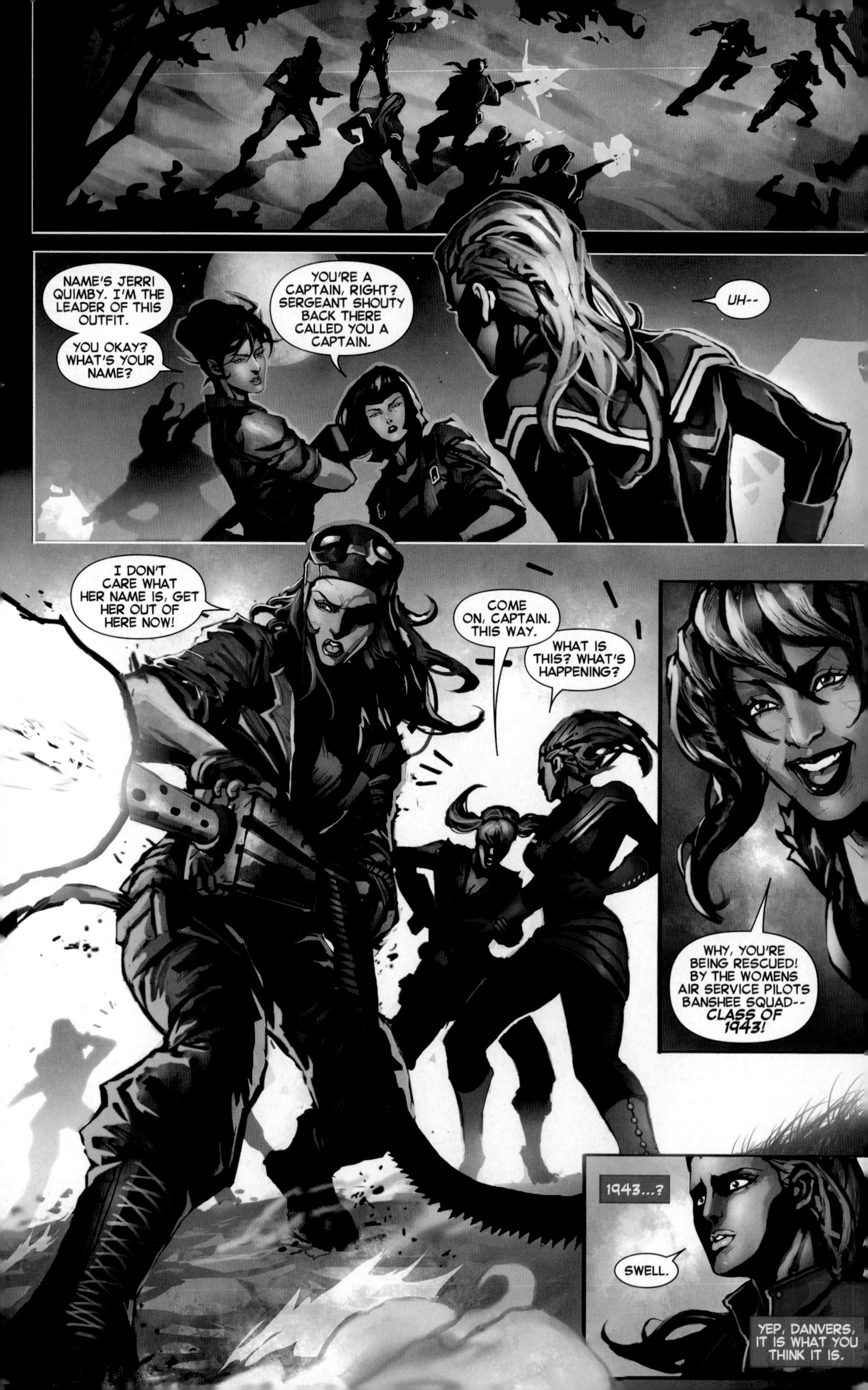
NAME'S JERRI QUIMBY. I'M THE LEADER OF THIS OUTFIT.
YOU OKAY? WHAT'S YOUR NAME?
YOU'RE A CAPTAIN, RIGHT? SERGEANT SHOUTY BACK THERE CALLED YOU A CAPTAIN.
UH--
I DON'T CARE WHAT HER NAME IS, GET HER OUT OF HERE NOW!
COME ON, CAPTAIN. THIS WAY.
WHAT IS THIS? WHAT'S HAPPENING?
WHY, YOU'RE BEING RESCUED! BY THE WOMENS AIR SERVICE PILOTS BANSHEE SQUAD-- CLASS OF 1943!
1943...?
SWELL.
YEP, DANVERS, IT IS WHAT YOU THINK IT IS.

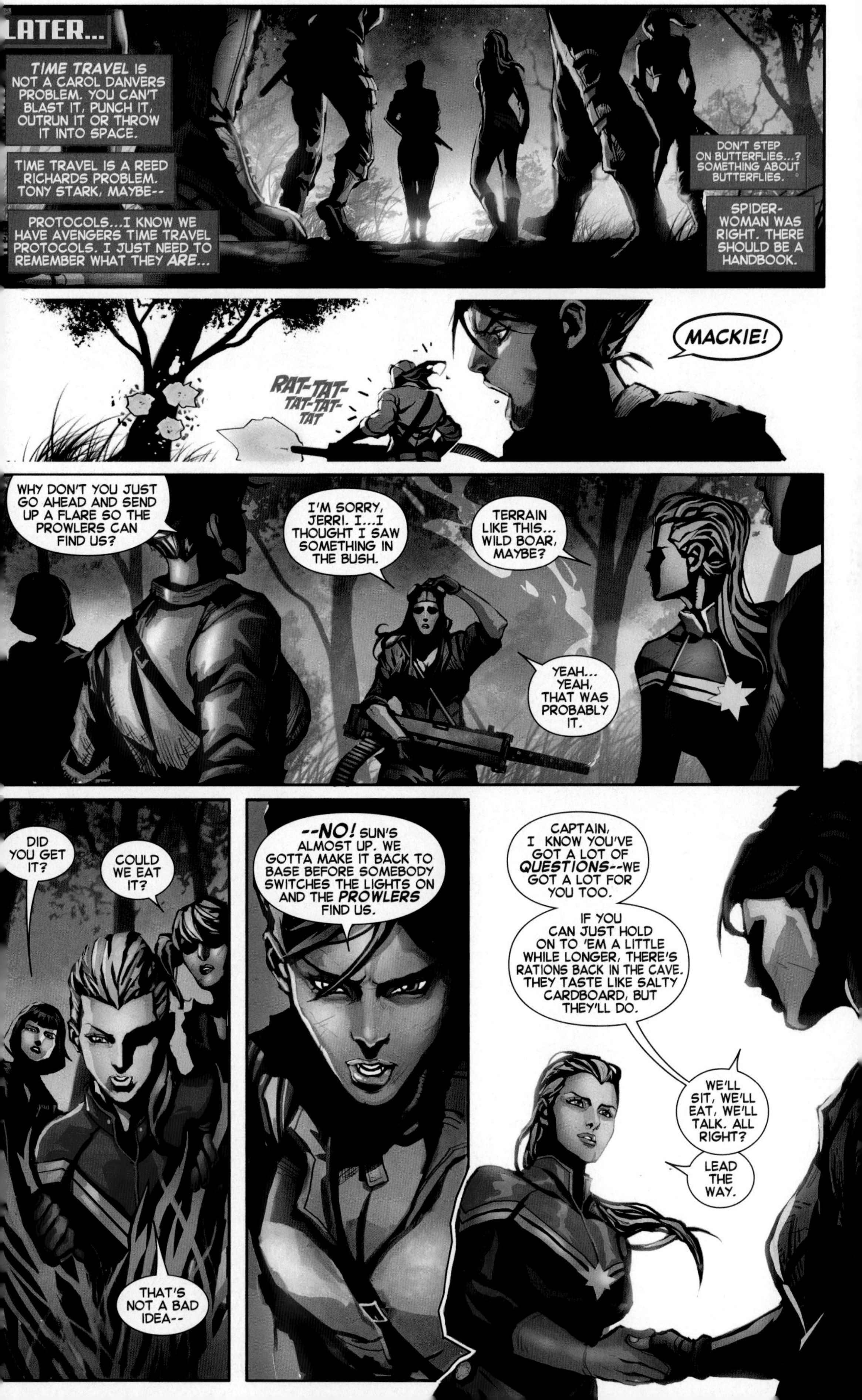
LATER...
TIME TRAVEL IS NOT A CAROL DANVERS PROBLEM. YOU CAN'T BLAST IT, PUNCH IT, OUTRUN IT OR THROW IT INTO SPACE.
TIME TRAVEL IS A REED RICHARDS PROBLEM. TONY STARK, MAYBE--
PROTOCOLS...I KNOW WE HAVE AVENGERS TIME TRAVEL PROTOCOLS. I JUST NEED TO REMEMBER WHAT THEY ARE...
DON'T STEP ON BUTTERFLIES...? SOMETHING ABOUT BUTTERFLIES.
SPIDER-WOMAN WAS RIGHT. THERE SHOULD BE A HANDBOOK.
RAT-TAT-TAT-TAT-TAT
MACKIE!
WHY DON'T YOU JUST GO AHEAD AND SEND UP A FLARE SO THE PROWLERS CAN FIND US?
I'M SORRY, JERRI. I...I THOUGHT I SAW SOMETHING IN THE BUSH.
TERRAIN LIKE THIS... WILD BOAR, MAYBE?
YEAH... YEAH, THAT WAS PROBABLY IT.
DID YOU GET IT?
COULD WE EAT IT?
THAT'S NOT A BAD IDEA--
--NO! SUN'S ALMOST UP. WE GOTTA MAKE IT BACK TO BASE BEFORE SOMEBODY SWITCHES THE LIGHTS ON AND THE PROWLERS FIND US.
CAPTAIN, I KNOW YOU'VE GOT A LOT OF QUESTIONS--WE GOT A LOT FOR YOU TOO.
IF YOU CAN JUST HOLD ON TO 'EM A LITTLE WHILE LONGER, THERE'S RATIONS BACK IN THE CAVE. THEY TASTE LIKE SALTY CARDBOARD, BUT THEY'LL DO.
WE'LL SIT, WE'LL EAT, WE'LL TALK. ALL RIGHT?
LEAD THE WAY.

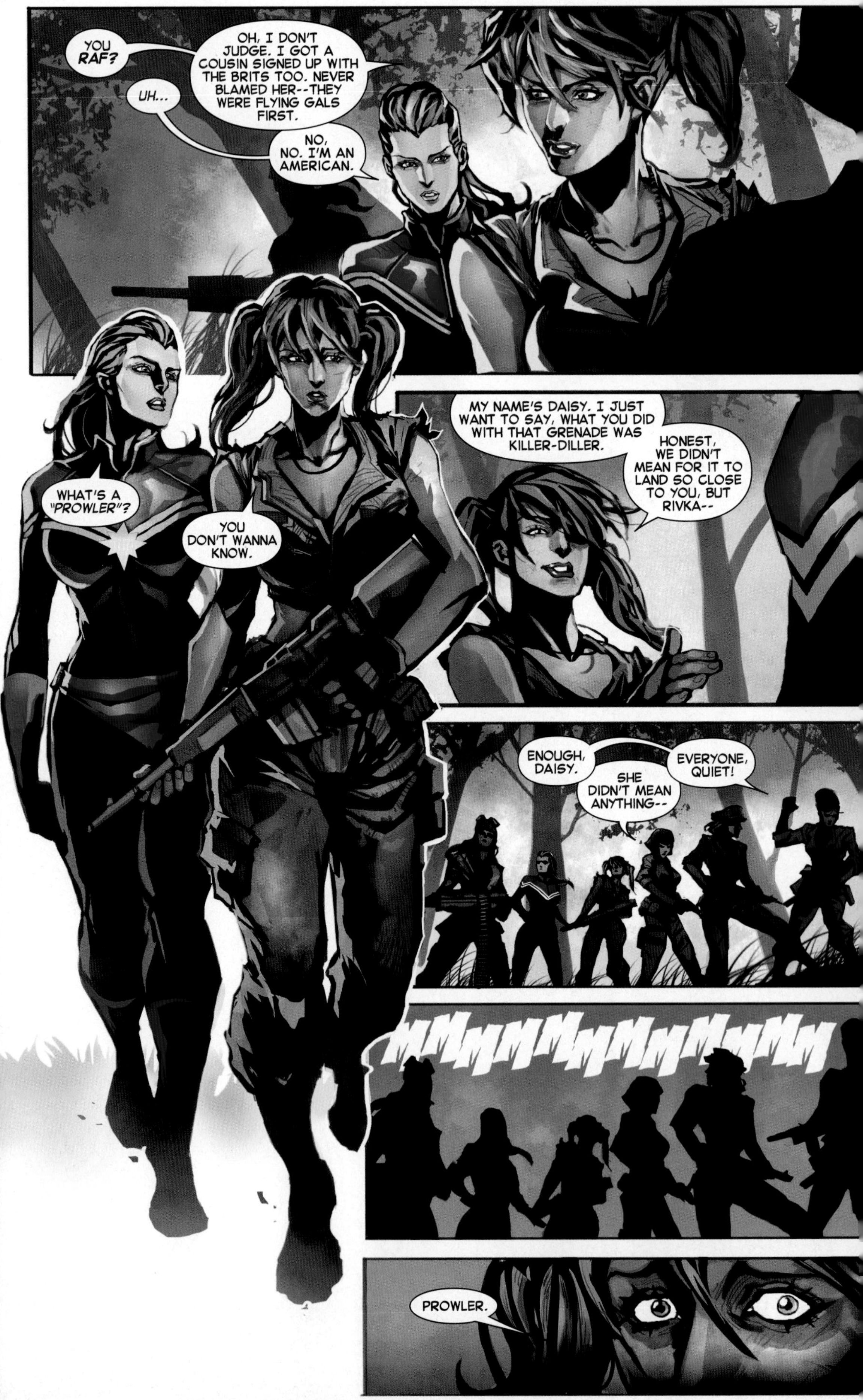
YOU RAF?
OH, I DON'T JUDGE. I GOT A COUSIN SIGNED UP WITH THE BRITS TOO. NEVER BLAMED HER--THEY WERE FLYING GALS FIRST.
UH...
NO, NO. I'M AN AMERICAN.
WHAT'S A "PROWLER"?
YOU DON'T WANNA KNOW.
MY NAME'S DAISY. I JUST WANT TO SAY, WHAT YOU DID WITH THAT GRENADE WAS KILLER-DILLER.
HONEST, WE DIDN'T MEAN FOR IT TO LAND SO CLOSE TO YOU, BUT RIVKA--
ENOUGH, DAISY.
SHE DIDN'T MEAN ANYTHING--
EVERYONE, QUIET!
MMMMMMMMMMMMMMMM
PROWLER.

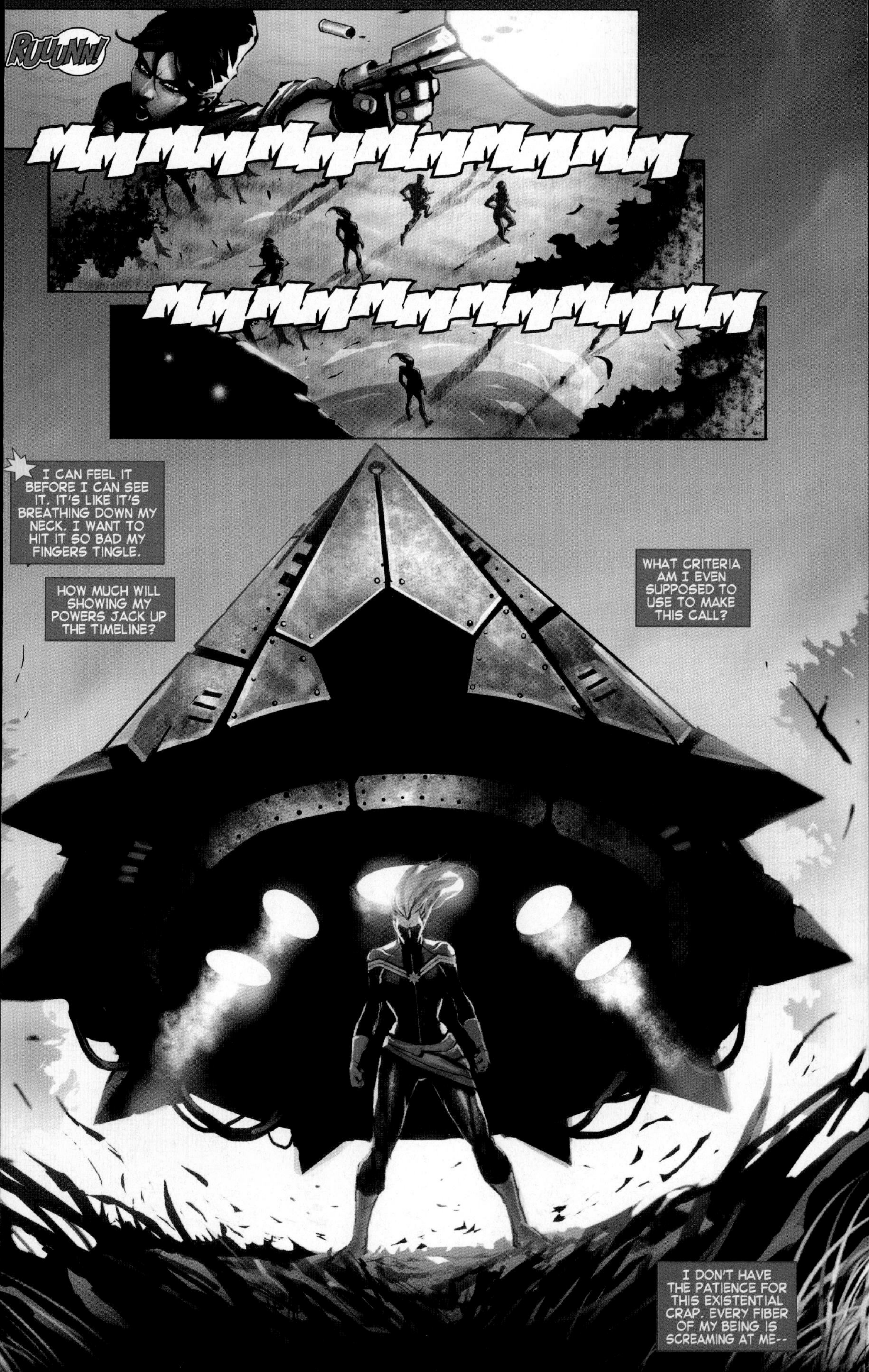
RUUUNN!
MMMMMMMMMMMMMMMM
MMMMMMMMMMMMMMMMMM
I CAN FEEL IT BEFORE I CAN SEE IT. IT'S LIKE IT'S BREATHING DOWN MY NECK. I WANT TO HIT IT SO BAD MY FINGERS TINGLE.
HOW MUCH WILL SHOWING MY POWERS JACK UP THE TIMELINE?
WHAT CRITERIA AM I EVEN SUPPOSED TO USE TO MAKE THIS CALL?
I DON'T HAVE THE PATIENCE FOR THIS EXISTENTIAL CRAP. EVERY FIBER OF MY BEING IS SCREAMING AT ME--

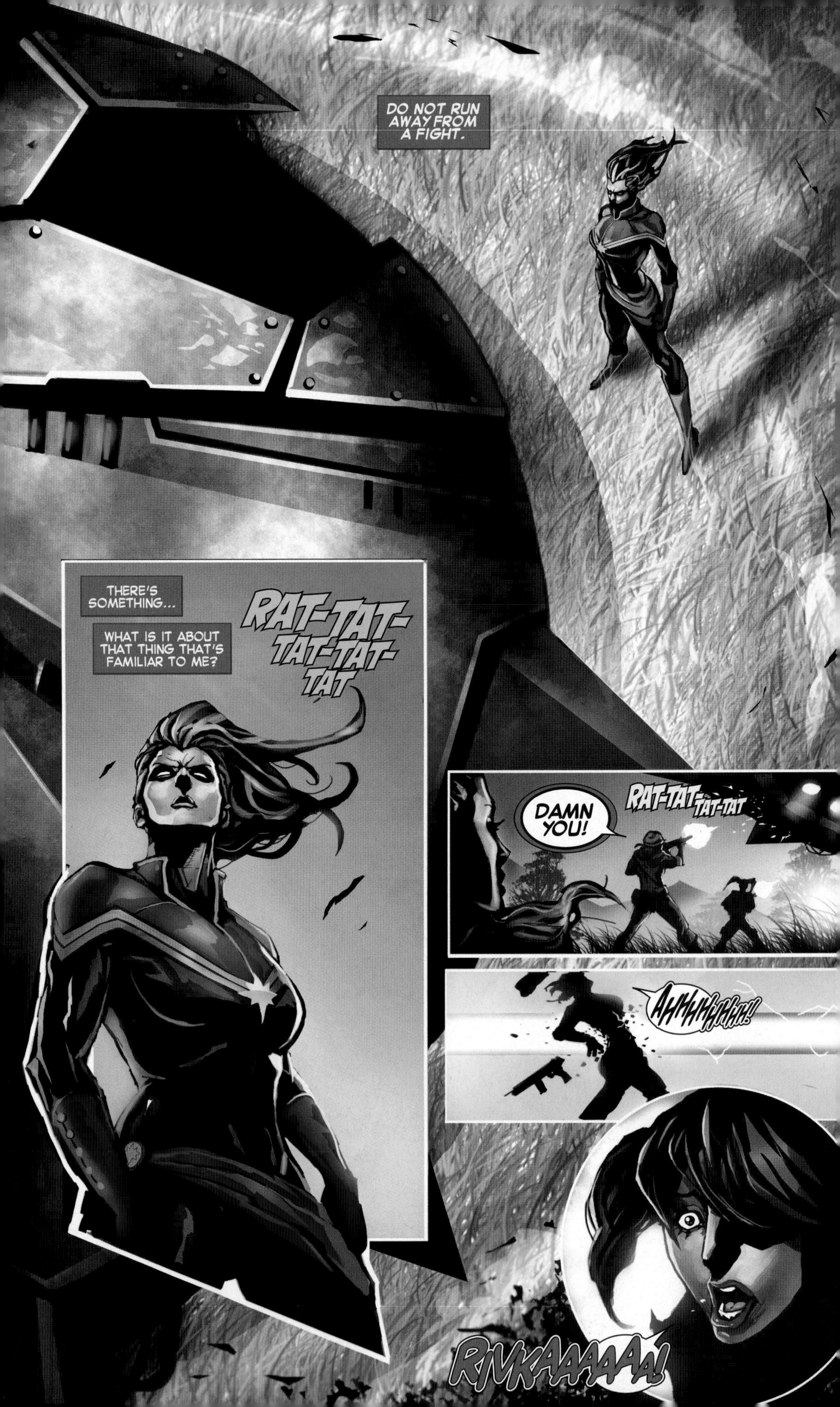
DO NOT RUN AWAY FROM A FIGHT.
THERE'S SOMETHING...
WHAT IS IT ABOUT THAT THING THAT'S FAMILIAR TO ME?
RAT-TAT-TAT-TAT-TAT
DAMN YOU!
RAT-TAT-TAT-TAT
RINKAAAAAA!

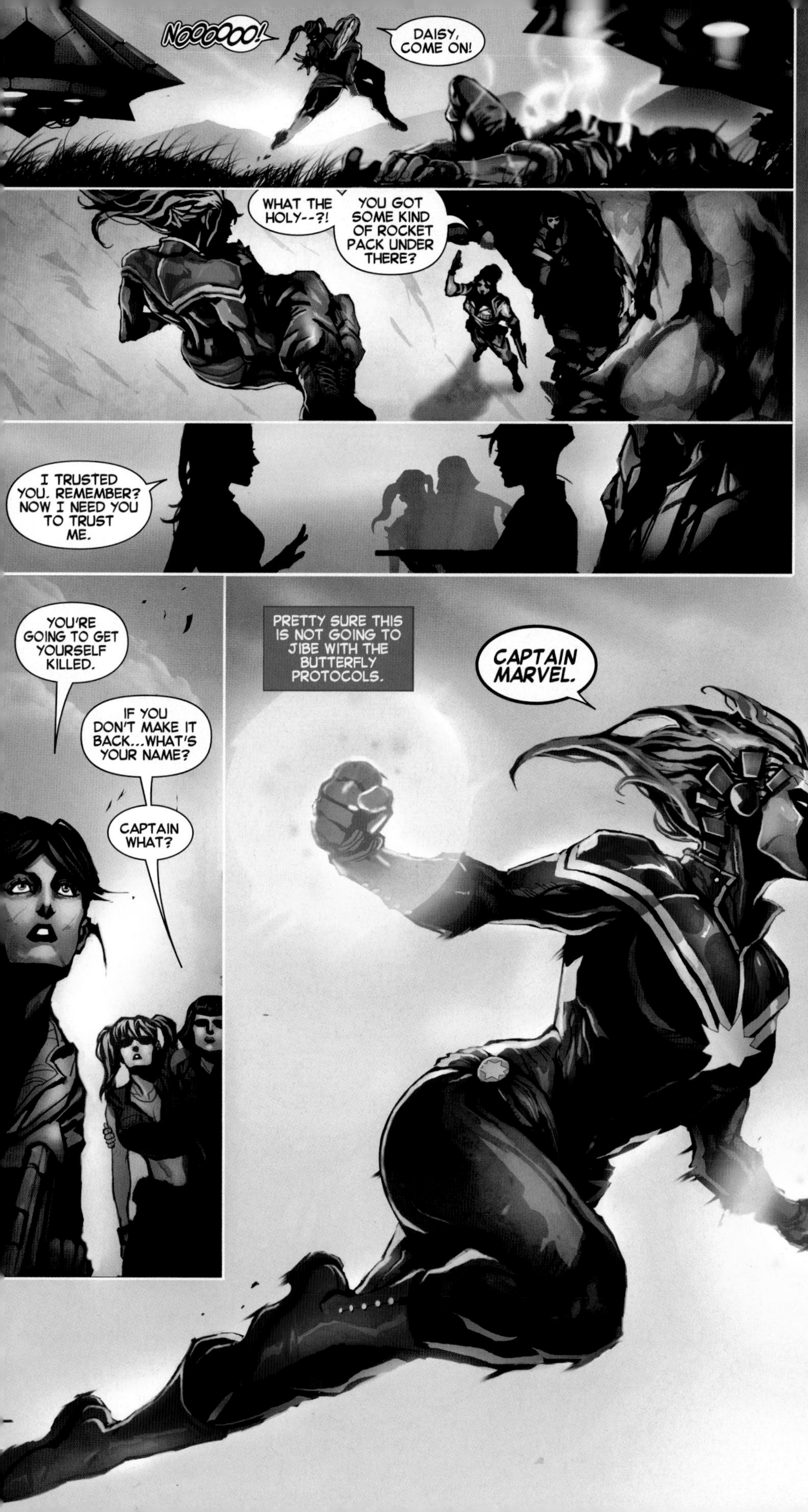
NOOOOOO!
DAISY, COME ON!
WHAT THE HOLY--?!
YOU GOT SOME KIND OF ROCKET PACK UNDER THERE?
I TRUSTED YOU. REMEMBER? NOW I NEED YOU TO TRUST ME.
YOU'RE GOING TO GET YOURSELF KILLED.
IF YOU DON'T MAKE IT BACK...WHAT'S YOUR NAME?
CAPTAIN WHAT?
PRETTY SURE THIS IS NOT GOING TO JIBE WITH THE BUTTERFLY PROTOCOLS.
CAPTAIN MARVEL.

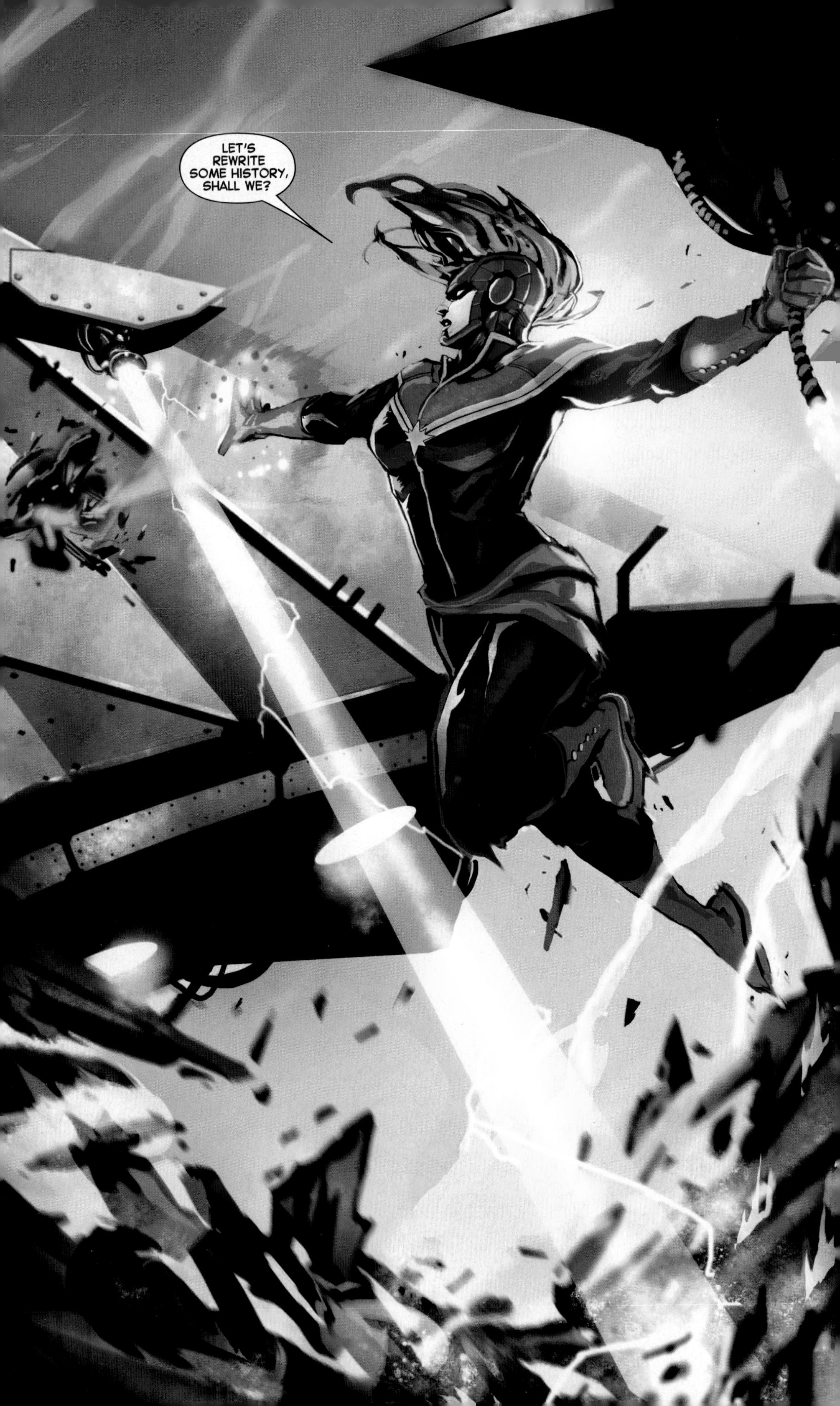
LET'S REWRITE SOME HISTORY, SHALL WE?

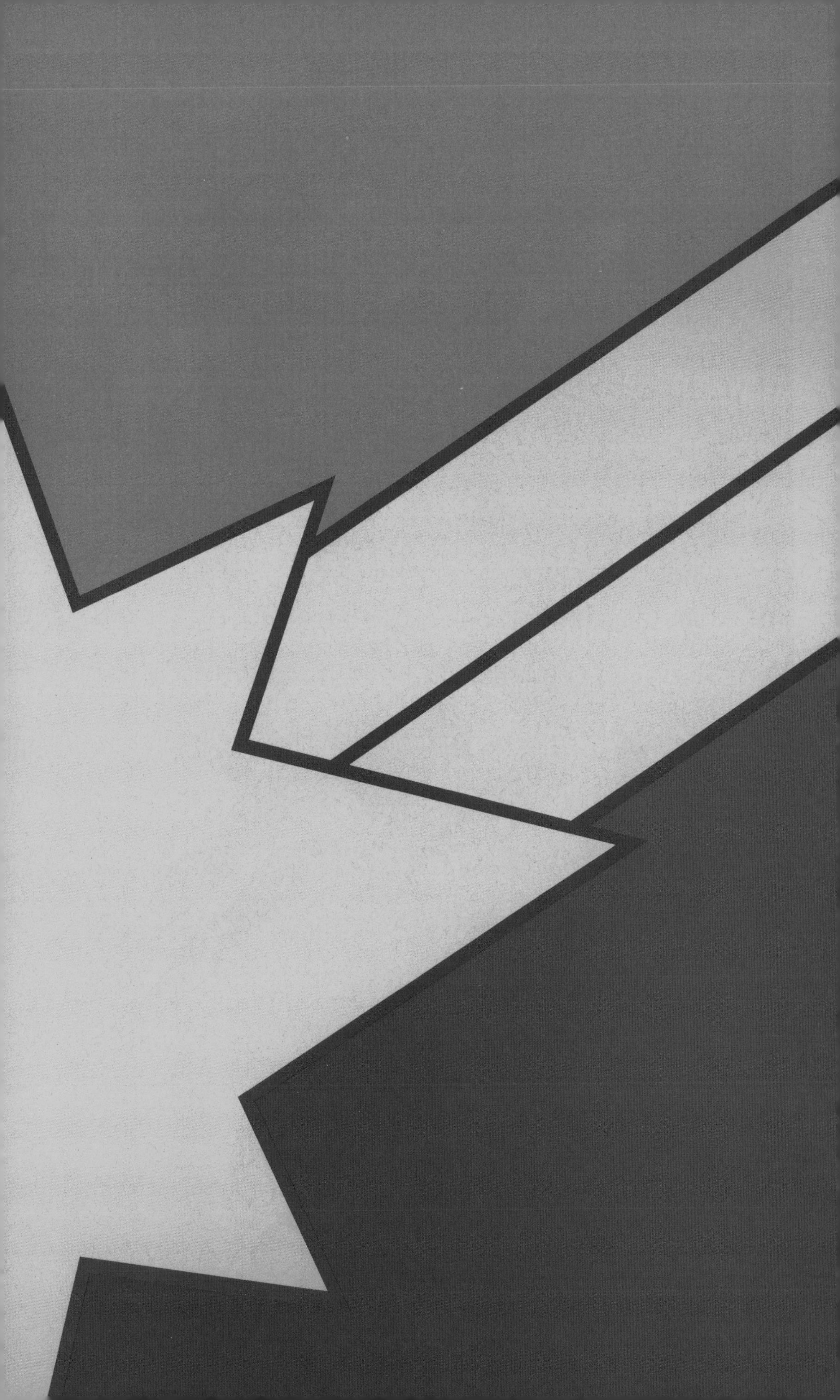

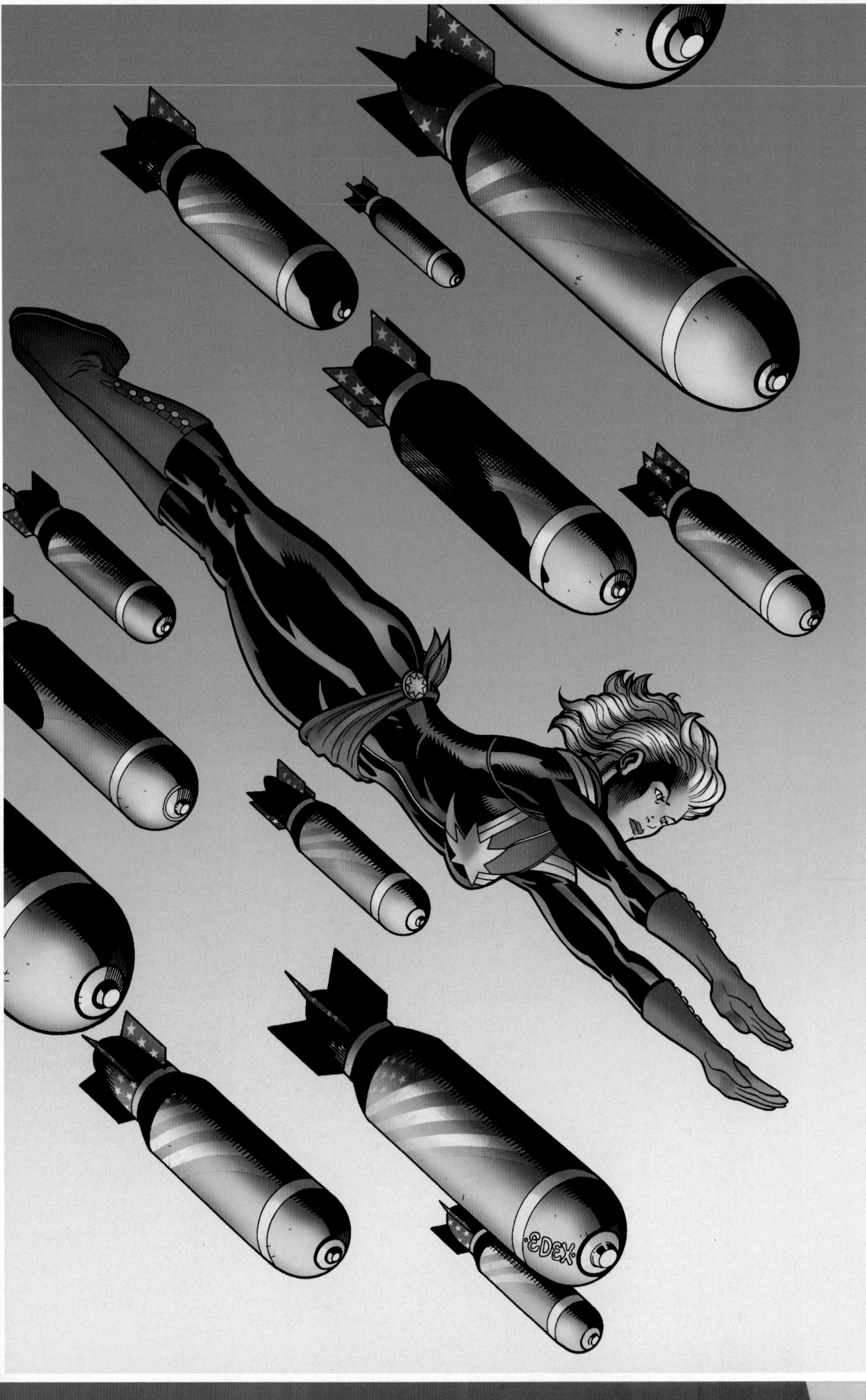
EDEX

THREE

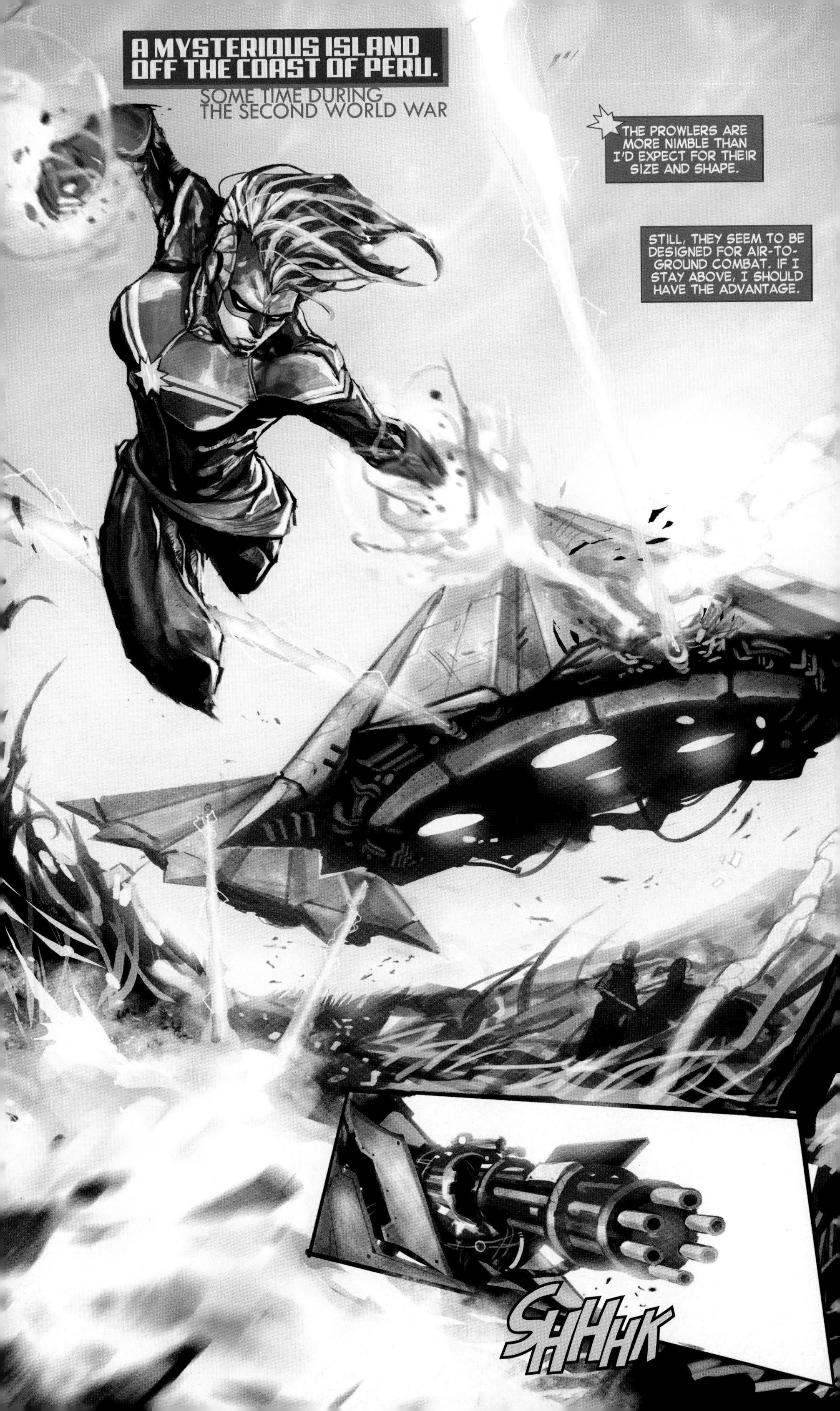
A MYSTERIOUS ISLAND OFF THE COAST OF PERU.
SOME TIME DURING THE SECOND WORLD WAR
THE PROWLERS ARE MORE NIMBLE THAN I'D EXPECT FOR THEIR SIZE AND SHAPE.
STILL, THEY SEEM TO BE DESIGNED FOR AIR-TO-GROUND COMBAT. IF I STAY ABOVE, I SHOULD HAVE THE ADVANTAGE.
SHHHK

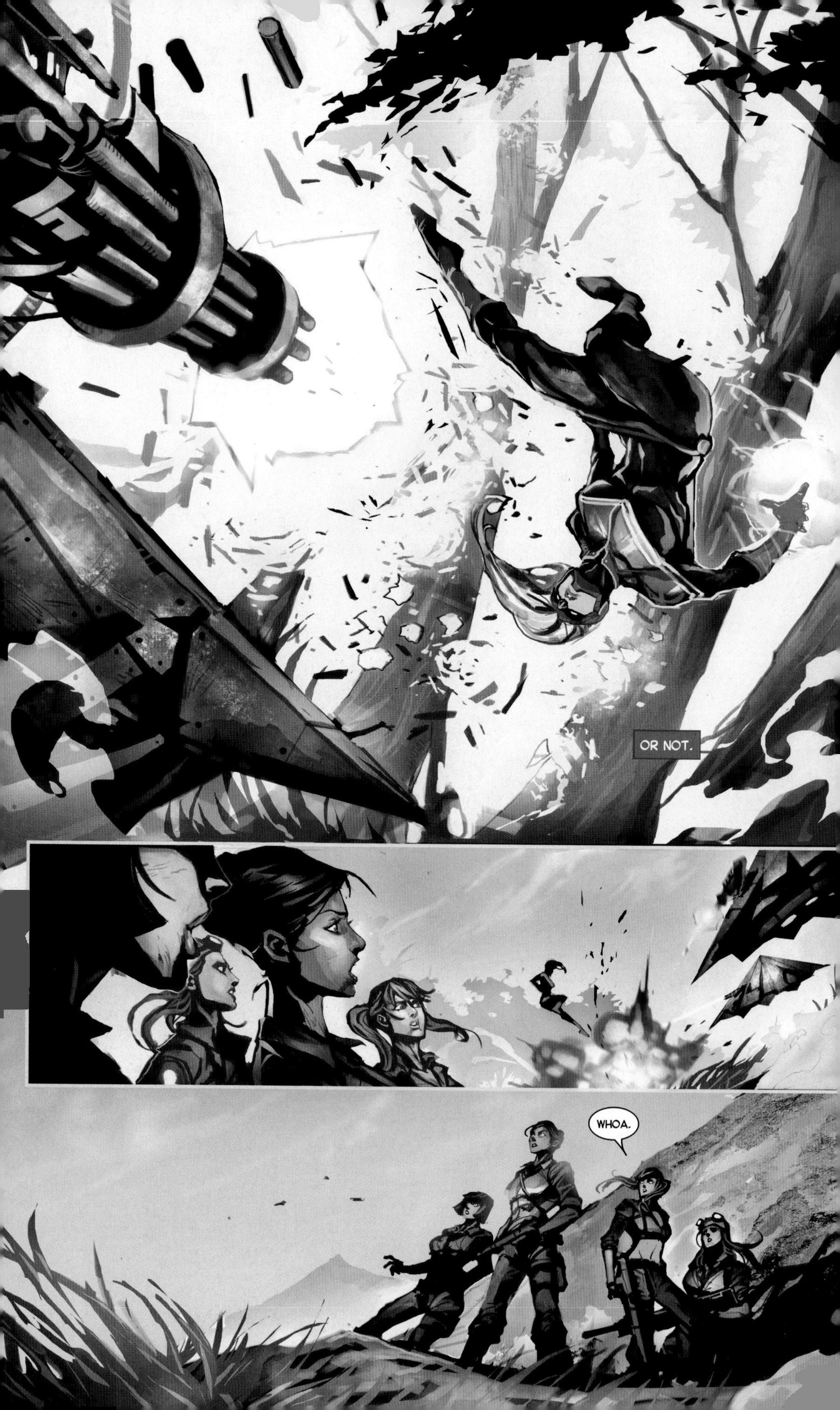
OR NOT.
WHOA.

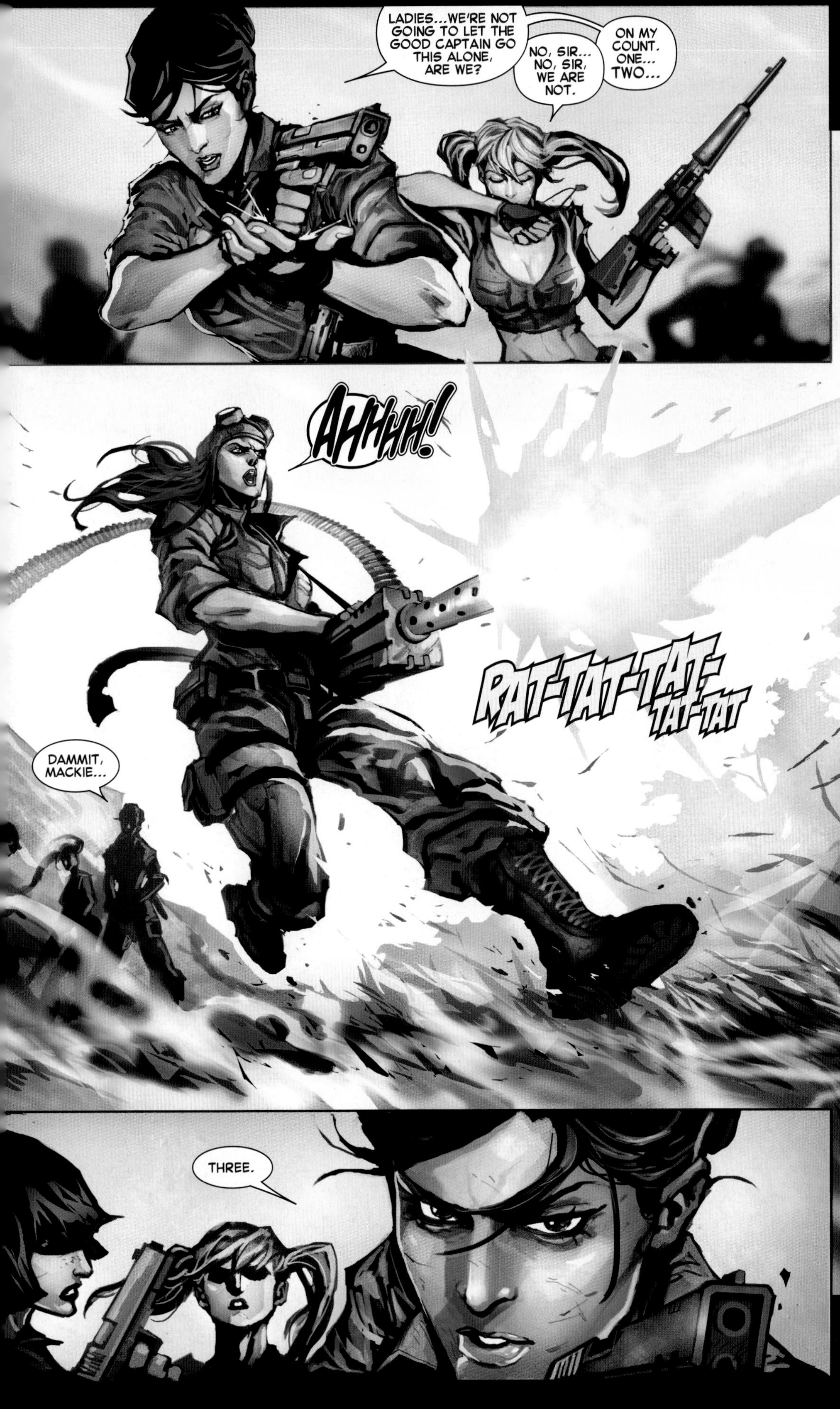
LADIES...WE'RE NOT GOING TO LET THE GOOD CAPTAIN GO THIS ALONE, ARE WE?
NO, SIR... NO, SIR, WE ARE NOT.
ON MY COUNT. ONE... TWO...
AHHHH!
RAT-TAT-TAT-TAT-TAT
DAMMIT, MACKIE...
THREE.

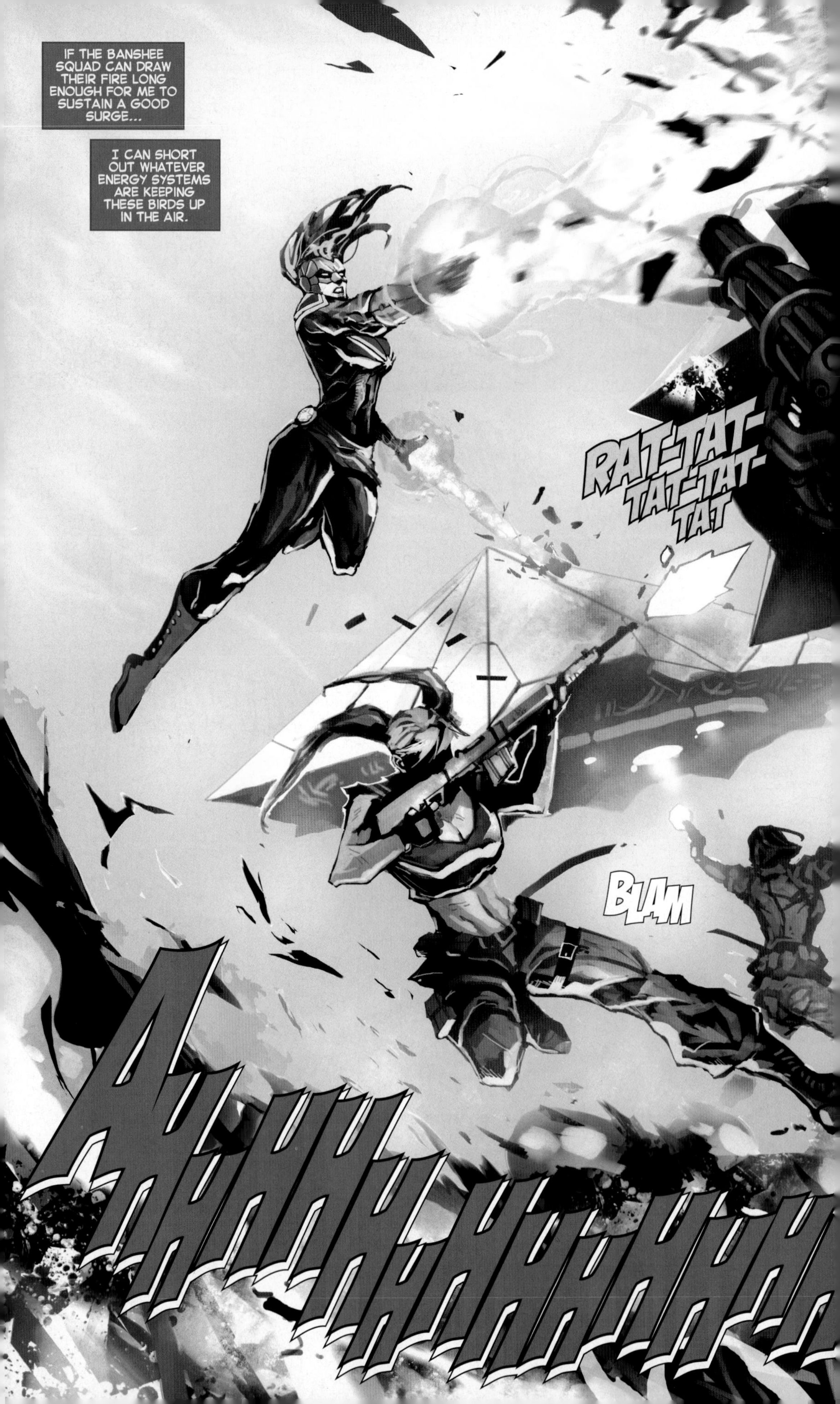
IF THE BANSHEE SQUAD CAN DRAW THEIR FIRE LONG ENOUGH FOR ME TO SUSTAIN A GOOD SURGE...
I CAN SHORT OUT WHATEVER ENERGY SYSTEMS ARE KEEPING THESE BIRDS UP IN THE AIR.
RAT-TAT-TAT-TAT-TAT
BLAM
AHHHHHHHHHHH

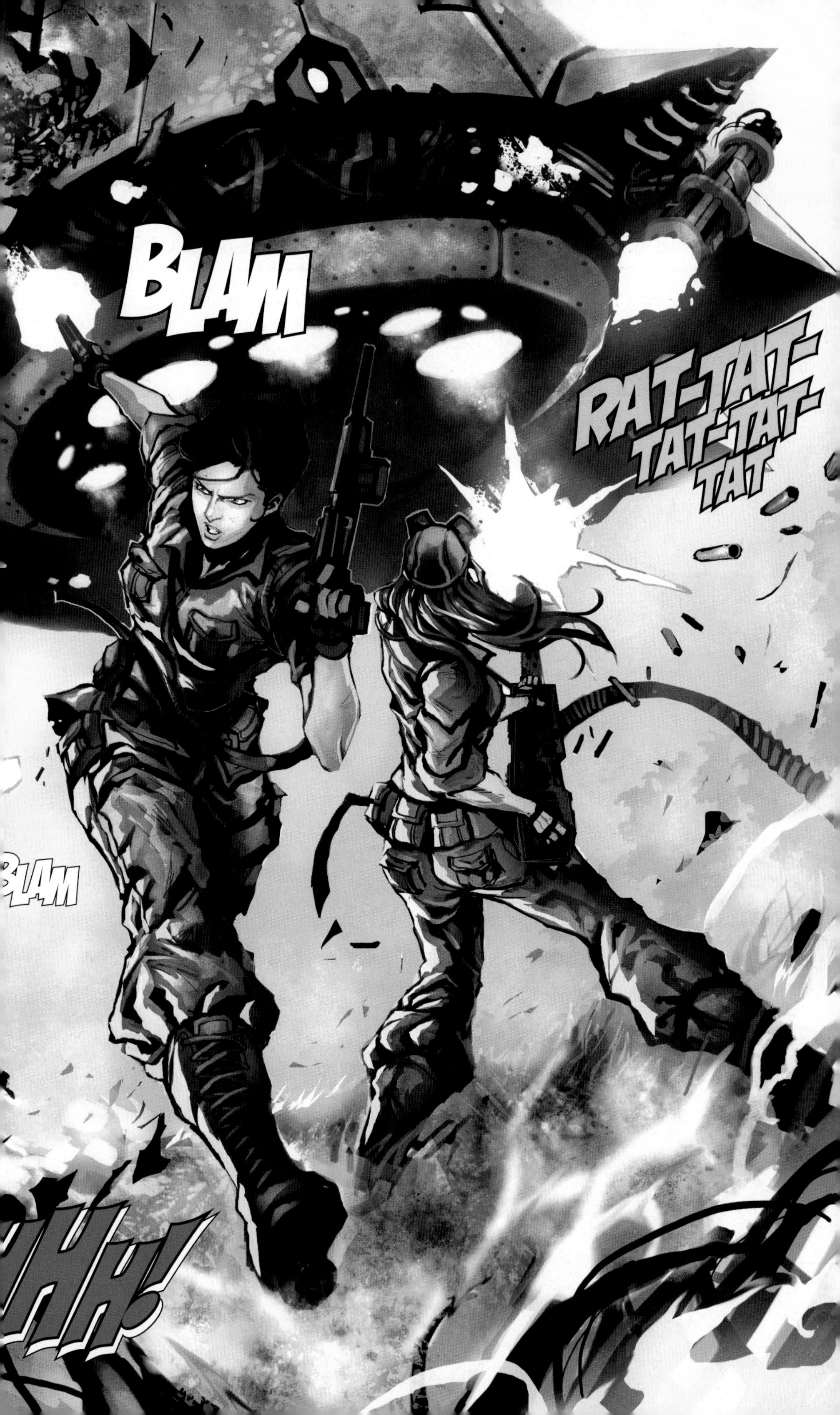
BLAM
RAT-TAT-TAT-TAT-TAT
BLAM

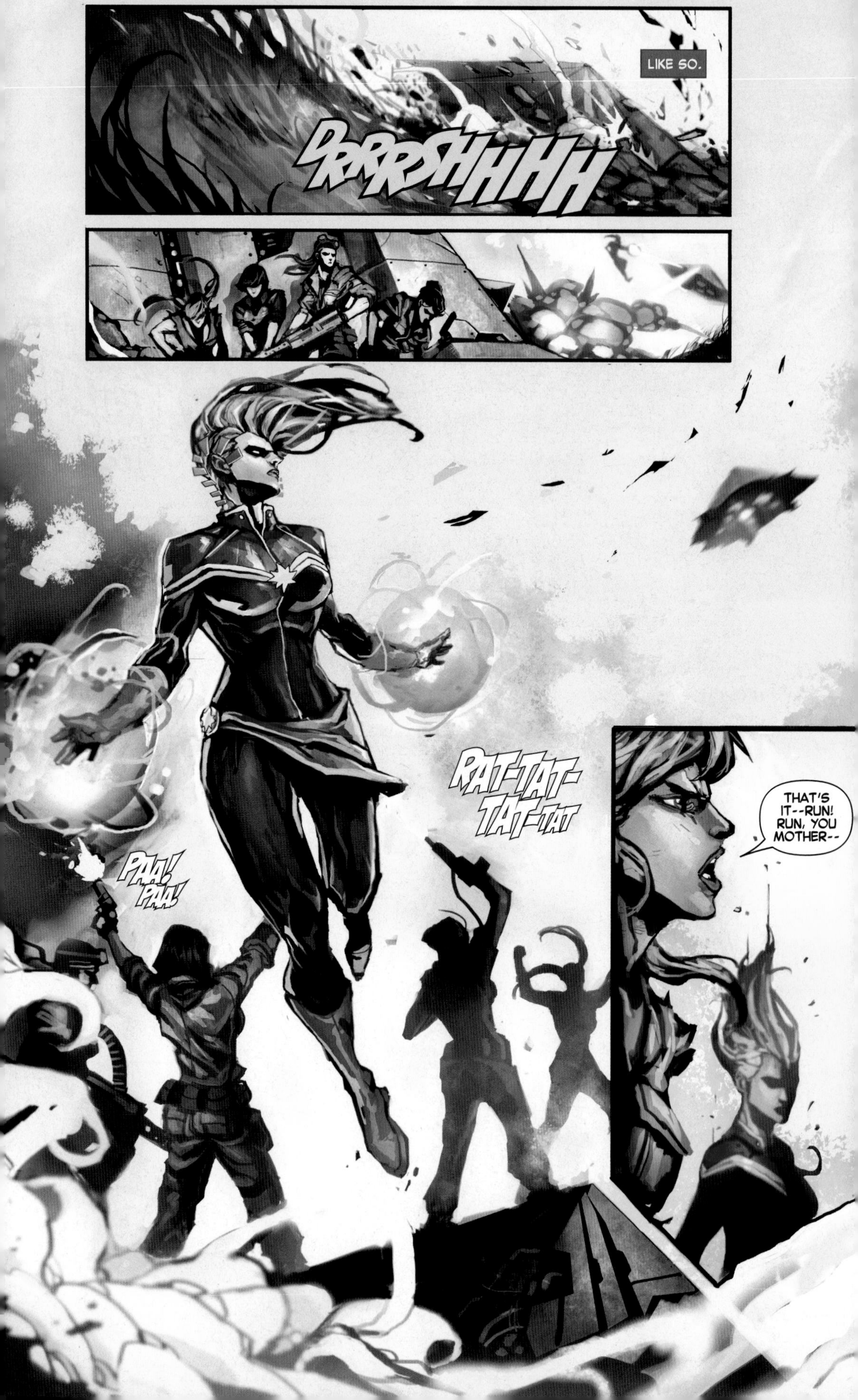
LIKE SO.
DRRRSHHHHH
RAT-TAT-TAT-TAT
PAA! PAA!
THAT'S IT--RUN! RUN, YOU MOTHER--

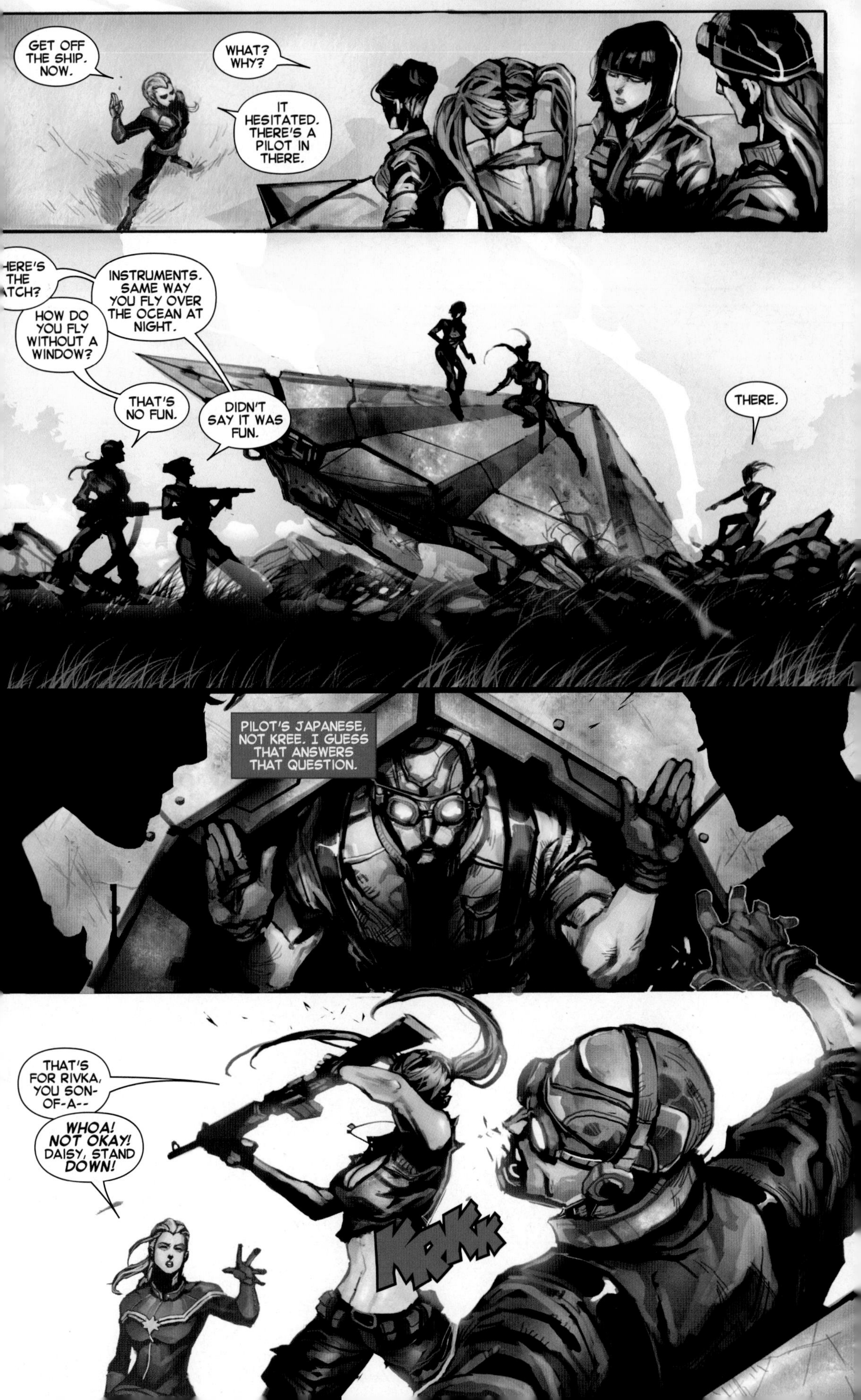

GET OFF THE SHIP. NOW.
WHAT? WHY?
IT HESITATED. THERE'S A PILOT IN THERE.
HERE'S THE ATCH?
INSTRUMENTS. SAME WAY YOU FLY OVER THE OCEAN AT NIGHT.
HOW DO YOU FLY WITHOUT A WINDOW?
THAT'S NO FUN.
DIDN'T SAY IT WAS FUN.
THERE.
PILOT'S JAPANESE, NOT KREE. I GUESS THAT ANSWERS THAT QUESTION.
THAT'S FOR RIVKA, YOU SON-OF-A--
WHOA! NOT OKAY! DAISY, STAND DOWN!
KRAKK

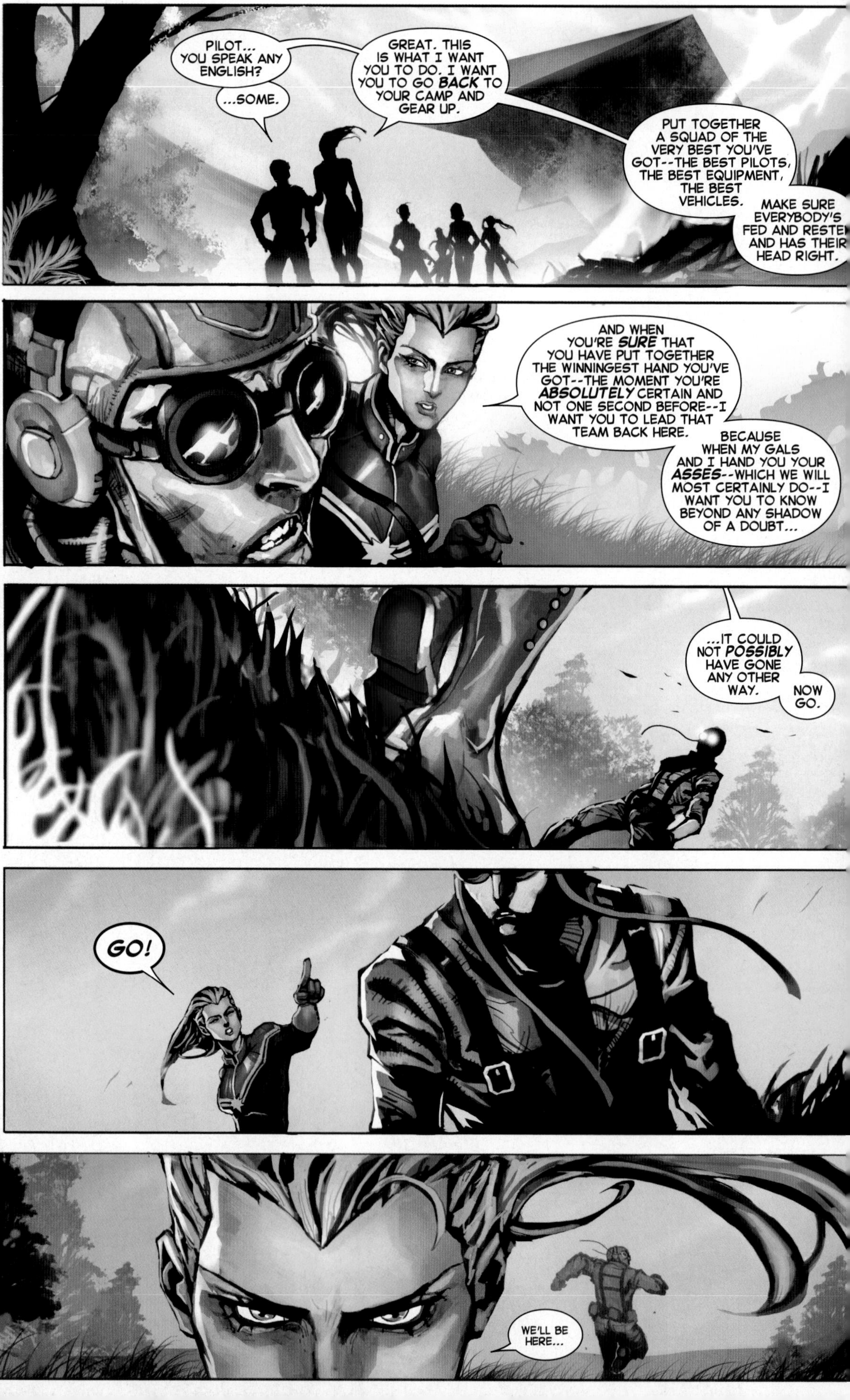
PILOT... YOU SPEAK ANY ENGLISH?
...SOME.
GREAT. THIS IS WHAT I WANT YOU TO DO. I WANT YOU TO GO BACK TO YOUR CAMP AND GEAR UP.
PUT TOGETHER A SQUAD OF THE VERY BEST YOU'VE GOT--THE BEST PILOTS, THE BEST EQUIPMENT, THE BEST VEHICLES.
MAKE SURE EVERYBODY'S FED AND RESTE AND HAS THEIR HEAD RIGHT.
AND WHEN YOU'RE SURE THAT YOU HAVE PUT TOGETHER THE WINNINGEST HAND YOU'VE GOT--THE MOMENT YOU'RE ABSOLUTELY CERTAIN AND NOT ONE SECOND BEFORE--I WANT YOU TO LEAD THAT TEAM BACK HERE.
BECAUSE WHEN MY GALS AND I HAND YOU YOUR ASSES--WHICH WE WILL MOST CERTAINLY DO--I WANT YOU TO KNOW BEYOND ANY SHADOW OF A DOUBT...
...IT COULD NOT POSSIBLY HAVE GONE ANY OTHER WAY.
NOW GO.
GO!
WE'LL BE HERE...

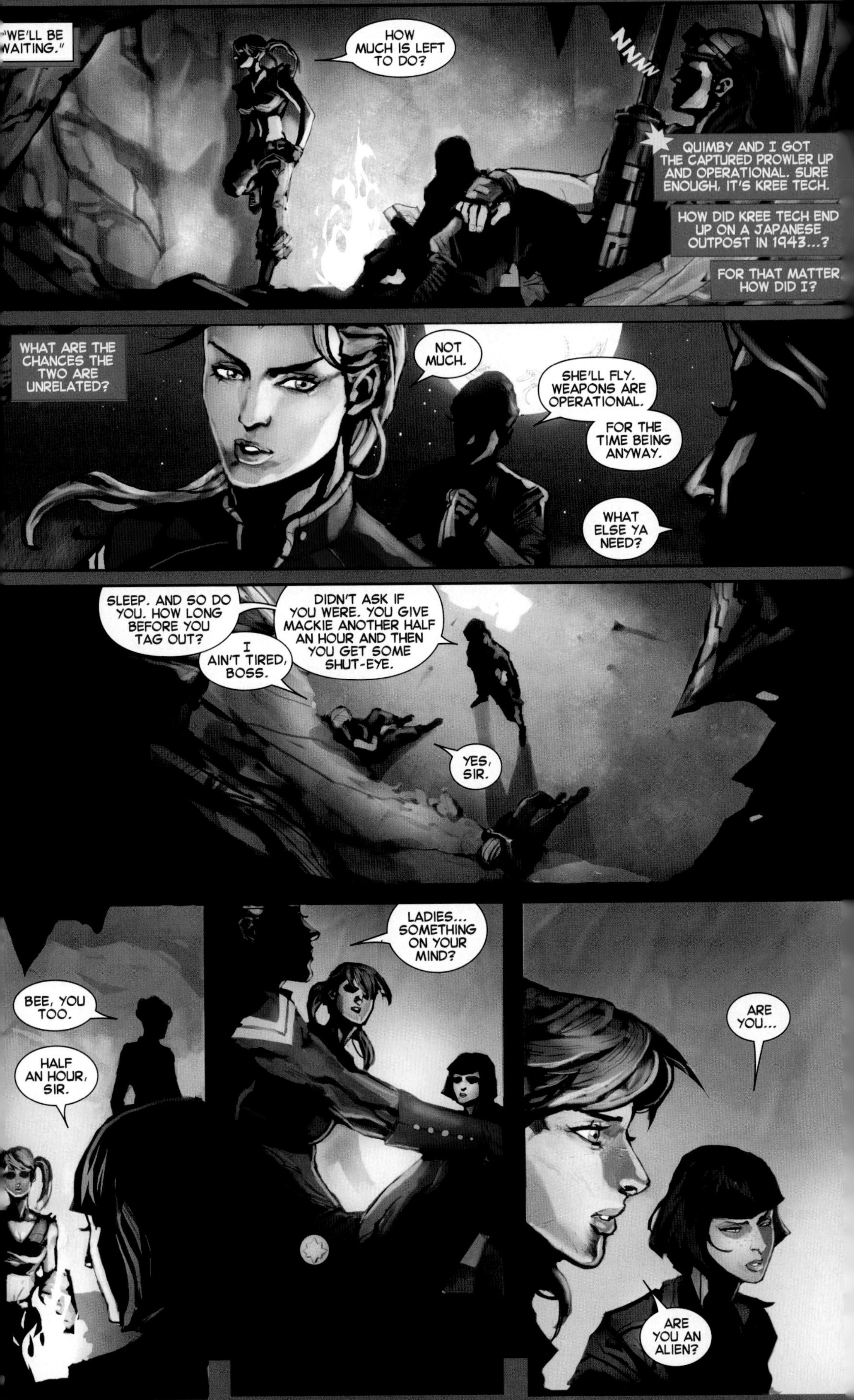

"WE'LL BE WAITING."
HOW MUCH IS LEFT TO DO?
NNNN
QUIMBY AND I GOT THE CAPTURED PROWLER UP AND OPERATIONAL. SURE ENOUGH, IT'S KREE TECH.
HOW DID KREE TECH END UP ON A JAPANESE OUTPOST IN 1943...?
FOR THAT MATTER, HOW DID I?
WHAT ARE THE CHANCES THE TWO ARE UNRELATED?
NOT MUCH.
SHE'LL FLY. WEAPONS ARE OPERATIONAL.
FOR THE TIME BEING ANYWAY.
WHAT ELSE YA NEED?
SLEEP. AND SO DO YOU. HOW LONG BEFORE YOU TAG OUT?
I AIN'T TIRED, BOSS.
DIDN'T ASK IF YOU WERE. YOU GIVE MACKIE ANOTHER HALF AN HOUR AND THEN YOU GET SOME SHUT-EYE.
YES, SIR.
BEE, YOU TOO.
HALF AN HOUR, SIR.
LADIES... SOMETHING ON YOUR MIND?
ARE YOU...
ARE YOU AN ALIEN?

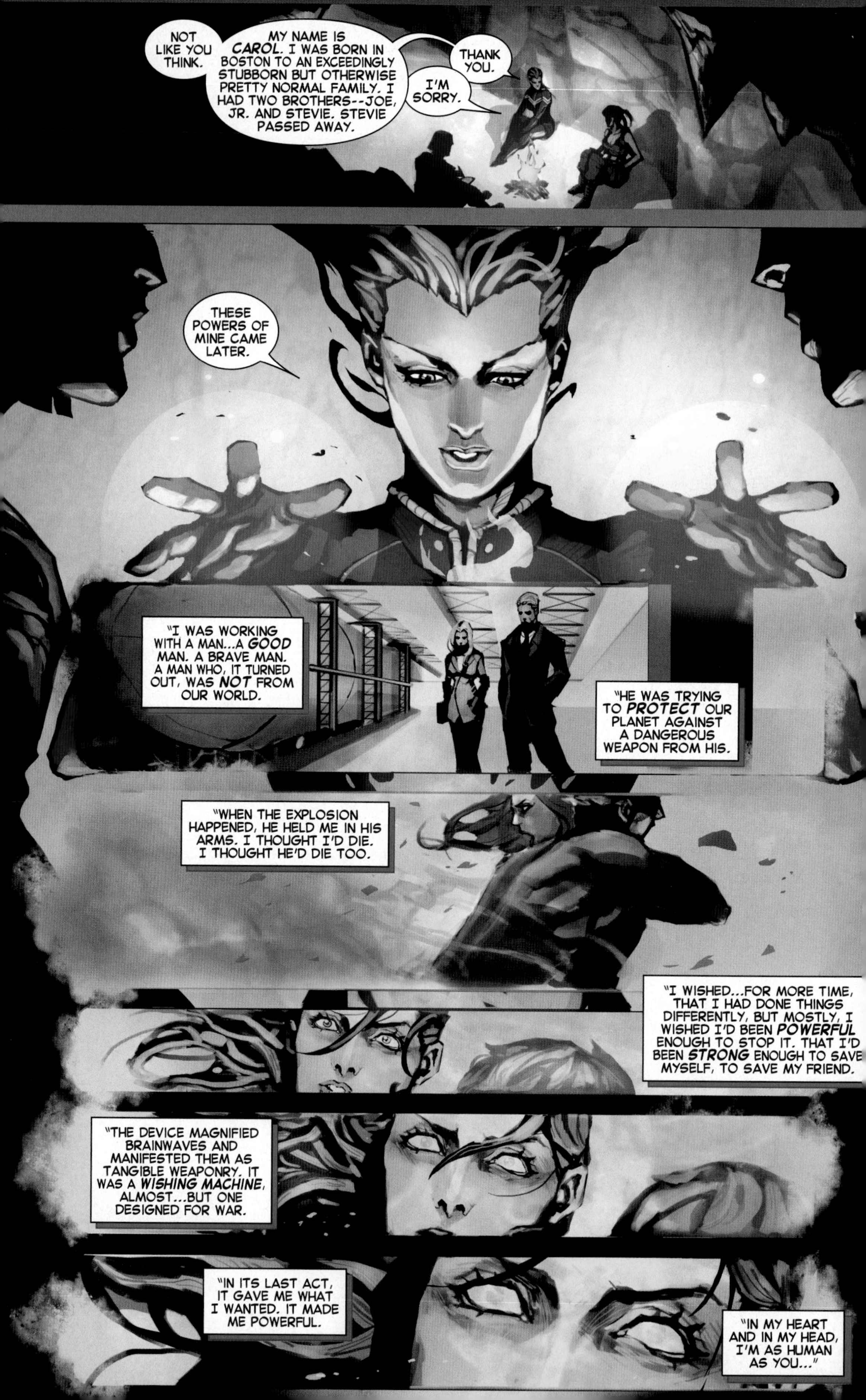

NOT LIKE YOU THINK.
MY NAME IS CAROL. I WAS BORN IN BOSTON TO AN EXCEEDINGLY STUBBORN BUT OTHERWISE PRETTY NORMAL FAMILY. I HAD TWO BROTHERS--JOE, JR. AND STEVIE. STEVIE PASSED AWAY.
THANK YOU.
I'M SORRY.
THESE POWERS OF MINE CAME LATER.
"I WAS WORKING WITH A MAN...A GOOD MAN. A BRAVE MAN. A MAN WHO, IT TURNED OUT, WAS NOT FROM OUR WORLD.
"HE WAS TRYING TO PROTECT OUR PLANET AGAINST A DANGEROUS WEAPON FROM HIS.
"WHEN THE EXPLOSION HAPPENED, HE HELD ME IN HIS ARMS. I THOUGHT I'D DIE. I THOUGHT HE'D DIE TOO.
"I WISHED...FOR MORE TIME, THAT I HAD DONE THINGS DIFFERENTLY, BUT MOSTLY, I WISHED I'D BEEN POWERFUL ENOUGH TO STOP IT. THAT I'D BEEN STRONG ENOUGH TO SAVE MYSELF, TO SAVE MY FRIEND.
"THE DEVICE MAGNIFIED BRAINWAVES AND MANIFESTED THEM AS TANGIBLE WEAPONRY. IT WAS A WISHING MACHINE, ALMOST...BUT ONE DESIGNED FOR WAR.
"IN ITS LAST ACT, IT GAVE ME WHAT I WANTED. IT MADE ME POWERFUL.
"IN MY HEART AND IN MY HEAD, I'M AS HUMAN AS YOU..."

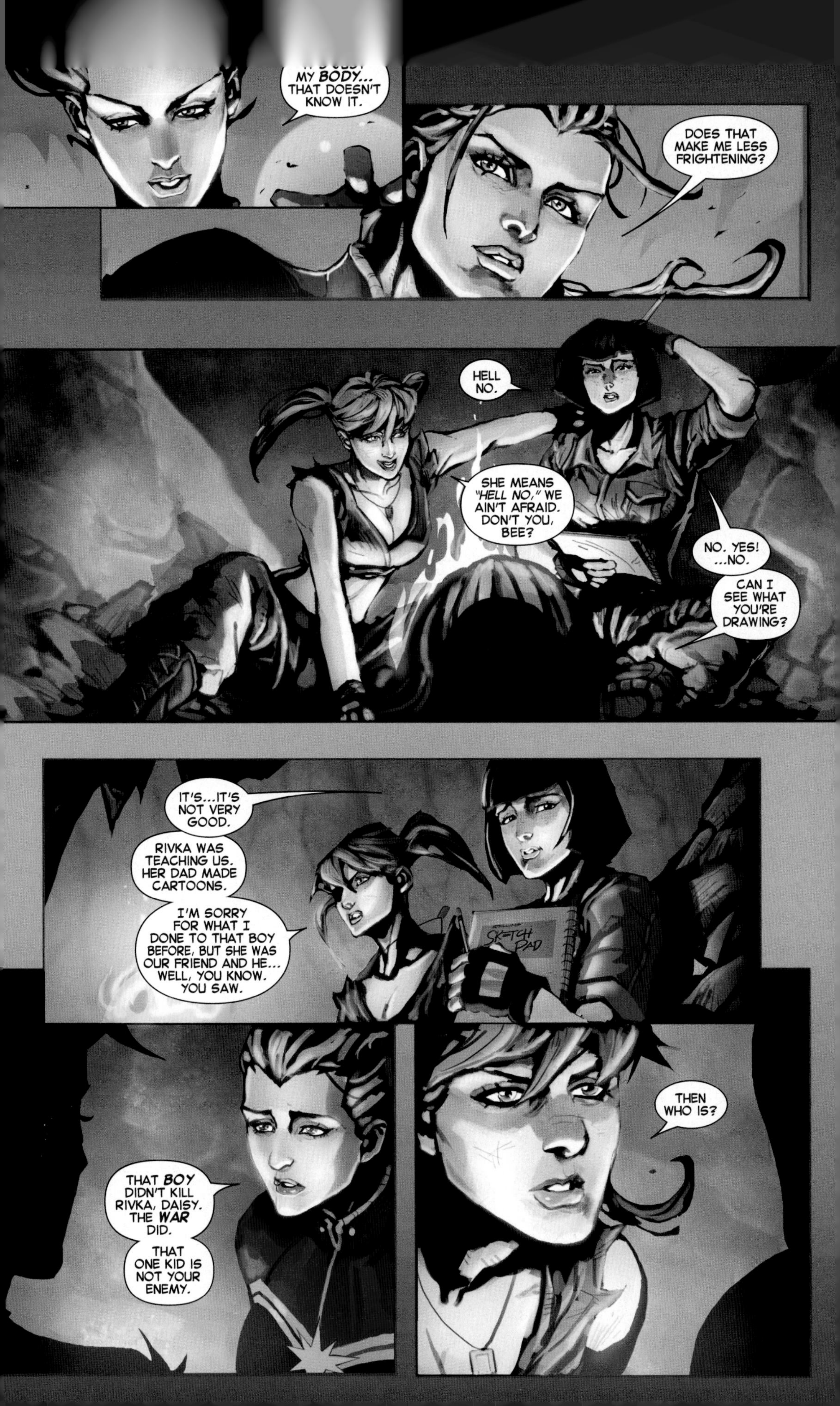

MY BODY... THAT DOESN'T KNOW IT.
DOES THAT MAKE ME LESS FRIGHTENING?
HELL NO.
SHE MEANS "HELL NO," WE AIN'T AFRAID. DON'T YOU, BEE?
NO. YES! ...NO.
CAN I SEE WHAT YOU'RE DRAWING?
IT'S...IT'S NOT VERY GOOD.
RIVKA WAS TEACHING US. HER DAD MADE CARTOONS.
I'M SORRY FOR WHAT I DONE TO THAT BOY BEFORE, BUT SHE WAS OUR FRIEND AND HE... WELL, YOU KNOW. YOU SAW.
SK-TCH PAD
THAT BOY DIDN'T KILL RIVKA, DAISY. THE WAR DID.
THAT ONE KID IS NOT YOUR ENEMY.
THEN WHO IS?

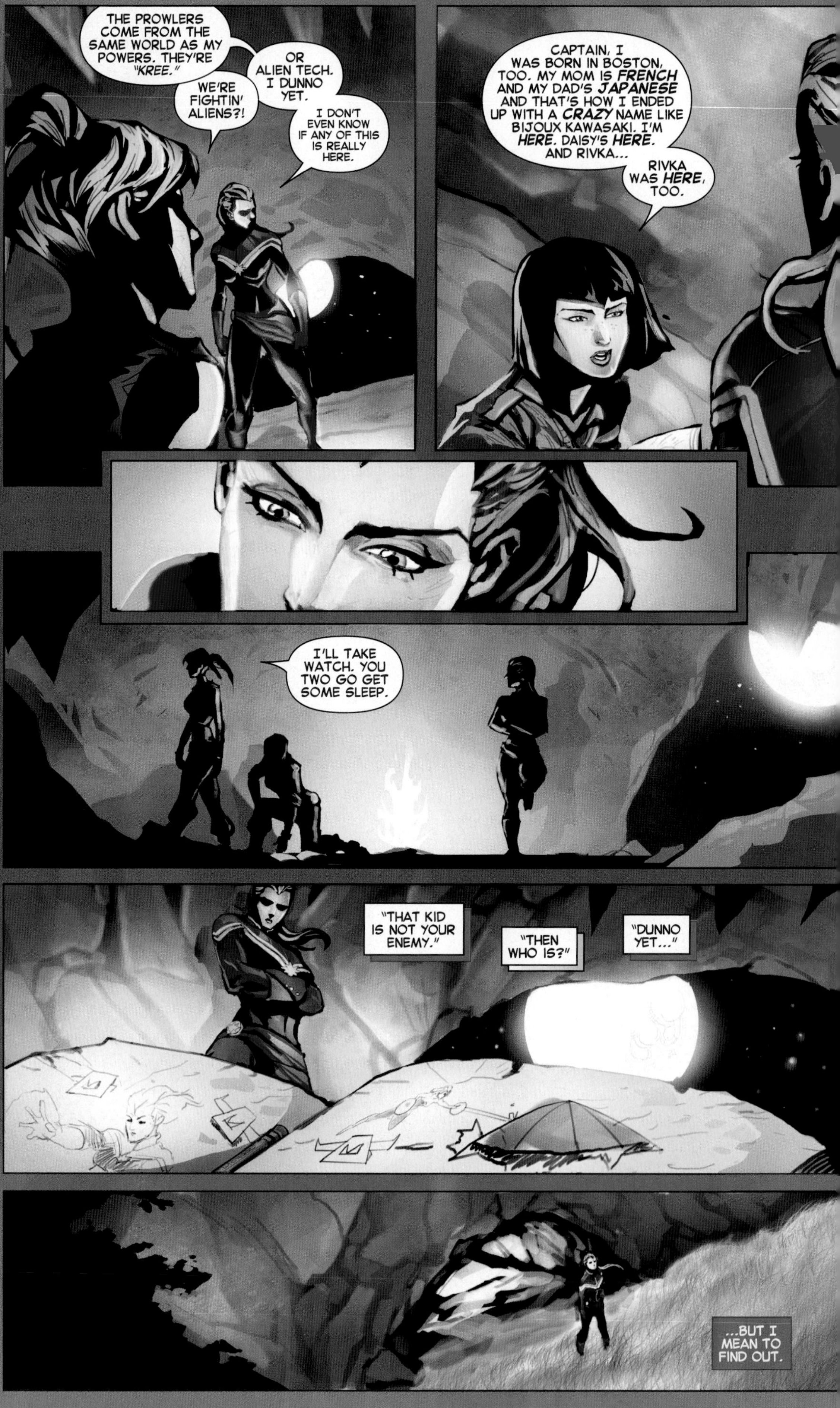
THE PROWLERS COME FROM THE SAME WORLD AS MY POWERS. THEY'RE "KREE."
WE'RE FIGHTIN' ALIENS?!
OR ALIEN TECH. I DUNNO YET.
I DON'T EVEN KNOW IF ANY OF THIS IS REALLY HERE.
CAPTAIN, I WAS BORN IN BOSTON, TOO. MY MOM IS FRENCH AND MY DAD'S JAPANESE AND THAT'S HOW I ENDED UP WITH A CRAZY NAME LIKE BIJOUX KAWASAKI. I'M HERE. DAISY'S HERE. AND RIVKA...
RIVKA WAS HERE, TOO.
I'LL TAKE WATCH. YOU TWO GO GET SOME SLEEP.
"THAT KID IS NOT YOUR ENEMY."
"THEN WHO IS?"
"DUNNO YET..."
...BUT I MEAN TO FIND OUT.

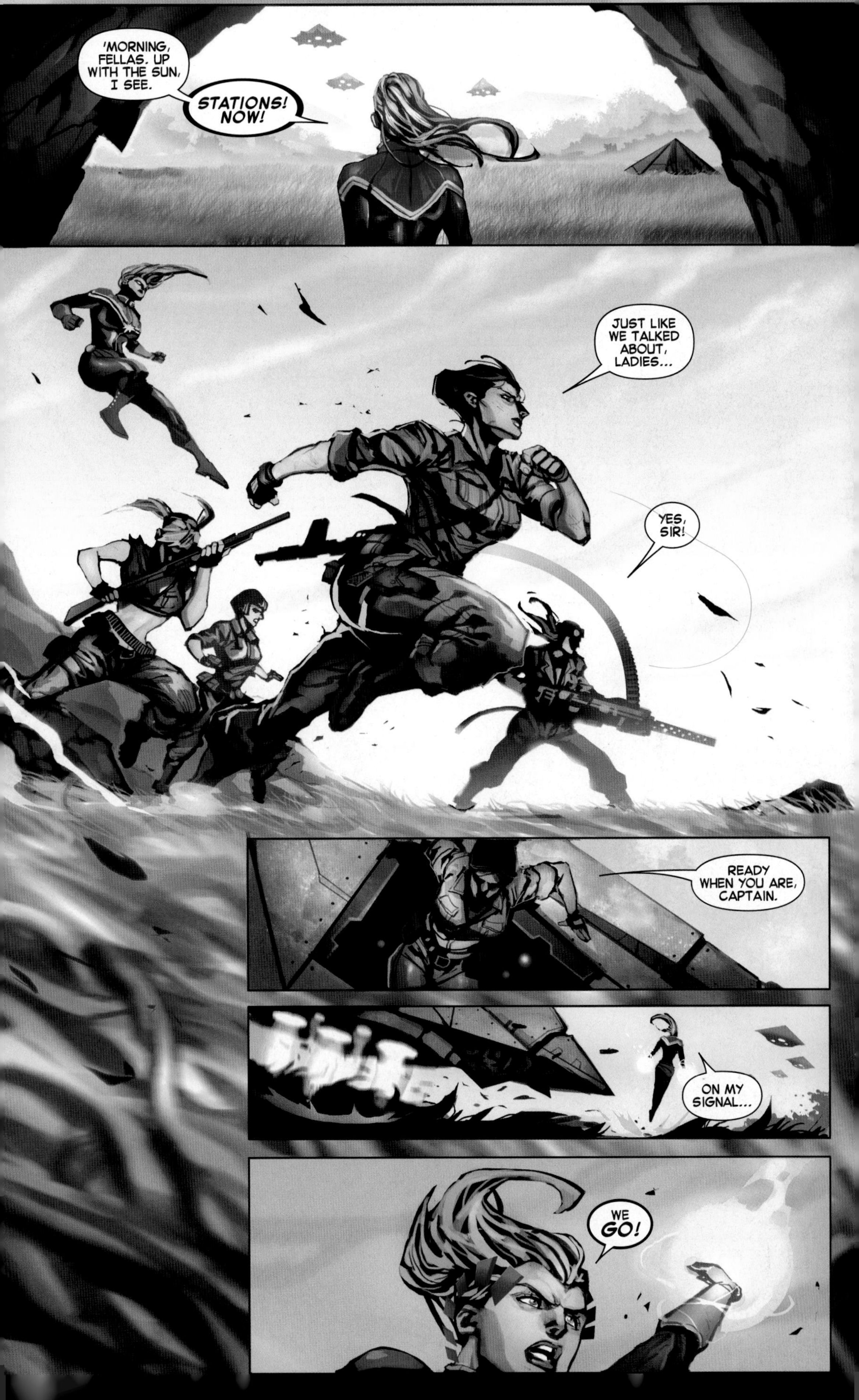
'MORNING, FELLAS. UP WITH THE SUN, I SEE.
STATIONS! NOW!
JUST LIKE WE TALKED ABOUT, LADIES...
YES, SIR!
READY WHEN YOU ARE, CAPTAIN.
ON MY SIGNAL...
WE GO!

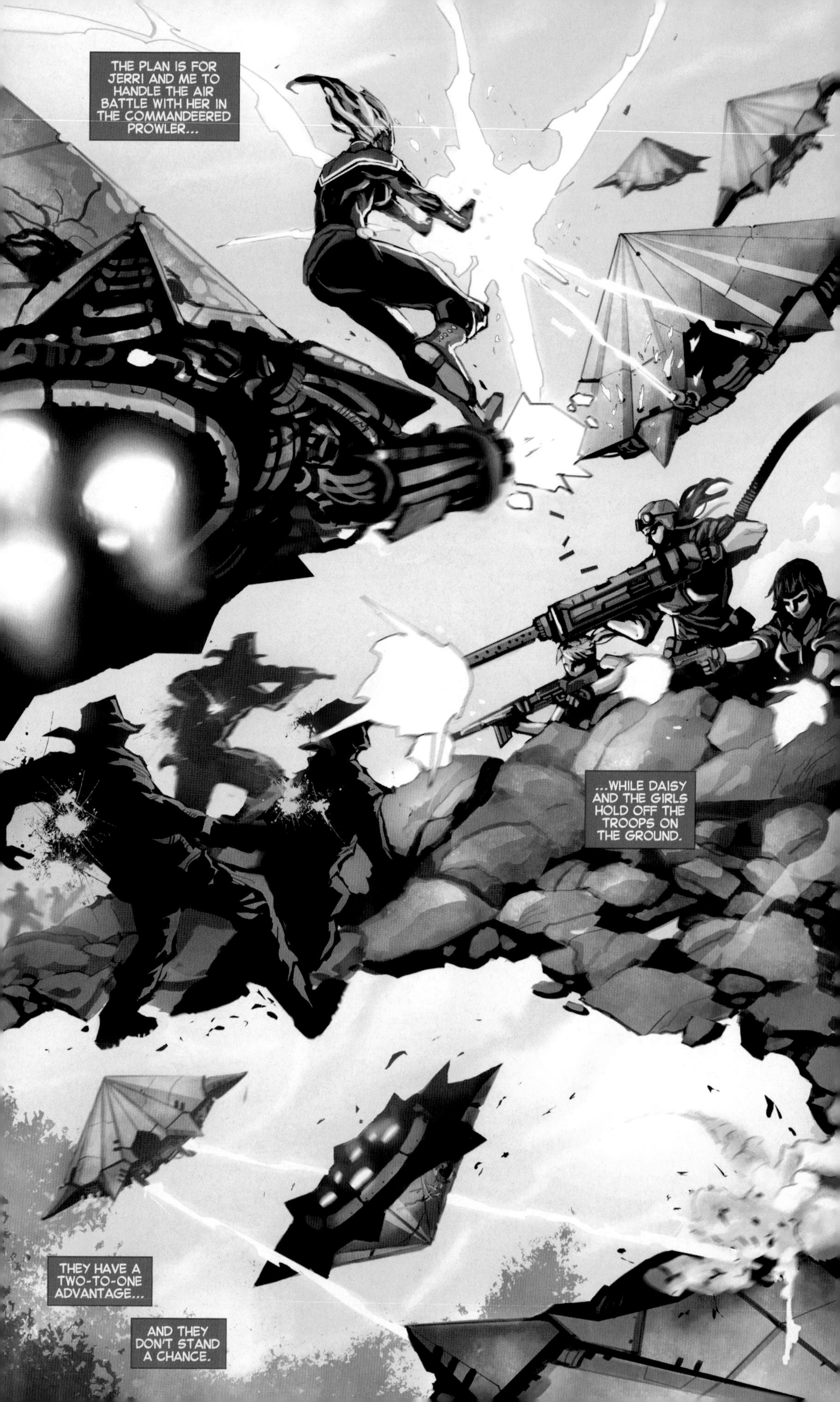
THE PLAN IS FOR JERRI AND ME TO HANDLE THE AIR BATTLE WITH HER IN THE COMMANDEERED PROWLER...
...WHILE DAISY AND THE GIRLS HOLD OFF THE TROOPS ON THE GROUND.
THEY HAVE A TWO-TO-ONE ADVANTAGE...
AND THEY DON'T STAND A CHANCE.

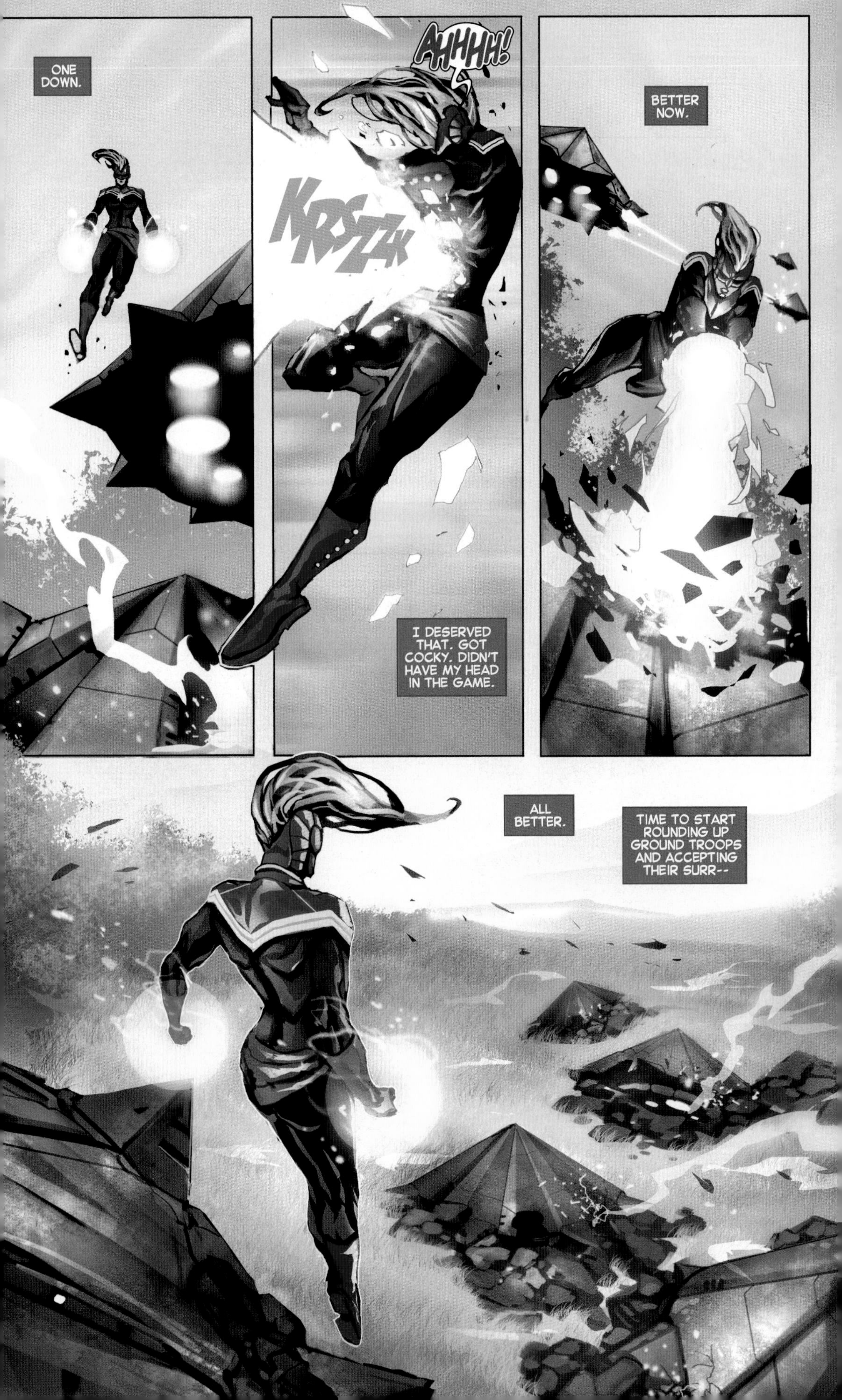
ONE DOWN.
AHHHH!
KRSZZK
I DESERVED THAT. GOT COCKY. DIDN'T HAVE MY HEAD IN THE GAME.
BETTER NOW.
ALL BETTER.
TIME TO START ROUNDING UP GROUND TROOPS AND ACCEPTING THEIR SURR--

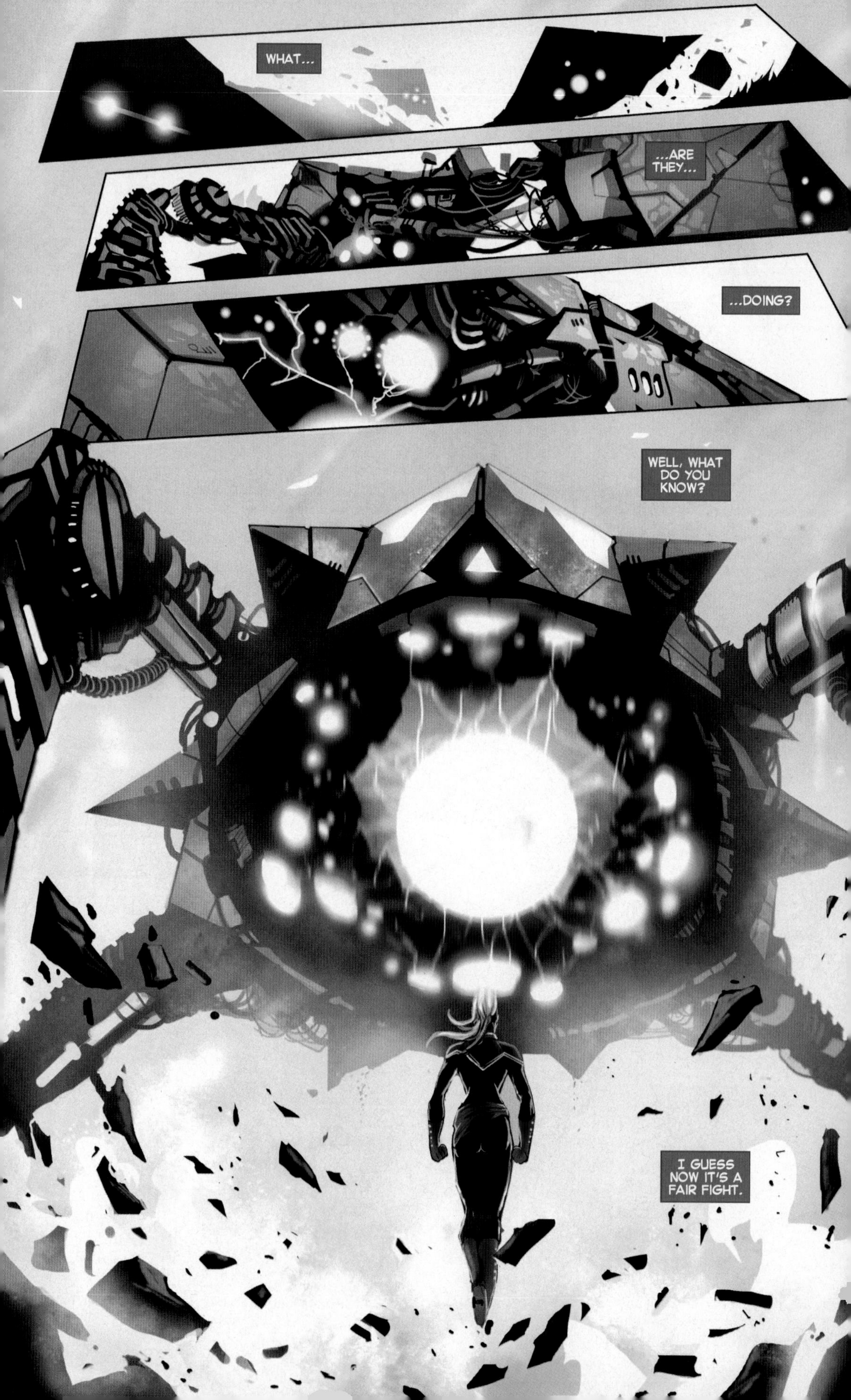
WHAT...
...ARE THEY...
...DOING?
WELL, WHAT DO YOU KNOW?
I GUESS NOW IT'S A FAIR FIGHT.

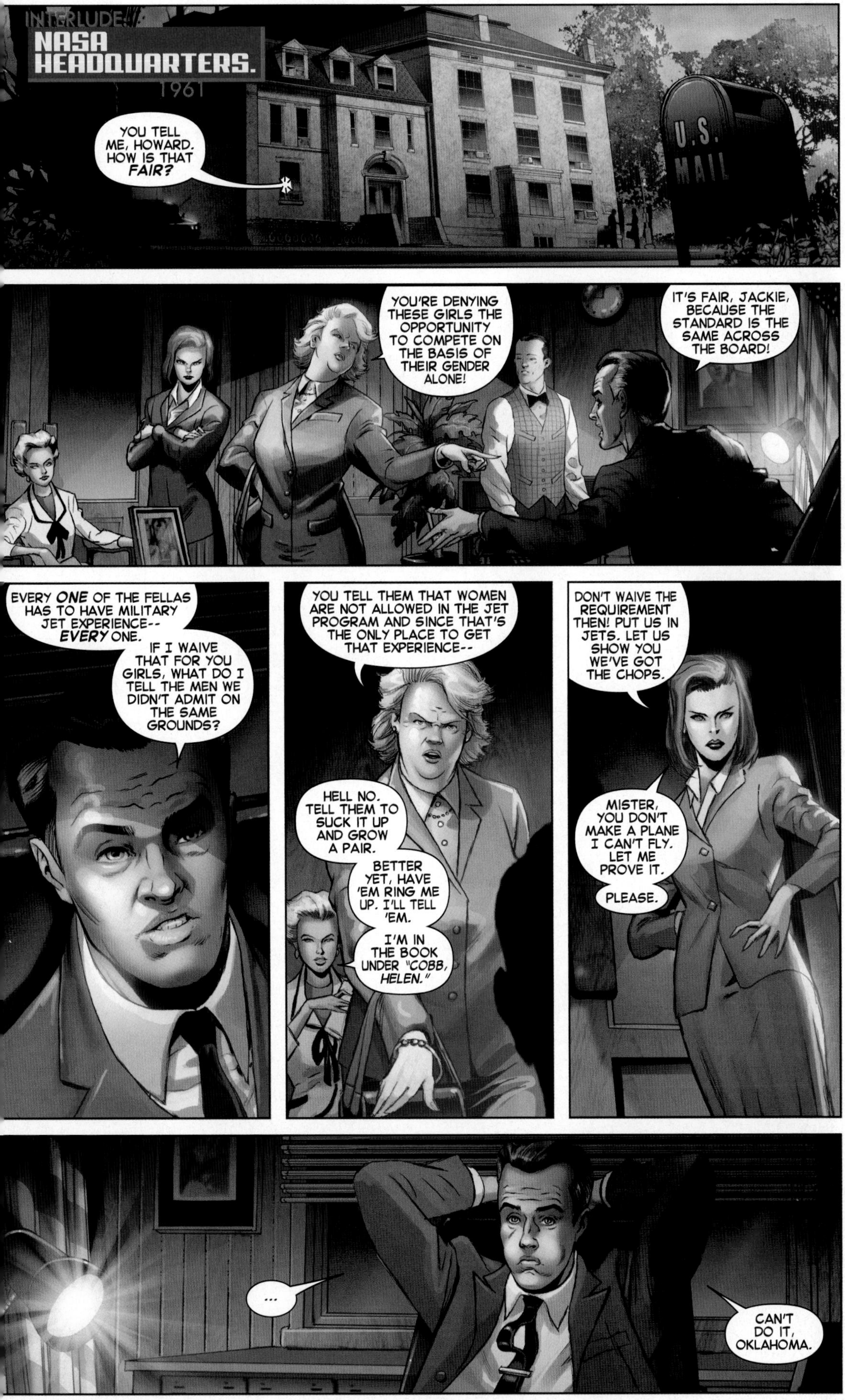
INTERLUDE:
NASA HEADQUARTERS.
1961
YOU TELL ME, HOWARD. HOW IS THAT FAIR?
U.S. MAIL
YOU'RE DENYING THESE GIRLS THE OPPORTUNITY TO COMPETE ON THE BASIS OF THEIR GENDER ALONE!
IT'S FAIR, JACKIE, BECAUSE THE STANDARD IS THE SAME ACROSS THE BOARD!
EVERY ONE OF THE FELLAS HAS TO HAVE MILITARY JET EXPERIENCE-- EVERY ONE.
IF I WAIVE THAT FOR YOU GIRLS, WHAT DO I TELL THE MEN WE DIDN'T ADMIT ON THE SAME GROUNDS?
YOU TELL THEM THAT WOMEN ARE NOT ALLOWED IN THE JET PROGRAM AND SINCE THAT'S THE ONLY PLACE TO GET THAT EXPERIENCE--
HELL NO. TELL THEM TO SUCK IT UP AND GROW A PAIR.
BETTER YET, HAVE 'EM RING ME UP. I'LL TELL 'EM.
I'M IN THE BOOK UNDER "COBB, HELEN."
DON'T WAIVE THE REQUIREMENT THEN! PUT US IN JETS. LET US SHOW YOU WE'VE GOT THE CHOPS.
MISTER, YOU DON'T MAKE A PLANE I CAN'T FLY. LET ME PROVE IT.
PLEASE.
...
CAN'T DO IT, OKLAHOMA.

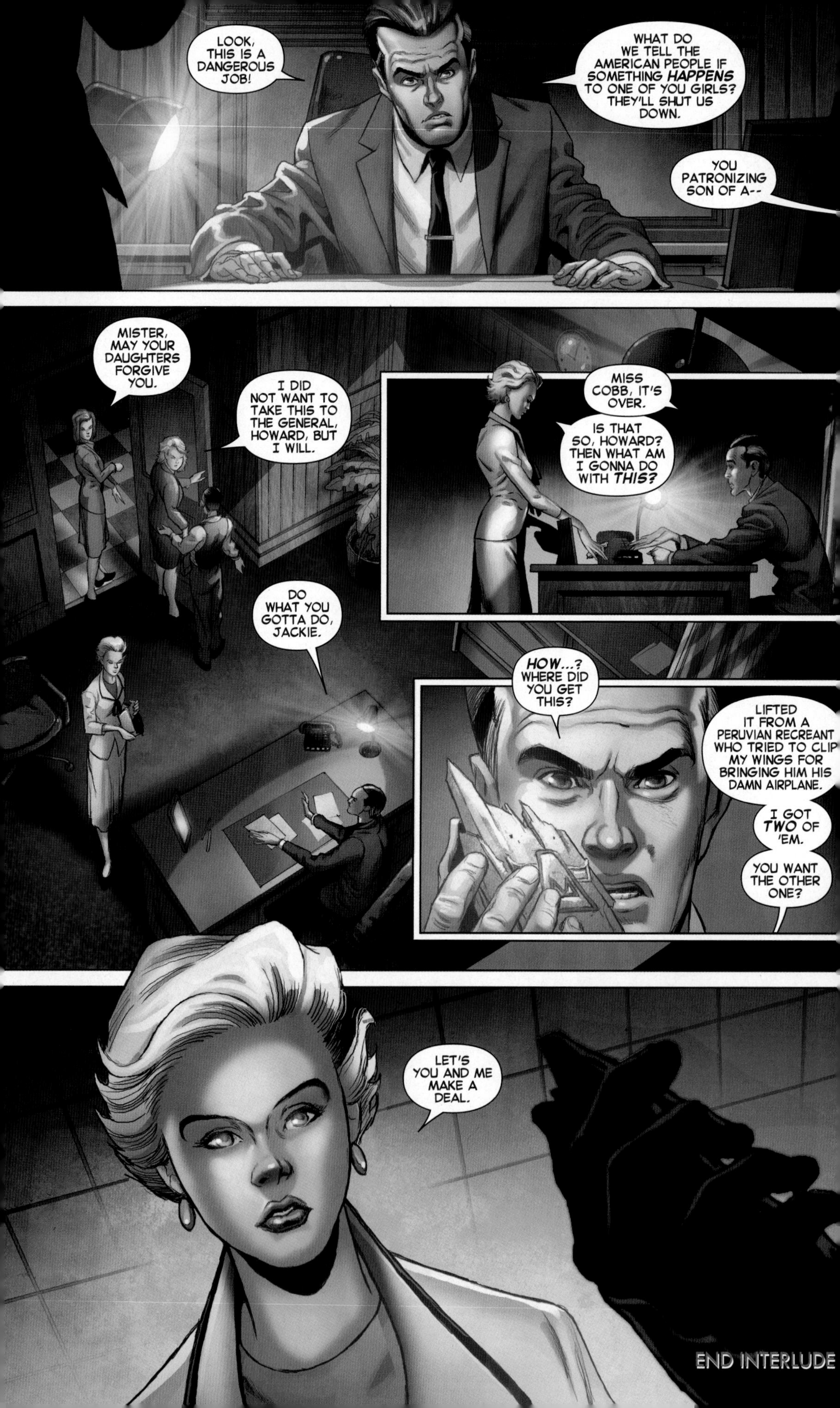

LOOK, THIS IS A DANGEROUS JOB!
WHAT DO WE TELL THE AMERICAN PEOPLE IF SOMETHING *HAPPENS* TO ONE OF YOU GIRLS? THEY'LL SHUT US DOWN.
YOU PATRONIZING SON OF A--
MISTER, MAY YOUR DAUGHTERS FORGIVE YOU.
I DID NOT WANT TO TAKE THIS TO THE GENERAL, HOWARD, BUT I WILL.
MISS COBB, IT'S OVER.
IS THAT SO, HOWARD? THEN WHAT AM I GONNA DO WITH *THIS?*
DO WHAT YOU GOTTA DO, JACKIE.
HOW...? WHERE DID YOU GET THIS?
LIFTED IT FROM A PERUVIAN RECREANT WHO TRIED TO CLIP MY WINGS FOR BRINGING HIM HIS DAMN AIRPLANE.
I GOT *TWO* OF 'EM.
YOU WANT THE OTHER ONE?
LET'S YOU AND ME MAKE A DEAL.
END INTERLUDE

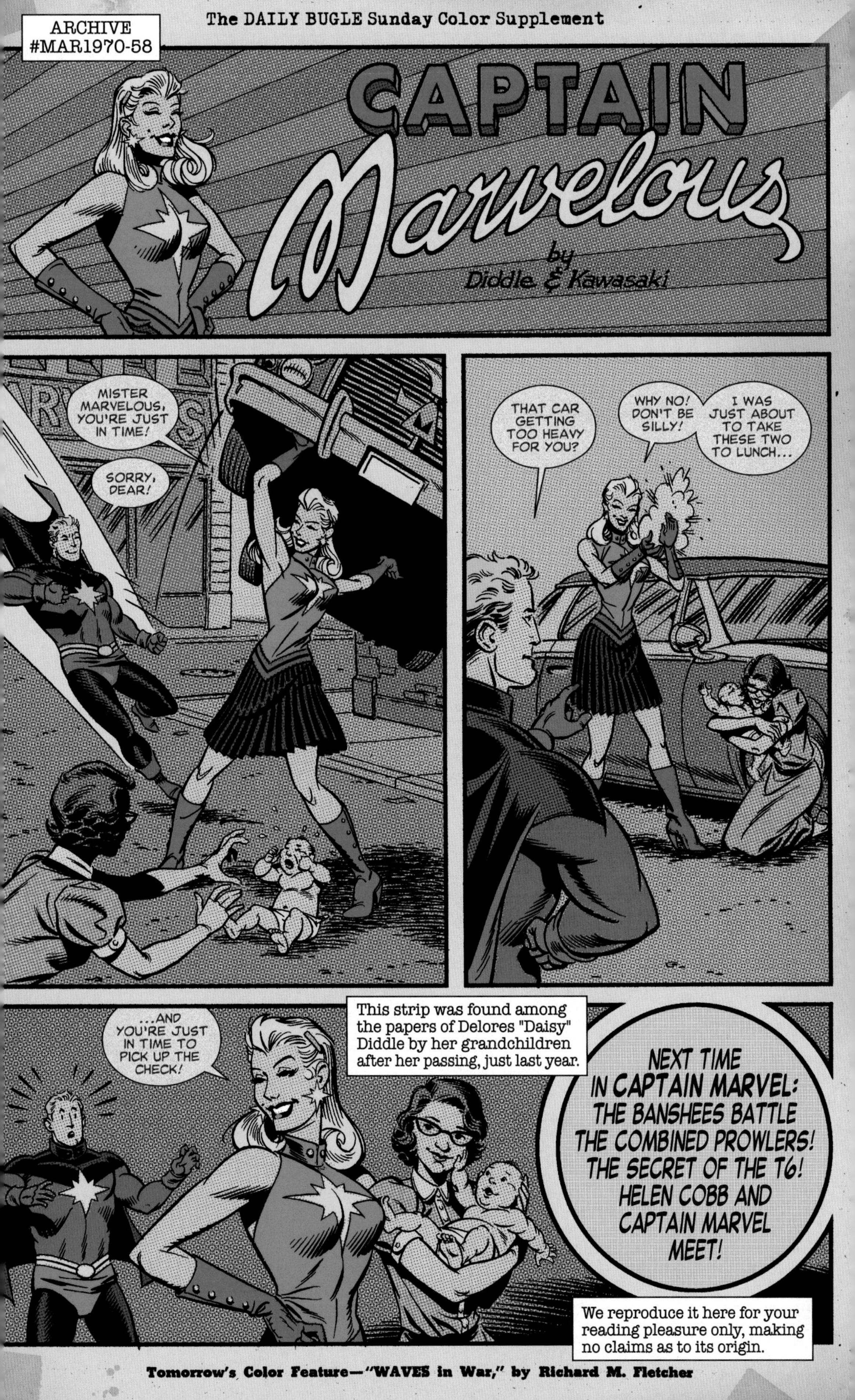

ARCHIVE #MAR1970-58
The DAILY BUGLE Sunday Color Supplement
CAPTAIN Marvelous
by Diddle & Kawasaki
MISTER MARVELOUS, YOU'RE JUST IN TIME!
SORRY, DEAR!
THAT CAR GETTING TOO HEAVY FOR YOU?
WHY NO! DON'T BE SILLY!
I WAS JUST ABOUT TO TAKE THESE TWO TO LUNCH...
...AND YOU'RE JUST IN TIME TO PICK UP THE CHECK!
This strip was found among the papers of Delores "Daisy" Diddle by her grandchildren after her passing, just last year.
NEXT TIME IN CAPTAIN MARVEL: THE BANSHEES BATTLE THE COMBINED PROWLERS! THE SECRET OF THE T6! HELEN COBB AND CAPTAIN MARVEL MEET!
We reproduce it here for your reading pleasure only, making no claims as to its origin.
Tomorrow's Color Feature—"WAVES in War," by Richard M. Fletcher

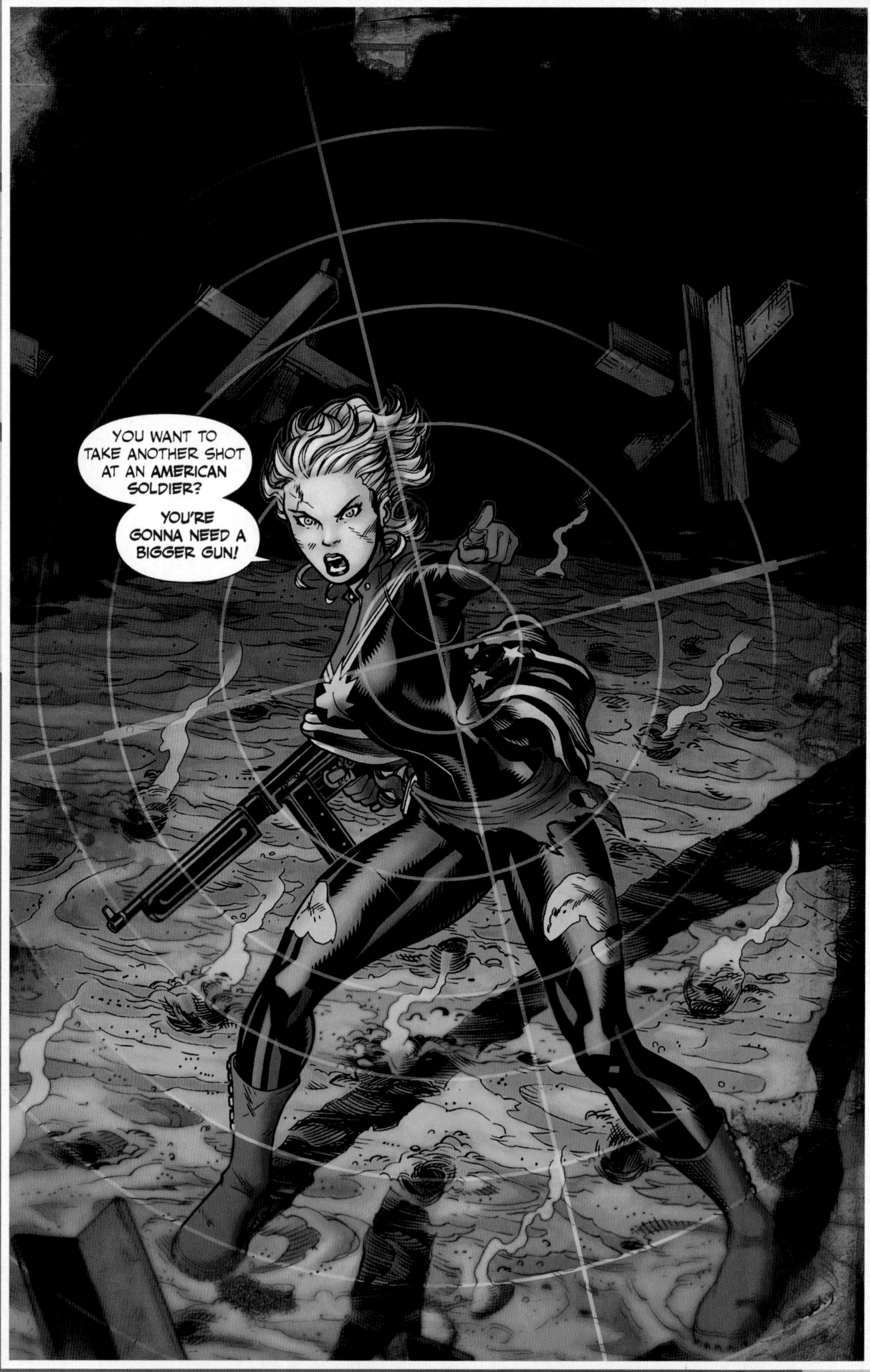

YOU WANT TO TAKE ANOTHER SHOT AT AN AMERICAN SOLDIER?
YOU'RE GONNA NEED A BIGGER GUN!

FOUR

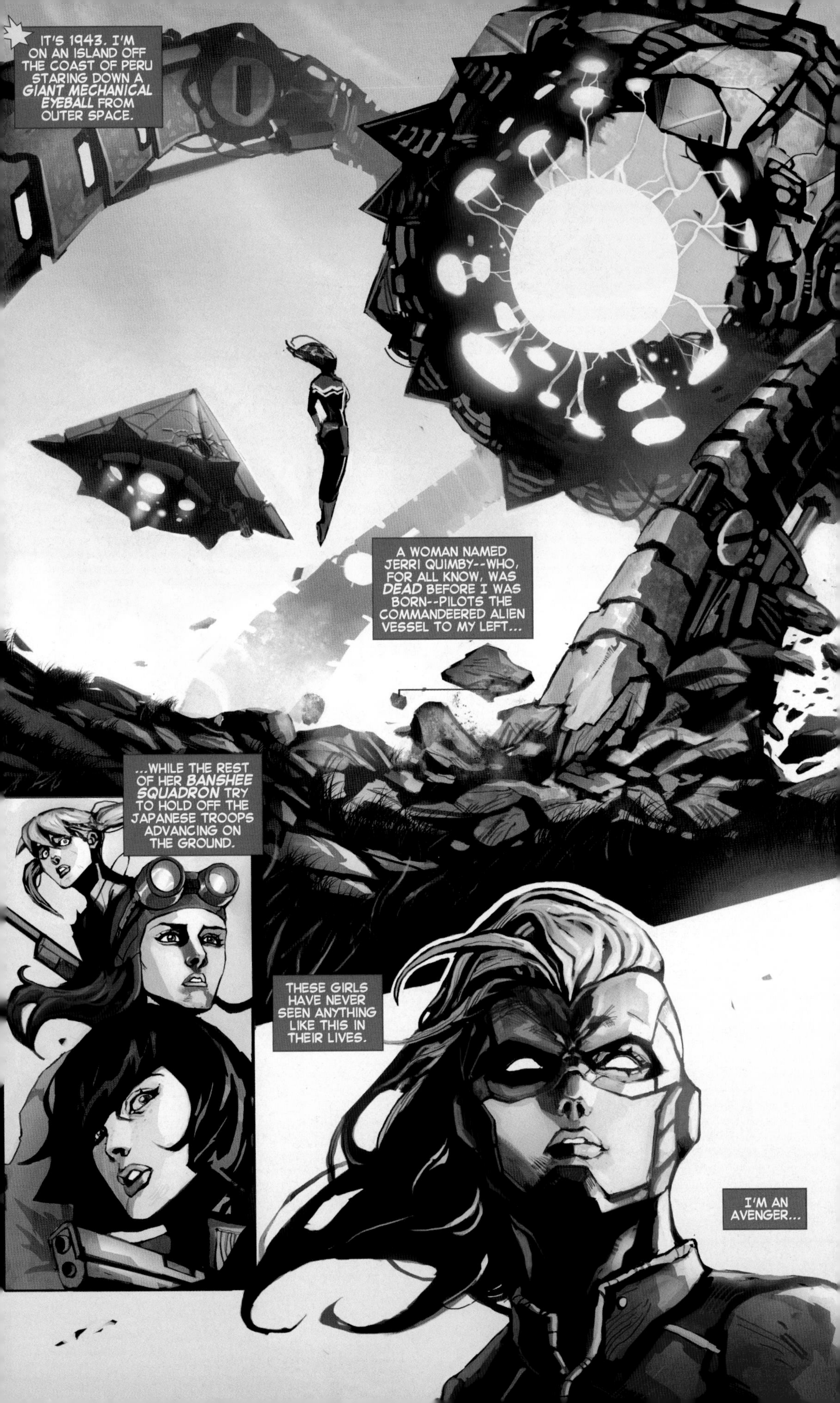
IT'S 1943. I'M ON AN ISLAND OFF THE COAST OF PERU STARING DOWN A GIANT MECHANICAL EYEBALL FROM OUTER SPACE.
A WOMAN NAMED JERRI QUIMBY--WHO, FOR ALL KNOW, WAS DEAD BEFORE I WAS BORN--PILOTS THE COMMANDEERED ALIEN VESSEL TO MY LEFT...
...WHILE THE REST OF HER BANSHEE SQUADRON TRY TO HOLD OFF THE JAPANESE TROOPS ADVANCING ON THE GROUND.
THESE GIRLS HAVE NEVER SEEN ANYTHING LIKE THIS IN THEIR LIVES.
I'M AN AVENGER...

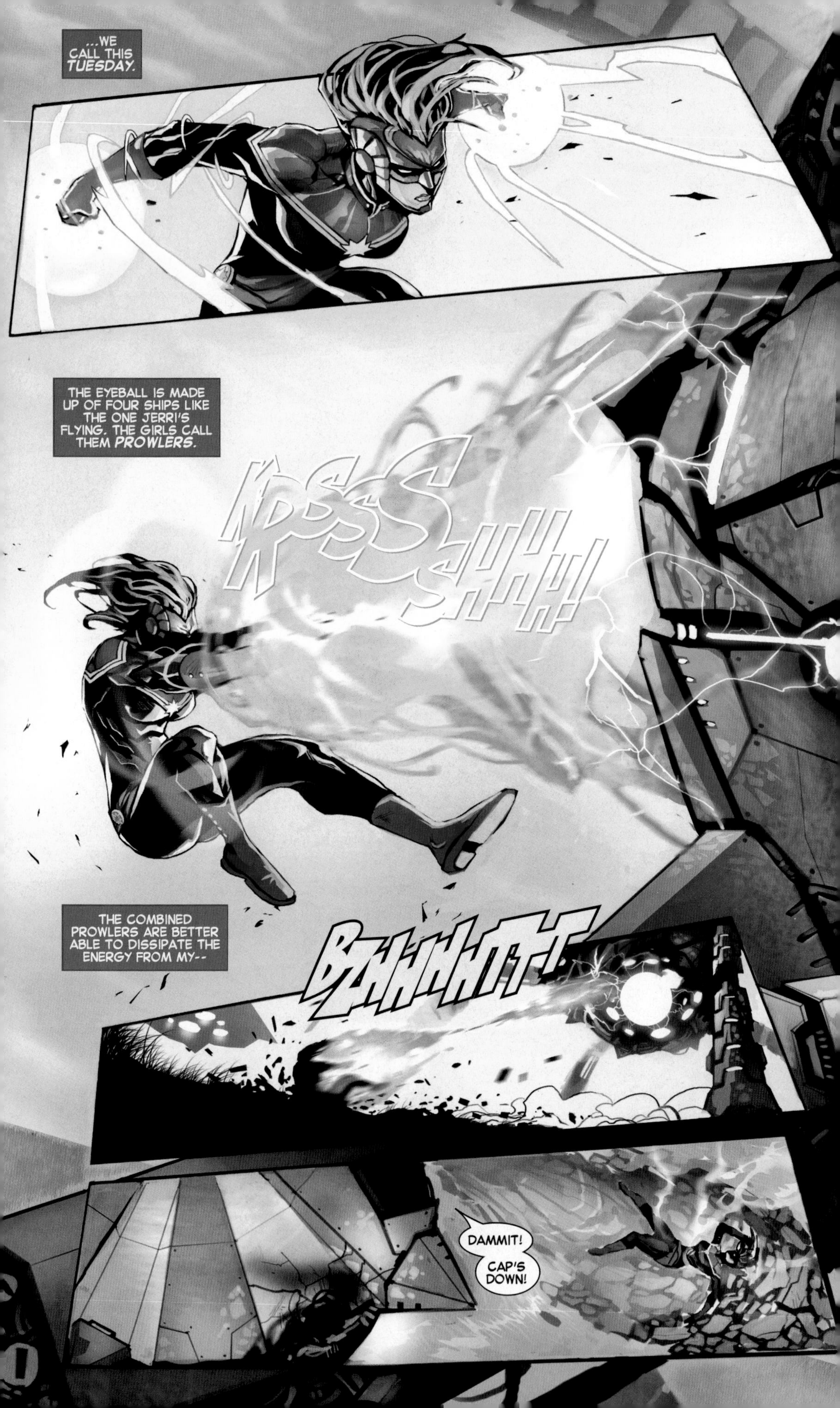
...WE CALL THIS *TUESDAY*.
THE EYEBALL IS MADE UP OF FOUR SHIPS LIKE THE ONE JERRI'S FLYING. THE GIRLS CALL THEM *PROWLERS*.
KRSSSHHH!
THE COMBINED PROWLERS ARE BETTER ABLE TO DISSIPATE THE ENERGY FROM MY--
BZHHHTT!
DAMMIT!
CAP'S DOWN!

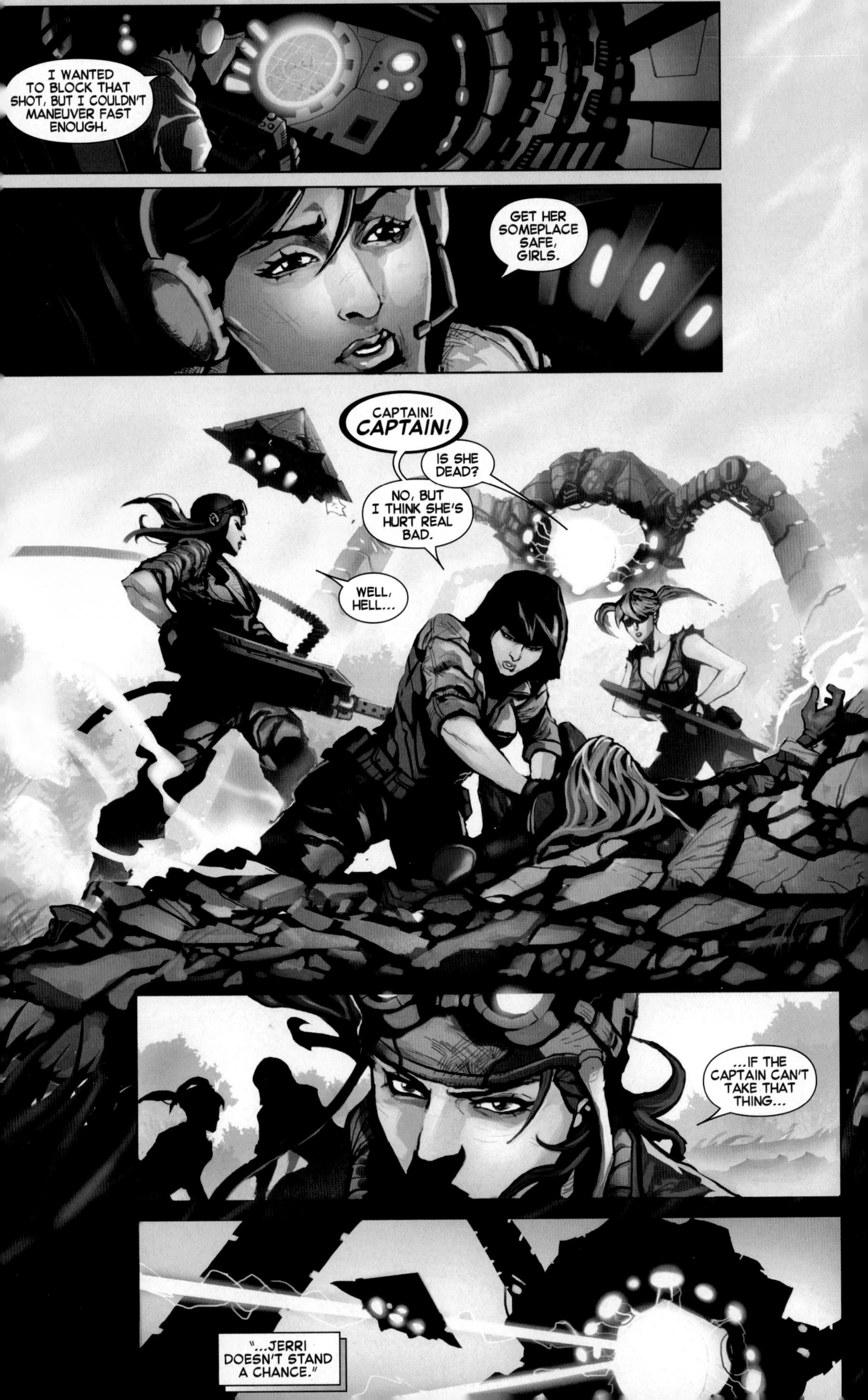

I WANTED TO BLOCK THAT SHOT, BUT I COULDN'T MANEUVER FAST ENOUGH.
GET HER SOMEPLACE SAFE, GIRLS.
CAPTAIN! CAPTAIN!
IS SHE DEAD?
NO, BUT I THINK SHE'S HURT REAL BAD.
WELL, HELL...
...IF THE CAPTAIN CAN'T TAKE THAT THING...
"...JERRI DOESN'T STAND A CHANCE."

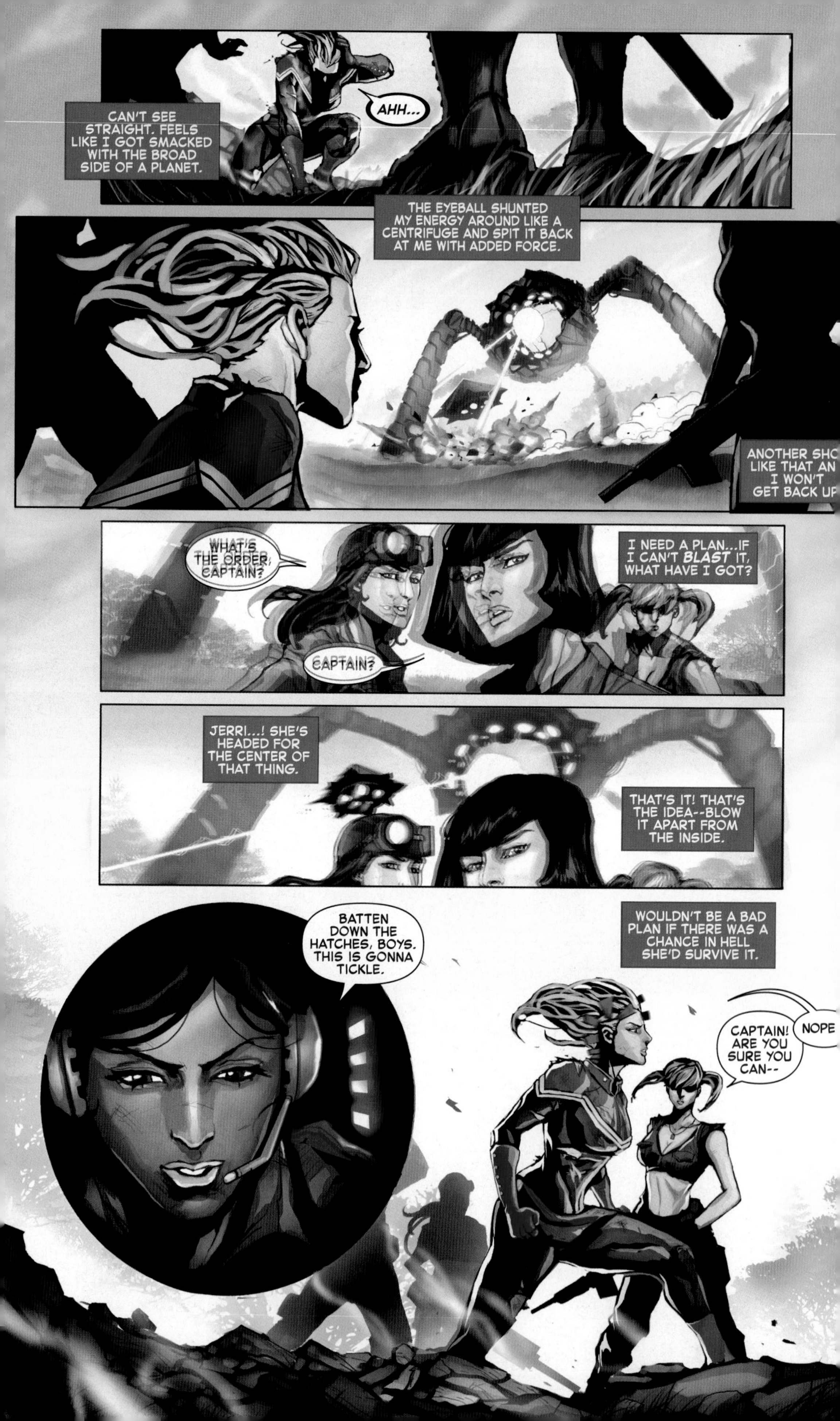
CAN'T SEE STRAIGHT. FEELS LIKE I GOT SMACKED WITH THE BROAD SIDE OF A PLANET.
AHH...
THE EYEBALL SHUNTED MY ENERGY AROUND LIKE A CENTRIFUGE AND SPIT IT BACK AT ME WITH ADDED FORCE.
ANOTHER SHO LIKE THAT AN I WON'T GET BACK UP
WHAT'S THE ORDER, CAPTAIN?
CAPTAIN?
I NEED A PLAN...IF I CAN'T BLAST IT, WHAT HAVE I GOT?
JERRI...! SHE'S HEADED FOR THE CENTER OF THAT THING.
THAT'S IT! THAT'S THE IDEA--BLOW IT APART FROM THE INSIDE.
BATTEN DOWN THE HATCHES, BOYS. THIS IS GONNA TICKLE.
WOULDN'T BE A BAD PLAN IF THERE WAS A CHANCE IN HELL SHE'D SURVIVE IT.
CAPTAIN! ARE YOU SURE YOU CAN--
NOPE

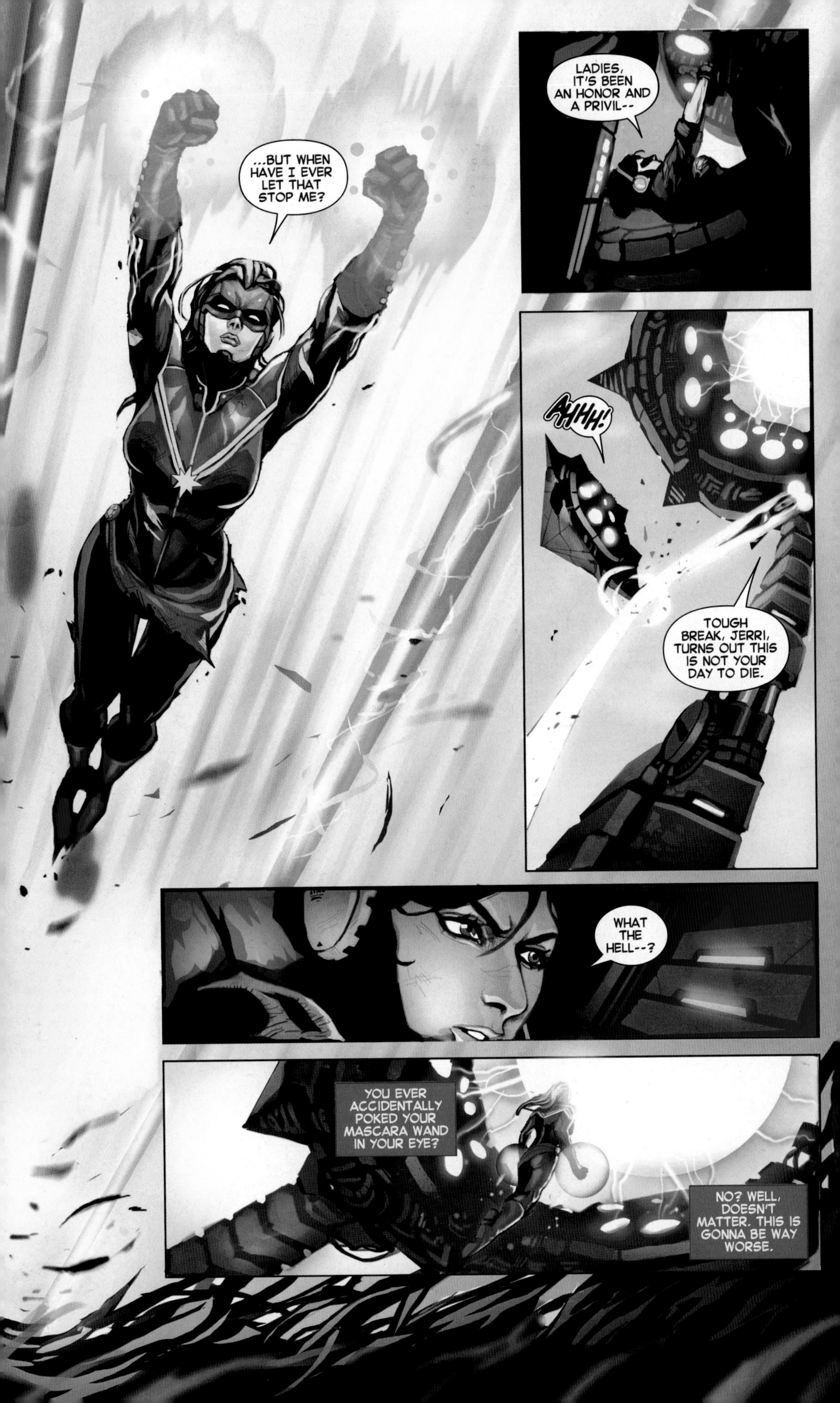
...BUT WHEN HAVE I EVER LET THAT STOP ME?
LADIES, IT'S BEEN AN HONOR AND A PRIVIL--
AHHH!
TOUGH BREAK, JERRI, TURNS OUT THIS IS NOT YOUR DAY TO DIE.
WHAT THE HELL--?
YOU EVER ACCIDENTALLY POKED YOUR MASCARA WAND IN YOUR EYE?
NO? WELL, DOESN'T MATTER. THIS IS GONNA BE WAY WORSE.

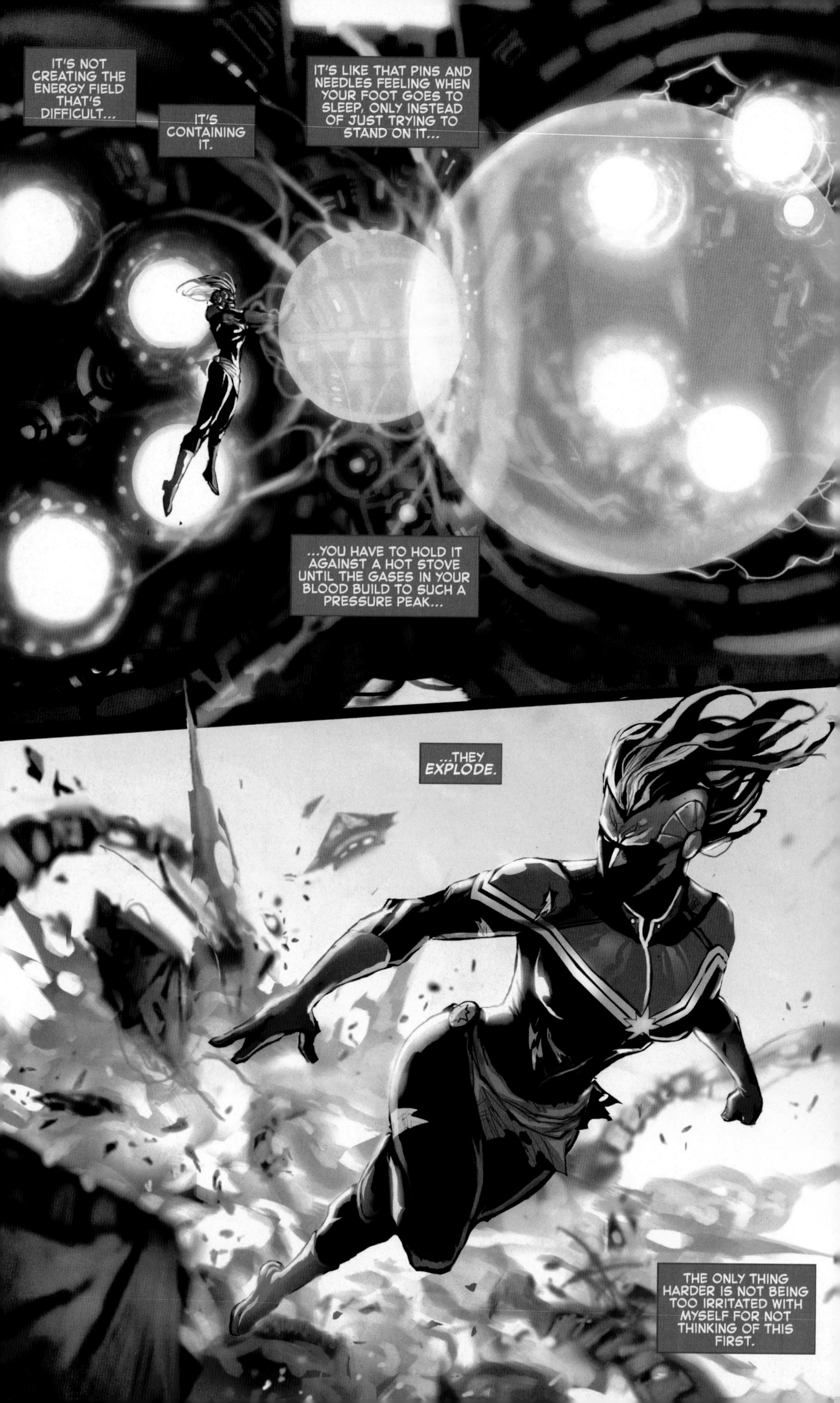
IT'S NOT CREATING THE ENERGY FIELD THAT'S DIFFICULT...
IT'S CONTAINING IT.
IT'S LIKE THAT PINS AND NEEDLES FEELING WHEN YOUR FOOT GOES TO SLEEP, ONLY INSTEAD OF JUST TRYING TO STAND ON IT...
...YOU HAVE TO HOLD IT AGAINST A HOT STOVE UNTIL THE GASES IN YOUR BLOOD BUILD TO SUCH A PRESSURE PEAK...
...THEY *EXPLODE.*
THE ONLY THING HARDER IS NOT BEING TOO IRRITATED WITH MYSELF FOR NOT THINKING OF THIS FIRST.

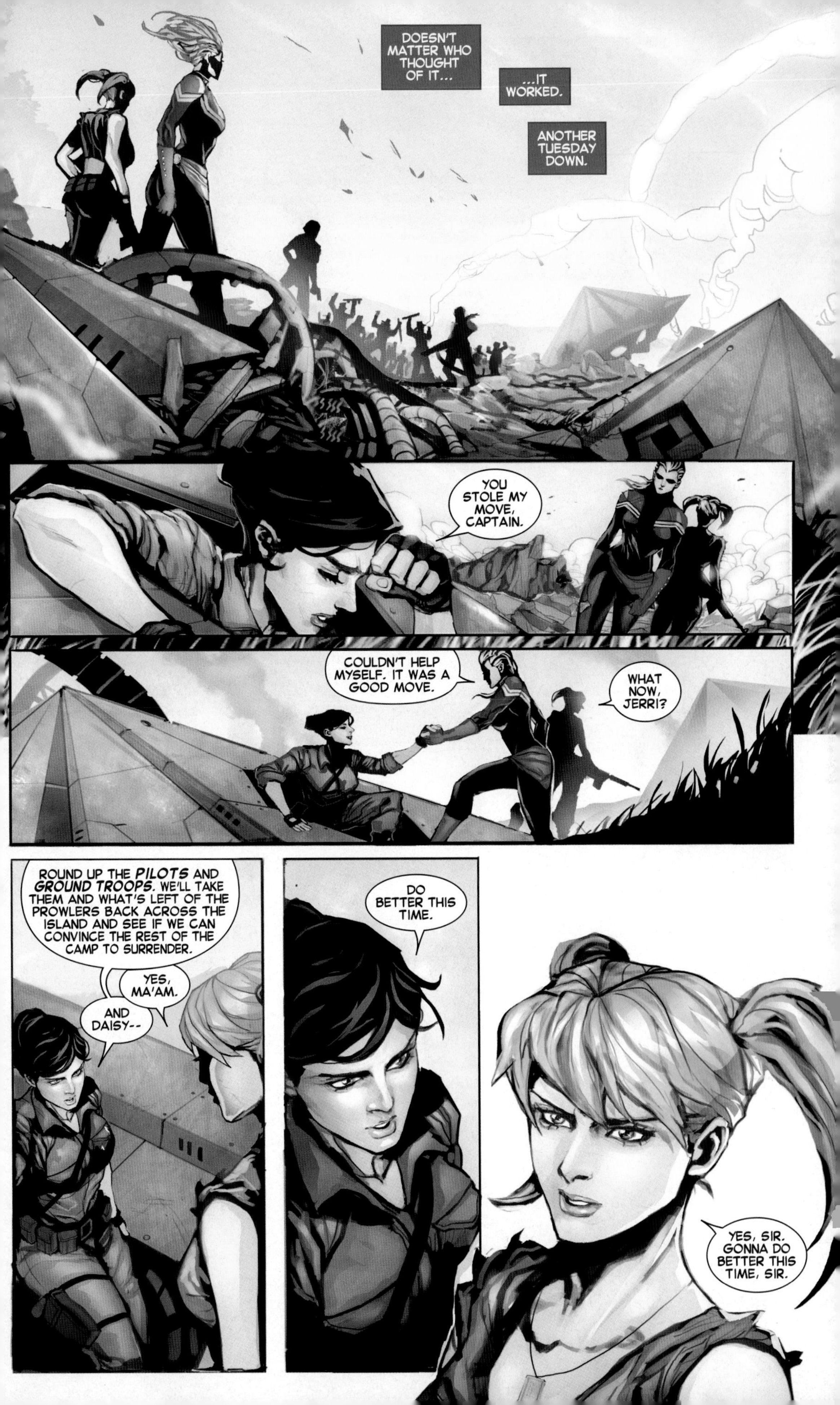
DOESN'T MATTER WHO THOUGHT OF IT...
...IT WORKED.
ANOTHER TUESDAY DOWN.
YOU STOLE MY MOVE, CAPTAIN.
COULDN'T HELP MYSELF. IT WAS A GOOD MOVE.
WHAT NOW, JERRI?
ROUND UP THE *PILOTS* AND *GROUND TROOPS*. WE'LL TAKE THEM AND WHAT'S LEFT OF THE PROWLERS BACK ACROSS THE ISLAND AND SEE IF WE CAN CONVINCE THE REST OF THE CAMP TO SURRENDER.
YES, MA'AM.
AND DAISY--
DO BETTER THIS TIME.
YES, SIR. GONNA DO BETTER THIS TIME, SIR.

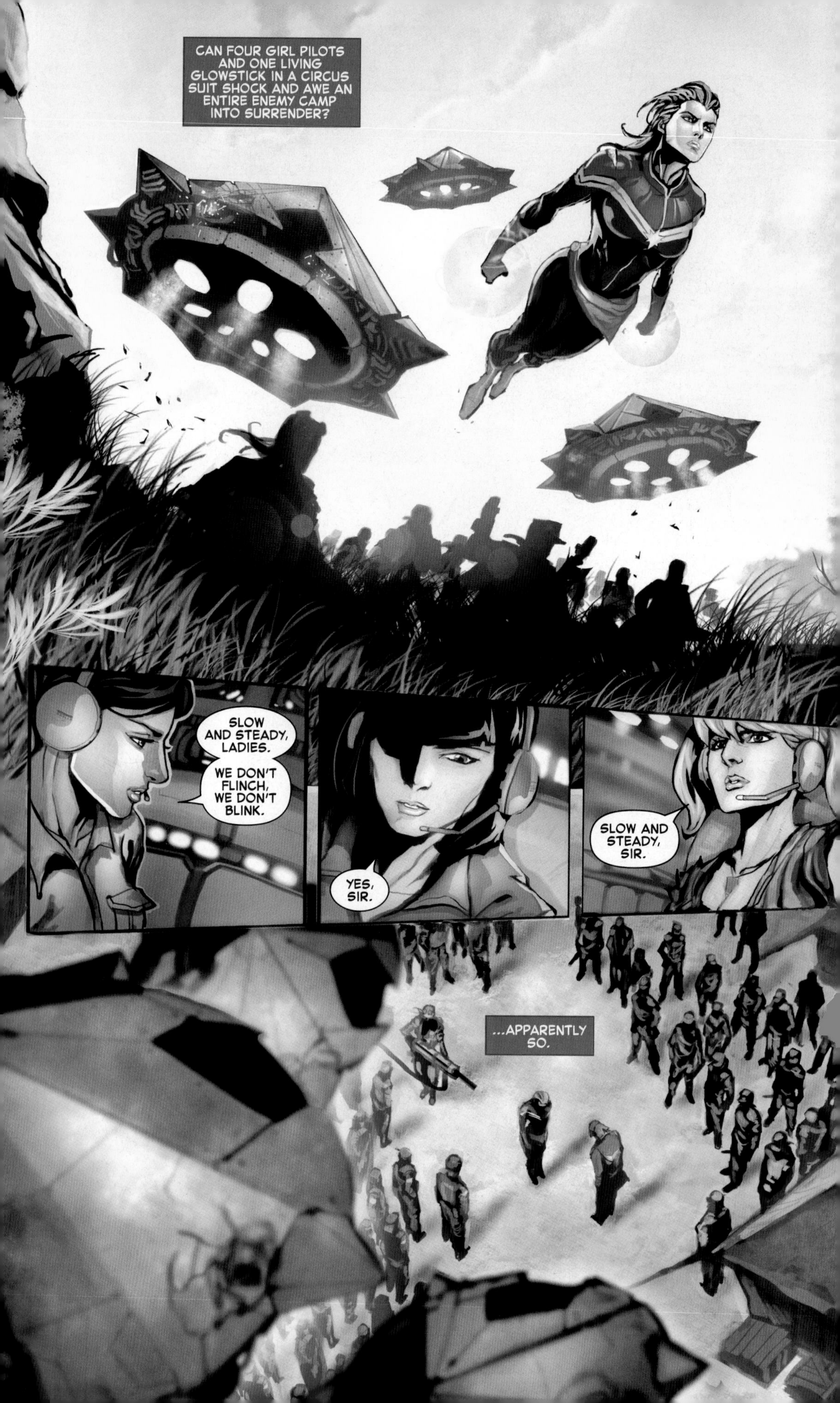
CAN FOUR GIRL PILOTS AND ONE LIVING GLOWSTICK IN A CIRCUS SUIT SHOCK AND AWE AN ENTIRE ENEMY CAMP INTO SURRENDER?
SLOW AND STEADY, LADIES.
WE DON'T FLINCH, WE DON'T BLINK.
YES, SIR.
SLOW AND STEADY, SIR.
...APPARENTLY SO.

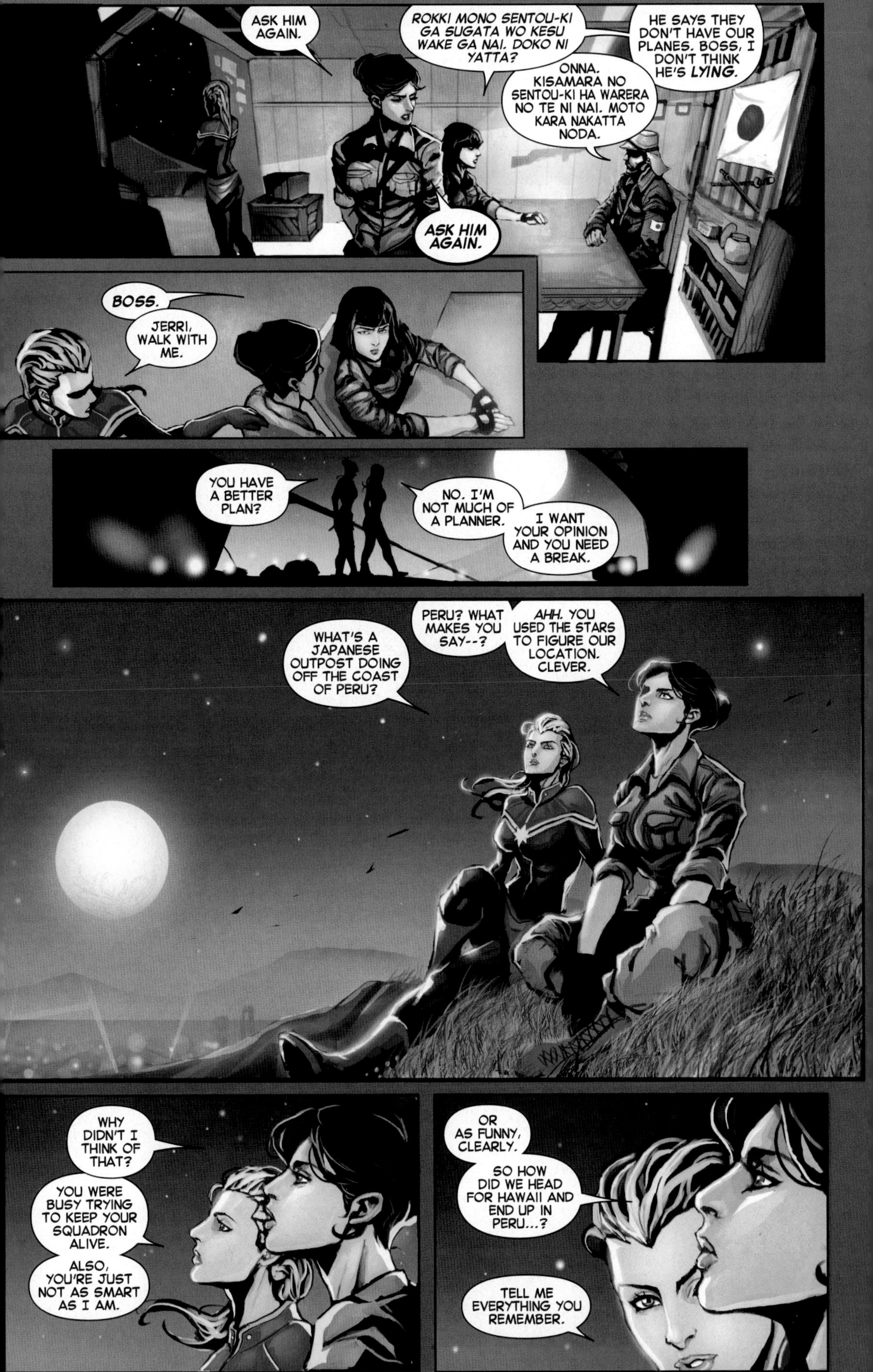
ASK HIM AGAIN.
ROKKI MONO SENTOU-KI GA SUGATA WO KESU WAKE GA NAI. DOKO NI YATTA?
HE SAYS THEY DON'T HAVE OUR PLANES. BOSS, I DON'T THINK HE'S *LYING*.
ONNA. KISAMARA NO SENTOU-KI HA WARERA NO TE NI NAI. MOTO KARA NAKATTA NODA.
ASK HIM AGAIN.
BOSS.
JERRI, WALK WITH ME.
YOU HAVE A BETTER PLAN?
NO. I'M NOT MUCH OF A PLANNER.
I WANT YOUR OPINION AND YOU NEED A BREAK.
WHAT'S A JAPANESE OUTPOST DOING OFF THE COAST OF PERU?
PERU? WHAT MAKES YOU SAY--?
AHH. YOU USED THE STARS TO FIGURE OUR LOCATION. CLEVER.
WHY DIDN'T I THINK OF THAT?
YOU WERE BUSY TRYING TO KEEP YOUR SQUADRON ALIVE.
ALSO, YOU'RE JUST NOT AS SMART AS I AM.
OR AS FUNNY, CLEARLY.
SO HOW DID WE HEAD FOR HAWAII AND END UP IN PERU...?
TELL ME EVERYTHING YOU REMEMBER.

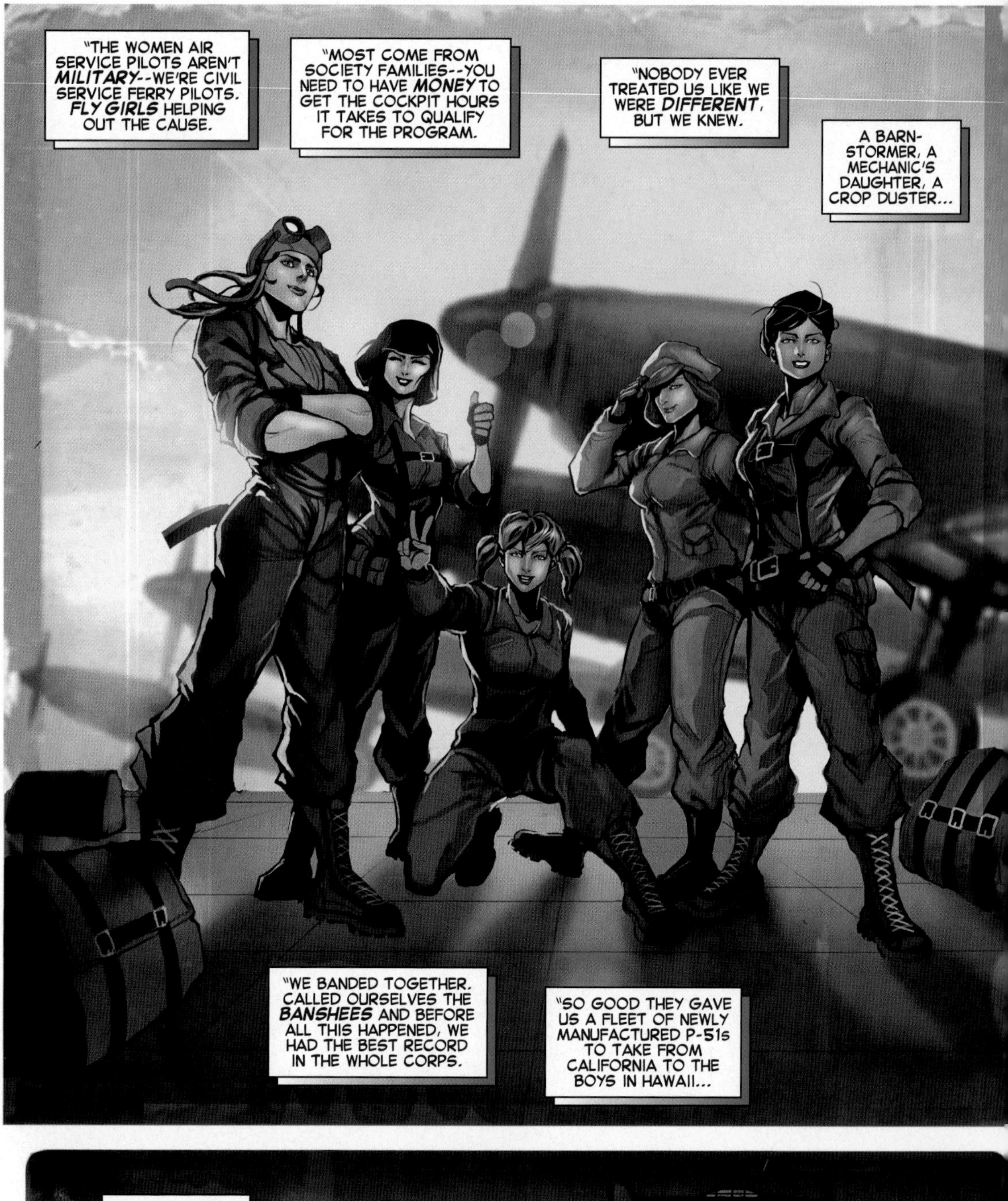
"THE WOMEN AIR SERVICE PILOTS AREN'T MILITARY--WE'RE CIVIL SERVICE FERRY PILOTS. FLY GIRLS HELPING OUT THE CAUSE.
"MOST COME FROM SOCIETY FAMILIES--YOU NEED TO HAVE MONEY TO GET THE COCKPIT HOURS IT TAKES TO QUALIFY FOR THE PROGRAM.
"NOBODY EVER TREATED US LIKE WE WERE DIFFERENT, BUT WE KNEW.
A BARN-STORMER, A MECHANIC'S DAUGHTER, A CROP DUSTER...
"WE BANDED TOGETHER. CALLED OURSELVES THE BANSHEES AND BEFORE ALL THIS HAPPENED, WE HAD THE BEST RECORD IN THE WHOLE CORPS.
"SO GOOD THEY GAVE US A FLEET OF NEWLY MANUFACTURED P-51s TO TAKE FROM CALIFORNIA TO THE BOYS IN HAWAII...

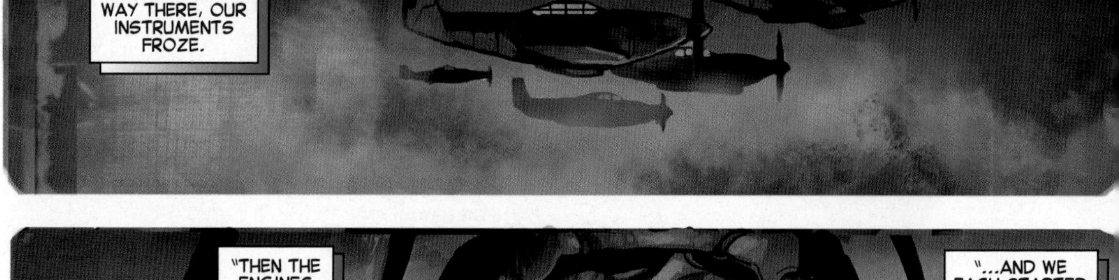
"ABOUT HALF-WAY THERE, OUR INSTRUMENTS FROZE.

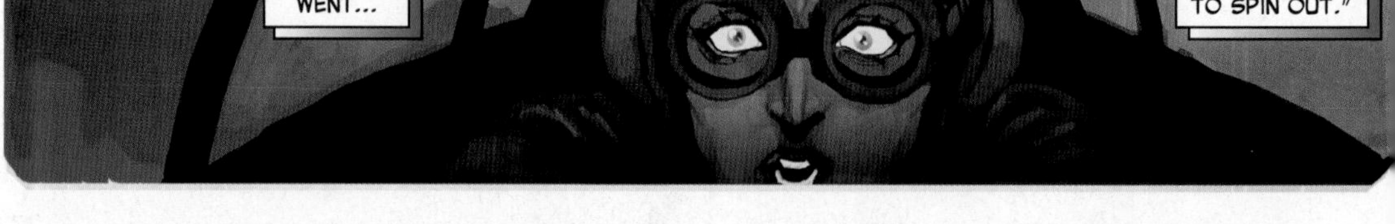
"THEN THE ENGINES WENT...
"...AND WE EACH STARTED TO SPIN OUT."

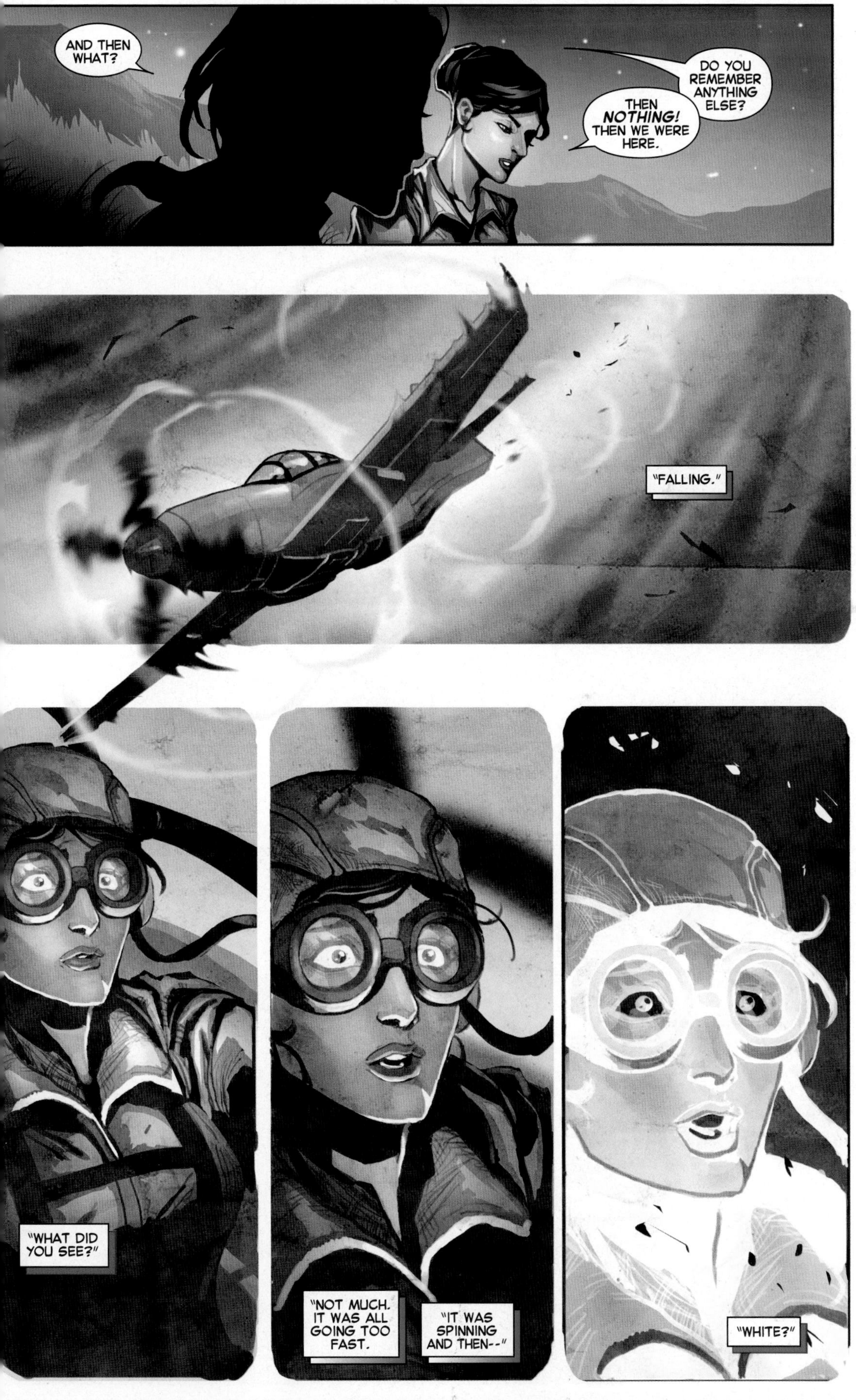
AND THEN WHAT?
DO YOU REMEMBER ANYTHING ELSE?
THEN NOTHING! THEN WE WERE HERE.
"FALLING."
"WHAT DID YOU SEE?"
"NOT MUCH. IT WAS ALL GOING TOO FAST.
"IT WAS SPINNING AND THEN--"
"WHITE?"

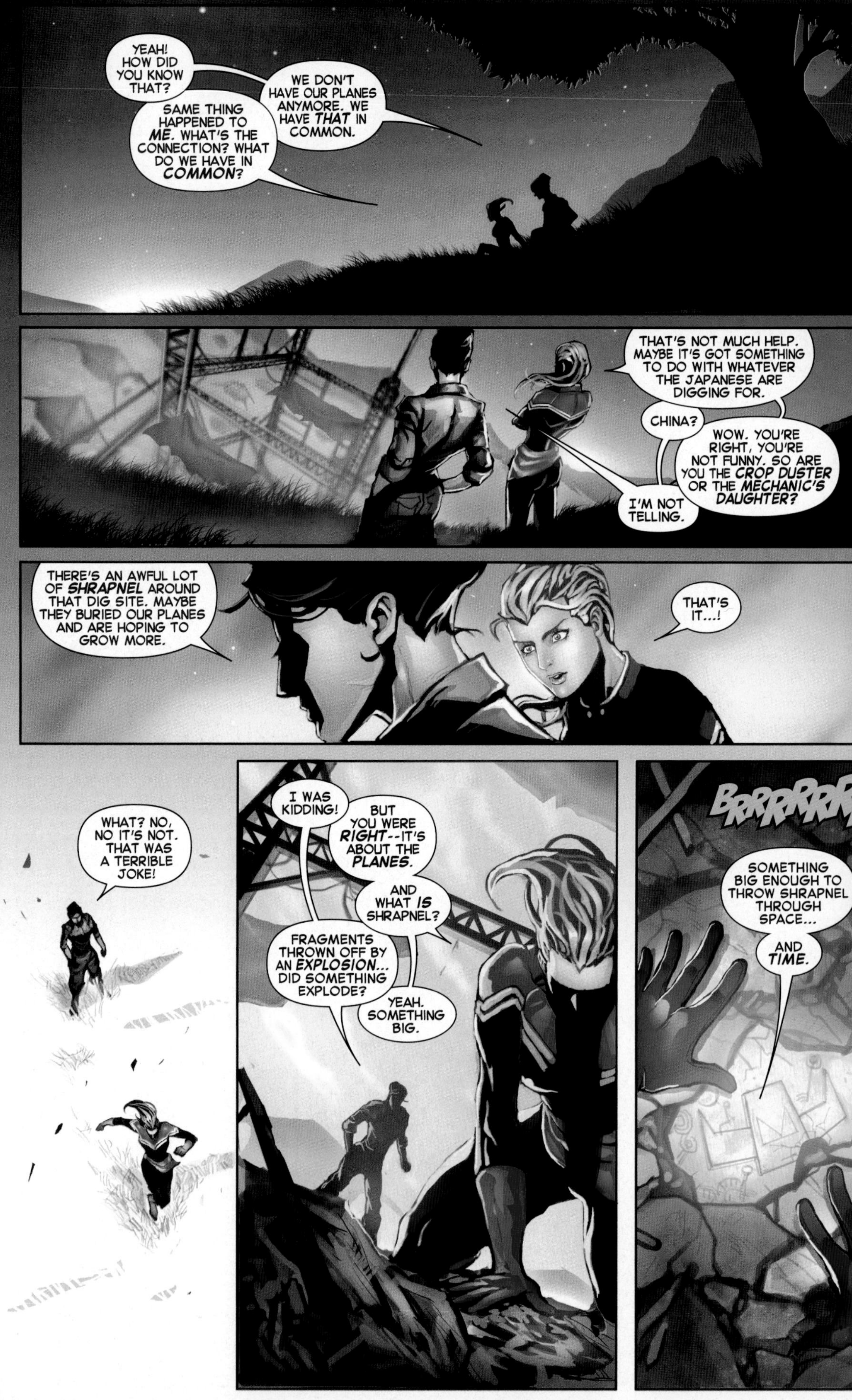

YEAH! HOW DID YOU KNOW THAT?
WE DON'T HAVE OUR PLANES ANYMORE. WE HAVE THAT IN COMMON.
SAME THING HAPPENED TO ME. WHAT'S THE CONNECTION? WHAT DO WE HAVE IN COMMON?
THAT'S NOT MUCH HELP. MAYBE IT'S GOT SOMETHING TO DO WITH WHATEVER THE JAPANESE ARE DIGGING FOR.
CHINA?
WOW. YOU'RE RIGHT, YOU'RE NOT FUNNY. SO ARE YOU THE CROP DUSTER OR THE MECHANIC'S DAUGHTER?
I'M NOT TELLING.
THERE'S AN AWFUL LOT OF SHRAPNEL AROUND THAT DIG SITE. MAYBE THEY BURIED OUR PLANES AND ARE HOPING TO GROW MORE.
THAT'S IT...!
WHAT? NO, NO IT'S NOT. THAT WAS A TERRIBLE JOKE!
I WAS KIDDING!
BUT YOU WERE RIGHT--IT'S ABOUT THE PLANES.
AND WHAT IS SHRAPNEL?
FRAGMENTS THROWN OFF BY AN EXPLOSION... DID SOMETHING EXPLODE?
YEAH. SOMETHING BIG.
BRRRRRR
SOMETHING BIG ENOUGH TO THROW SHRAPNEL THROUGH SPACE...
AND TIME.

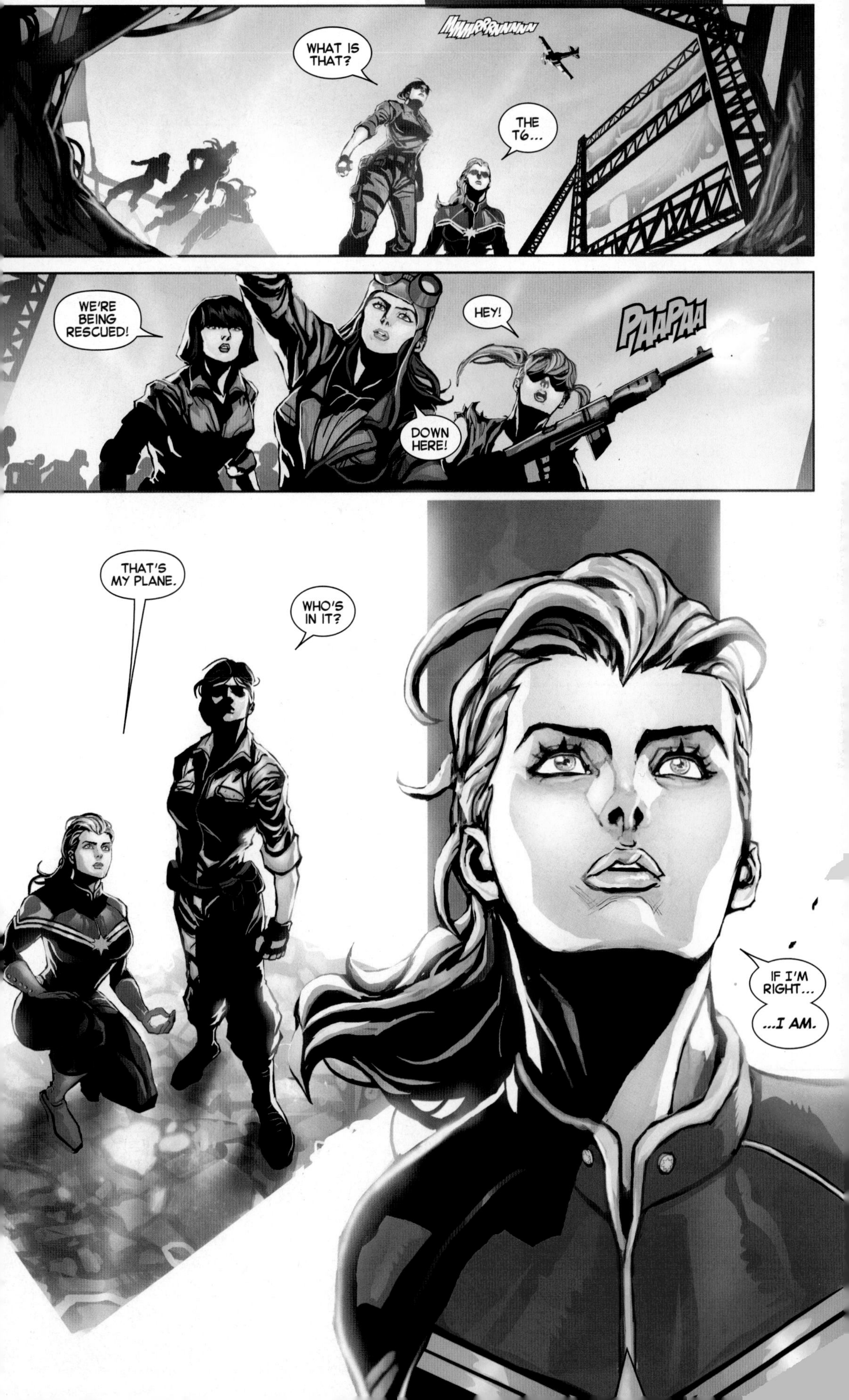
MMMRRRNNNNN
WHAT IS THAT?
THE T6...
WE'RE BEING RESCUED!
HEY!
PAAPAA
DOWN HERE!
THAT'S MY PLANE.
WHO'S IN IT?
IF I'M RIGHT...
...I AM.

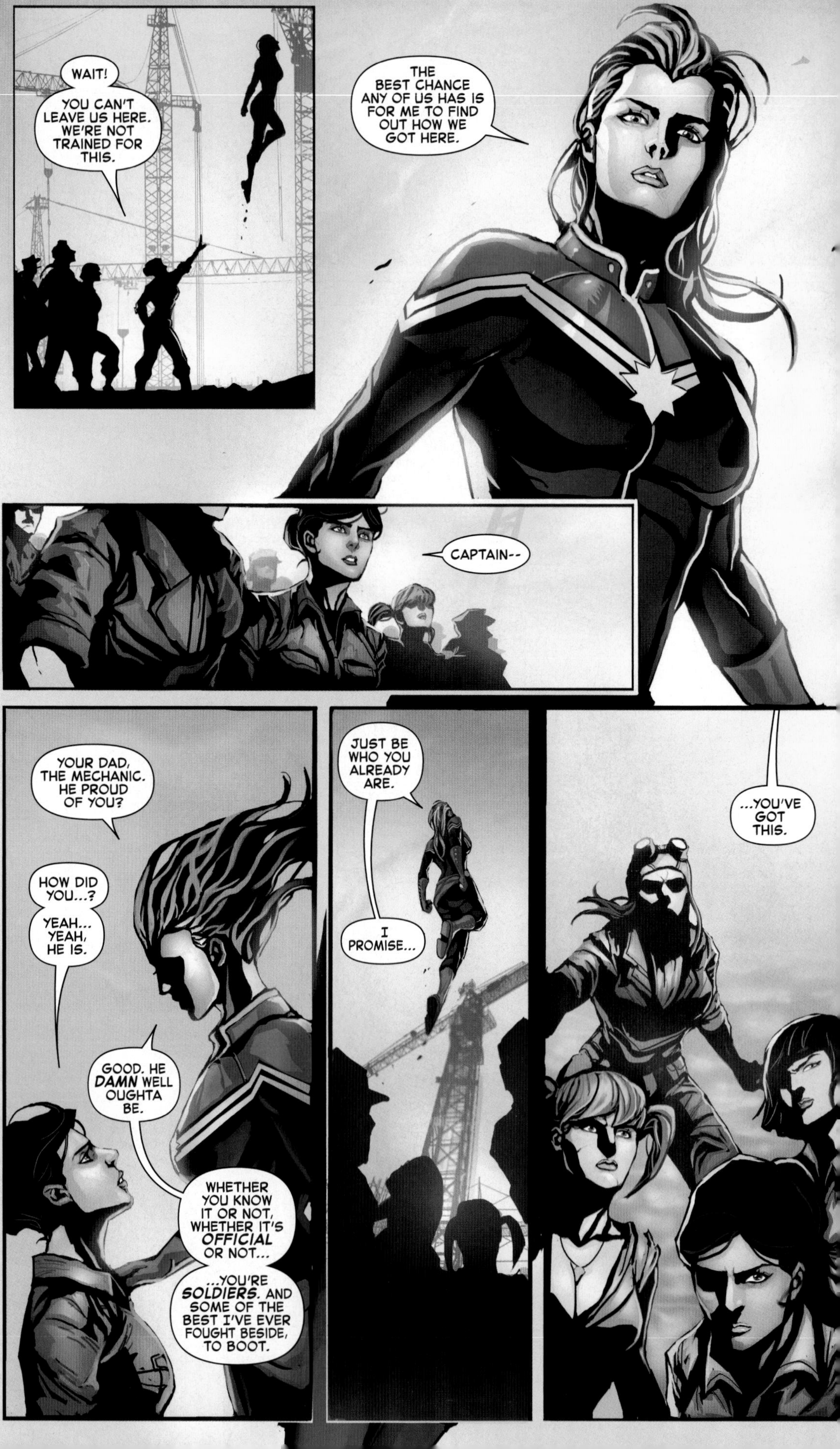
WAIT!
YOU CAN'T LEAVE US HERE. WE'RE NOT TRAINED FOR THIS.
THE BEST CHANCE ANY OF US HAS IS FOR ME TO FIND OUT HOW WE GOT HERE.
CAPTAIN--
YOUR DAD, THE MECHANIC. HE PROUD OF YOU?
HOW DID YOU...?
YEAH... YEAH, HE IS.
GOOD. HE DAMN WELL OUGHTA BE.
WHETHER YOU KNOW IT OR NOT, WHETHER IT'S OFFICIAL OR NOT...
...YOU'RE SOLDIERS. AND SOME OF THE BEST I'VE EVER FOUGHT BESIDE, TO BOOT.
JUST BE WHO YOU ALREADY ARE.
I PROMISE...
...YOU'VE GOT THIS.

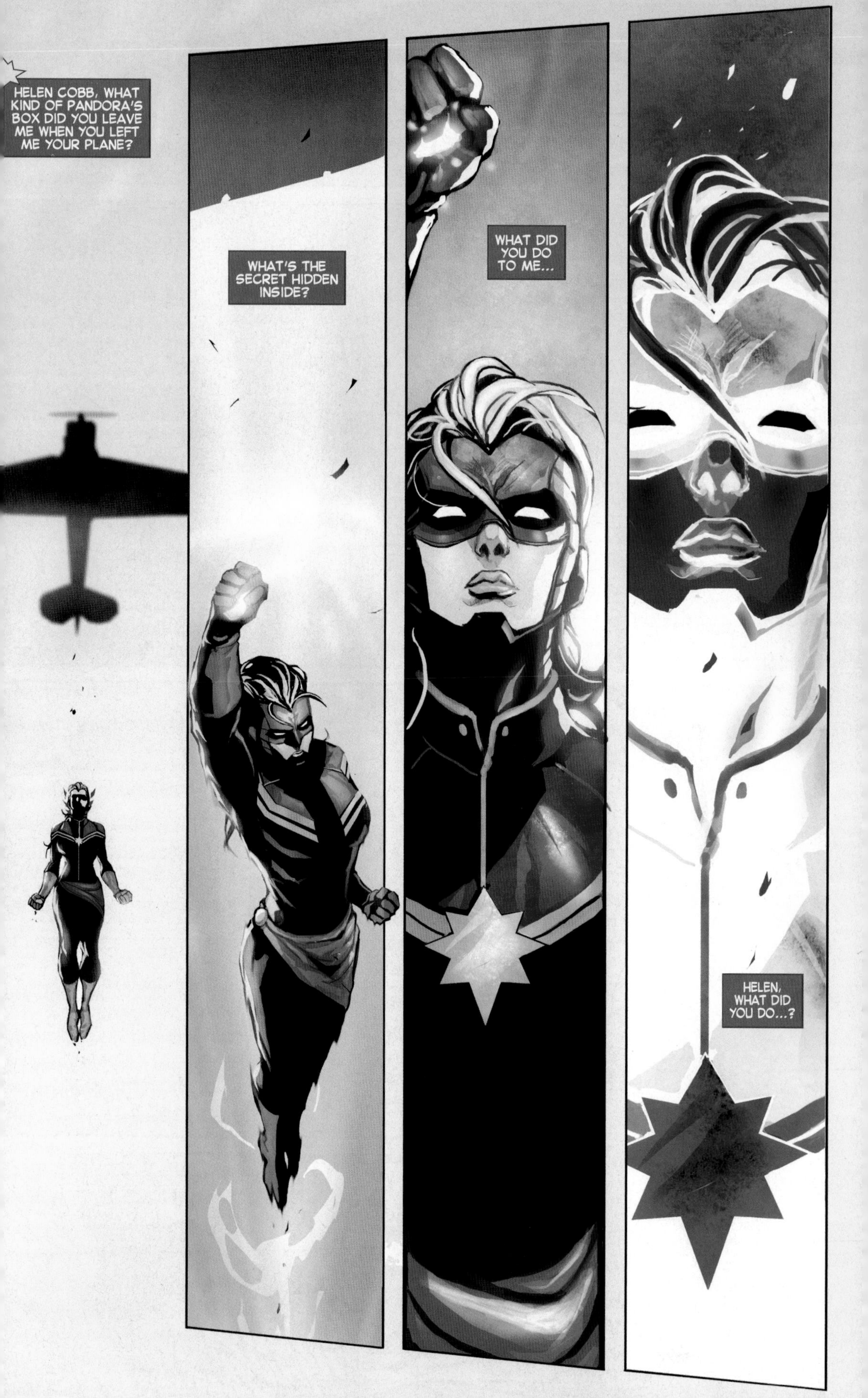

HELEN COBB, WHAT KIND OF PANDORA'S BOX DID YOU LEAVE ME WHEN YOU LEFT ME YOUR PLANE?
WHAT'S THE SECRET HIDDEN INSIDE?
WHAT DID YOU DO TO ME...
HELEN, WHAT DID YOU DO...?

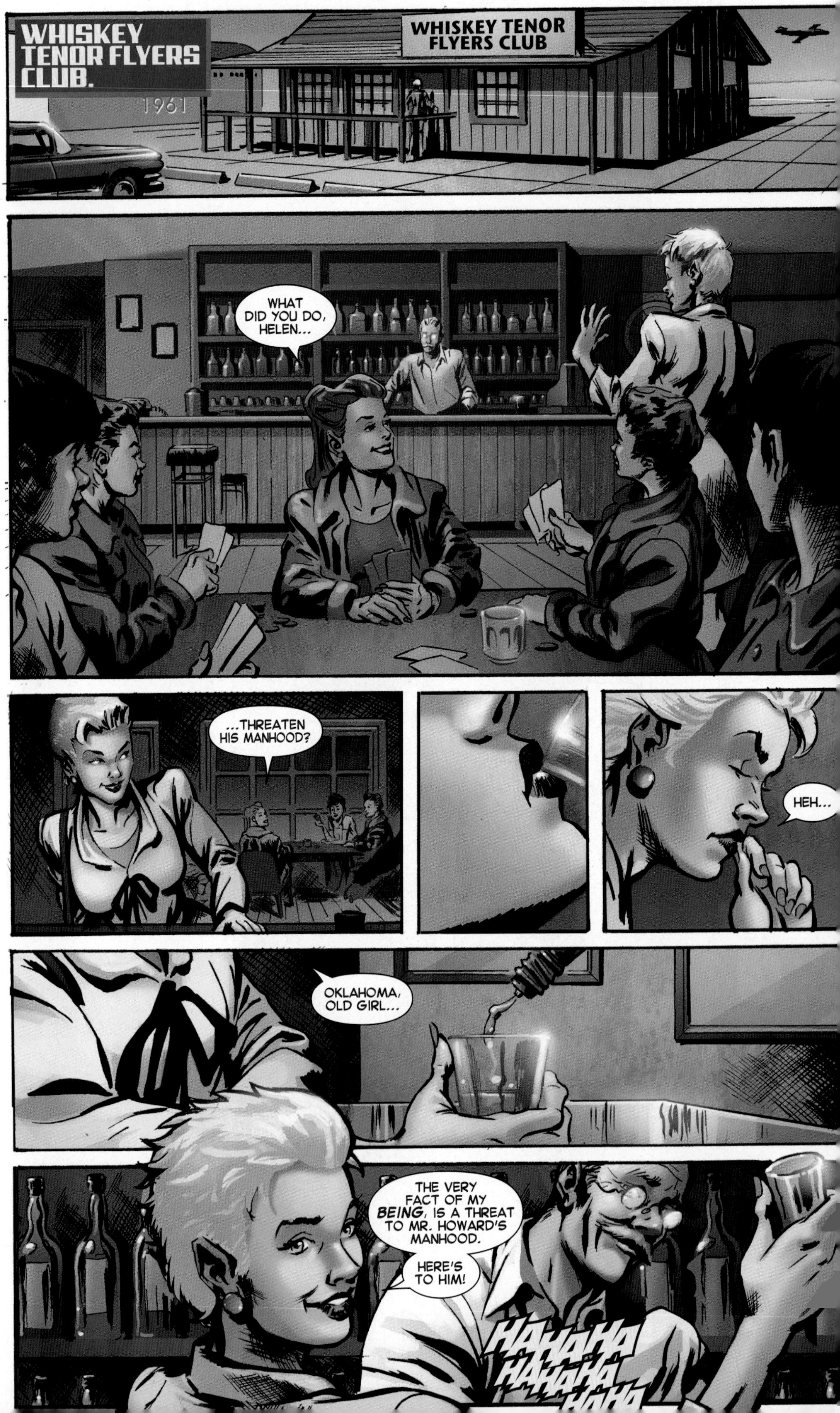
WHISKEY TENOR FLYERS CLUB.
1961
WHISKEY TENOR FLYERS CLUB
WHAT DID YOU DO, HELEN...
...THREATEN HIS MANHOOD?
HEH...
OKLAHOMA, OLD GIRL...
THE VERY FACT OF MY BEING, IS A THREAT TO MR. HOWARD'S MANHOOD.
HERE'S TO HIM!
HAHAHA HAHAHA

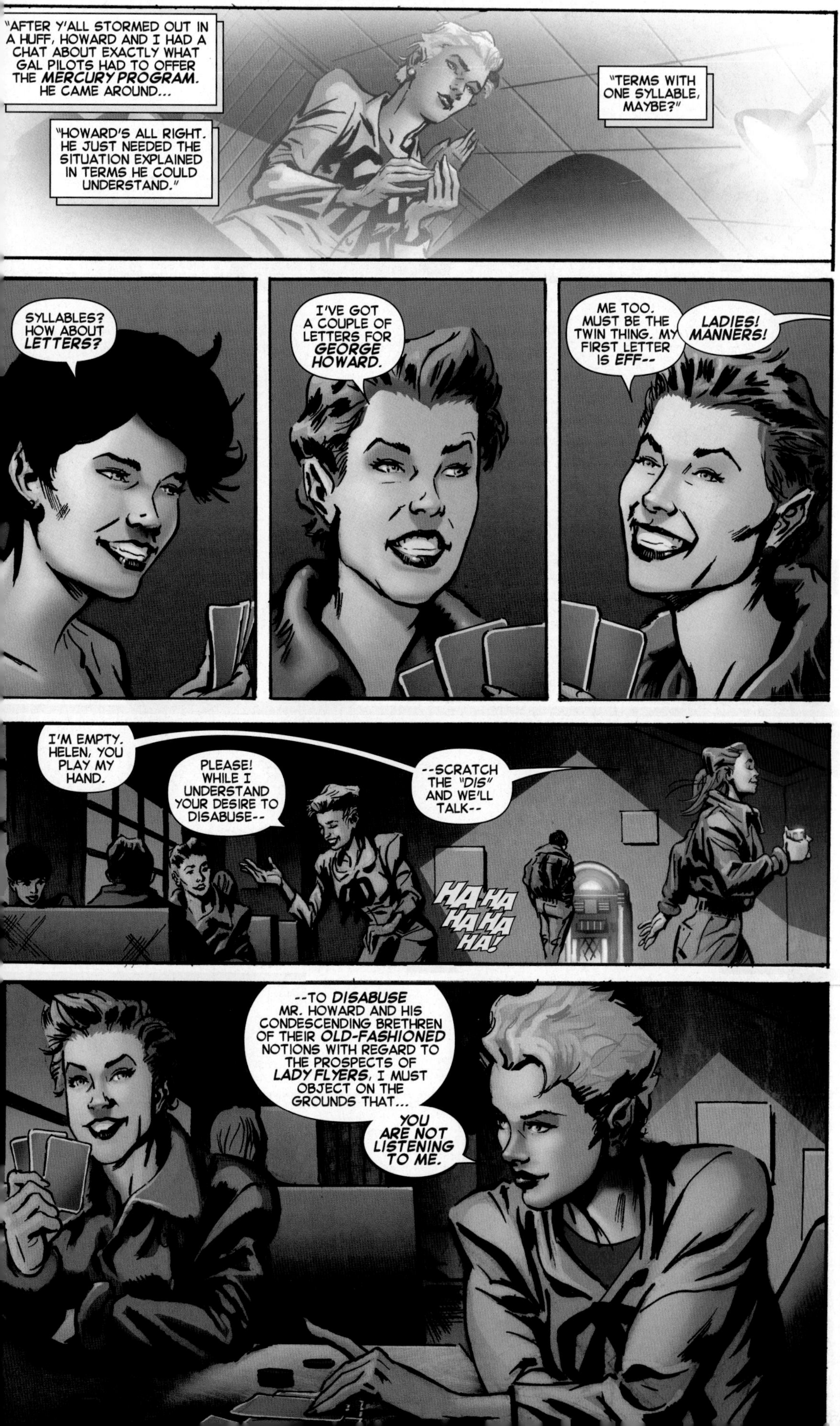
"AFTER Y'ALL STORMED OUT IN A HUFF, HOWARD AND I HAD A CHAT ABOUT EXACTLY WHAT GAL PILOTS HAD TO OFFER THE MERCURY PROGRAM. HE CAME AROUND...
"HOWARD'S ALL RIGHT. HE JUST NEEDED THE SITUATION EXPLAINED IN TERMS HE COULD UNDERSTAND."
"TERMS WITH ONE SYLLABLE, MAYBE?"
SYLLABLES? HOW ABOUT LETTERS?
I'VE GOT A COUPLE OF LETTERS FOR GEORGE HOWARD.
ME TOO. MUST BE THE TWIN THING. MY FIRST LETTER IS EFF--
LADIES! MANNERS!
I'M EMPTY. HELEN, YOU PLAY MY HAND.
PLEASE! WHILE I UNDERSTAND YOUR DESIRE TO DISABUSE--
--SCRATCH THE "DIS" AND WE'LL TALK--
HA HA HA HA HA!
--TO DISABUSE MR. HOWARD AND HIS CONDESCENDING BRETHREN OF THEIR OLD-FASHIONED NOTIONS WITH REGARD TO THE PROSPECTS OF LADY FLYERS, I MUST OBJECT ON THE GROUNDS THAT...
YOU ARE NOT LISTENING TO ME.

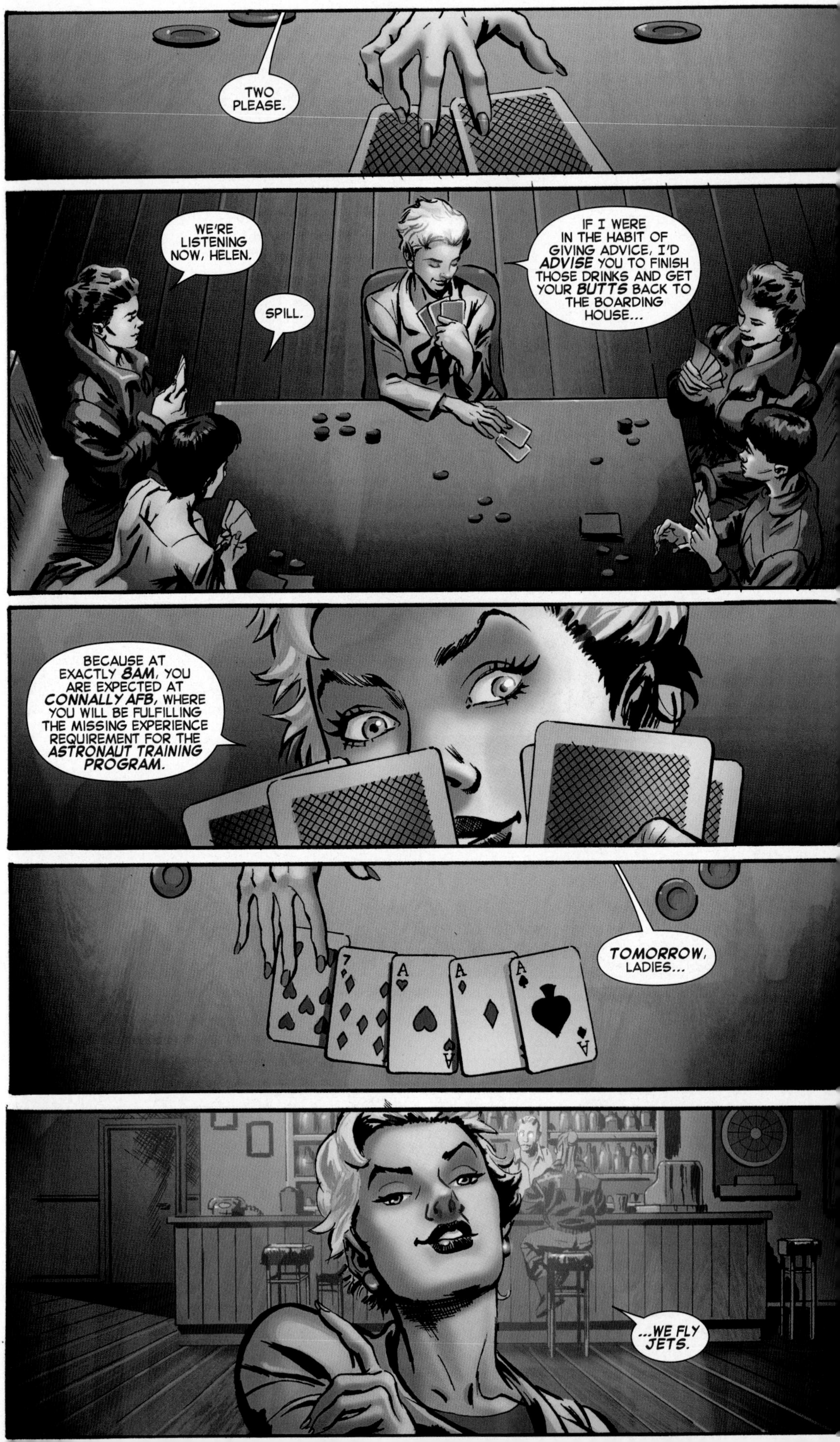
TWO PLEASE.
WE'RE LISTENING NOW, HELEN.
SPILL.
IF I WERE IN THE HABIT OF GIVING ADVICE, I'D ADVISE YOU TO FINISH THOSE DRINKS AND GET YOUR BUTTS BACK TO THE BOARDING HOUSE...
BECAUSE AT EXACTLY 8AM, YOU ARE EXPECTED AT CONNALLY AFB, WHERE YOU WILL BE FULFILLING THE MISSING EXPERIENCE REQUIREMENT FOR THE ASTRONAUT TRAINING PROGRAM.
TOMORROW, LADIES...
...WE FLY JETS.

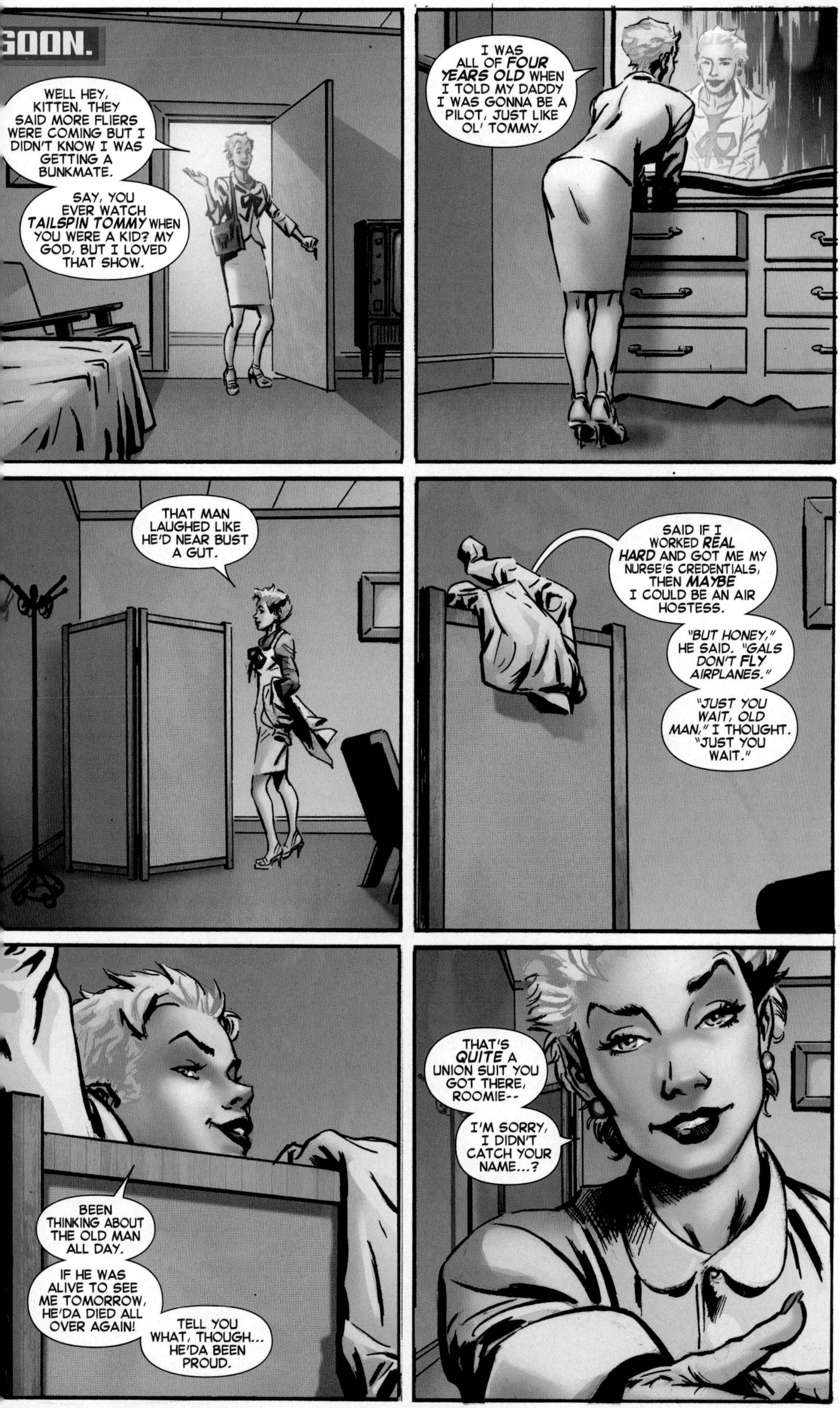

GOON.
WELL HEY, KITTEN. THEY SAID MORE FLIERS WERE COMING BUT I DIDN'T KNOW I WAS GETTING A BUNKMATE.
SAY, YOU EVER WATCH TAILSPIN TOMMY WHEN YOU WERE A KID? MY GOD, BUT I LOVED THAT SHOW.
I WAS ALL OF FOUR YEARS OLD WHEN I TOLD MY DADDY I WAS GONNA BE A PILOT, JUST LIKE OL' TOMMY.
THAT MAN LAUGHED LIKE HE'D NEAR BUST A GUT.
SAID IF I WORKED REAL HARD AND GOT ME MY NURSE'S CREDENTIALS, THEN MAYBE I COULD BE AN AIR HOSTESS.
"BUT HONEY," HE SAID. "GALS DON'T FLY AIRPLANES."
"JUST YOU WAIT, OLD MAN," I THOUGHT. "JUST YOU WAIT."
BEEN THINKING ABOUT THE OLD MAN ALL DAY.
IF HE WAS ALIVE TO SEE ME TOMORROW, HE'DA DIED ALL OVER AGAIN!
TELL YOU WHAT, THOUGH... HE'DA BEEN PROUD.
THAT'S QUITE A UNION SUIT YOU GOT THERE, ROOMIE--
I'M SORRY, I DIDN'T CATCH YOUR NAME...?

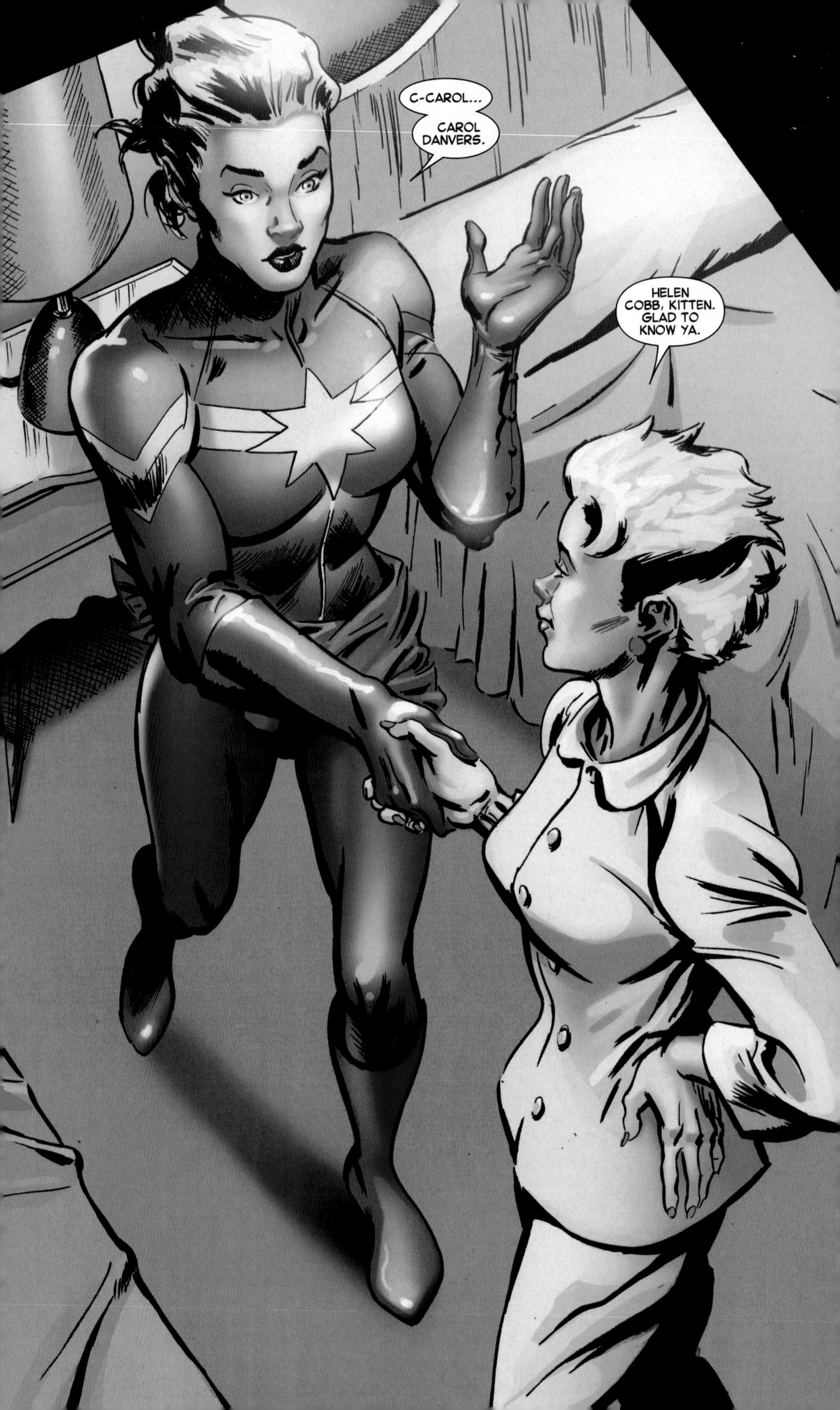
C-CAROL...
CAROL DANVERS.
HELEN COBB, KITTEN. GLAD TO KNOW YA.

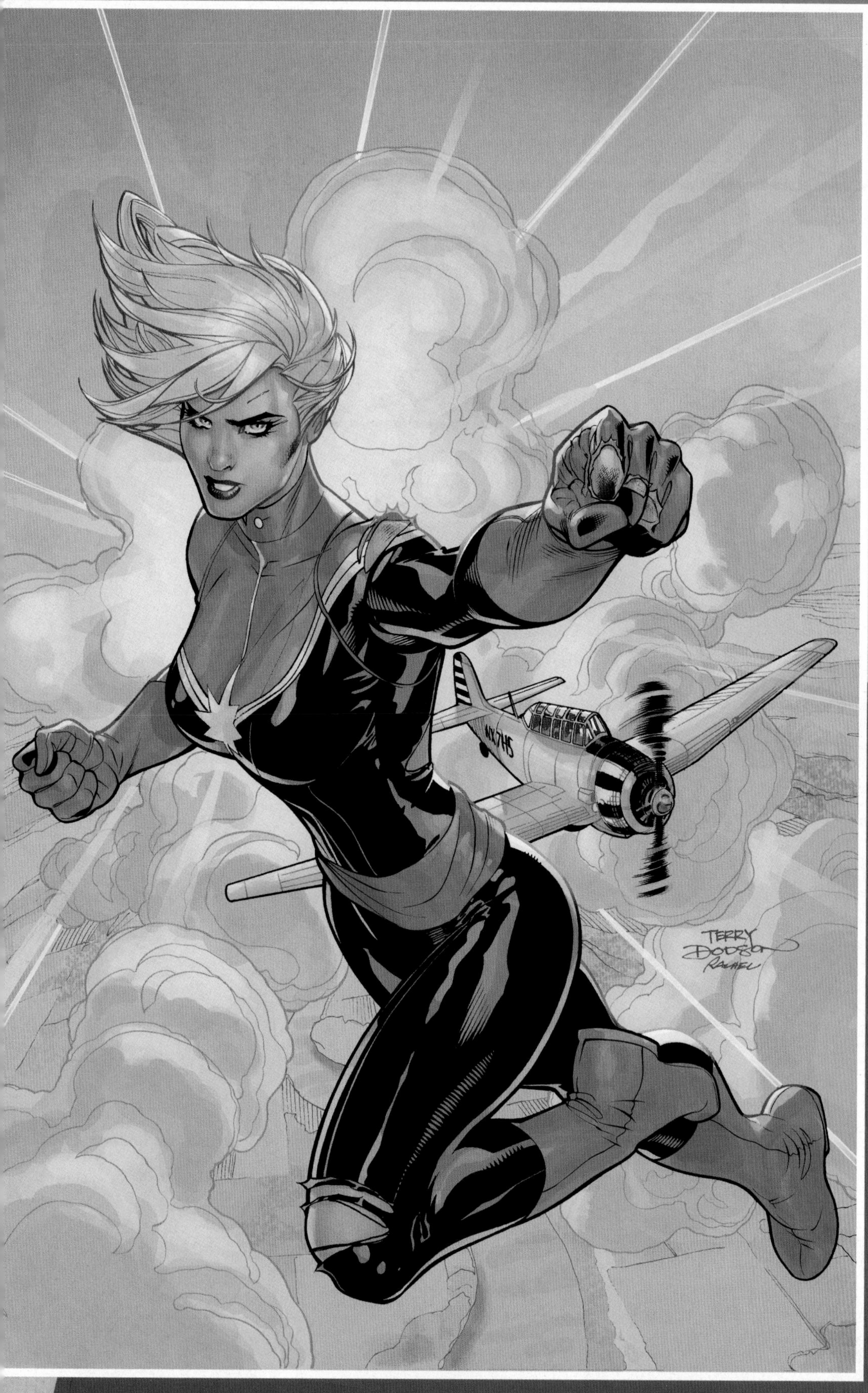
NX7HS
TERRY DODSON RACHEL

FIVE

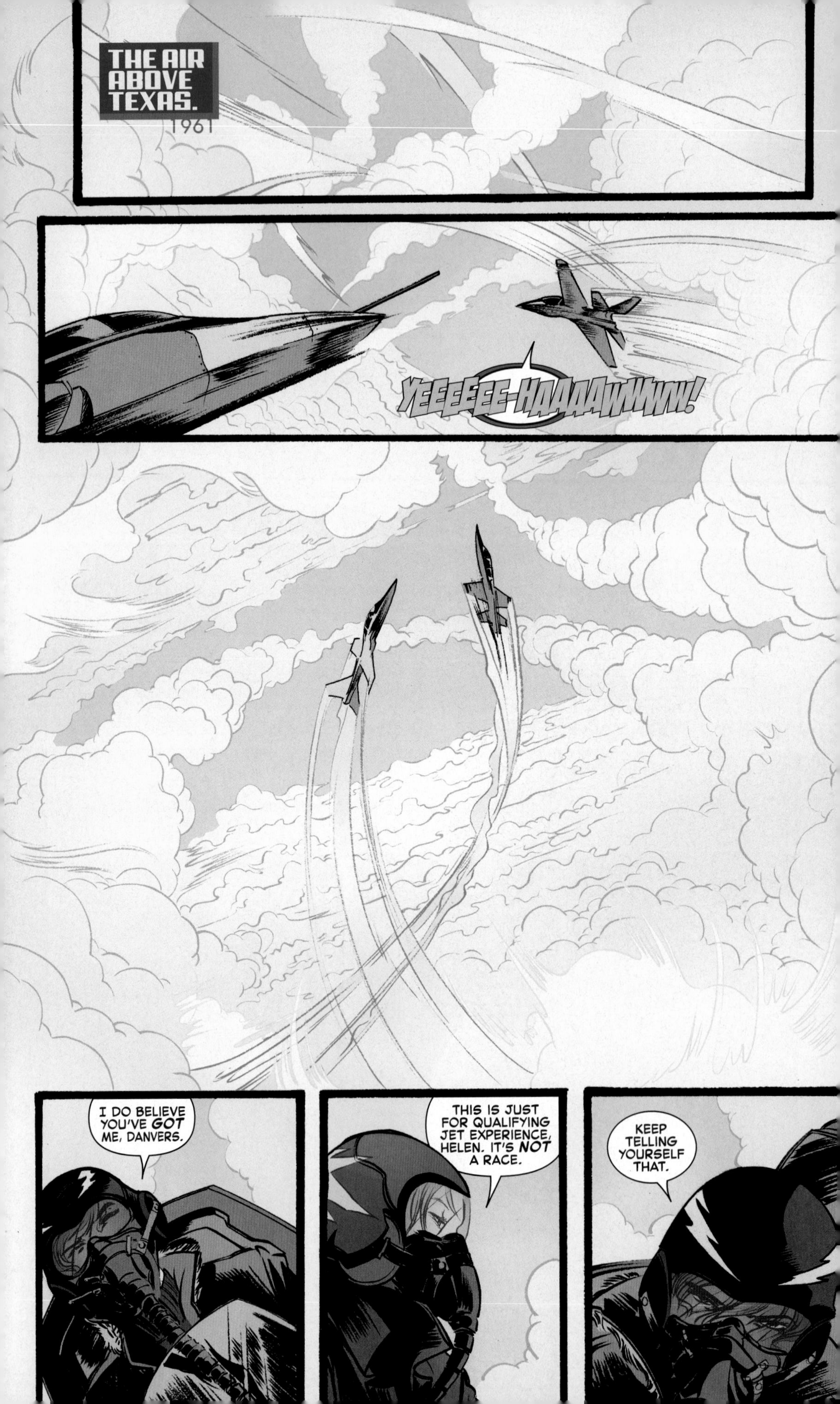
THE AIR ABOVE TEXAS.
1961
YEEEEEE-HAAAAWWWW!
I DO BELIEVE YOU'VE GOT ME, DANVERS.
THIS IS JUST FOR QUALIFYING JET EXPERIENCE, HELEN. IT'S NOT A RACE.
KEEP TELLING YOURSELF THAT.

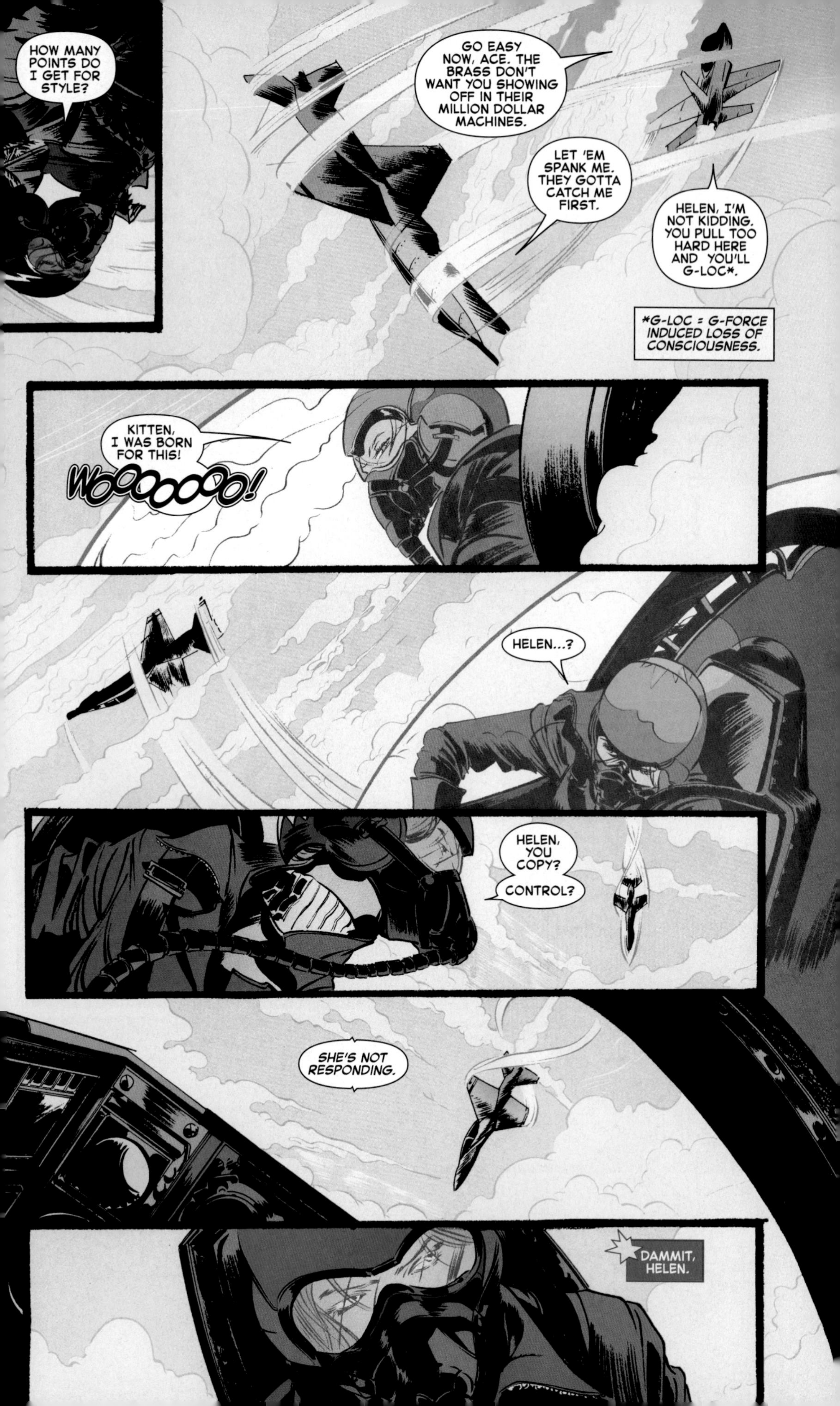
HOW MANY POINTS DO I GET FOR STYLE?
GO EASY NOW, ACE. THE BRASS DON'T WANT YOU SHOWING OFF IN THEIR MILLION DOLLAR MACHINES.
LET 'EM SPANK ME. THEY GOTTA CATCH ME FIRST.
HELEN, I'M NOT KIDDING. YOU PULL TOO HARD HERE AND YOU'LL G-LOC*.
*G-LOC = G-FORCE INDUCED LOSS OF CONSCIOUSNESS.
KITTEN, I WAS BORN FOR THIS!
WOOOOOOOO!
HELEN...?
HELEN, YOU COPY?
CONTROL?
SHE'S NOT RESPONDING.
DAMMIT, HELEN.

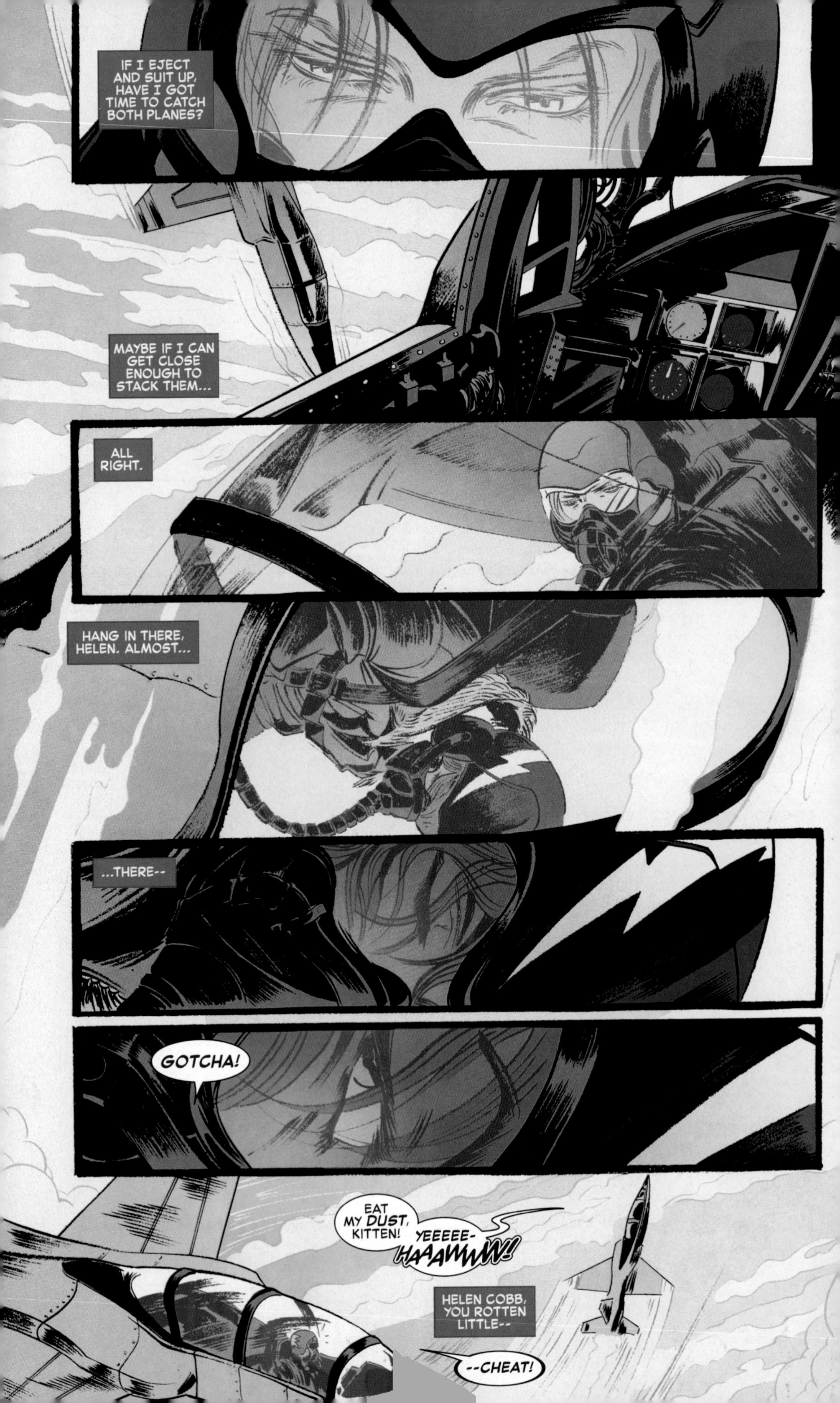
IF I EJECT AND SUIT UP, HAVE I GOT TIME TO CATCH BOTH PLANES?
MAYBE IF I CAN GET CLOSE ENOUGH TO STACK THEM...
ALL RIGHT.
HANG IN THERE, HELEN. ALMOST...
...THERE--
GOTCHA!
EAT MY DUST, KITTEN!
YEEEEE-HAAAWWW!
HELEN COBB, YOU ROTTEN LITTLE--
--CHEAT!

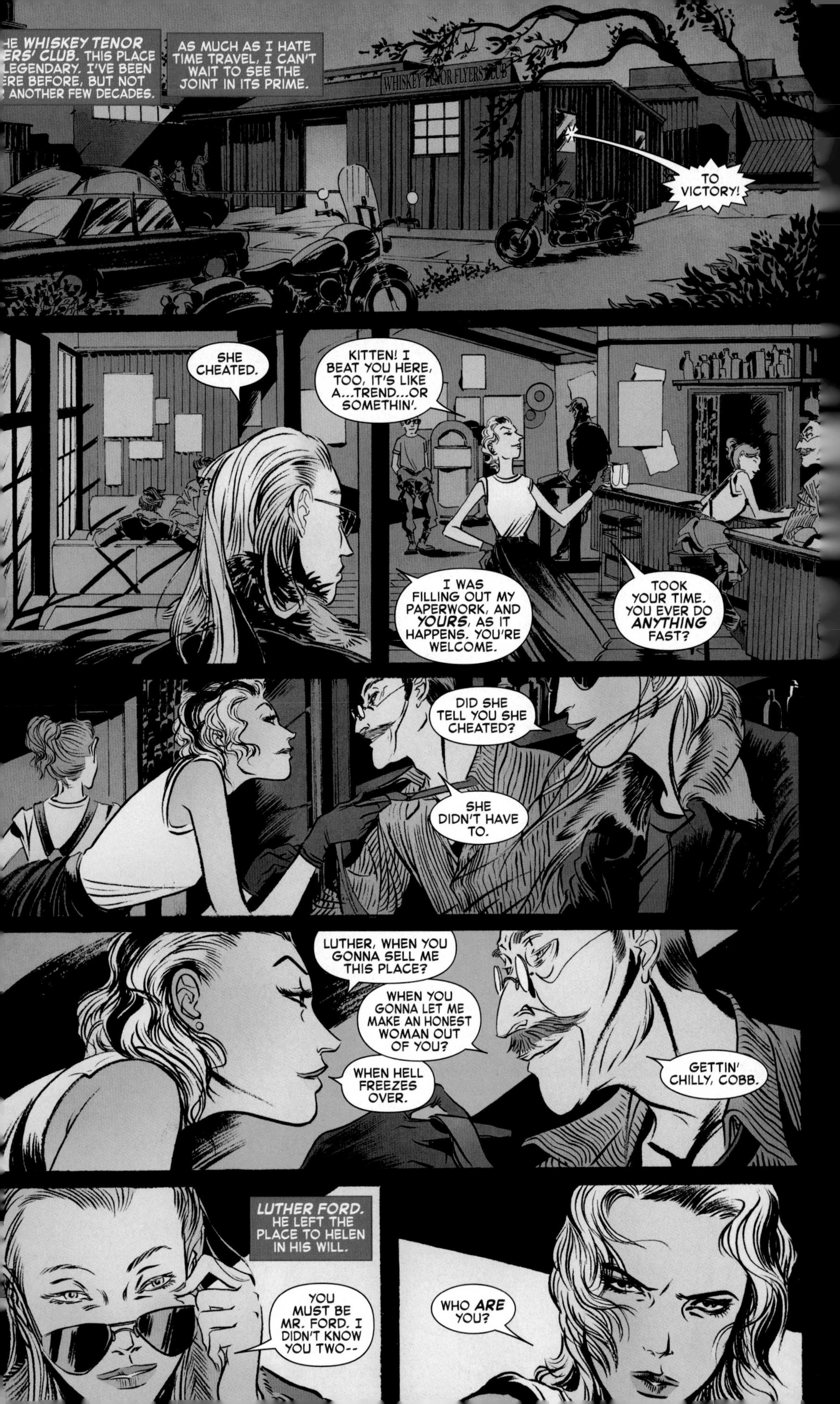
HE WHISKEY TENOR ERS' CLUB. THIS PLACE LEGENDARY. I'VE BEEN ERE BEFORE, BUT NOT ANOTHER FEW DECADES.
AS MUCH AS I HATE TIME TRAVEL, I CAN'T WAIT TO SEE THE JOINT IN ITS PRIME.
WHISKEY TENOR FLYERS CLUB
TO VICTORY!
SHE CHEATED.
KITTEN! I BEAT YOU HERE, TOO, IT'S LIKE A...TREND...OR SOMETHIN'.
I WAS FILLING OUT MY PAPERWORK, AND YOURS, AS IT HAPPENS. YOU'RE WELCOME.
TOOK YOUR TIME. YOU EVER DO ANYTHING FAST?
DID SHE TELL YOU SHE CHEATED?
SHE DIDN'T HAVE TO.
LUTHER, WHEN YOU GONNA SELL ME THIS PLACE?
WHEN YOU GONNA LET ME MAKE AN HONEST WOMAN OUT OF YOU?
WHEN HELL FREEZES OVER.
GETTIN' CHILLY, COBB.
LUTHER FORD. HE LEFT THE PLACE TO HELEN IN HIS WILL.
YOU MUST BE MR. FORD. I DIDN'T KNOW YOU TWO--
WHO ARE YOU?

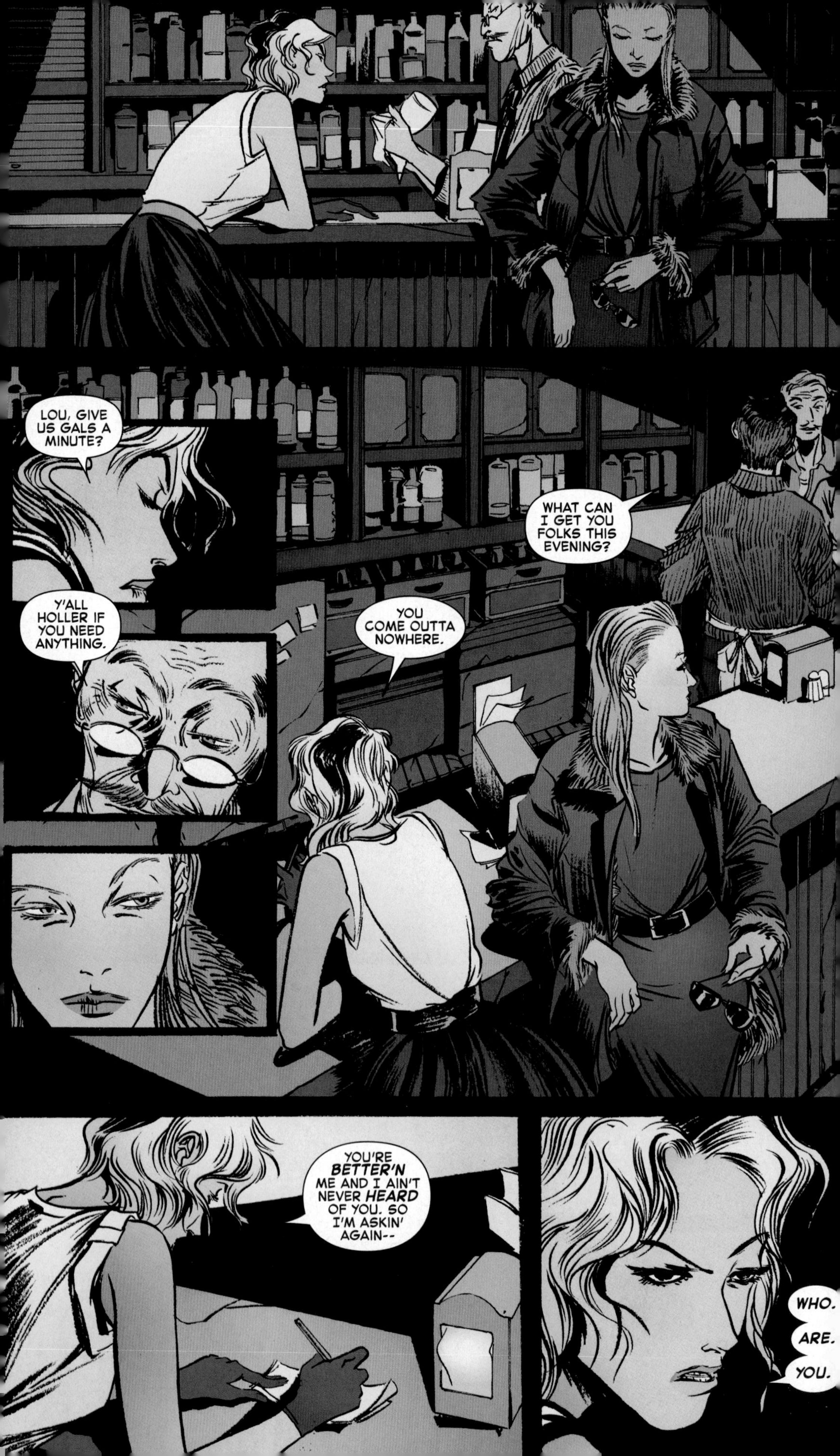
LOU, GIVE US GALS A MINUTE?
Y'ALL HOLLER IF YOU NEED ANYTHING.
WHAT CAN I GET YOU FOLKS THIS EVENING?
YOU COME OUTTA NOWHERE.
YOU'RE BETTER'N ME AND I AIN'T NEVER HEARD OF YOU. SO I'M ASKIN' AGAIN--
WHO.
ARE.
YOU.

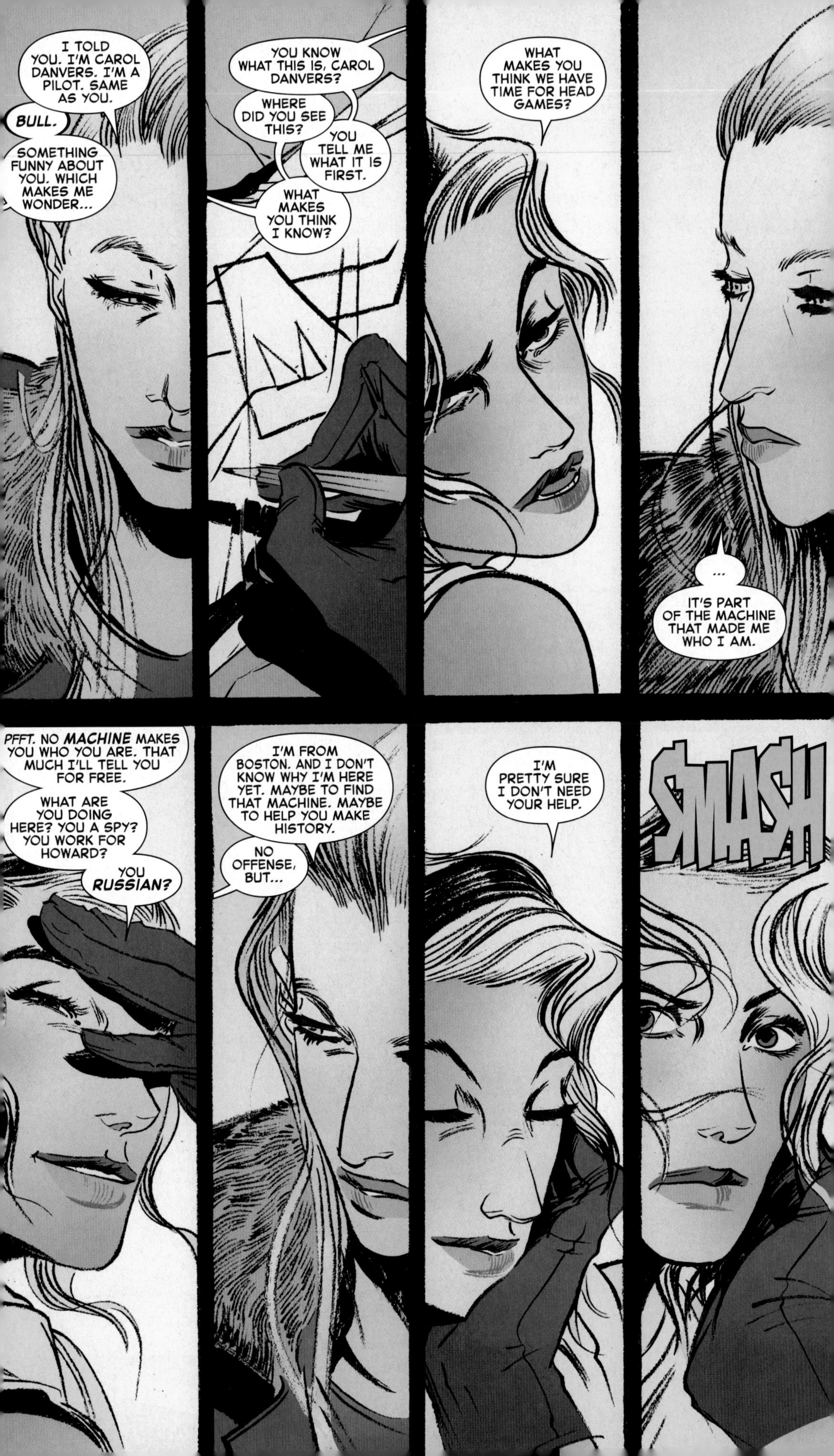
I TOLD YOU. I'M CAROL DANVERS. I'M A PILOT. SAME AS YOU.
BULL.
SOMETHING FUNNY ABOUT YOU. WHICH MAKES ME WONDER...
YOU KNOW WHAT THIS IS, CAROL DANVERS?
WHERE DID YOU SEE THIS?
YOU TELL ME WHAT IT IS FIRST.
WHAT MAKES YOU THINK I KNOW?
WHAT MAKES YOU THINK WE HAVE TIME FOR HEAD GAMES?
...
IT'S PART OF THE MACHINE THAT MADE ME WHO I AM.
PFFT. NO MACHINE MAKES YOU WHO YOU ARE. THAT MUCH I'LL TELL YOU FOR FREE.
WHAT ARE YOU DOING HERE? YOU A SPY? YOU WORK FOR HOWARD?
YOU RUSSIAN?
I'M FROM BOSTON. AND I DON'T KNOW WHY I'M HERE YET. MAYBE TO FIND THAT MACHINE. MAYBE TO HELP YOU MAKE HISTORY.
NO OFFENSE, BUT...
I'M PRETTY SURE I DON'T NEED YOUR HELP.
SMASH

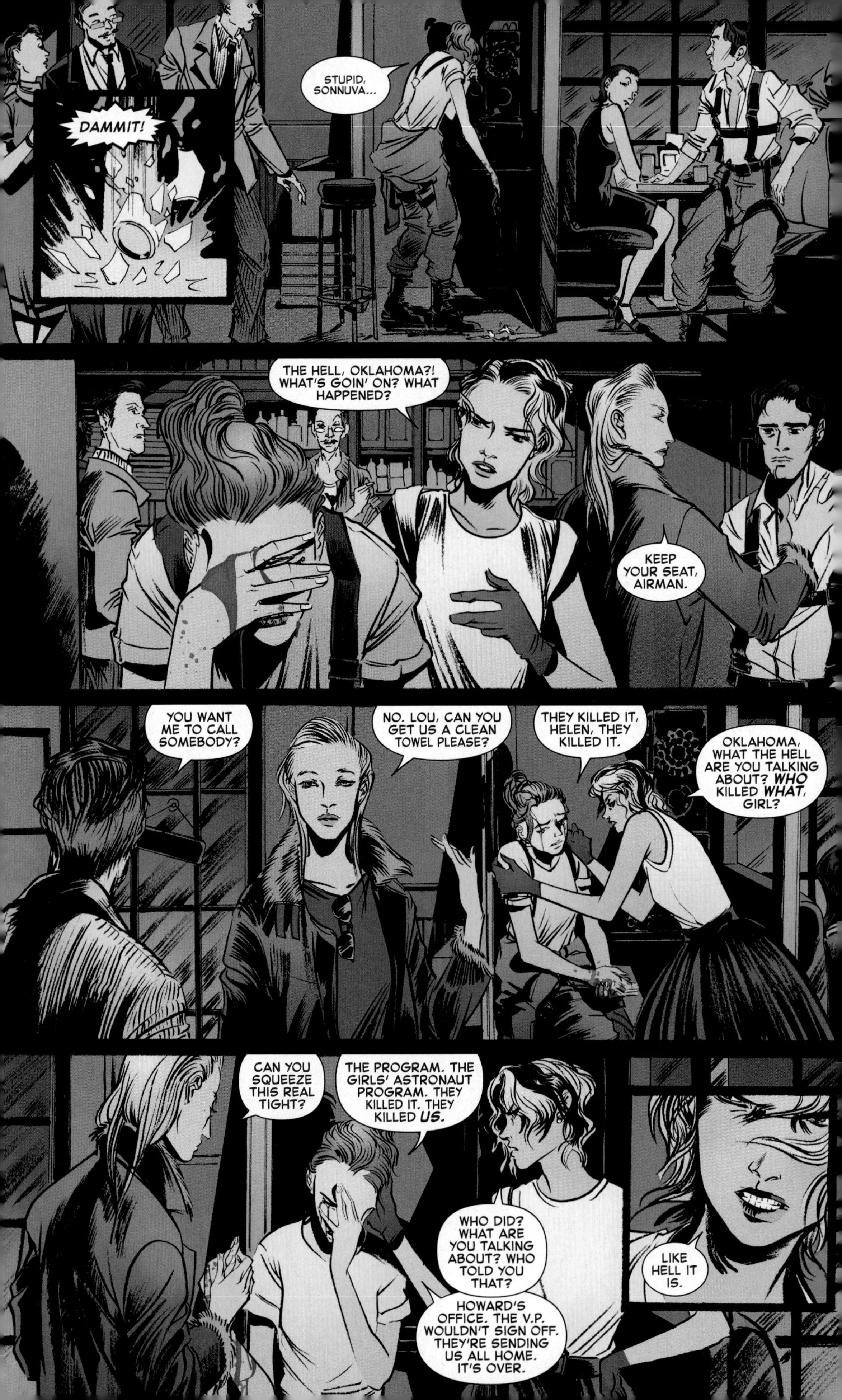
DAMMIT!
STUPID, SONNUVA...
THE HELL, OKLAHOMA?! WHAT'S GOIN' ON? WHAT HAPPENED?
KEEP YOUR SEAT, AIRMAN.
YOU WANT ME TO CALL SOMEBODY?
NO. LOU, CAN YOU GET US A CLEAN TOWEL PLEASE?
THEY KILLED IT, HELEN, THEY KILLED IT.
OKLAHOMA, WHAT THE HELL ARE YOU TALKING ABOUT? WHO KILLED WHAT, GIRL?
CAN YOU SQUEEZE THIS REAL TIGHT?
THE PROGRAM. THE GIRLS' ASTRONAUT PROGRAM. THEY KILLED IT. THEY KILLED US.
WHO DID? WHAT ARE YOU TALKING ABOUT? WHO TOLD YOU THAT?
HOWARD'S OFFICE. THE V.P. WOULDN'T SIGN OFF. THEY'RE SENDING US ALL HOME. IT'S OVER.
LIKE HELL IT IS.

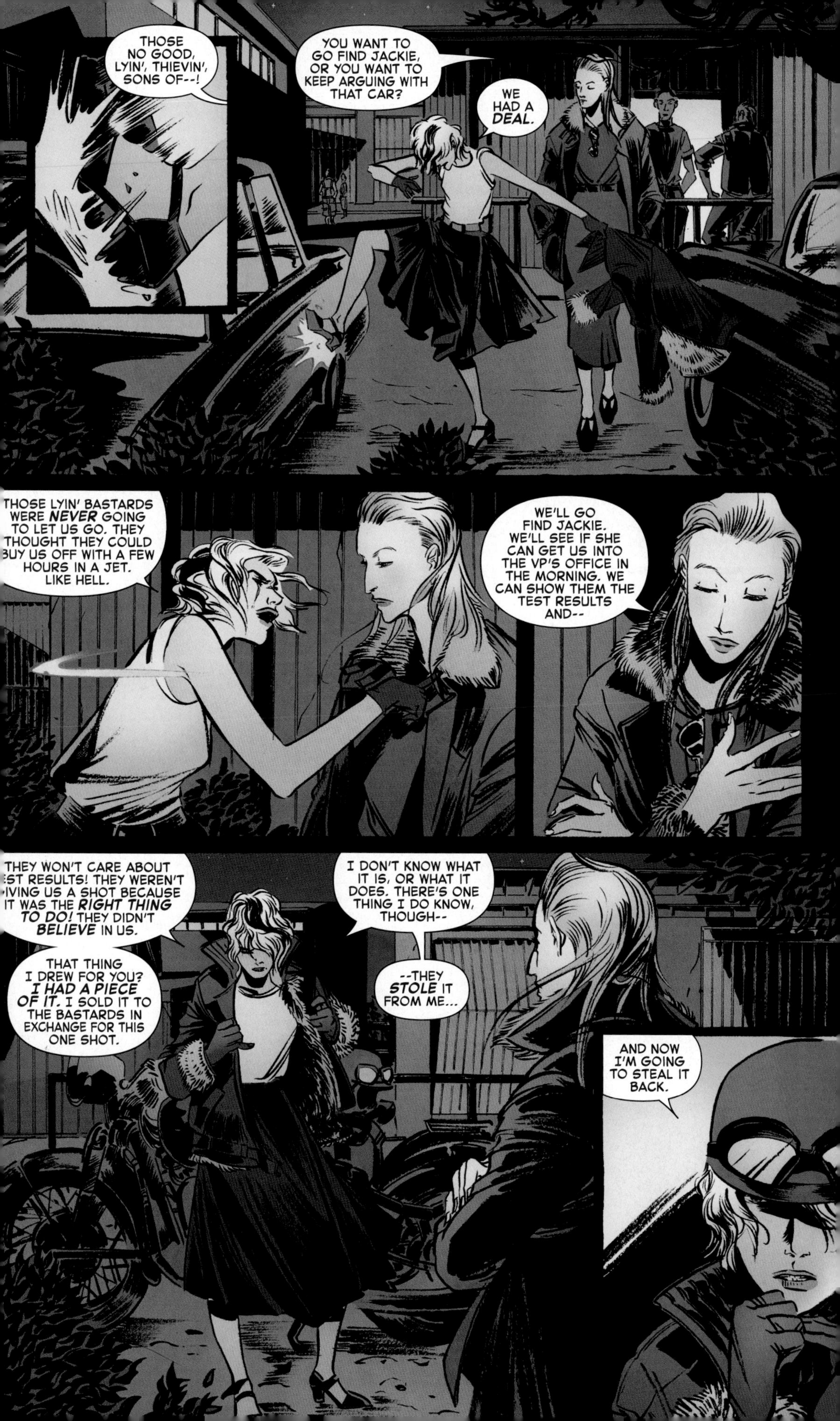
THOSE NO GOOD, LYIN', THIEVIN', SONS OF--!
YOU WANT TO GO FIND JACKIE, OR YOU WANT TO KEEP ARGUING WITH THAT CAR?
WE HAD A ***DEAL.***
THOSE LYIN' BASTARDS WERE ***NEVER*** GOING TO LET US GO. THEY THOUGHT THEY COULD BUY US OFF WITH A FEW HOURS IN A JET. LIKE HELL.
WE'LL GO FIND JACKIE. WE'LL SEE IF SHE CAN GET US INTO THE VP'S OFFICE IN THE MORNING. WE CAN SHOW THEM THE TEST RESULTS AND--
THEY WON'T CARE ABOUT TEST RESULTS! THEY WEREN'T GIVING US A SHOT BECAUSE IT WAS THE ***RIGHT THING TO DO!*** THEY DIDN'T ***BELIEVE*** IN US.
THAT THING I DREW FOR YOU? ***I HAD A PIECE OF IT.*** I SOLD IT TO THE BASTARDS IN EXCHANGE FOR THIS ONE SHOT.
I DON'T KNOW WHAT IT IS, OR WHAT IT DOES. THERE'S ONE THING I DO KNOW, THOUGH--
--THEY ***STOLE*** IT FROM ME...
AND NOW I'M GOING TO STEAL IT BACK.

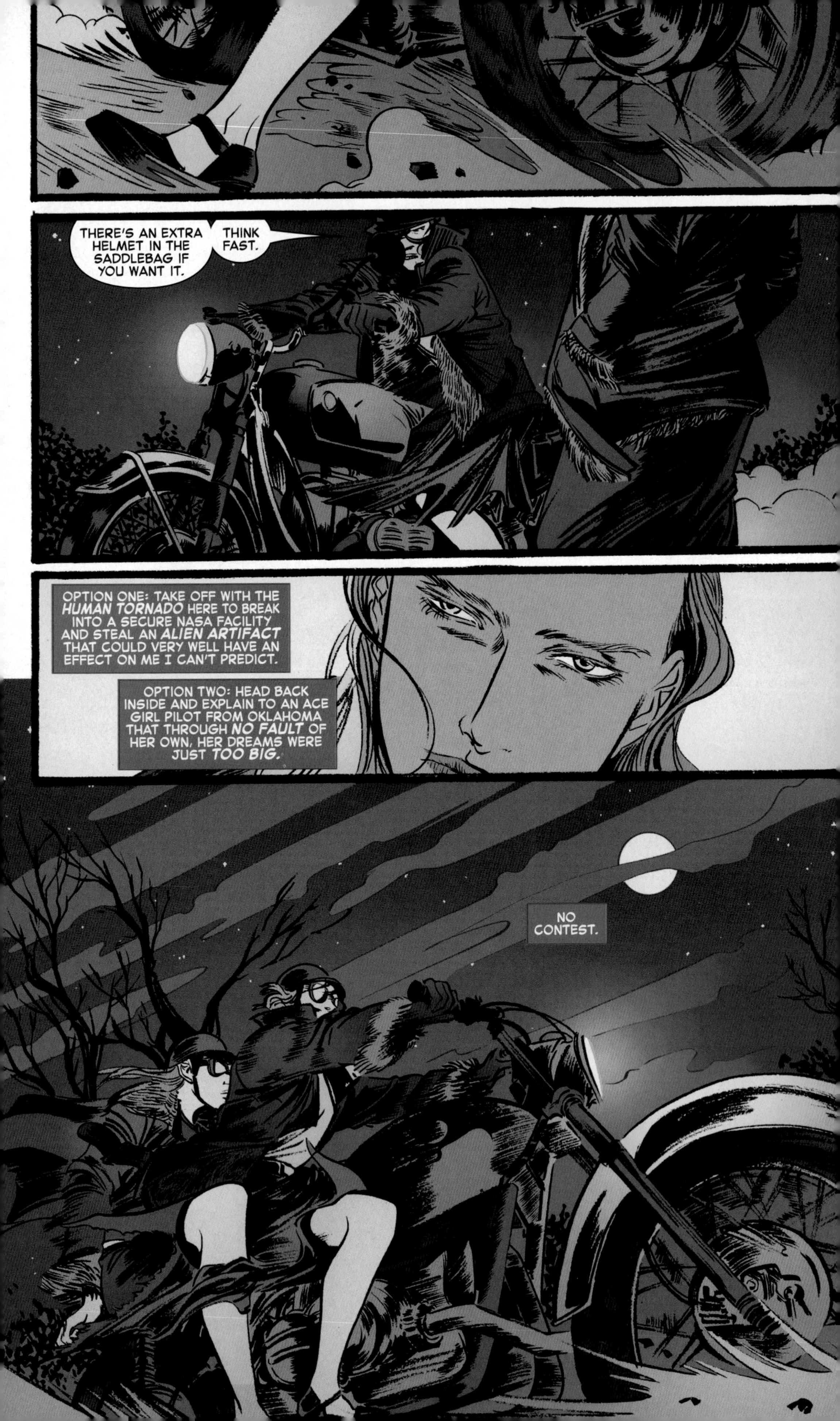

THERE'S AN EXTRA HELMET IN THE SADDLEBAG IF YOU WANT IT.
THINK FAST.
OPTION ONE: TAKE OFF WITH THE HUMAN TORNADO HERE TO BREAK INTO A SECURE NASA FACILITY AND STEAL AN ALIEN ARTIFACT THAT COULD VERY WELL HAVE AN EFFECT ON ME I CAN'T PREDICT.
OPTION TWO: HEAD BACK INSIDE AND EXPLAIN TO AN ACE GIRL PILOT FROM OKLAHOMA THAT THROUGH NO FAULT OF HER OWN, HER DREAMS WERE JUST TOO BIG.
NO CONTEST.

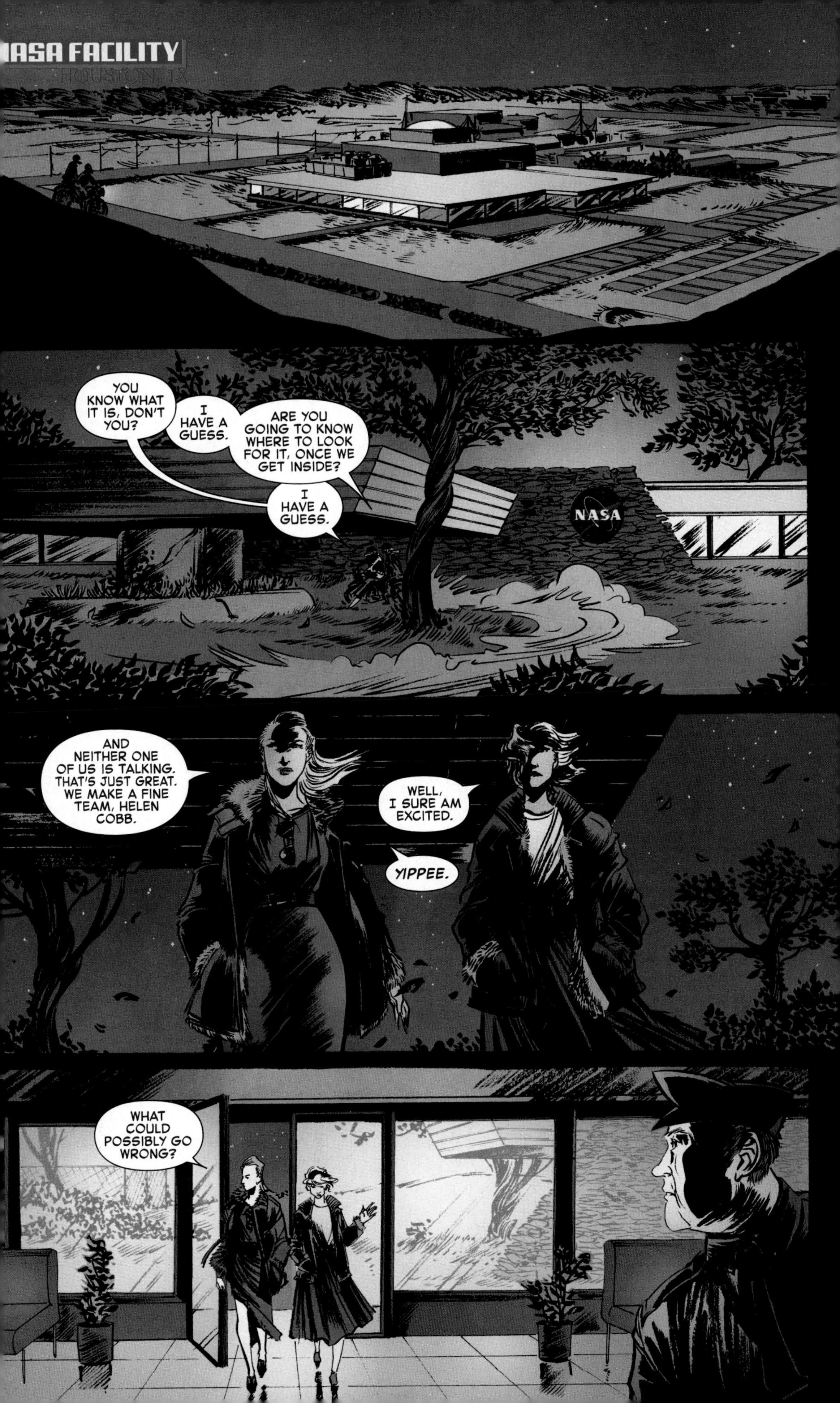
NASA FACILITY
HOUSTON, TX
YOU KNOW WHAT IT IS, DON'T YOU?
I HAVE A GUESS.
ARE YOU GOING TO KNOW WHERE TO LOOK FOR IT, ONCE WE GET INSIDE?
I HAVE A GUESS.
NASA
AND NEITHER ONE OF US IS TALKING. THAT'S JUST GREAT. WE MAKE A FINE TEAM, HELEN COBB.
WELL, I SURE AM EXCITED.
YIPPEE.
WHAT COULD POSSIBLY GO WRONG?

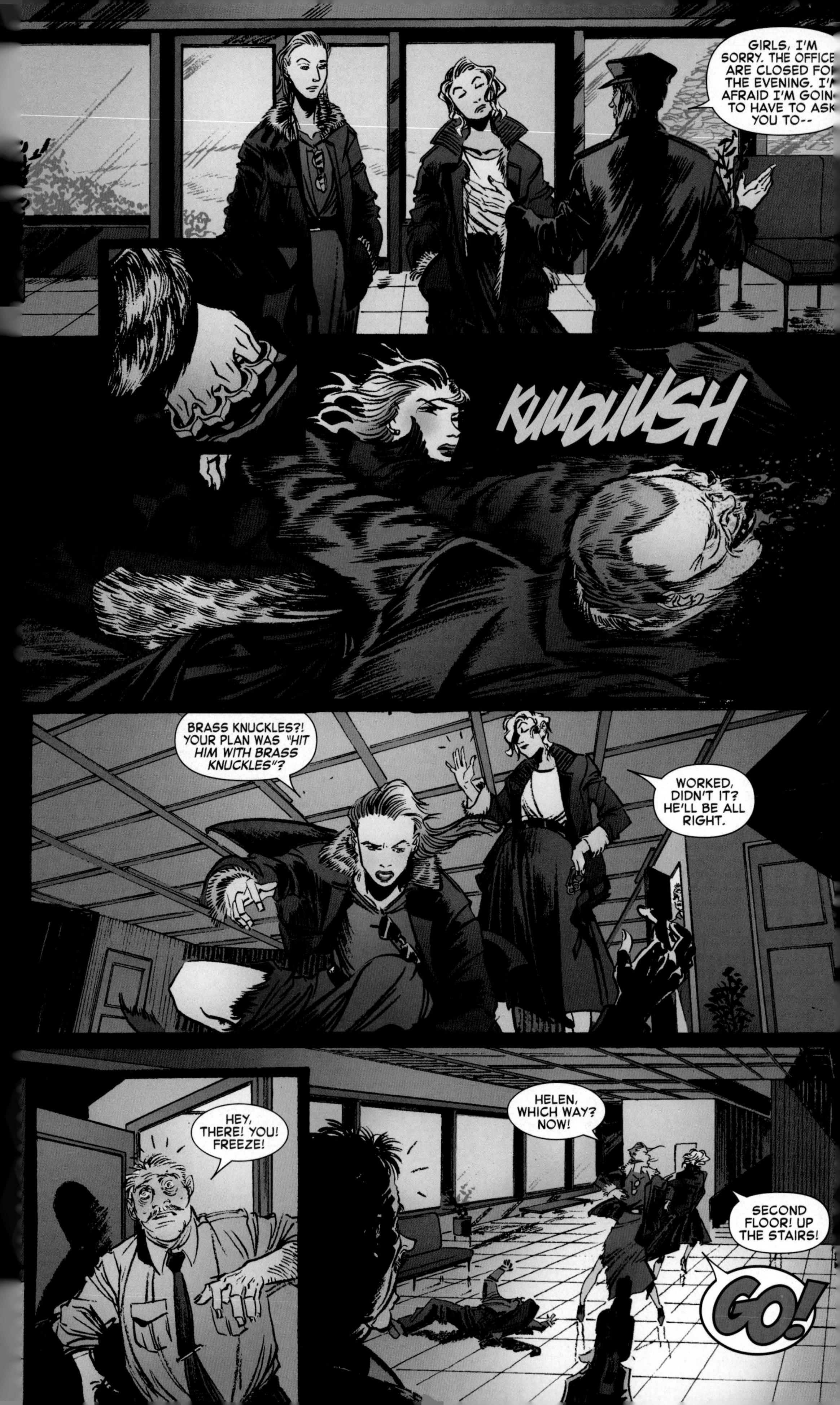
GIRLS, I'M SORRY. THE OFFICE ARE CLOSED FO THE EVENING. I' AFRAID I'M GOIN TO HAVE TO ASK YOU TO--
KUUDUUSH
BRASS KNUCKLES?! YOUR PLAN WAS "HIT HIM WITH BRASS KNUCKLES"?
WORKED, DIDN'T IT? HE'LL BE ALL RIGHT.
HEY, THERE! YOU! FREEZE!
HELEN, WHICH WAY? NOW!
SECOND FLOOR! UP THE STAIRS!
GO!

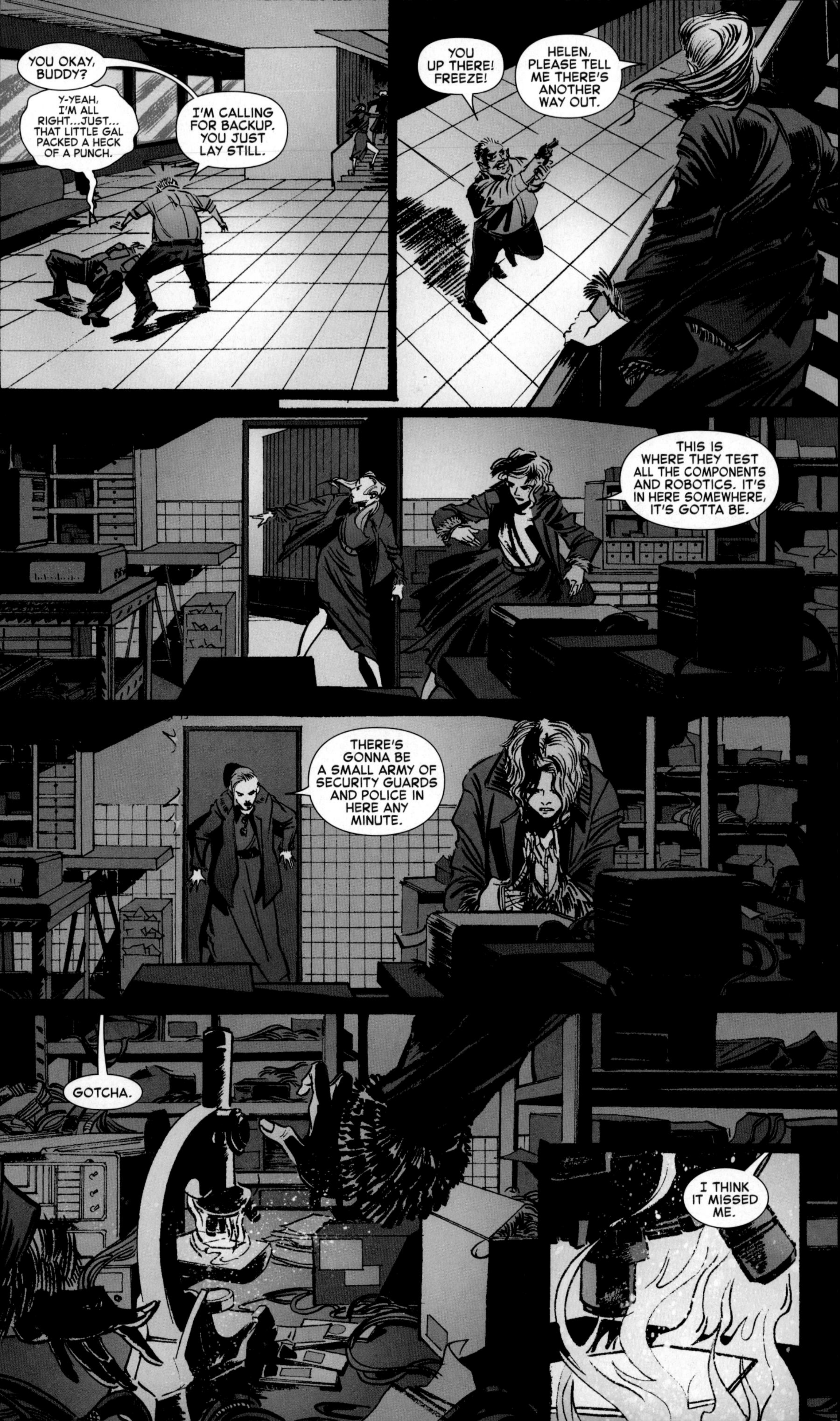
YOU OKAY, BUDDY?
Y-YEAH, I'M ALL RIGHT...JUST... THAT LITTLE GAL PACKED A HECK OF A PUNCH.
I'M CALLING FOR BACKUP. YOU JUST LAY STILL.
YOU UP THERE! FREEZE!
HELEN, PLEASE TELL ME THERE'S ANOTHER WAY OUT.
THIS IS WHERE THEY TEST ALL THE COMPONENTS AND ROBOTICS. IT'S IN HERE SOMEWHERE, IT'S GOTTA BE.
THERE'S GONNA BE A SMALL ARMY OF SECURITY GUARDS AND POLICE IN HERE ANY MINUTE.
GOTCHA.
I THINK IT MISSED ME.

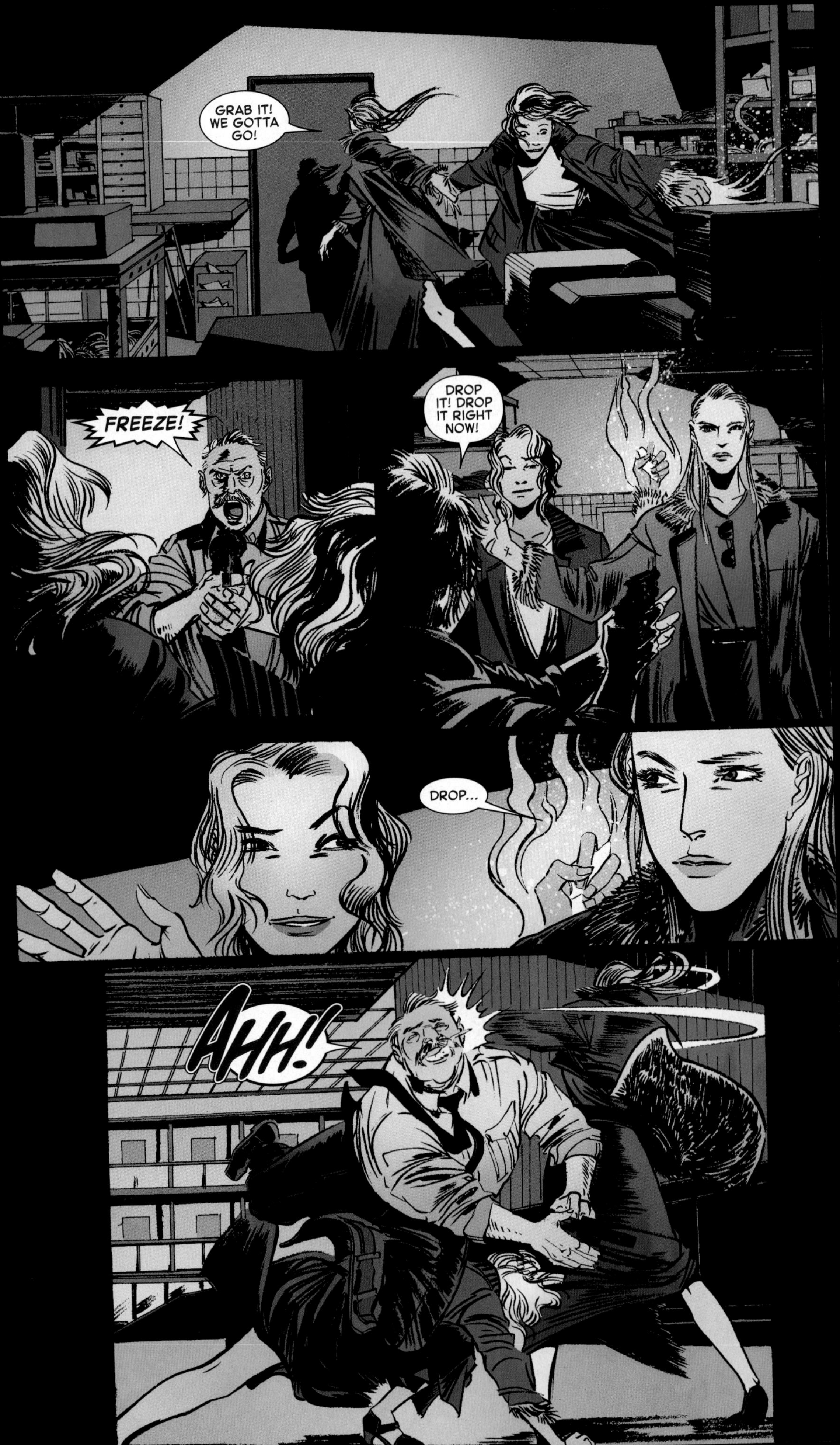
GRAB IT! WE GOTTA GO!
FREEZE!
DROP IT! DROP IT RIGHT NOW!
DROP...
AHH!

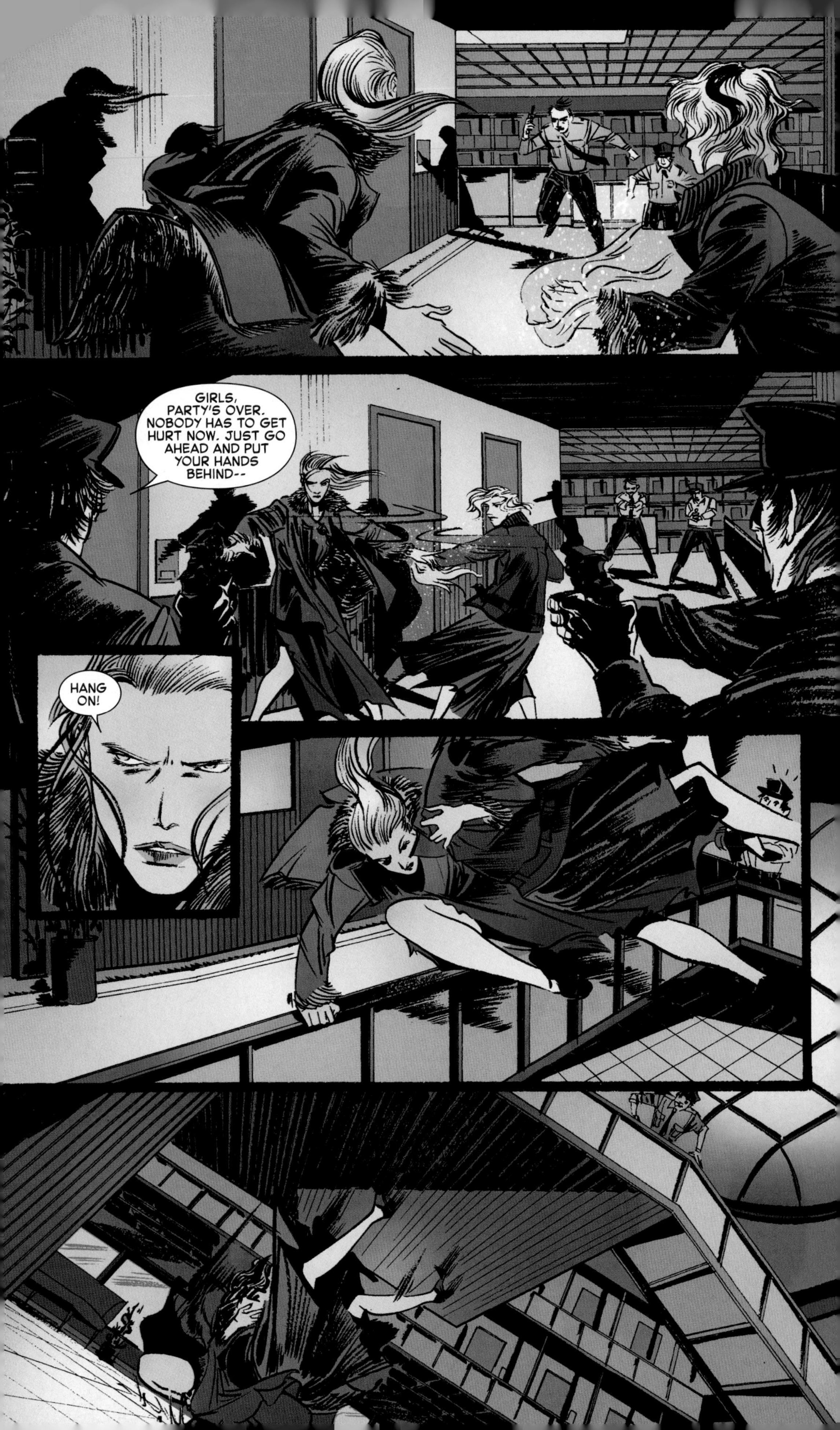
GIRLS, PARTY'S OVER. NOBODY HAS TO GET HURT NOW. JUST GO AHEAD AND PUT YOUR HANDS BEHIND--
HANG ON!

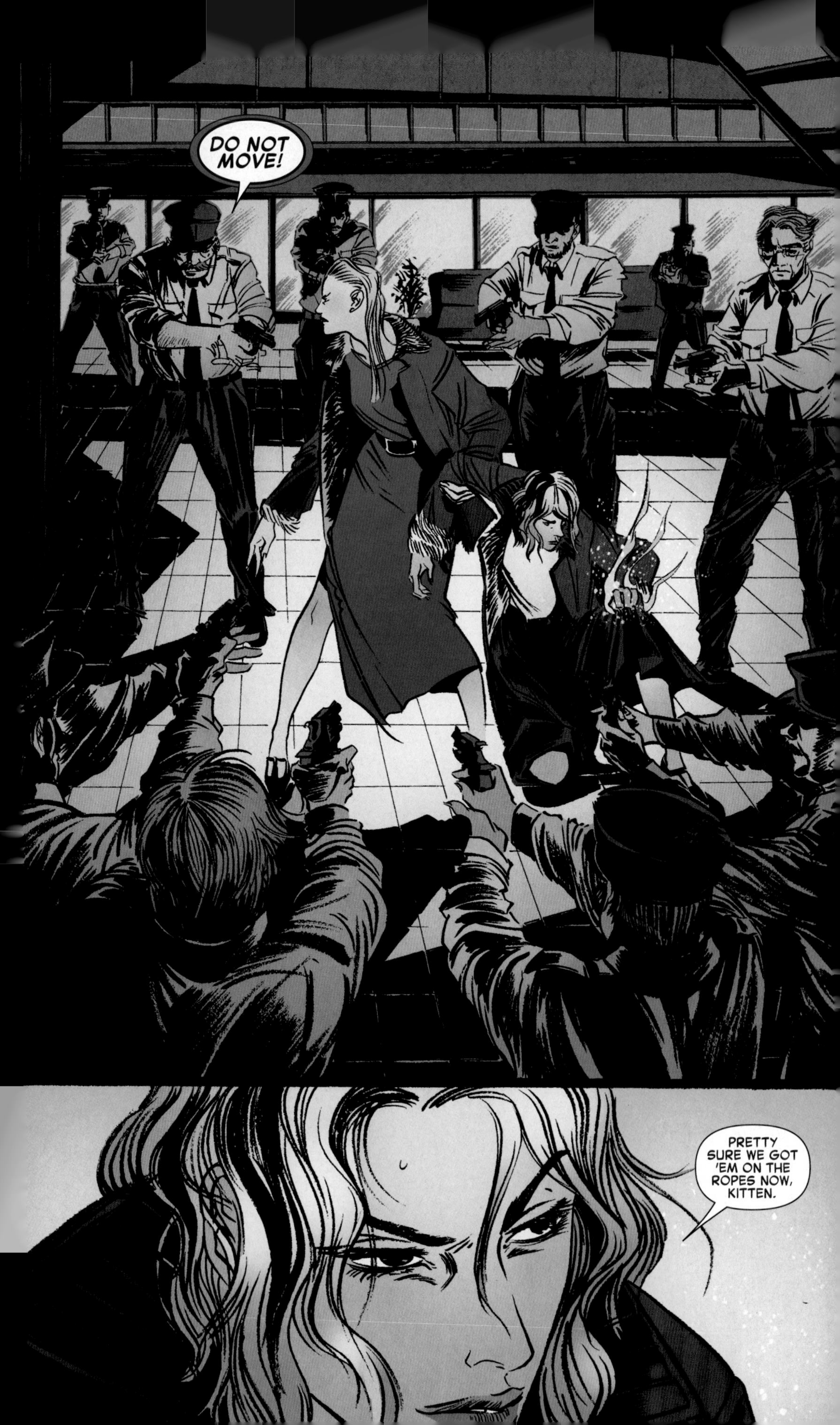
DO NOT MOVE!
PRETTY SURE WE GOT 'EM ON THE ROPES NOW, KITTEN.

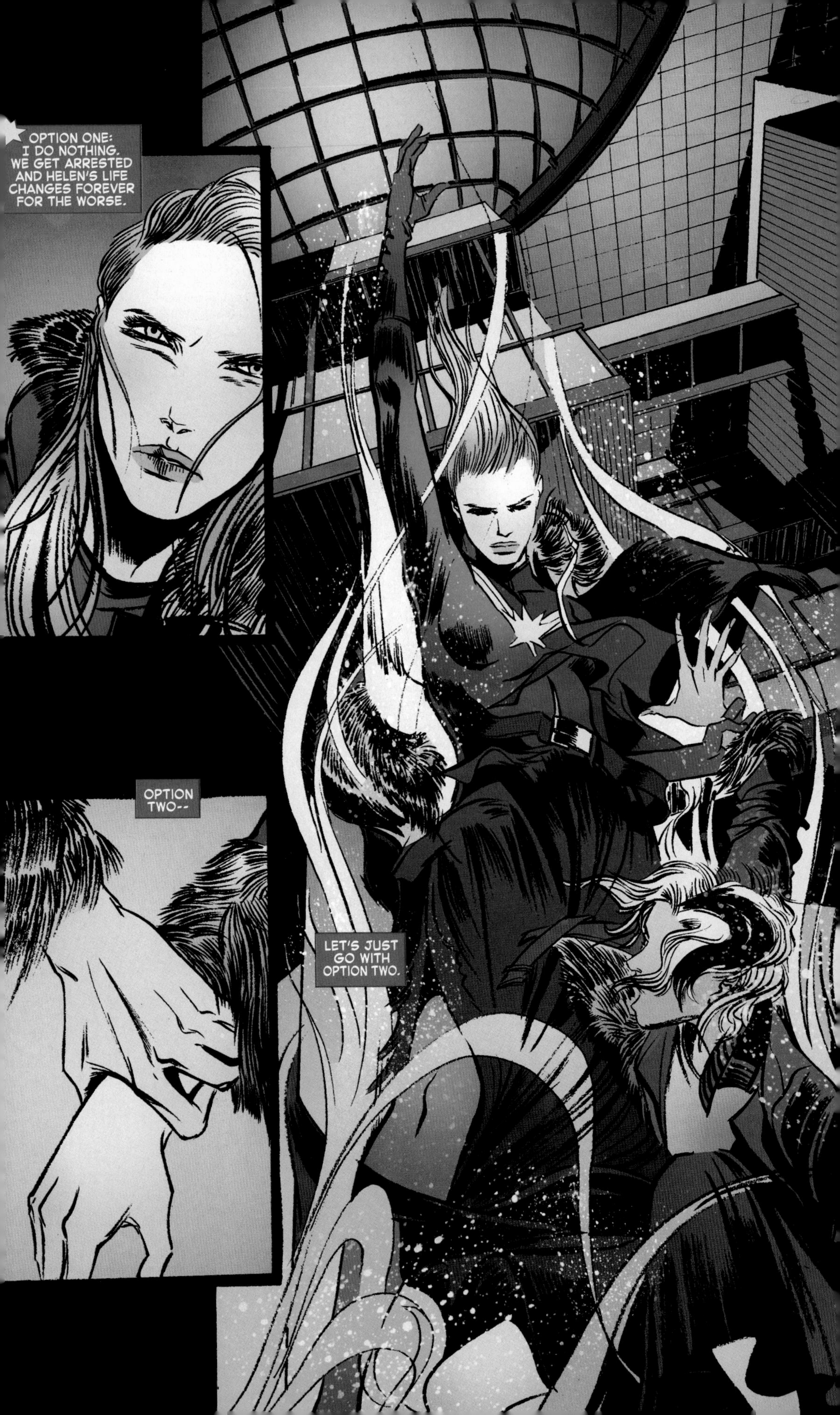
OPTION ONE: I DO NOTHING. WE GET ARRESTED AND HELEN'S LIFE CHANGES FOREVER FOR THE WORSE.
OPTION TWO--
LET'S JUST GO WITH OPTION TWO.

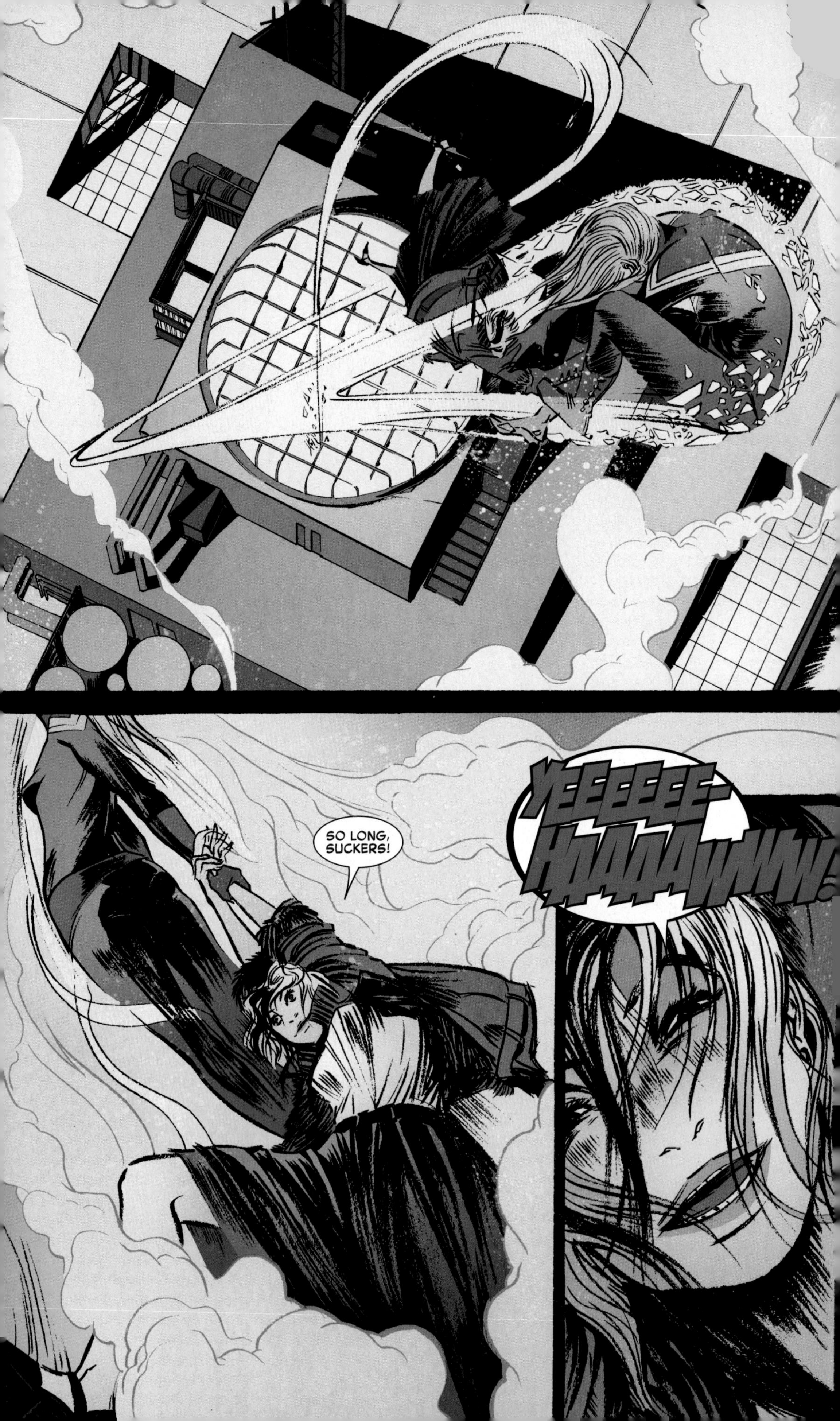
SO LONG, SUCKERS!
YEEEEEE-HAAAAWWW!

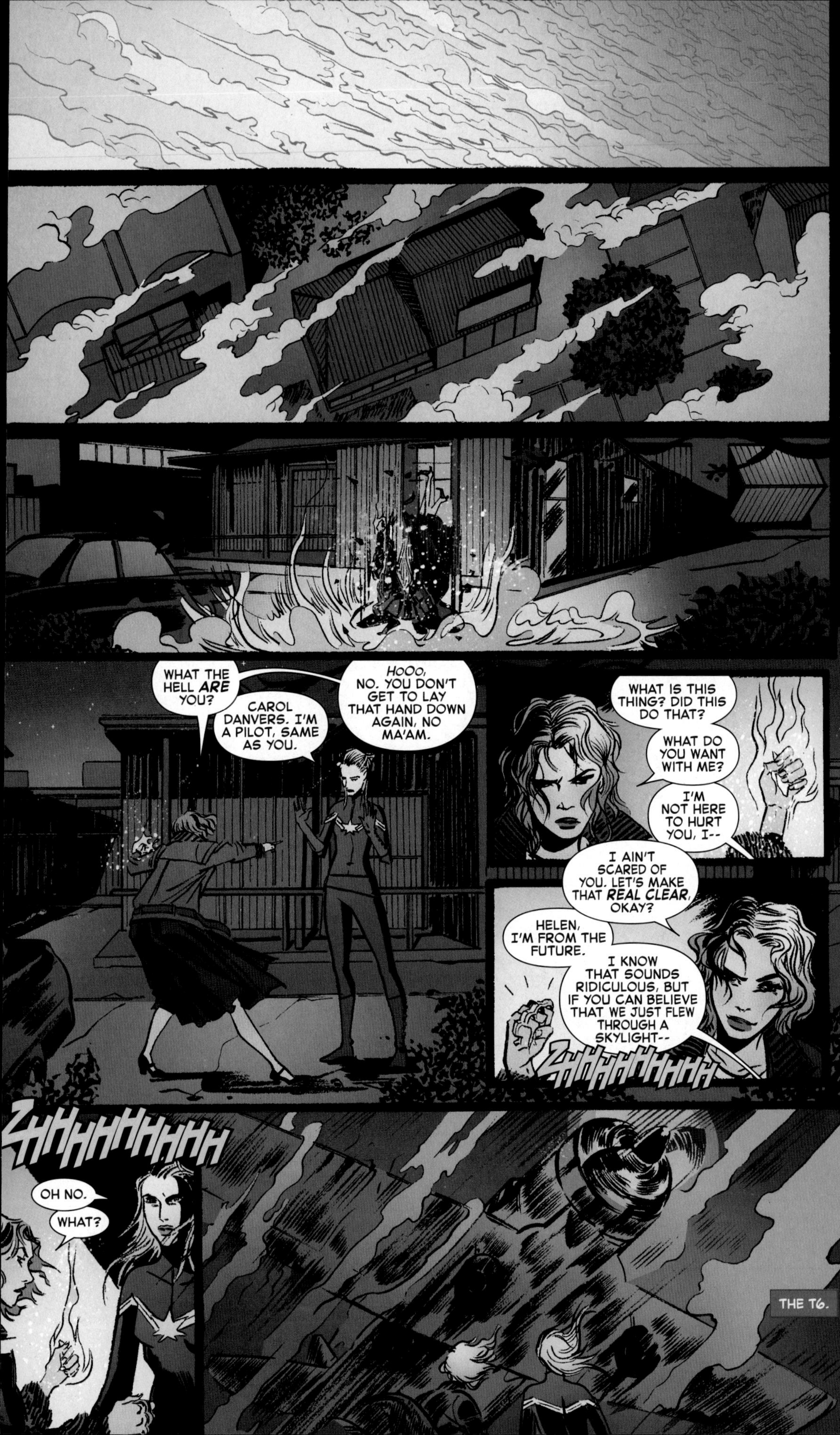
WHAT THE HELL *ARE* YOU?
CAROL DANVERS. I'M A PILOT, SAME AS YOU.
HOOO, NO. YOU DON'T GET TO LAY THAT HAND DOWN AGAIN, NO MA'AM.
WHAT IS THIS THING? DID THIS DO THAT?
WHAT DO YOU WANT WITH ME?
I'M NOT HERE TO HURT YOU, I--
I AIN'T SCARED OF YOU. LET'S MAKE THAT *REAL CLEAR,* OKAY?
HELEN, I'M FROM THE FUTURE.
I KNOW THAT SOUNDS RIDICULOUS, BUT IF YOU CAN BELIEVE THAT WE JUST FLEW THROUGH A SKYLIGHT--
ZHHHHHHHHHH
ZHHHHHHHHHH
OH NO.
WHAT?
THE T6.

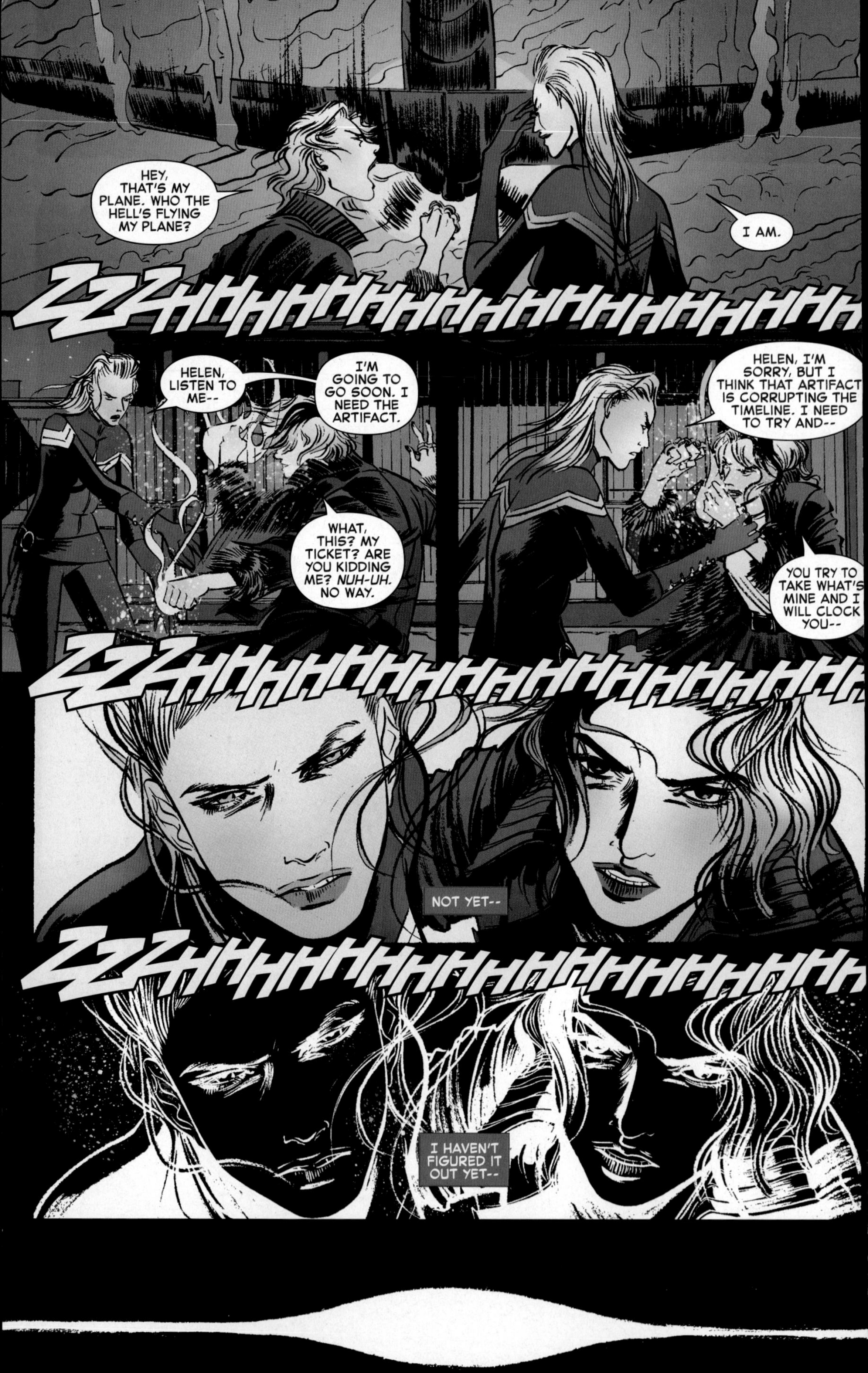
HEY, THAT'S MY PLANE. WHO THE HELL'S FLYING MY PLANE?
I AM.
ZZZHHHHHHHHHHHHHHHHHHHHHH
HELEN, LISTEN TO ME--
I'M GOING TO GO SOON. I NEED THE ARTIFACT.
WHAT, THIS? MY TICKET? ARE YOU KIDDING ME? *NUH-UH.* NO WAY.
HELEN, I'M SORRY, BUT I THINK THAT ARTIFACT IS CORRUPTING THE TIMELINE. I NEED TO TRY AND--
YOU TRY TO TAKE WHAT'S MINE AND I WILL CLOCK YOU--
ZZZHHHHHHHHHHHHHHHHHHHHHH
NOT YET--
ZZZHHHHHHHHHHHHHHHHHHHHHH
I HAVEN'T FIGURED IT OUT YET--

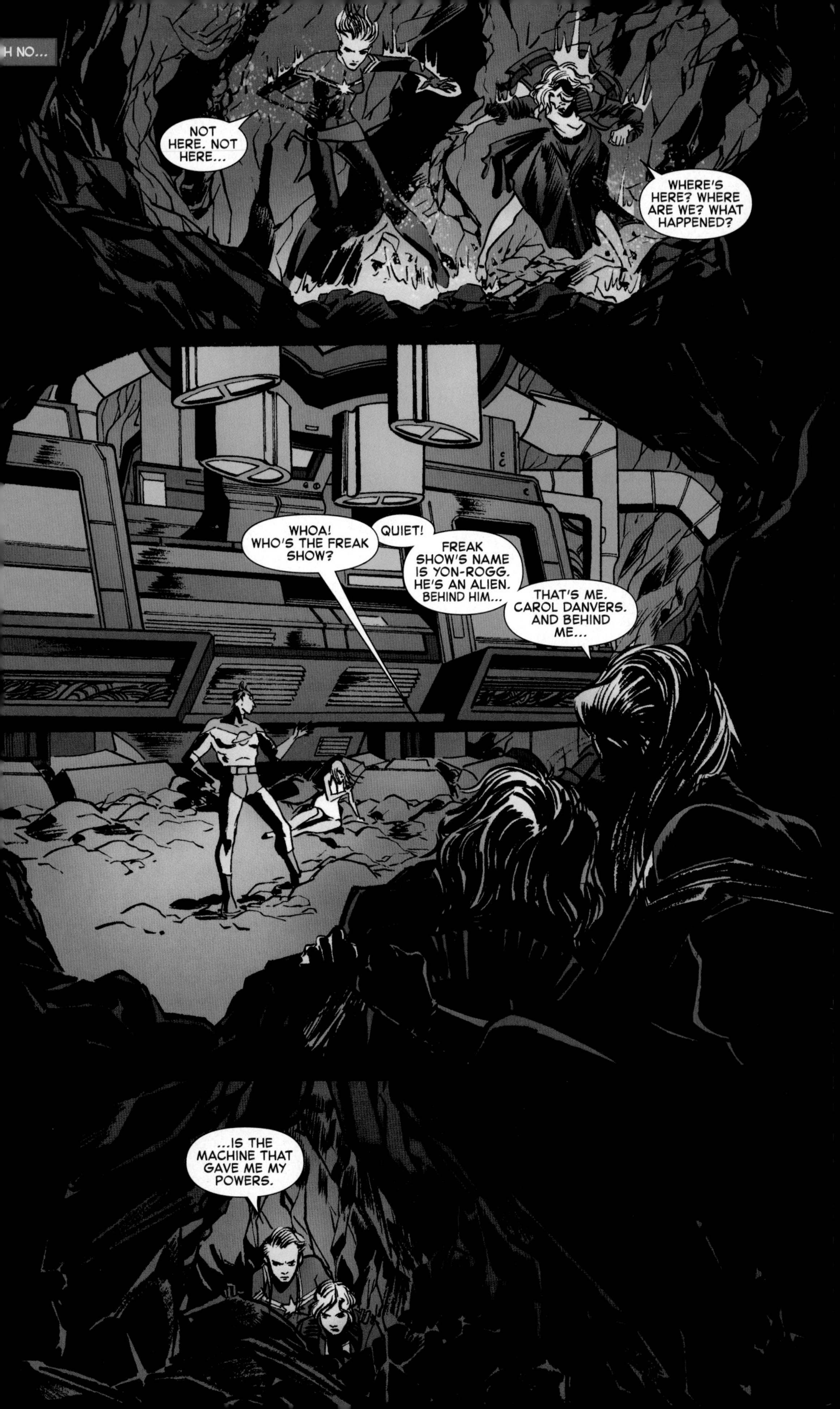
H NO...
NOT HERE. NOT HERE...
WHERE'S HERE? WHERE ARE WE? WHAT HAPPENED?
WHOA! WHO'S THE FREAK SHOW?
QUIET!
FREAK SHOW'S NAME IS YON-ROGG. HE'S AN ALIEN. BEHIND HIM...
THAT'S ME. CAROL DANVERS. AND BEHIND ME...
...IS THE MACHINE THAT GAVE ME MY POWERS.

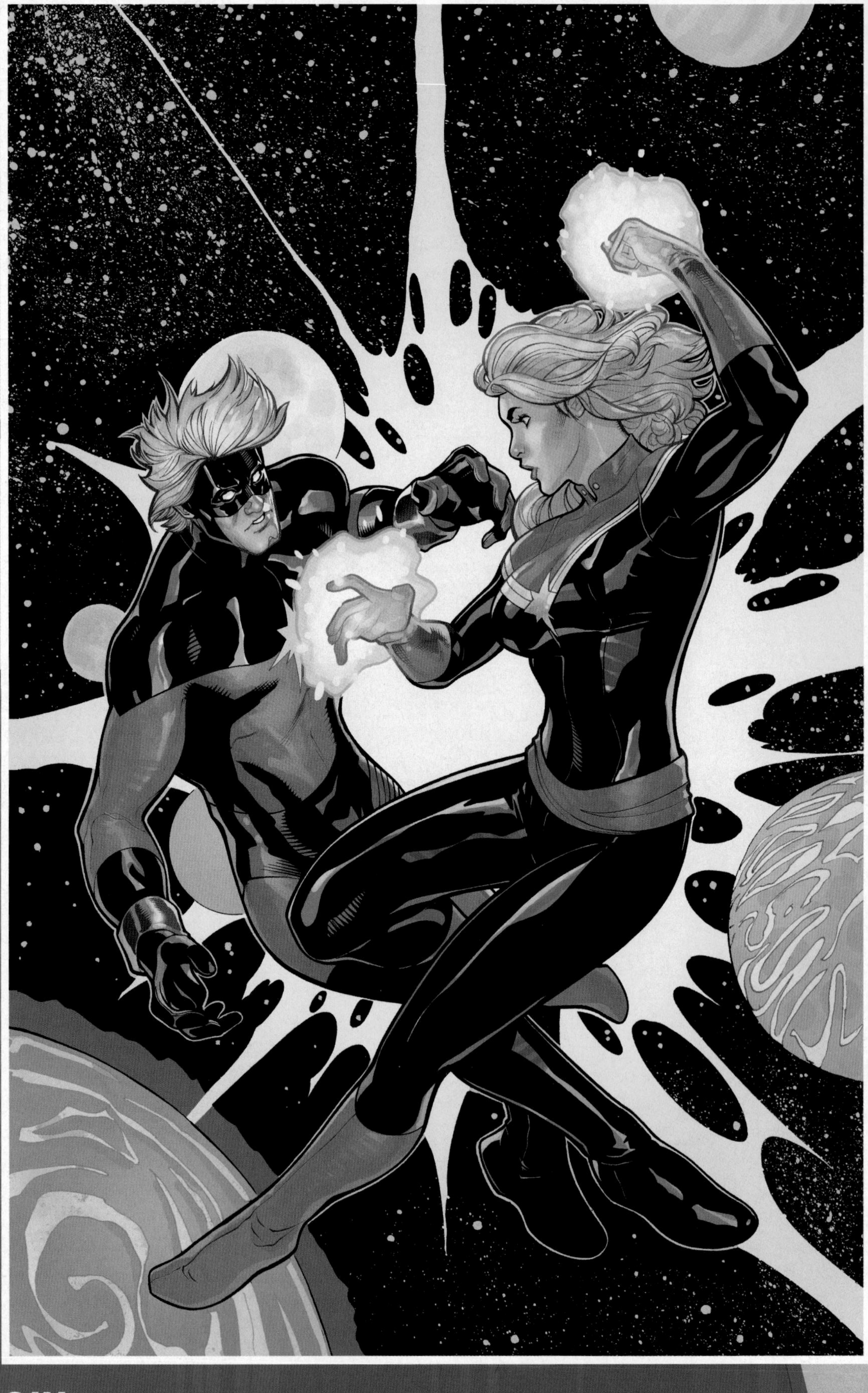

SIX

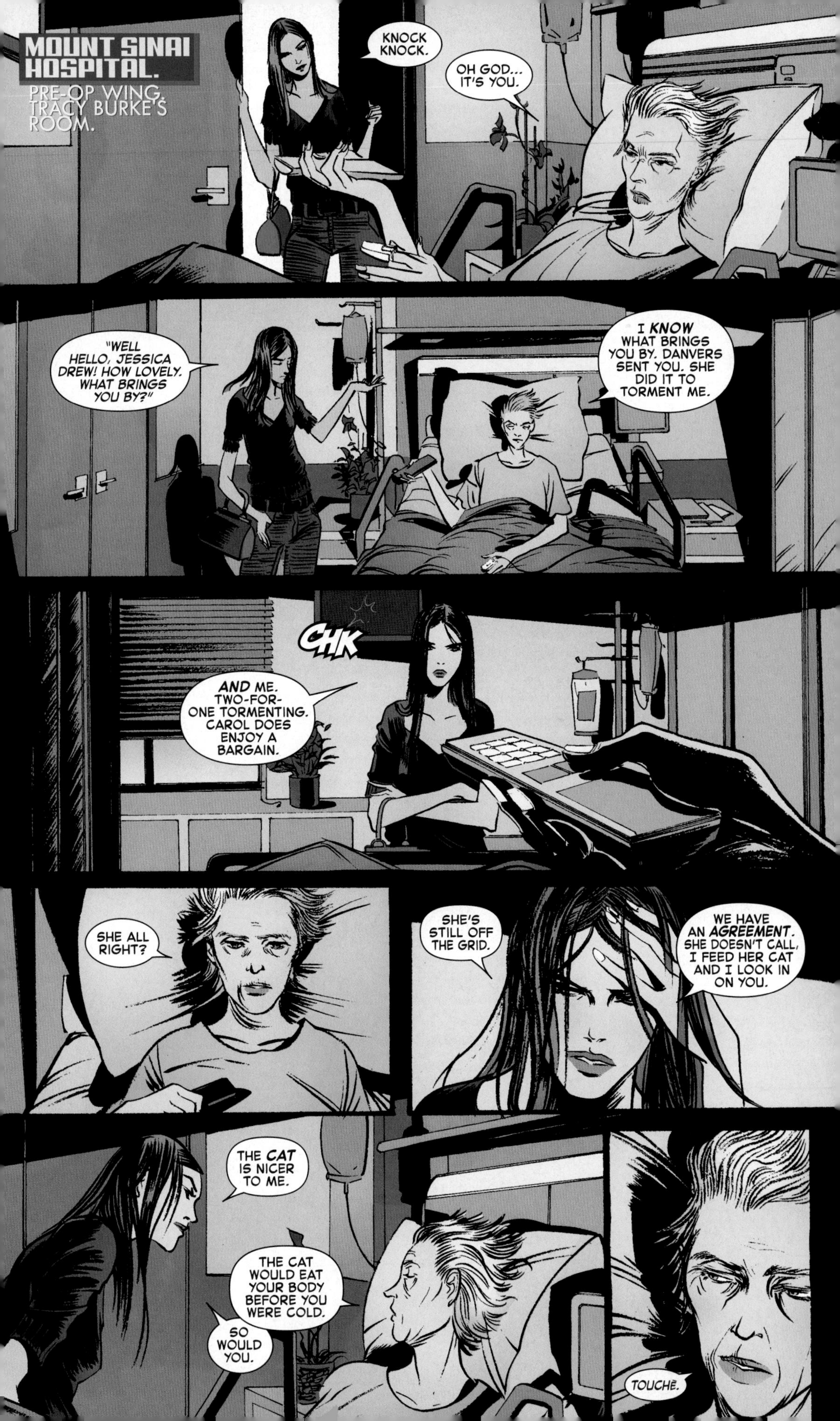
MOUNT SINAI HOSPITAL.
PRE-OP WING, TRACY BURKE'S ROOM.
KNOCK KNOCK.
OH GOD... IT'S YOU.
"WELL HELLO, JESSICA DREW! HOW LOVELY. WHAT BRINGS YOU BY?"
I KNOW WHAT BRINGS YOU BY. DANVERS SENT YOU. SHE DID IT TO TORMENT ME.
CHK
AND ME. TWO-FOR-ONE TORMENTING. CAROL DOES ENJOY A BARGAIN.
SHE ALL RIGHT?
SHE'S STILL OFF THE GRID.
WE HAVE AN AGREEMENT. SHE DOESN'T CALL, I FEED HER CAT AND I LOOK IN ON YOU.
THE CAT IS NICER TO ME.
THE CAT WOULD EAT YOUR BODY BEFORE YOU WERE COLD.
SO WOULD YOU.
TOUCHÉ.

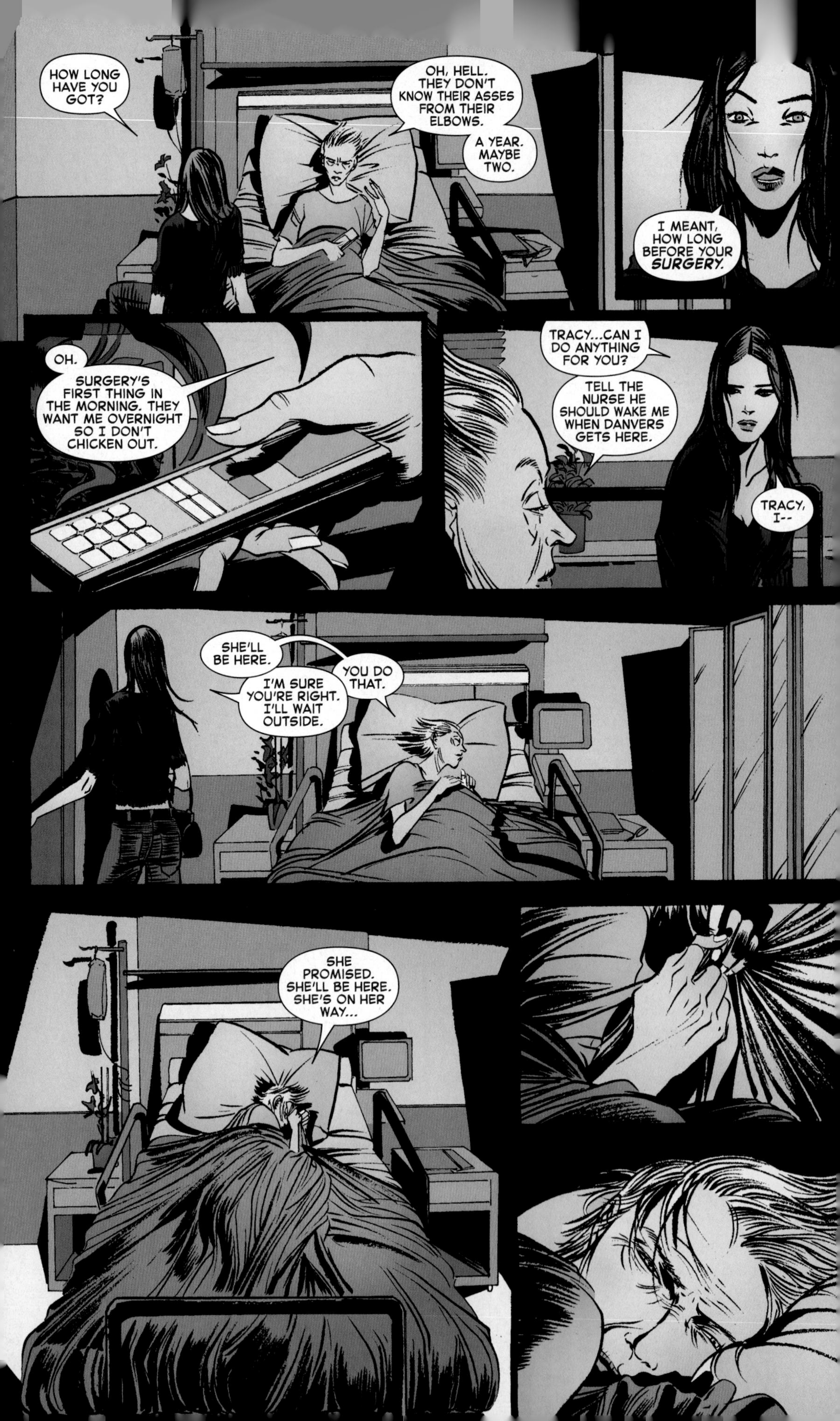
HOW LONG HAVE YOU GOT?
OH, HELL. THEY DON'T KNOW THEIR ASSES FROM THEIR ELBOWS.
A YEAR. MAYBE TWO.
I MEANT, HOW LONG BEFORE YOUR *SURGERY*.
OH.
SURGERY'S FIRST THING IN THE MORNING. THEY WANT ME OVERNIGHT SO I DON'T CHICKEN OUT.
TRACY...CAN I DO ANYTHING FOR YOU?
TELL THE NURSE HE SHOULD WAKE ME WHEN DANVERS GETS HERE.
TRACY, I--
SHE'LL BE HERE.
YOU DO THAT.
I'M SURE YOU'RE RIGHT. I'LL WAIT OUTSIDE.
SHE PROMISED. SHE'LL BE HERE. SHE'S ON HER WAY...

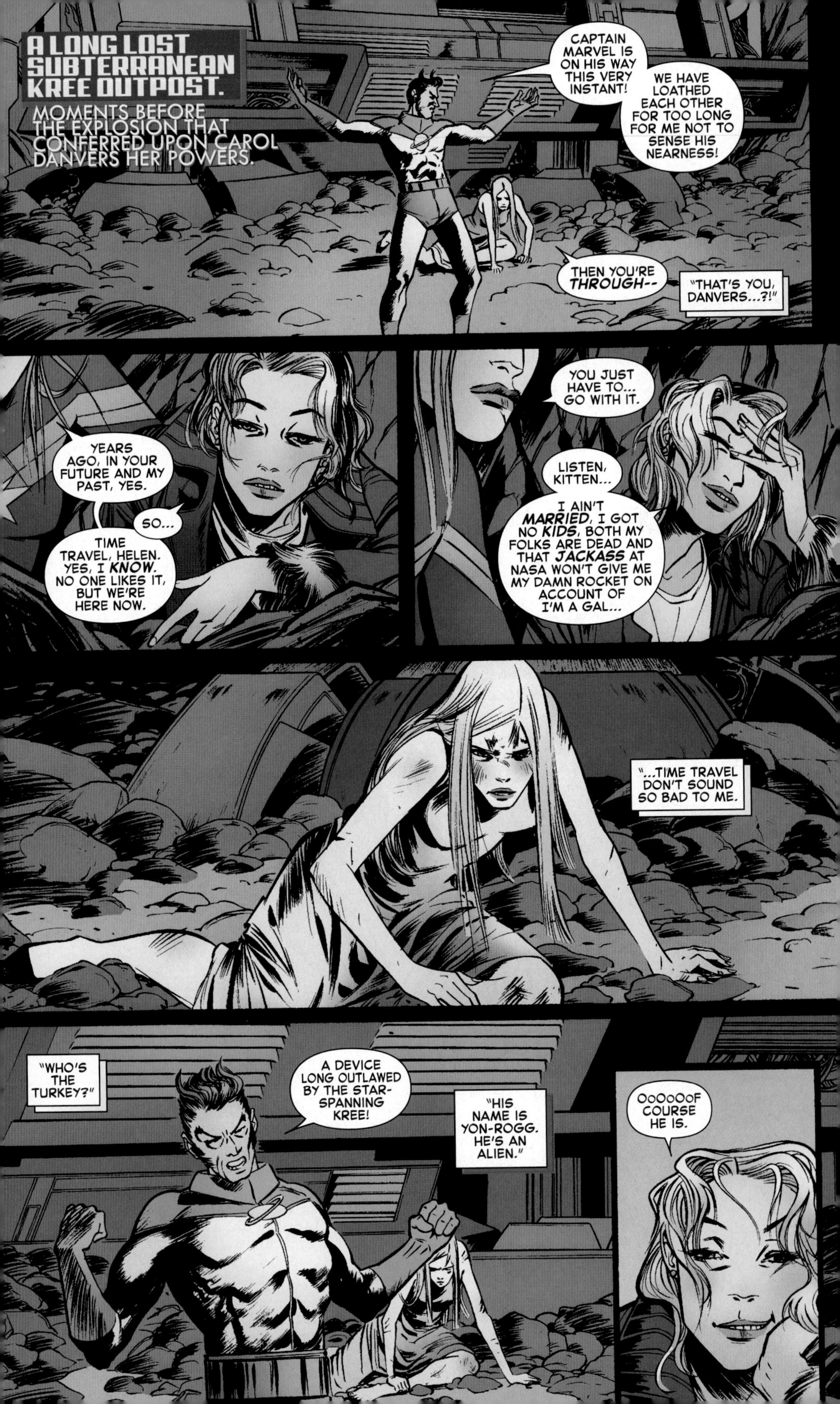
A LONG LOST SUBTERRANEAN KREE OUTPOST.
MOMENTS BEFORE THE EXPLOSION THAT CONFERRED UPON CAROL DANVERS HER POWERS.
CAPTAIN MARVEL IS ON HIS WAY THIS VERY INSTANT!
WE HAVE LOATHED EACH OTHER FOR TOO LONG FOR ME NOT TO SENSE HIS NEARNESS!
THEN YOU'RE THROUGH--
"THAT'S YOU, DANVERS...?!"
YEARS AGO, IN YOUR FUTURE AND MY PAST, YES.
SO...
TIME TRAVEL, HELEN. YES, I KNOW. NO ONE LIKES IT, BUT WE'RE HERE NOW.
YOU JUST HAVE TO... GO WITH IT.
LISTEN, KITTEN...
I AIN'T MARRIED, I GOT NO KIDS, BOTH MY FOLKS ARE DEAD AND THAT JACKASS AT NASA WON'T GIVE ME MY DAMN ROCKET ON ACCOUNT OF I'M A GAL...
"...TIME TRAVEL DON'T SOUND SO BAD TO ME.
"WHO'S THE TURKEY?"
A DEVICE LONG OUTLAWED BY THE STAR-SPANNING KREE!
"HIS NAME IS YON-ROGG. HE'S AN ALIEN."
OOOOOOF COURSE HE IS.

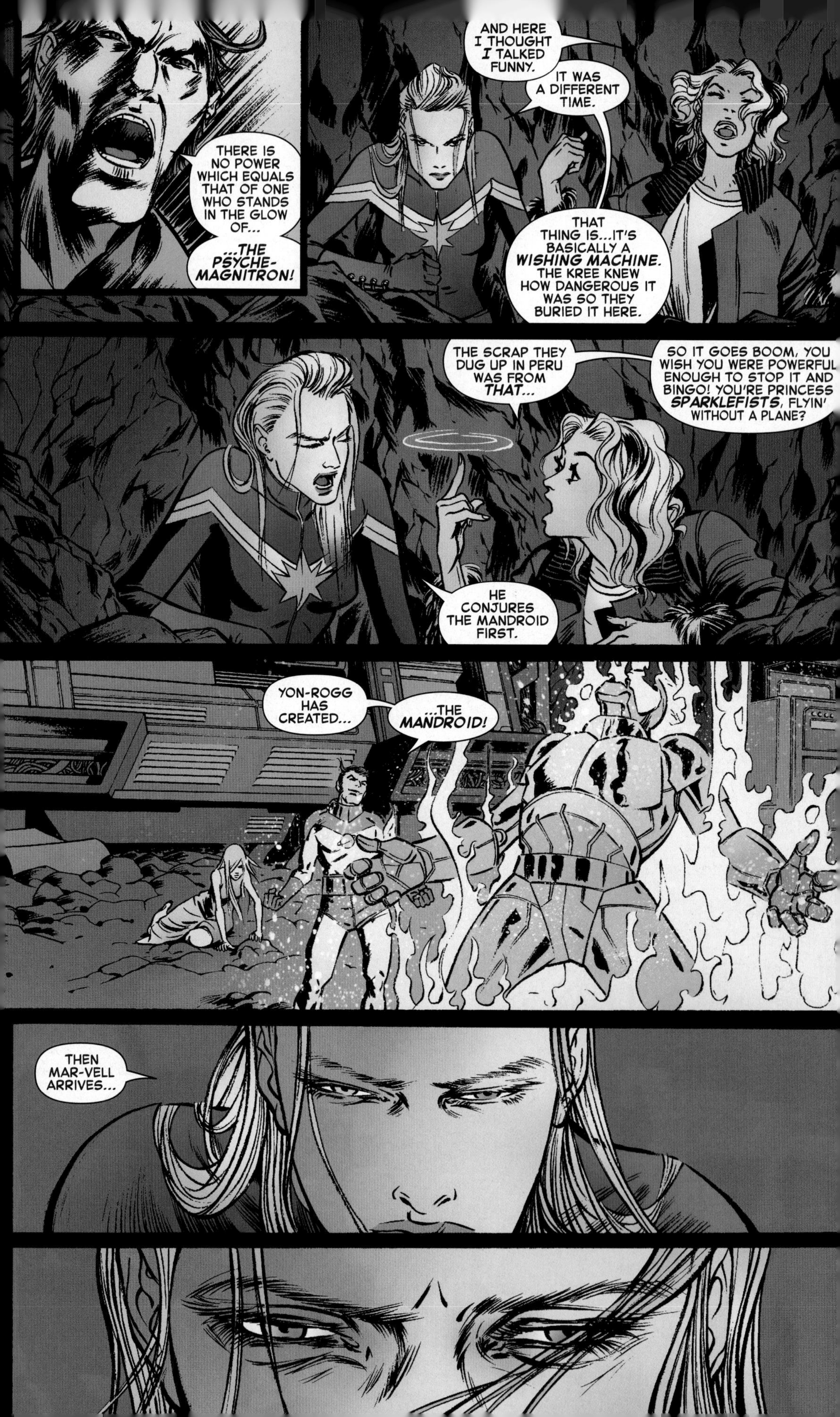
THERE IS NO POWER WHICH EQUALS THAT OF ONE WHO STANDS IN THE GLOW OF...
...THE PSYCHE-MAGNITRON!
AND HERE I THOUGHT I TALKED FUNNY.
IT WAS A DIFFERENT TIME.
THAT THING IS...IT'S BASICALLY A WISHING MACHINE. THE KREE KNEW HOW DANGEROUS IT WAS SO THEY BURIED IT HERE.
THE SCRAP THEY DUG UP IN PERU WAS FROM THAT...
SO IT GOES BOOM, YOU WISH YOU WERE POWERFUL ENOUGH TO STOP IT AND BINGO! YOU'RE PRINCESS SPARKLEFISTS, FLYIN' WITHOUT A PLANE?
HE CONJURES THE MANDROID FIRST.
YON-ROGG HAS CREATED...
...THE MANDROID!
THEN MAR-VELL ARRIVES...

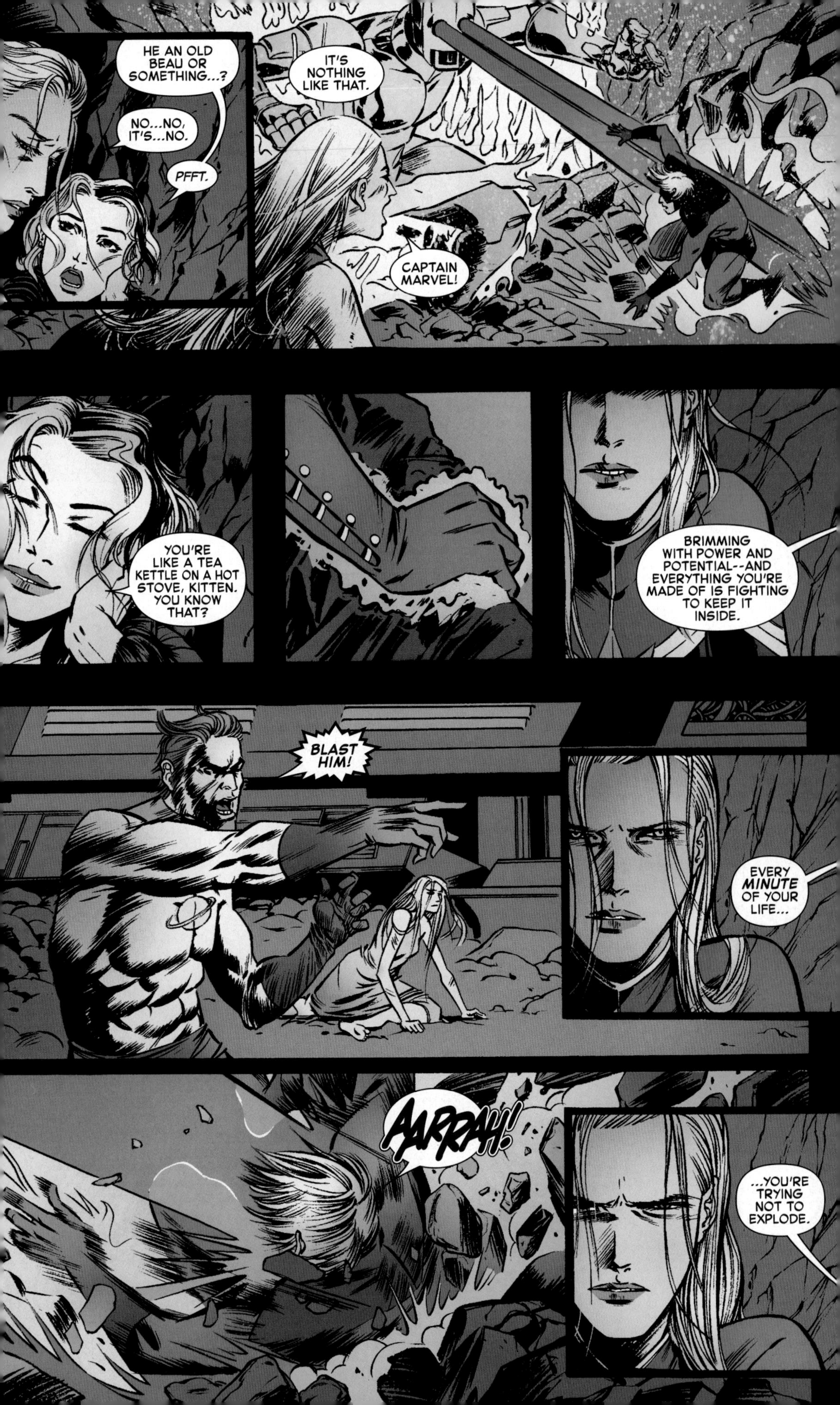

HE AN OLD BEAU OR SOMETHING...?
NO...NO, IT'S...NO.
PFFT.
IT'S NOTHING LIKE THAT.
CAPTAIN MARVEL!
YOU'RE LIKE A TEA KETTLE ON A HOT STOVE, KITTEN. YOU KNOW THAT?
BRIMMING WITH POWER AND POTENTIAL--AND EVERYTHING YOU'RE MADE OF IS FIGHTING TO KEEP IT INSIDE.
BLAST HIM!
EVERY MINUTE OF YOUR LIFE...
AARRAH!
...YOU'RE TRYING NOT TO EXPLODE.

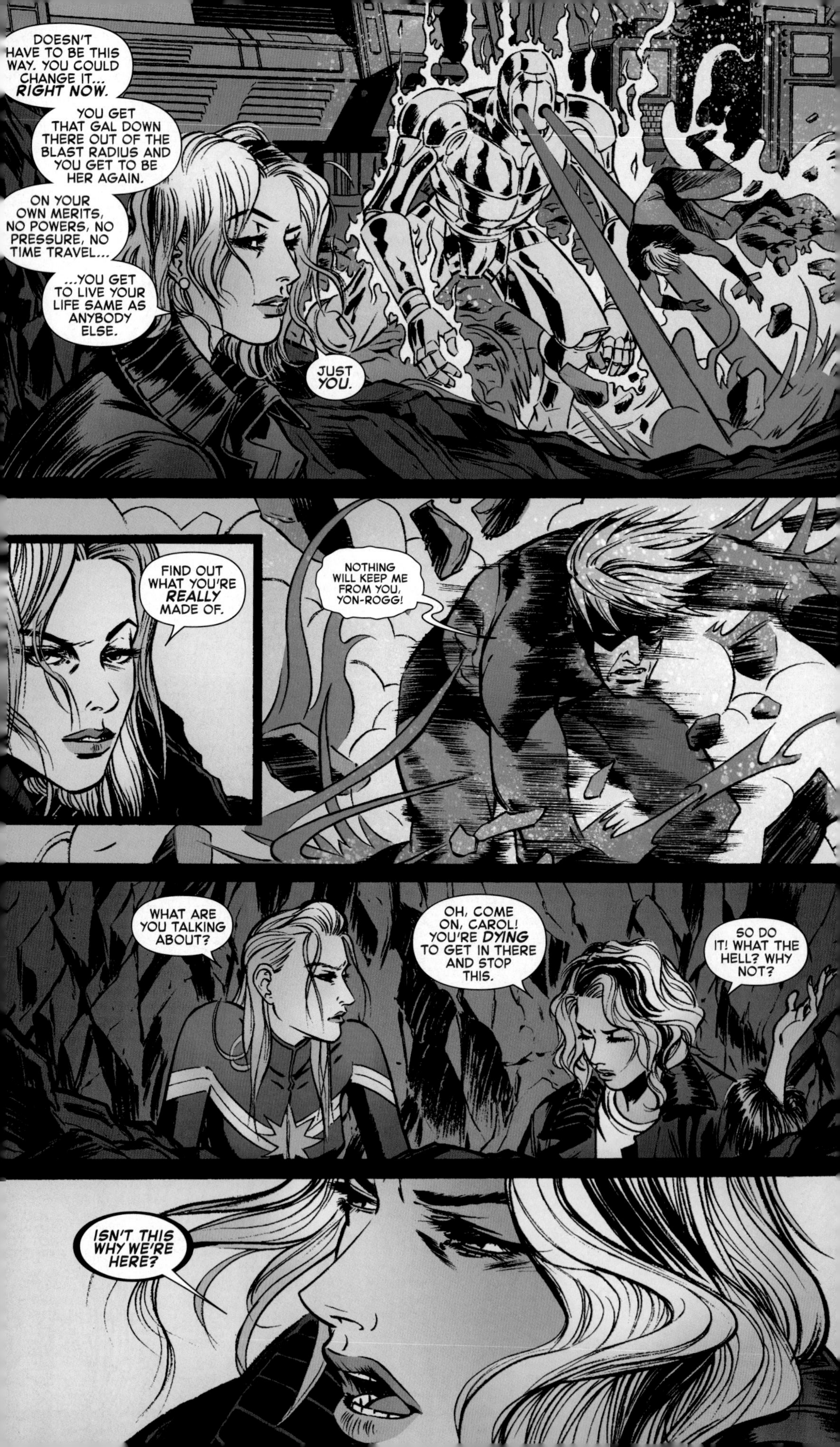

DOESN'T HAVE TO BE THIS WAY. YOU COULD CHANGE IT... RIGHT NOW.
YOU GET THAT GAL DOWN THERE OUT OF THE BLAST RADIUS AND YOU GET TO BE HER AGAIN.
ON YOUR OWN MERITS, NO POWERS, NO PRESSURE, NO TIME TRAVEL...
...YOU GET TO LIVE YOUR LIFE SAME AS ANYBODY ELSE.
JUST YOU.
FIND OUT WHAT YOU'RE REALLY MADE OF.
NOTHING WILL KEEP ME FROM YOU, YON-ROGG!
WHAT ARE YOU TALKING ABOUT?
OH, COME ON, CAROL! YOU'RE DYING TO GET IN THERE AND STOP THIS.
SO DO IT! WHAT THE HELL? WHY NOT?
ISN'T THIS WHY WE'RE HERE?

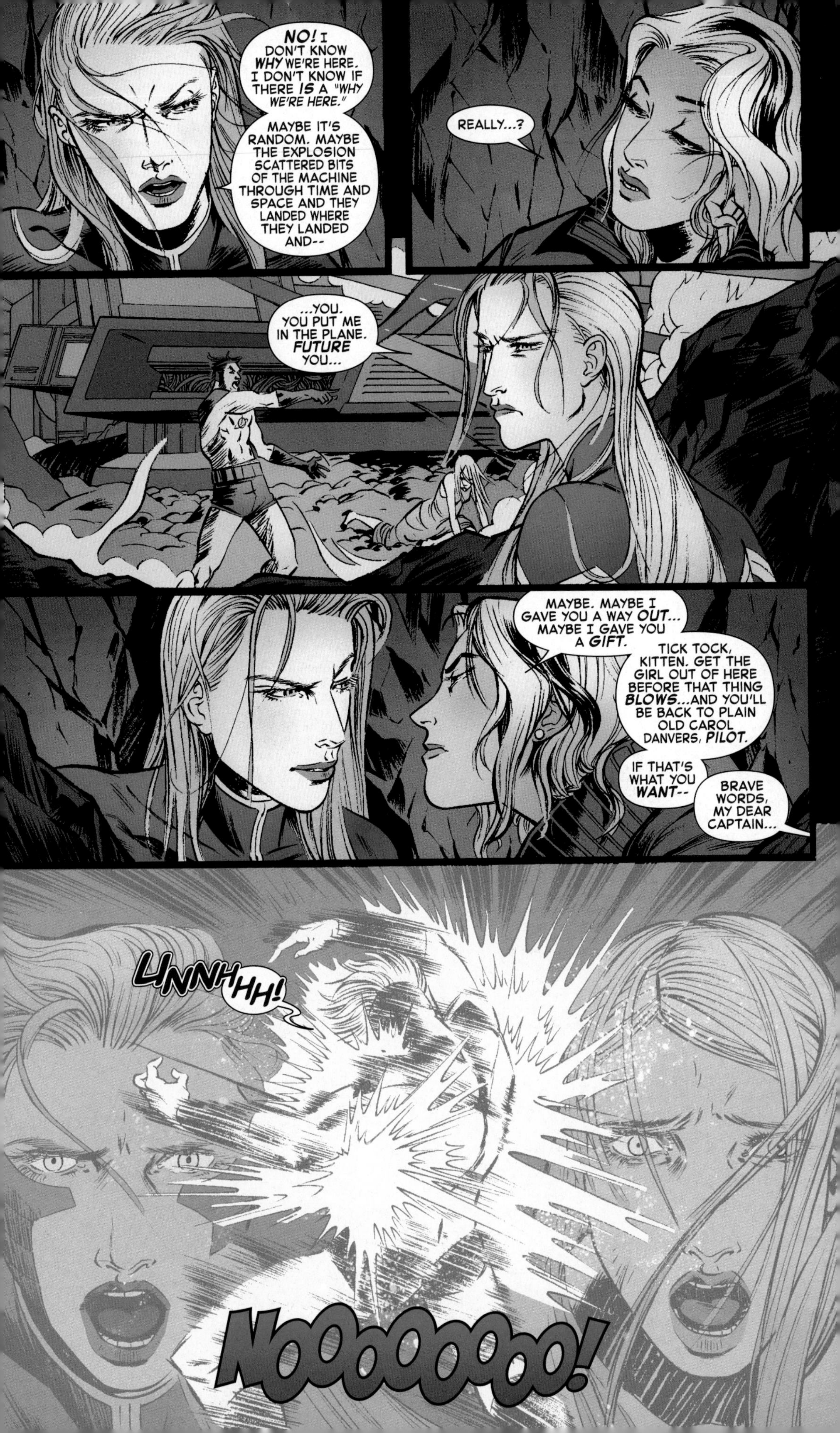
NO! I DON'T KNOW WHY WE'RE HERE. I DON'T KNOW IF THERE IS A "WHY WE'RE HERE."
MAYBE IT'S RANDOM. MAYBE THE EXPLOSION SCATTERED BITS OF THE MACHINE THROUGH TIME AND SPACE AND THEY LANDED WHERE THEY LANDED AND--
REALLY...?
...YOU. YOU PUT ME IN THE PLANE. FUTURE YOU...
MAYBE. MAYBE I GAVE YOU A WAY OUT... MAYBE I GAVE YOU A GIFT.
TICK TOCK, KITTEN. GET THE GIRL OUT OF HERE BEFORE THAT THING BLOWS...AND YOU'LL BE BACK TO PLAIN OLD CAROL DANVERS, PILOT.
IF THAT'S WHAT YOU WANT--
BRAVE WORDS, MY DEAR CAPTAIN...
UNNHHH!
NOOOOOOOO!

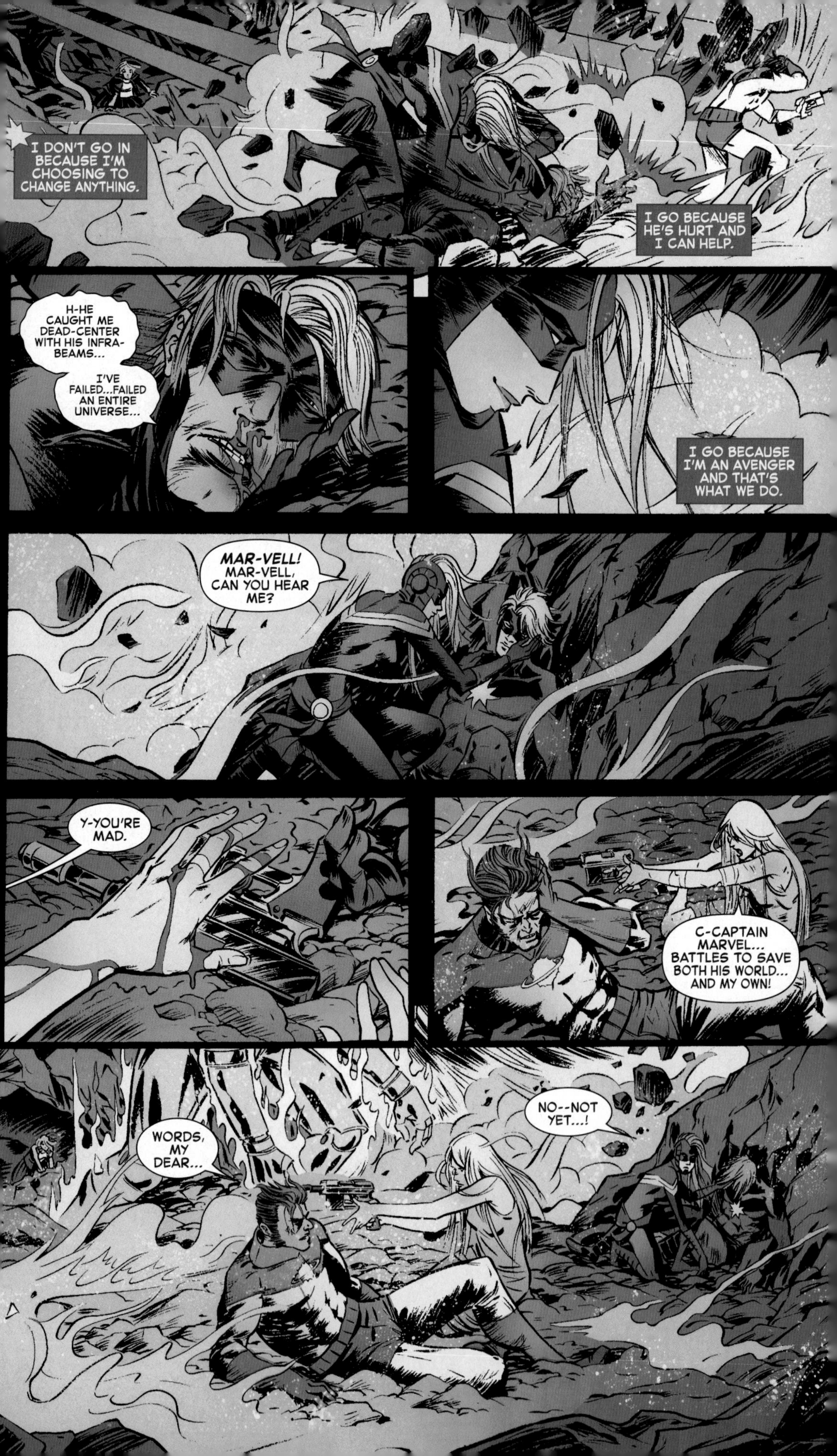
I DON'T GO IN BECAUSE I'M CHOOSING TO CHANGE ANYTHING.
I GO BECAUSE HE'S HURT AND I CAN HELP.
H-HE CAUGHT ME DEAD-CENTER WITH HIS INFRA-BEAMS...
I'VE FAILED...FAILED AN ENTIRE UNIVERSE...
I GO BECAUSE I'M AN AVENGER AND THAT'S WHAT WE DO.
MAR-VELL! MAR-VELL, CAN YOU HEAR ME?
Y-YOU'RE MAD.
C-CAPTAIN MARVEL... BATTLES TO SAVE BOTH HIS WORLD... AND MY OWN!
WORDS, MY DEAR...
NO--NOT YET...!

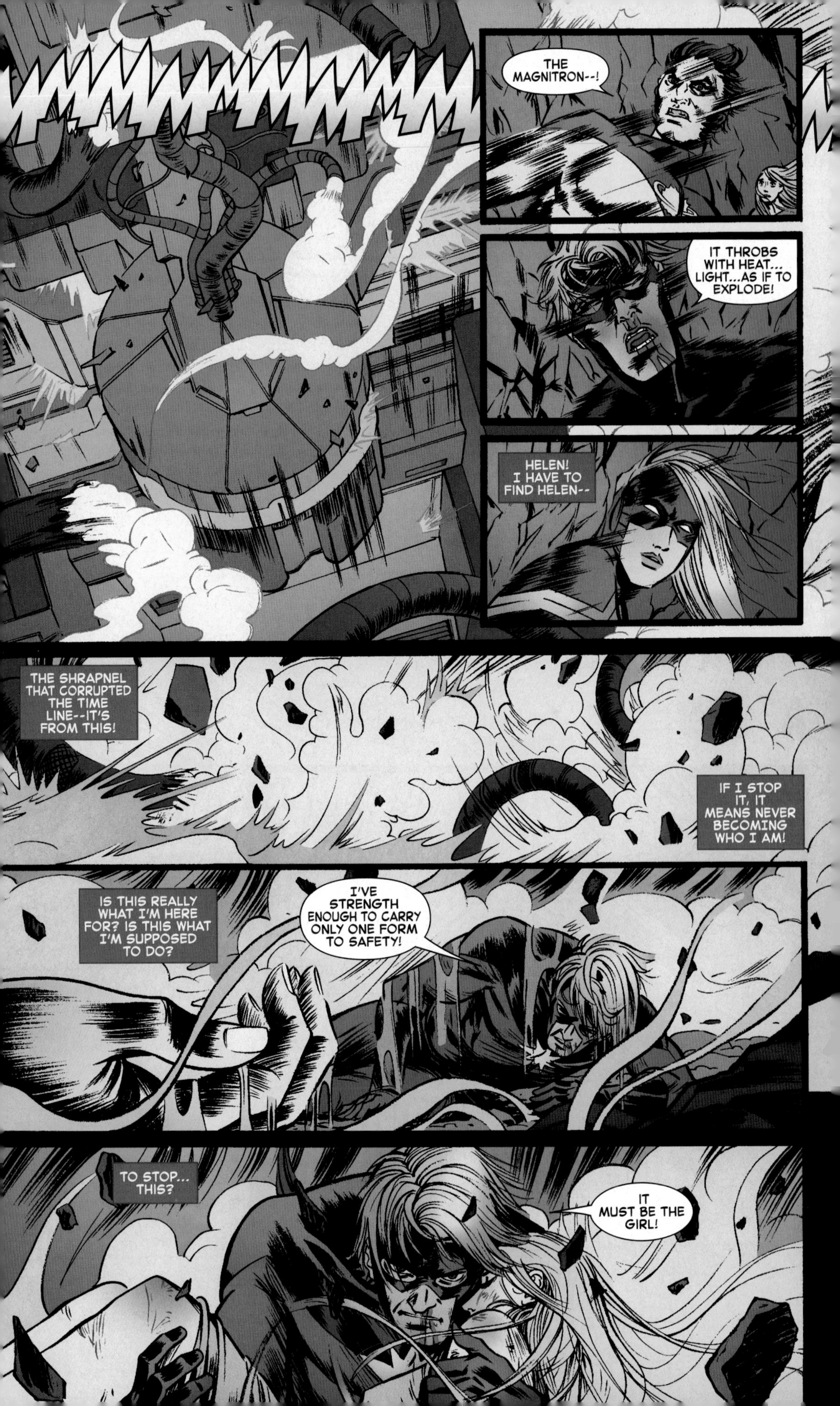
THE MAGNITRON--!
IT THROBS WITH HEAT... LIGHT...AS IF TO EXPLODE!
HELEN! I HAVE TO FIND HELEN--
THE SHRAPNEL THAT CORRUPTED THE TIME LINE--IT'S FROM THIS!
IF I STOP IT, IT MEANS NEVER BECOMING WHO I AM!
IS THIS REALLY WHAT I'M HERE FOR? IS THIS WHAT I'M SUPPOSED TO DO?
I'VE STRENGTH ENOUGH TO CARRY ONLY ONE FORM TO SAFETY!
TO STOP... THIS?
IT MUST BE THE GIRL!

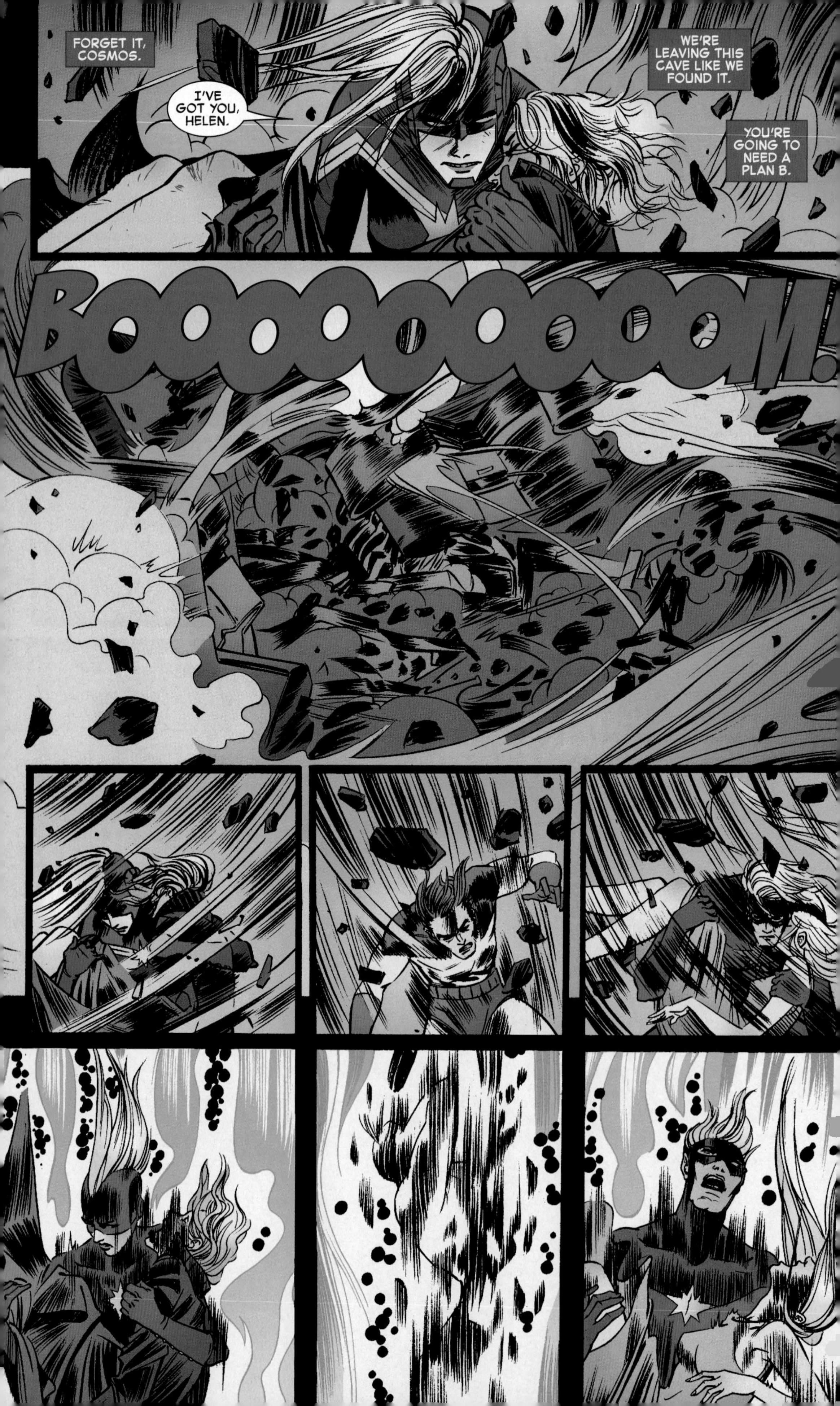

FORGET IT, COSMOS.
I'VE GOT YOU, HELEN.
WE'RE LEAVING THIS CAVE LIKE WE FOUND IT.
YOU'RE GOING TO NEED A PLAN B.
BOOOOOOOOOM!!

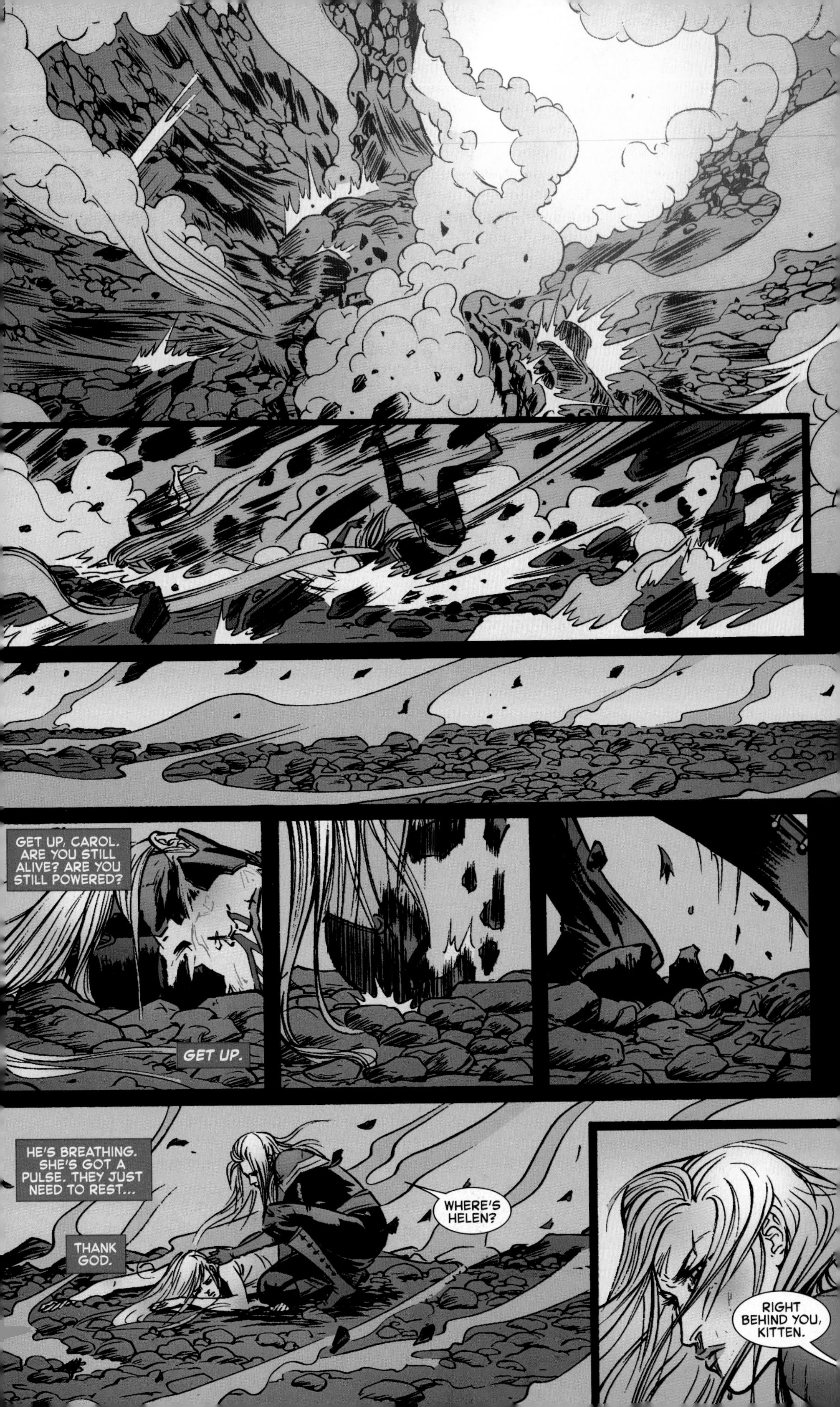
GET UP, CAROL. ARE YOU STILL ALIVE? ARE YOU STILL POWERED?
GET UP.
HE'S BREATHING. SHE'S GOT A PULSE. THEY JUST NEED TO REST...
THANK GOD.
WHERE'S HELEN?
RIGHT BEHIND YOU, KITTEN.

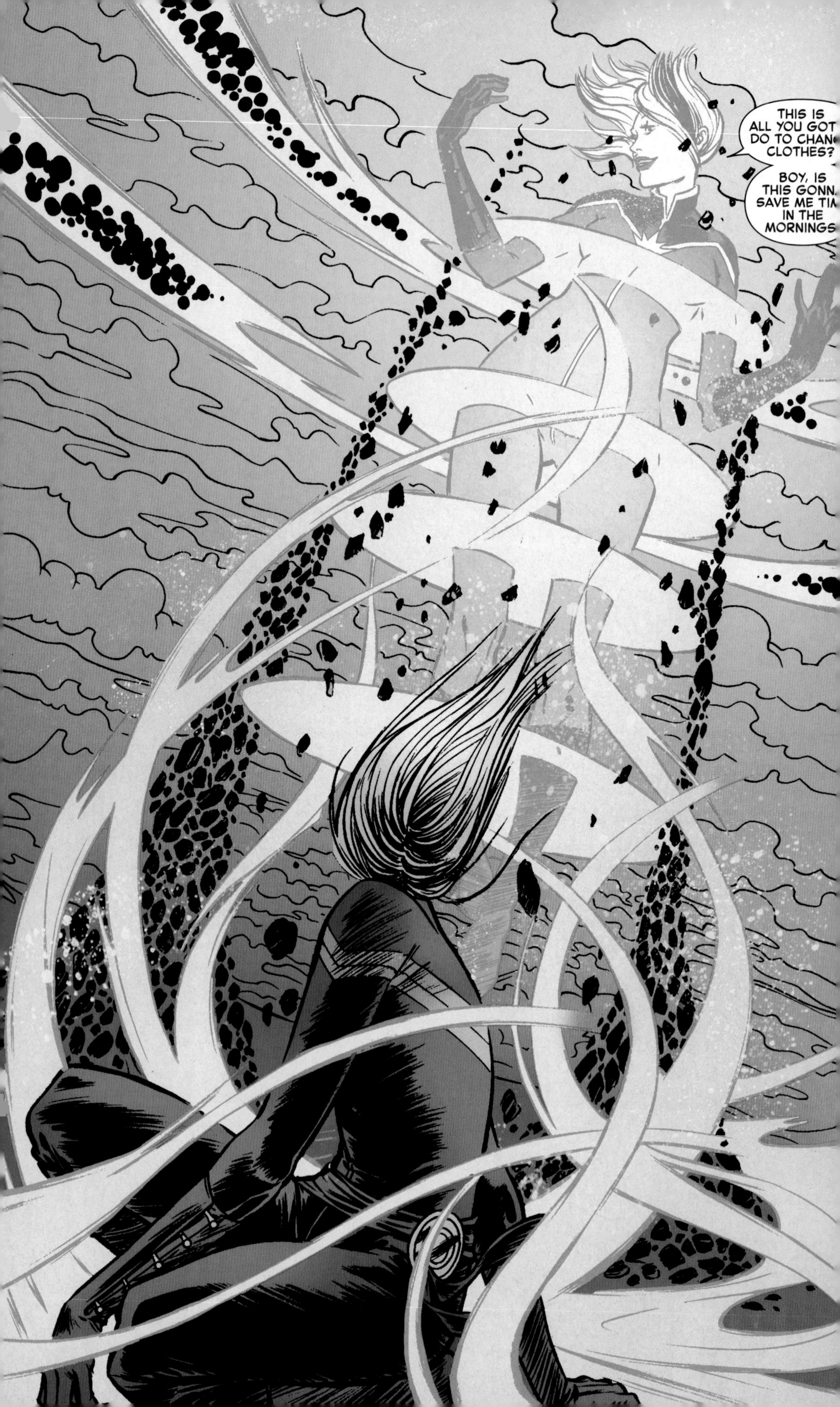
THIS IS ALL YOU GOT DO TO CHAN CLOTHES?
BOY, IS THIS GONN SAVE ME TI IN THE MORNINGS

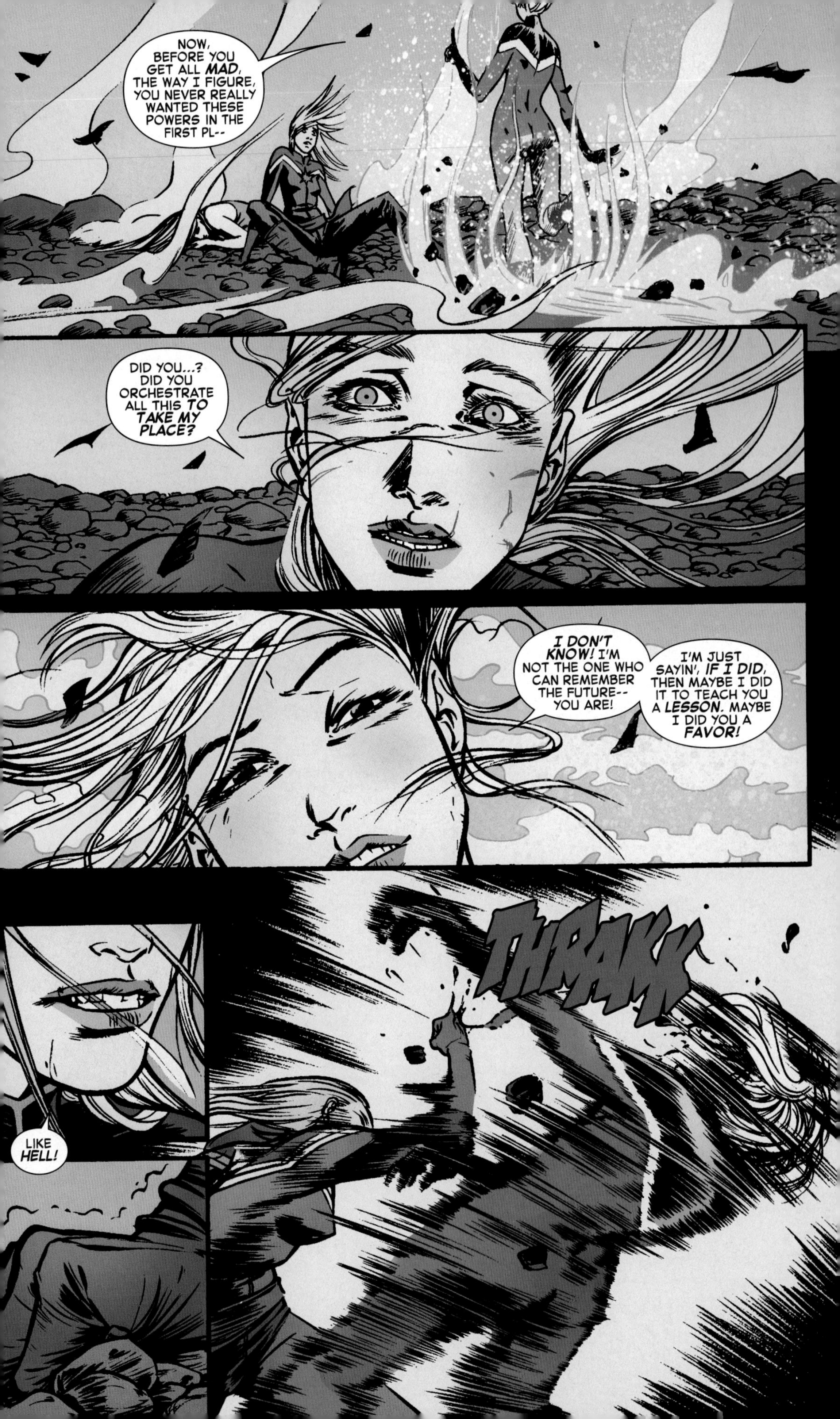
NOW, BEFORE YOU GET ALL MAD, THE WAY I FIGURE, YOU NEVER REALLY WANTED THESE POWERS IN THE FIRST PL--
DID YOU...? DID YOU ORCHESTRATE ALL THIS TO TAKE MY PLACE?
I DON'T KNOW! I'M NOT THE ONE WHO CAN REMEMBER THE FUTURE-- YOU ARE!
I'M JUST SAYIN', IF I DID, THEN MAYBE I DID IT TO TEACH YOU A LESSON. MAYBE I DID YOU A FAVOR!
LIKE HELL!
THRAKK

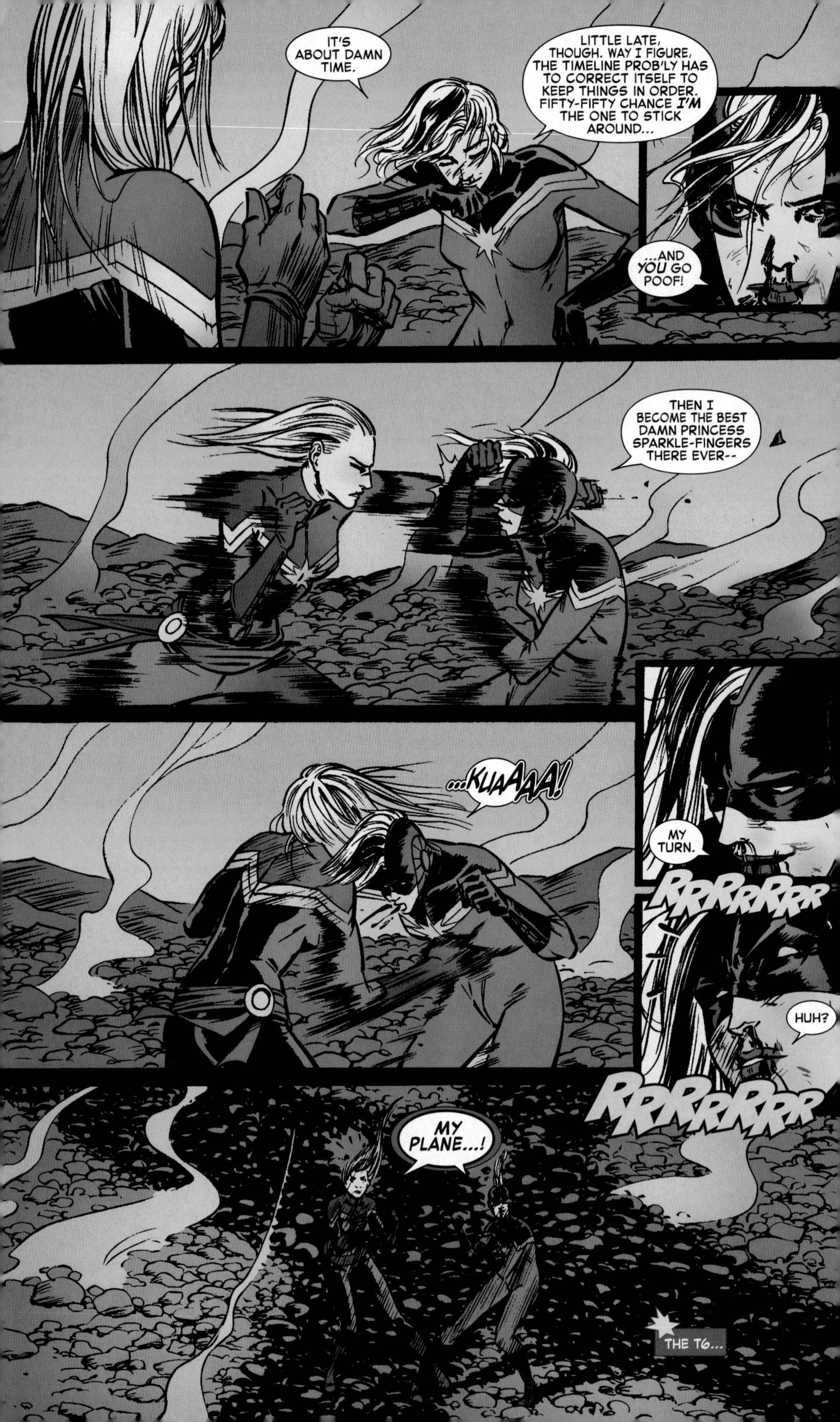
IT'S ABOUT DAMN TIME.
LITTLE LATE, THOUGH. WAY I FIGURE, THE TIMELINE PROB'LY HAS TO CORRECT ITSELF TO KEEP THINGS IN ORDER. FIFTY-FIFTY CHANCE I'M THE ONE TO STICK AROUND...
...AND YOU GO POOF!
THEN I BECOME THE BEST DAMN PRINCESS SPARKLE-FINGERS THERE EVER--
...KLIAAAA!
MY TURN.
RRRRRRRR
HUH?
RRRRRRRR
MY PLANE...!
THE T6...

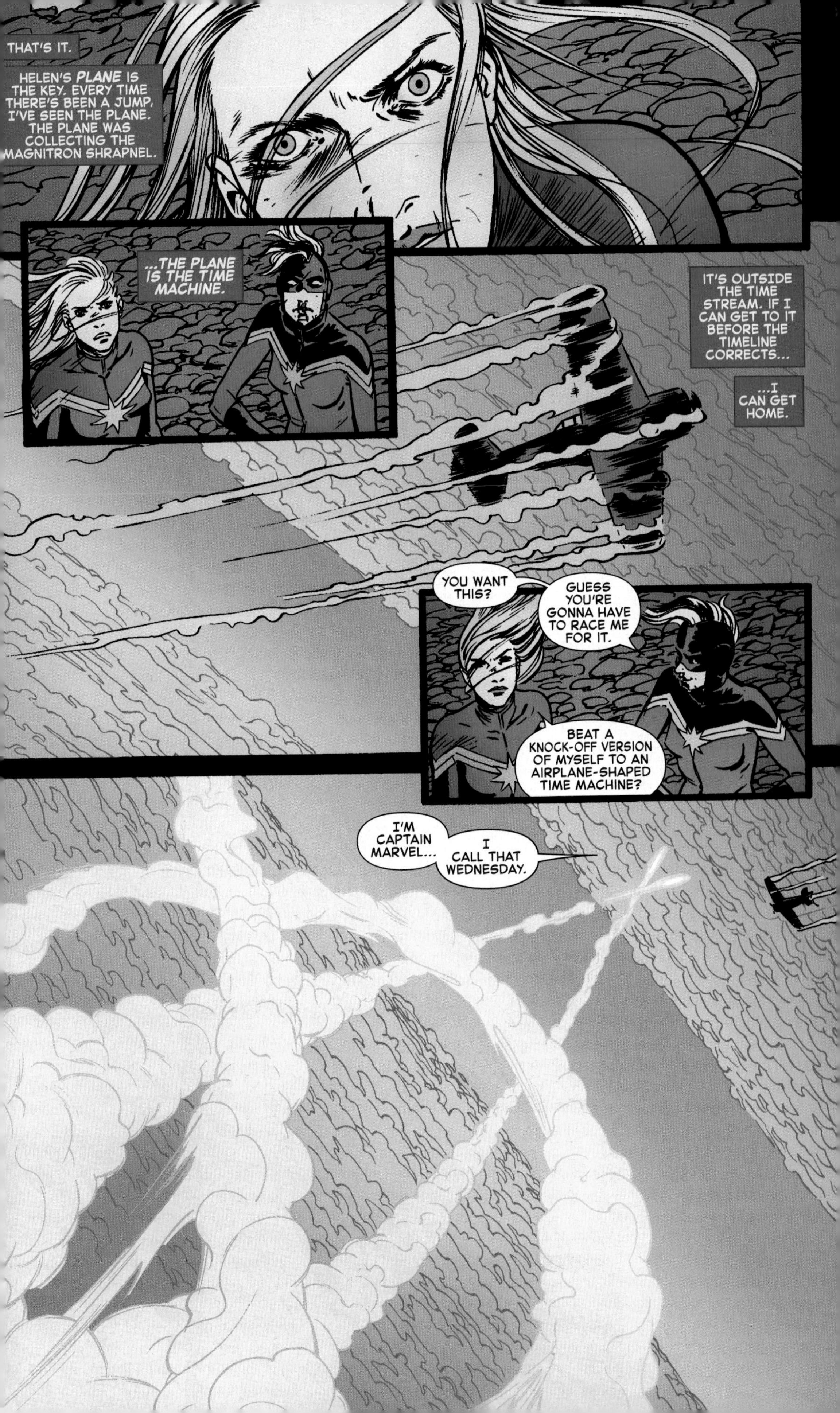
THAT'S IT.
HELEN'S PLANE IS THE KEY. EVERY TIME THERE'S BEEN A JUMP, I'VE SEEN THE PLANE. THE PLANE WAS COLLECTING THE MAGNITRON SHRAPNEL.
...THE PLANE IS THE TIME MACHINE.
IT'S OUTSIDE THE TIME STREAM. IF I CAN GET TO IT BEFORE THE TIMELINE CORRECTS...
...I CAN GET HOME.
YOU WANT THIS?
GUESS YOU'RE GONNA HAVE TO RACE ME FOR IT.
BEAT A KNOCK-OFF VERSION OF MYSELF TO AN AIRPLANE-SHAPED TIME MACHINE?
I'M CAPTAIN MARVEL...
I CALL THAT WEDNESDAY.

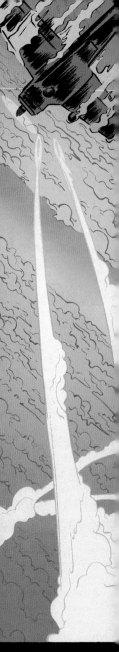

GOT IT.

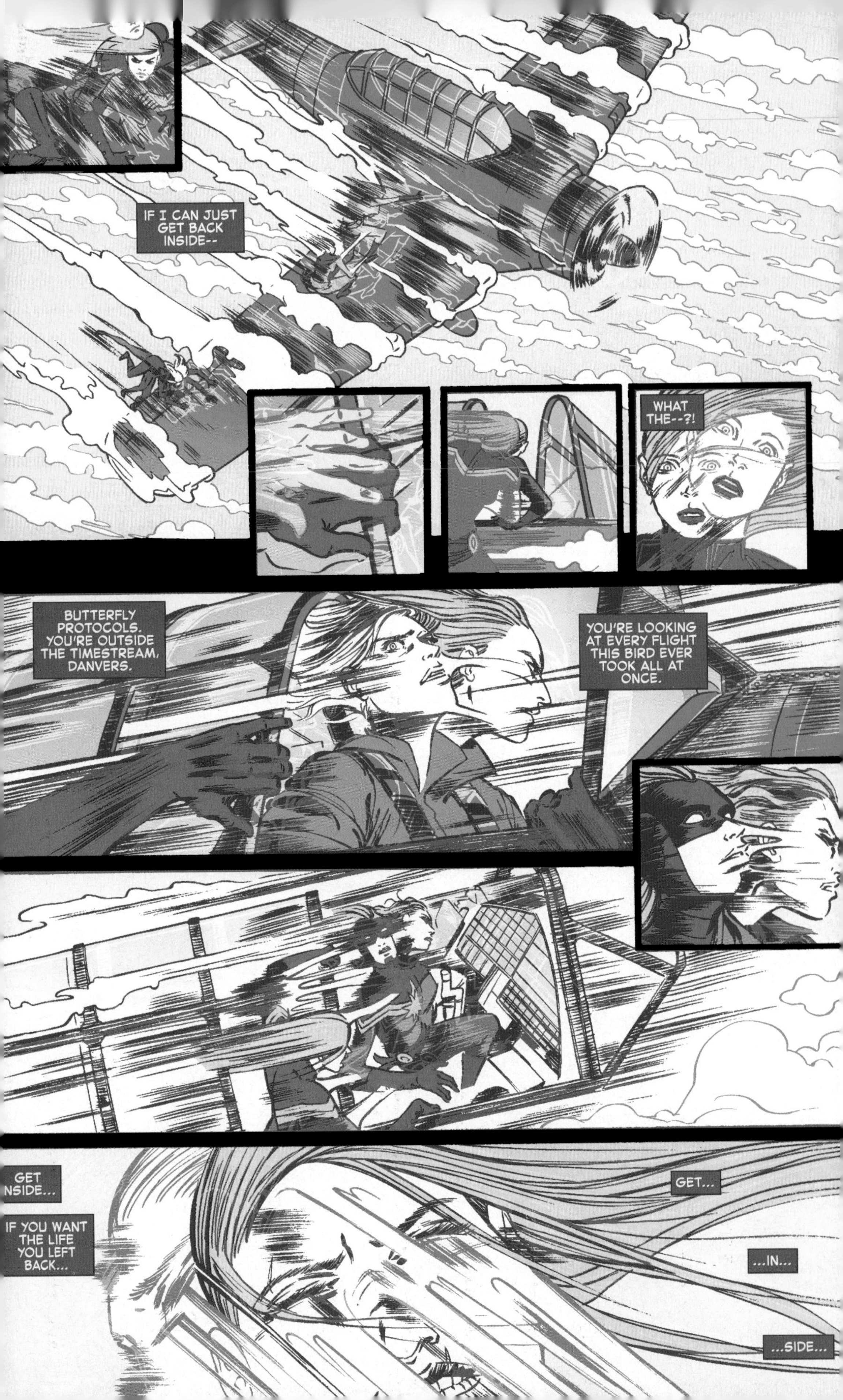
IF I CAN JUST GET BACK INSIDE--
WHAT THE--?!
BUTTERFLY PROTOCOLS. YOU'RE OUTSIDE THE TIMESTREAM, DANVERS.
YOU'RE LOOKING AT EVERY FLIGHT THIS BIRD EVER TOOK ALL AT ONCE.
GET INSIDE...
IF YOU WANT THE LIFE YOU LEFT BACK...
GET...
...IN...
...SIDE...

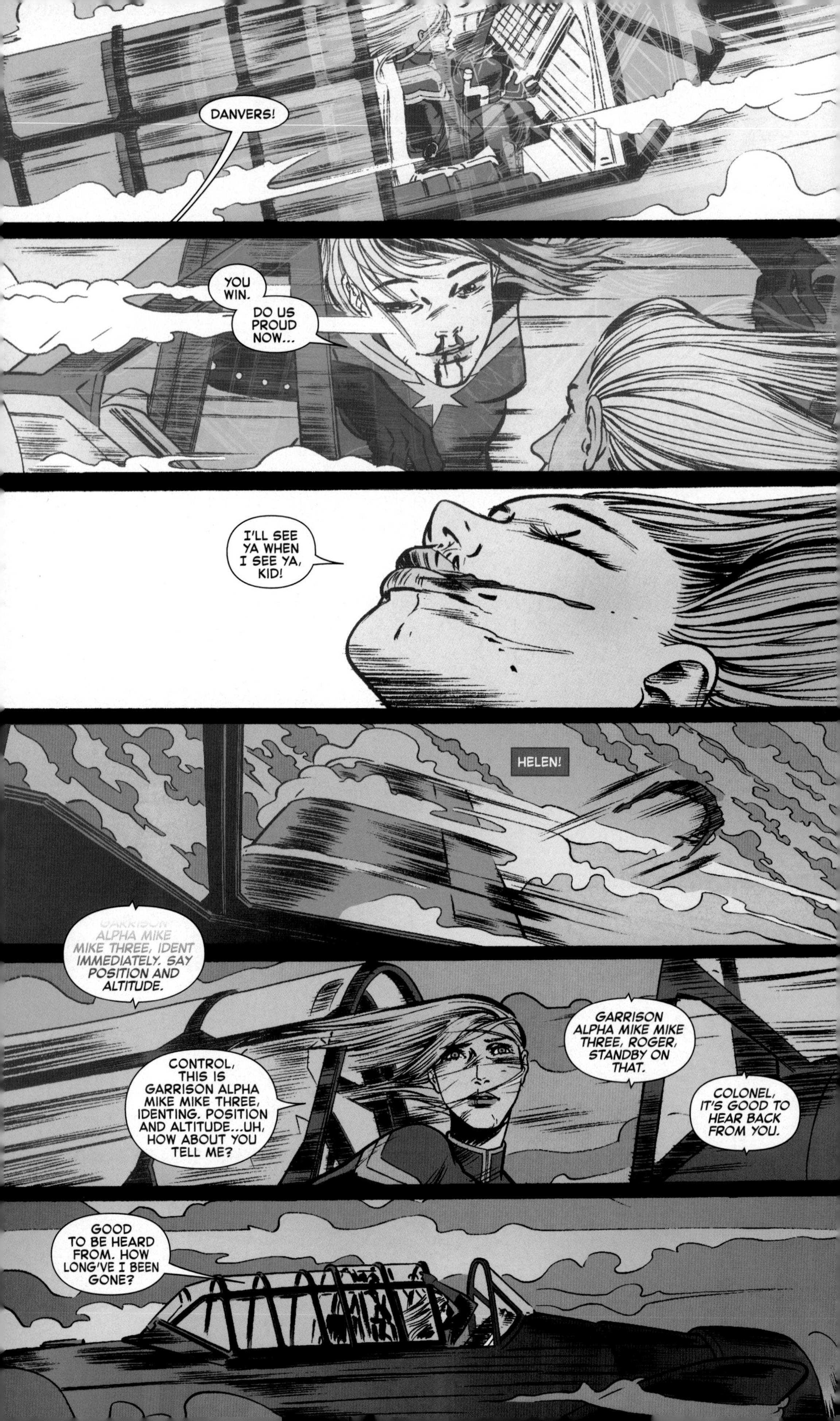
DANVERS!
YOU WIN.
DO US PROUD NOW...
I'LL SEE YA WHEN I SEE YA, KID!
HELEN!
GARRISON ALPHA MIKE MIKE THREE, IDENT IMMEDIATELY. SAY POSITION AND ALTITUDE.
CONTROL, THIS IS GARRISON ALPHA MIKE MIKE THREE, IDENTING. POSITION AND ALTITUDE...UH, HOW ABOUT YOU TELL ME?
GARRISON ALPHA MIKE MIKE THREE, ROGER, STANDBY ON THAT.
COLONEL, IT'S GOOD TO HEAR BACK FROM YOU.
GOOD TO BE HEARD FROM. HOW LONG'VE I BEEN GONE?

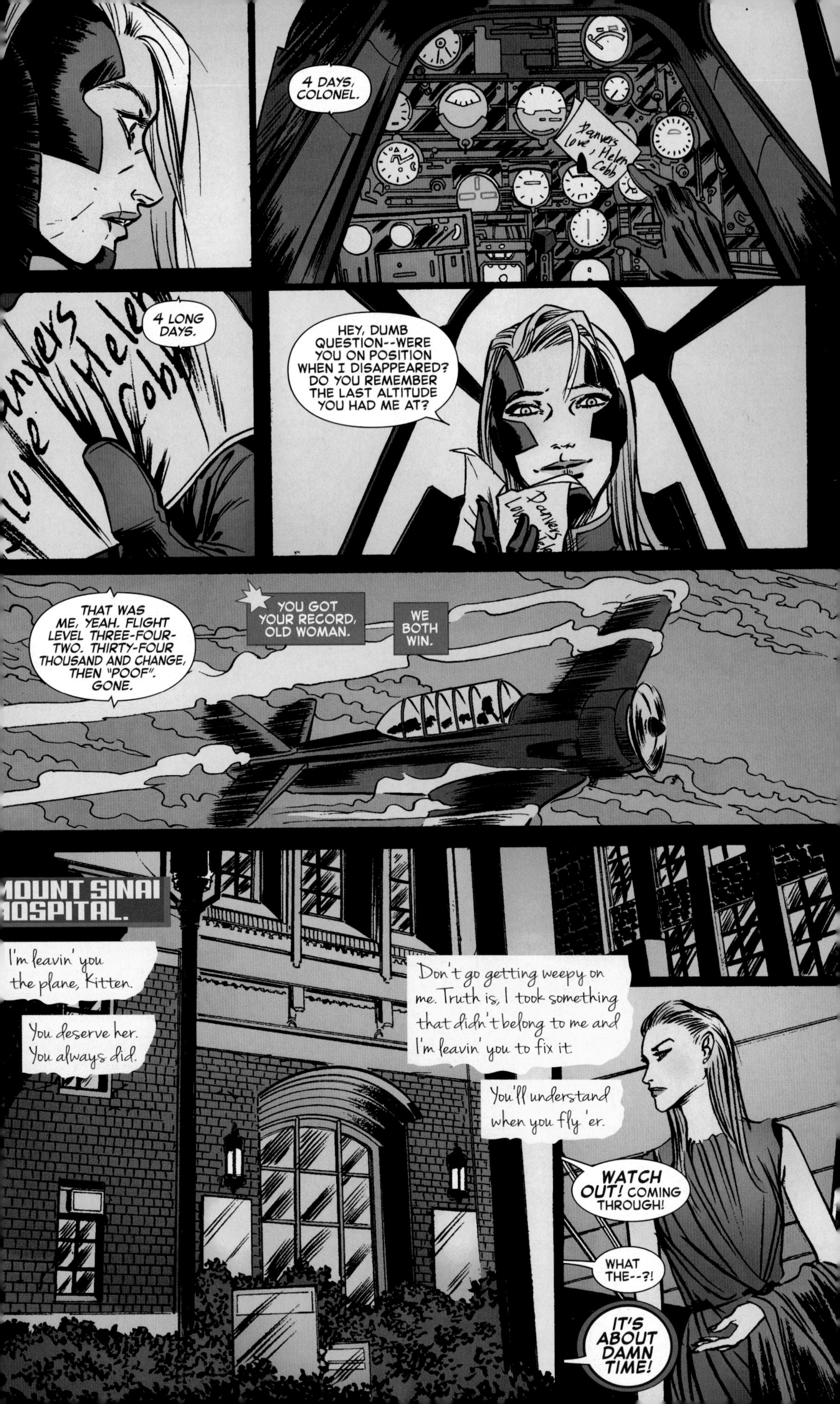
4 DAYS, COLONEL.
Danvers Love, Helen Cobb
4 LONG DAYS.
HEY, DUMB QUESTION--WERE YOU ON POSITION WHEN I DISAPPEARED? DO YOU REMEMBER THE LAST ALTITUDE YOU HAD ME AT?
THAT WAS ME, YEAH. FLIGHT LEVEL THREE-FOUR-TWO. THIRTY-FOUR THOUSAND AND CHANGE, THEN "POOF". GONE.
YOU GOT YOUR RECORD, OLD WOMAN.
WE BOTH WIN.
MOUNT SINAI HOSPITAL.
I'm leavin' you the plane, Kitten.
You deserve her. You always did.
Don't go getting weepy on me. Truth is, I took something that didn't belong to me and I'm leavin' you to fix it.
You'll understand when you fly 'er.
WATCH OUT! COMING THROUGH!
WHAT THE--?!
IT'S ABOUT DAMN TIME!

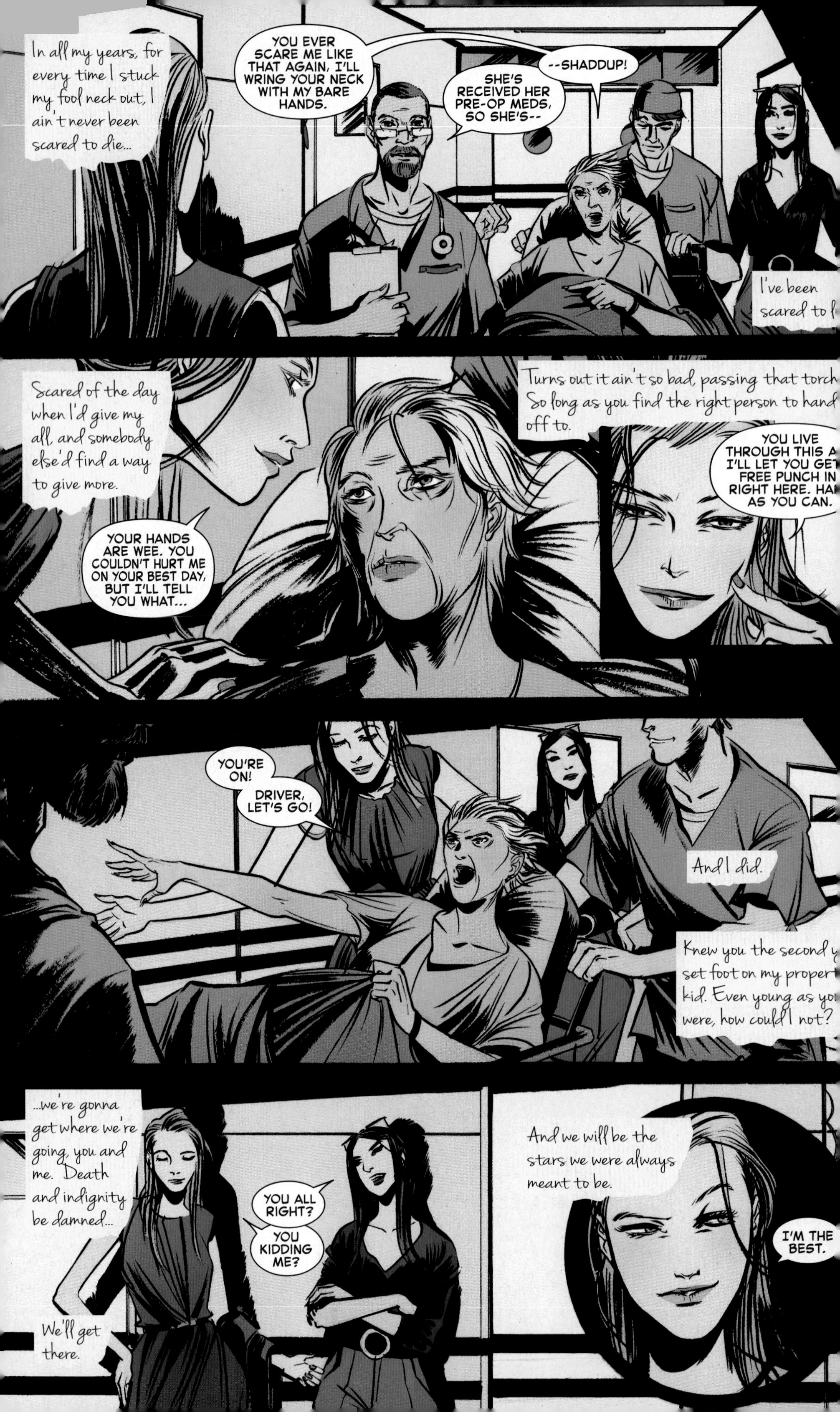

In all my years, for every time I stuck my fool neck out, I ain't never been scared to die...
YOU EVER SCARE ME LIKE THAT AGAIN, I'LL WRING YOUR NECK WITH MY BARE HANDS.
SHE'S RECEIVED HER PRE-OP MEDS, SO SHE'S--
--SHADDUP!
I've been scared to
Scared of the day when I'd give my all, and somebody else'd find a way to give more.
YOUR HANDS ARE WEE. YOU COULDN'T HURT ME ON YOUR BEST DAY, BUT I'LL TELL YOU WHAT...
Turns out it ain't so bad, passing that torch. So long as you find the right person to hand off to.
YOU LIVE THROUGH THIS A I'LL LET YOU GET FREE PUNCH IN RIGHT HERE. HA AS YOU CAN.
YOU'RE ON!
DRIVER, LET'S GO!
And I did.
Knew you the second y set foot on my proper kid. Even young as yo were, how could I not?
...we're gonna get where we're going, you and me. Death and indignity be damned...
YOU ALL RIGHT?
YOU KIDDING ME?
We'll get there.
And we will be the stars we were always meant to be.
I'M THE BEST.

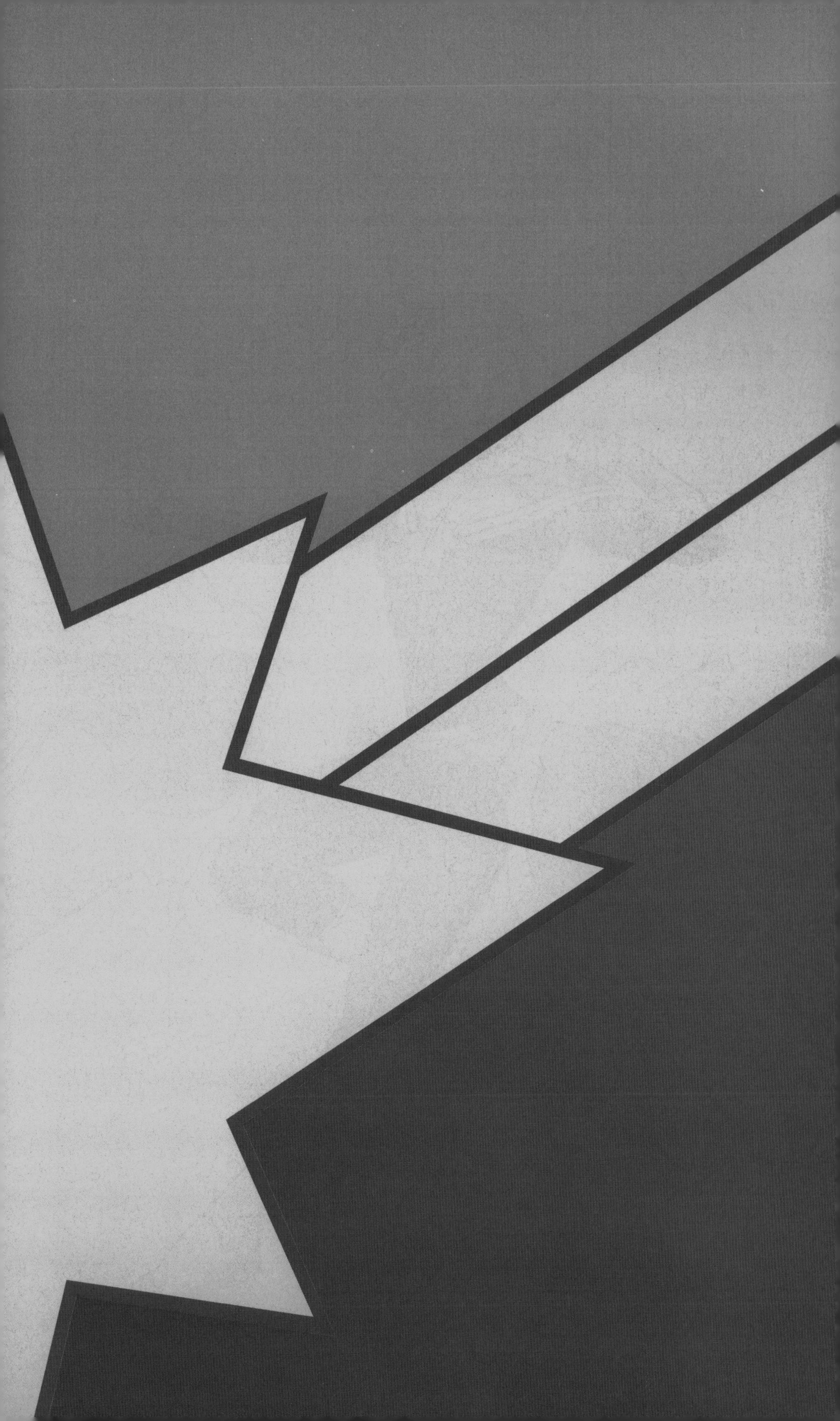

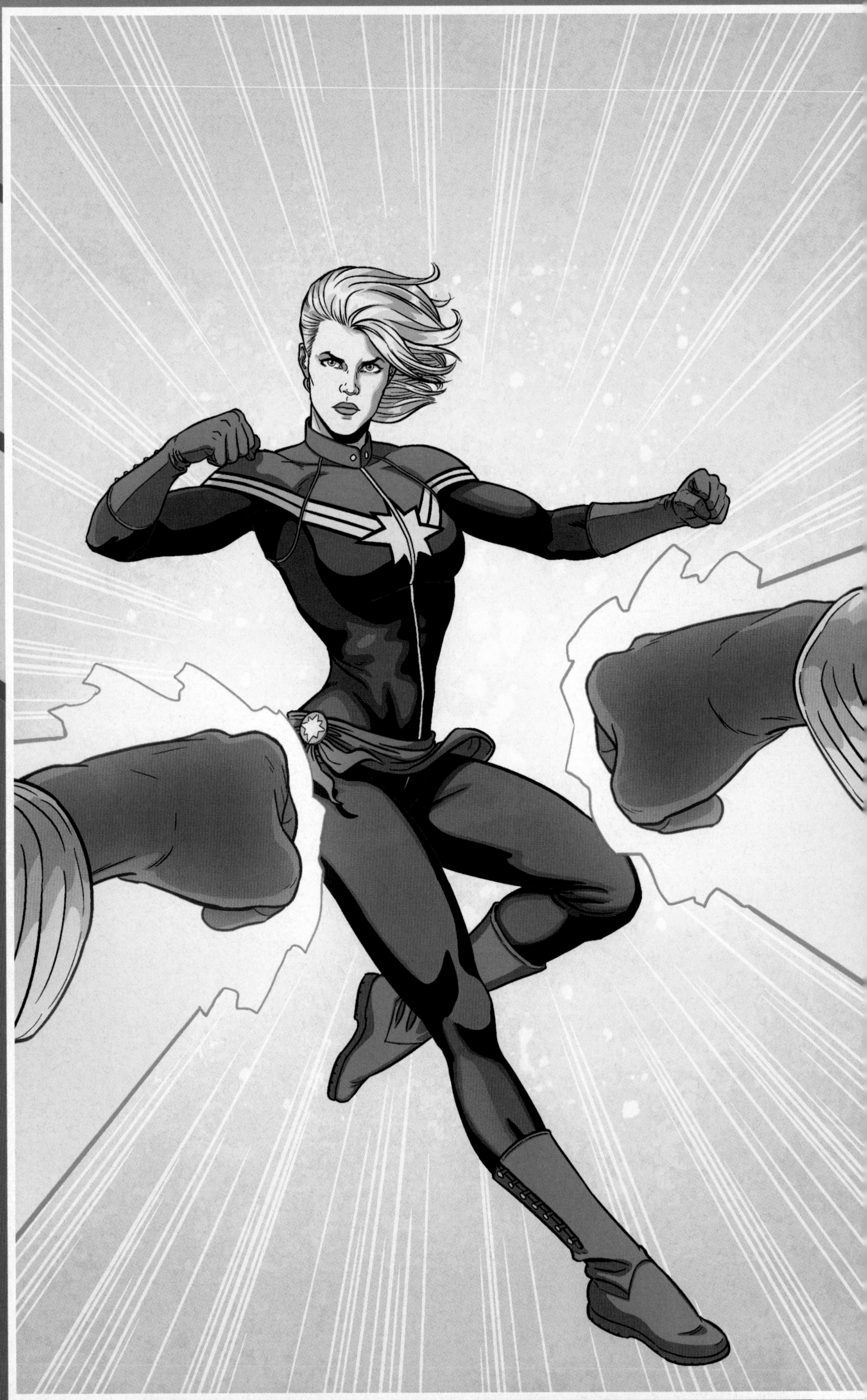

SEVEN

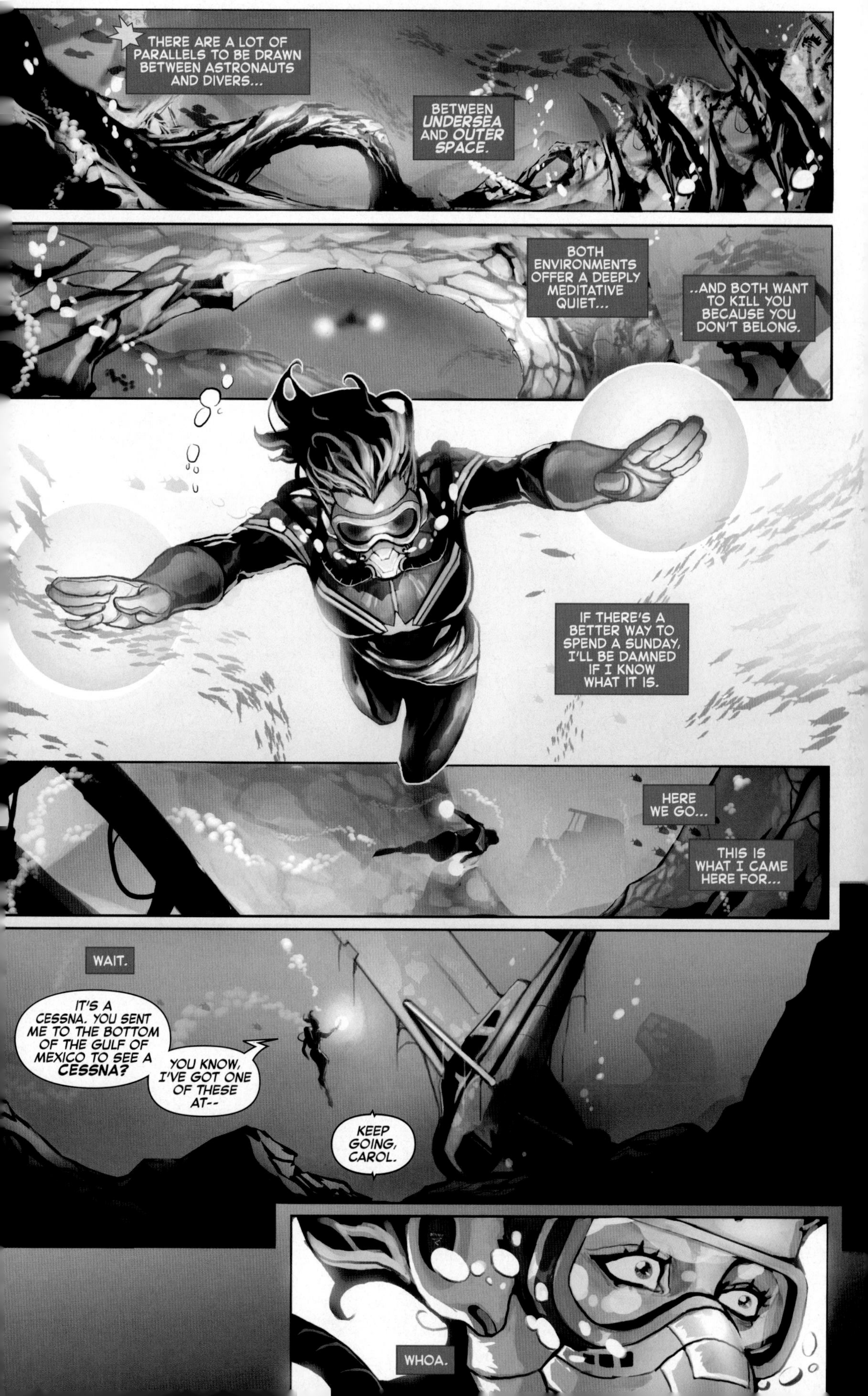
THERE ARE A LOT OF PARALLELS TO BE DRAWN BETWEEN ASTRONAUTS AND DIVERS...
BETWEEN *UNDERSEA* AND *OUTER SPACE.*
BOTH ENVIRONMENTS OFFER A DEEPLY MEDITATIVE QUIET...
..AND BOTH WANT TO KILL YOU BECAUSE YOU DON'T BELONG.
IF THERE'S A BETTER WAY TO SPEND A SUNDAY, I'LL BE DAMNED IF I KNOW WHAT IT IS.
HERE WE GO...
THIS IS WHAT I CAME HERE FOR...
WAIT.
IT'S A CESSNA. YOU SENT ME TO THE BOTTOM OF THE GULF OF MEXICO TO SEE A **CESSNA?**
YOU KNOW, I'VE GOT ONE OF THESE AT--
KEEP GOING, CAROL.
WHOA.

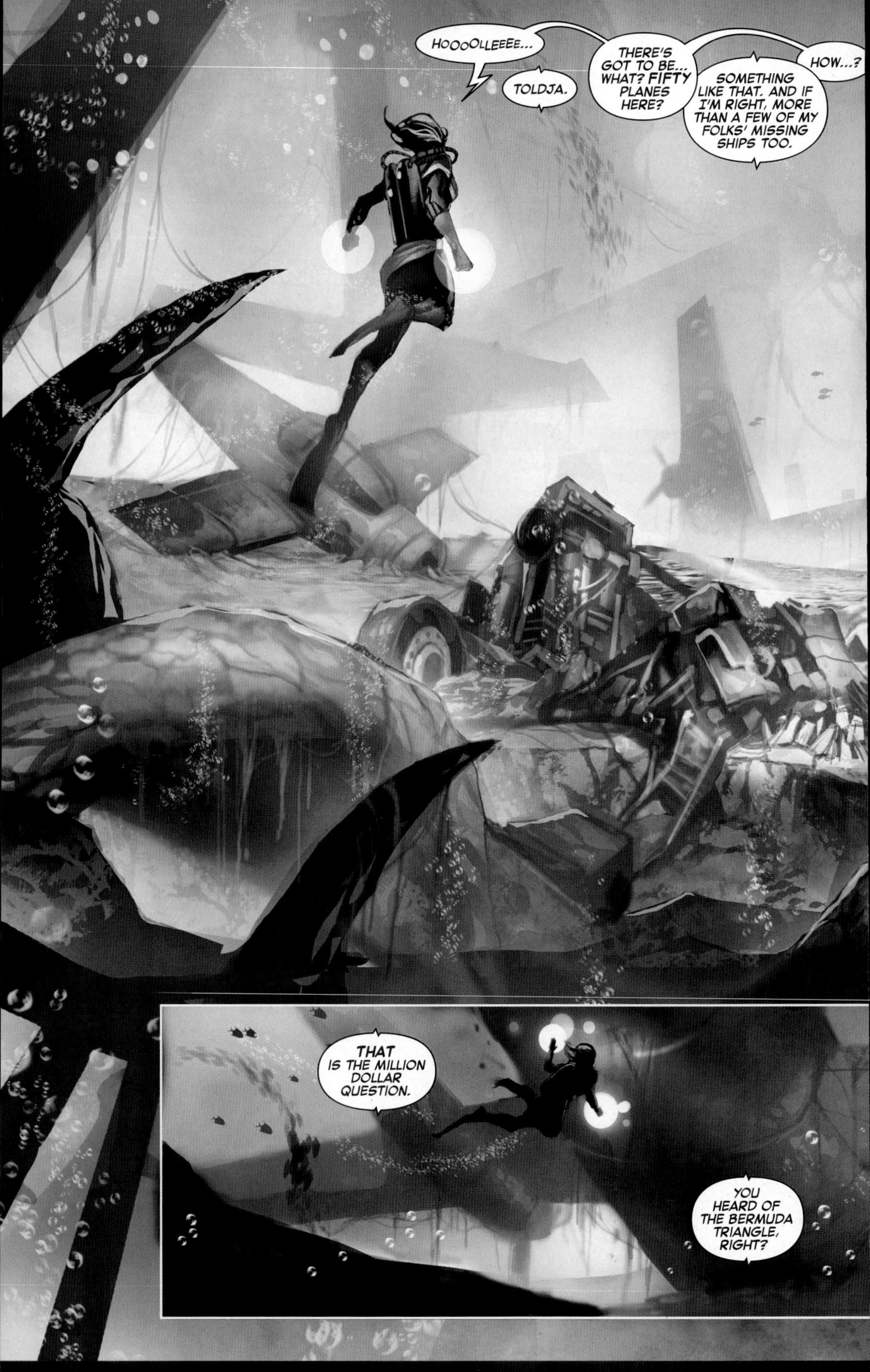
HOOOOLLEEEE...
TOLDJA.
THERE'S GOT TO BE... WHAT? FIFTY PLANES HERE?
SOMETHING LIKE THAT. AND IF I'M RIGHT, MORE THAN A FEW OF MY FOLKS' MISSING SHIPS TOO.
HOW...?
THAT IS THE MILLION DOLLAR QUESTION.
YOU HEARD OF THE BERMUDA TRIANGLE, RIGHT?

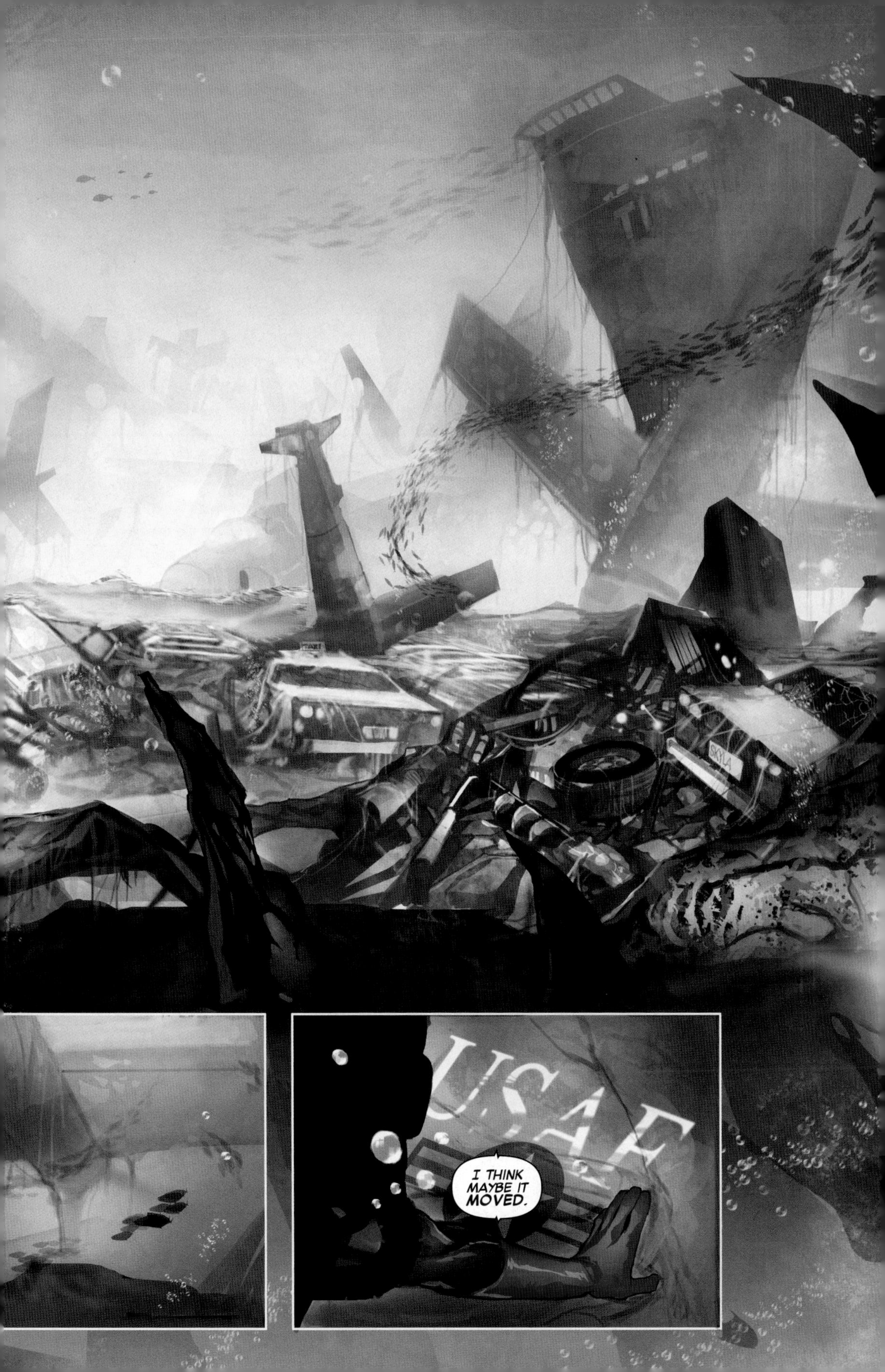
USAF
I THINK MAYBE IT MOVED.

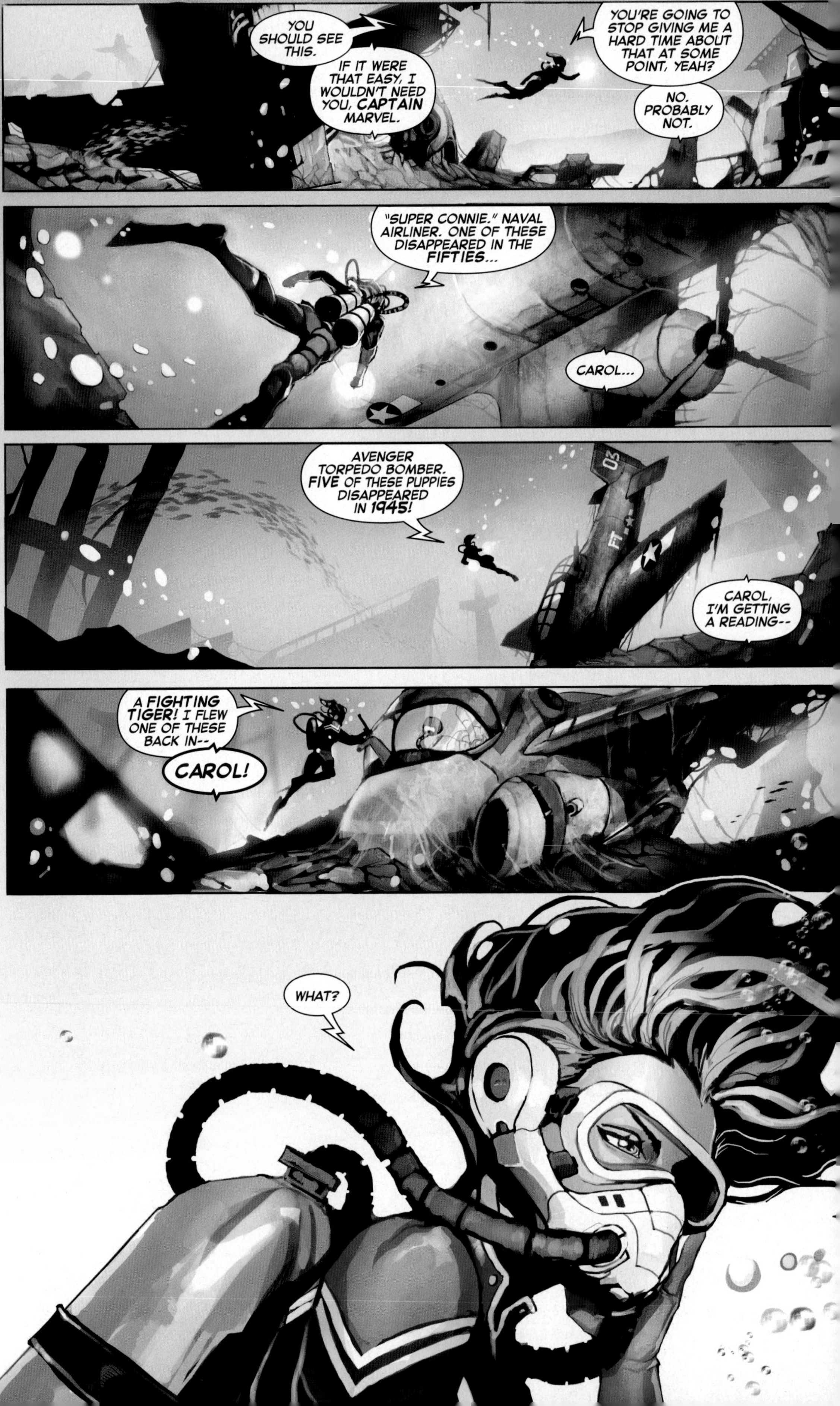
YOU SHOULD SEE THIS.
IF IT WERE THAT EASY, I WOULDN'T NEED YOU, CAPTAIN MARVEL.
YOU'RE GOING TO STOP GIVING ME A HARD TIME ABOUT THAT AT SOME POINT, YEAH?
NO. PROBABLY NOT.
"SUPER CONNIE." NAVAL AIRLINER. ONE OF THESE DISAPPEARED IN THE FIFTIES...
CAROL...
AVENGER TORPEDO BOMBER. FIVE OF THESE PUPPIES DISAPPEARED IN 1945!
CAROL, I'M GETTING A READING--
A FIGHTING TIGER! I FLEW ONE OF THESE BACK IN--
CAROL!
WHAT?

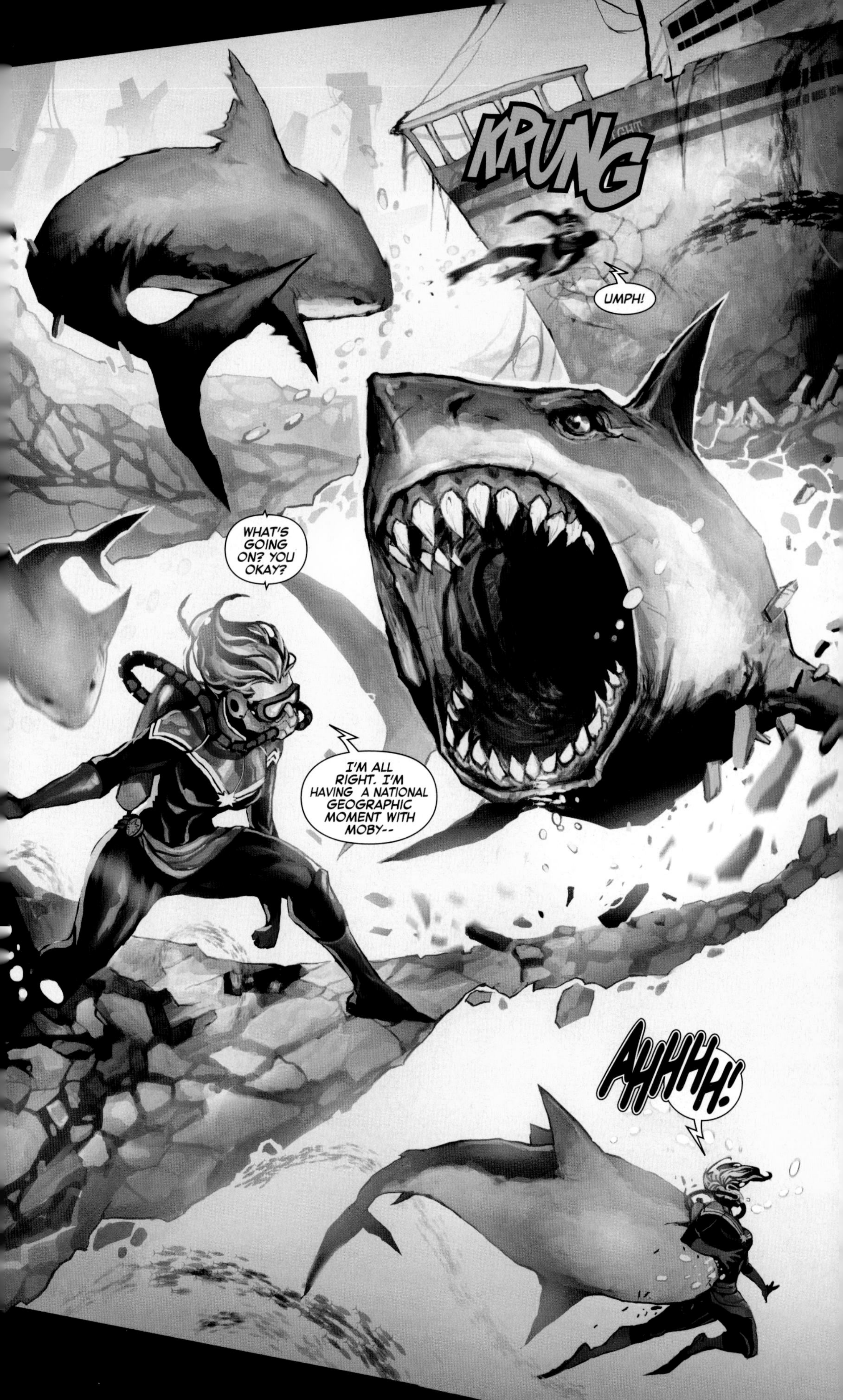
KRUNG
UMPH!
WHAT'S GOING ON? YOU OKAY?
I'M ALL RIGHT. I'M HAVING A NATIONAL GEOGRAPHIC MOMENT WITH MOBY--
AHHHH!

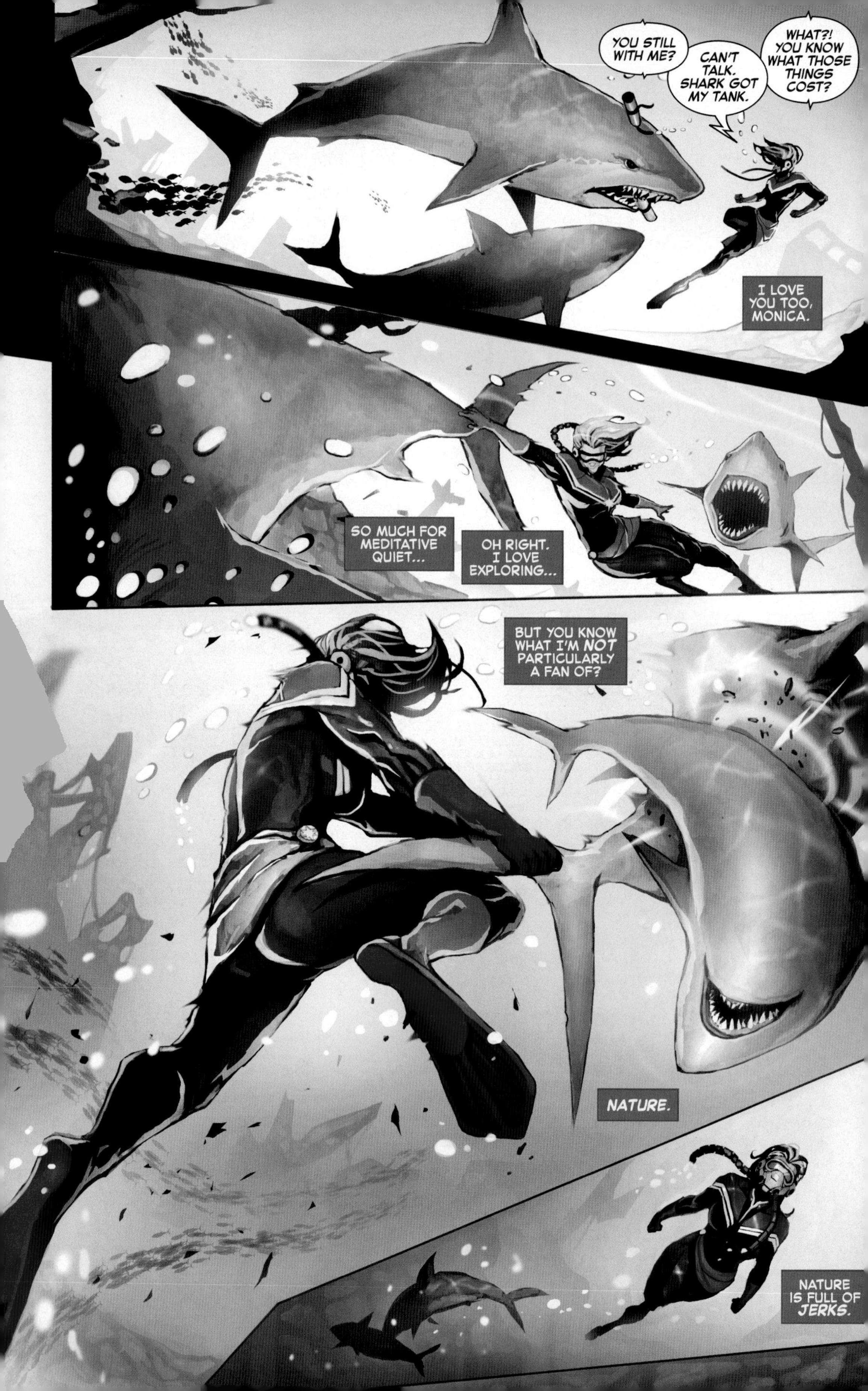
YOU STILL WITH ME?
CAN'T TALK. SHARK GOT MY TANK.
WHAT?! YOU KNOW WHAT THOSE THINGS COST?
I LOVE YOU TOO, MONICA.
SO MUCH FOR MEDITATIVE QUIET...
OH RIGHT. I LOVE EXPLORING...
BUT YOU KNOW WHAT I'M NOT PARTICULARLY A FAN OF?
NATURE.
NATURE IS FULL OF JERKS.

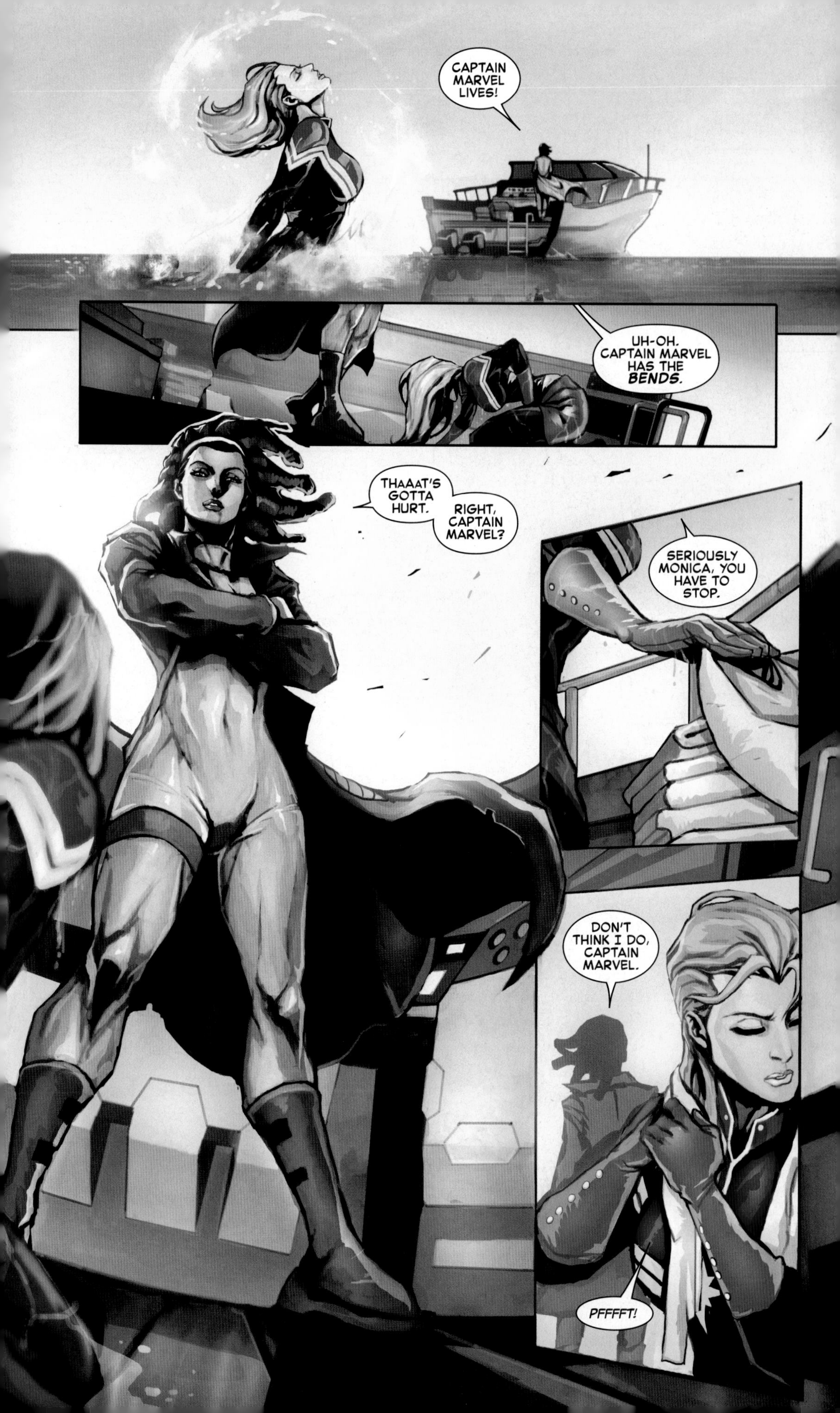
CAPTAIN MARVEL LIVES!
UH-OH. CAPTAIN MARVEL HAS THE *BENDS.*
THAAAT'S GOTTA HURT.
RIGHT, CAPTAIN MARVEL?
SERIOUSLY MONICA, YOU HAVE TO STOP.
DON'T THINK I DO, CAPTAIN MARVEL.
PFFFFT!

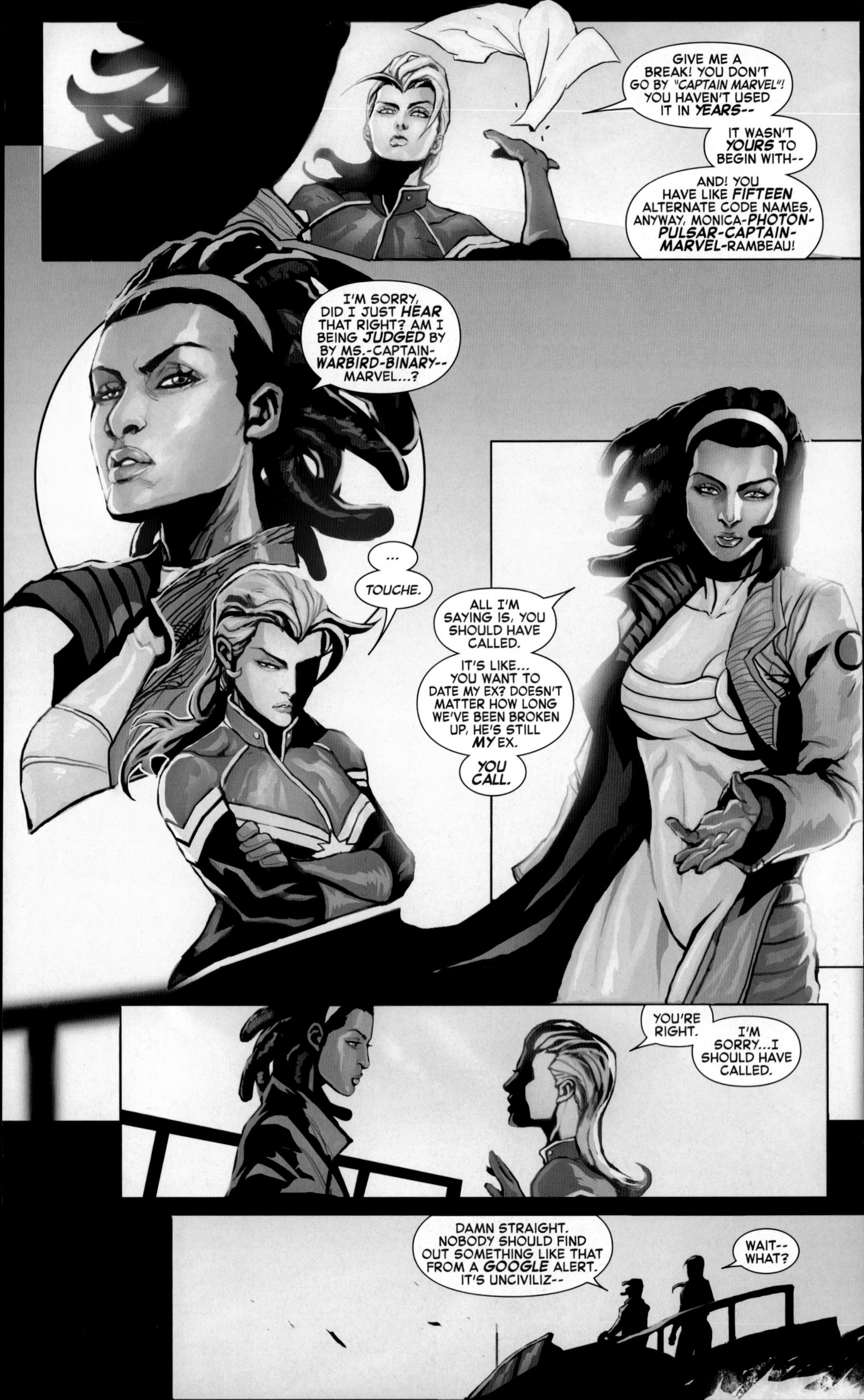
GIVE ME A BREAK! YOU DON'T GO BY "CAPTAIN MARVEL"! YOU HAVEN'T USED IT IN YEARS--
IT WASN'T YOURS TO BEGIN WITH--
AND! YOU HAVE LIKE FIFTEEN ALTERNATE CODE NAMES, ANYWAY, MONICA-PHOTON-PULSAR-CAPTAIN-MARVEL-RAMBEAU!
I'M SORRY, DID I JUST HEAR THAT RIGHT? AM I BEING JUDGED BY BY MS.-CAPTAIN-WARBIRD-BINARY--MARVEL...?
...
TOUCHE.
ALL I'M SAYING IS, YOU SHOULD HAVE CALLED.
IT'S LIKE... YOU WANT TO DATE MY EX? DOESN'T MATTER HOW LONG WE'VE BEEN BROKEN UP, HE'S STILL MY EX.
YOU CALL.
YOU'RE RIGHT.
I'M SORRY...I SHOULD HAVE CALLED.
DAMN STRAIGHT. NOBODY SHOULD FIND OUT SOMETHING LIKE THAT FROM A GOOGLE ALERT. IT'S UNCIVILIZ--
WAIT-- WHAT?

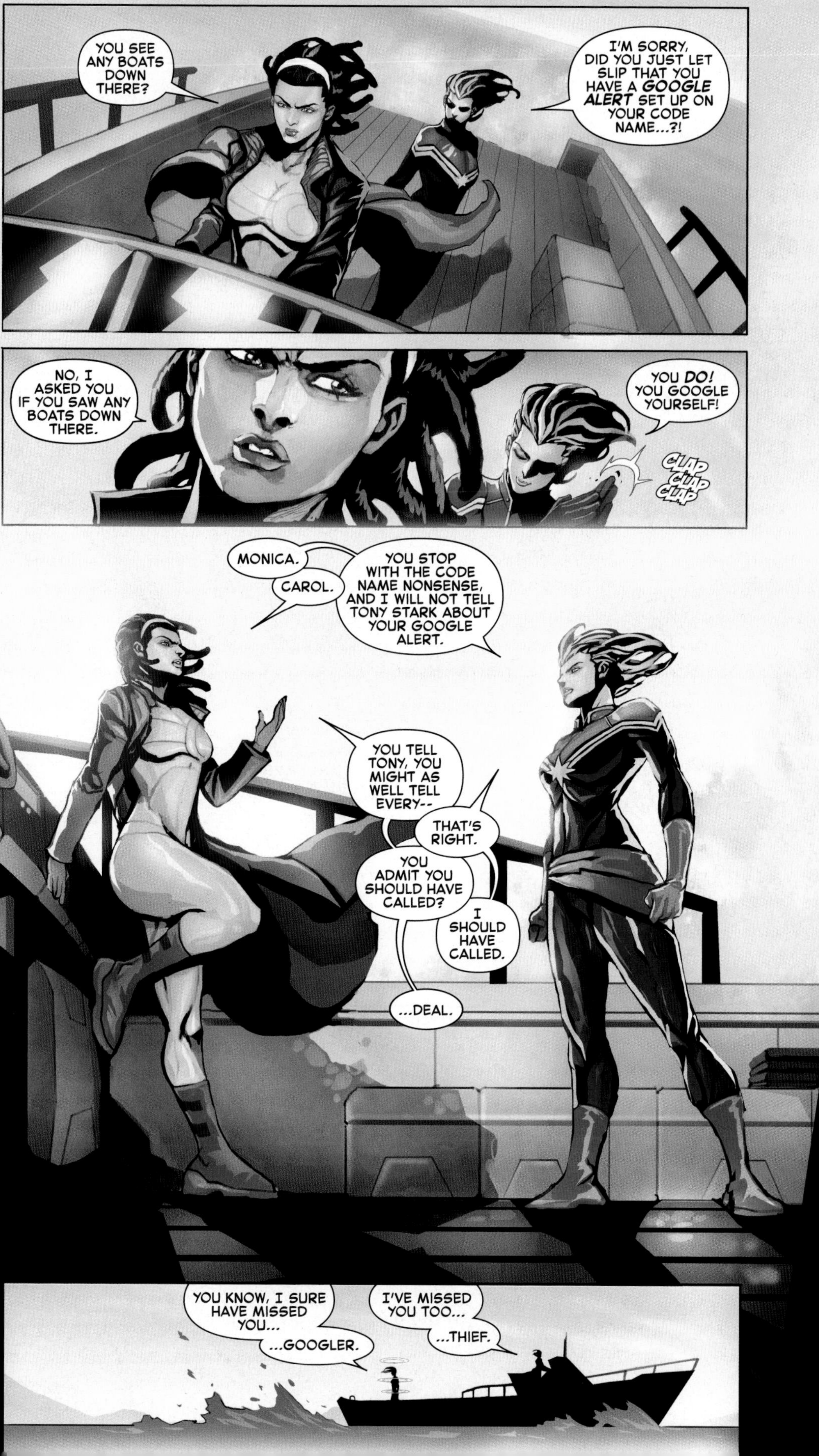
YOU SEE ANY BOATS DOWN THERE?
I'M SORRY, DID YOU JUST LET SLIP THAT YOU HAVE A GOOGLE ALERT SET UP ON YOUR CODE NAME...?!
NO, I ASKED YOU IF YOU SAW ANY BOATS DOWN THERE.
YOU DO! YOU GOOGLE YOURSELF!
CLAP CLAP CLAP
MONICA.
CAROL.
YOU STOP WITH THE CODE NAME NONSENSE, AND I WILL NOT TELL TONY STARK ABOUT YOUR GOOGLE ALERT.
YOU TELL TONY, YOU MIGHT AS WELL TELL EVERY--
THAT'S RIGHT.
YOU ADMIT YOU SHOULD HAVE CALLED?
I SHOULD HAVE CALLED.
...DEAL.
YOU KNOW, I SURE HAVE MISSED YOU...
...GOOGLER.
I'VE MISSED YOU TOO...
...THIEF.

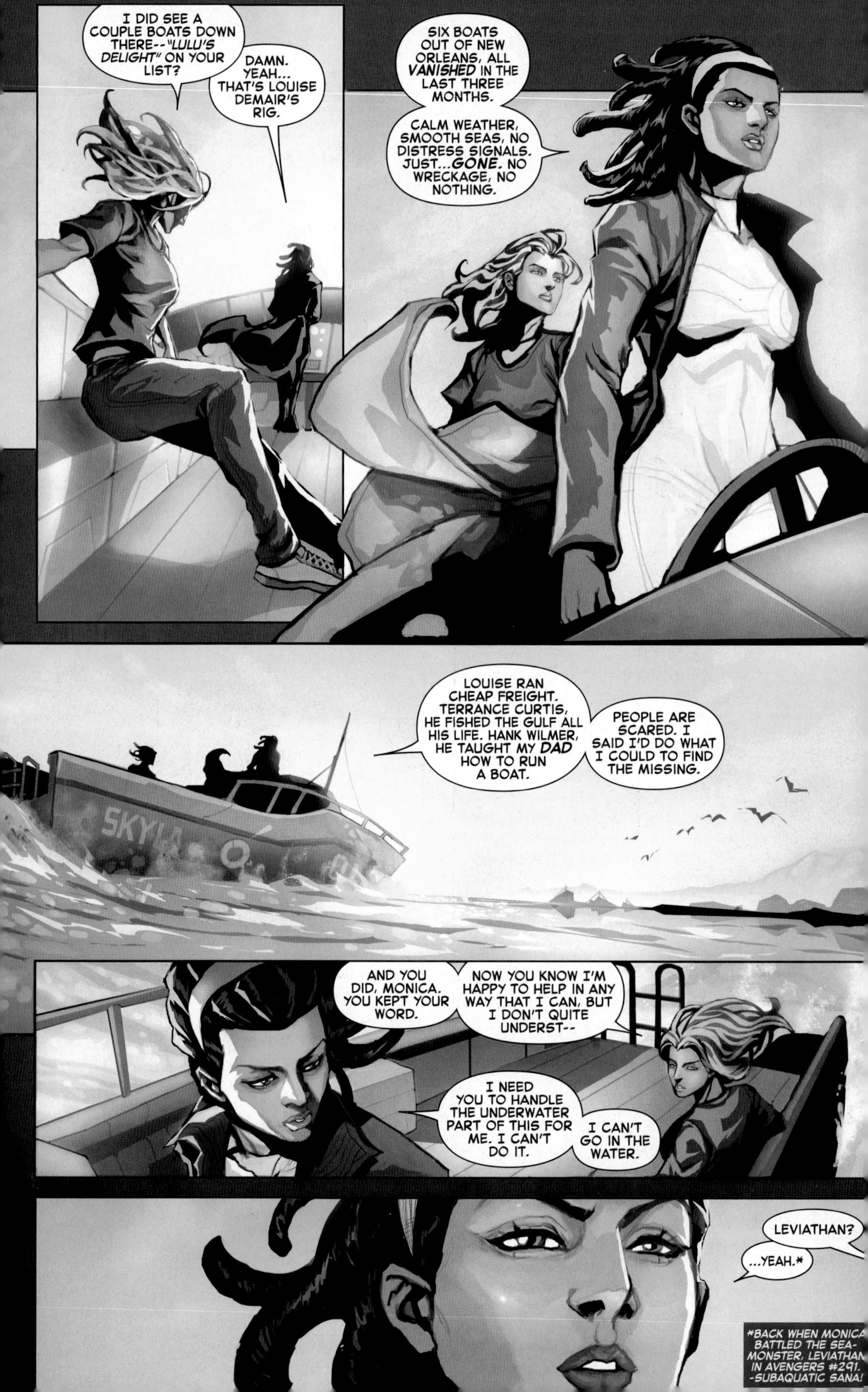
I DID SEE A COUPLE BOATS DOWN THERE--"LULU'S DELIGHT" ON YOUR LIST?
DAMN. YEAH... THAT'S LOUISE DEMAIR'S RIG.
SIX BOATS OUT OF NEW ORLEANS, ALL VANISHED IN THE LAST THREE MONTHS.
CALM WEATHER, SMOOTH SEAS, NO DISTRESS SIGNALS. JUST...GONE. NO WRECKAGE, NO NOTHING.
LOUISE RAN CHEAP FREIGHT. TERRANCE CURTIS, HE FISHED THE GULF ALL HIS LIFE. HANK WILMER, HE TAUGHT MY DAD HOW TO RUN A BOAT.
PEOPLE ARE SCARED. I SAID I'D DO WHAT I COULD TO FIND THE MISSING.
AND YOU DID, MONICA. YOU KEPT YOUR WORD.
NOW YOU KNOW I'M HAPPY TO HELP IN ANY WAY THAT I CAN, BUT I DON'T QUITE UNDERST--
I NEED YOU TO HANDLE THE UNDERWATER PART OF THIS FOR ME. I CAN'T DO IT.
I CAN'T GO IN THE WATER.
LEVIATHAN?
...YEAH.*
*BACK WHEN MONICA BATTLED THE SEA-MONSTER, LEVIATHAN IN AVENGERS #291. -SUBAQUATIC SANA!

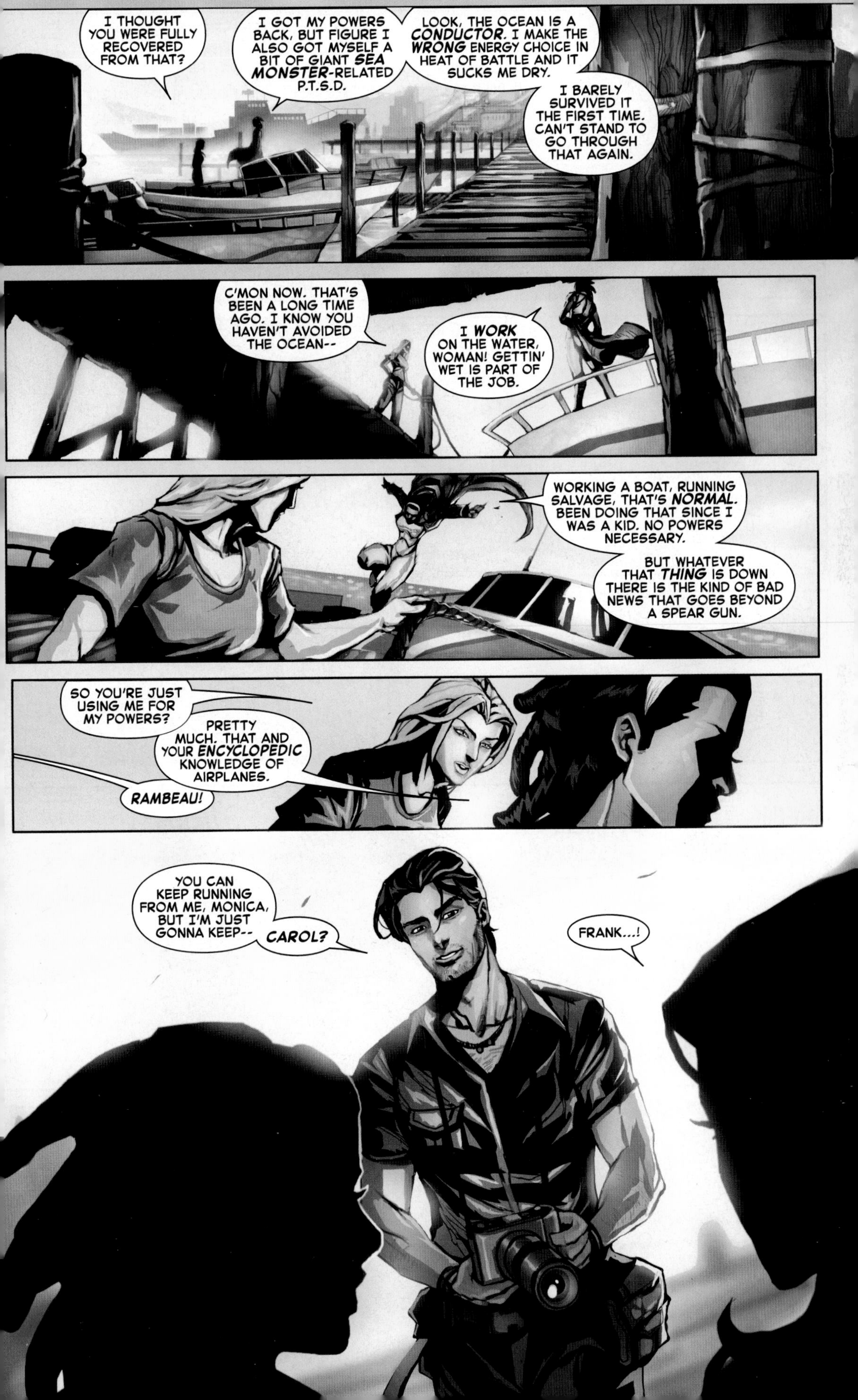

I THOUGHT YOU WERE FULLY RECOVERED FROM THAT?
I GOT MY POWERS BACK, BUT FIGURE I ALSO GOT MYSELF A BIT OF GIANT SEA MONSTER-RELATED P.T.S.D.
LOOK, THE OCEAN IS A CONDUCTOR. I MAKE THE WRONG ENERGY CHOICE IN HEAT OF BATTLE AND IT SUCKS ME DRY.
I BARELY SURVIVED IT THE FIRST TIME. CAN'T STAND TO GO THROUGH THAT AGAIN.
C'MON NOW. THAT'S BEEN A LONG TIME AGO. I KNOW YOU HAVEN'T AVOIDED THE OCEAN--
I WORK ON THE WATER, WOMAN! GETTIN' WET IS PART OF THE JOB.
WORKING A BOAT, RUNNING SALVAGE, THAT'S NORMAL. BEEN DOING THAT SINCE I WAS A KID. NO POWERS NECESSARY.
BUT WHATEVER THAT THING IS DOWN THERE IS THE KIND OF BAD NEWS THAT GOES BEYOND A SPEAR GUN.
SO YOU'RE JUST USING ME FOR MY POWERS?
PRETTY MUCH. THAT AND YOUR ENCYCLOPEDIC KNOWLEDGE OF AIRPLANES.
RAMBEAU!
YOU CAN KEEP RUNNING FROM ME, MONICA, BUT I'M JUST GONNA KEEP--
CAROL?
FRANK...!

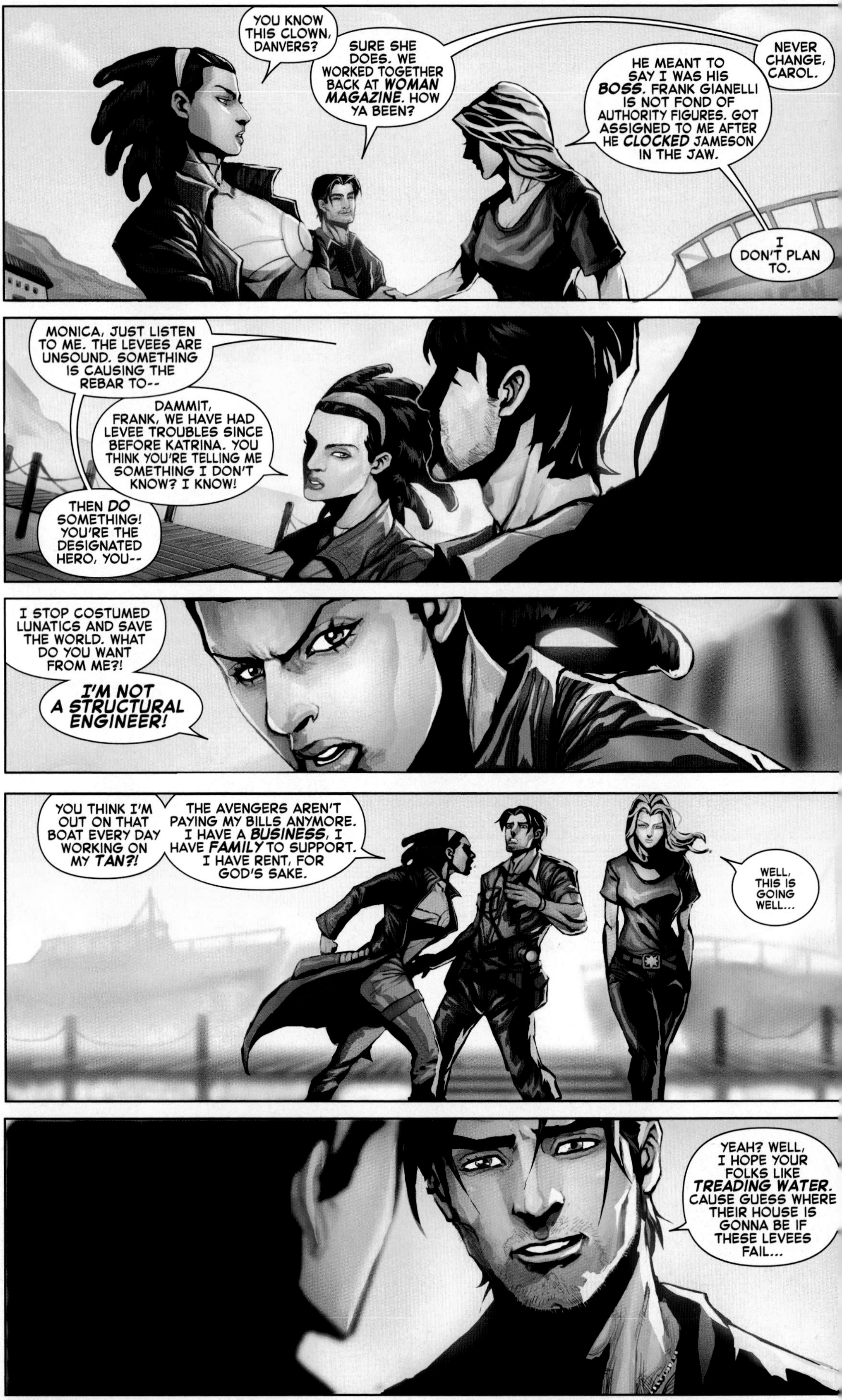

YOU KNOW THIS CLOWN, DANVERS?
SURE SHE DOES. WE WORKED TOGETHER BACK AT WOMAN MAGAZINE. HOW YA BEEN?
HE MEANT TO SAY I WAS HIS BOSS. FRANK GIANELLI IS NOT FOND OF AUTHORITY FIGURES. GOT ASSIGNED TO ME AFTER HE CLOCKED JAMESON IN THE JAW.
NEVER CHANGE, CAROL.
I DON'T PLAN TO.
MONICA, JUST LISTEN TO ME. THE LEVEES ARE UNSOUND. SOMETHING IS CAUSING THE REBAR TO--
DAMMIT, FRANK, WE HAVE HAD LEVEE TROUBLES SINCE BEFORE KATRINA. YOU THINK YOU'RE TELLING ME SOMETHING I DON'T KNOW? I KNOW!
THEN DO SOMETHING! YOU'RE THE DESIGNATED HERO, YOU--
I STOP COSTUMED LUNATICS AND SAVE THE WORLD. WHAT DO YOU WANT FROM ME?!
I'M NOT A STRUCTURAL ENGINEER!
YOU THINK I'M OUT ON THAT BOAT EVERY DAY WORKING ON MY TAN?!
THE AVENGERS AREN'T PAYING MY BILLS ANYMORE. I HAVE A BUSINESS, I HAVE FAMILY TO SUPPORT. I HAVE RENT, FOR GOD'S SAKE.
WELL, THIS IS GOING WELL...
YEAH? WELL, I HOPE YOUR FOLKS LIKE TREADING WATER. CAUSE GUESS WHERE THEIR HOUSE IS GONNA BE IF THESE LEVEES FAIL...

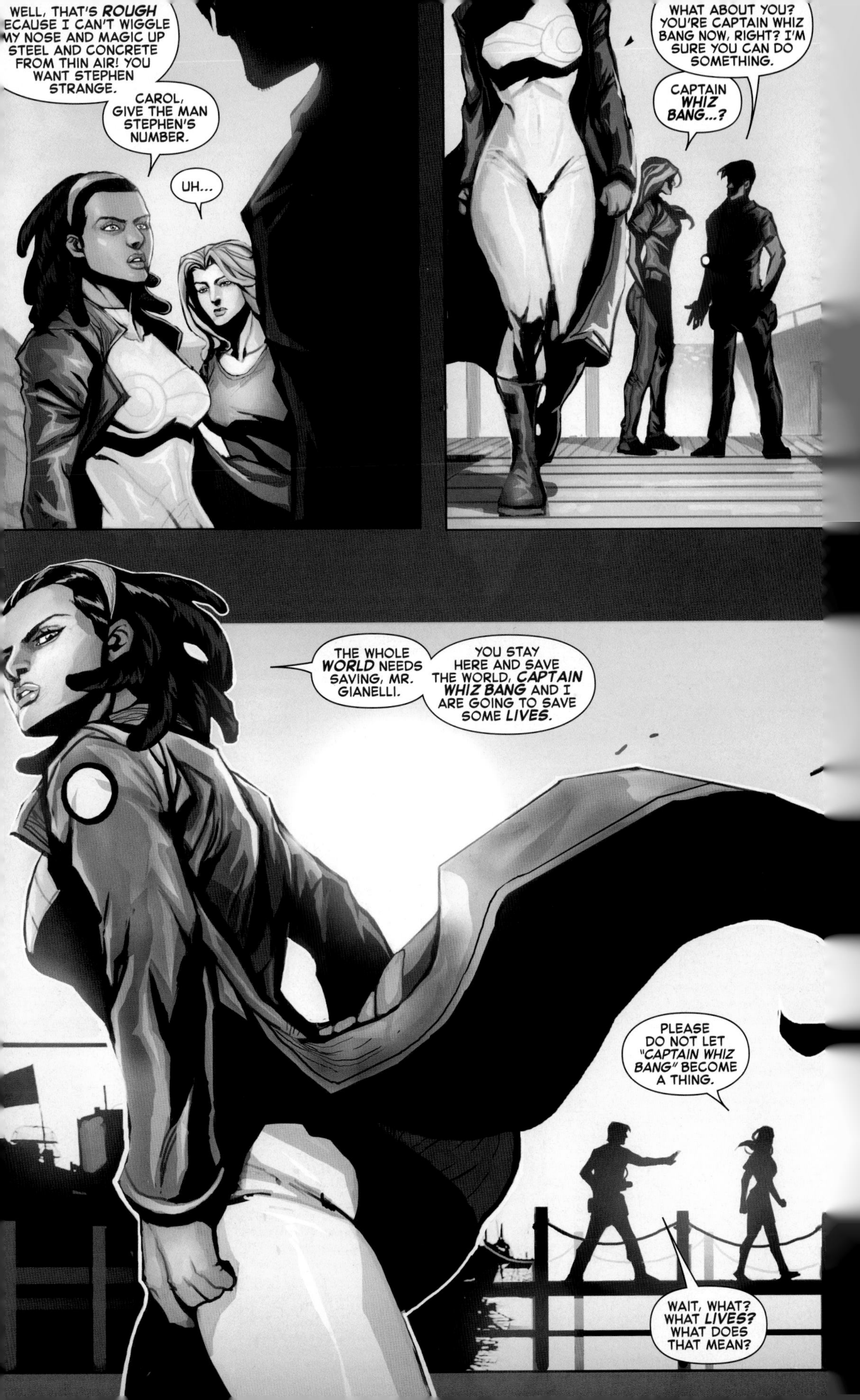
WELL, THAT'S ROUGH ECAUSE I CAN'T WIGGLE MY NOSE AND MAGIC UP STEEL AND CONCRETE FROM THIN AIR! YOU WANT STEPHEN STRANGE.
CAROL, GIVE THE MAN STEPHEN'S NUMBER.
UH...
WHAT ABOUT YOU? YOU'RE CAPTAIN WHIZ BANG NOW, RIGHT? I'M SURE YOU CAN DO SOMETHING.
CAPTAIN WHIZ BANG...?
THE WHOLE WORLD NEEDS SAVING, MR. GIANELLI.
YOU STAY HERE AND SAVE THE WORLD, CAPTAIN WHIZ BANG AND I ARE GOING TO SAVE SOME LIVES.
PLEASE DO NOT LET "CAPTAIN WHIZ BANG" BECOME A THING.
WAIT, WHAT? WHAT LIVES? WHAT DOES THAT MEAN?

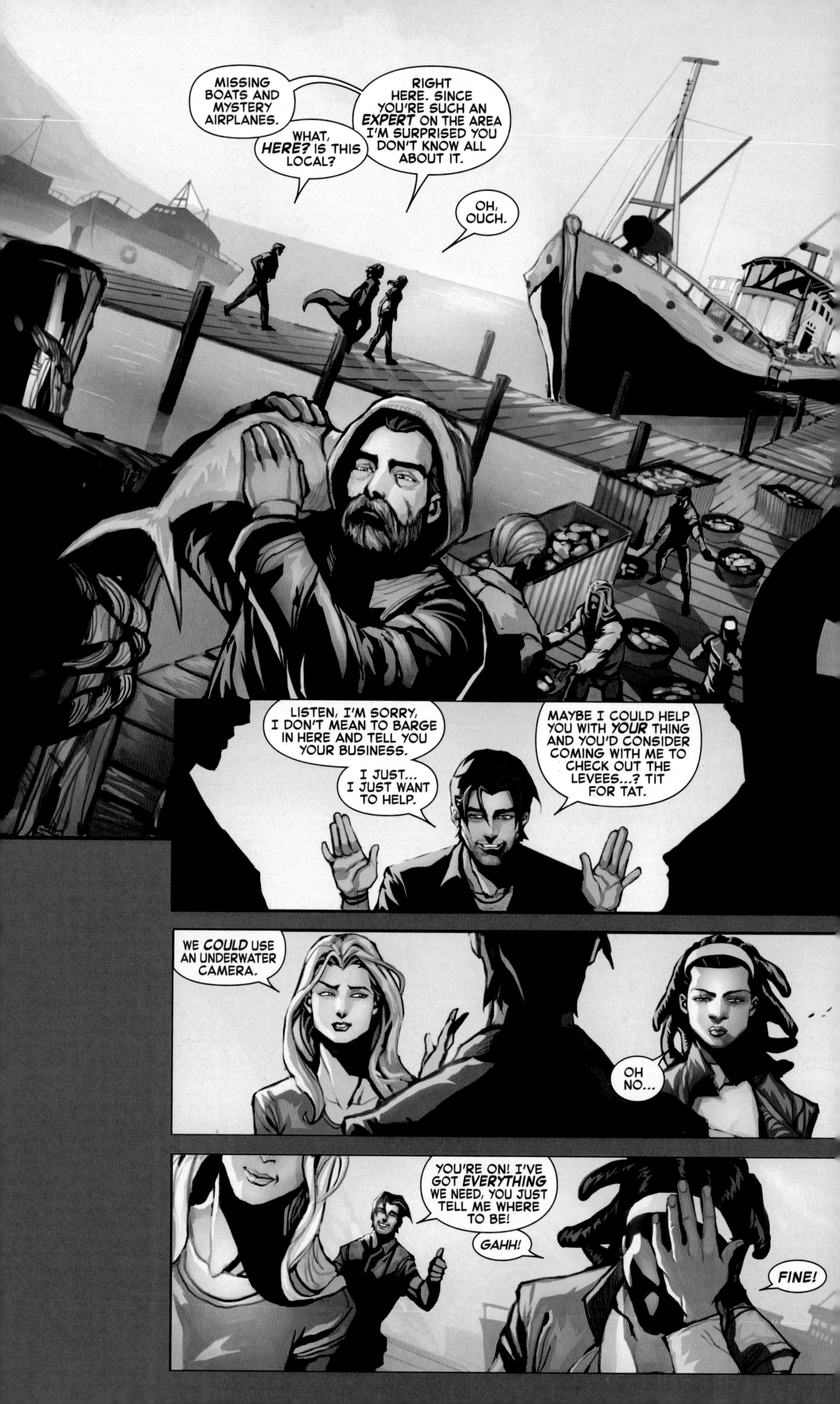
MISSING BOATS AND MYSTERY AIRPLANES.
WHAT, HERE? IS THIS LOCAL?
RIGHT HERE. SINCE YOU'RE SUCH AN EXPERT ON THE AREA I'M SURPRISED YOU DON'T KNOW ALL ABOUT IT.
OH, OUCH.
LISTEN, I'M SORRY, I DON'T MEAN TO BARGE IN HERE AND TELL YOU YOUR BUSINESS.
I JUST... I JUST WANT TO HELP.
MAYBE I COULD HELP YOU WITH YOUR THING AND YOU'D CONSIDER COMING WITH ME TO CHECK OUT THE LEVEES...? TIT FOR TAT.
WE COULD USE AN UNDERWATER CAMERA.
OH NO...
YOU'RE ON! I'VE GOT EVERYTHING WE NEED, YOU JUST TELL ME WHERE TO BE!
GAHH!
FINE!

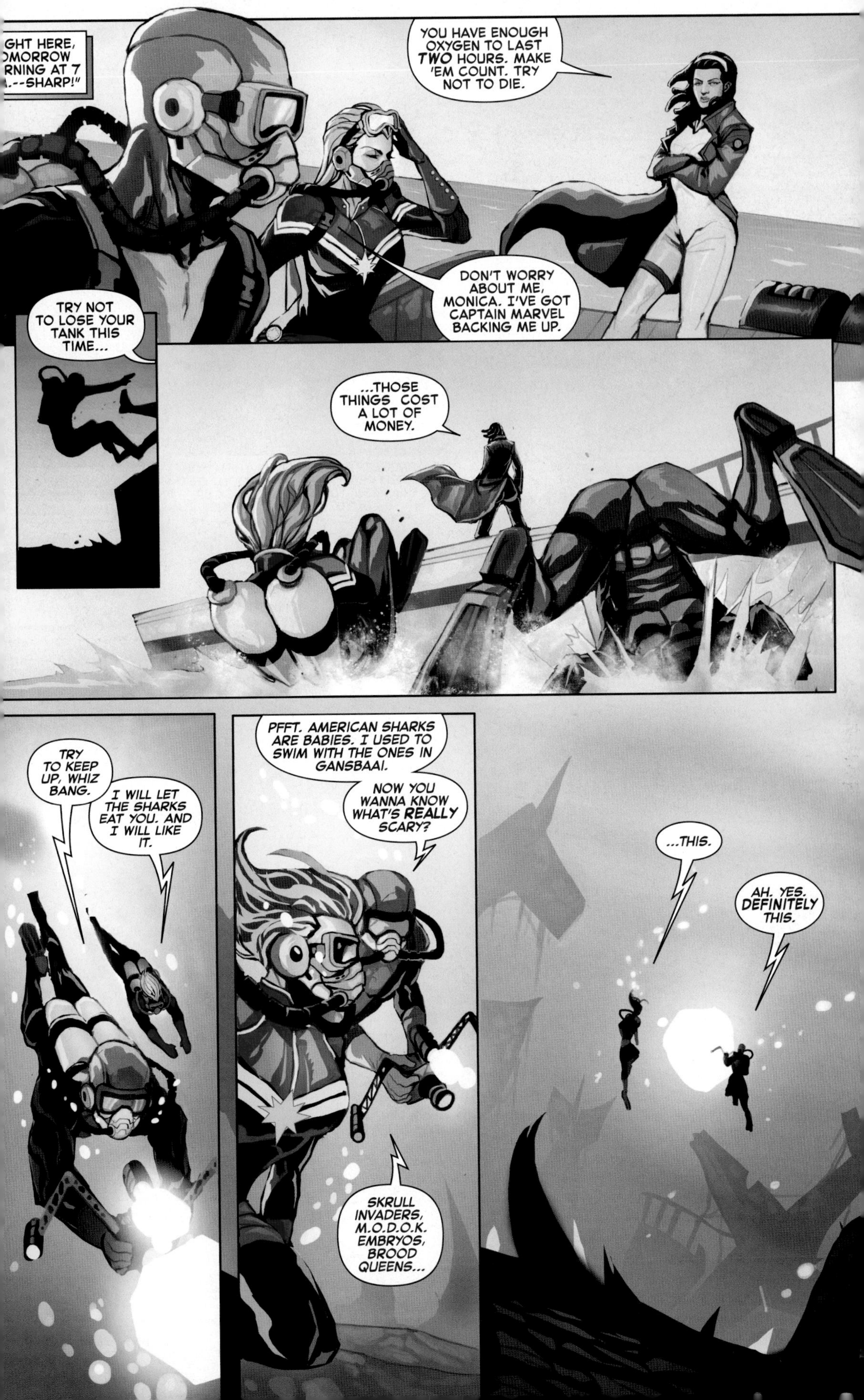

GHT HERE, OMORROW RNING AT 7 .--SHARP!"
YOU HAVE ENOUGH OXYGEN TO LAST **TWO** HOURS. MAKE 'EM COUNT. TRY NOT TO DIE.
DON'T WORRY ABOUT ME, MONICA. I'VE GOT CAPTAIN MARVEL BACKING ME UP.
TRY NOT TO LOSE YOUR TANK THIS TIME...
...THOSE THINGS COST A LOT OF MONEY.
TRY TO KEEP UP, WHIZ BANG.
I WILL LET THE SHARKS EAT YOU. AND I WILL LIKE IT.
PFFT. AMERICAN SHARKS ARE BABIES. I USED TO SWIM WITH THE ONES IN GANSBAAI.
NOW YOU WANNA KNOW WHAT'S **REALLY** SCARY?
SKRULL INVADERS, M.O.D.O.K. EMBRYOS, BROOD QUEENS...
...THIS.
AH. YES. DEFINITELY THIS.

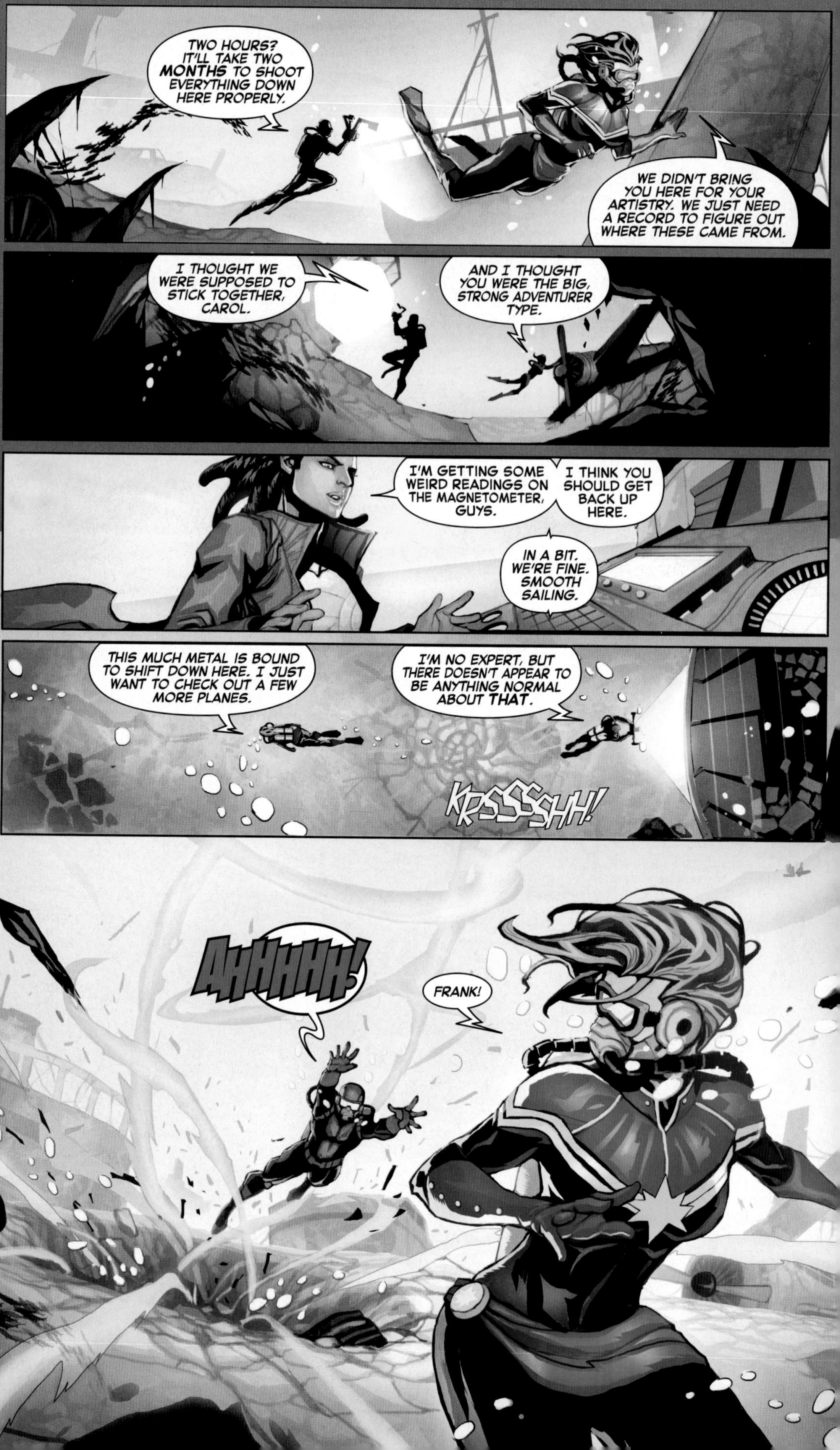
TWO HOURS? IT'LL TAKE TWO MONTHS TO SHOOT EVERYTHING DOWN HERE PROPERLY.
WE DIDN'T BRING YOU HERE FOR YOUR ARTISTRY. WE JUST NEED A RECORD TO FIGURE OUT WHERE THESE CAME FROM.
I THOUGHT WE WERE SUPPOSED TO STICK TOGETHER, CAROL.
AND I THOUGHT YOU WERE THE BIG, STRONG ADVENTURER TYPE.
I'M GETTING SOME WEIRD READINGS ON THE MAGNETOMETER, GUYS.
I THINK YOU SHOULD GET BACK UP HERE.
IN A BIT. WE'RE FINE. SMOOTH SAILING.
THIS MUCH METAL IS BOUND TO SHIFT DOWN HERE. I JUST WANT TO CHECK OUT A FEW MORE PLANES.
I'M NO EXPERT, BUT THERE DOESN'T APPEAR TO BE ANYTHING NORMAL ABOUT THAT.
KRSSSSHH!
AHHHHH!
FRANK!

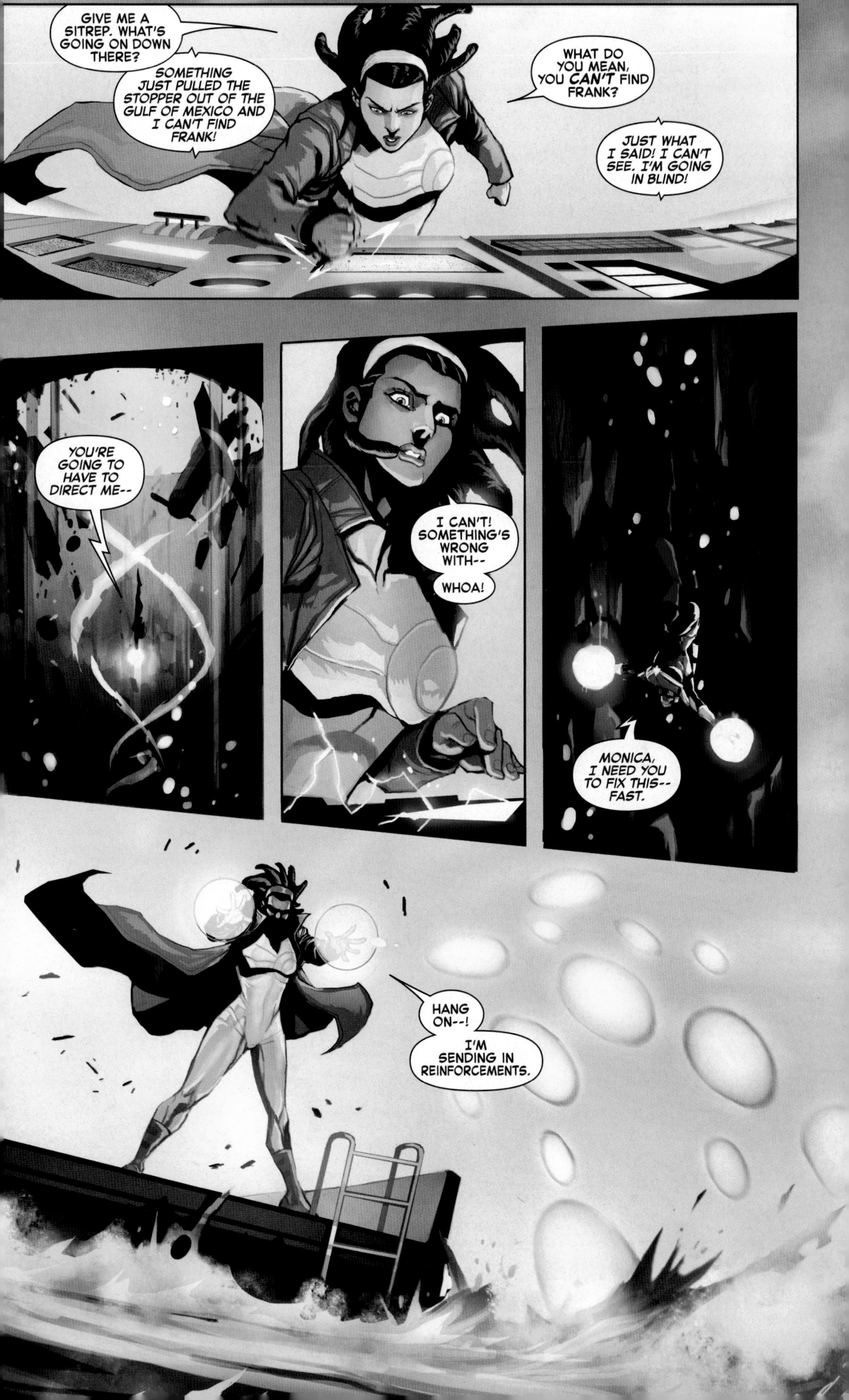

GIVE ME A SITREP. WHAT'S GOING ON DOWN THERE?
SOMETHING JUST PULLED THE STOPPER OUT OF THE GULF OF MEXICO AND I CAN'T FIND FRANK!
WHAT DO YOU MEAN, YOU CAN'T FIND FRANK?
JUST WHAT I SAID! I CAN'T SEE. I'M GOING IN BLIND!
YOU'RE GOING TO HAVE TO DIRECT ME--
I CAN'T! SOMETHING'S WRONG WITH--
WHOA!
MONICA, I NEED YOU TO FIX THIS-- FAST.
HANG ON--!
I'M SENDING IN REINFORCEMENTS.

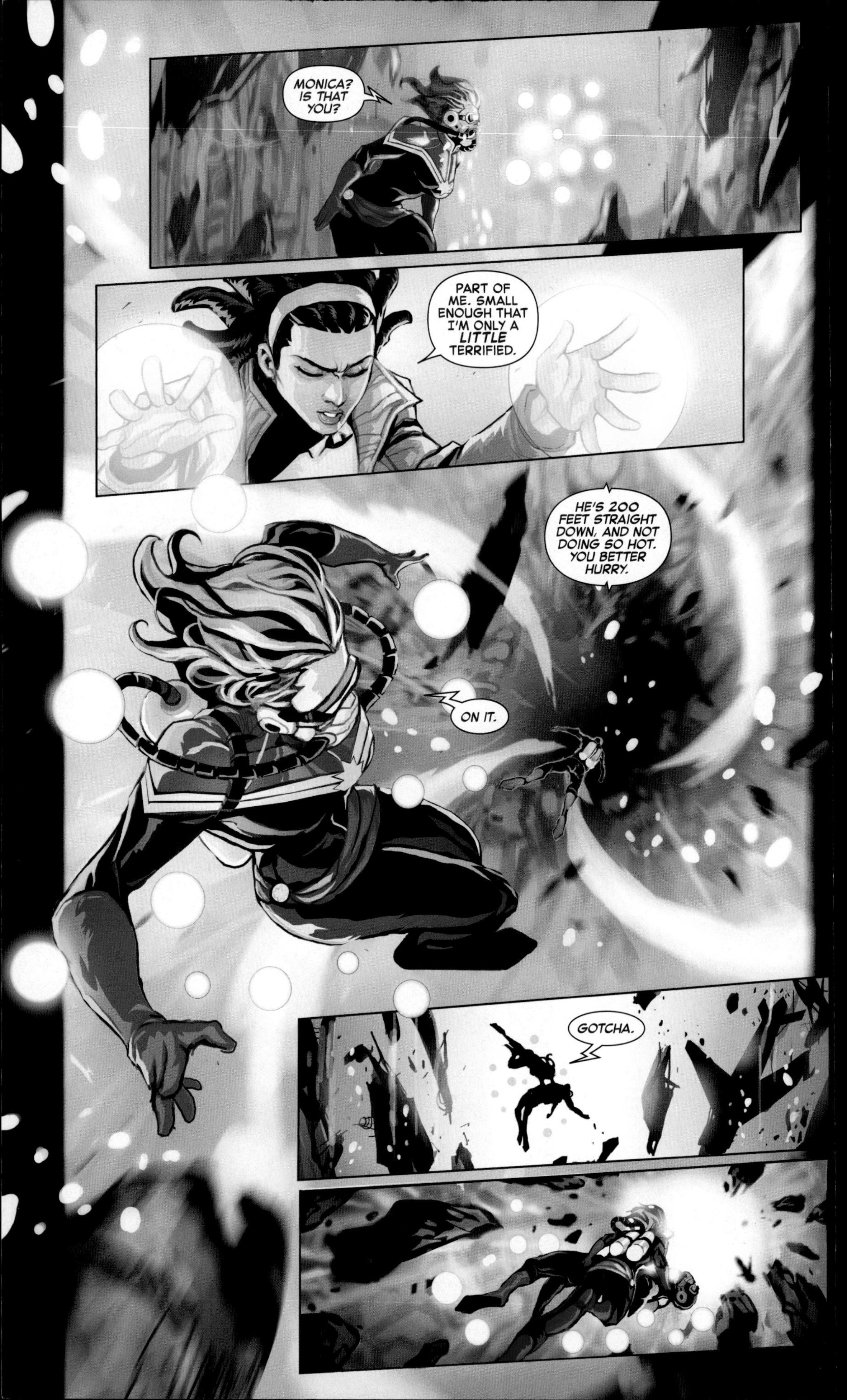
MONICA? IS THAT YOU?
PART OF ME. SMALL ENOUGH THAT I'M ONLY A *LITTLE* TERRIFIED.
HE'S 200 FEET STRAIGHT DOWN, AND NOT DOING SO HOT. YOU BETTER HURRY.
ON IT.
GOTCHA.

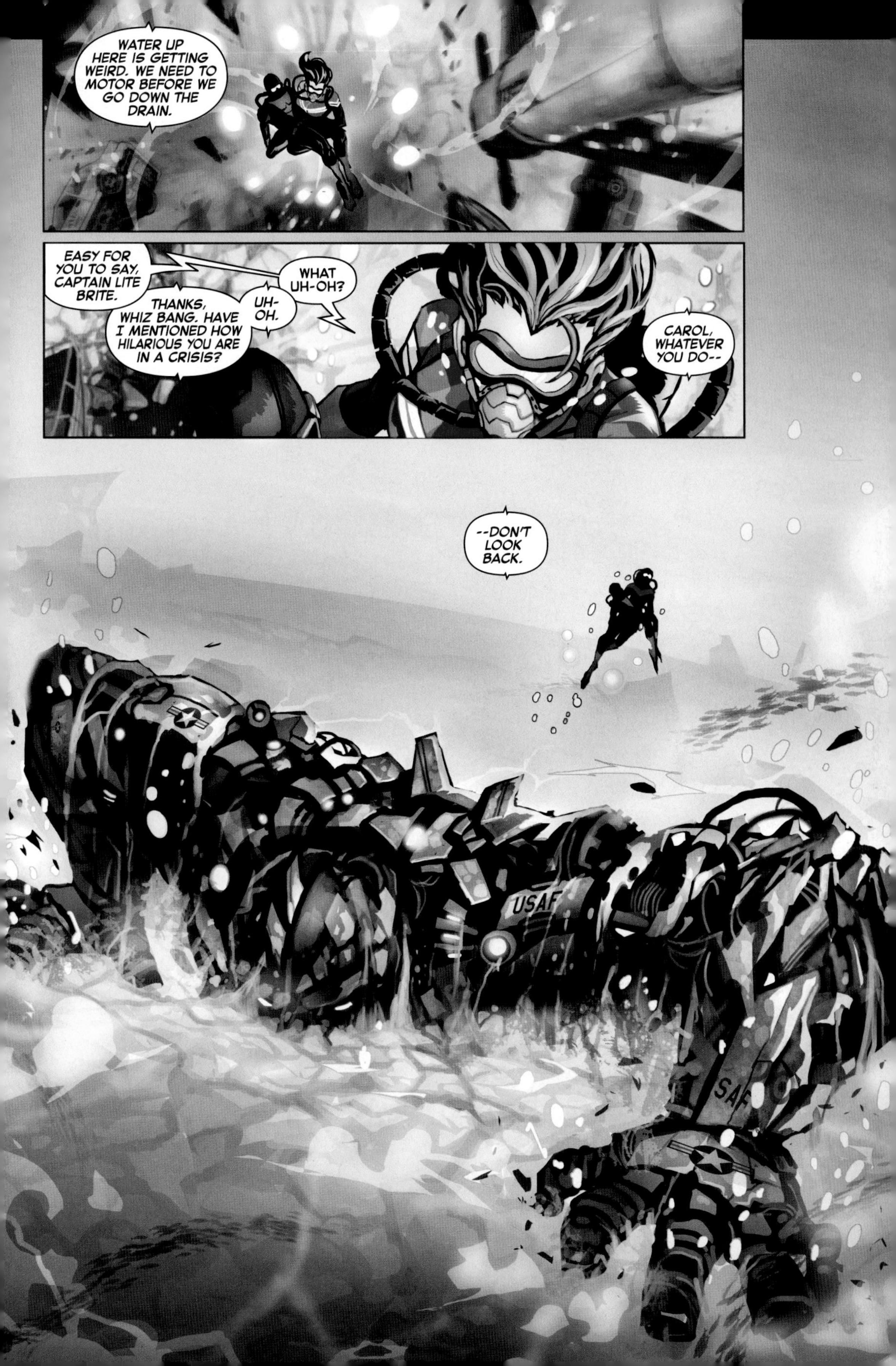
WATER UP HERE IS GETTING WEIRD. WE NEED TO MOTOR BEFORE WE GO DOWN THE DRAIN.
EASY FOR YOU TO SAY, CAPTAIN LITE BRITE.
THANKS, WHIZ BANG. HAVE I MENTIONED HOW HILARIOUS YOU ARE IN A CRISIS?
UH-OH.
WHAT UH-OH?
CAROL, WHATEVER YOU DO--
--DON'T LOOK BACK.
USAF
SAF

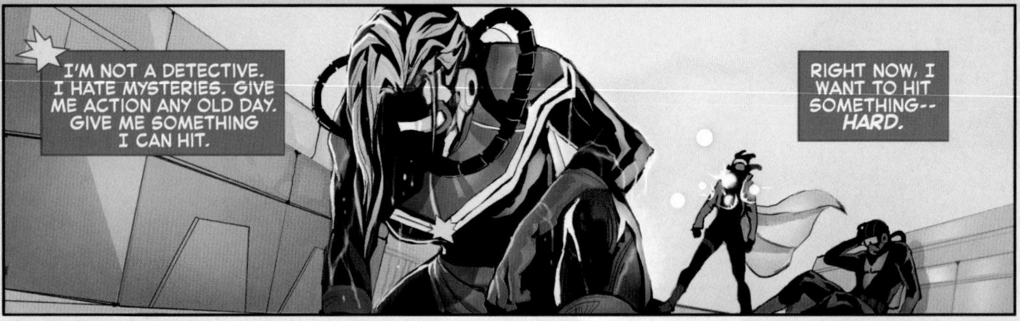
I'M NOT A DETECTIVE. I HATE MYSTERIES. GIVE ME ACTION ANY OLD DAY. GIVE ME SOMETHING I CAN HIT.
RIGHT NOW, I WANT TO HIT SOMETHING-- HARD.
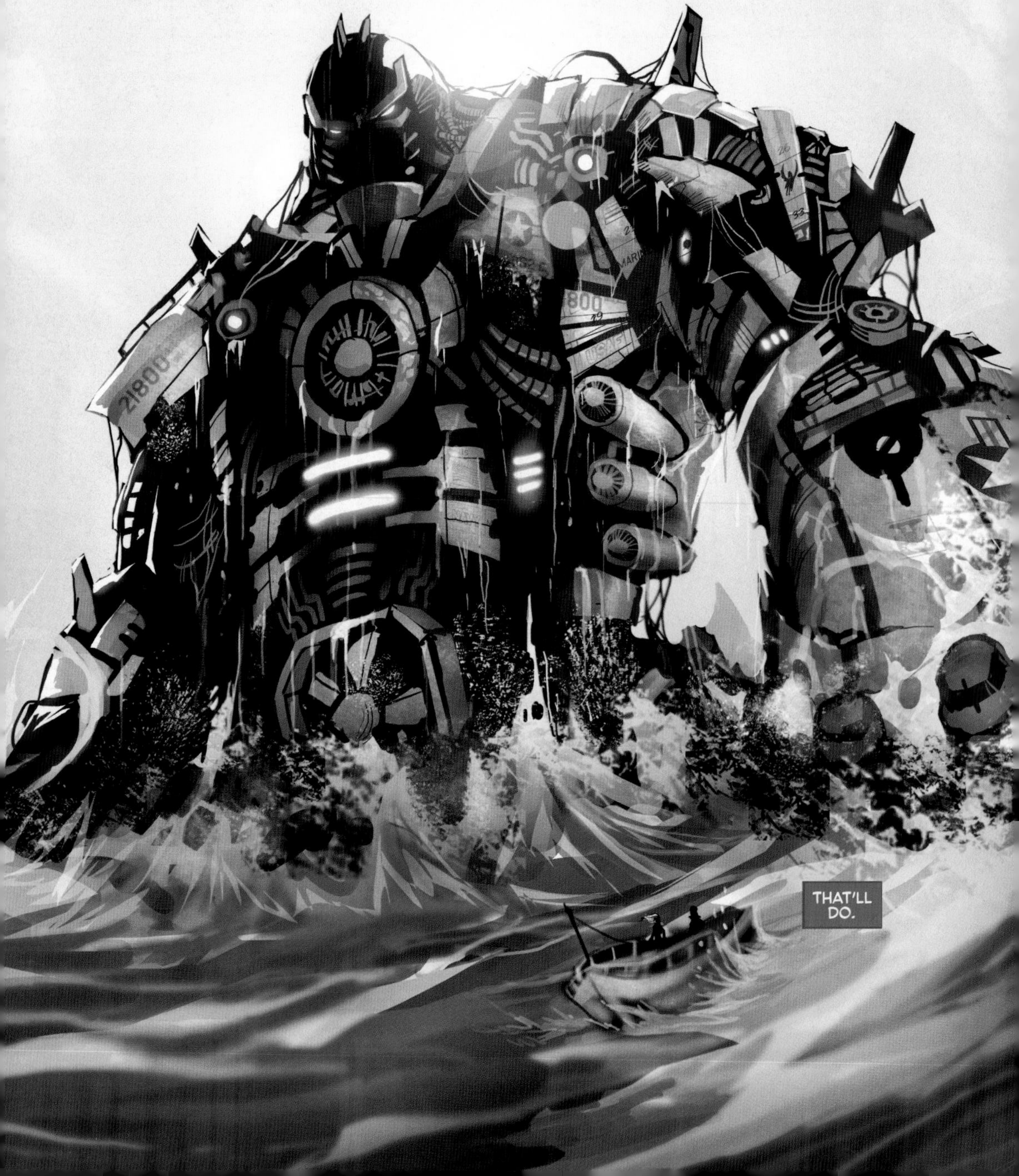
THAT'LL DO.

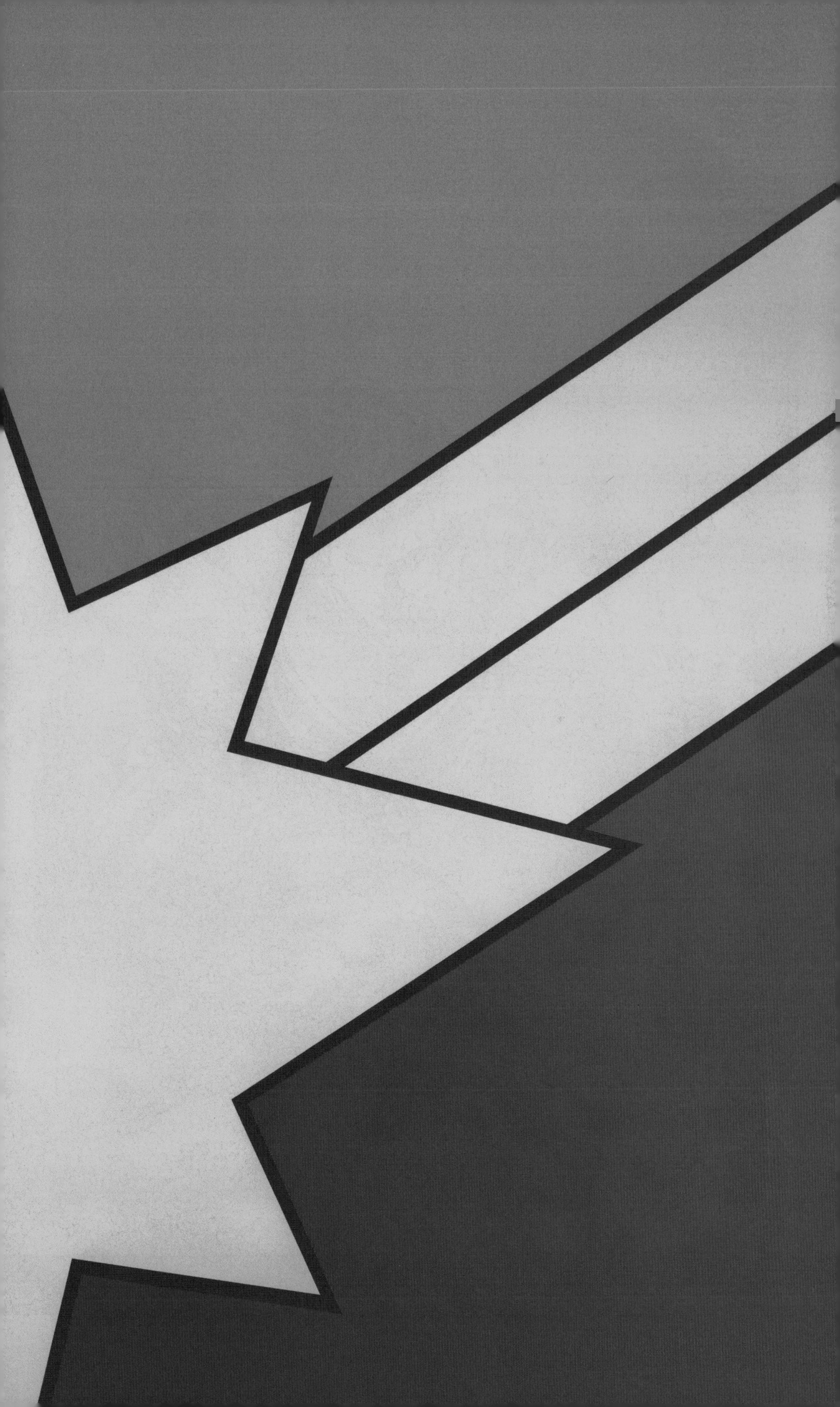

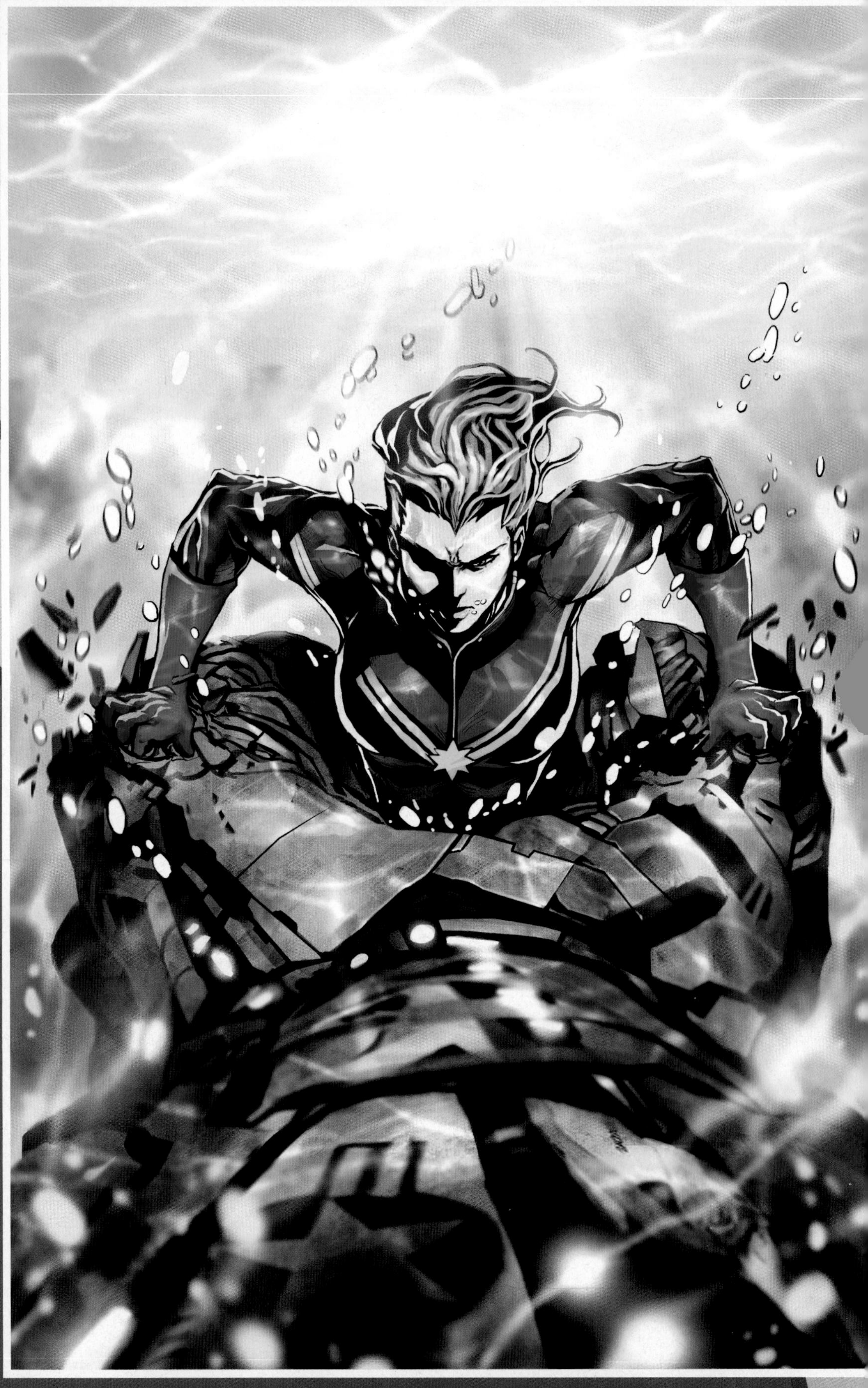

EIGHT

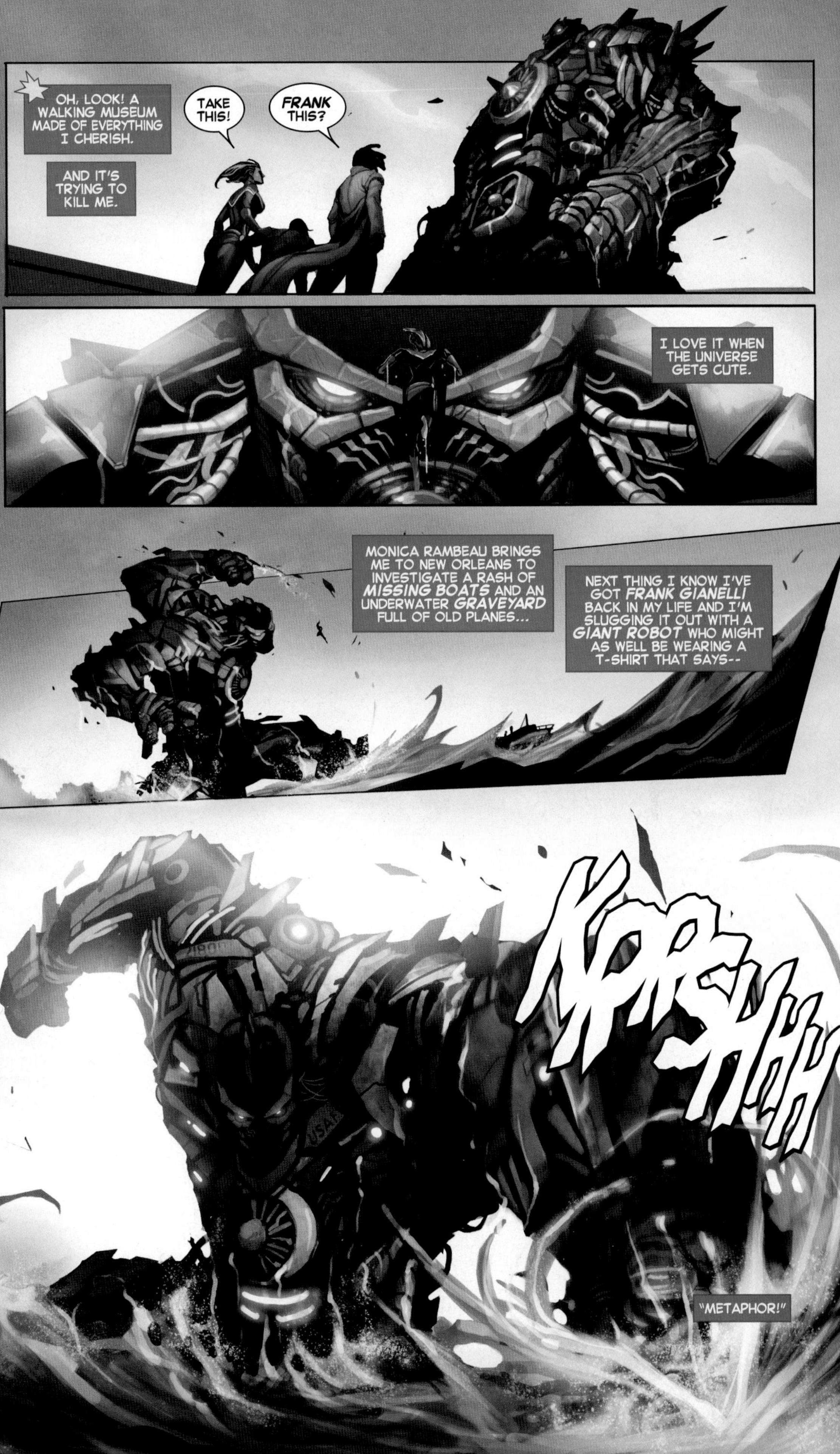
OH, LOOK! A WALKING MUSEUM MADE OF EVERYTHING I CHERISH.
AND IT'S TRYING TO KILL ME.
TAKE THIS!
FRANK THIS?
I LOVE IT WHEN THE UNIVERSE GETS CUTE.
MONICA RAMBEAU BRINGS ME TO NEW ORLEANS TO INVESTIGATE A RASH OF MISSING BOATS AND AN UNDERWATER GRAVEYARD FULL OF OLD PLANES...
NEXT THING I KNOW I'VE GOT FRANK GIANELLI BACK IN MY LIFE AND I'M SLUGGING IT OUT WITH A GIANT ROBOT WHO MIGHT AS WELL BE WEARING A T-SHIRT THAT SAYS--
KRRSHHH
"METAPHOR!"

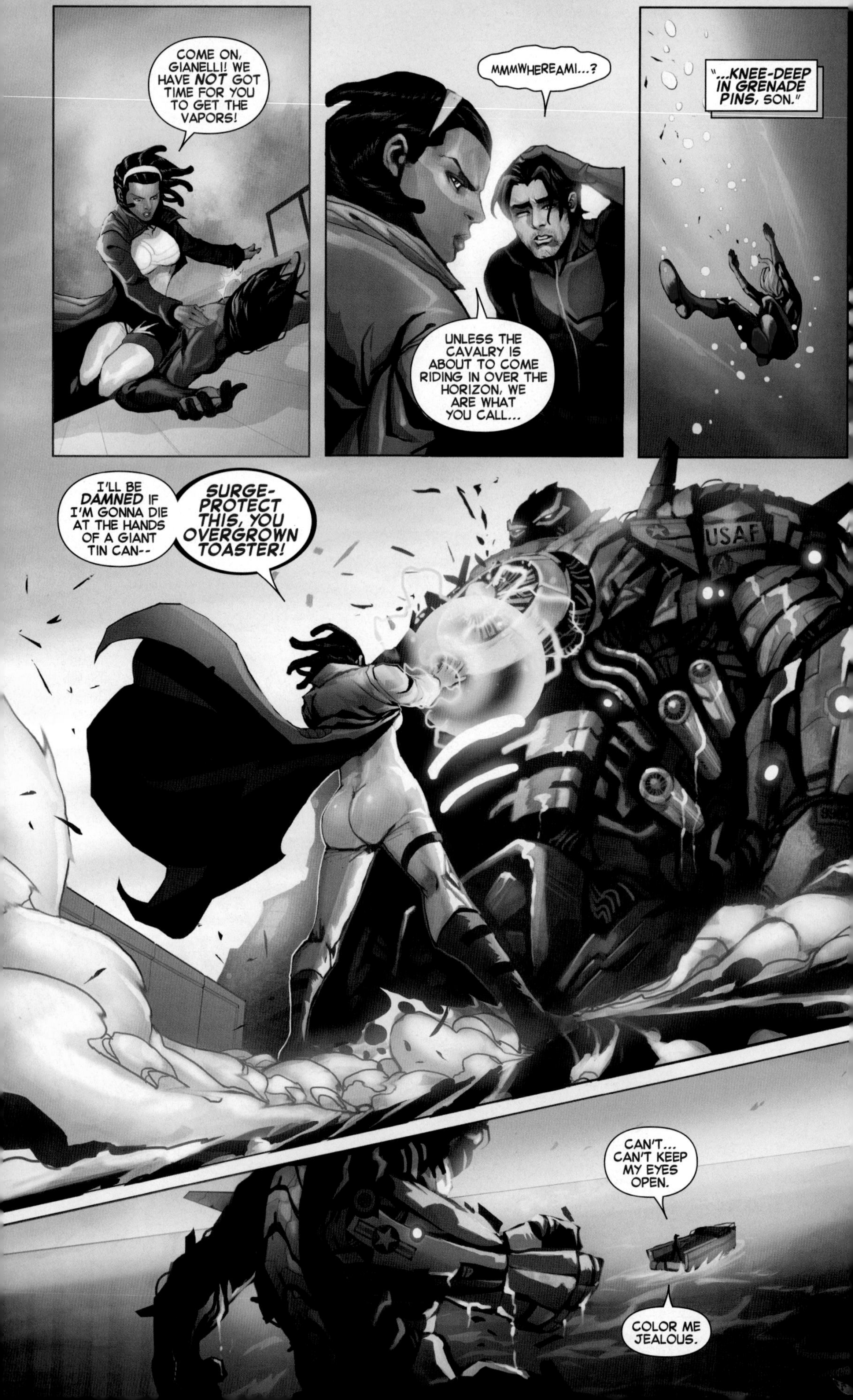
COME ON, GIANELLI! WE HAVE NOT GOT TIME FOR YOU TO GET THE VAPORS!
MMMWHEREAMI...?
UNLESS THE CAVALRY IS ABOUT TO COME RIDING IN OVER THE HORIZON, WE ARE WHAT YOU CALL...
"...KNEE-DEEP IN GRENADE PINS, SON."
I'LL BE DAMNED IF I'M GONNA DIE AT THE HANDS OF A GIANT TIN CAN--
SURGE-PROTECT THIS, YOU OVERGROWN TOASTER!
USAF
CAN'T... CAN'T KEEP MY EYES OPEN.
COLOR ME JEALOUS.

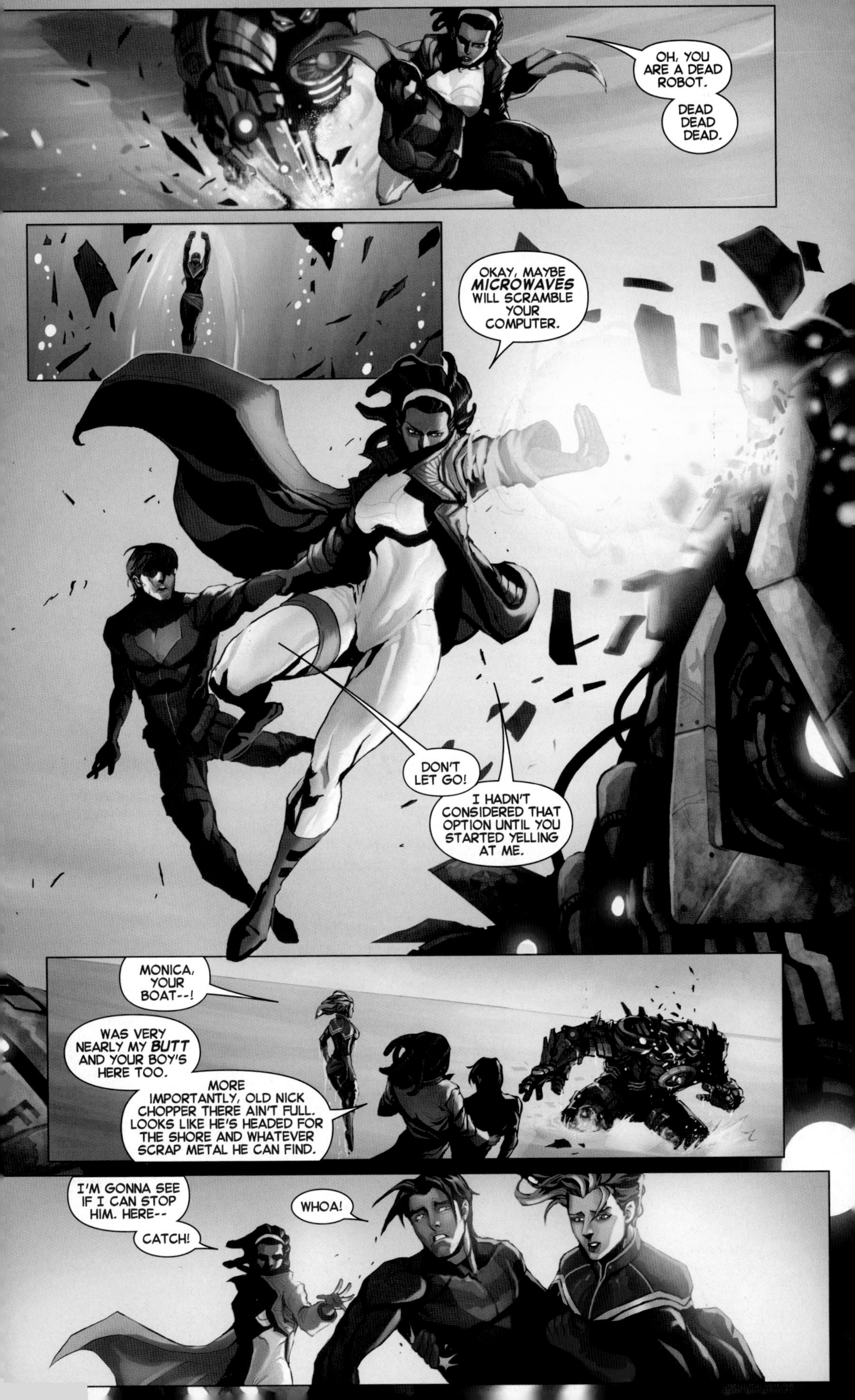
OH, YOU ARE A DEAD ROBOT.
DEAD DEAD DEAD.
OKAY, MAYBE *MICROWAVES* WILL SCRAMBLE YOUR COMPUTER.
DON'T LET GO!
I HADN'T CONSIDERED THAT OPTION UNTIL YOU STARTED YELLING AT ME.
MONICA, YOUR BOAT--!
WAS VERY NEARLY MY *BUTT* AND YOUR BOY'S HERE TOO.
MORE IMPORTANTLY, OLD NICK CHOPPER THERE AIN'T FULL. LOOKS LIKE HE'S HEADED FOR THE SHORE AND WHATEVER SCRAP METAL HE CAN FIND.
I'M GONNA SEE IF I CAN STOP HIM. HERE--
CATCH!
WHOA!

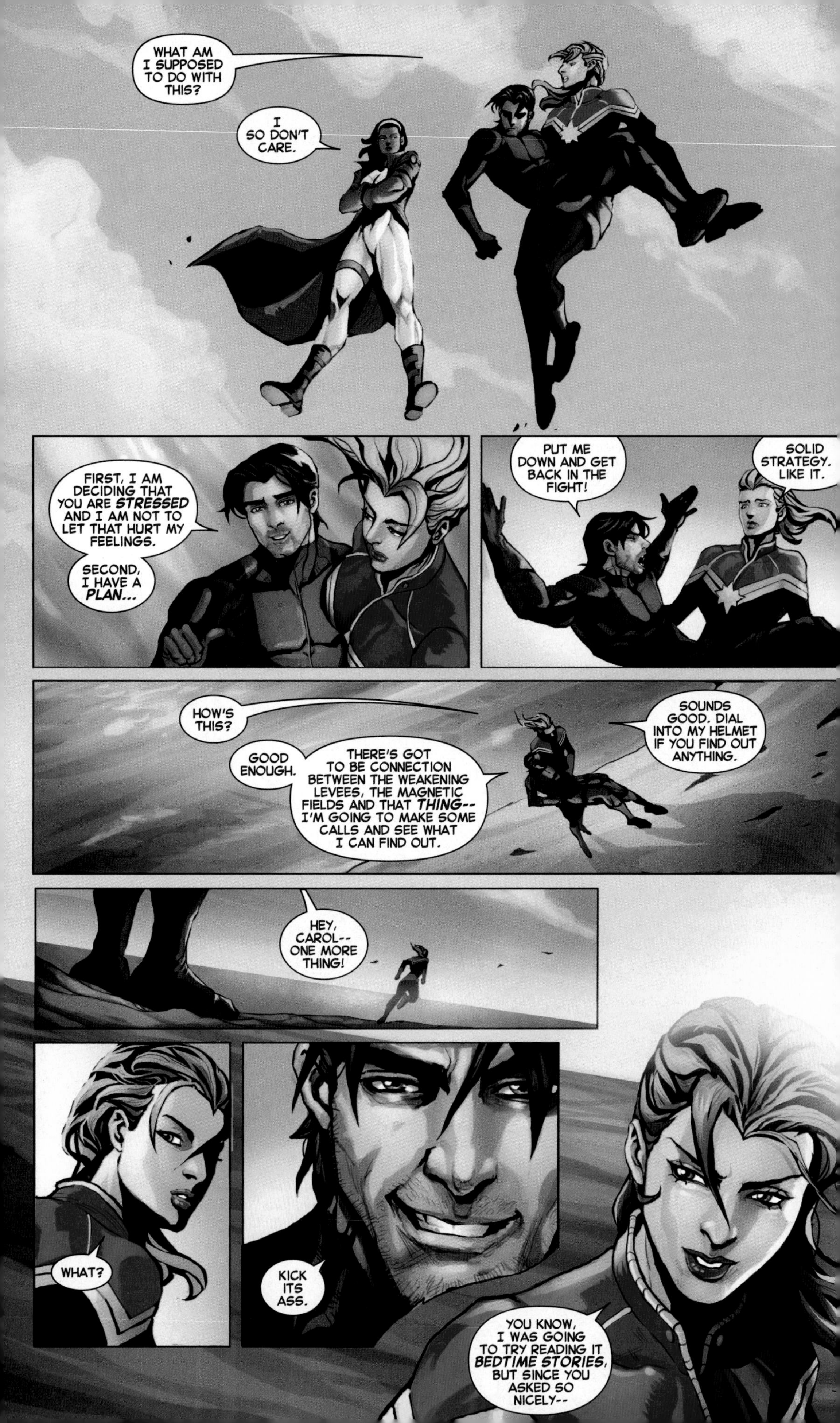
WHAT AM I SUPPOSED TO DO WITH THIS?
I SO DON'T CARE.
FIRST, I AM DECIDING THAT YOU ARE STRESSED AND I AM NOT TO LET THAT HURT MY FEELINGS.
SECOND, I HAVE A PLAN...
PUT ME DOWN AND GET BACK IN THE FIGHT!
SOLID STRATEGY. LIKE IT.
HOW'S THIS?
GOOD ENOUGH.
THERE'S GOT TO BE CONNECTION BETWEEN THE WEAKENING LEVEES, THE MAGNETIC FIELDS AND THAT THING-- I'M GOING TO MAKE SOME CALLS AND SEE WHAT I CAN FIND OUT.
SOUNDS GOOD. DIAL INTO MY HELMET IF YOU FIND OUT ANYTHING.
HEY, CAROL-- ONE MORE THING!
WHAT?
KICK ITS ASS.
YOU KNOW, I WAS GOING TO TRY READING IT BEDTIME STORIES, BUT SINCE YOU ASKED SO NICELY--

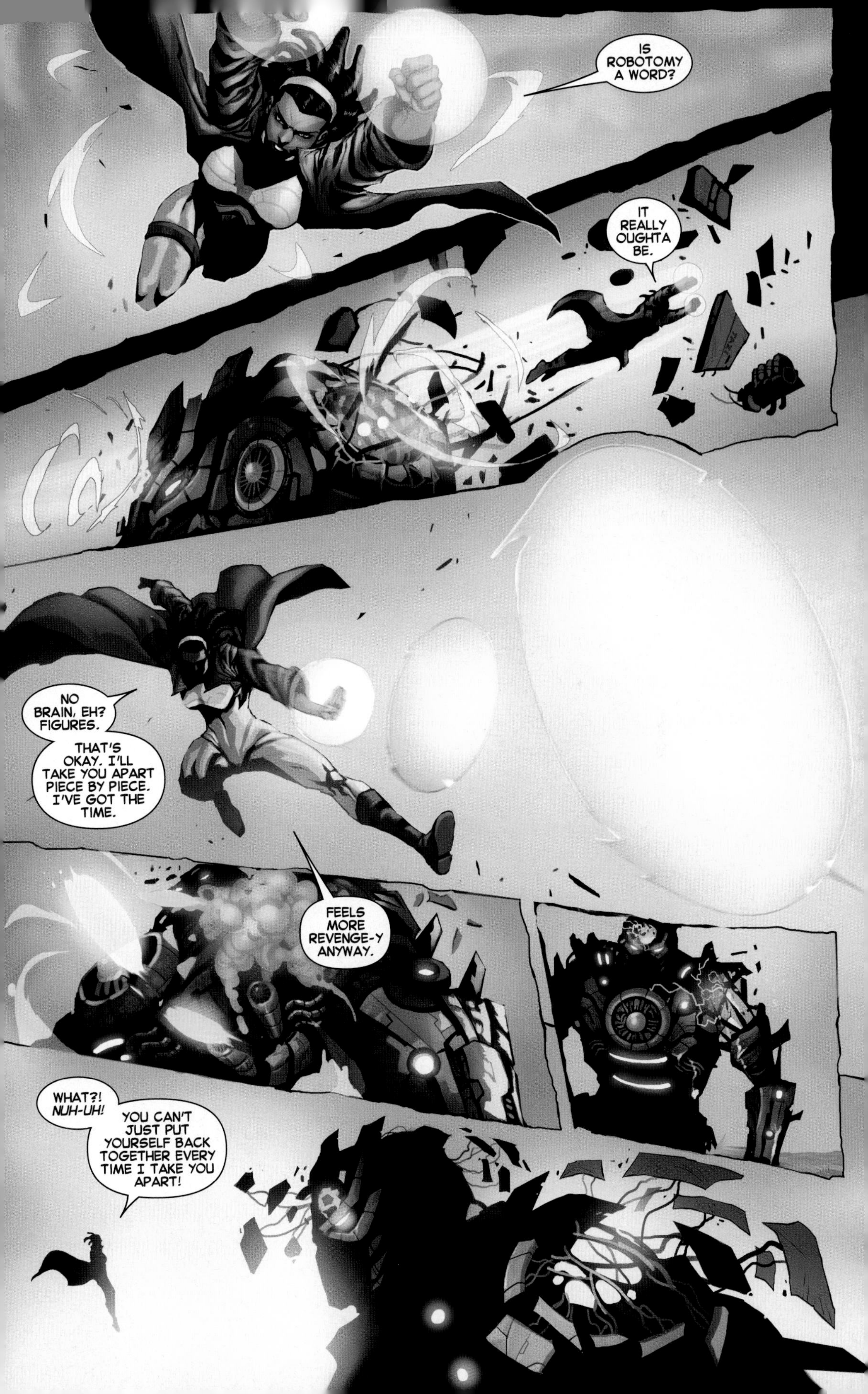
IS ROBOTOMY A WORD?
IT REALLY OUGHTA BE.
NO BRAIN, EH? FIGURES.
THAT'S OKAY. I'LL TAKE YOU APART PIECE BY PIECE. I'VE GOT THE TIME.
FEELS MORE REVENGE-Y ANYWAY.
WHAT?! *NUH-UH!*
YOU CAN'T JUST PUT YOURSELF BACK TOGETHER EVERY TIME I TAKE YOU APART!

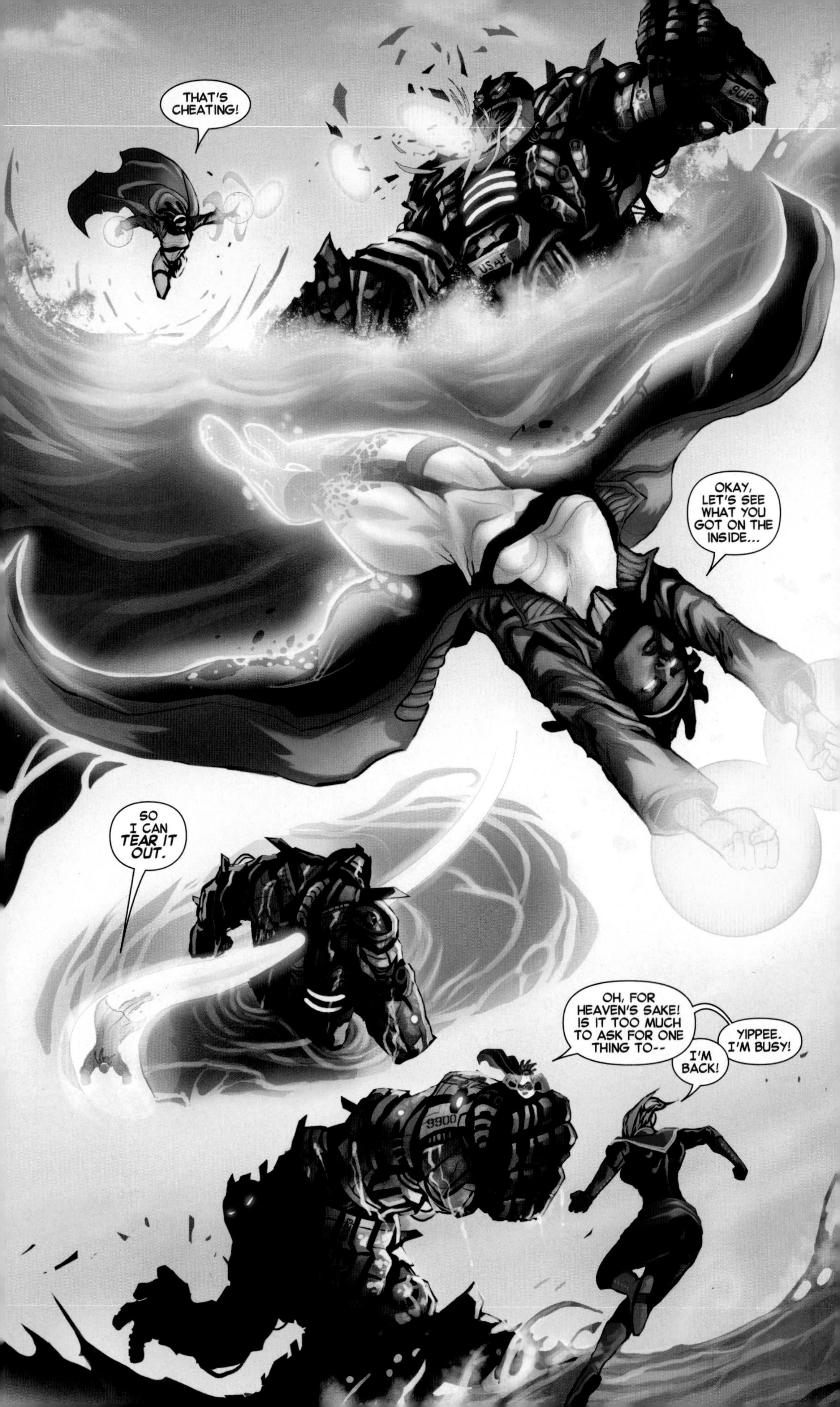
THAT'S CHEATING!
OKAY, LET'S SEE WHAT YOU GOT ON THE INSIDE...
SO I CAN TEAR IT OUT.
OH, FOR HEAVEN'S SAKE! IS IT TOO MUCH TO ASK FOR ONE THING TO--
YIPPEE. I'M BUSY!
I'M BACK!

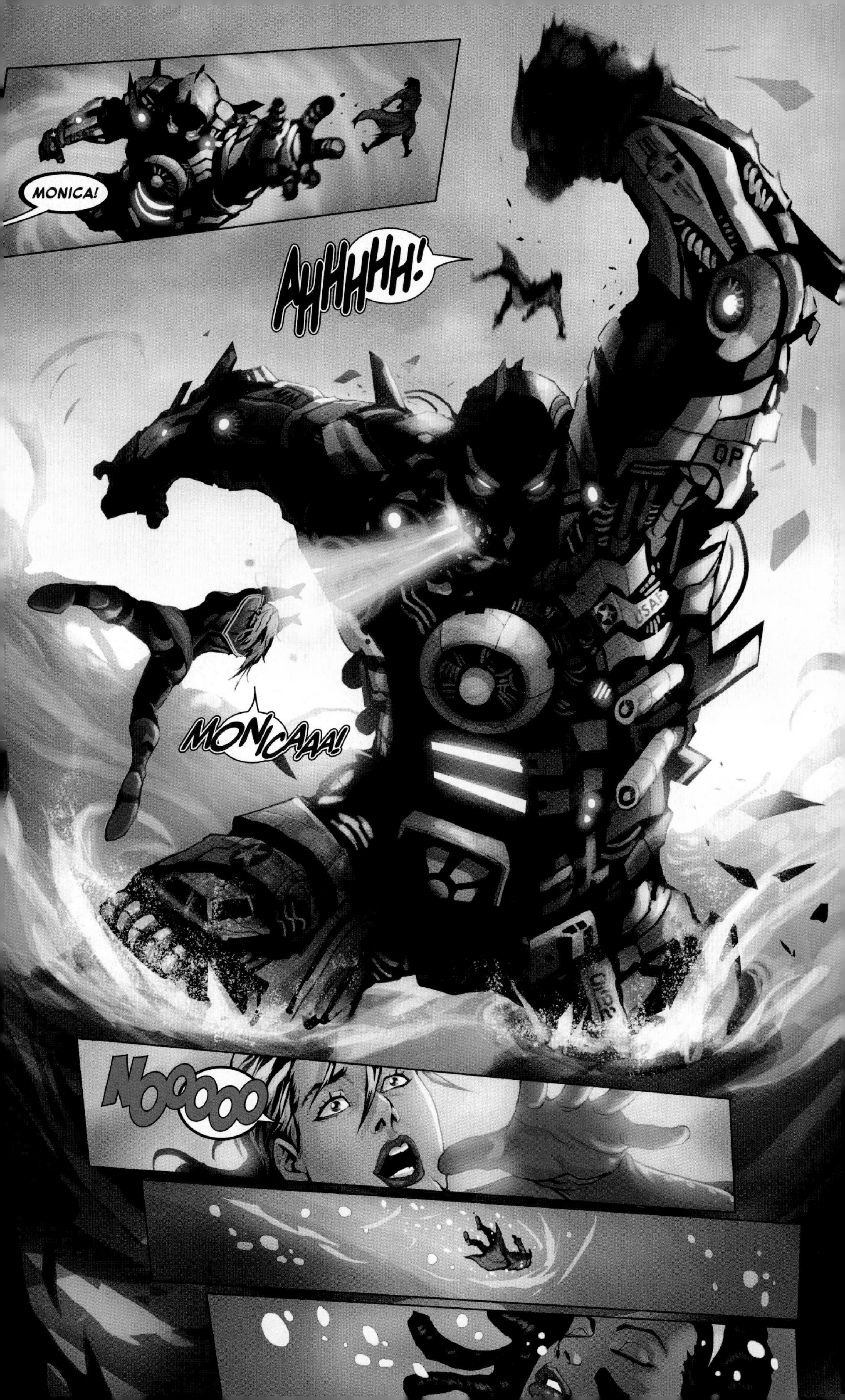
MONICA!
AHHHHH!
MONICAAA!
NOOOOO

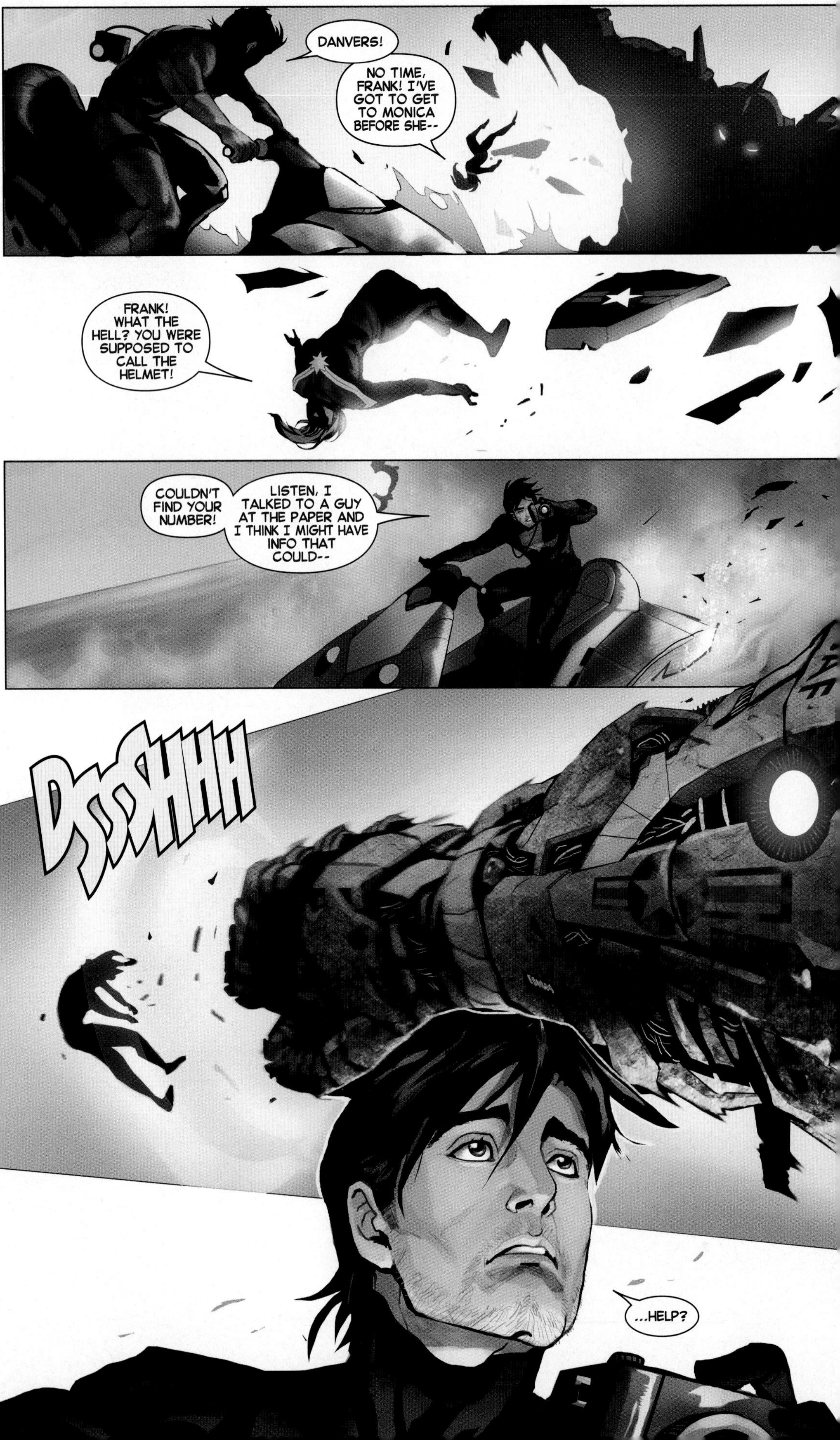
DANVERS!
NO TIME, FRANK! I'VE GOT TO GET TO MONICA BEFORE SHE--
FRANK! WHAT THE HELL? YOU WERE SUPPOSED TO CALL THE HELMET!
COULDN'T FIND YOUR NUMBER!
LISTEN, I TALKED TO A GUY AT THE PAPER AND I THINK I MIGHT HAVE INFO THAT COULD--
DSSSHHH
...HELP?

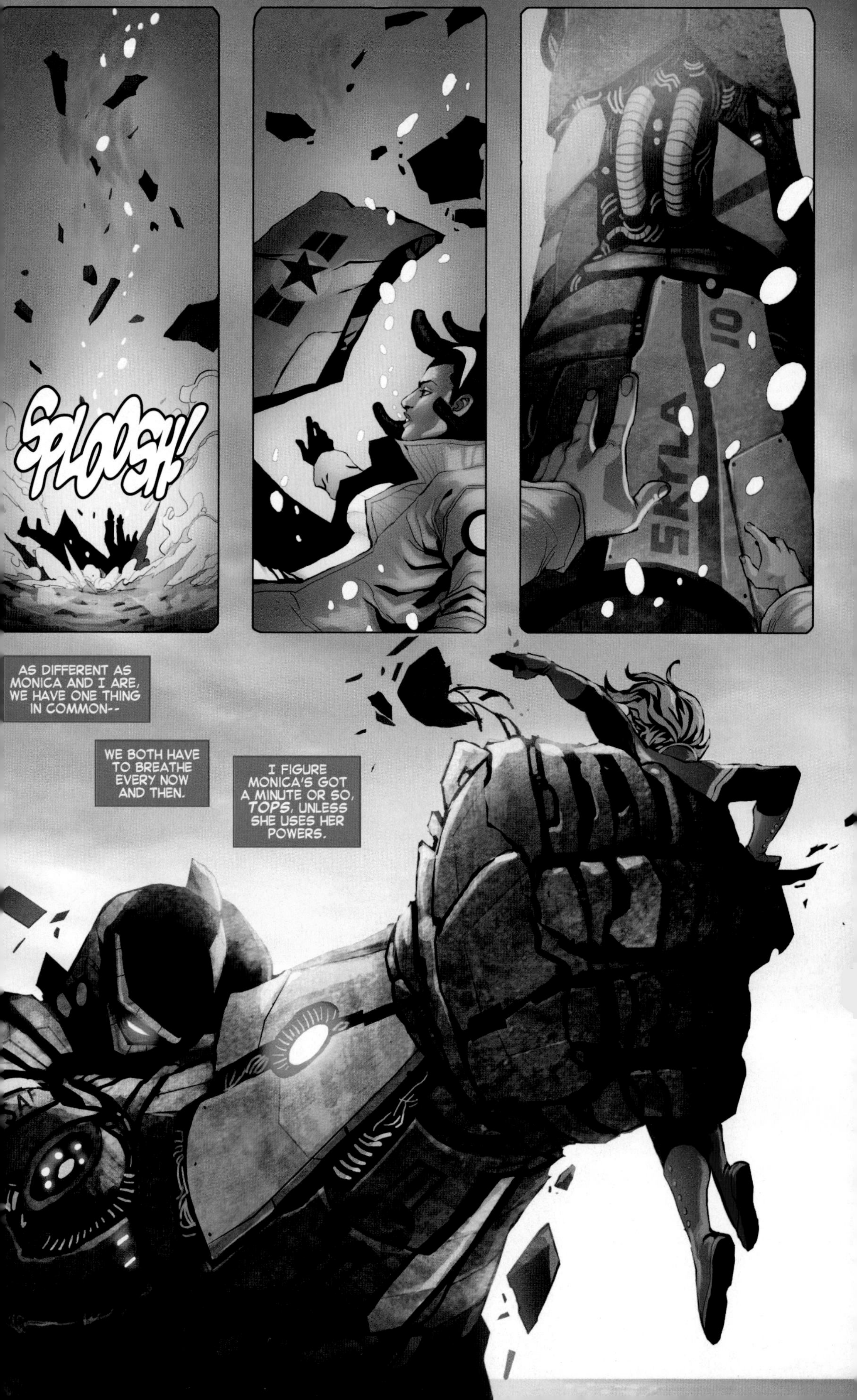
SPLOOSH!
SKYLA 10
AS DIFFERENT AS MONICA AND I ARE, WE HAVE ONE THING IN COMMON--
WE BOTH HAVE TO BREATHE EVERY NOW AND THEN.
I FIGURE MONICA'S GOT A MINUTE OR SO, TOPS, UNLESS SHE USES HER POWERS.

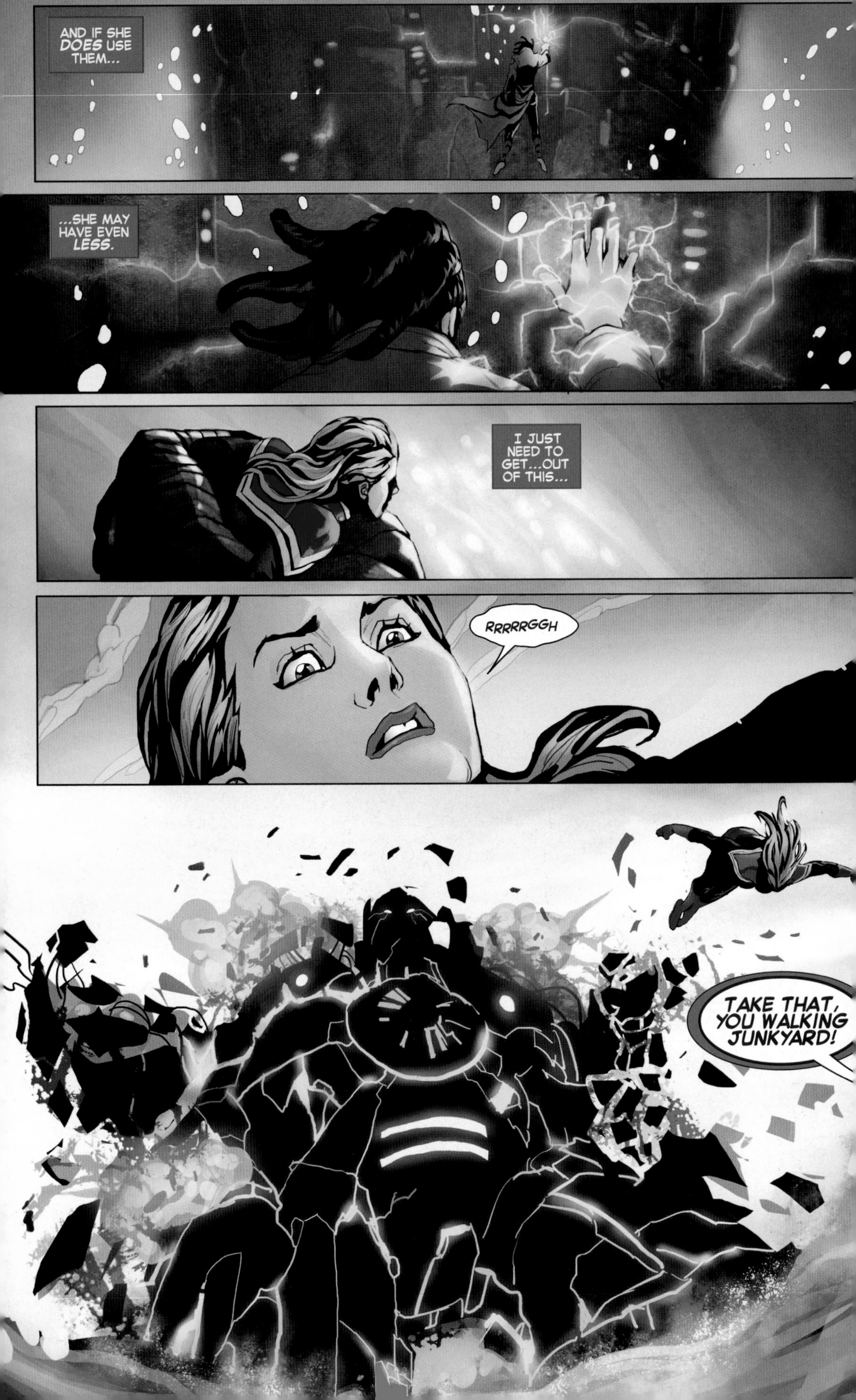
AND IF SHE DOES USE THEM...
...SHE MAY HAVE EVEN LESS.
I JUST NEED TO GET...OUT OF THIS...
RRRRRGGH
TAKE THAT, YOU WALKING JUNKYARD!

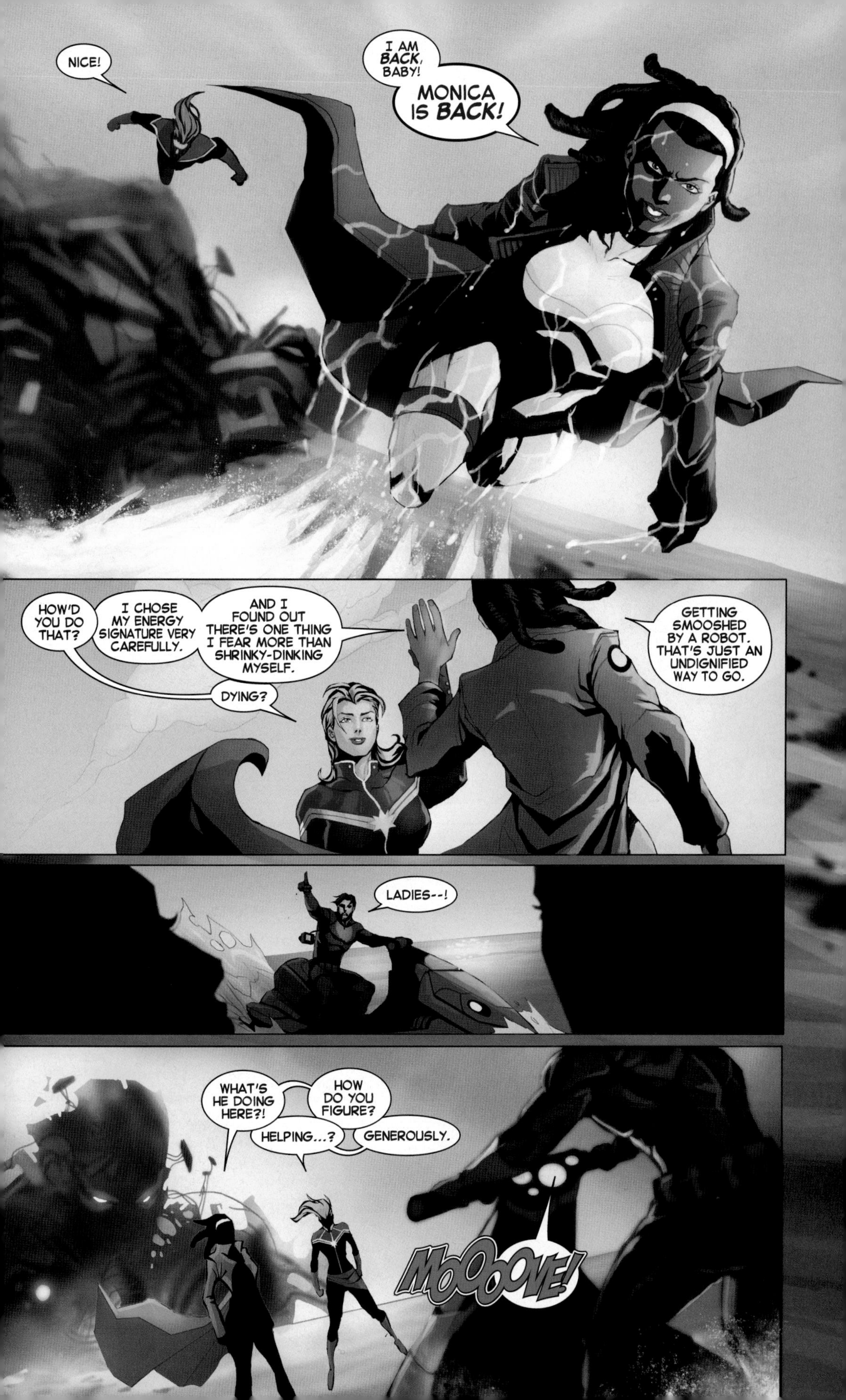
NICE!
I AM BACK, BABY!
MONICA IS BACK!
HOW'D YOU DO THAT?
I CHOSE MY ENERGY SIGNATURE VERY CAREFULLY.
AND I FOUND OUT THERE'S ONE THING I FEAR MORE THAN SHRINKY-DINKING MYSELF.
DYING?
GETTING SMOOSHED BY A ROBOT. THAT'S JUST AN UNDIGNIFIED WAY TO GO.
LADIES--!
WHAT'S HE DOING HERE?!
HOW DO YOU FIGURE?
HELPING...?
GENEROUSLY.
MOOOOOVE!

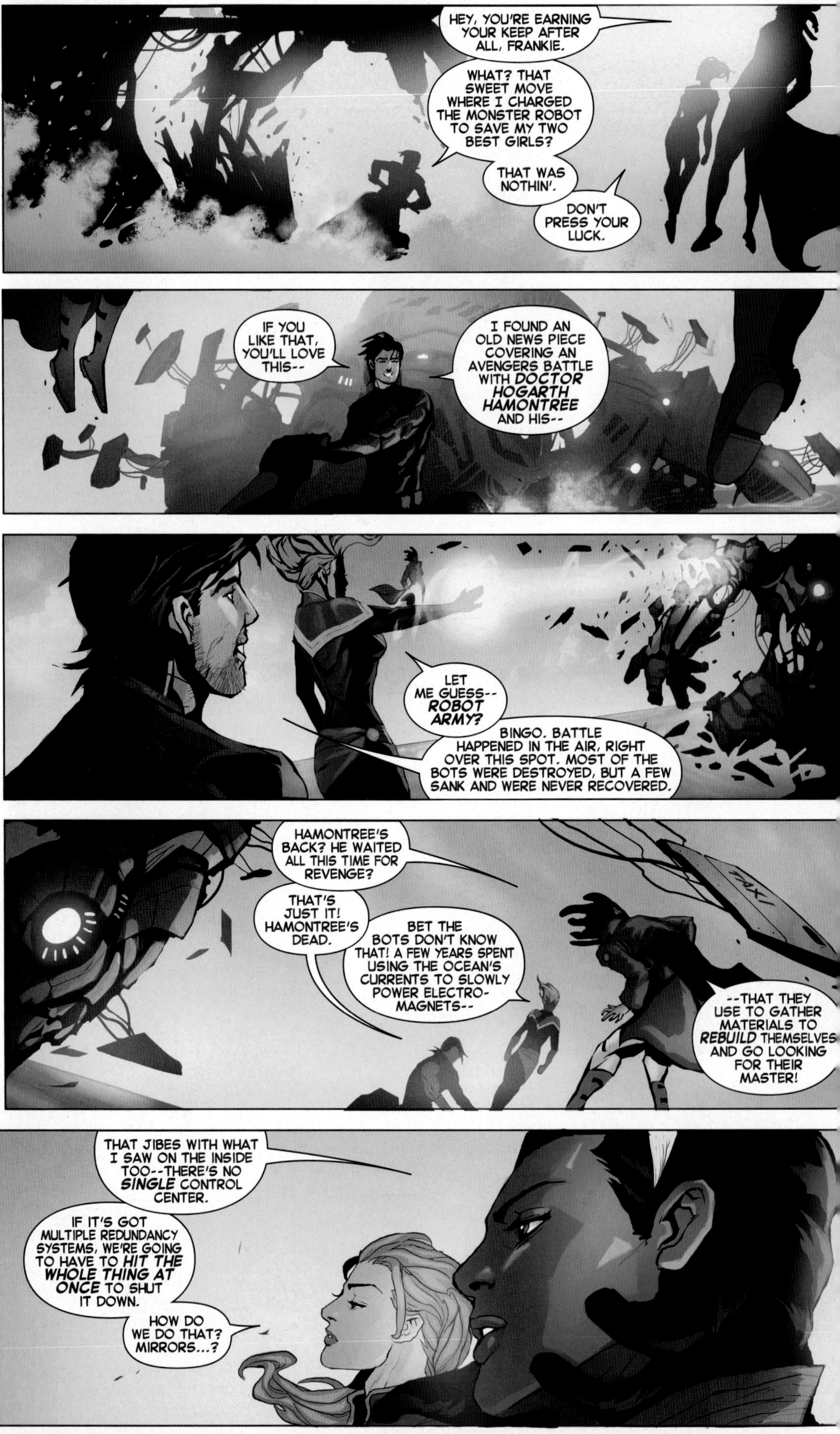
HEY, YOU'RE EARNING YOUR KEEP AFTER ALL, FRANKIE.
WHAT? THAT SWEET MOVE WHERE I CHARGED THE MONSTER ROBOT TO SAVE MY TWO BEST GIRLS?
THAT WAS NOTHIN'.
DON'T PRESS YOUR LUCK.
IF YOU LIKE THAT, YOU'LL LOVE THIS--
I FOUND AN OLD NEWS PIECE COVERING AN AVENGERS BATTLE WITH DOCTOR HOGARTH HAMONTREE AND HIS--
LET ME GUESS-- ROBOT ARMY?
BINGO. BATTLE HAPPENED IN THE AIR, RIGHT OVER THIS SPOT. MOST OF THE BOTS WERE DESTROYED, BUT A FEW SANK AND WERE NEVER RECOVERED.
HAMONTREE'S BACK? HE WAITED ALL THIS TIME FOR REVENGE?
THAT'S JUST IT! HAMONTREE'S DEAD.
BET THE BOTS DON'T KNOW THAT! A FEW YEARS SPENT USING THE OCEAN'S CURRENTS TO SLOWLY POWER ELECTRO-MAGNETS--
--THAT THEY USE TO GATHER MATERIALS TO REBUILD THEMSELVES AND GO LOOKING FOR THEIR MASTER!
THAT JIBES WITH WHAT I SAW ON THE INSIDE TOO--THERE'S NO SINGLE CONTROL CENTER.
IF IT'S GOT MULTIPLE REDUNDANCY SYSTEMS, WE'RE GOING TO HAVE TO HIT THE WHOLE THING AT ONCE TO SHUT IT DOWN.
HOW DO WE DO THAT? MIRRORS...?

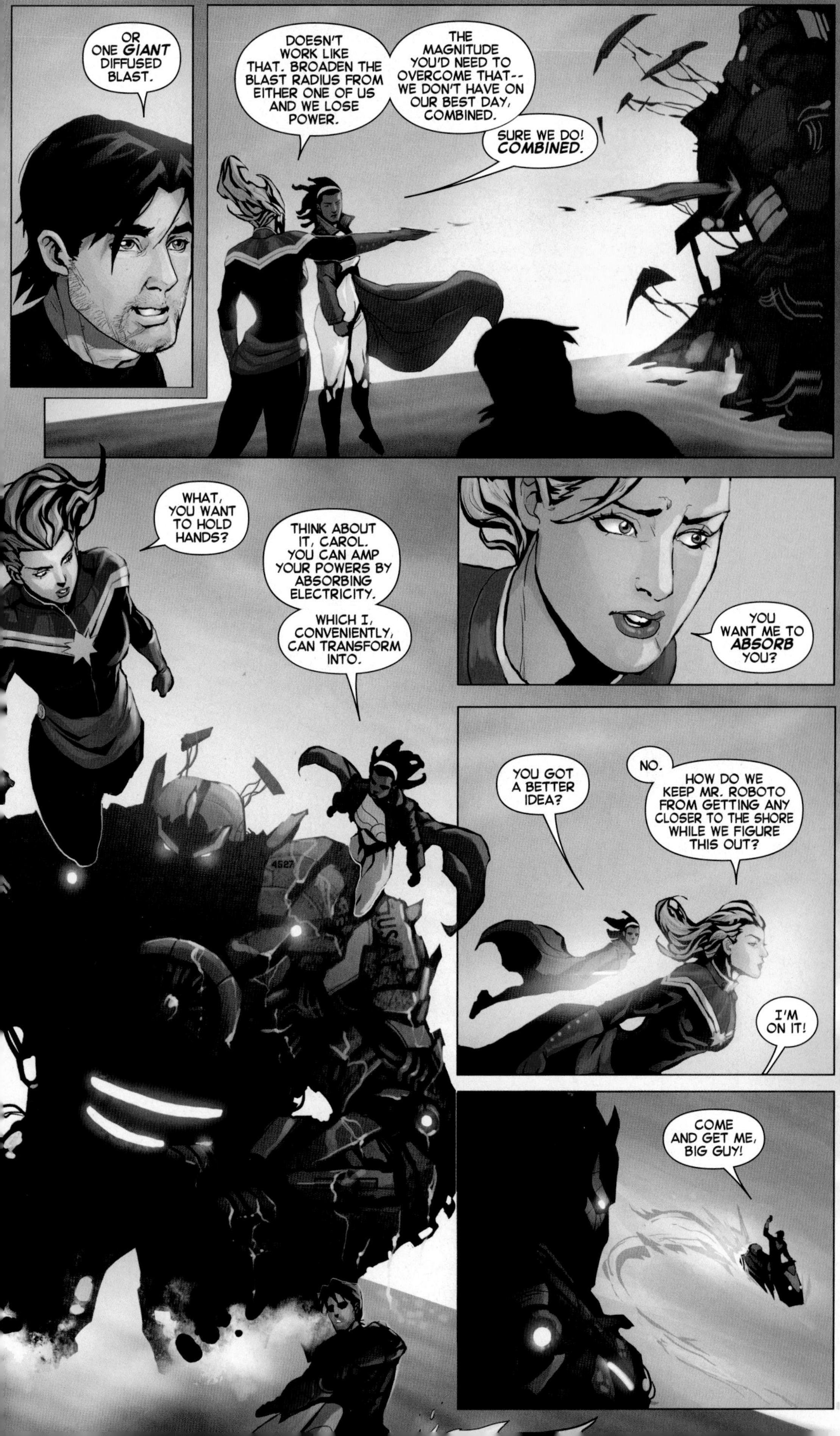
OR ONE GIANT DIFFUSED BLAST.
DOESN'T WORK LIKE THAT. BROADEN THE BLAST RADIUS FROM EITHER ONE OF US AND WE LOSE POWER.
THE MAGNITUDE YOU'D NEED TO OVERCOME THAT-- WE DON'T HAVE ON OUR BEST DAY, COMBINED.
SURE WE DO! COMBINED.
WHAT, YOU WANT TO HOLD HANDS?
THINK ABOUT IT, CAROL. YOU CAN AMP YOUR POWERS BY ABSORBING ELECTRICITY.
WHICH I, CONVENIENTLY, CAN TRANSFORM INTO.
4527
USA
YOU WANT ME TO ABSORB YOU?
YOU GOT A BETTER IDEA?
NO.
HOW DO WE KEEP MR. ROBOTO FROM GETTING ANY CLOSER TO THE SHORE WHILE WE FIGURE THIS OUT?
I'M ON IT!
COME AND GET ME, BIG GUY!

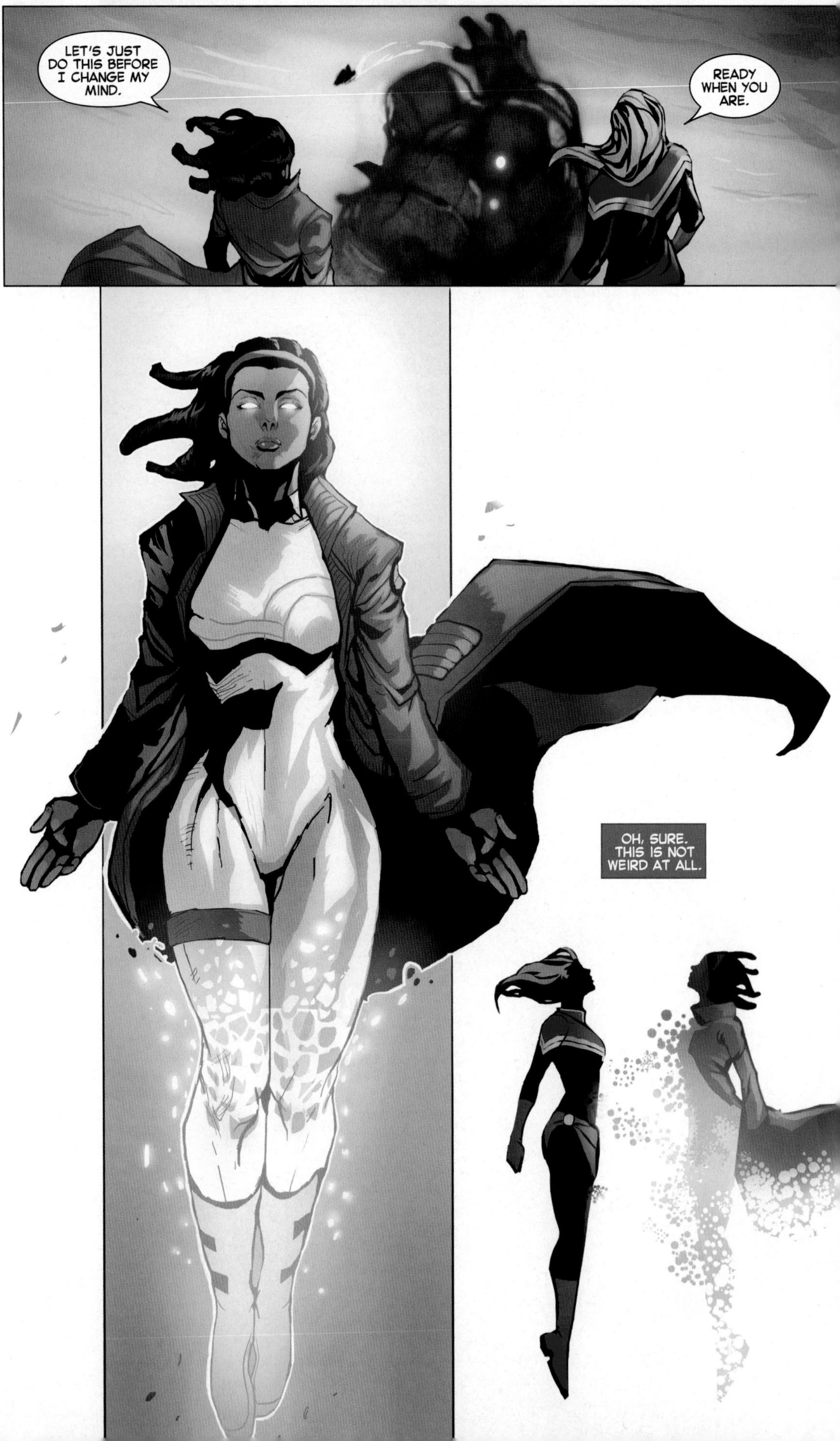
LET'S JUST DO THIS BEFORE I CHANGE MY MIND.
READY WHEN YOU ARE.
OH, SURE. THIS IS NOT WEIRD AT ALL.

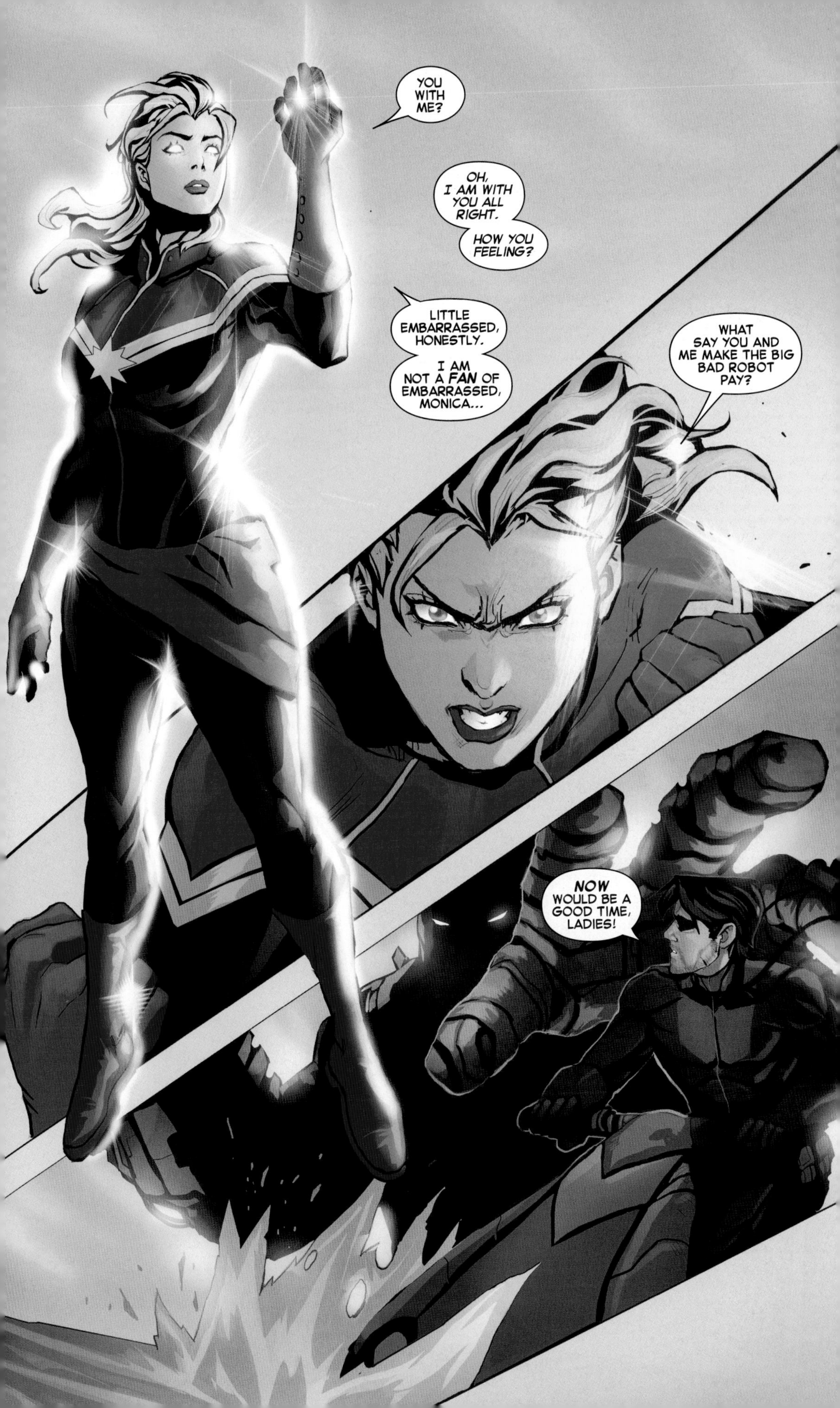
YOU WITH ME?
OH, I AM WITH YOU ALL RIGHT.
HOW YOU FEELING?
LITTLE EMBARRASSED, HONESTLY.
I AM NOT A FAN OF EMBARRASSED, MONICA...
WHAT SAY YOU AND ME MAKE THE BIG BAD ROBOT PAY?
NOW WOULD BE A GOOD TIME, LADIES!

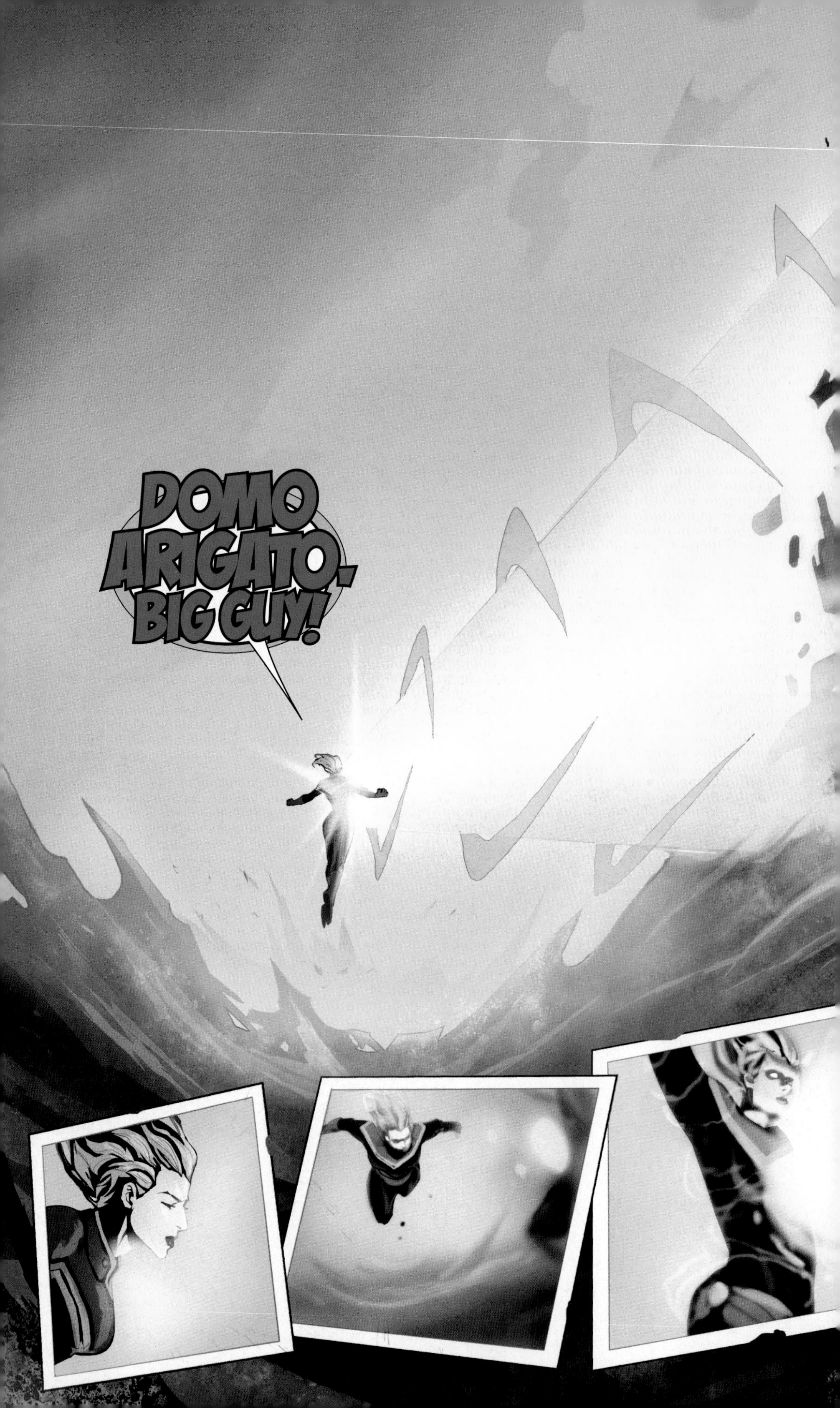
DOMO ARIGATO, BIG GUY!

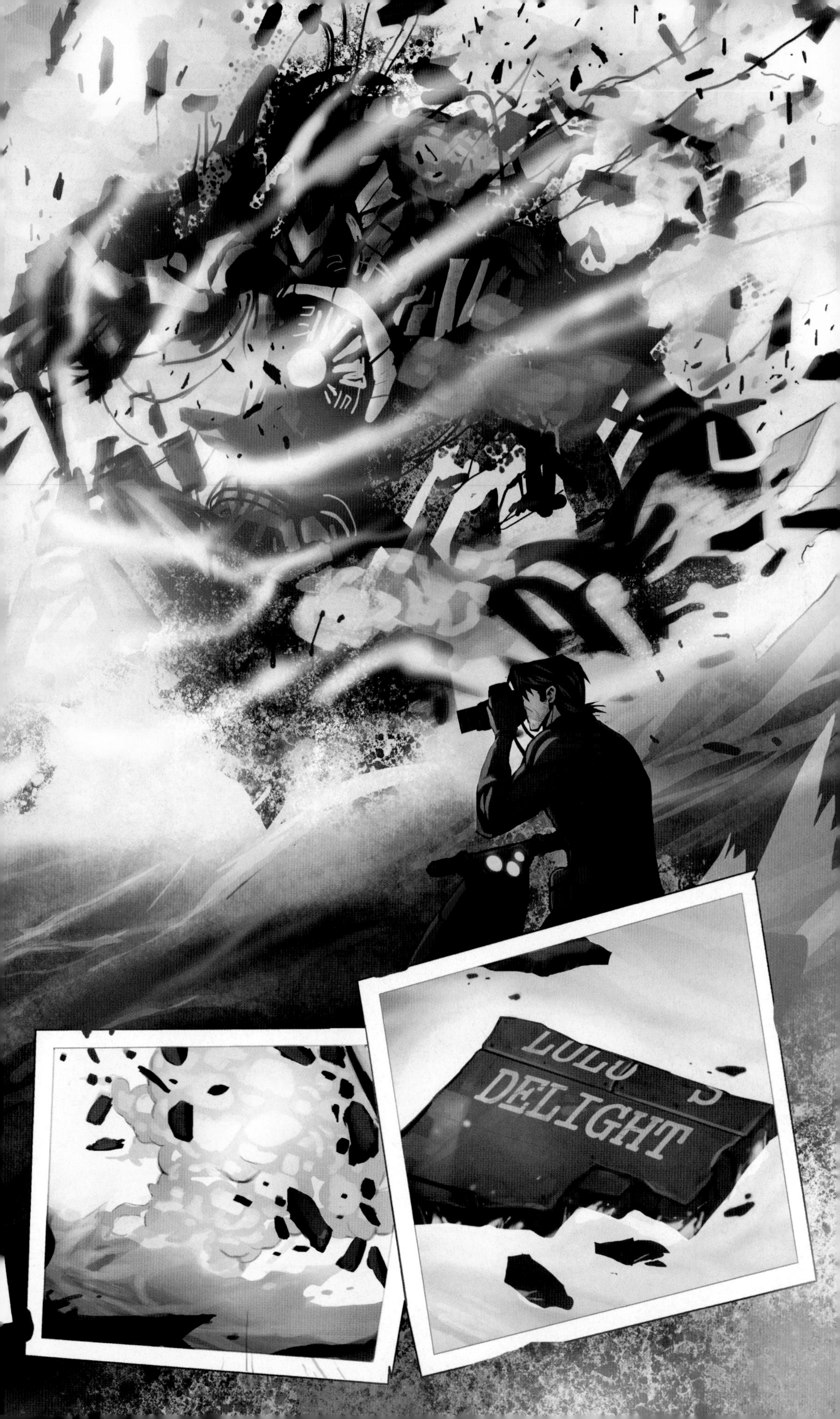
DELIGHT

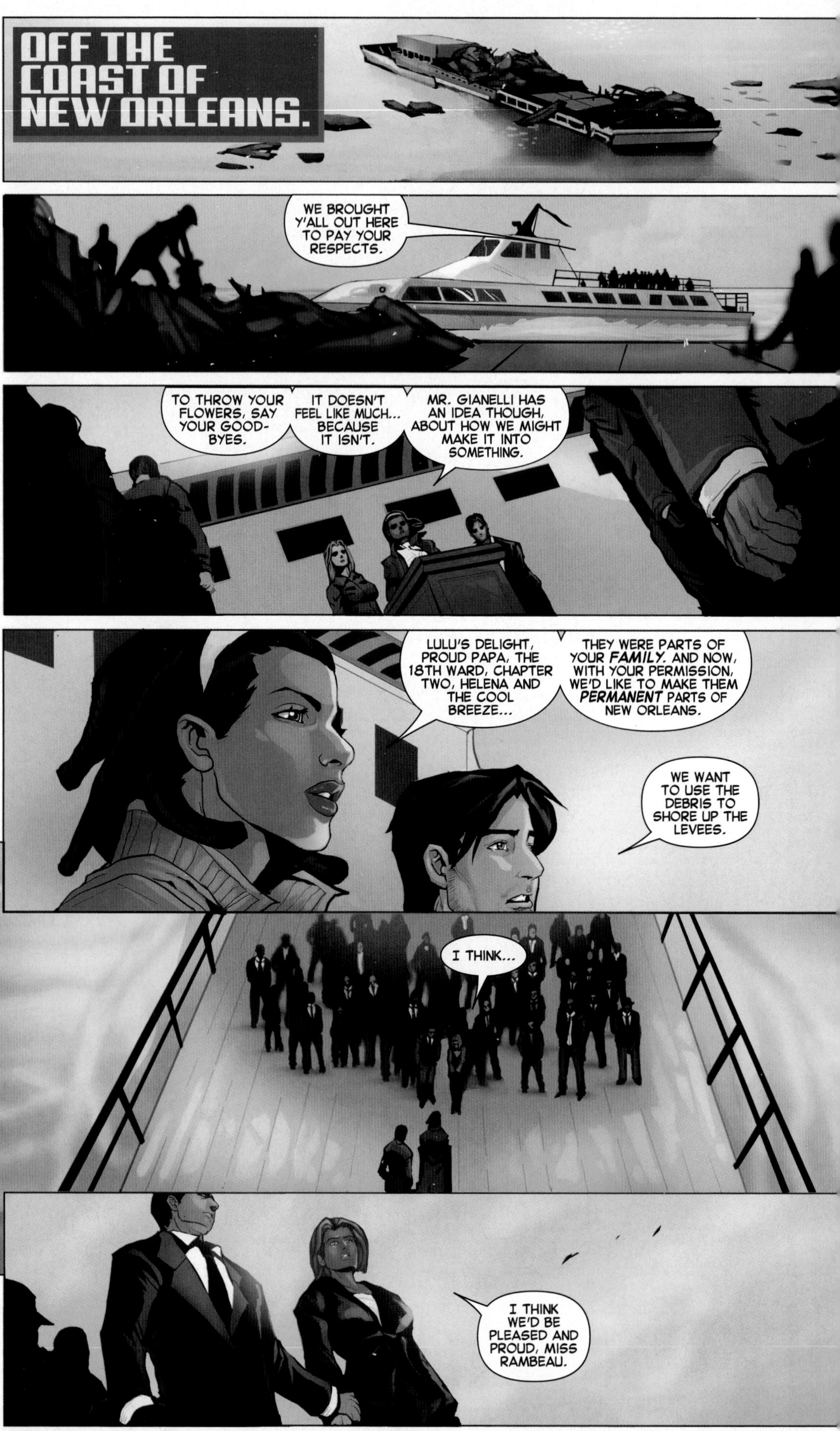
OFF THE COAST OF NEW ORLEANS.
WE BROUGHT Y'ALL OUT HERE TO PAY YOUR RESPECTS.
TO THROW YOUR FLOWERS, SAY YOUR GOOD-BYES.
IT DOESN'T FEEL LIKE MUCH... BECAUSE IT ISN'T.
MR. GIANELLI HAS AN IDEA THOUGH, ABOUT HOW WE MIGHT MAKE IT INTO SOMETHING.
LULU'S DELIGHT, PROUD PAPA, THE 18TH WARD, CHAPTER TWO, HELENA AND THE COOL BREEZE...
THEY WERE PARTS OF YOUR FAMILY. AND NOW, WITH YOUR PERMISSION, WE'D LIKE TO MAKE THEM PERMANENT PARTS OF NEW ORLEANS.
WE WANT TO USE THE DEBRIS TO SHORE UP THE LEVEES.
I THINK...
I THINK WE'D BE PLEASED AND PROUD, MISS RAMBEAU.

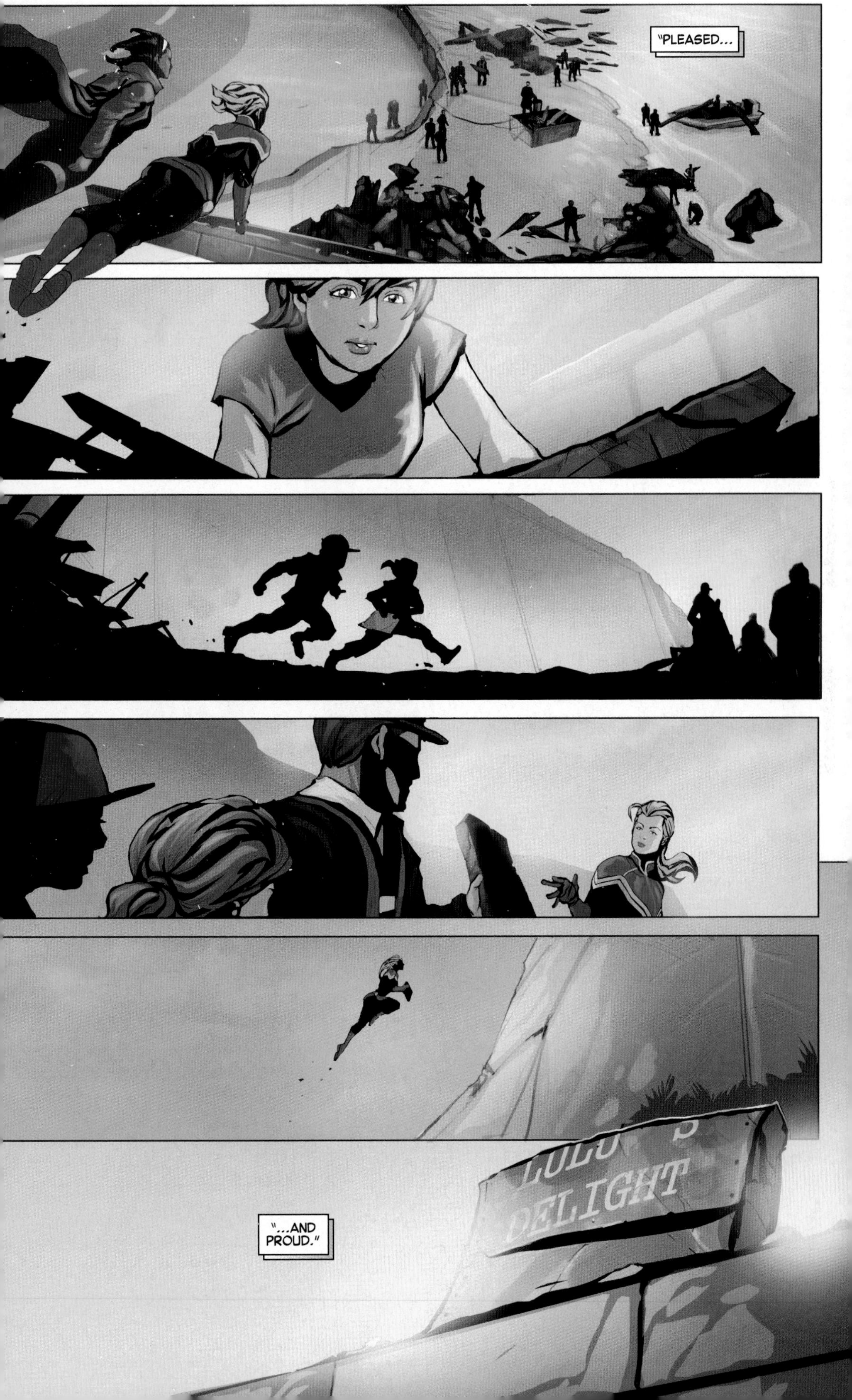
"PLEASED...
LULU S
DELIGHT
"...AND PROUD."

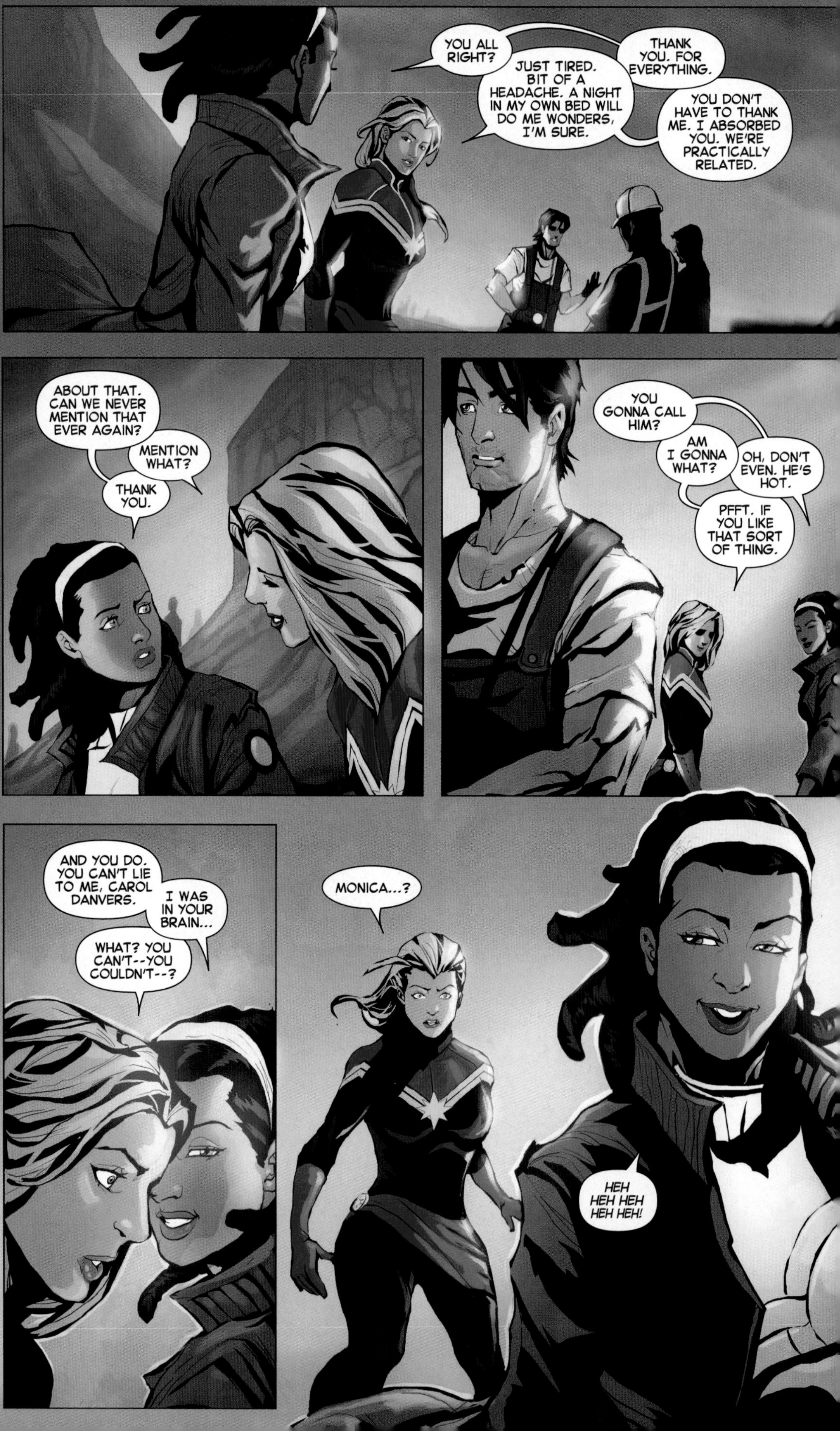
YOU ALL RIGHT?
JUST TIRED. BIT OF A HEADACHE. A NIGHT IN MY OWN BED WILL DO ME WONDERS, I'M SURE.
THANK YOU. FOR EVERYTHING.
YOU DON'T HAVE TO THANK ME. I ABSORBED YOU. WE'RE PRACTICALLY RELATED.
ABOUT THAT. CAN WE NEVER MENTION THAT EVER AGAIN?
MENTION WHAT?
THANK YOU.
YOU GONNA CALL HIM?
AM I GONNA WHAT?
OH, DON'T EVEN. HE'S HOT.
PFFT. IF YOU LIKE THAT SORT OF THING.
AND YOU DO. YOU CAN'T LIE TO ME, CAROL DANVERS.
I WAS IN YOUR BRAIN...
WHAT? YOU CAN'T--YOU COULDN'T--?
MONICA...?
HEH HEH HEH HEH HEH!

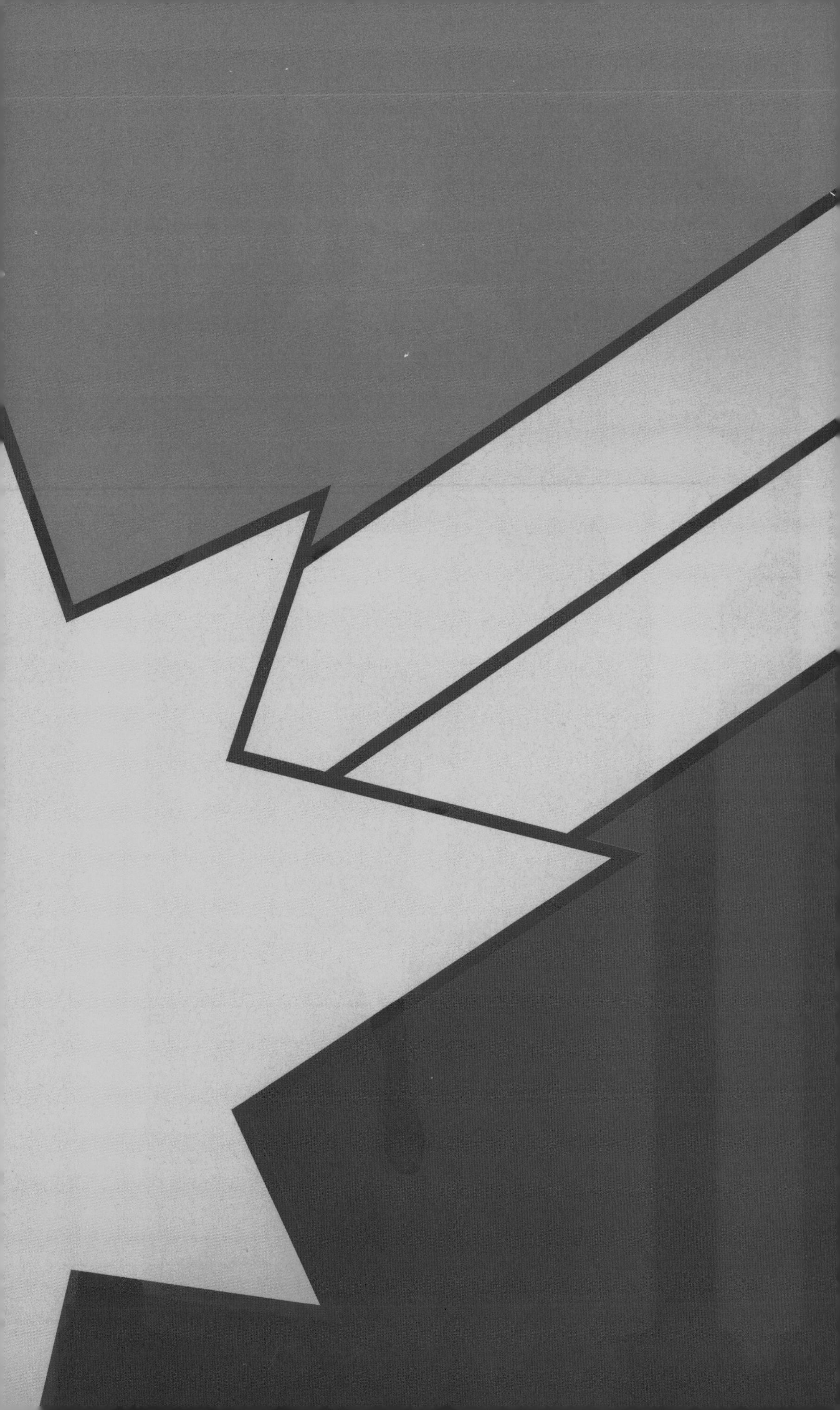

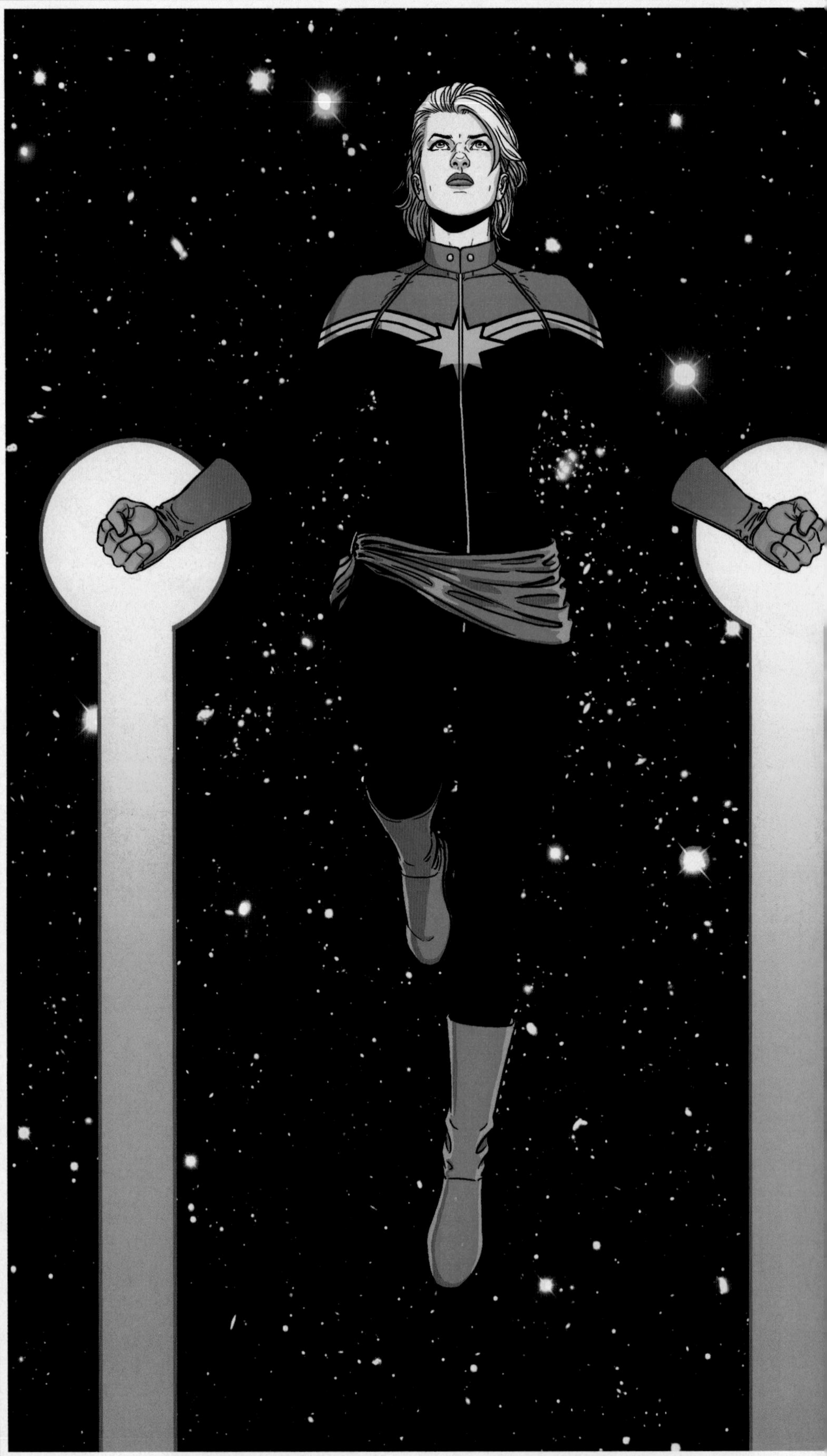

NINE

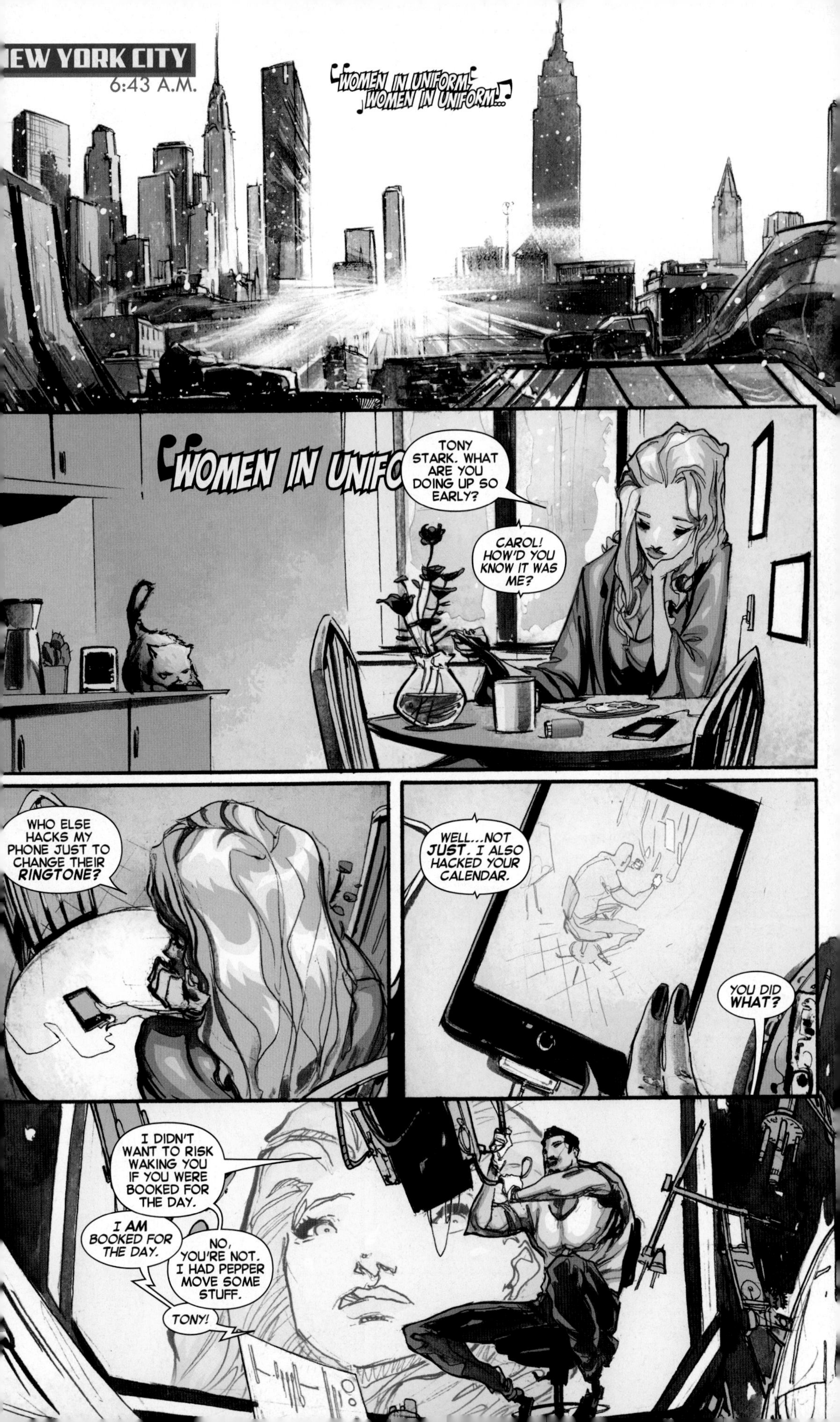
NEW YORK CITY
6:43 A.M.
WOMEN IN UNIFORM, WOMEN IN UNIFORM...
WOMEN IN UNIFO
TONY STARK. WHAT ARE YOU DOING UP SO EARLY?
CAROL! HOW'D YOU KNOW IT WAS ME?
WHO ELSE HACKS MY PHONE JUST TO CHANGE THEIR RINGTONE?
WELL...NOT JUST. I ALSO HACKED YOUR CALENDAR.
YOU DID WHAT?
I DIDN'T WANT TO RISK WAKING YOU IF YOU WERE BOOKED FOR THE DAY.
I AM BOOKED FOR THE DAY.
NO, YOU'RE NOT. I HAD PEPPER MOVE SOME STUFF.
TONY!

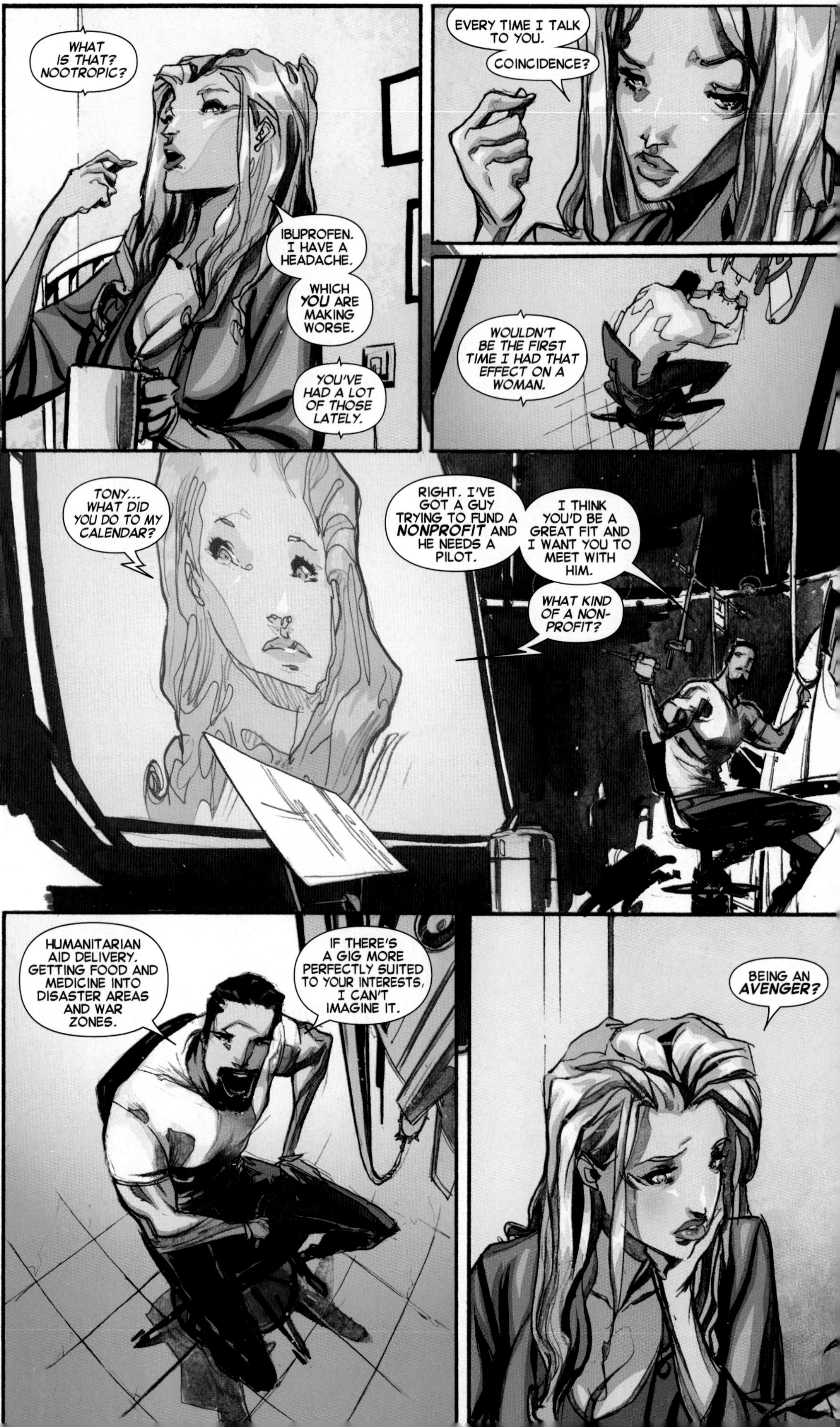
WHAT IS THAT? NOOTROPIC?
IBUPROFEN. I HAVE A HEADACHE.
WHICH YOU ARE MAKING WORSE.
YOU'VE HAD A LOT OF THOSE LATELY.
EVERY TIME I TALK TO YOU.
COINCIDENCE?
WOULDN'T BE THE FIRST TIME I HAD THAT EFFECT ON A WOMAN.
TONY... WHAT DID YOU DO TO MY CALENDAR?
RIGHT. I'VE GOT A GUY TRYING TO FUND A NONPROFIT AND HE NEEDS A PILOT.
I THINK YOU'D BE A GREAT FIT AND I WANT YOU TO MEET WITH HIM.
WHAT KIND OF A NON-PROFIT?
HUMANITARIAN AID DELIVERY. GETTING FOOD AND MEDICINE INTO DISASTER AREAS AND WAR ZONES.
IF THERE'S A GIG MORE PERFECTLY SUITED TO YOUR INTERESTS, I CAN'T IMAGINE IT.
BEING AN AVENGER?

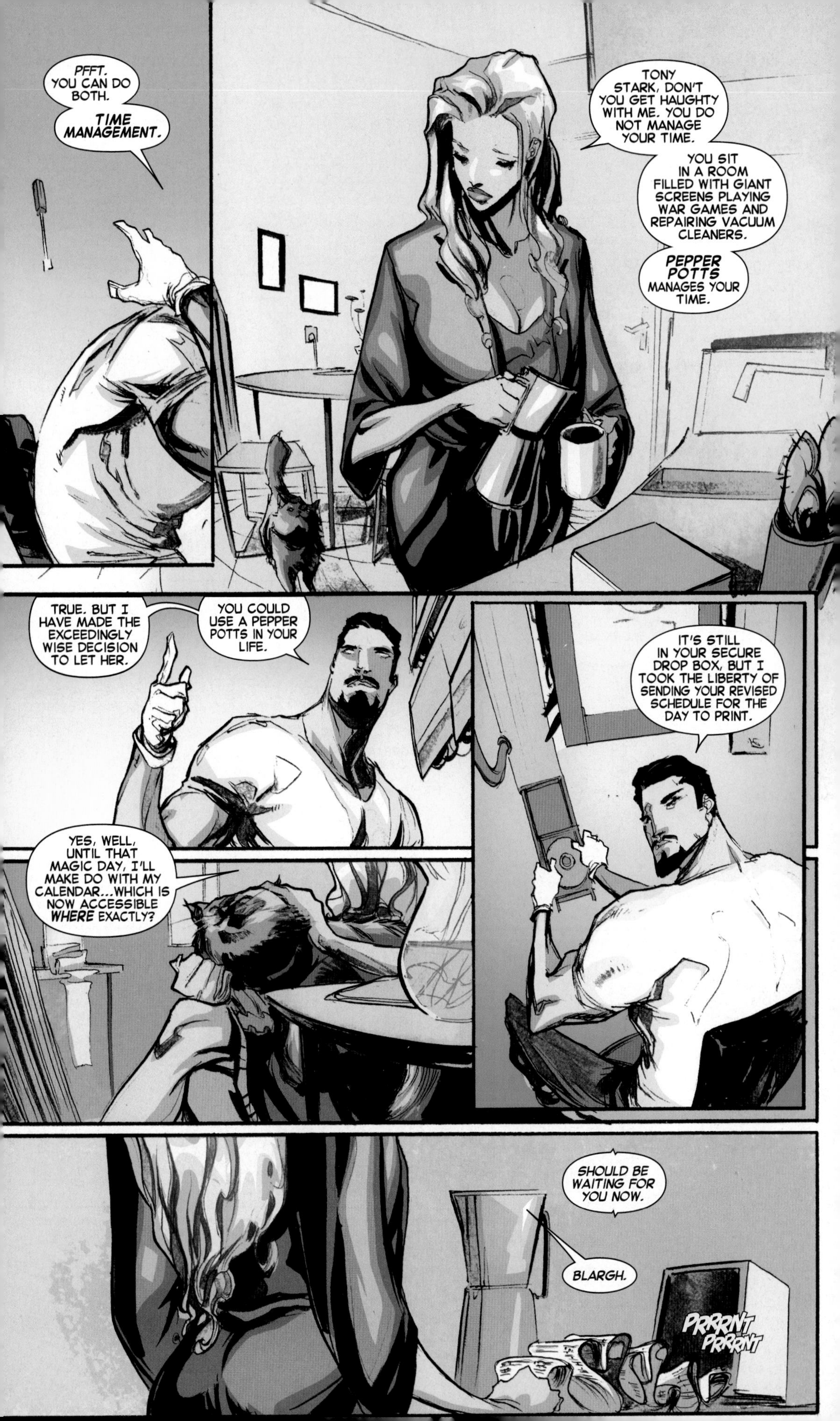
PFFT. YOU CAN DO BOTH.
TIME MANAGEMENT.
TONY STARK, DON'T YOU GET HAUGHTY WITH ME. YOU DO NOT MANAGE YOUR TIME.
YOU SIT IN A ROOM FILLED WITH GIANT SCREENS PLAYING WAR GAMES AND REPAIRING VACUUM CLEANERS.
PEPPER POTTS MANAGES YOUR TIME.
YOU COULD USE A PEPPER POTTS IN YOUR LIFE.
TRUE. BUT I HAVE MADE THE EXCEEDINGLY WISE DECISION TO LET HER.
YES, WELL, UNTIL THAT MAGIC DAY, I'LL MAKE DO WITH MY CALENDAR...WHICH IS NOW ACCESSIBLE WHERE EXACTLY?
IT'S STILL IN YOUR SECURE DROP BOX, BUT I TOOK THE LIBERTY OF SENDING YOUR REVISED SCHEDULE FOR THE DAY TO PRINT.
SHOULD BE WAITING FOR YOU NOW.
BLARGH.
PRRRNT PRRRNT

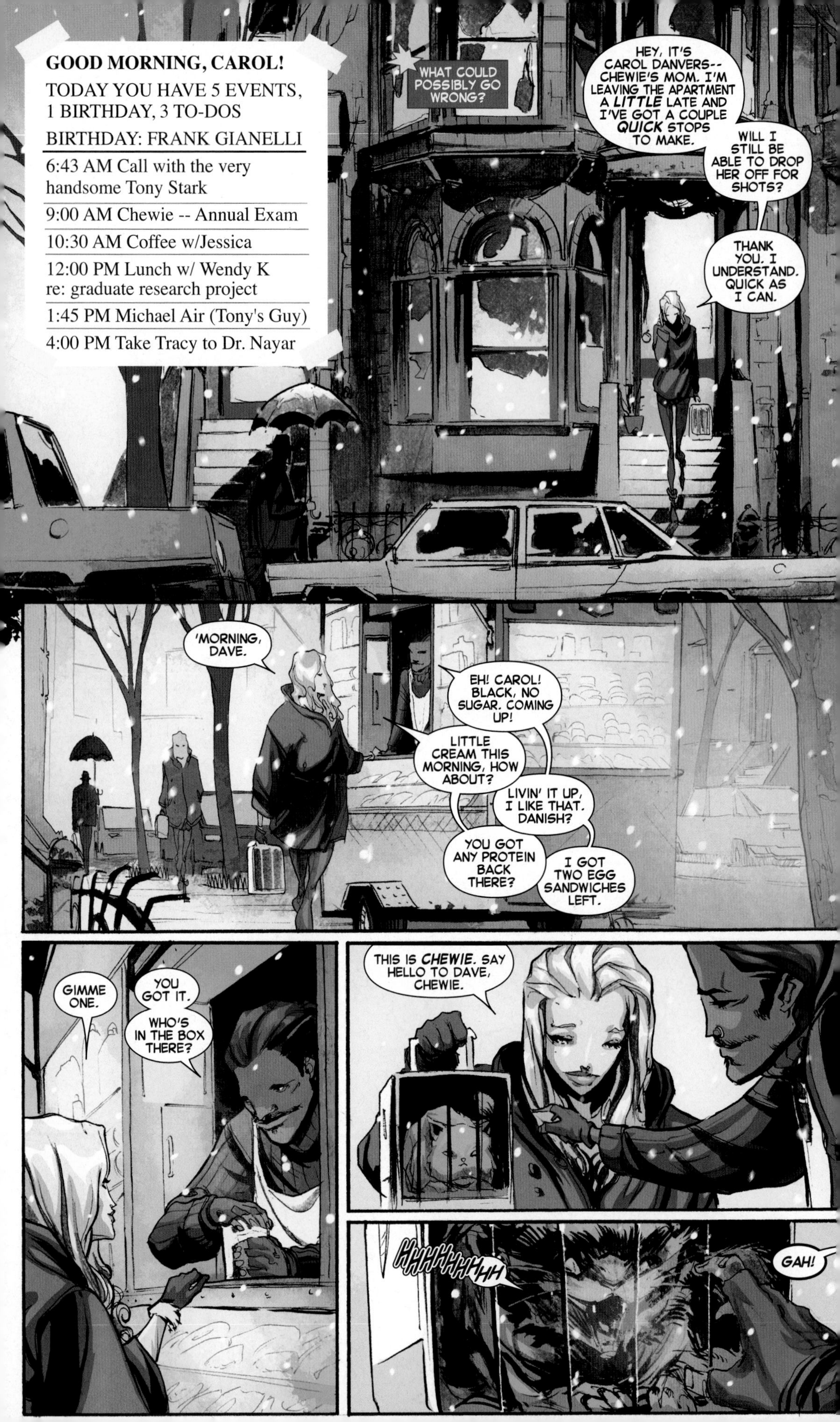
GOOD MORNING, CAROL!
TODAY YOU HAVE 5 EVENTS, 1 BIRTHDAY, 3 TO-DOS
BIRTHDAY: FRANK GIANELLI
6:43 AM Call with the very handsome Tony Stark
9:00 AM Chewie -- Annual Exam
10:30 AM Coffee w/Jessica
12:00 PM Lunch w/ Wendy K re: graduate research project
1:45 PM Michael Air (Tony's Guy)
4:00 PM Take Tracy to Dr. Nayar
WHAT COULD POSSIBLY GO WRONG?
HEY, IT'S CAROL DANVERS-- CHEWIE'S MOM. I'M LEAVING THE APARTMENT A LITTLE LATE AND I'VE GOT A COUPLE QUICK STOPS TO MAKE.
WILL I STILL BE ABLE TO DROP HER OFF FOR SHOTS?
THANK YOU. I UNDERSTAND. QUICK AS I CAN.
'MORNING, DAVE.
EH! CAROL! BLACK, NO SUGAR. COMING UP!
LITTLE CREAM THIS MORNING, HOW ABOUT?
LIVIN' IT UP, I LIKE THAT. DANISH?
YOU GOT ANY PROTEIN BACK THERE?
I GOT TWO EGG SANDWICHES LEFT.
GIMME ONE.
YOU GOT IT.
WHO'S IN THE BOX THERE?
THIS IS CHEWIE. SAY HELLO TO DAVE, CHEWIE.
HHHHHHHHH
GAH!

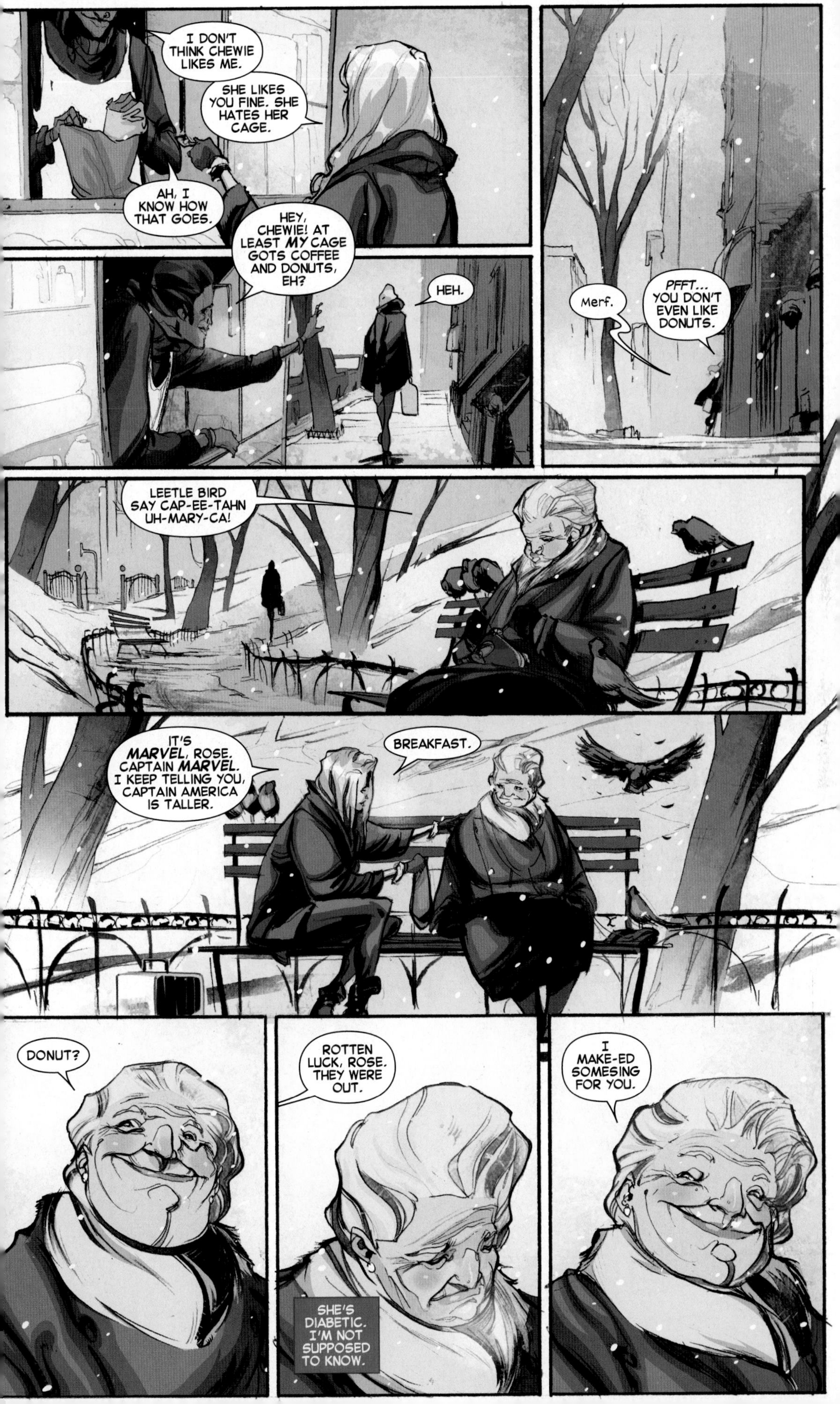
I DON'T THINK CHEWIE LIKES ME.
SHE LIKES YOU FINE. SHE HATES HER CAGE.
AH, I KNOW HOW THAT GOES.
HEY, CHEWIE! AT LEAST MY CAGE GOTS COFFEE AND DONUTS, EH?
HEH.
PFFT... YOU DON'T EVEN LIKE DONUTS.
Merf.
LEETLE BIRD SAY CAP-EE-TAHN UH-MARY-CA!
IT'S MARVEL, ROSE. CAPTAIN MARVEL. I KEEP TELLING YOU, CAPTAIN AMERICA IS TALLER.
BREAKFAST.
DONUT?
ROTTEN LUCK, ROSE. THEY WERE OUT.
SHE'S DIABETIC. I'M NOT SUPPOSED TO KNOW.
I MAKE-ED SOMESING FOR YOU.

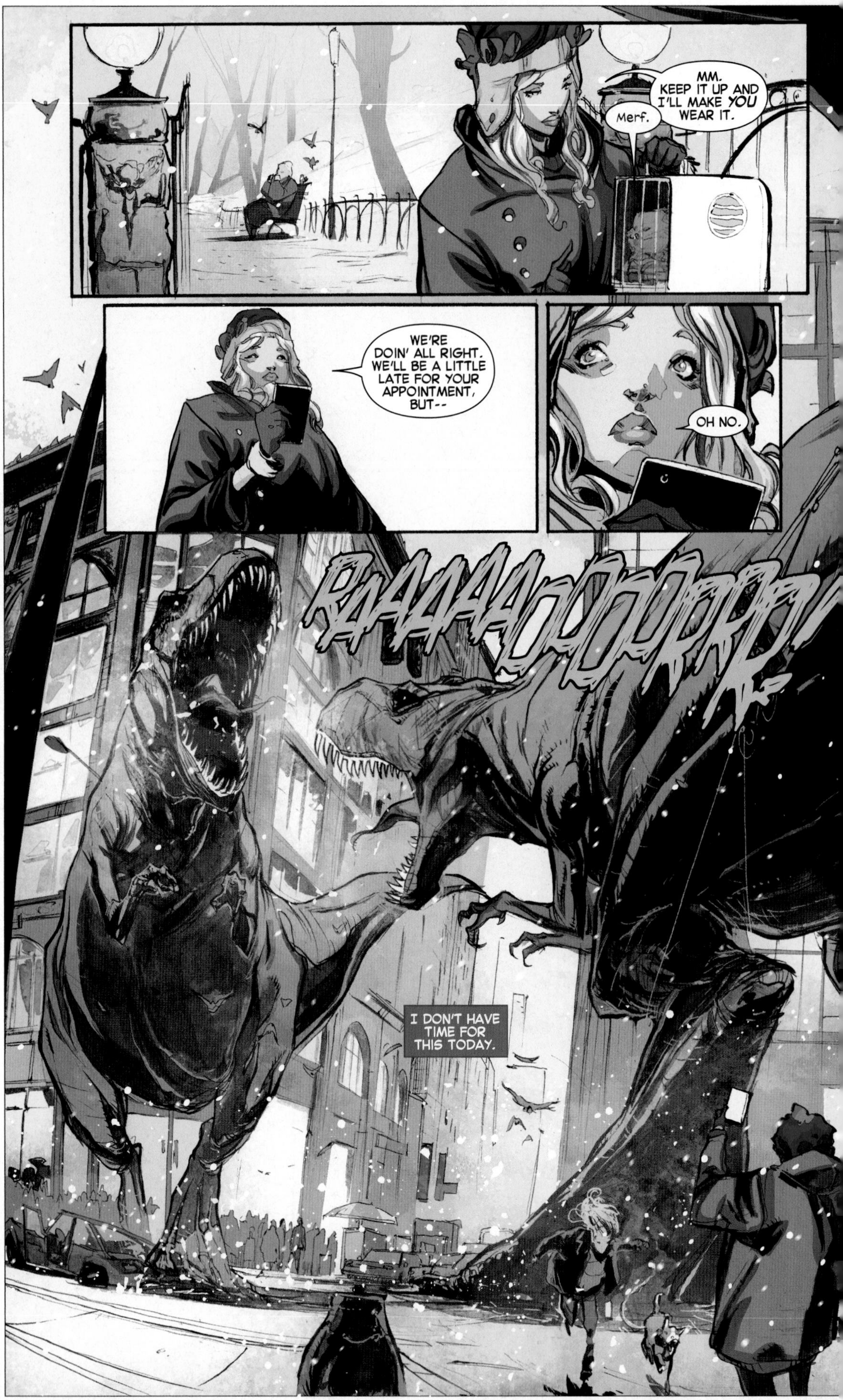
Merf.
MM. KEEP IT UP AND I'LL MAKE YOU WEAR IT.
WE'RE DOIN' ALL RIGHT. WE'LL BE A LITTLE LATE FOR YOUR APPOINTMENT, BUT--
OH NO.
RAAAAAOOORRR!
I DON'T HAVE TIME FOR THIS TODAY.

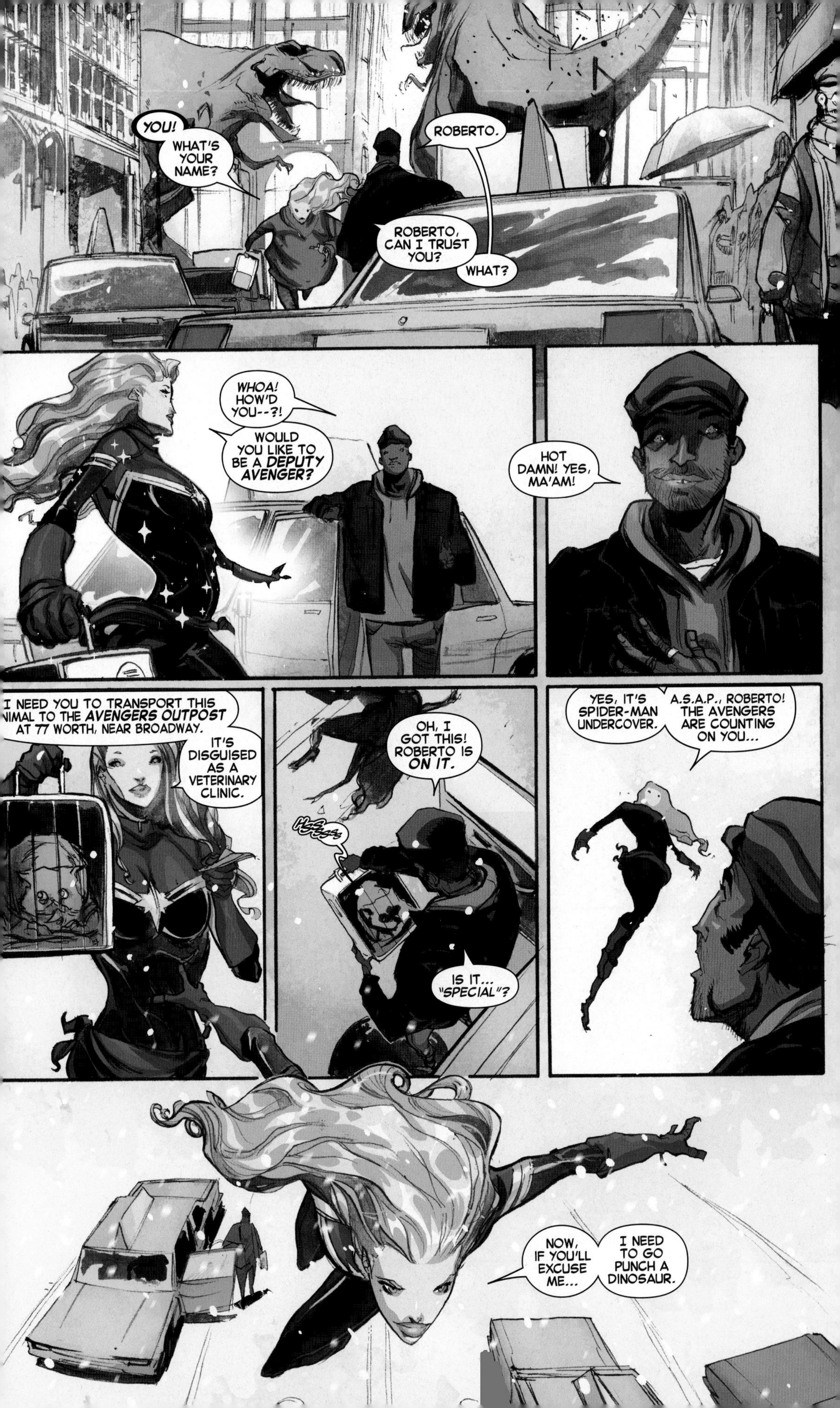

YOU! WHAT'S YOUR NAME?
ROBERTO.
ROBERTO, CAN I TRUST YOU?
WHAT?
WHOA! HOW'D YOU--?!
WOULD YOU LIKE TO BE A DEPUTY AVENGER?
HOT DAMN! YES, MA'AM!
I NEED YOU TO TRANSPORT THIS NIMAL TO THE AVENGERS OUTPOST AT 77 WORTH, NEAR BROADWAY.
IT'S DISGUISED AS A VETERINARY CLINIC.
OH, I GOT THIS! ROBERTO IS ON IT.
IS IT... "SPECIAL"?
YES, IT'S SPIDER-MAN UNDERCOVER.
A.S.A.P., ROBERTO! THE AVENGERS ARE COUNTING ON YOU...
NOW, IF YOU'LL EXCUSE ME...
I NEED TO GO PUNCH A DINOSAUR.

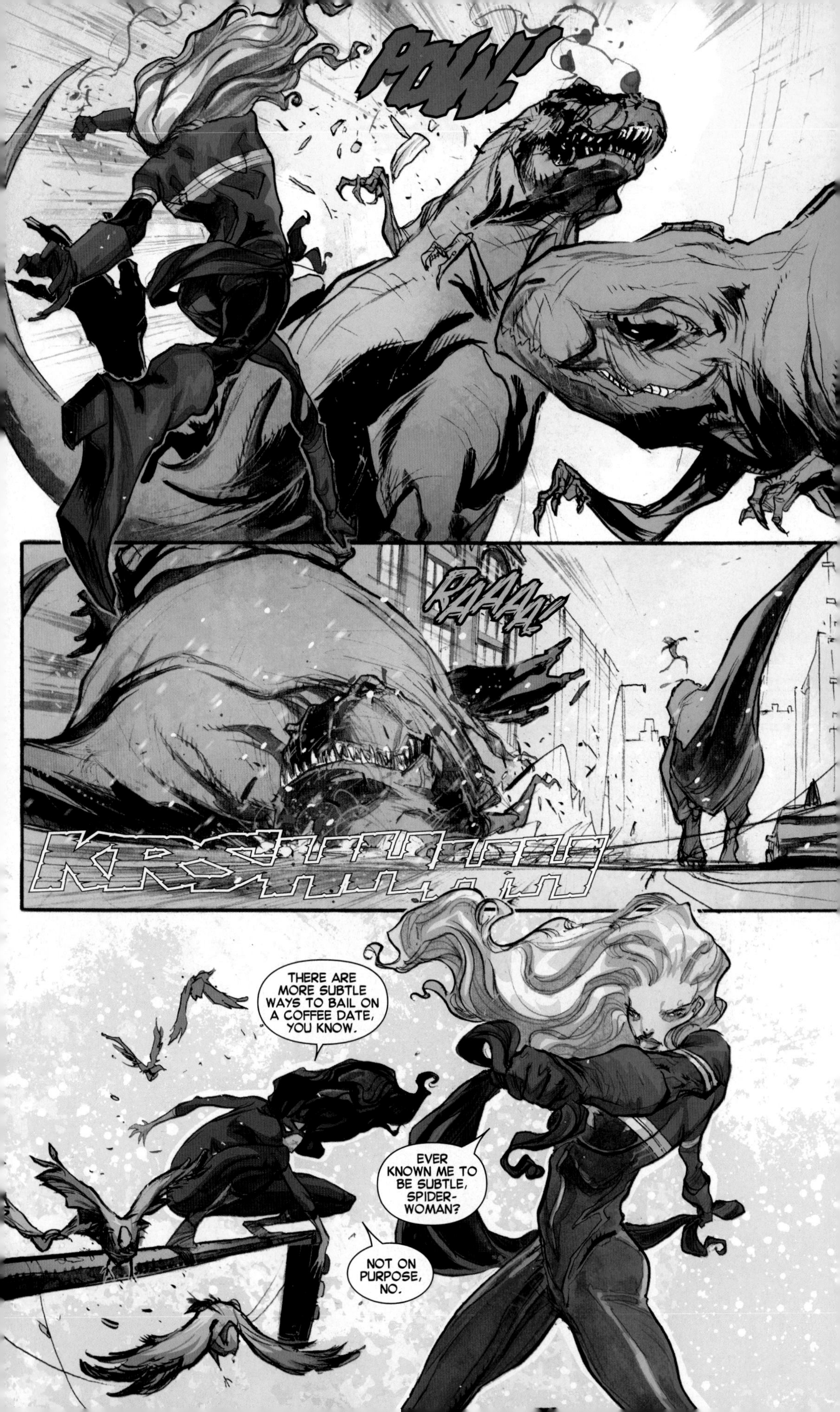
POW!
RAAAA!
KRSHHHHHH
THERE ARE MORE SUBTLE WAYS TO BAIL ON A COFFEE DATE, YOU KNOW.
EVER KNOWN ME TO BE SUBTLE, SPIDER-WOMAN?
NOT ON PURPOSE, NO.

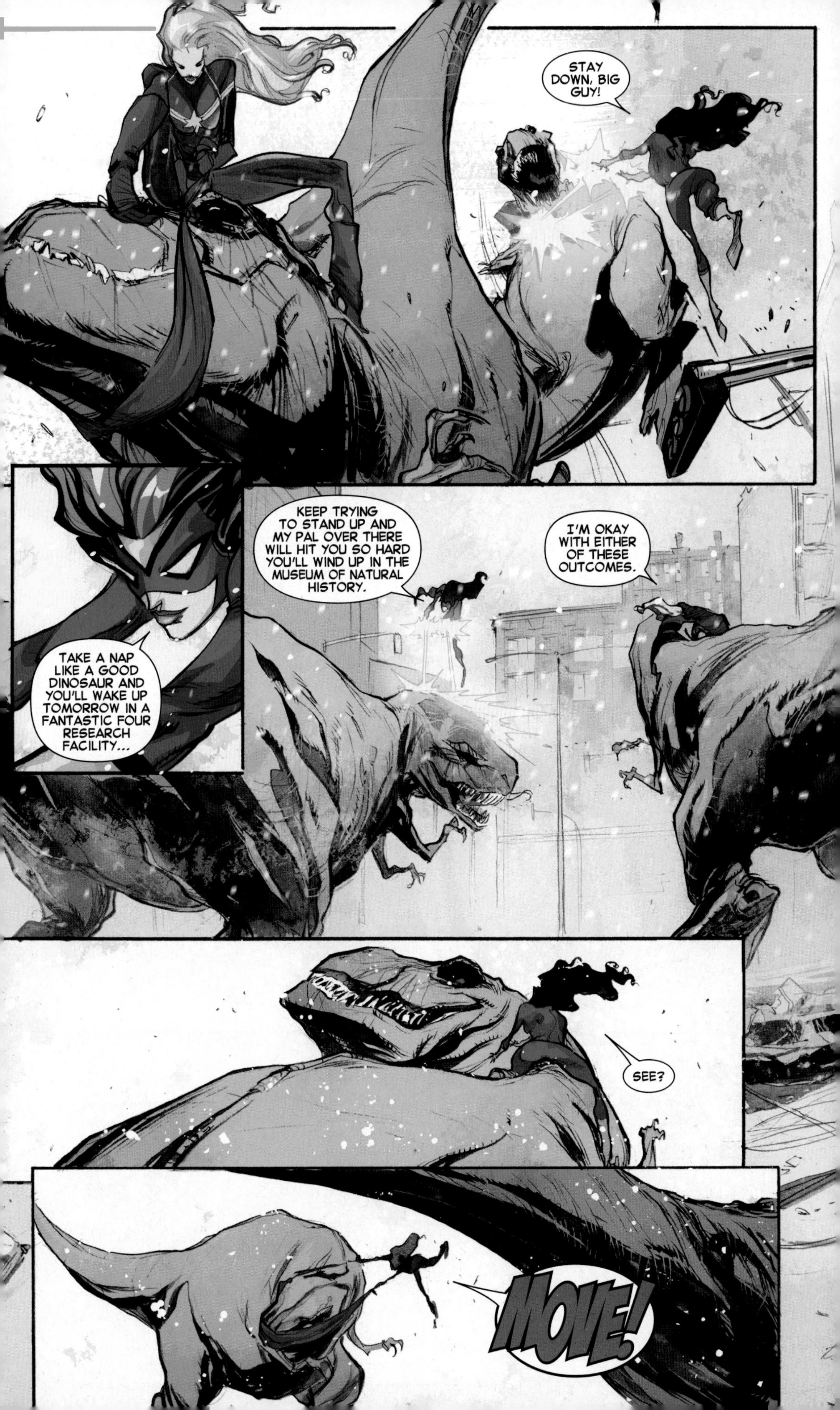
STAY DOWN, BIG GUY!
TAKE A NAP LIKE A GOOD DINOSAUR AND YOU'LL WAKE UP TOMORROW IN A FANTASTIC FOUR RESEARCH FACILITY...
KEEP TRYING TO STAND UP AND MY PAL OVER THERE WILL HIT YOU SO HARD YOU'LL WIND UP IN THE MUSEUM OF NATURAL HISTORY.
I'M OKAY WITH EITHER OF THESE OUTCOMES.
SEE?
MOVE!

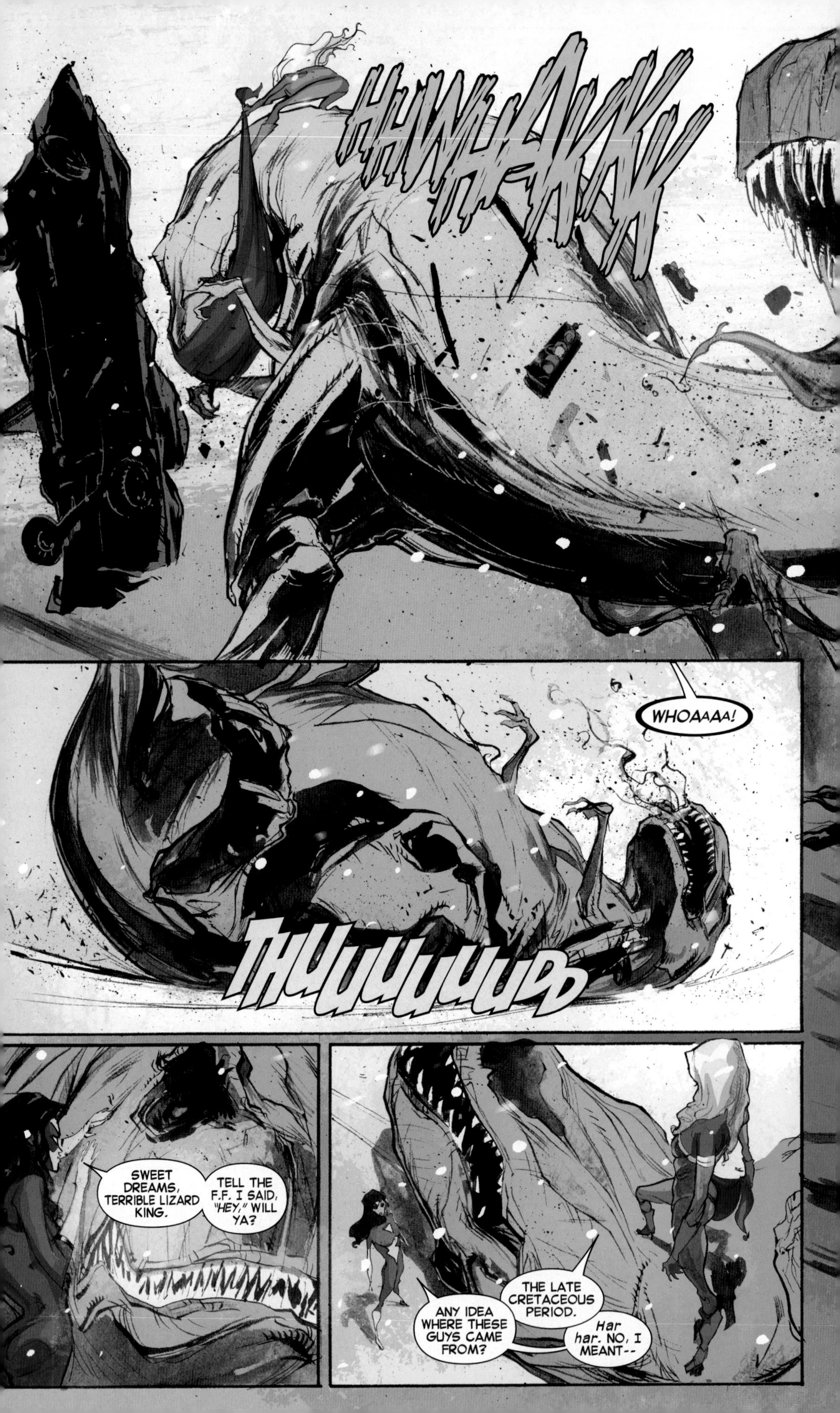
HHWHAKAKK
WHOAAAA!
THUUUUUUDD
SWEET DREAMS, TERRIBLE LIZARD KING.
TELL THE F.F. I SAID, "HEY," WILL YA?
ANY IDEA WHERE THESE GUYS CAME FROM?
THE LATE CRETACEOUS PERIOD.
Har har. NO, I MEANT--

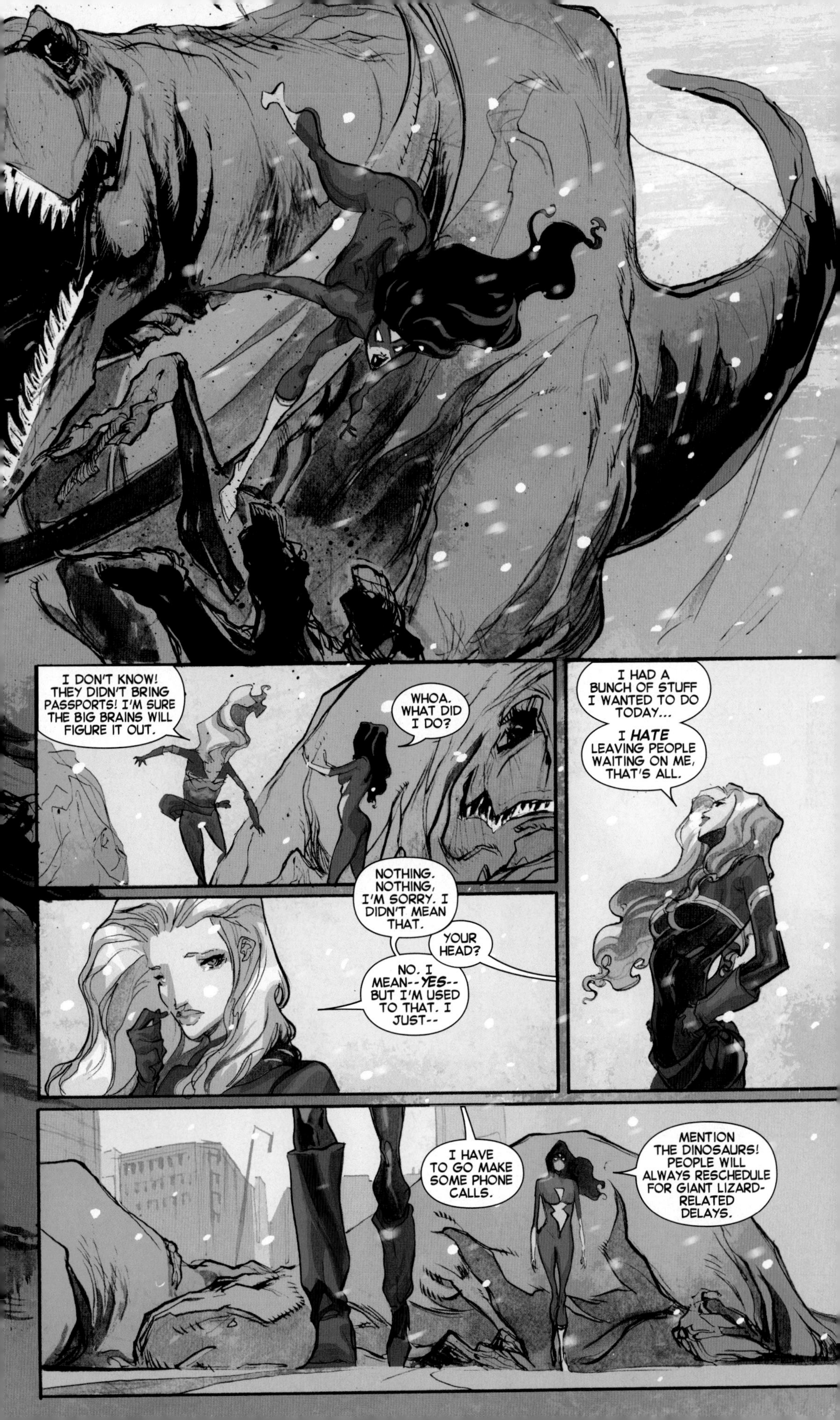

I DON'T KNOW! THEY DIDN'T BRING PASSPORTS! I'M SURE THE BIG BRAINS WILL FIGURE IT OUT.
WHOA. WHAT DID I DO?
I HAD A BUNCH OF STUFF I WANTED TO DO TODAY...
I *HATE* LEAVING PEOPLE WAITING ON ME, THAT'S ALL.
NOTHING. NOTHING, I'M SORRY. I DIDN'T MEAN THAT.
YOUR HEAD?
NO. I MEAN--*YES*--BUT I'M USED TO THAT. I JUST--
I HAVE TO GO MAKE SOME PHONE CALLS.
MENTION THE DINOSAURS! PEOPLE WILL ALWAYS RESCHEDULE FOR GIANT LIZARD-RELATED DELAYS.

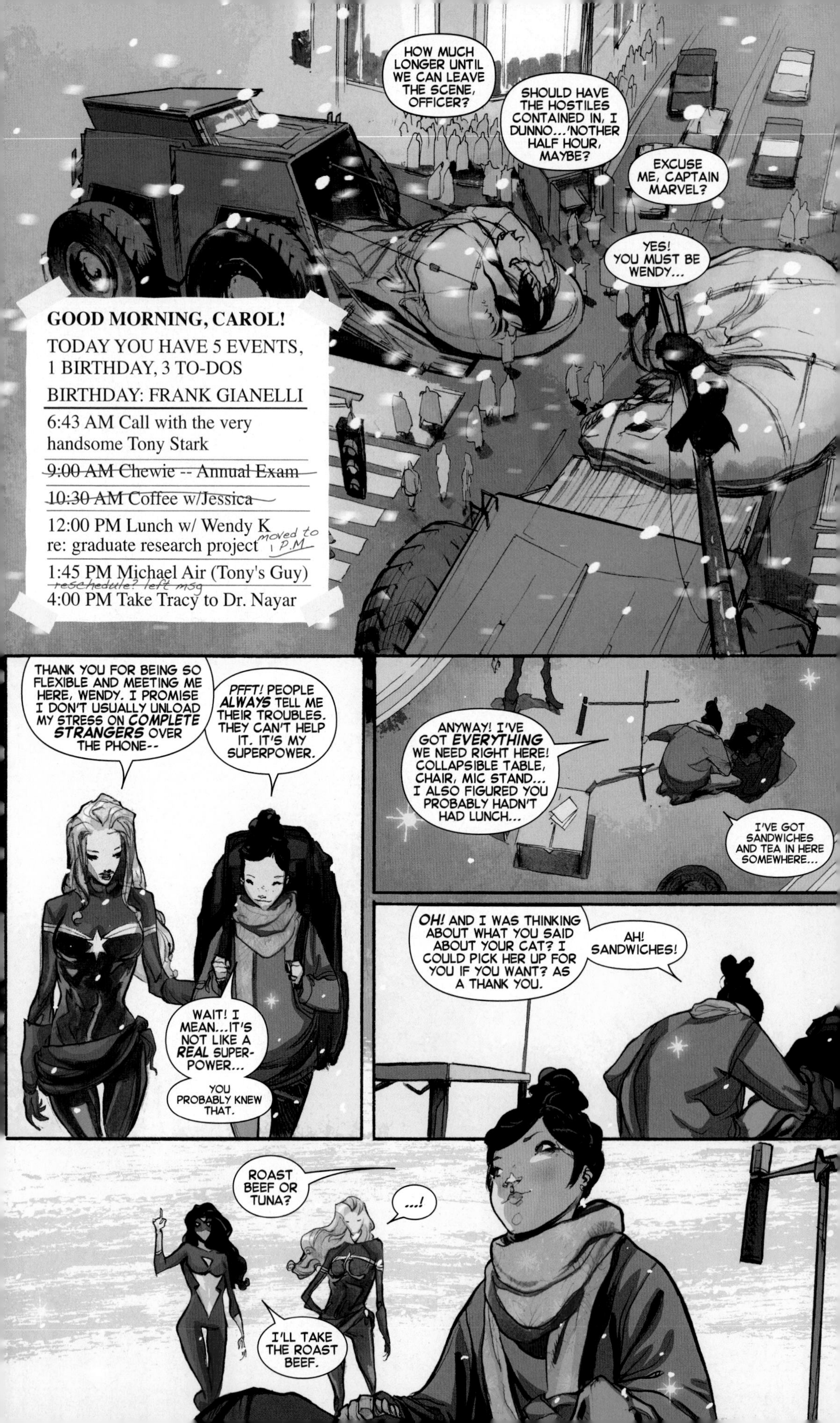
HOW MUCH LONGER UNTIL WE CAN LEAVE THE SCENE, OFFICER?
SHOULD HAVE THE HOSTILES CONTAINED IN, I DUNNO...'NOTHER HALF HOUR, MAYBE?
EXCUSE ME, CAPTAIN MARVEL?
YES! YOU MUST BE WENDY...
GOOD MORNING, CAROL!
TODAY YOU HAVE 5 EVENTS, 1 BIRTHDAY, 3 TO-DOS
BIRTHDAY: FRANK GIANELLI
6:43 AM Call with the very handsome Tony Stark
~~9:00 AM Chewie -- Annual Exam~~
~~10:30 AM Coffee w/Jessica~~
12:00 PM Lunch w/ Wendy K re: graduate research project ~~moved to 1 P.M~~
1:45 PM Michael Air (Tony's Guy) ~~reschedule? left msg~~
4:00 PM Take Tracy to Dr. Nayar
THANK YOU FOR BEING SO FLEXIBLE AND MEETING ME HERE, WENDY. I PROMISE I DON'T USUALLY UNLOAD MY STRESS ON COMPLETE STRANGERS OVER THE PHONE--
PFFT! PEOPLE ALWAYS TELL ME THEIR TROUBLES. THEY CAN'T HELP IT. IT'S MY SUPERPOWER.
WAIT! I MEAN...IT'S NOT LIKE A REAL SUPER-POWER...
YOU PROBABLY KNEW THAT.
ANYWAY! I'VE GOT EVERYTHING WE NEED RIGHT HERE! COLLAPSIBLE TABLE, CHAIR, MIC STAND... I ALSO FIGURED YOU PROBABLY HADN'T HAD LUNCH...
I'VE GOT SANDWICHES AND TEA IN HERE SOMEWHERE...
OH! AND I WAS THINKING ABOUT WHAT YOU SAID ABOUT YOUR CAT? I COULD PICK HER UP FOR YOU IF YOU WANT? AS A THANK YOU.
AH! SANDWICHES!
ROAST BEEF OR TUNA?
...!
I'LL TAKE THE ROAST BEEF.

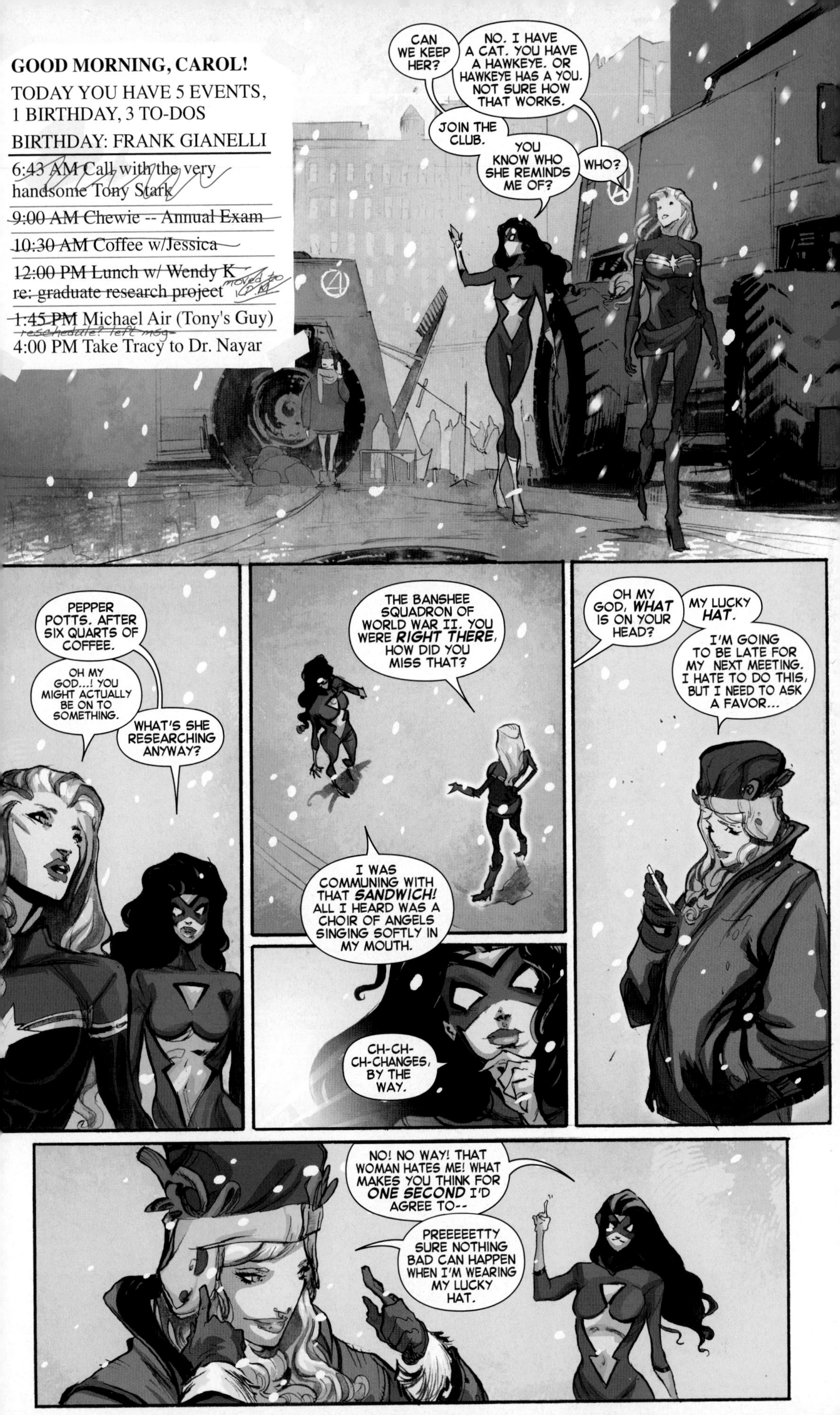
GOOD MORNING, CAROL!
TODAY YOU HAVE 5 EVENTS, 1 BIRTHDAY, 3 TO-DOS
BIRTHDAY: FRANK GIANELLI
6:43 AM Call with the very handsome Tony Stark
9:00 AM Chewie -- Annual Exam
10:30 AM Coffee w/Jessica
12:00 PM Lunch w/ Wendy K re: graduate research project
1:45 PM Michael Air (Tony's Guy)
reschedule? left msg
4:00 PM Take Tracy to Dr. Nayar
CAN WE KEEP HER?
NO. I HAVE A CAT. YOU HAVE A HAWKEYE. OR HAWKEYE HAS A YOU. NOT SURE HOW THAT WORKS.
JOIN THE CLUB.
YOU KNOW WHO SHE REMINDS ME OF?
WHO?
PEPPER POTTS. AFTER SIX QUARTS OF COFFEE.
OH MY GOD...! YOU MIGHT ACTUALLY BE ON TO SOMETHING.
WHAT'S SHE RESEARCHING ANYWAY?
THE BANSHEE SQUADRON OF WORLD WAR II. YOU WERE RIGHT THERE, HOW DID YOU MISS THAT?
I WAS COMMUNING WITH THAT SANDWICH! ALL I HEARD WAS A CHOIR OF ANGELS SINGING SOFTLY IN MY MOUTH.
CH-CH-CH-CHANGES, BY THE WAY.
OH MY GOD, WHAT IS ON YOUR HEAD?
MY LUCKY HAT.
I'M GOING TO BE LATE FOR MY NEXT MEETING. I HATE TO DO THIS, BUT I NEED TO ASK A FAVOR...
NO! NO WAY! THAT WOMAN HATES ME! WHAT MAKES YOU THINK FOR ONE SECOND I'D AGREE TO--
PREEEEETTY SURE NOTHING BAD CAN HAPPEN WHEN I'M WEARING MY LUCKY HAT.

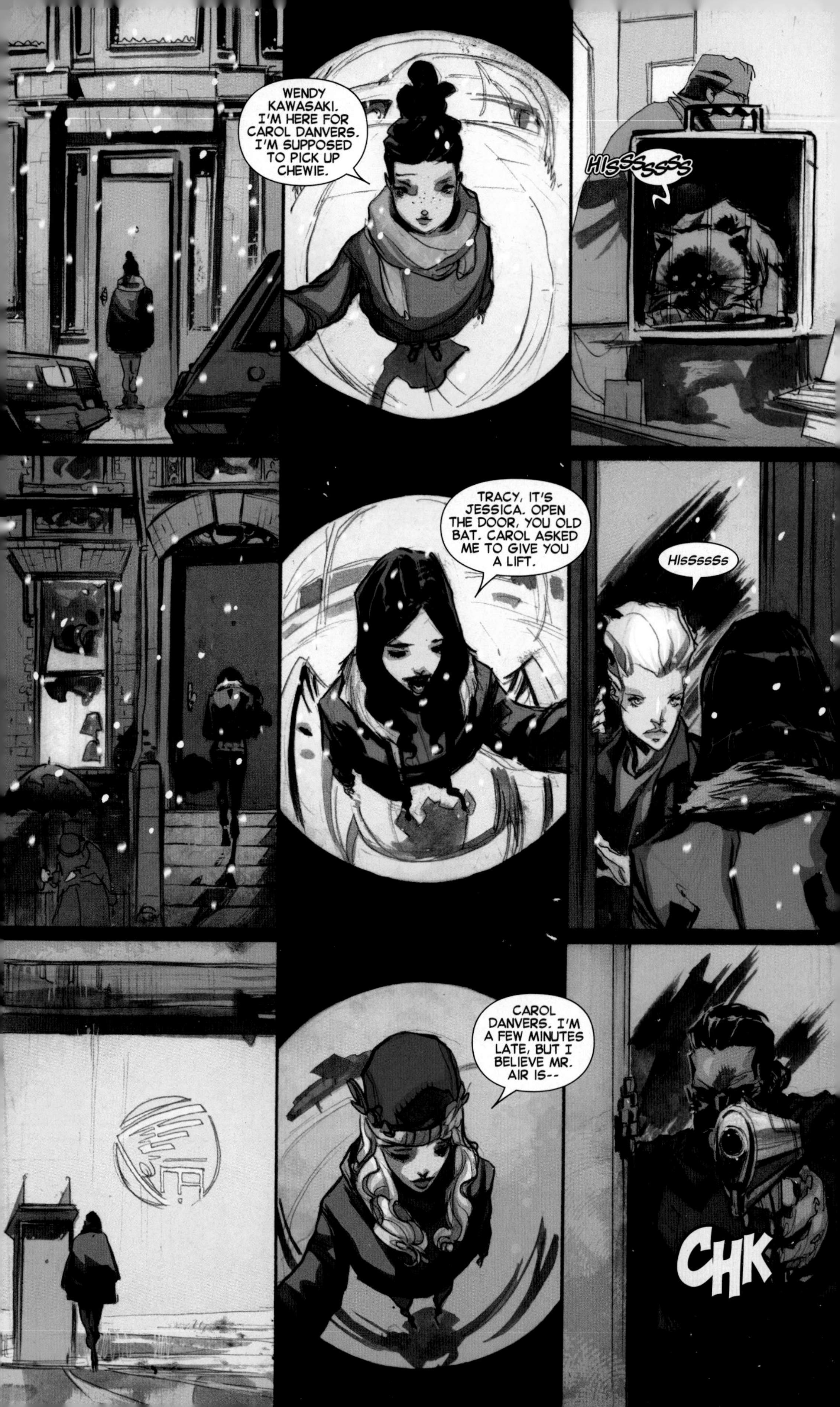
WENDY KAWASAKI. I'M HERE FOR CAROL DANVERS. I'M SUPPOSED TO PICK UP CHEWIE.
HISSSSSSS
TRACY, IT'S JESSICA. OPEN THE DOOR, YOU OLD BAT. CAROL ASKED ME TO GIVE YOU A LIFT.
HISSSSSS
CAROL DANVERS. I'M A FEW MINUTES LATE, BUT I BELIEVE MR. AIR IS--
CHK

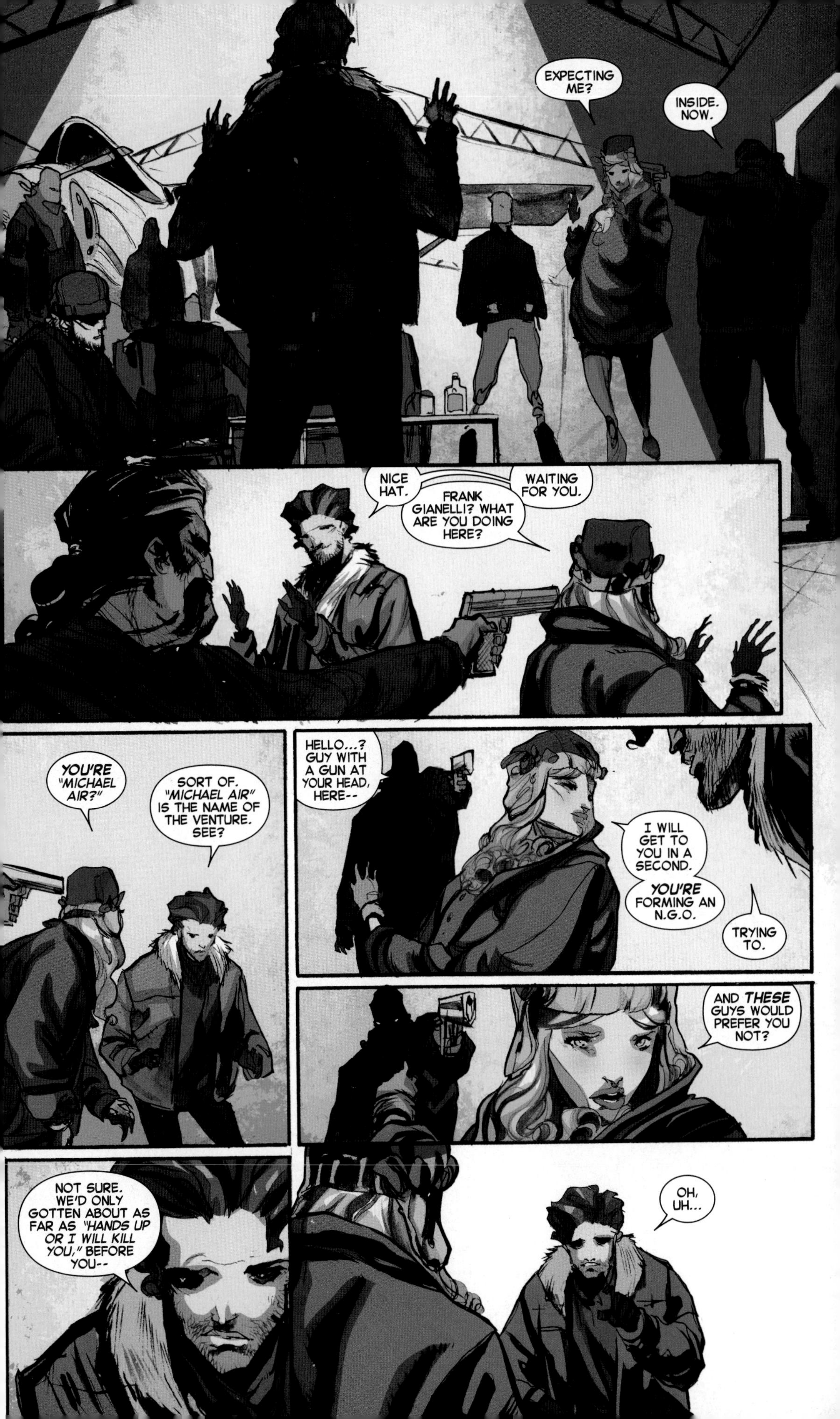
EXPECTING ME?
INSIDE. NOW.
NICE HAT.
WAITING FOR YOU.
FRANK GIANELLI? WHAT ARE YOU DOING HERE?
YOU'RE "MICHAEL AIR?"
SORT OF. "MICHAEL AIR" IS THE NAME OF THE VENTURE. SEE?
HELLO...? GUY WITH A GUN AT YOUR HEAD, HERE--
I WILL GET TO YOU IN A SECOND. YOU'RE FORMING AN N.G.O.
TRYING TO.
AND THESE GUYS WOULD PREFER YOU NOT?
NOT SURE. WE'D ONLY GOTTEN ABOUT AS FAR AS "HANDS UP OR I WILL KILL YOU," BEFORE YOU--
OH, UH...

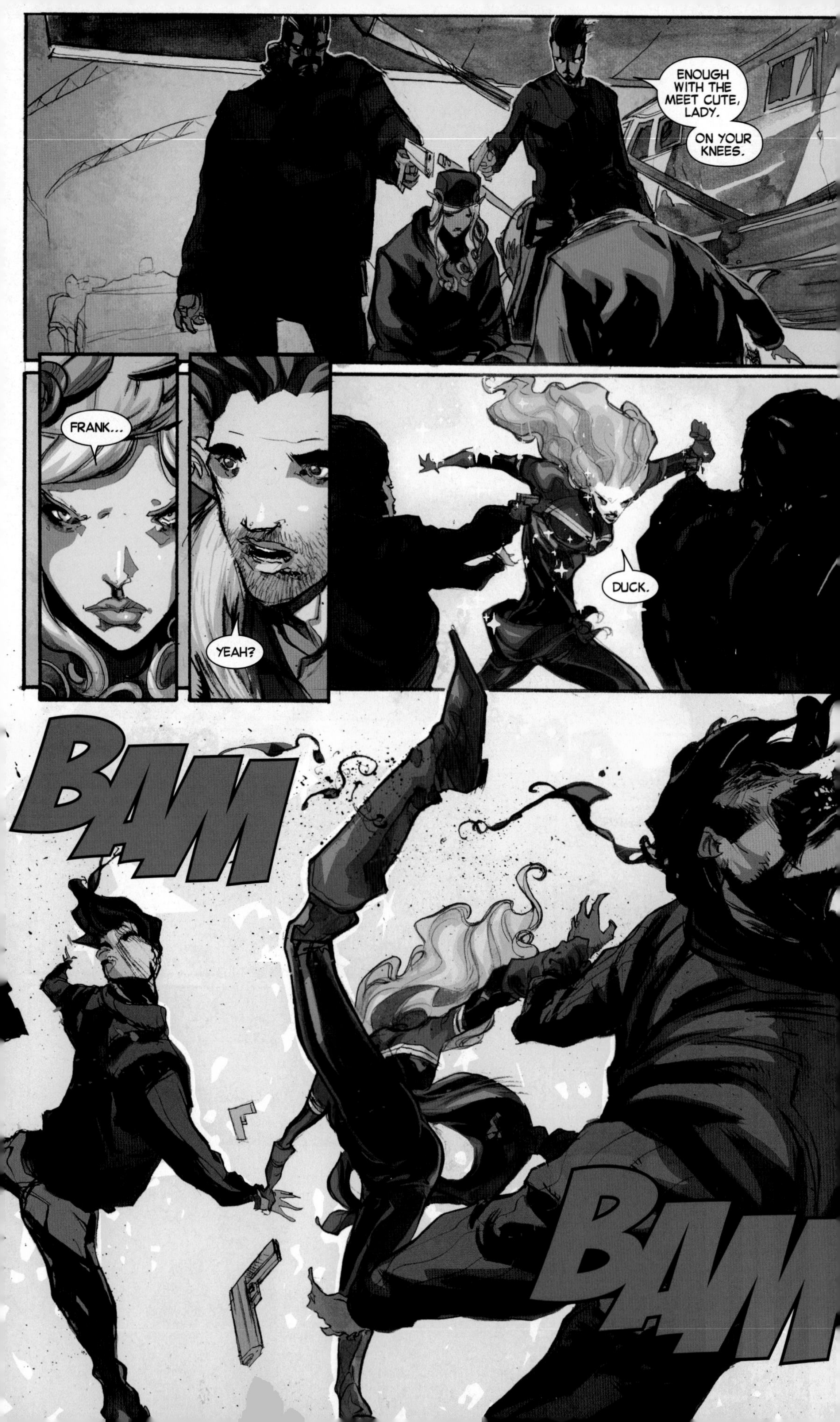
ENOUGH WITH THE MEET CUTE, LADY.
ON YOUR KNEES.
FRANK...
YEAH?
DUCK.
BAM
BAM

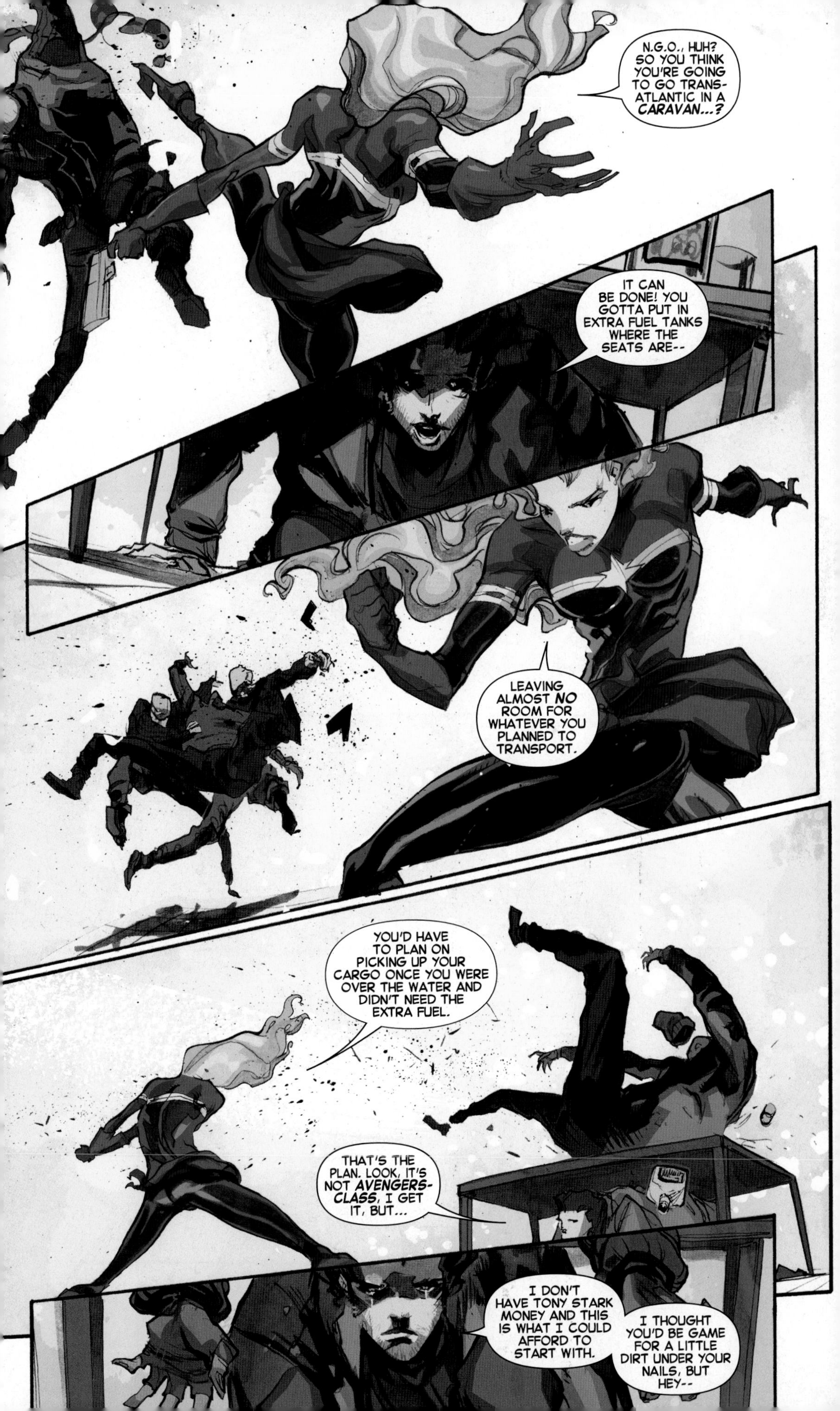
N.G.O., HUH? SO YOU THINK YOU'RE GOING TO GO TRANS-ATLANTIC IN A CARAVAN...?
IT CAN BE DONE! YOU GOTTA PUT IN EXTRA FUEL TANKS WHERE THE SEATS ARE--
LEAVING ALMOST NO ROOM FOR WHATEVER YOU PLANNED TO TRANSPORT.
YOU'D HAVE TO PLAN ON PICKING UP YOUR CARGO ONCE YOU WERE OVER THE WATER AND DIDN'T NEED THE EXTRA FUEL.
THAT'S THE PLAN. LOOK, IT'S NOT AVENGERS-CLASS, I GET IT, BUT...
I DON'T HAVE TONY STARK MONEY AND THIS IS WHAT I COULD AFFORD TO START WITH.
I THOUGHT YOU'D BE GAME FOR A LITTLE DIRT UNDER YOUR NAILS, BUT HEY--

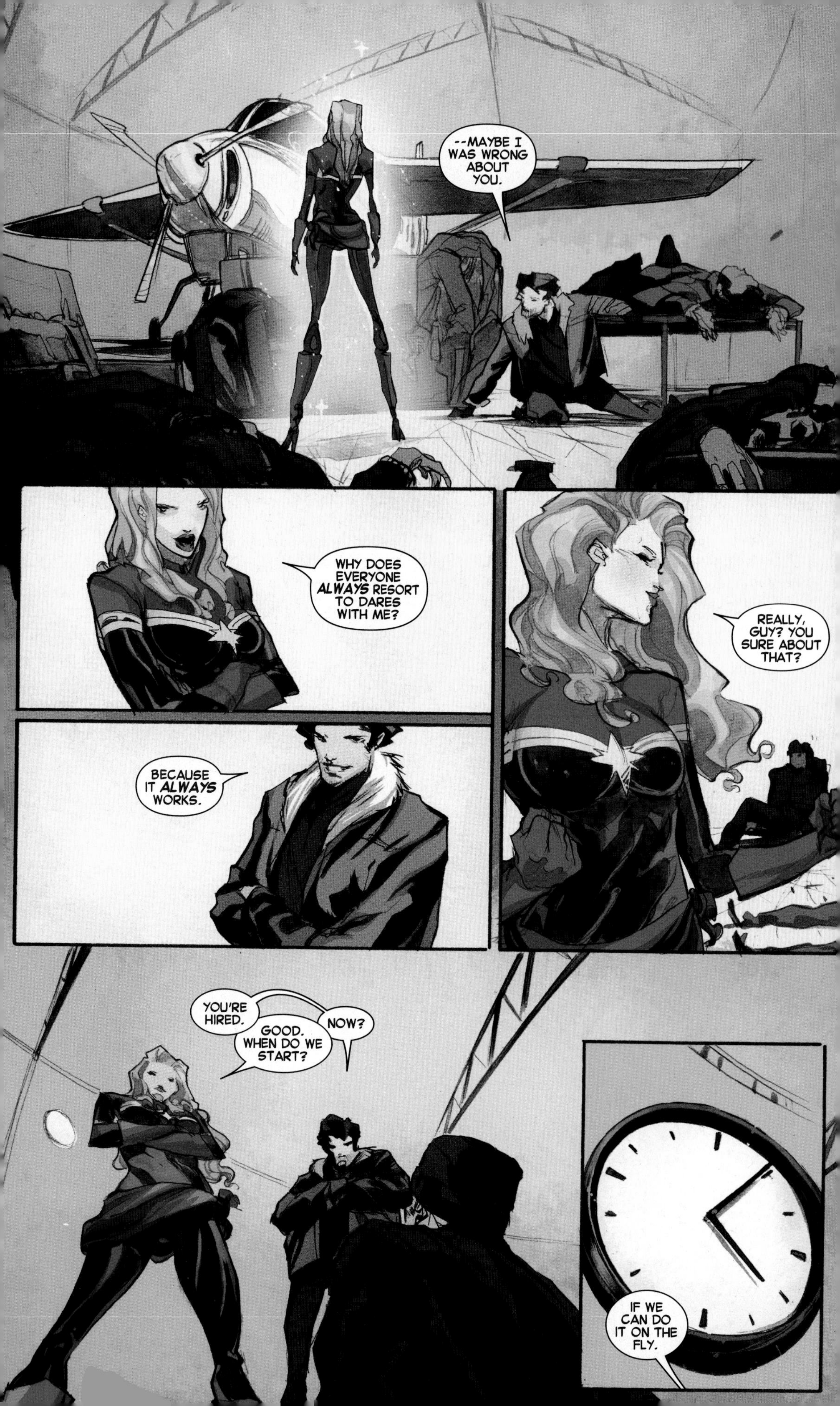
--MAYBE I WAS WRONG ABOUT YOU.
WHY DOES EVERYONE ALWAYS RESORT TO DARES WITH ME?
REALLY, GUY? YOU SURE ABOUT THAT?
BECAUSE IT ALWAYS WORKS.
YOU'RE HIRED.
GOOD. WHEN DO WE START?
NOW?
IF WE CAN DO IT ON THE FLY.

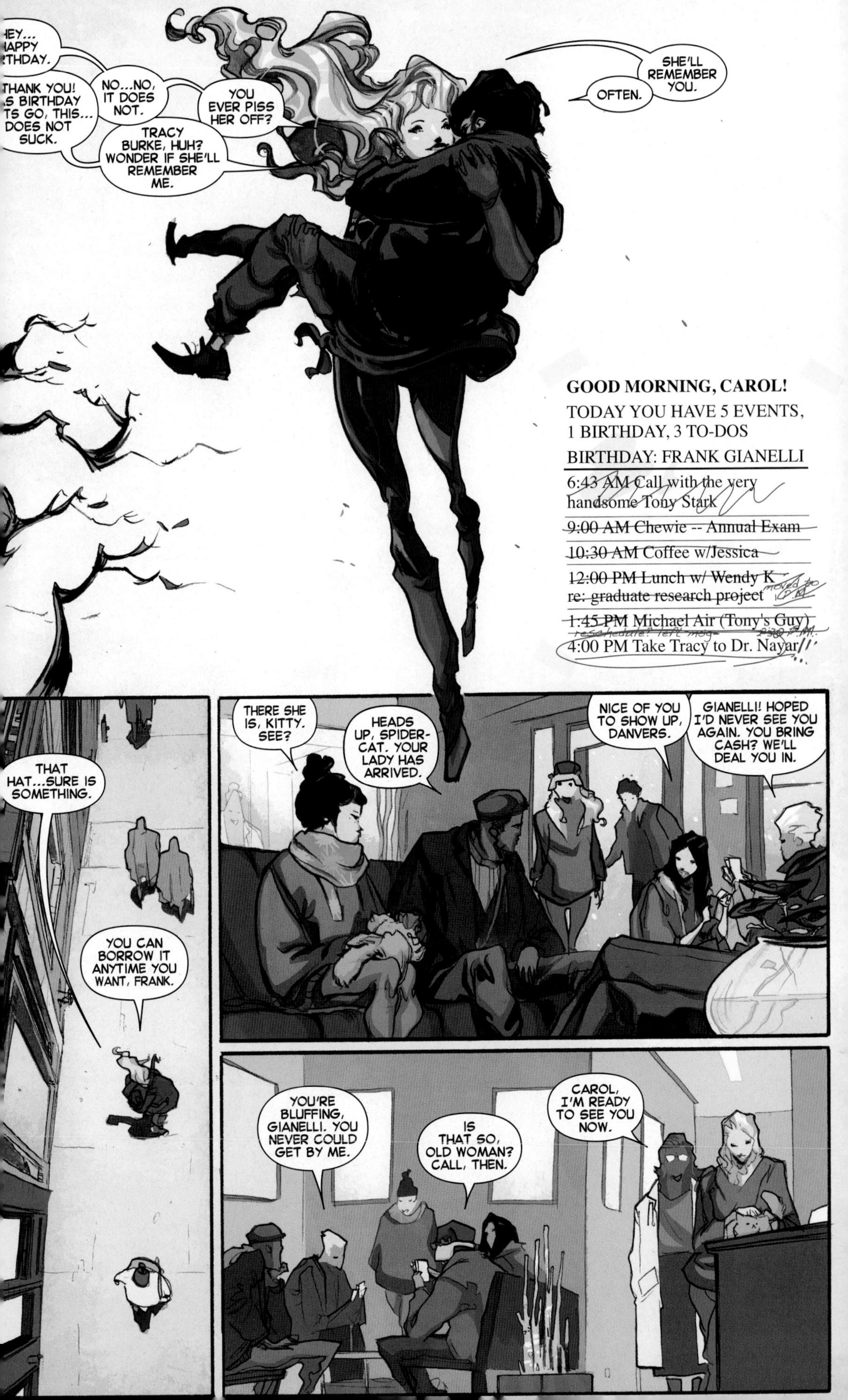

HEY... HAPPY BIRTHDAY.
THANK YOU! AS BIRTHDAYS GO, THIS... DOES NOT SUCK.
NO...NO, IT DOES NOT.
TRACY BURKE, HUH? WONDER IF SHE'LL REMEMBER ME.
YOU EVER PISS HER OFF?
SHE'LL REMEMBER YOU.
OFTEN.
GOOD MORNING, CAROL!
TODAY YOU HAVE 5 EVENTS, 1 BIRTHDAY, 3 TO-DOS
BIRTHDAY: FRANK GIANELLI
6:43 AM Call with the very handsome Tony Stark
9:00 AM Chewie -- Annual Exam
10:30 AM Coffee w/Jessica
12:00 PM Lunch w/ Wendy K re: graduate research project
1:45 PM Michael Air (Tony's Guy)
4:00 PM Take Tracy to Dr. Nayar!!!
THAT HAT...SURE IS SOMETHING.
YOU CAN BORROW IT ANYTIME YOU WANT, FRANK.
THERE SHE IS, KITTY. SEE?
HEADS UP, SPIDER-CAT. YOUR LADY HAS ARRIVED.
NICE OF YOU TO SHOW UP, DANVERS.
GIANELLI! HOPED I'D NEVER SEE YOU AGAIN. YOU BRING CASH? WE'LL DEAL YOU IN.
YOU'RE BLUFFING, GIANELLI. YOU NEVER COULD GET BY ME.
IS THAT SO, OLD WOMAN? CALL, THEN.
CAROL, I'M READY TO SEE YOU NOW.

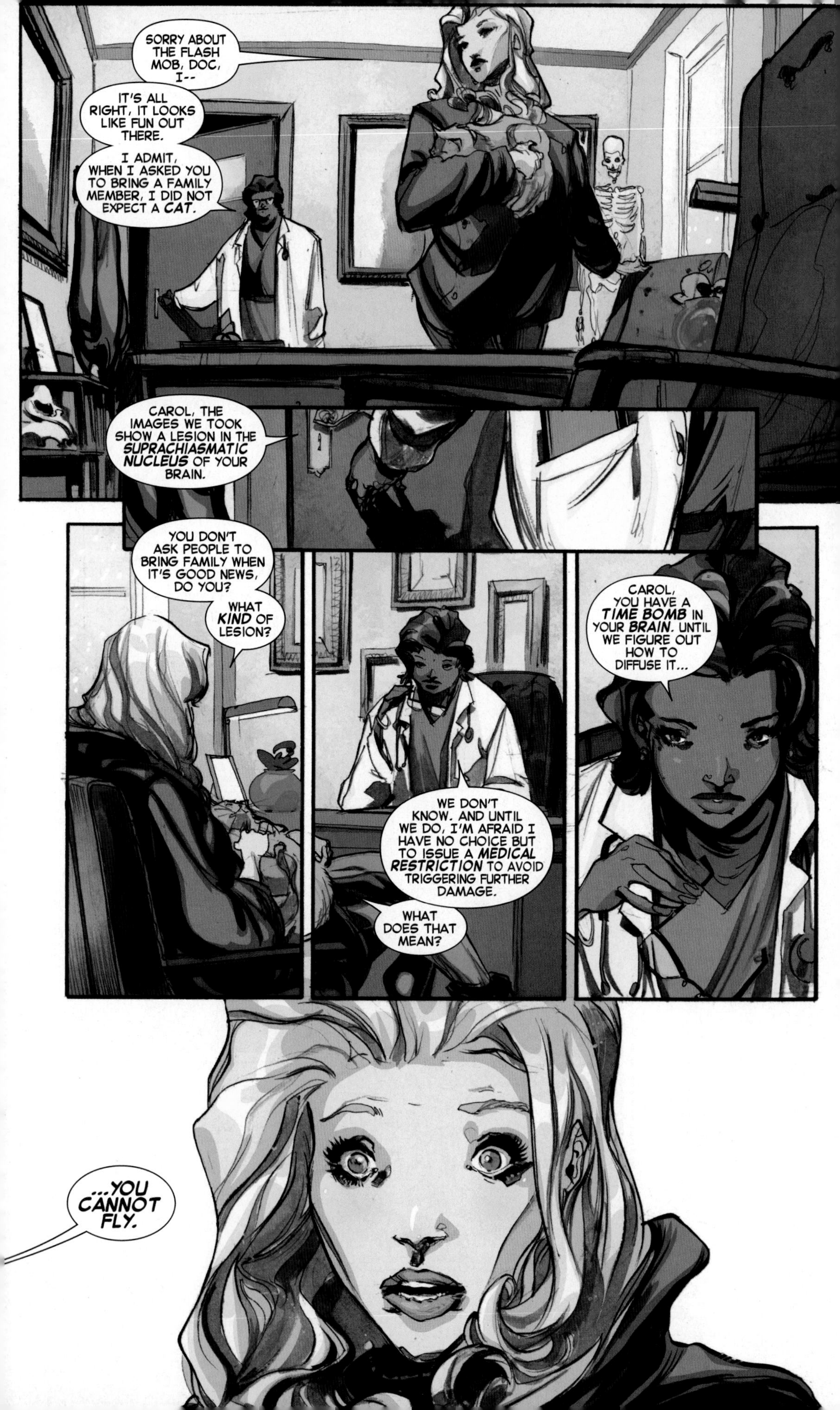

SORRY ABOUT THE FLASH MOB, DOC, I--
IT'S ALL RIGHT, IT LOOKS LIKE FUN OUT THERE.
I ADMIT, WHEN I ASKED YOU TO BRING A FAMILY MEMBER, I DID NOT EXPECT A CAT.
CAROL, THE IMAGES WE TOOK SHOW A LESION IN THE SUPRACHIASMATIC NUCLEUS OF YOUR BRAIN.
YOU DON'T ASK PEOPLE TO BRING FAMILY WHEN IT'S GOOD NEWS, DO YOU?
WHAT KIND OF LESION?
WE DON'T KNOW. AND UNTIL WE DO, I'M AFRAID I HAVE NO CHOICE BUT TO ISSUE A MEDICAL RESTRICTION TO AVOID TRIGGERING FURTHER DAMAGE.
WHAT DOES THAT MEAN?
CAROL, YOU HAVE A TIME BOMB IN YOUR BRAIN. UNTIL WE FIGURE OUT HOW TO DIFFUSE IT...
...YOU CANNOT FLY.

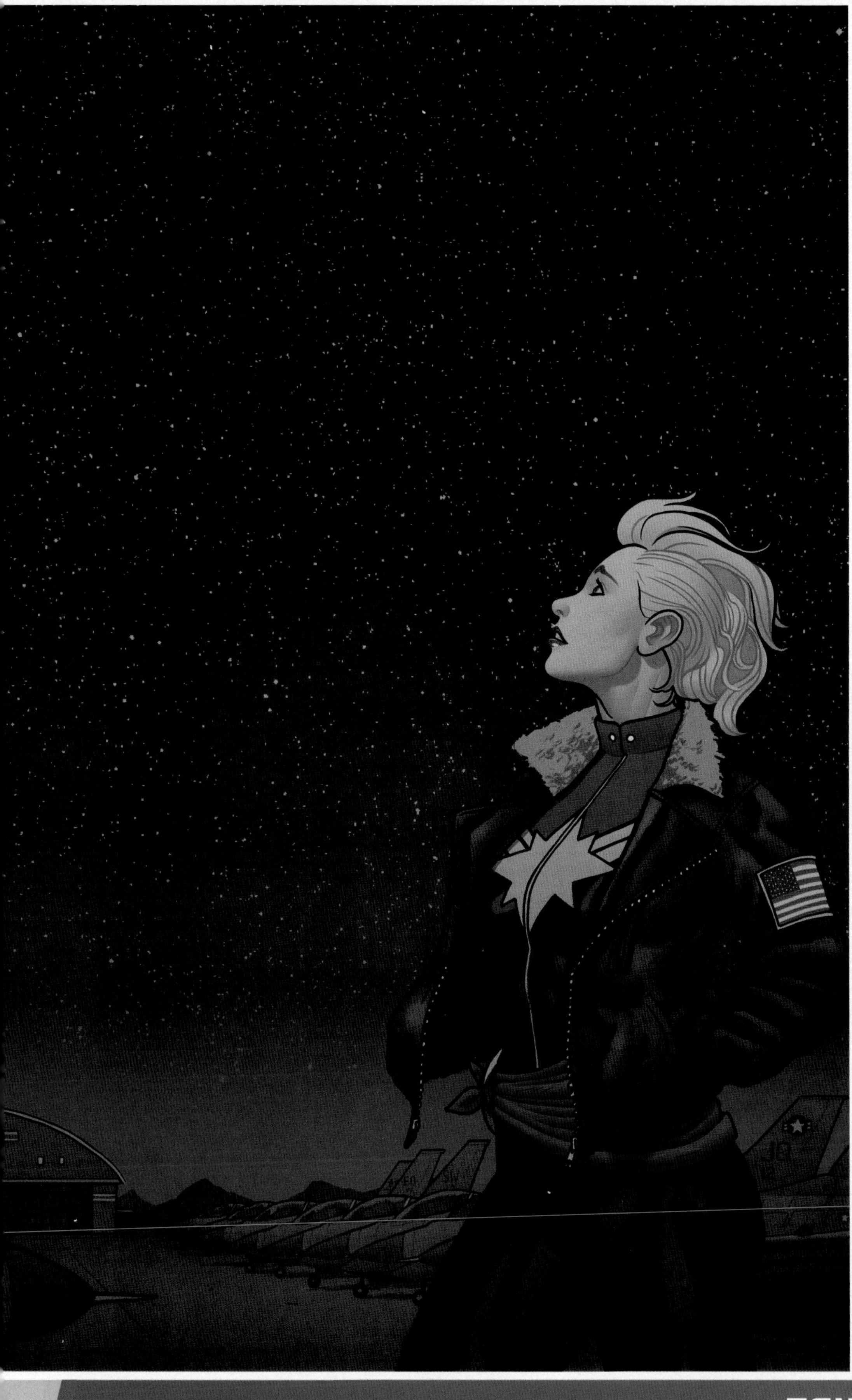

TEN

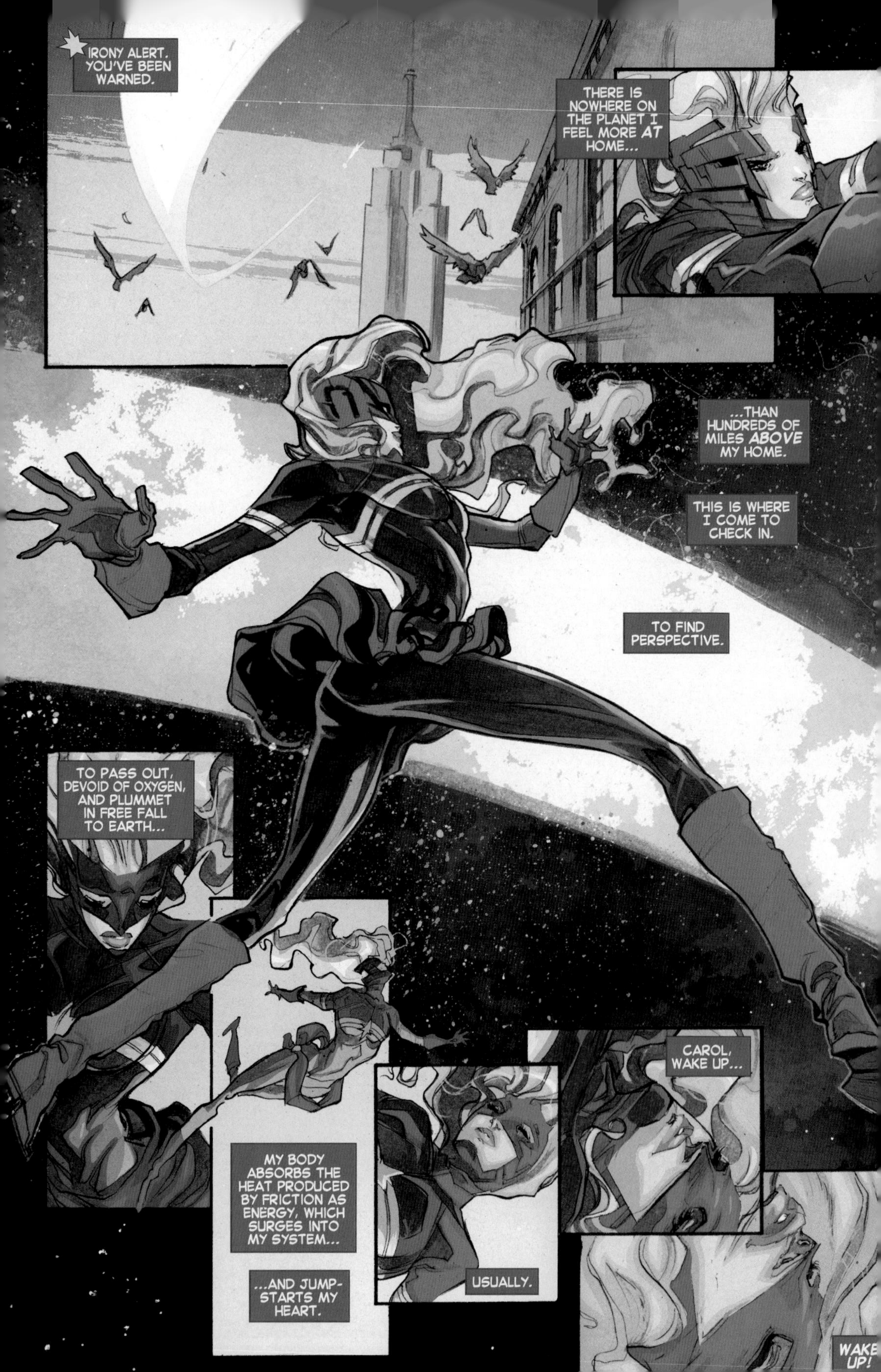

IRONY ALERT. YOU'VE BEEN WARNED.
THERE IS NOWHERE ON THE PLANET I FEEL MORE AT HOME...
...THAN HUNDREDS OF MILES ABOVE MY HOME.
THIS IS WHERE I COME TO CHECK IN.
TO FIND PERSPECTIVE.
TO PASS OUT, DEVOID OF OXYGEN, AND PLUMMET IN FREE FALL TO EARTH...
MY BODY ABSORBS THE HEAT PRODUCED BY FRICTION AS ENERGY, WHICH SURGES INTO MY SYSTEM...
...AND JUMP-STARTS MY HEART.
USUALLY.
CAROL, WAKE UP...
WAKE UP!

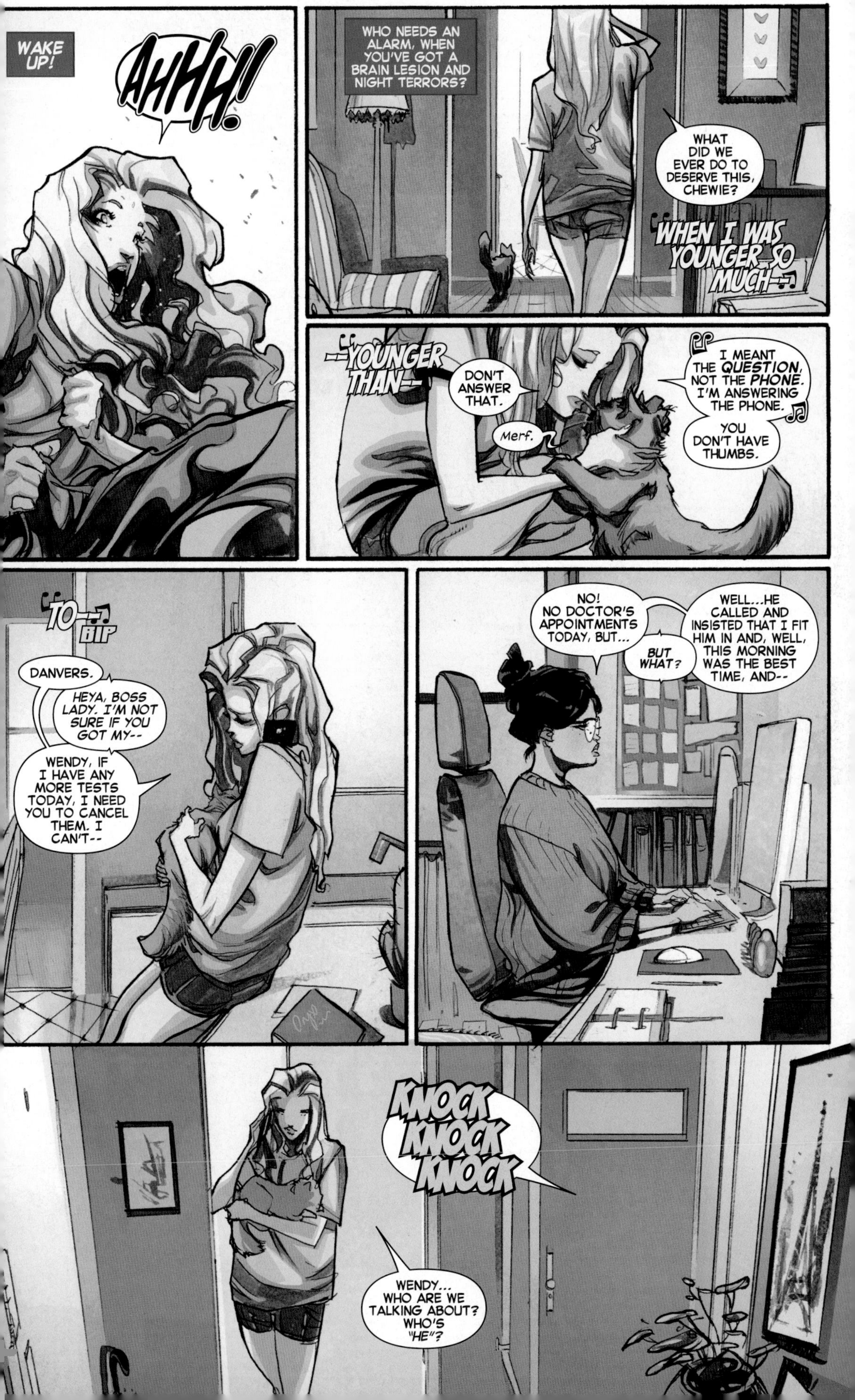
WAKE UP!
AHHH!
WHO NEEDS AN ALARM, WHEN YOU'VE GOT A BRAIN LESION AND NIGHT TERRORS?
WHAT DID WE EVER DO TO DESERVE THIS, CHEWIE?
WHEN I WAS YOUNGER SO MUCH
YOUNGER THAN
DON'T ANSWER THAT.
Merf.
I MEANT THE QUESTION, NOT THE PHONE. I'M ANSWERING THE PHONE.
YOU DON'T HAVE THUMBS.
TO BIP
DANVERS.
HEYA, BOSS LADY. I'M NOT SURE IF YOU GOT MY--
WENDY, IF I HAVE ANY MORE TESTS TODAY, I NEED YOU TO CANCEL THEM. I CAN'T--
NO! NO DOCTOR'S APPOINTMENTS TODAY, BUT...
BUT WHAT?
WELL...HE CALLED AND INSISTED THAT I FIT HIM IN AND, WELL, THIS MORNING WAS THE BEST TIME, AND--
KNOCK KNOCK KNOCK
WENDY... WHO ARE WE TALKING ABOUT? WHO'S "HE"?

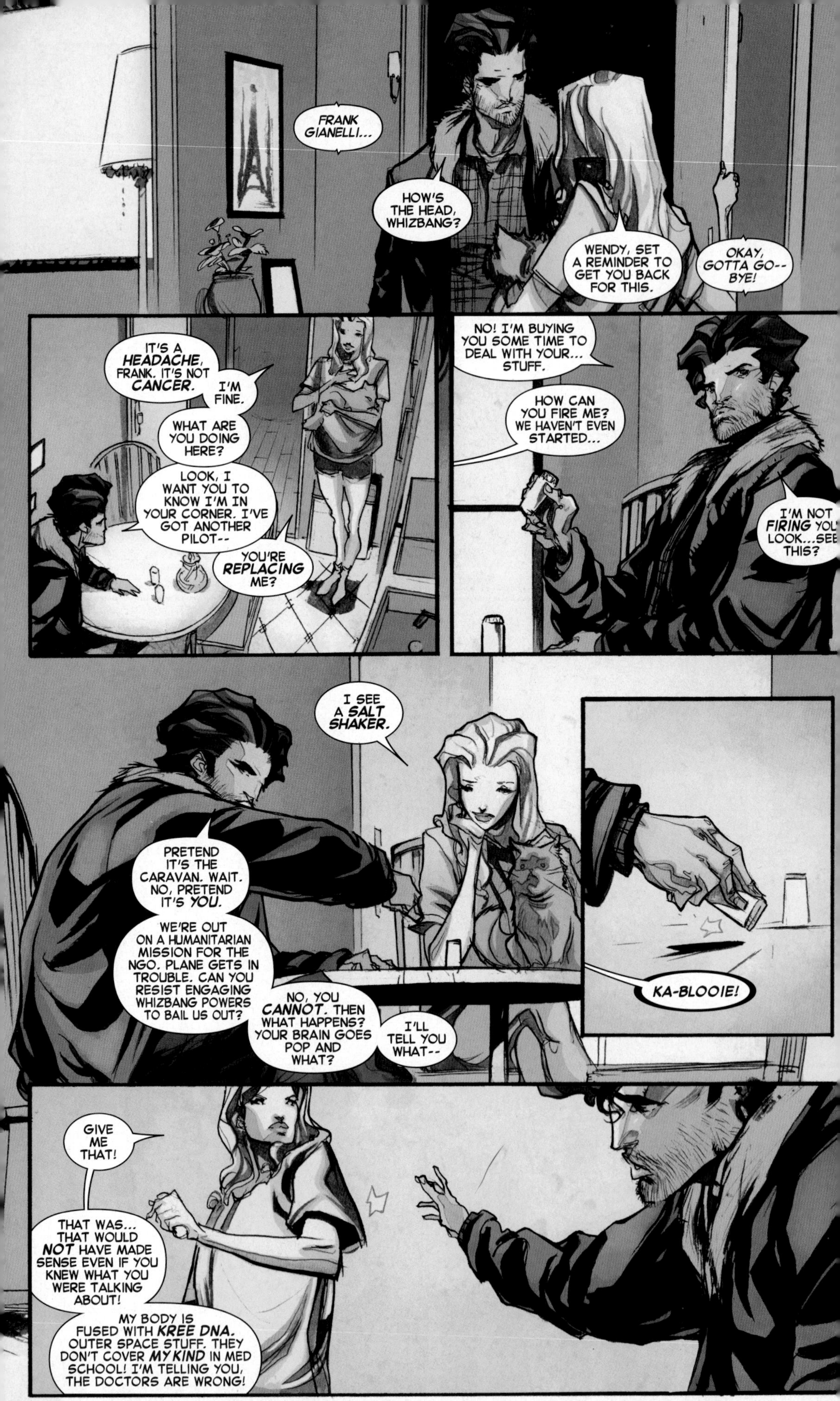
FRANK GIANELLI...
HOW'S THE HEAD, WHIZBANG?
WENDY, SET A REMINDER TO GET YOU BACK FOR THIS.
OKAY, GOTTA GO-- BYE!
IT'S A HEADACHE, FRANK. IT'S NOT CANCER.
I'M FINE.
WHAT ARE YOU DOING HERE?
LOOK, I WANT YOU TO KNOW I'M IN YOUR CORNER. I'VE GOT ANOTHER PILOT--
YOU'RE REPLACING ME?
NO! I'M BUYING YOU SOME TIME TO DEAL WITH YOUR... STUFF.
HOW CAN YOU FIRE ME? WE HAVEN'T EVEN STARTED...
I'M NOT FIRING YOU. LOOK...SEE THIS?
I SEE A SALT SHAKER.
PRETEND IT'S THE CARAVAN. WAIT. NO, PRETEND IT'S YOU.
WE'RE OUT ON A HUMANITARIAN MISSION FOR THE NGO. PLANE GETS IN TROUBLE. CAN YOU RESIST ENGAGING WHIZBANG POWERS TO BAIL US OUT?
NO, YOU CANNOT. THEN WHAT HAPPENS? YOUR BRAIN GOES POP AND WHAT?
I'LL TELL YOU WHAT--
KA-BLOOIE!
GIVE ME THAT!
THAT WAS... THAT WOULD NOT HAVE MADE SENSE EVEN IF YOU KNEW WHAT YOU WERE TALKING ABOUT!
MY BODY IS FUSED WITH KREE DNA. OUTER SPACE STUFF. THEY DON'T COVER MY KIND IN MED SCHOOL! I'M TELLING YOU, THE DOCTORS ARE WRONG!

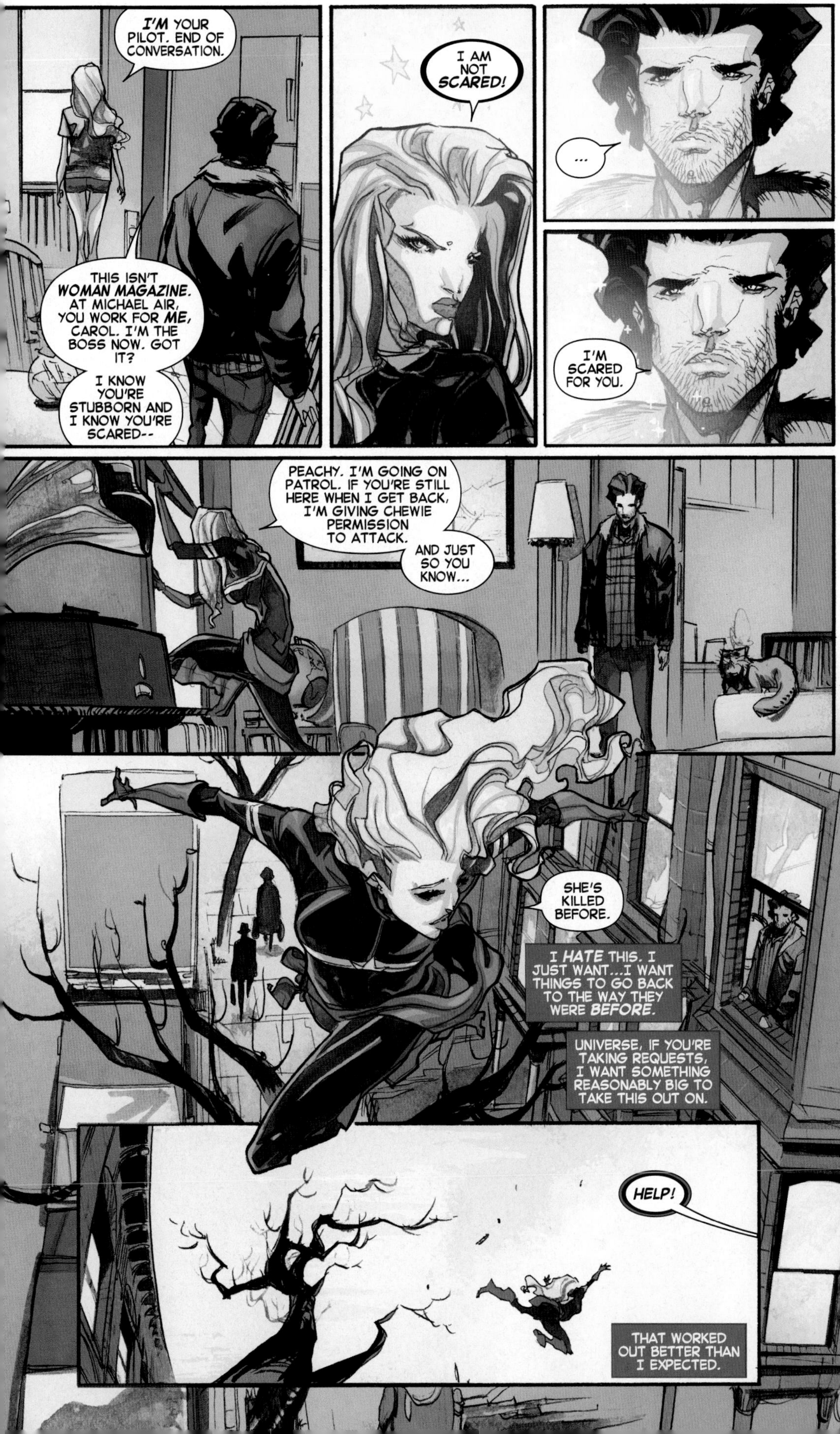

I'M YOUR PILOT. END OF CONVERSATION.
THIS ISN'T WOMAN MAGAZINE. AT MICHAEL AIR, YOU WORK FOR ME, CAROL. I'M THE BOSS NOW. GOT IT?
I KNOW YOU'RE STUBBORN AND I KNOW YOU'RE SCARED--
I AM NOT SCARED!
...
I'M SCARED FOR YOU.
PEACHY. I'M GOING ON PATROL. IF YOU'RE STILL HERE WHEN I GET BACK, I'M GIVING CHEWIE PERMISSION TO ATTACK.
AND JUST SO YOU KNOW...
SHE'S KILLED BEFORE.
I HATE THIS. I JUST WANT...I WANT THINGS TO GO BACK TO THE WAY THEY WERE BEFORE.
UNIVERSE, IF YOU'RE TAKING REQUESTS, I WANT SOMETHING REASONABLY BIG TO TAKE THIS OUT ON.
HELP!
THAT WORKED OUT BETTER THAN I EXPECTED.

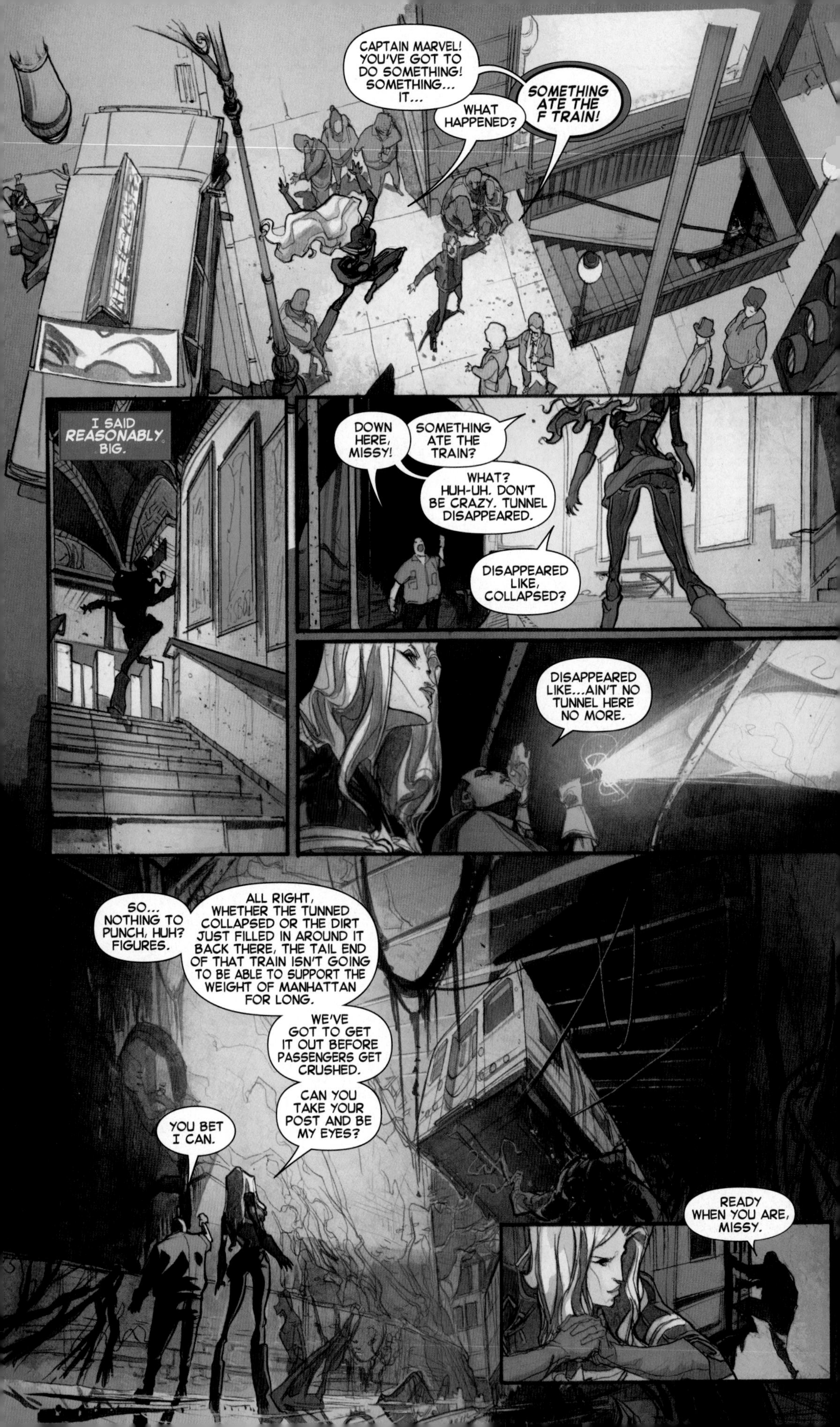
CAPTAIN MARVEL! YOU'VE GOT TO DO SOMETHING! SOMETHING... IT...
WHAT HAPPENED?
SOMETHING ATE THE F TRAIN!
I SAID REASONABLY BIG.
DOWN HERE, MISSY!
SOMETHING ATE THE TRAIN?
WHAT? HUH-UH. DON'T BE CRAZY. TUNNEL DISAPPEARED.
DISAPPEARED LIKE, COLLAPSED?
DISAPPEARED LIKE...AIN'T NO TUNNEL HERE NO MORE.
SO... NOTHING TO PUNCH, HUH? FIGURES.
ALL RIGHT, WHETHER THE TUNNED COLLAPSED OR THE DIRT JUST FILLED IN AROUND IT BACK THERE, THE TAIL END OF THAT TRAIN ISN'T GOING TO BE ABLE TO SUPPORT THE WEIGHT OF MANHATTAN FOR LONG.
WE'VE GOT TO GET IT OUT BEFORE PASSENGERS GET CRUSHED.
CAN YOU TAKE YOUR POST AND BE MY EYES?
YOU BET I CAN.
READY WHEN YOU ARE, MISSY.

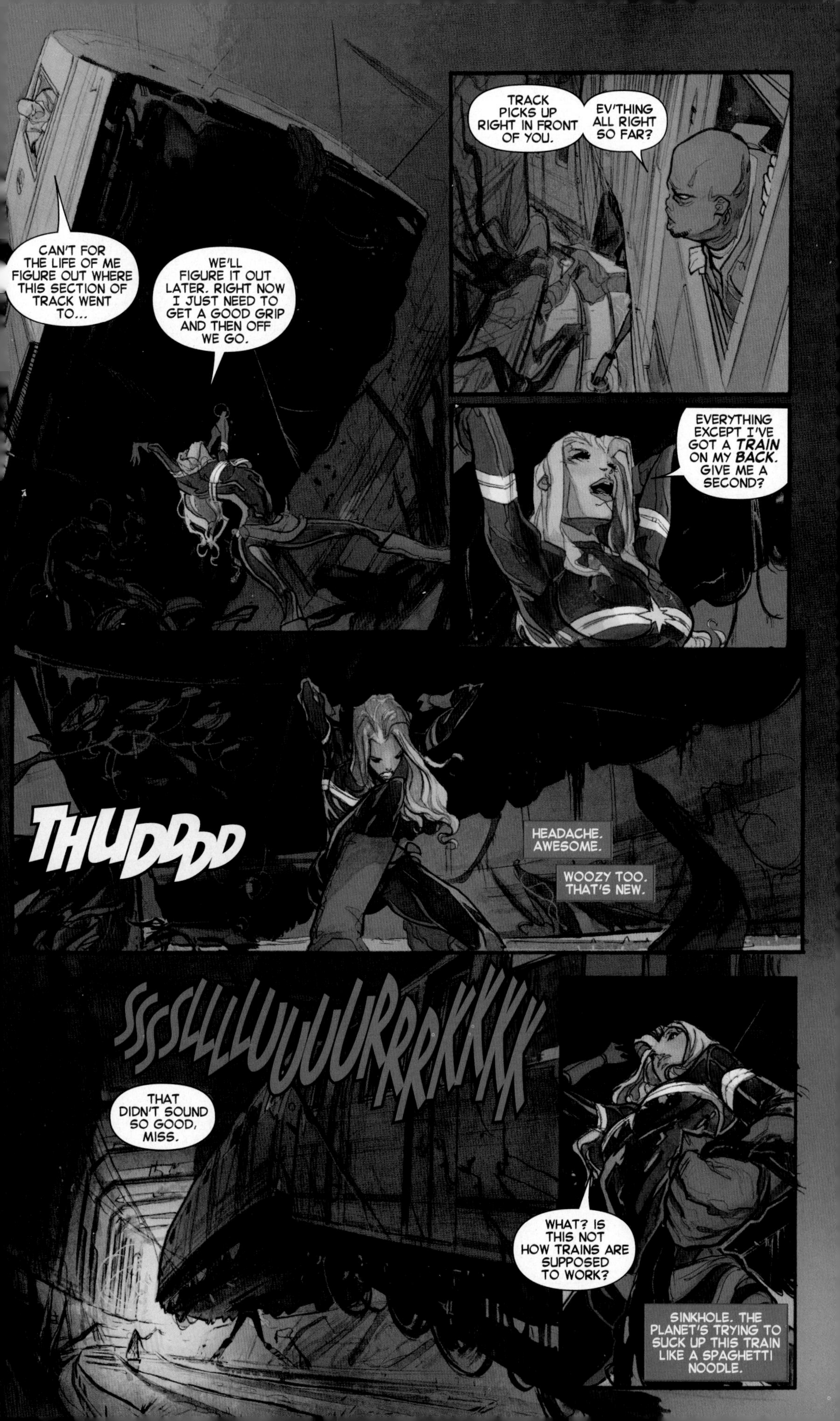
CAN'T FOR THE LIFE OF ME FIGURE OUT WHERE THIS SECTION OF TRACK WENT TO...
WE'LL FIGURE IT OUT LATER. RIGHT NOW I JUST NEED TO GET A GOOD GRIP AND THEN OFF WE GO.
TRACK PICKS UP RIGHT IN FRONT OF YOU.
EV'THING ALL RIGHT SO FAR?
EVERYTHING EXCEPT I'VE GOT A *TRAIN* ON MY *BACK*. GIVE ME A SECOND?
THUDDDD
HEADACHE. AWESOME.
WOOZY TOO. THAT'S NEW.
SSSSLLLLUUUURRRKKKK
THAT DIDN'T SOUND SO GOOD, MISS.
WHAT? IS THIS NOT HOW TRAINS ARE SUPPOSED TO WORK?
SINKHOLE. THE PLANET'S TRYING TO SUCK UP THIS TRAIN LIKE A SPAGHETTI NOODLE.

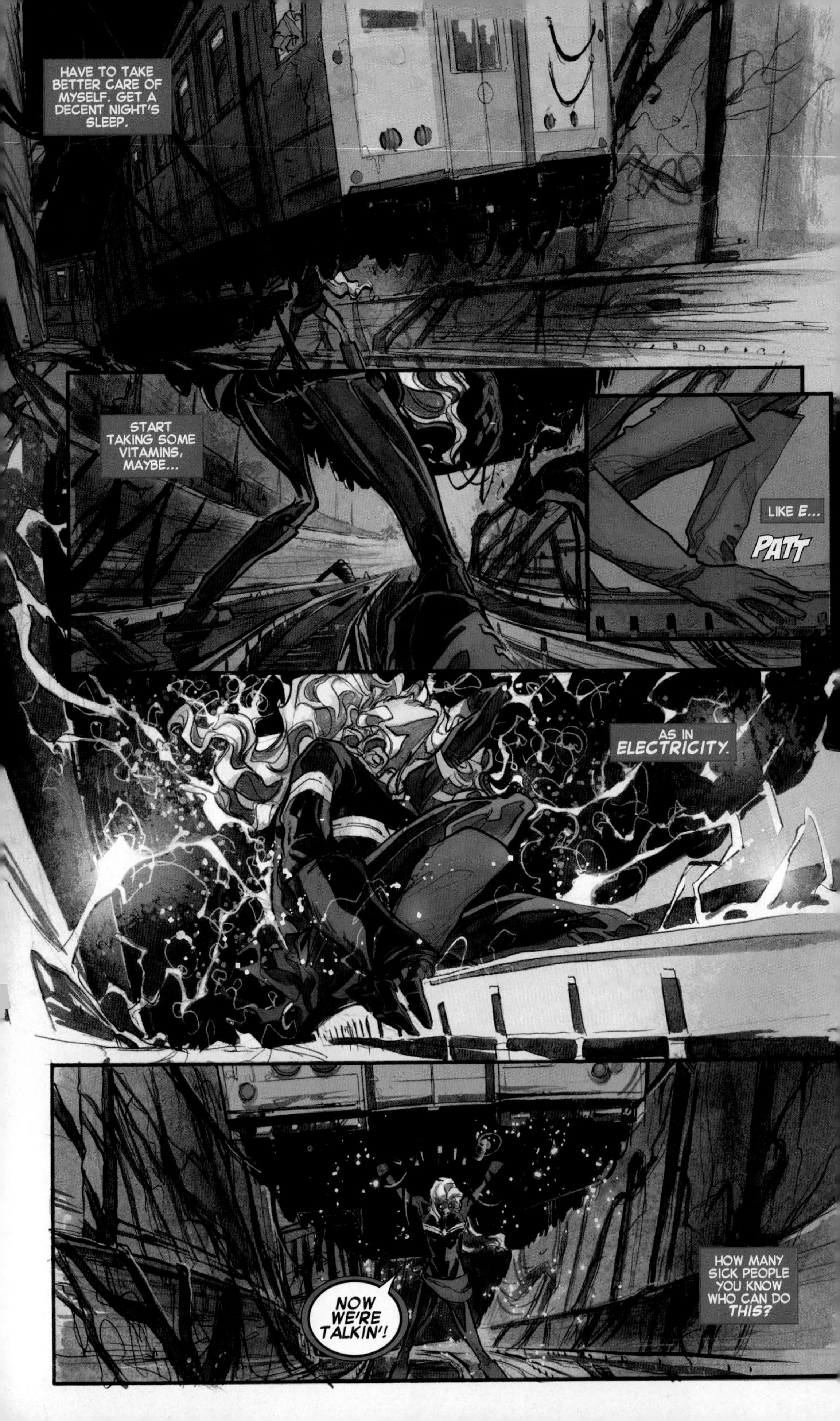

HAVE TO TAKE BETTER CARE OF MYSELF. GET A DECENT NIGHT'S SLEEP.
START TAKING SOME VITAMINS, MAYBE...
LIKE E...
PATT
AS IN ELECTRICITY.
NOW WE'RE TALKIN'!
HOW MANY SICK PEOPLE YOU KNOW WHO CAN DO THIS?

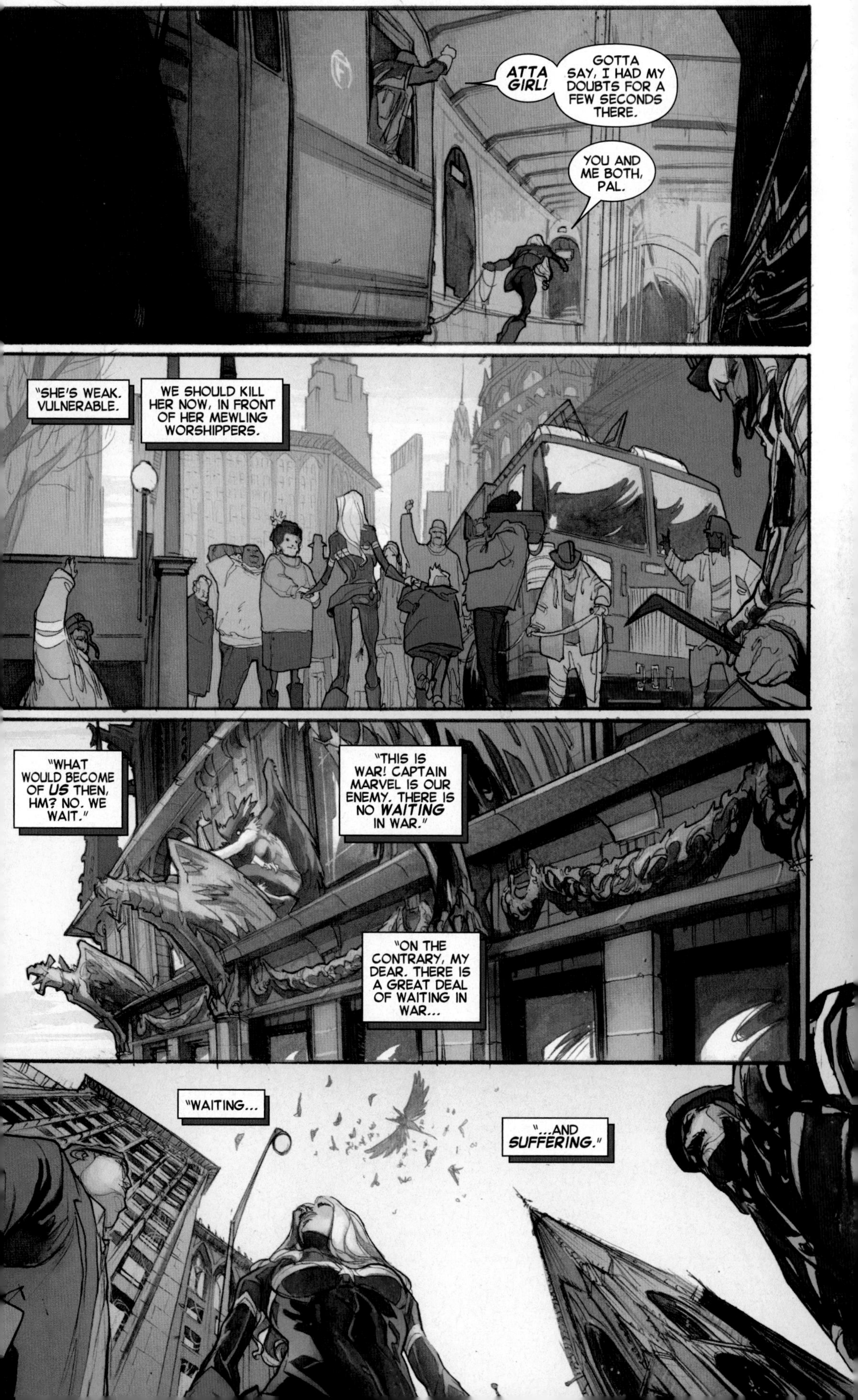
ATTA GIRL!
GOTTA SAY, I HAD MY DOUBTS FOR A FEW SECONDS THERE.
YOU AND ME BOTH, PAL.
"SHE'S WEAK. VULNERABLE.
WE SHOULD KILL HER NOW, IN FRONT OF HER MEWLING WORSHIPPERS.
"WHAT WOULD BECOME OF US THEN, HM? NO. WE WAIT."
"THIS IS WAR! CAPTAIN MARVEL IS OUR ENEMY. THERE IS NO WAITING IN WAR."
"ON THE CONTRARY, MY DEAR. THERE IS A GREAT DEAL OF WAITING IN WAR...
"WAITING...
"...AND SUFFERING."

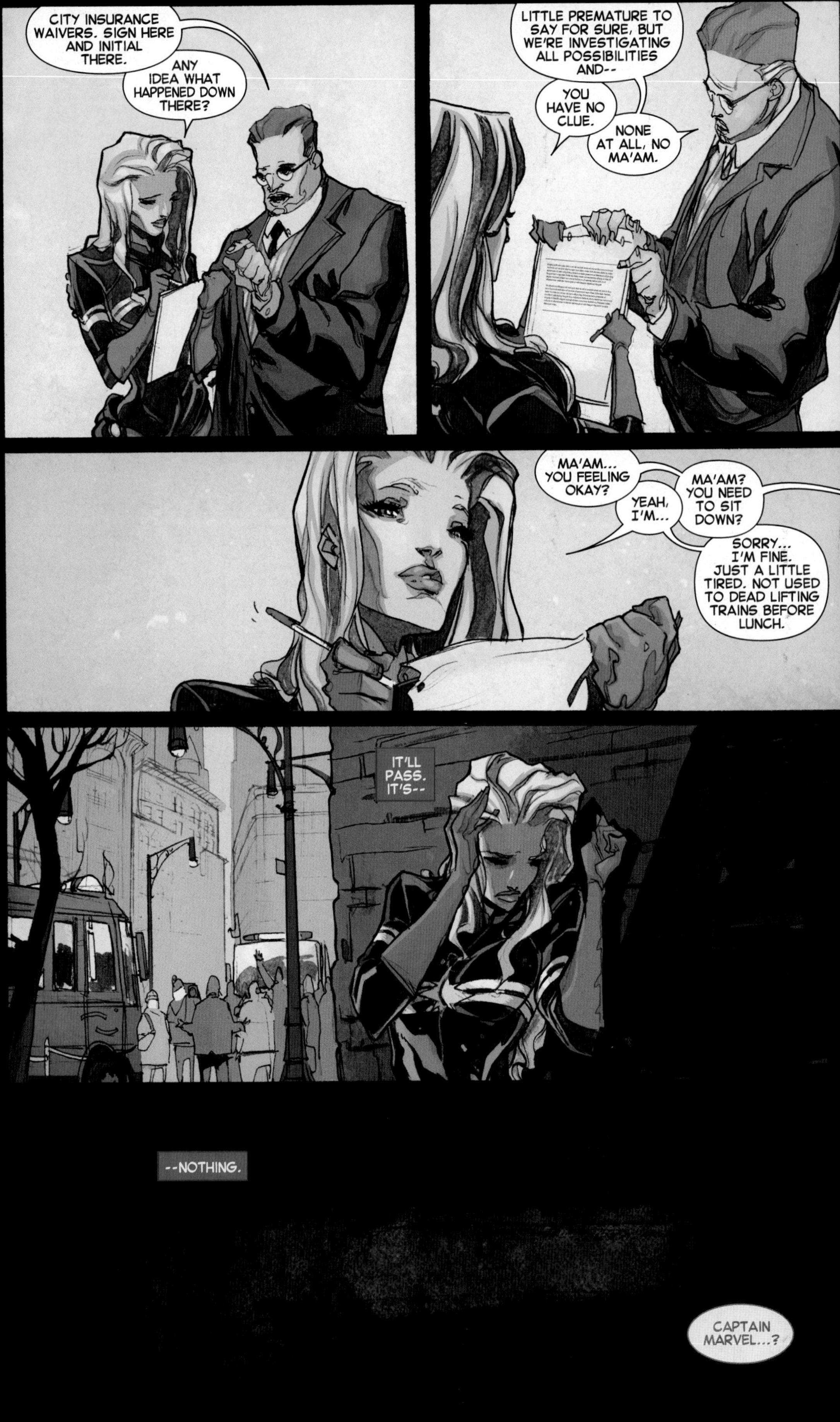

CITY INSURANCE WAIVERS. SIGN HERE AND INITIAL THERE.
ANY IDEA WHAT HAPPENED DOWN THERE?
LITTLE PREMATURE TO SAY FOR SURE, BUT WE'RE INVESTIGATING ALL POSSIBILITIES AND--
YOU HAVE NO CLUE.
NONE AT ALL, NO MA'AM.
MA'AM... YOU FEELING OKAY?
YEAH, I'M...
MA'AM? YOU NEED TO SIT DOWN?
SORRY... I'M FINE. JUST A LITTLE TIRED. NOT USED TO DEAD LIFTING TRAINS BEFORE LUNCH.
IT'LL PASS. IT'S--
--NOTHING.
CAPTAIN MARVEL...?

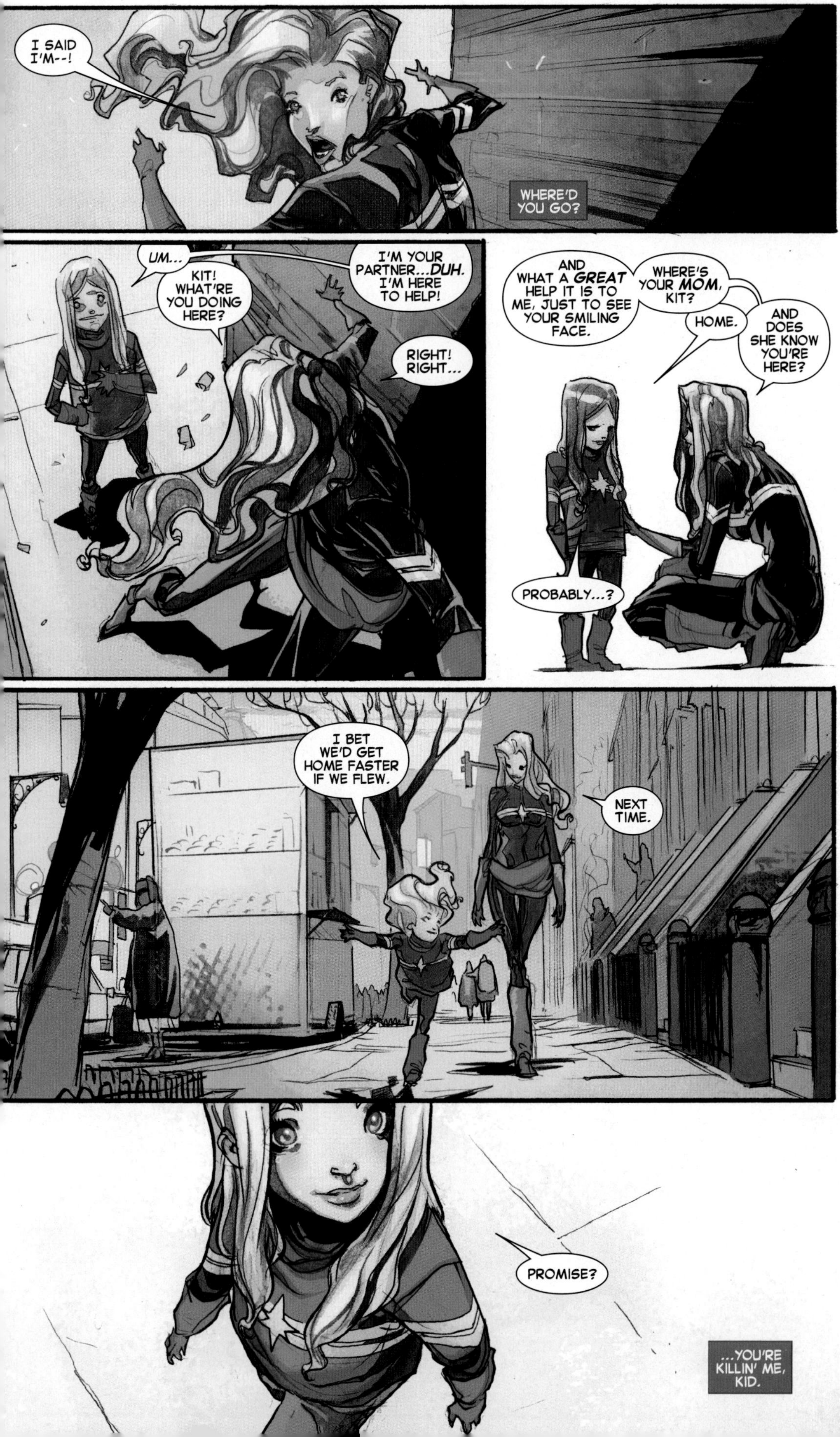
I SAID I'M--!
WHERE'D YOU GO?
UM...
KIT! WHAT'RE YOU DOING HERE?
I'M YOUR PARTNER...DUH. I'M HERE TO HELP!
RIGHT! RIGHT...
AND WHAT A GREAT HELP IT IS TO ME, JUST TO SEE YOUR SMILING FACE.
WHERE'S YOUR MOM, KIT?
HOME.
AND DOES SHE KNOW YOU'RE HERE?
PROBABLY...?
I BET WE'D GET HOME FASTER IF WE FLEW.
NEXT TIME.
PROMISE?
...YOU'RE KILLIN' ME, KID.

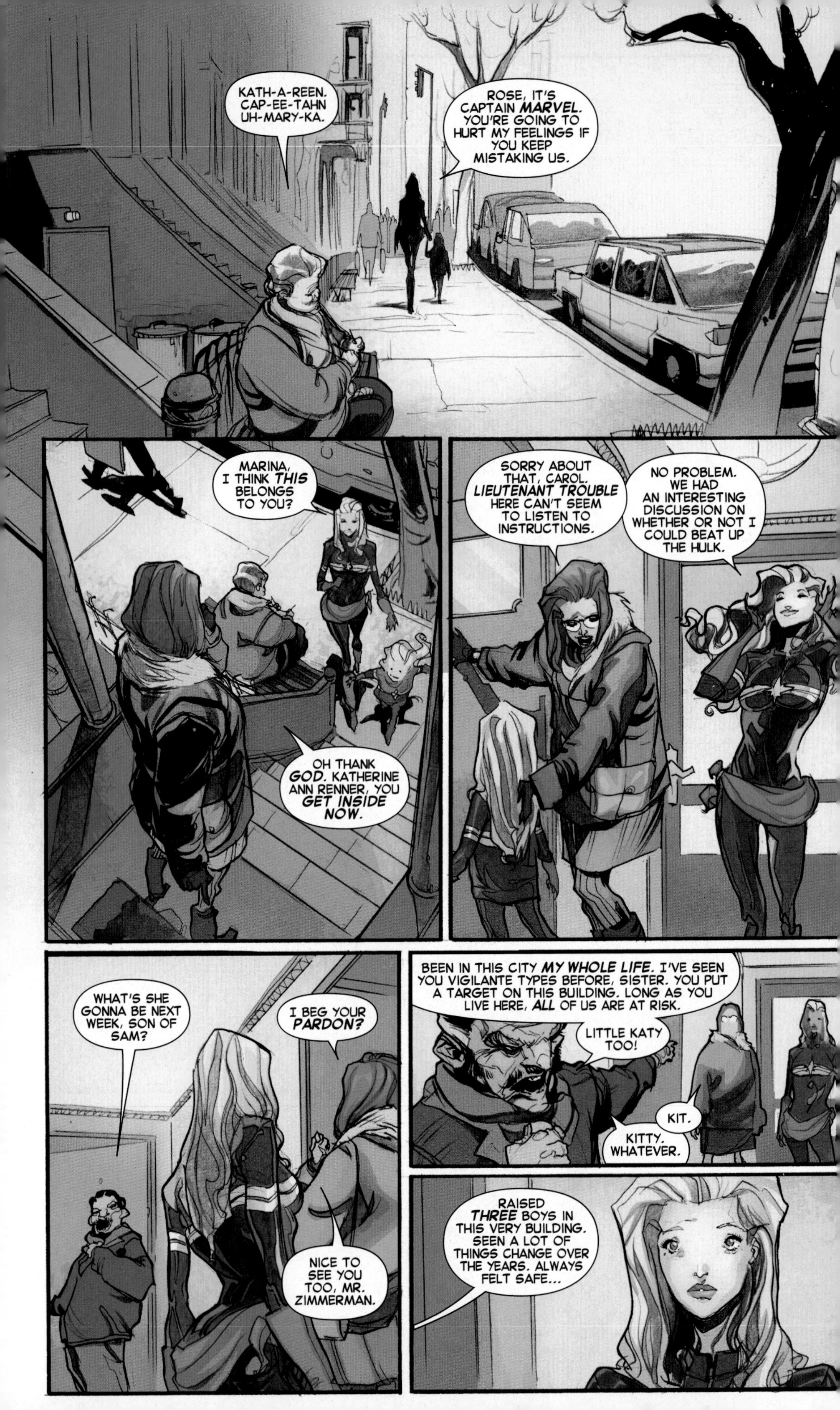
KATH-A-REEN. CAP-EE-TAHN UH-MARY-KA.
ROSE, IT'S CAPTAIN MARVEL. YOU'RE GOING TO HURT MY FEELINGS IF YOU KEEP MISTAKING US.
MARINA, I THINK THIS BELONGS TO YOU?
OH THANK GOD. KATHERINE ANN RENNER, YOU GET INSIDE NOW.
SORRY ABOUT THAT, CAROL. LIEUTENANT TROUBLE HERE CAN'T SEEM TO LISTEN TO INSTRUCTIONS.
NO PROBLEM. WE HAD AN INTERESTING DISCUSSION ON WHETHER OR NOT I COULD BEAT UP THE HULK.
WHAT'S SHE GONNA BE NEXT WEEK, SON OF SAM?
I BEG YOUR PARDON?
NICE TO SEE YOU TOO, MR. ZIMMERMAN.
BEEN IN THIS CITY MY WHOLE LIFE. I'VE SEEN YOU VIGILANTE TYPES BEFORE, SISTER. YOU PUT A TARGET ON THIS BUILDING. LONG AS YOU LIVE HERE, ALL OF US ARE AT RISK.
LITTLE KATY TOO!
KIT.
KITTY. WHATEVER.
RAISED THREE BOYS IN THIS VERY BUILDING. SEEN A LOT OF THINGS CHANGE OVER THE YEARS. ALWAYS FELT SAFE...

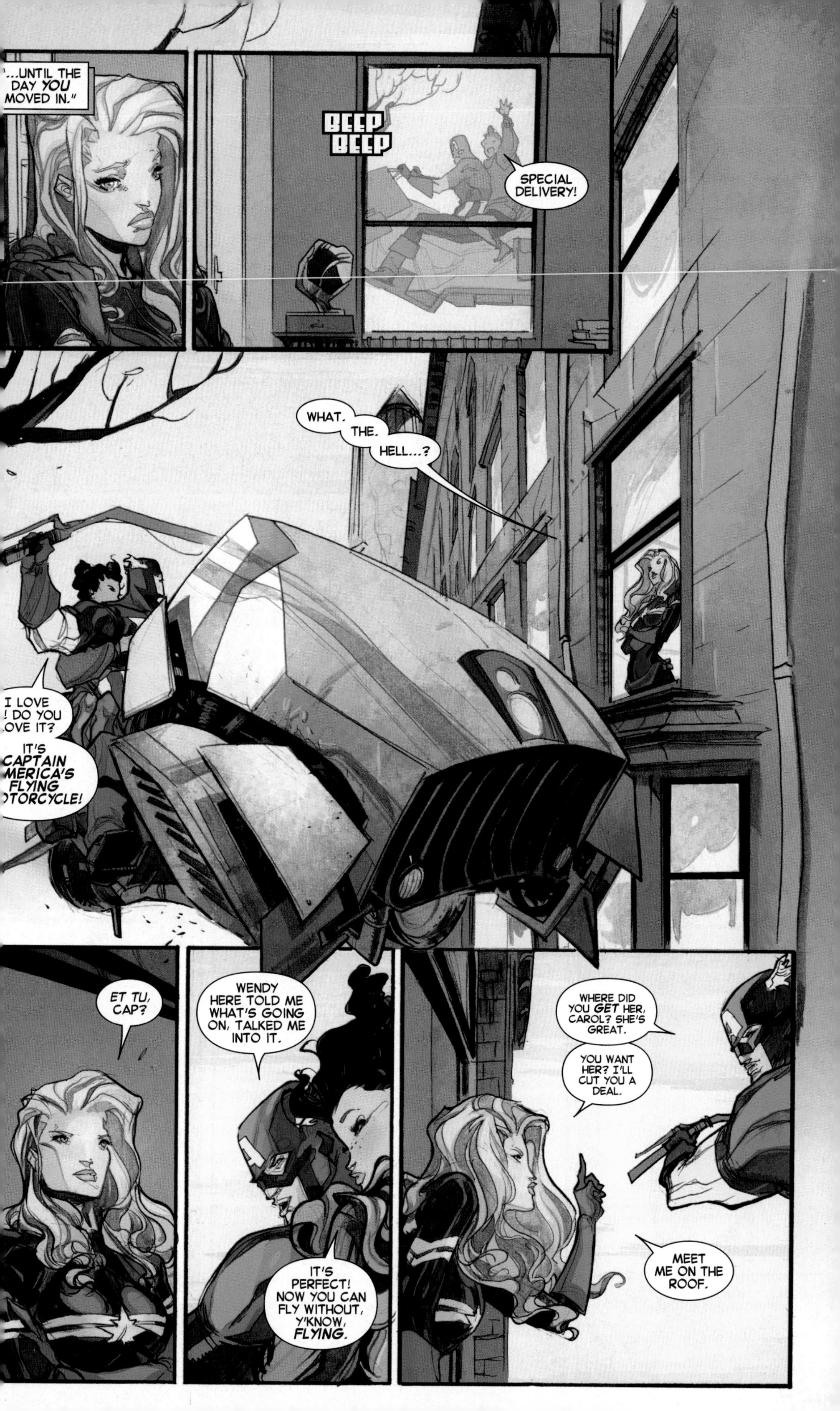
"...UNTIL THE DAY YOU MOVED IN."
BEEP BEEP
SPECIAL DELIVERY!
WHAT.
THE.
HELL...?
I LOVE ! DO YOU OVE IT?
IT'S CAPTAIN MERICA'S FLYING OTORCYCLE!
ET TU, CAP?
WENDY HERE TOLD ME WHAT'S GOING ON, TALKED ME INTO IT.
IT'S PERFECT! NOW YOU CAN FLY WITHOUT, Y'KNOW, FLYING.
WHERE DID YOU GET HER, CAROL? SHE'S GREAT.
YOU WANT HER? I'LL CUT YOU A DEAL.
MEET ME ON THE ROOF.

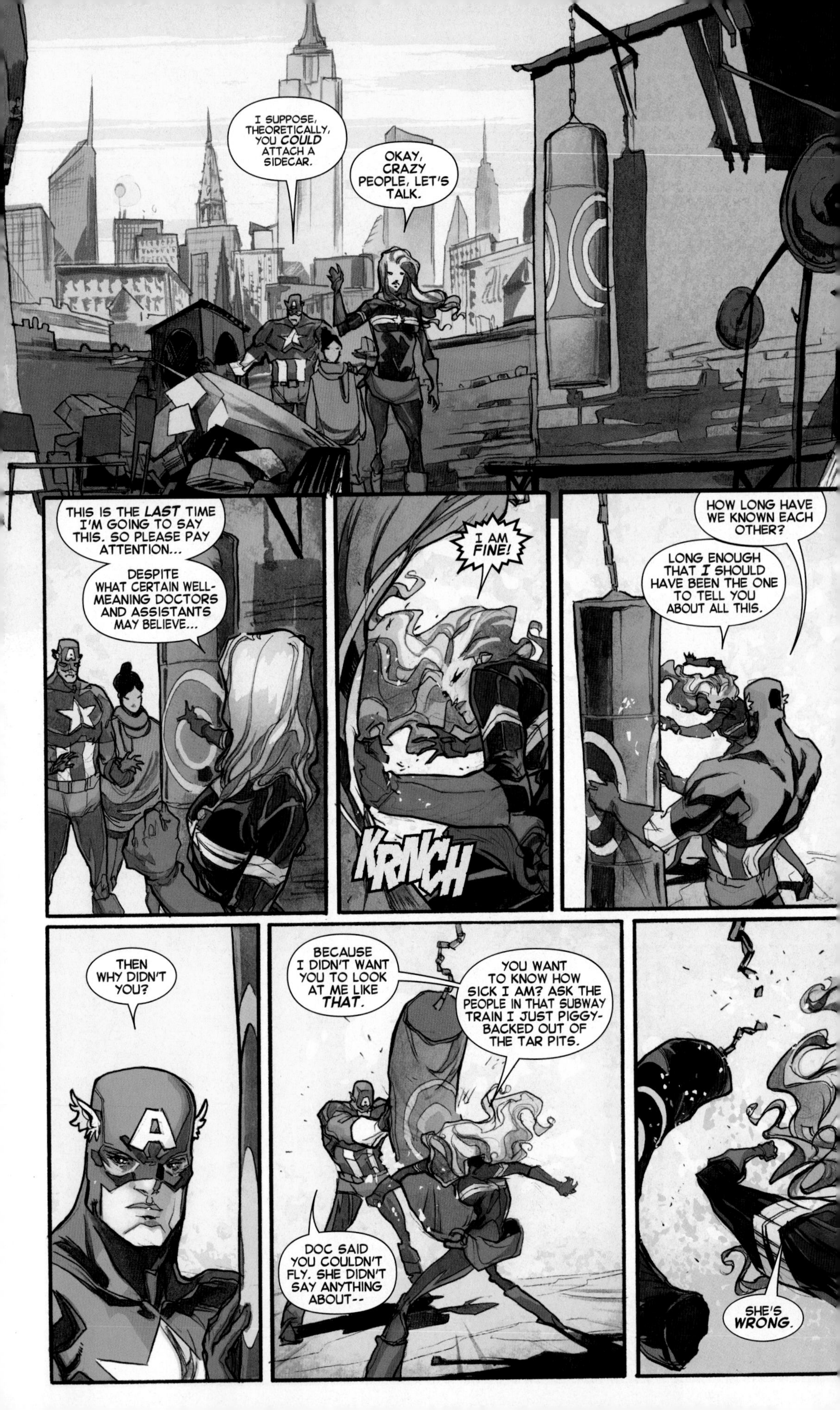

I SUPPOSE, THEORETICALLY, YOU COULD ATTACH A SIDECAR.
OKAY, CRAZY PEOPLE, LET'S TALK.
THIS IS THE LAST TIME I'M GOING TO SAY THIS. SO PLEASE PAY ATTENTION...
DESPITE WHAT CERTAIN WELL-MEANING DOCTORS AND ASSISTANTS MAY BELIEVE...
I AM FINE!
KRNCH
HOW LONG HAVE WE KNOWN EACH OTHER?
LONG ENOUGH THAT I SHOULD HAVE BEEN THE ONE TO TELL YOU ABOUT ALL THIS.
THEN WHY DIDN'T YOU?
BECAUSE I DIDN'T WANT YOU TO LOOK AT ME LIKE THAT.
YOU WANT TO KNOW HOW SICK I AM? ASK THE PEOPLE IN THAT SUBWAY TRAIN I JUST PIGGY-BACKED OUT OF THE TAR PITS.
DOC SAID YOU COULDN'T FLY. SHE DIDN'T SAY ANYTHING ABOUT--
SHE'S WRONG.

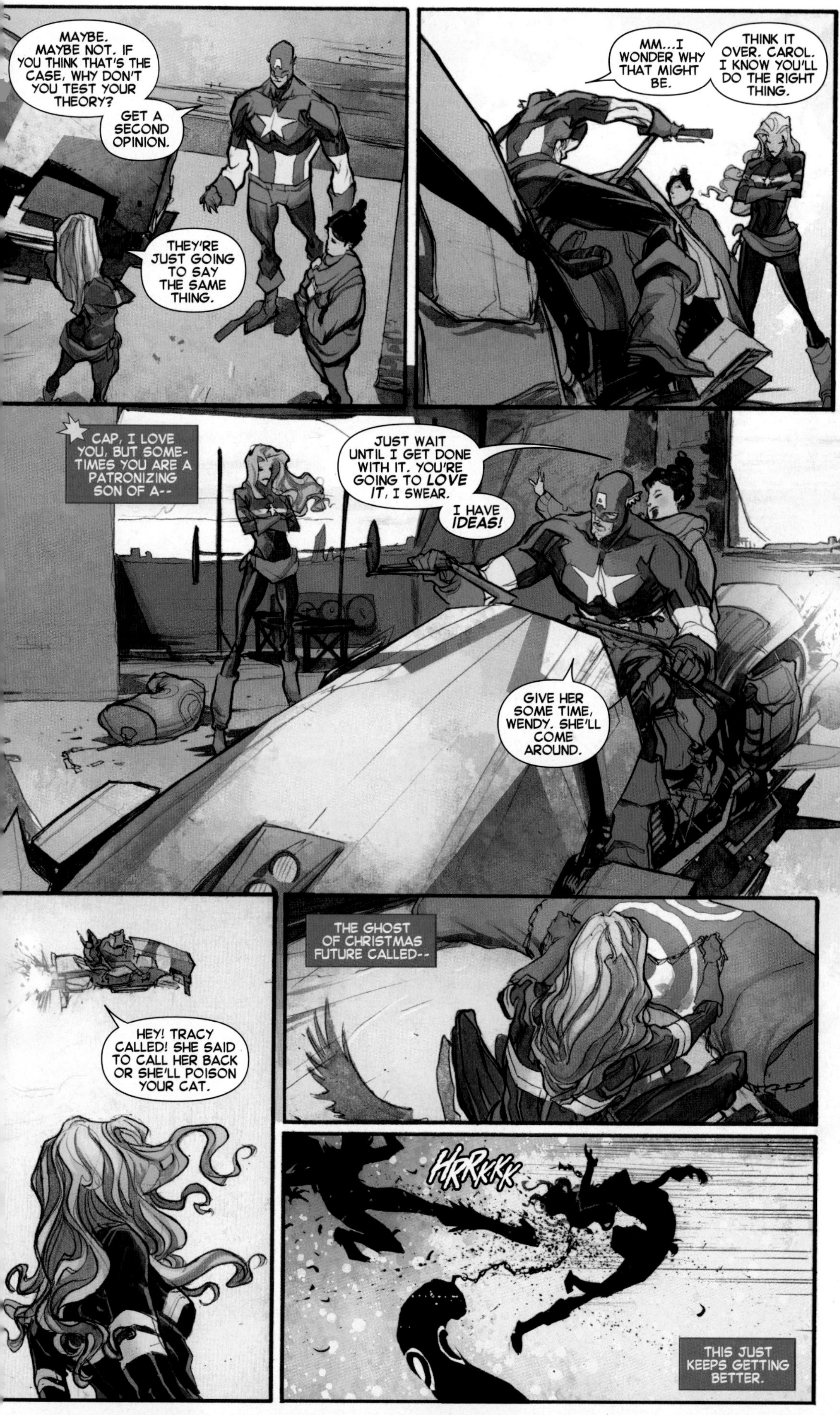

MAYBE. MAYBE NOT. IF YOU THINK THAT'S THE CASE, WHY DON'T YOU TEST YOUR THEORY?
GET A SECOND OPINION.
THEY'RE JUST GOING TO SAY THE SAME THING.
THINK IT OVER. CAROL. I KNOW YOU'LL DO THE RIGHT THING.
MM...I WONDER WHY THAT MIGHT BE.
CAP, I LOVE YOU, BUT SOME-TIMES YOU ARE A PATRONIZING SON OF A--
JUST WAIT UNTIL I GET DONE WITH IT. YOU'RE GOING TO LOVE IT, I SWEAR.
I HAVE IDEAS!
GIVE HER SOME TIME, WENDY. SHE'LL COME AROUND.
HEY! TRACY CALLED! SHE SAID TO CALL HER BACK OR SHE'LL POISON YOUR CAT.
THE GHOST OF CHRISTMAS FUTURE CALLED--
HRRKKK
THIS JUST KEEPS GETTING BETTER.

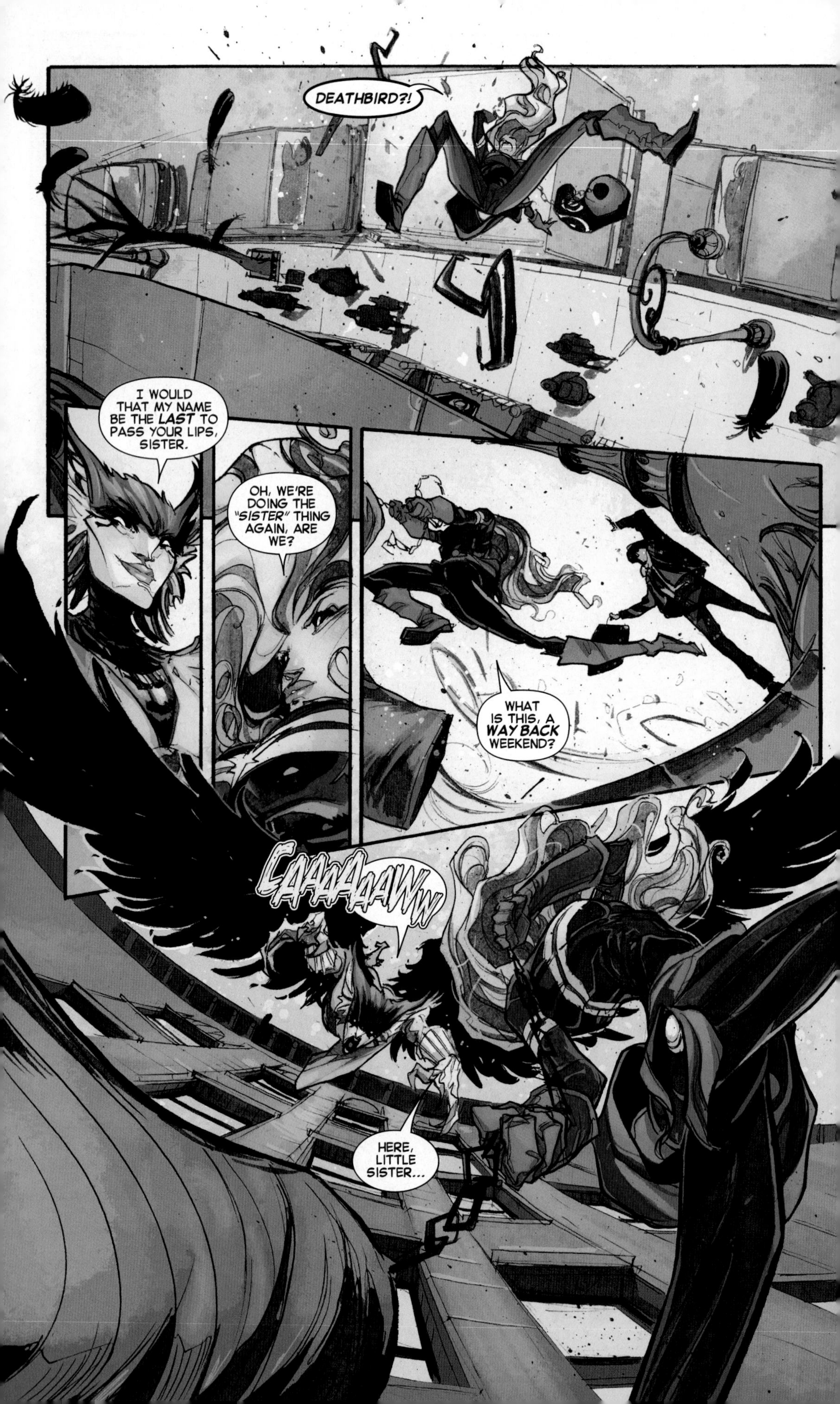

DEATHBIRD?!
I WOULD THAT MY NAME BE THE LAST TO PASS YOUR LIPS, SISTER.
OH, WE'RE DOING THE "SISTER" THING AGAIN, ARE WE?
WHAT IS THIS, A WAY BACK WEEKEND?
CAAAAAAAWW
HERE, LITTLE SISTER...

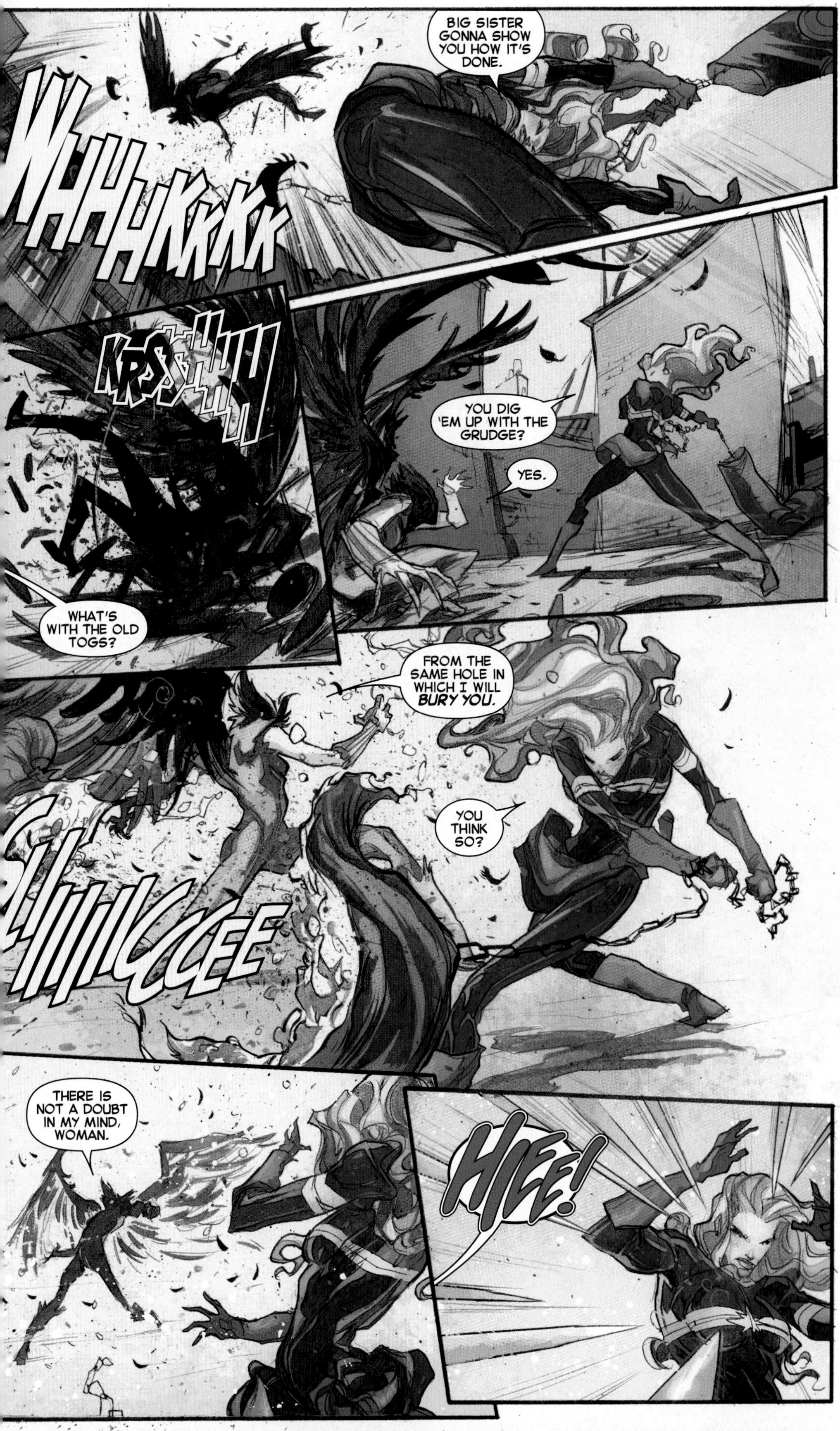
WHHHKKKKK
BIG SISTER GONNA SHOW YOU HOW IT'S DONE.
KRSSHH!
WHAT'S WITH THE OLD TOGS?
YOU DIG 'EM UP WITH THE GRUDGE?
YES.
FROM THE SAME HOLE IN WHICH I WILL BURY YOU.
SHHHHCCEE
YOU THINK SO?
THERE IS NOT A DOUBT IN MY MIND, WOMAN.
HEE!

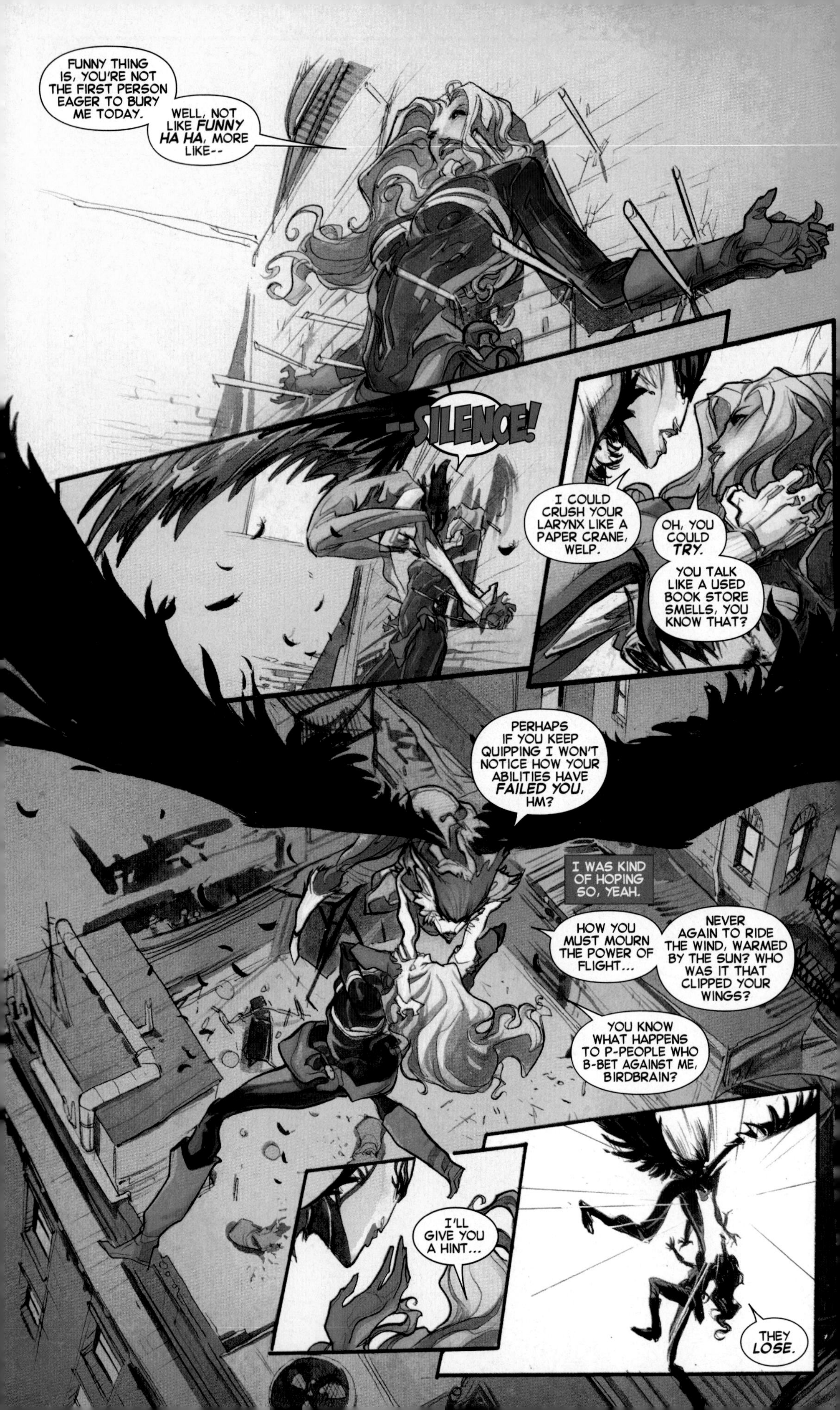
FUNNY THING IS, YOU'RE NOT THE FIRST PERSON EAGER TO BURY ME TODAY.
WELL, NOT LIKE FUNNY HA HA, MORE LIKE--
--SILENCE!
I COULD CRUSH YOUR LARYNX LIKE A PAPER CRANE, WELP.
OH, YOU COULD TRY.
YOU TALK LIKE A USED BOOK STORE SMELLS, YOU KNOW THAT?
PERHAPS IF YOU KEEP QUIPPING I WON'T NOTICE HOW YOUR ABILITIES HAVE FAILED YOU, HM?
I WAS KIND OF HOPING SO, YEAH.
HOW YOU MUST MOURN THE POWER OF FLIGHT...
NEVER AGAIN TO RIDE THE WIND, WARMED BY THE SUN? WHO WAS IT THAT CLIPPED YOUR WINGS?
YOU KNOW WHAT HAPPENS TO P-PEOPLE WHO B-BET AGAINST ME, BIRDBRAIN?
I'LL GIVE YOU A HINT...
THEY LOSE.

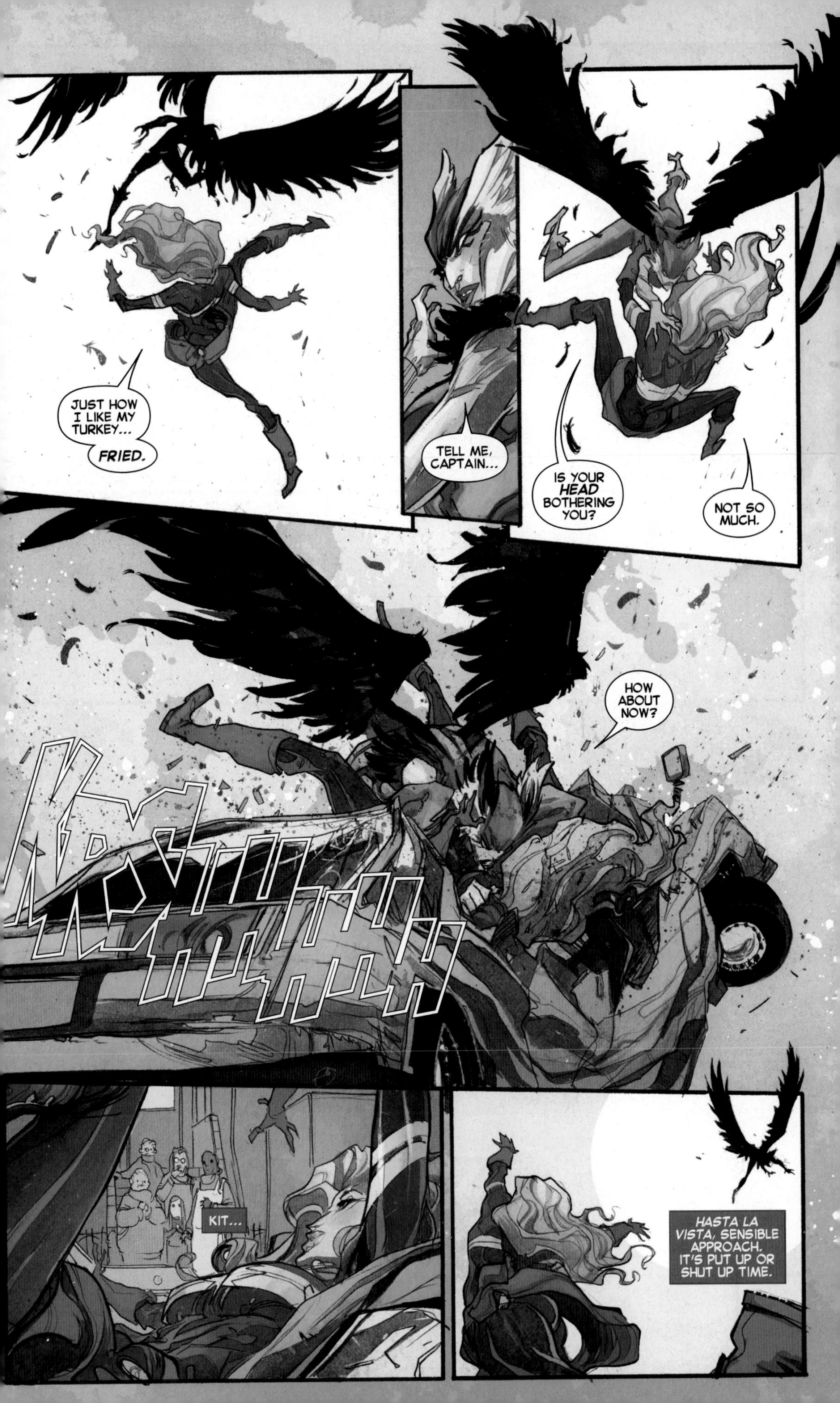
JUST HOW I LIKE MY TURKEY... FRIED.
TELL ME, CAPTAIN...
IS YOUR HEAD BOTHERING YOU?
NOT SO MUCH.
HOW ABOUT NOW?
KIT...
HASTA LA VISTA, SENSIBLE APPROACH. IT'S PUT UP OR SHUT UP TIME.

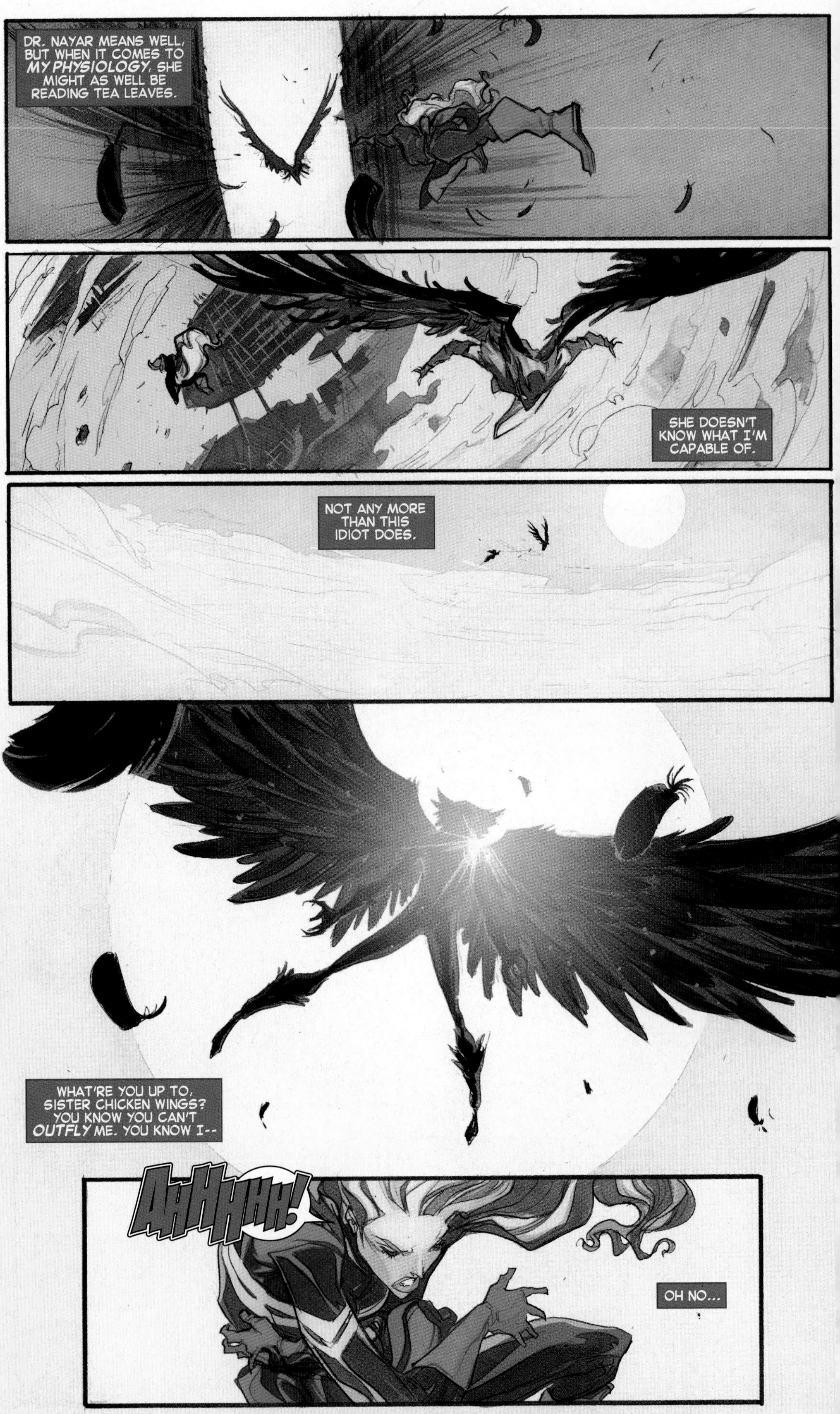
DR. NAYAR MEANS WELL, BUT WHEN IT COMES TO MY PHYSIOLOGY, SHE MIGHT AS WELL BE READING TEA LEAVES.
SHE DOESN'T KNOW WHAT I'M CAPABLE OF.
NOT ANY MORE THAN THIS IDIOT DOES.
WHAT'RE YOU UP TO, SISTER CHICKEN WINGS? YOU KNOW YOU CAN'T OUTFLY ME. YOU KNOW I--
AHHHHHH!
OH NO...

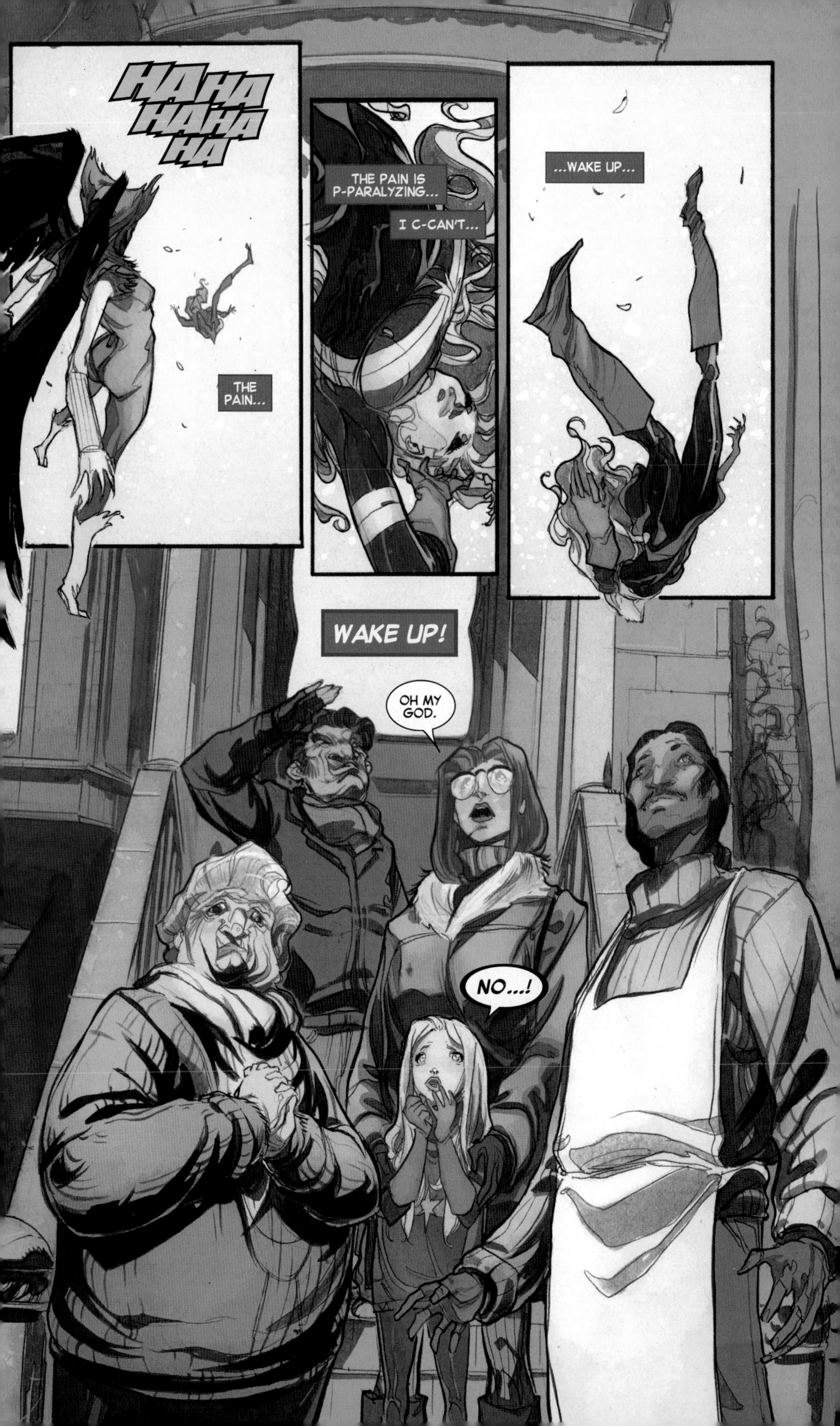
HA HA HA HA HA
THE PAIN...
THE PAIN IS P-PARALYZING...
I C-CAN'T...
...WAKE UP...
WAKE UP!
OH MY GOD.
NO...!

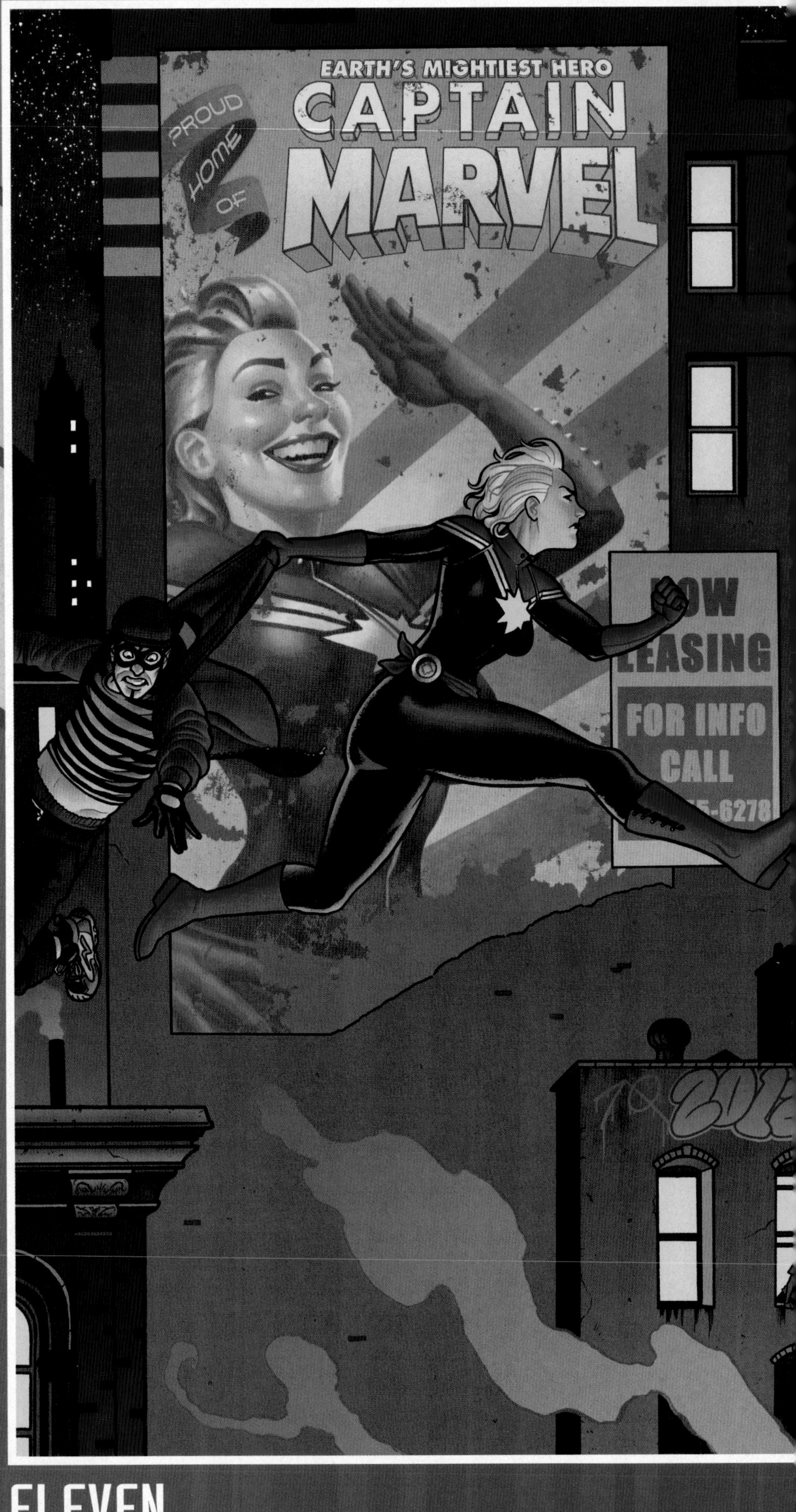
EARTH'S MIGHTIEST HERO
CAPTAIN MARVEL
PROUD HOME OF
FOR INFO CALL

ELEVEN

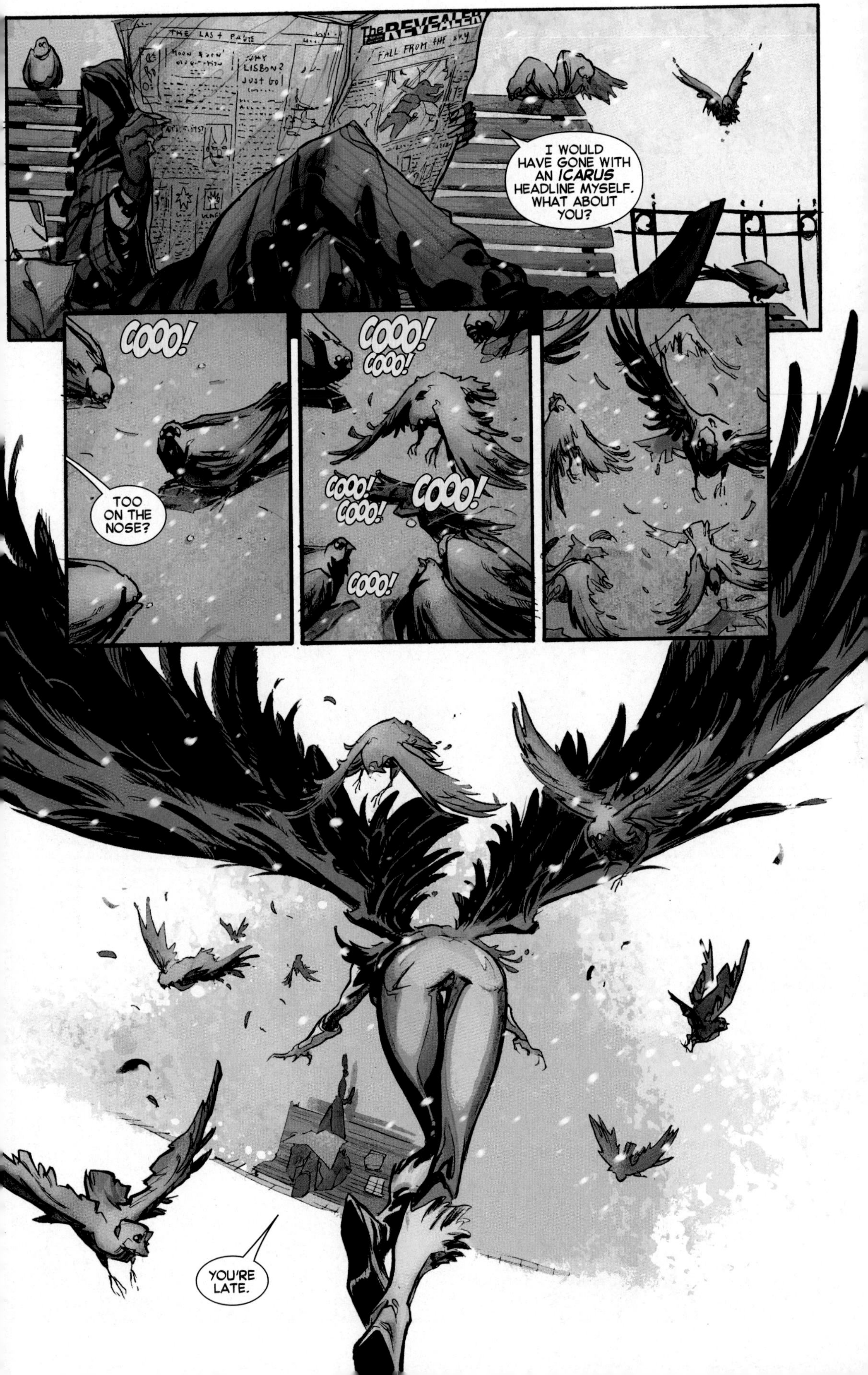

The REVEALER
FALL FROM THE SKY
THE LAST PAGE
WHY LISBON? JUST GO!
I WOULD HAVE GONE WITH AN *ICARUS* HEADLINE MYSELF. WHAT ABOUT YOU?
COOO!
TOO ON THE NOSE?
COOO! COOO!
COOO! COOO!
COOO!
COOO!
YOU'RE LATE.

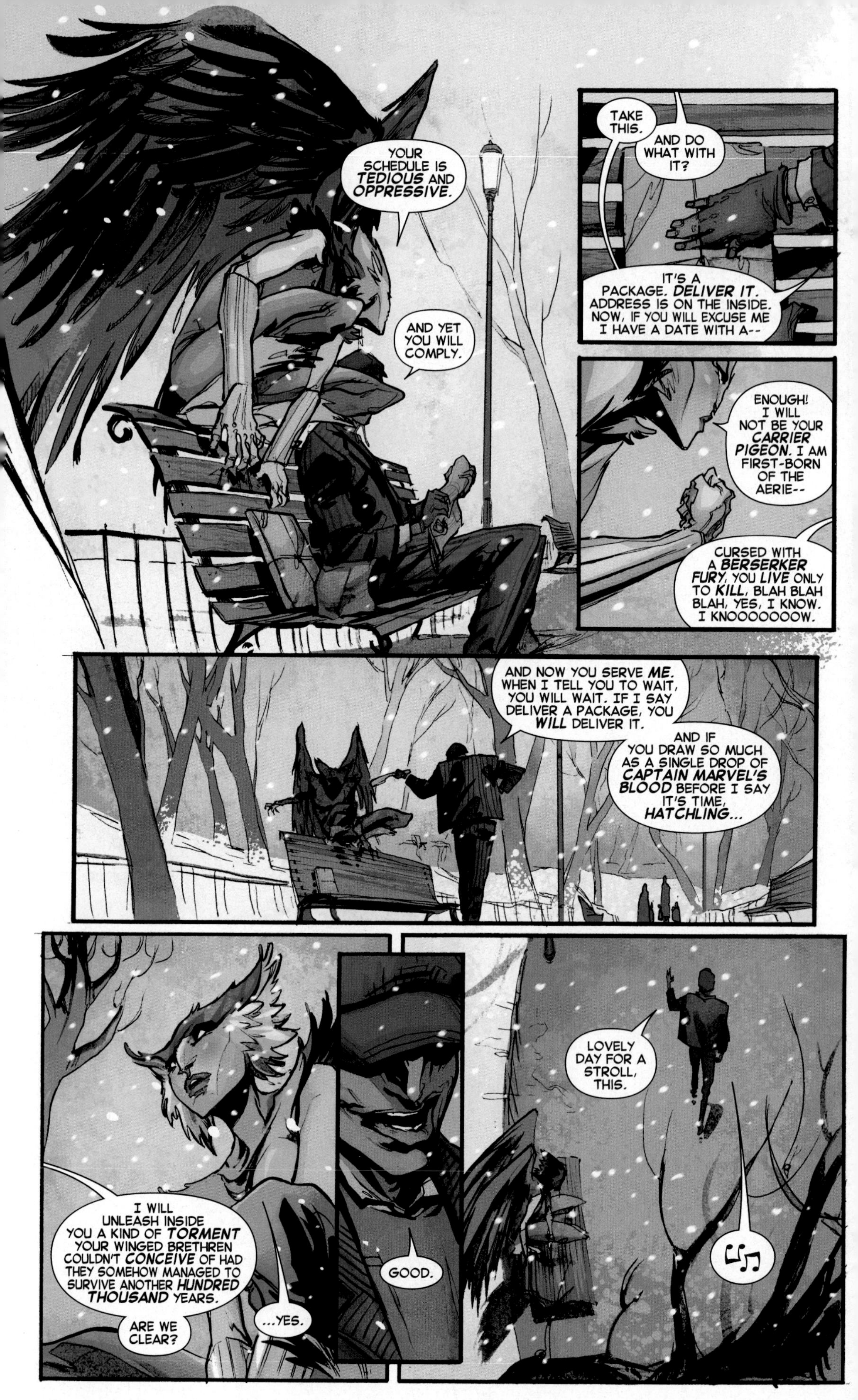

YOUR SCHEDULE IS TEDIOUS AND OPPRESSIVE.
AND YET YOU WILL COMPLY.
TAKE THIS.
AND DO WHAT WITH IT?
IT'S A PACKAGE. DELIVER IT. ADDRESS IS ON THE INSIDE. NOW, IF YOU WILL EXCUSE ME I HAVE A DATE WITH A--
ENOUGH! I WILL NOT BE YOUR CARRIER PIGEON. I AM FIRST-BORN OF THE AERIE--
CURSED WITH A BERSERKER FURY, YOU LIVE ONLY TO KILL, BLAH BLAH BLAH, YES, I KNOW. I KNOOOOOOOW.
AND NOW YOU SERVE ME. WHEN I TELL YOU TO WAIT, YOU WILL WAIT. IF I SAY DELIVER A PACKAGE, YOU WILL DELIVER IT.
AND IF YOU DRAW SO MUCH AS A SINGLE DROP OF CAPTAIN MARVEL'S BLOOD BEFORE I SAY IT'S TIME, HATCHLING...
I WILL UNLEASH INSIDE YOU A KIND OF TORMENT YOUR WINGED BRETHREN COULDN'T CONCEIVE OF HAD THEY SOMEHOW MANAGED TO SURVIVE ANOTHER HUNDRED THOUSAND YEARS.
ARE WE CLEAR?
...YES.
GOOD.
LOVELY DAY FOR A STROLL, THIS.

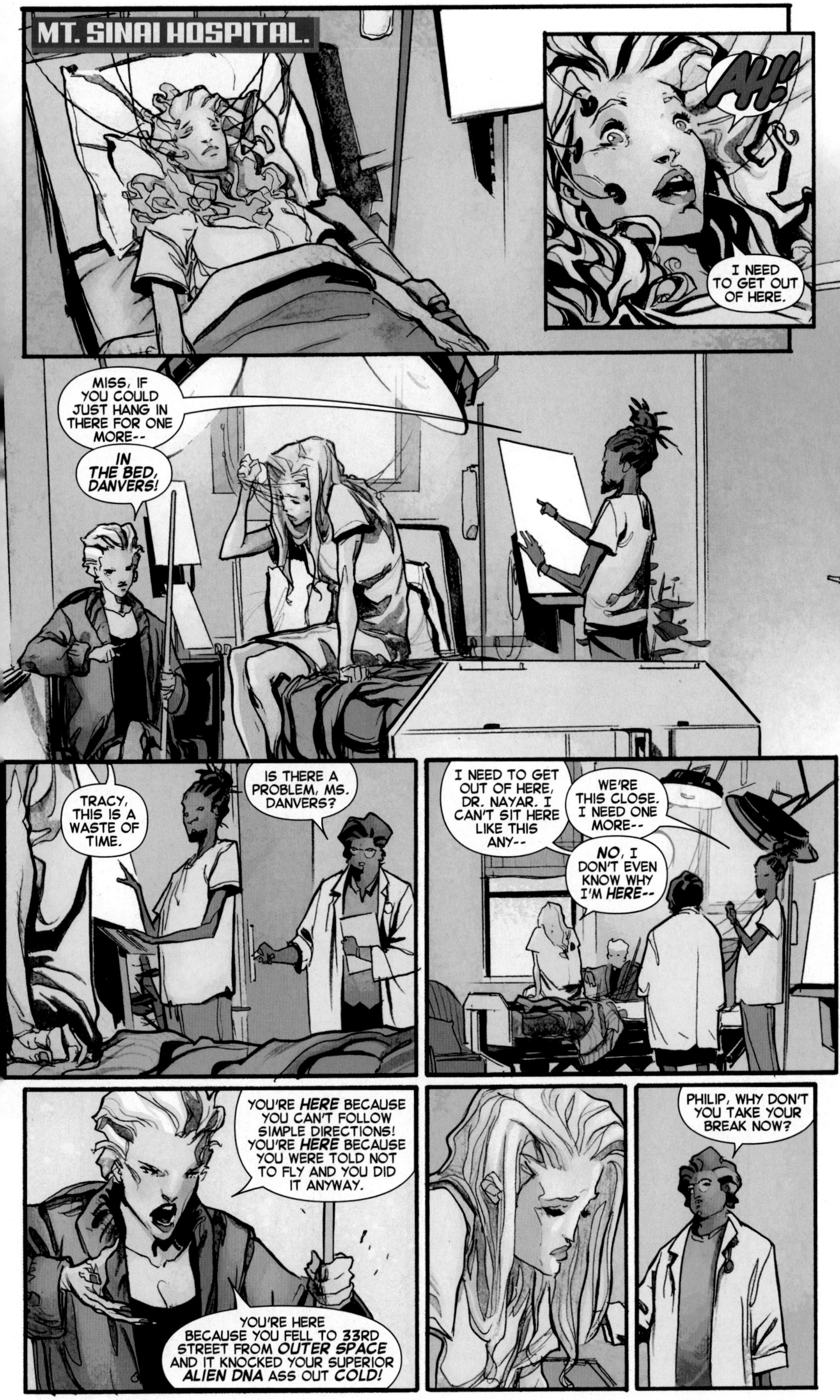

MT. SINAI HOSPITAL.
AH!
I NEED TO GET OUT OF HERE.
MISS, IF YOU COULD JUST HANG IN THERE FOR ONE MORE--
IN THE BED, DANVERS!
TRACY, THIS IS A WASTE OF TIME.
IS THERE A PROBLEM, MS. DANVERS?
I NEED TO GET OUT OF HERE, DR. NAYAR. I CAN'T SIT HERE LIKE THIS ANY--
WE'RE THIS CLOSE. I NEED ONE MORE--
NO, I DON'T EVEN KNOW WHY I'M HERE--
YOU'RE HERE BECAUSE YOU CAN'T FOLLOW SIMPLE DIRECTIONS! YOU'RE HERE BECAUSE YOU WERE TOLD NOT TO FLY AND YOU DID IT ANYWAY.
YOU'RE HERE BECAUSE YOU FELL TO 33RD STREET FROM OUTER SPACE AND IT KNOCKED YOUR SUPERIOR ALIEN DNA ASS OUT COLD!
PHILIP, WHY DON'T YOU TAKE YOUR BREAK NOW?

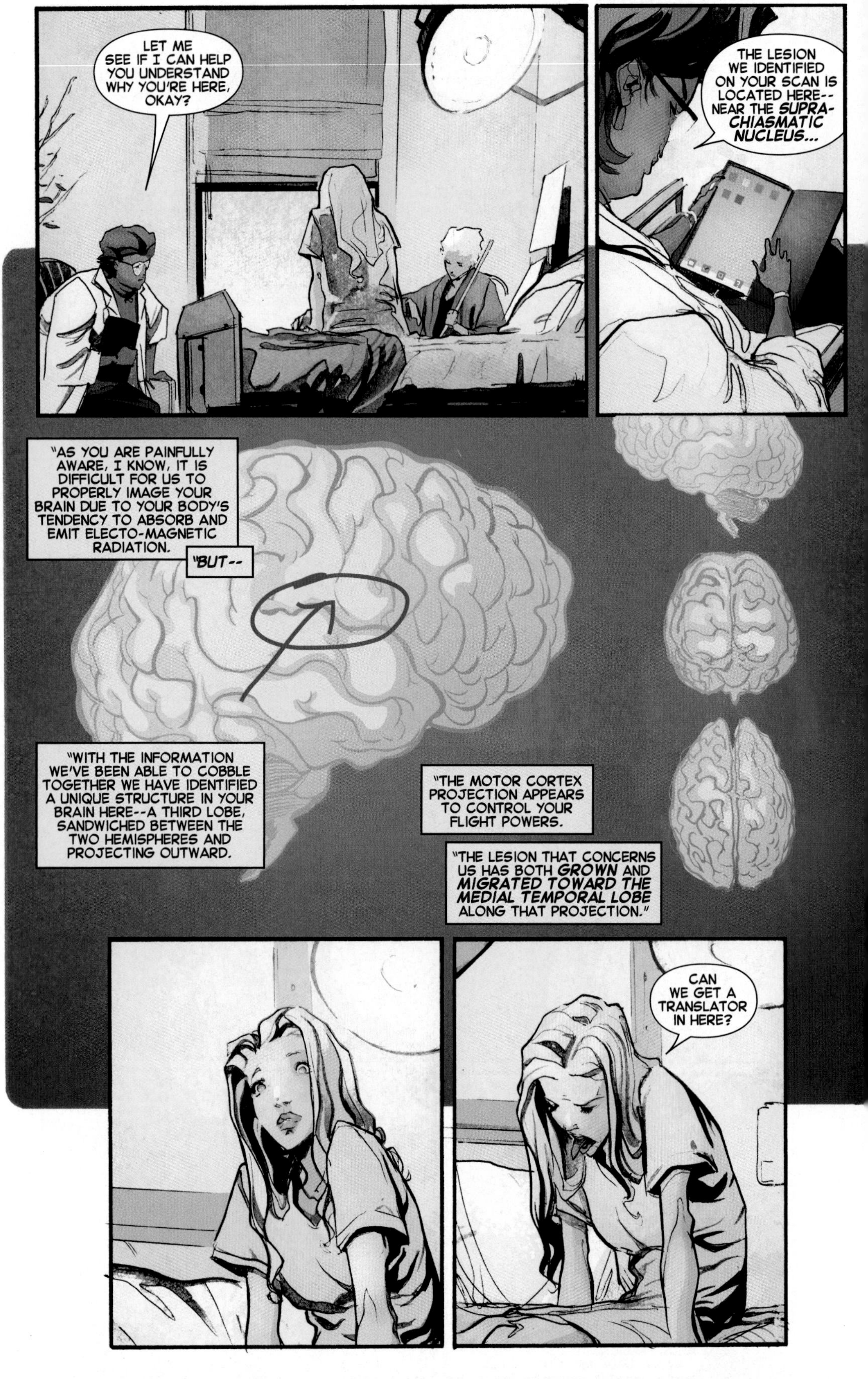
LET ME SEE IF I CAN HELP YOU UNDERSTAND WHY YOU'RE HERE, OKAY?
THE LESION WE IDENTIFIED ON YOUR SCAN IS LOCATED HERE-- NEAR THE SUPRA-CHIASMATIC NUCLEUS...
"AS YOU ARE PAINFULLY AWARE, I KNOW, IT IS DIFFICULT FOR US TO PROPERLY IMAGE YOUR BRAIN DUE TO YOUR BODY'S TENDENCY TO ABSORB AND EMIT ELECTO-MAGNETIC RADIATION.
"BUT--
"WITH THE INFORMATION WE'VE BEEN ABLE TO COBBLE TOGETHER WE HAVE IDENTIFIED A UNIQUE STRUCTURE IN YOUR BRAIN HERE--A THIRD LOBE, SANDWICHED BETWEEN THE TWO HEMISPHERES AND PROJECTING OUTWARD.
"THE MOTOR CORTEX PROJECTION APPEARS TO CONTROL YOUR FLIGHT POWERS.
"THE LESION THAT CONCERNS US HAS BOTH GROWN AND MIGRATED TOWARD THE MEDIAL TEMPORAL LOBE ALONG THAT PROJECTION."
CAN WE GET A TRANSLATOR IN HERE?

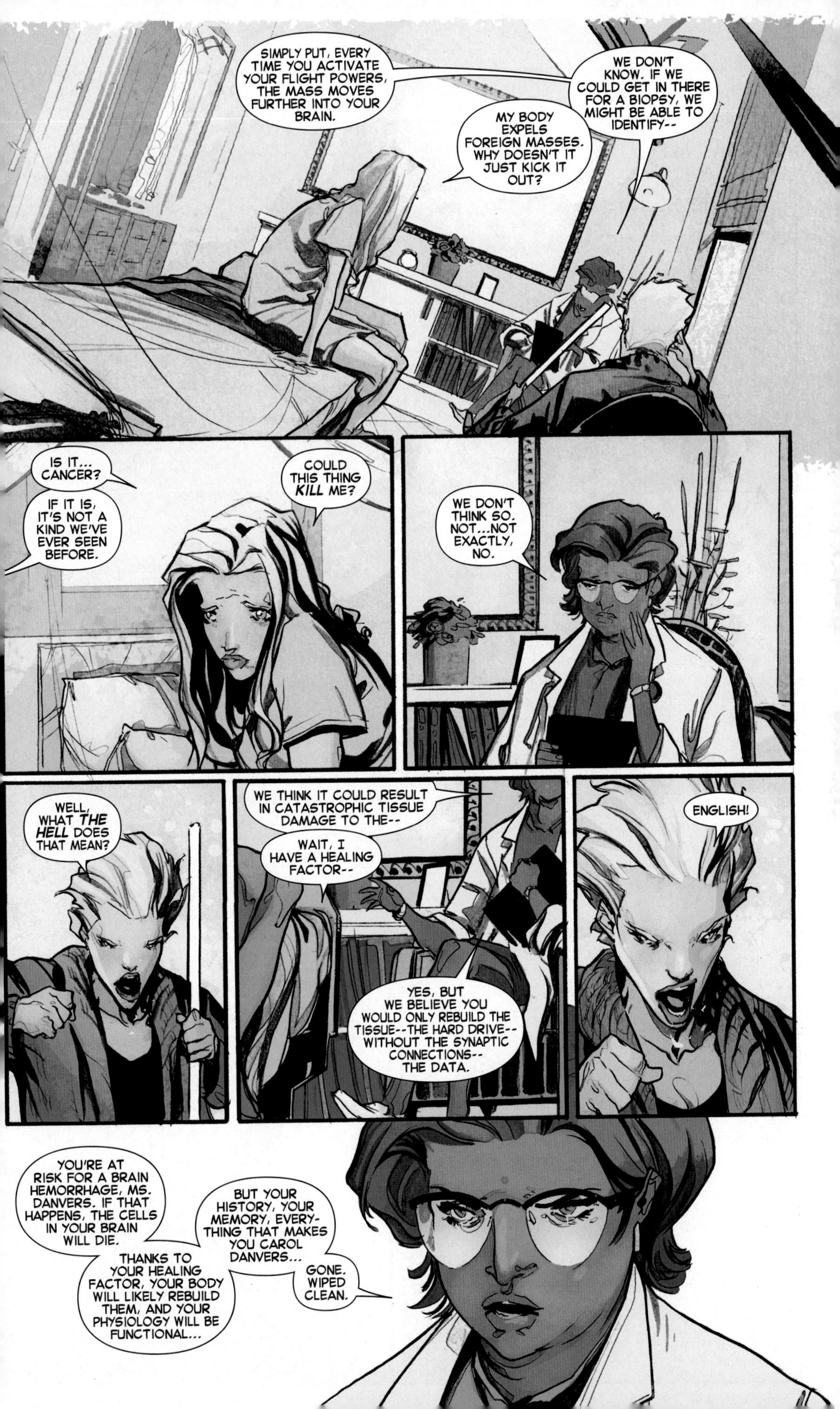
SIMPLY PUT, EVERY TIME YOU ACTIVATE YOUR FLIGHT POWERS, THE MASS MOVES FURTHER INTO YOUR BRAIN.
MY BODY EXPELS FOREIGN MASSES. WHY DOESN'T IT JUST KICK IT OUT?
WE DON'T KNOW. IF WE COULD GET IN THERE FOR A BIOPSY, WE MIGHT BE ABLE TO IDENTIFY--
IS IT... CANCER?
IF IT IS, IT'S NOT A KIND WE'VE EVER SEEN BEFORE.
COULD THIS THING *KILL* ME?
WE DON'T THINK SO. NOT...NOT EXACTLY, NO.
WELL, WHAT *THE HELL* DOES THAT MEAN?
WE THINK IT COULD RESULT IN CATASTROPHIC TISSUE DAMAGE TO THE--
WAIT, I HAVE A HEALING FACTOR--
YES, BUT WE BELIEVE YOU WOULD ONLY REBUILD THE TISSUE--THE HARD DRIVE--WITHOUT THE SYNAPTIC CONNECTIONS--THE DATA.
ENGLISH!
YOU'RE AT RISK FOR A BRAIN HEMORRHAGE, MS. DANVERS. IF THAT HAPPENS, THE CELLS IN YOUR BRAIN WILL DIE.
THANKS TO YOUR HEALING FACTOR, YOUR BODY WILL LIKELY REBUILD THEM, AND YOUR PHYSIOLOGY WILL BE FUNCTIONAL...
BUT YOUR HISTORY, YOUR MEMORY, EVERYTHING THAT MAKES YOU CAROL DANVERS...
GONE. WIPED CLEAN.

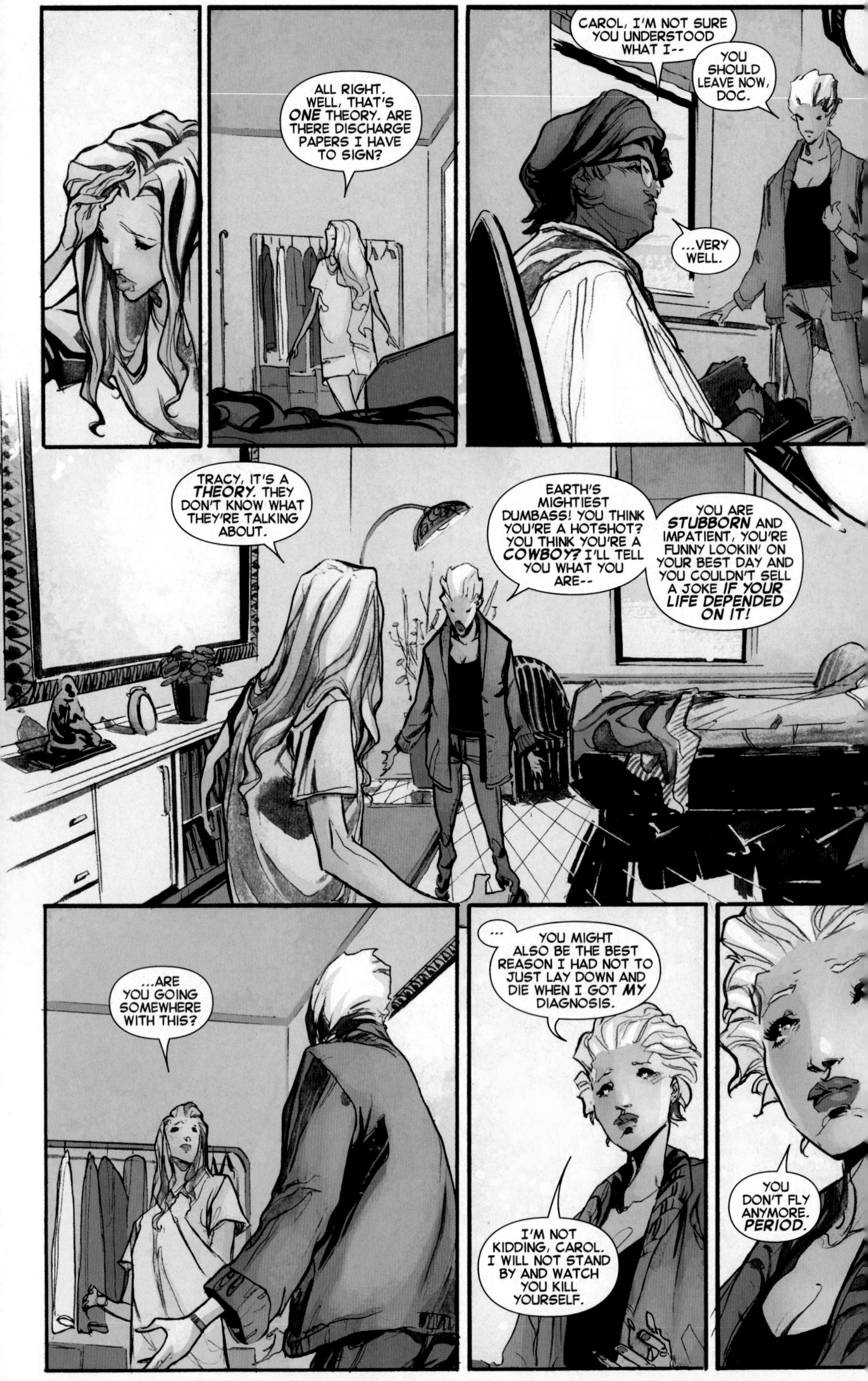
ALL RIGHT. WELL, THAT'S ONE THEORY. ARE THERE DISCHARGE PAPERS I HAVE TO SIGN?
CAROL, I'M NOT SURE YOU UNDERSTOOD WHAT I--
YOU SHOULD LEAVE NOW, DOC.
...VERY WELL.
TRACY, IT'S A THEORY. THEY DON'T KNOW WHAT THEY'RE TALKING ABOUT.
EARTH'S MIGHTIEST DUMBASS! YOU THINK YOU'RE A HOTSHOT? YOU THINK YOU'RE A COWBOY? I'LL TELL YOU WHAT YOU ARE--
YOU ARE STUBBORN AND IMPATIENT, YOU'RE FUNNY LOOKIN' ON YOUR BEST DAY AND YOU COULDN'T SELL A JOKE IF YOUR LIFE DEPENDED ON IT!
...ARE YOU GOING SOMEWHERE WITH THIS?
...
YOU MIGHT ALSO BE THE BEST REASON I HAD NOT TO JUST LAY DOWN AND DIE WHEN I GOT MY DIAGNOSIS.
I'M NOT KIDDING, CAROL. I WILL NOT STAND BY AND WATCH YOU KILL YOURSELF.
YOU DON'T FLY ANYMORE. PERIOD.

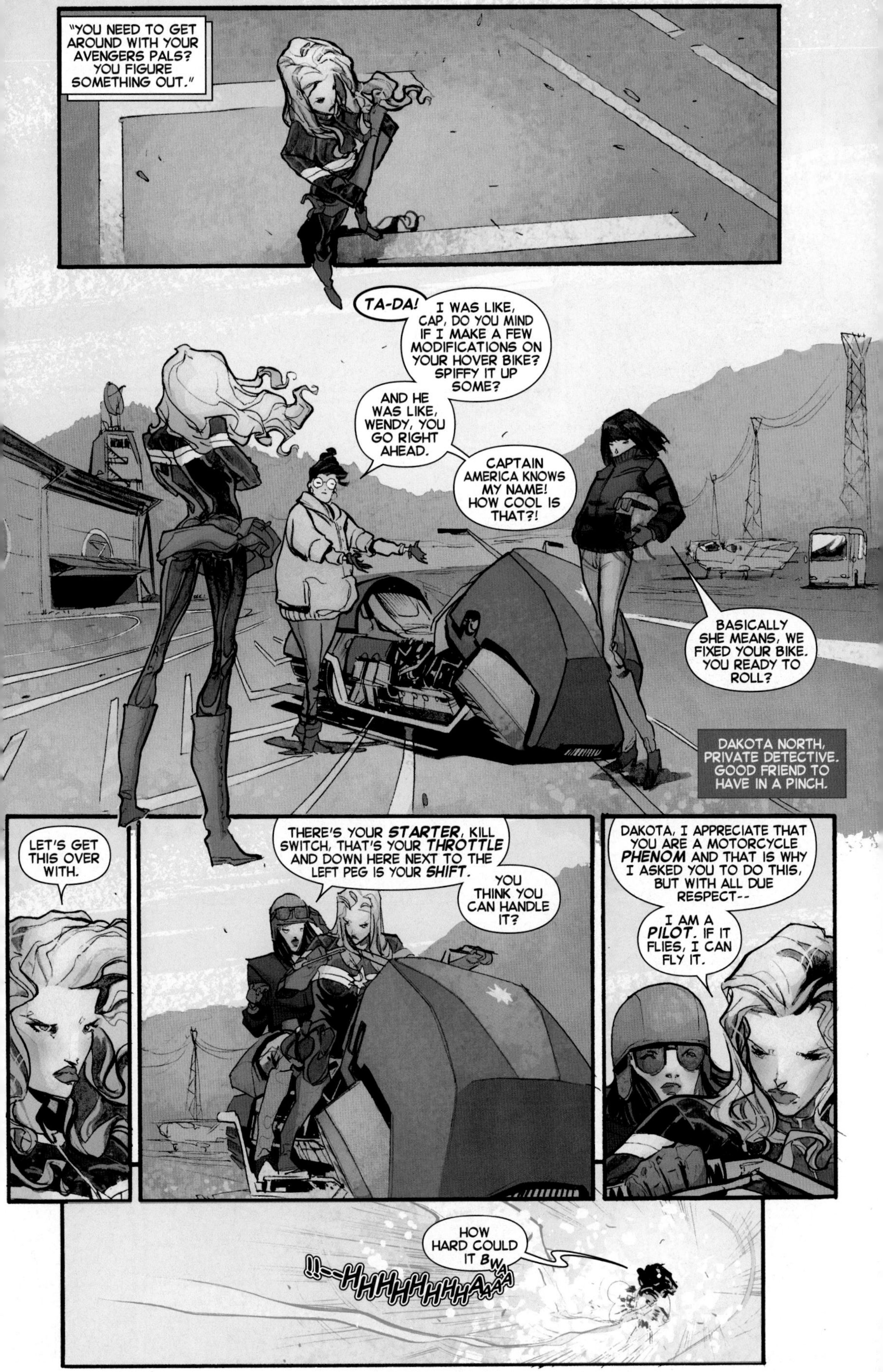
"YOU NEED TO GET AROUND WITH YOUR AVENGERS PALS? YOU FIGURE SOMETHING OUT."
TA-DA!
I WAS LIKE, CAP, DO YOU MIND IF I MAKE A FEW MODIFICATIONS ON YOUR HOVER BIKE? SPIFFY IT UP SOME?
AND HE WAS LIKE, WENDY, YOU GO RIGHT AHEAD.
CAPTAIN AMERICA KNOWS MY NAME! HOW COOL IS THAT?!
BASICALLY SHE MEANS, WE FIXED YOUR BIKE. YOU READY TO ROLL?
DAKOTA NORTH, PRIVATE DETECTIVE. GOOD FRIEND TO HAVE IN A PINCH.
LET'S GET THIS OVER WITH.
THERE'S YOUR STARTER, KILL SWITCH, THAT'S YOUR THROTTLE AND DOWN HERE NEXT TO THE LEFT PEG IS YOUR SHIFT.
YOU THINK YOU CAN HANDLE IT?
DAKOTA, I APPRECIATE THAT YOU ARE A MOTORCYCLE PHENOM AND THAT IS WHY I ASKED YOU TO DO THIS, BUT WITH ALL DUE RESPECT--
I AM A PILOT. IF IT FLIES, I CAN FLY IT.
HOW HARD COULD IT BWAAA
!!--HHHHHHHHAAAA

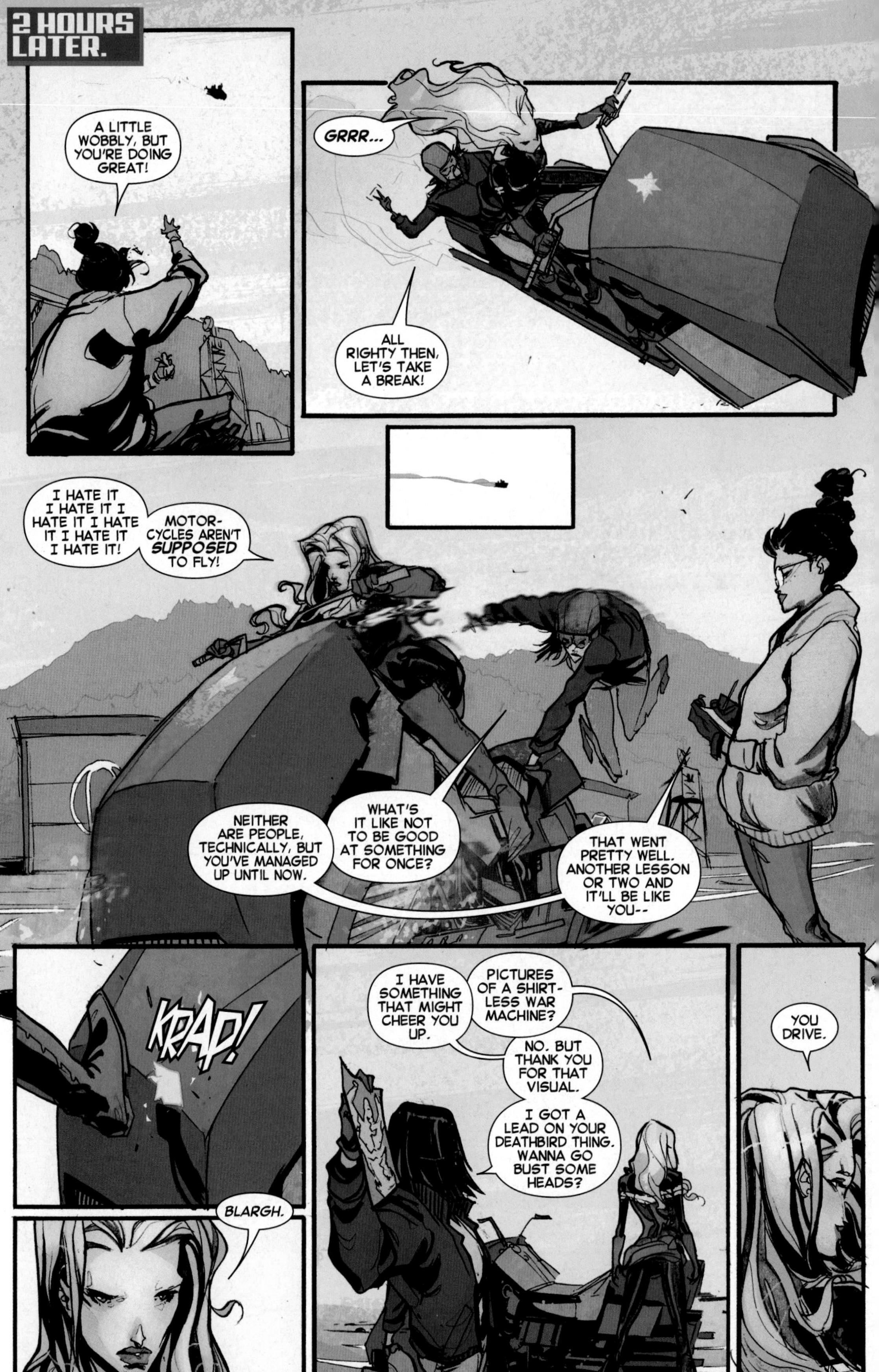
2 HOURS LATER.
A LITTLE WOBBLY, BUT YOU'RE DOING GREAT!
GRRR...
ALL RIGHTY THEN, LET'S TAKE A BREAK!
I HATE IT I HATE IT I HATE IT I HATE IT I HATE IT I HATE IT!
MOTOR-CYCLES AREN'T *SUPPOSED* TO FLY!
NEITHER ARE PEOPLE, TECHNICALLY, BUT YOU'VE MANAGED UP UNTIL NOW.
WHAT'S IT LIKE NOT TO BE GOOD AT SOMETHING FOR ONCE?
THAT WENT PRETTY WELL. ANOTHER LESSON OR TWO AND IT'LL BE LIKE YOU--
KRAP!
BLARGH.
I HAVE SOMETHING THAT MIGHT CHEER YOU UP.
PICTURES OF A SHIRT-LESS WAR MACHINE?
NO. BUT THANK YOU FOR THAT VISUAL.
I GOT A LEAD ON YOUR DEATHBIRD THING. WANNA GO BUST SOME HEADS?
YOU DRIVE.

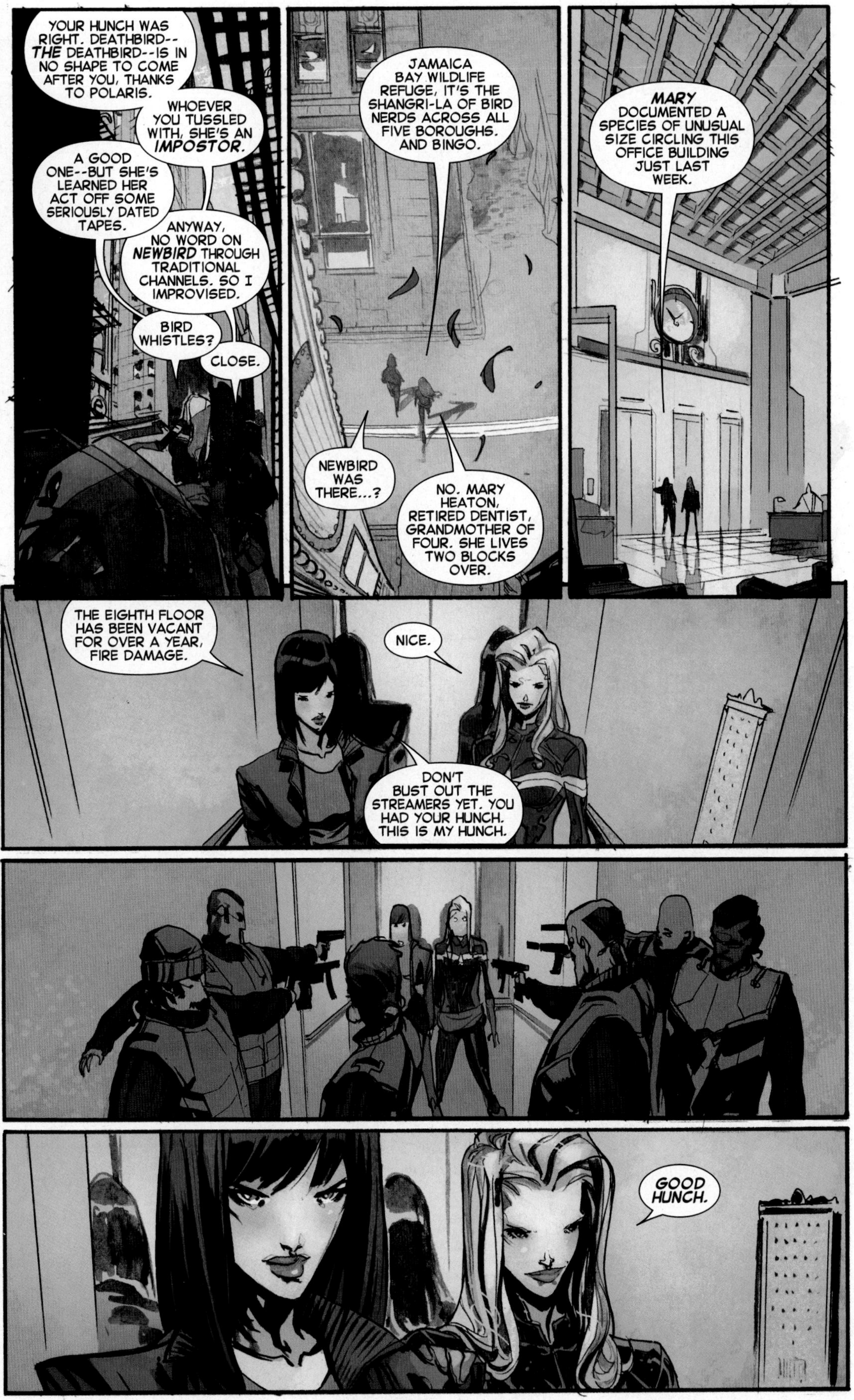
YOUR HUNCH WAS RIGHT. DEATHBIRD-- THE DEATHBIRD--IS IN NO SHAPE TO COME AFTER YOU, THANKS TO POLARIS.
WHOEVER YOU TUSSLED WITH, SHE'S AN IMPOSTOR.
A GOOD ONE--BUT SHE'S LEARNED HER ACT OFF SOME SERIOUSLY DATED TAPES.
ANYWAY, NO WORD ON NEWBIRD THROUGH TRADITIONAL CHANNELS. SO I IMPROVISED.
BIRD WHISTLES?
CLOSE.
JAMAICA BAY WILDLIFE REFUGE, IT'S THE SHANGRI-LA OF BIRD NERDS ACROSS ALL FIVE BOROUGHS. AND BINGO.
NEWBIRD WAS THERE...?
NO. MARY HEATON, RETIRED DENTIST, GRANDMOTHER OF FOUR. SHE LIVES TWO BLOCKS OVER.
MARY DOCUMENTED A SPECIES OF UNUSUAL SIZE CIRCLING THIS OFFICE BUILDING JUST LAST WEEK.
THE EIGHTH FLOOR HAS BEEN VACANT FOR OVER A YEAR, FIRE DAMAGE.
NICE.
DON'T BUST OUT THE STREAMERS YET. YOU HAD YOUR HUNCH. THIS IS MY HUNCH.
GOOD HUNCH.

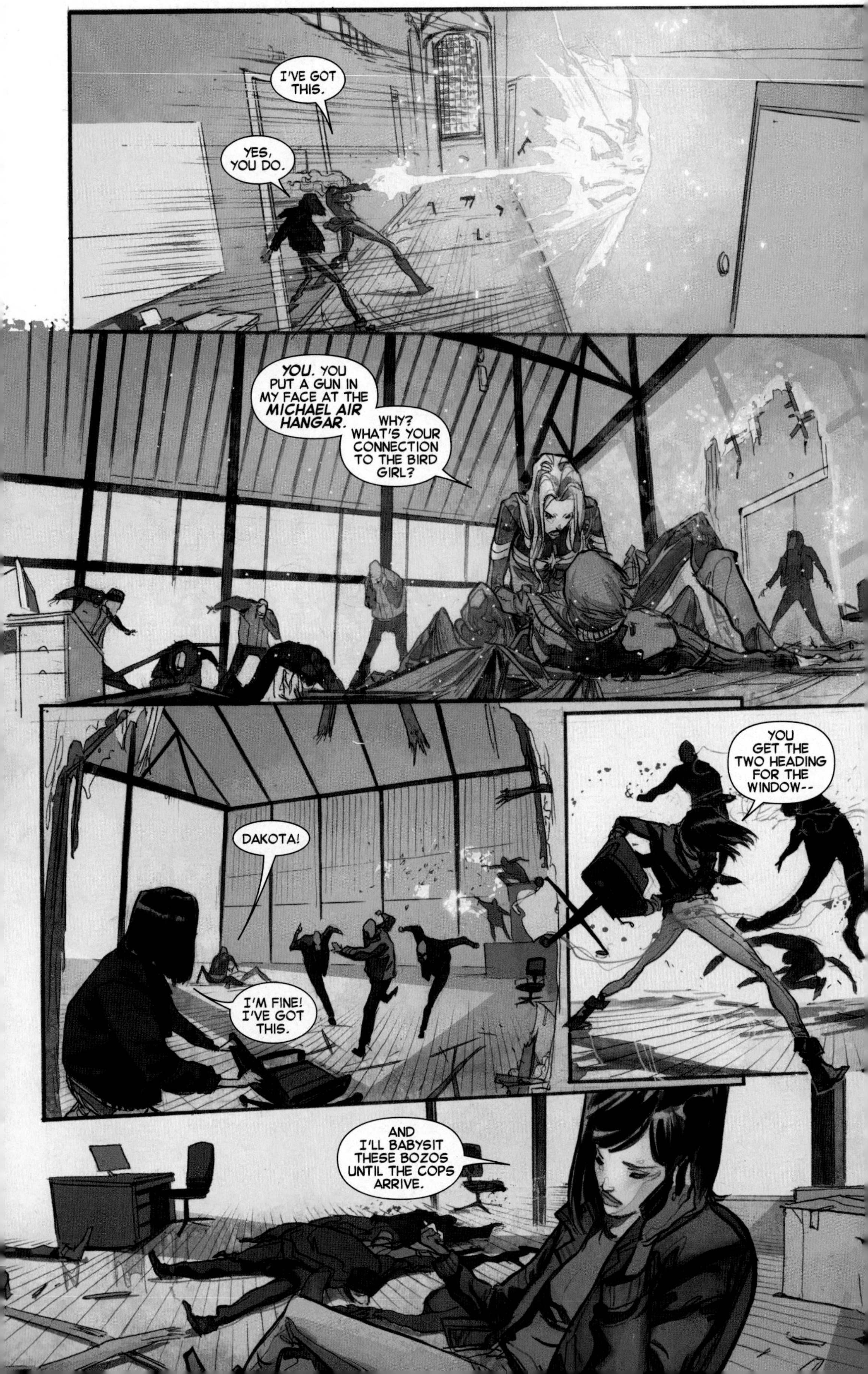
I'VE GOT THIS.
YES, YOU DO.
YOU. YOU PUT A GUN IN MY FACE AT THE MICHAEL AIR HANGAR.
WHY? WHAT'S YOUR CONNECTION TO THE BIRD GIRL?
DAKOTA!
I'M FINE! I'VE GOT THIS.
YOU GET THE TWO HEADING FOR THE WINDOW--
AND I'LL BABYSIT THESE BOZOS UNTIL THE COPS ARRIVE.

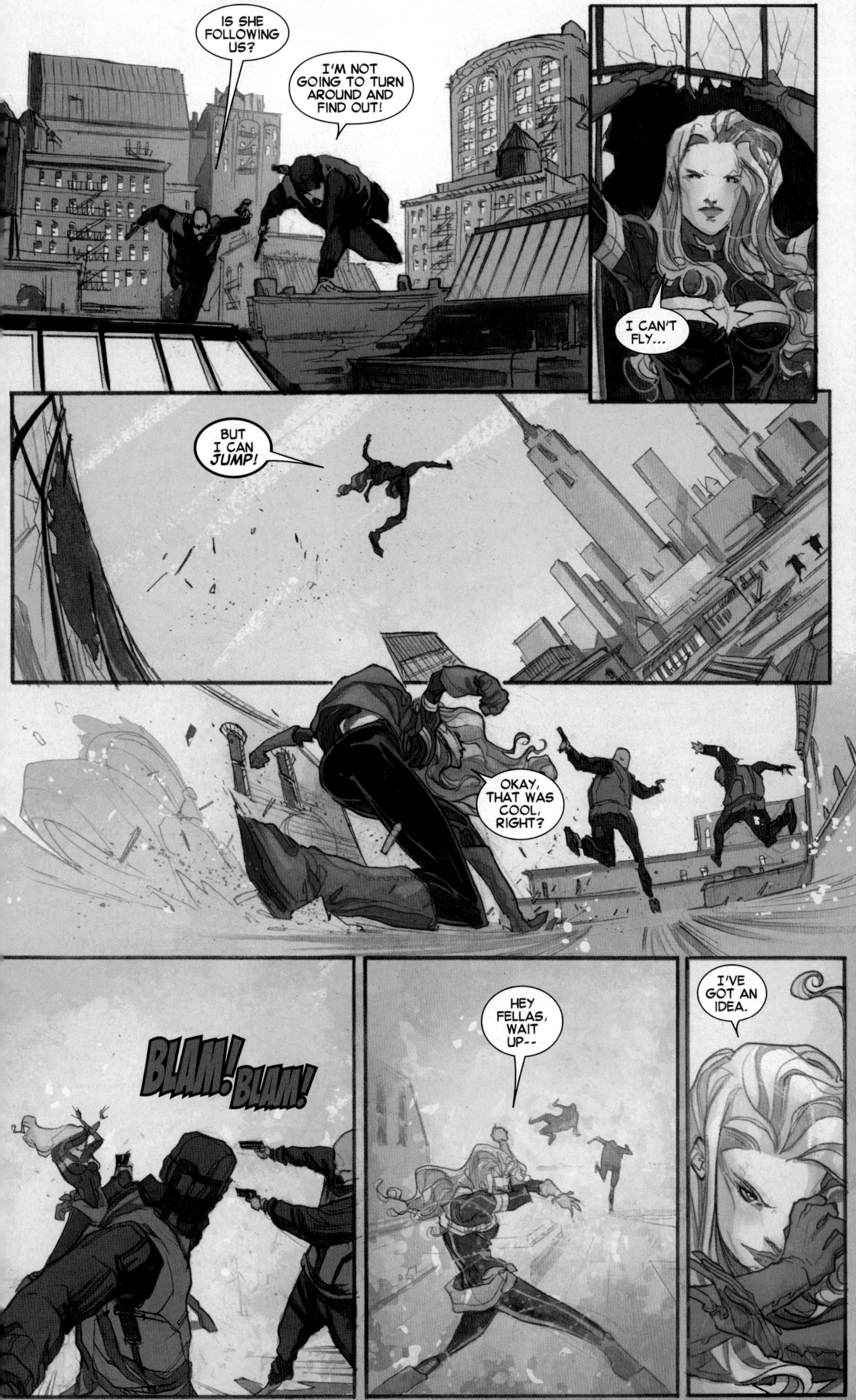
IS SHE FOLLOWING US?
I'M NOT GOING TO TURN AROUND AND FIND OUT!
I CAN'T FLY...
BUT I CAN JUMP!
OKAY, THAT WAS COOL, RIGHT?
BLAM! BLAM!
HEY FELLAS, WAIT UP--
I'VE GOT AN IDEA.

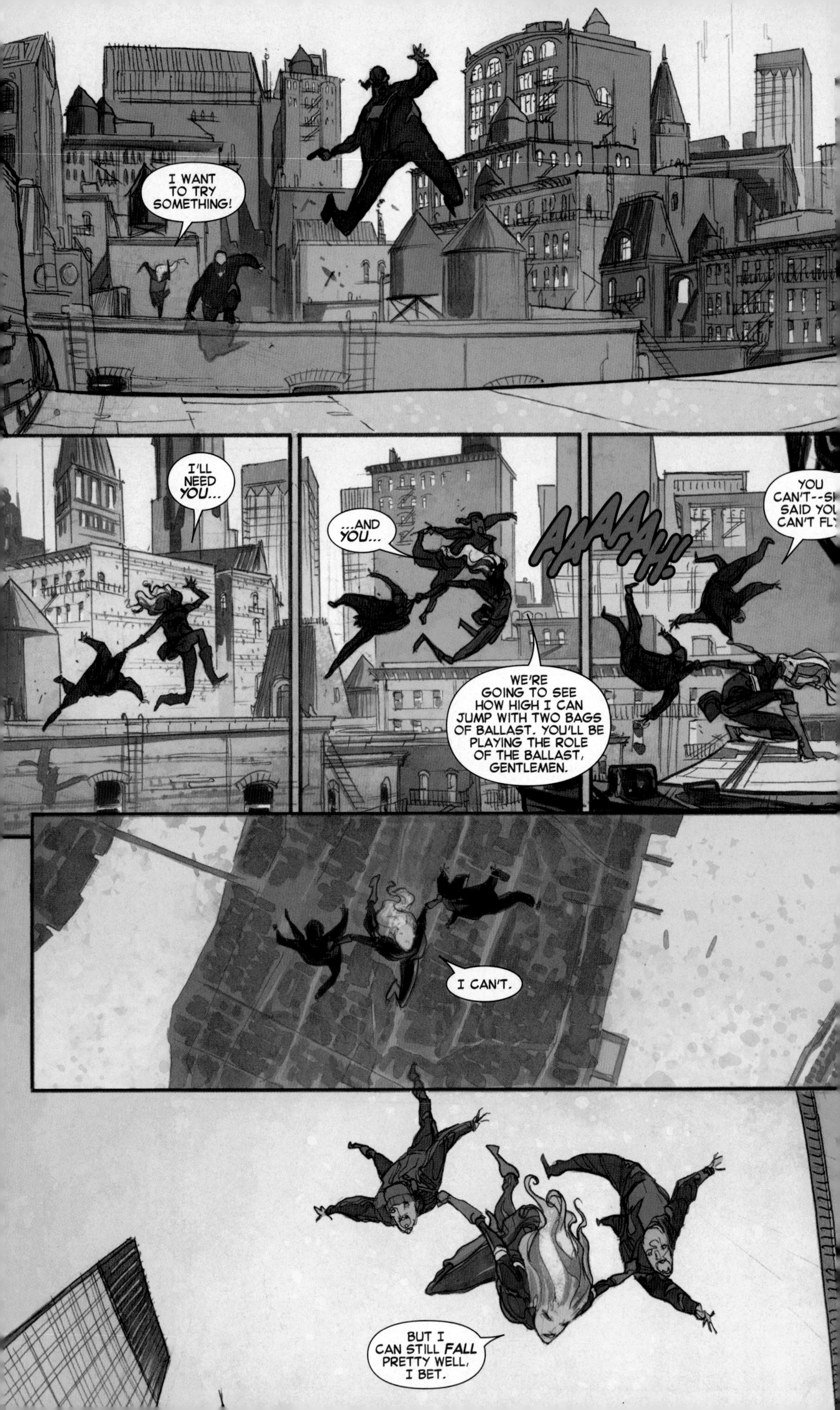
I WANT TO TRY SOMETHING!
I'LL NEED *YOU*...
...AND *YOU*...
WE'RE GOING TO SEE HOW HIGH I CAN JUMP WITH TWO BAGS OF BALLAST. YOU'LL BE PLAYING THE ROLE OF THE BALLAST, GENTLEMEN.
AAAAAAH!
YOU CAN'T--S
SAID YO
CAN'T FL
I CAN'T.
BUT I CAN STILL *FALL* PRETTY WELL, I BET.

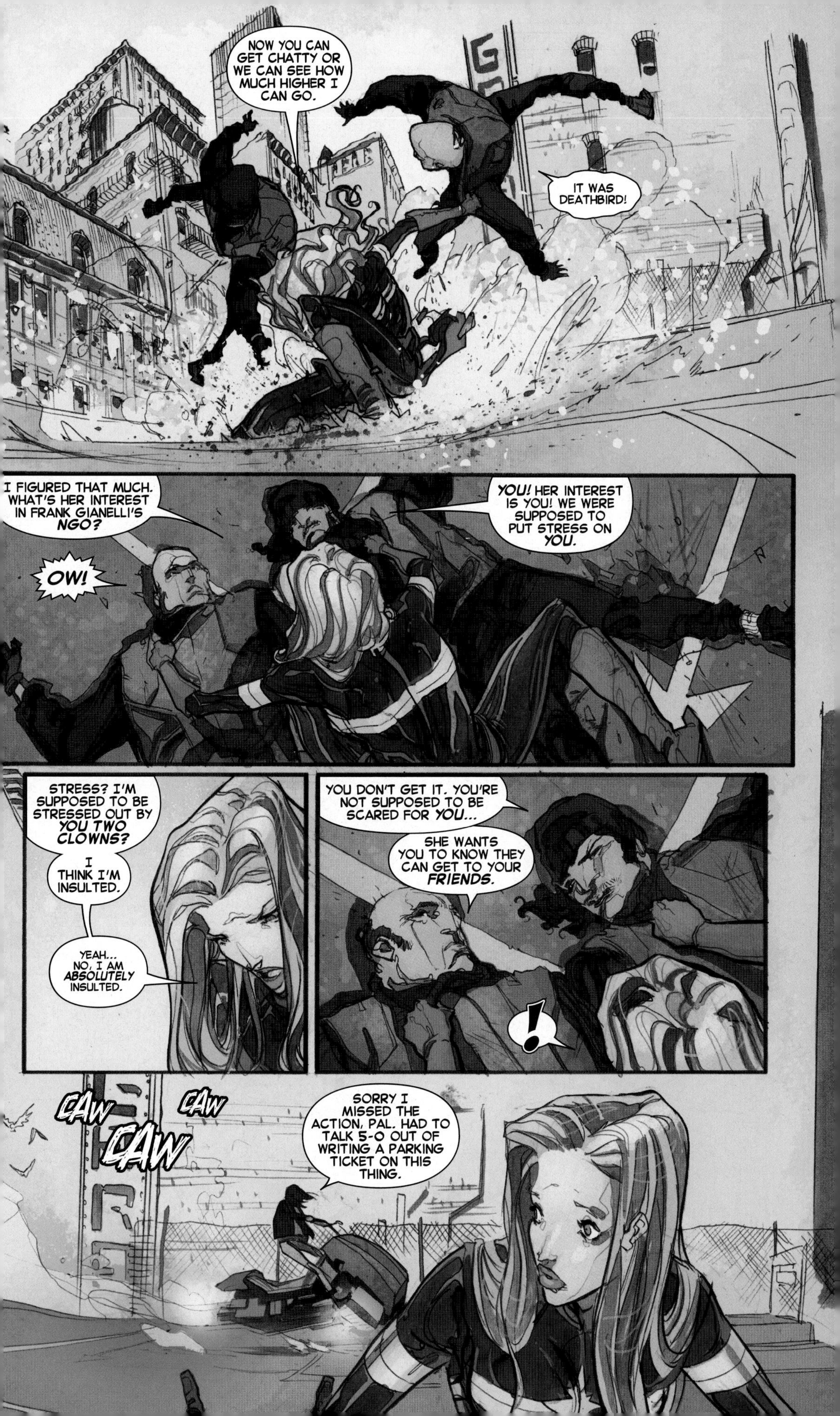
NOW YOU CAN GET CHATTY OR WE CAN SEE HOW MUCH HIGHER I CAN GO.
IT WAS DEATHBIRD!
I FIGURED THAT MUCH. WHAT'S HER INTEREST IN FRANK GIANELLI'S NGO?
OW!
YOU! HER INTEREST IS YOU! WE WERE SUPPOSED TO PUT STRESS ON YOU.
STRESS? I'M SUPPOSED TO BE STRESSED OUT BY YOU TWO CLOWNS?
I THINK I'M INSULTED.
YEAH... NO, I AM ABSOLUTELY INSULTED.
YOU DON'T GET IT. YOU'RE NOT SUPPOSED TO BE SCARED FOR YOU...
SHE WANTS YOU TO KNOW THEY CAN GET TO YOUR FRIENDS.
!
CAW
CAW
CAW
SORRY I MISSED THE ACTION, PAL. HAD TO TALK 5-O OUT OF WRITING A PARKING TICKET ON THIS THING.

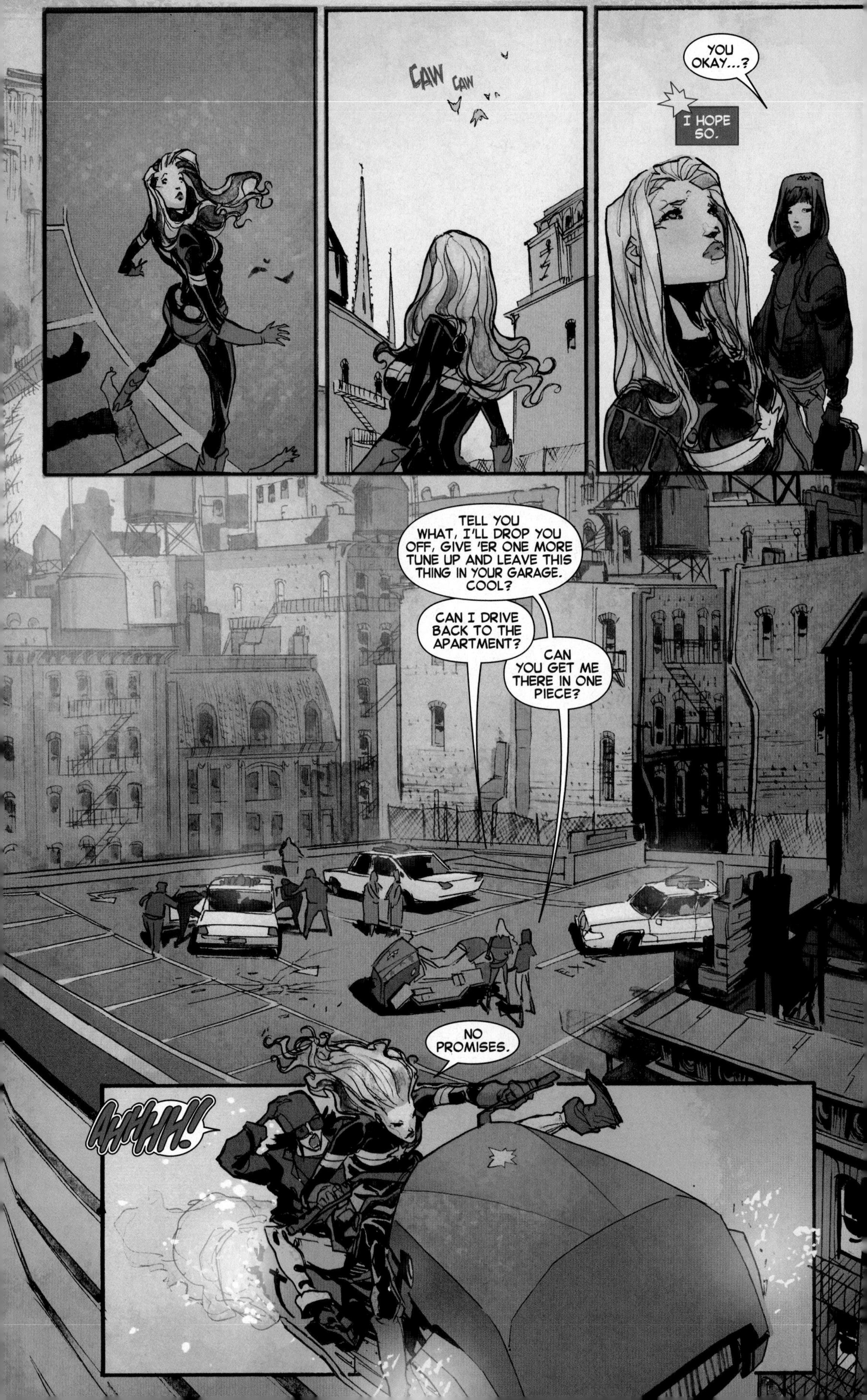
CAW CAW
YOU OKAY...?
I HOPE SO.
TELL YOU WHAT, I'LL DROP YOU OFF, GIVE 'ER ONE MORE TUNE UP AND LEAVE THIS THING IN YOUR GARAGE. COOL?
CAN I DRIVE BACK TO THE APARTMENT?
CAN YOU GET ME THERE IN ONE PIECE?
NO PROMISES.
AHHHH!

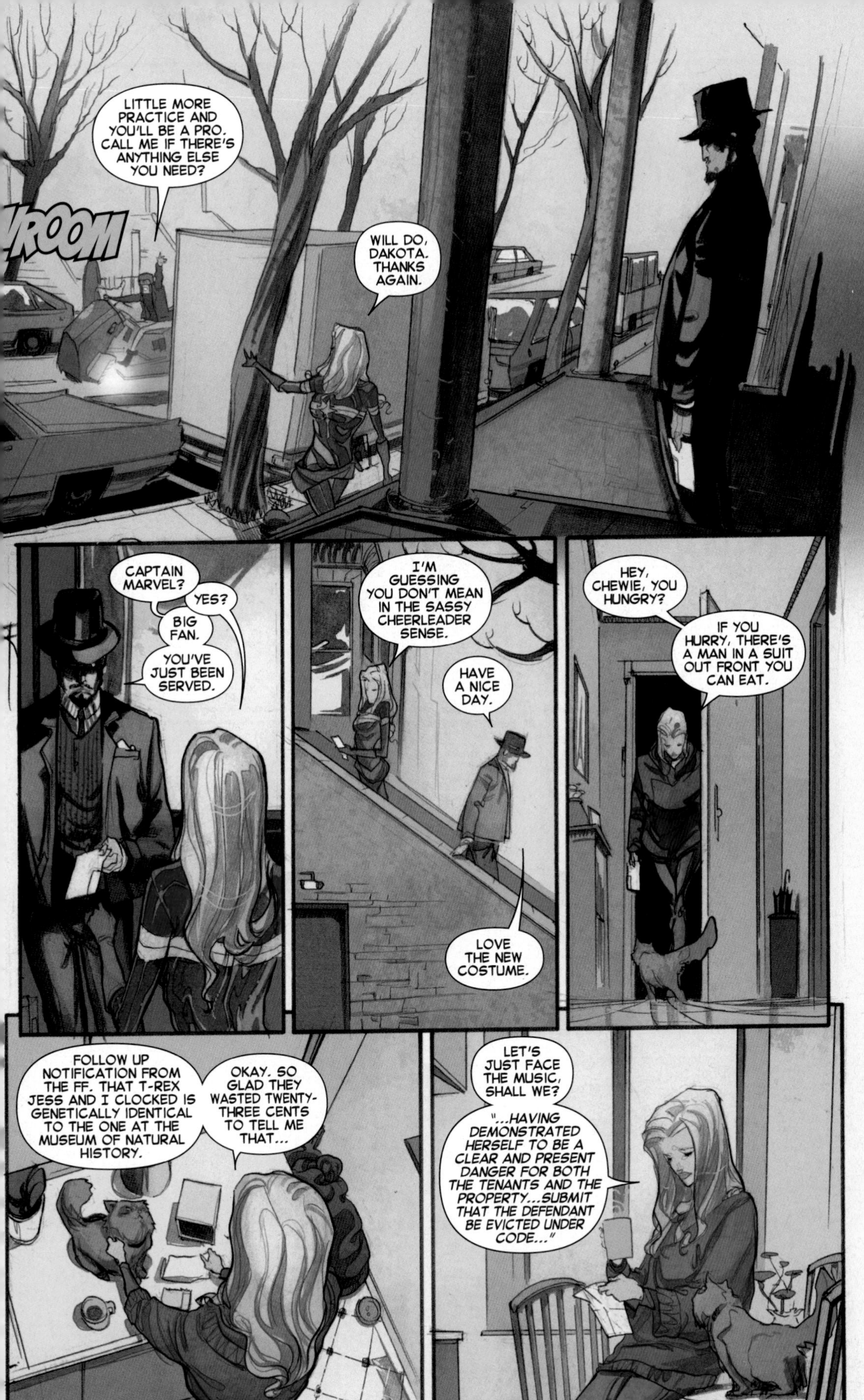
LITTLE MORE PRACTICE AND YOU'LL BE A PRO. CALL ME IF THERE'S ANYTHING ELSE YOU NEED?
VROOM
WILL DO, DAKOTA. THANKS AGAIN.
CAPTAIN MARVEL?
YES?
BIG FAN.
YOU'VE JUST BEEN SERVED.
I'M GUESSING YOU DON'T MEAN IN THE SASSY CHEERLEADER SENSE.
HAVE A NICE DAY.
LOVE THE NEW COSTUME.
HEY, CHEWIE, YOU HUNGRY?
IF YOU HURRY, THERE'S A MAN IN A SUIT OUT FRONT YOU CAN EAT.
FOLLOW UP NOTIFICATION FROM THE FF. THAT T-REX JESS AND I CLOCKED IS GENETICALLY IDENTICAL TO THE ONE AT THE MUSEUM OF NATURAL HISTORY.
OKAY. SO GLAD THEY WASTED TWENTY-THREE CENTS TO TELL ME THAT...
LET'S JUST FACE THE MUSIC, SHALL WE?
"...HAVING DEMONSTRATED HERSELF TO BE A CLEAR AND PRESENT DANGER FOR BOTH THE TENANTS AND THE PROPERTY...SUBMIT THAT THE DEFENDANT BE EVICTED UNDER CODE..."

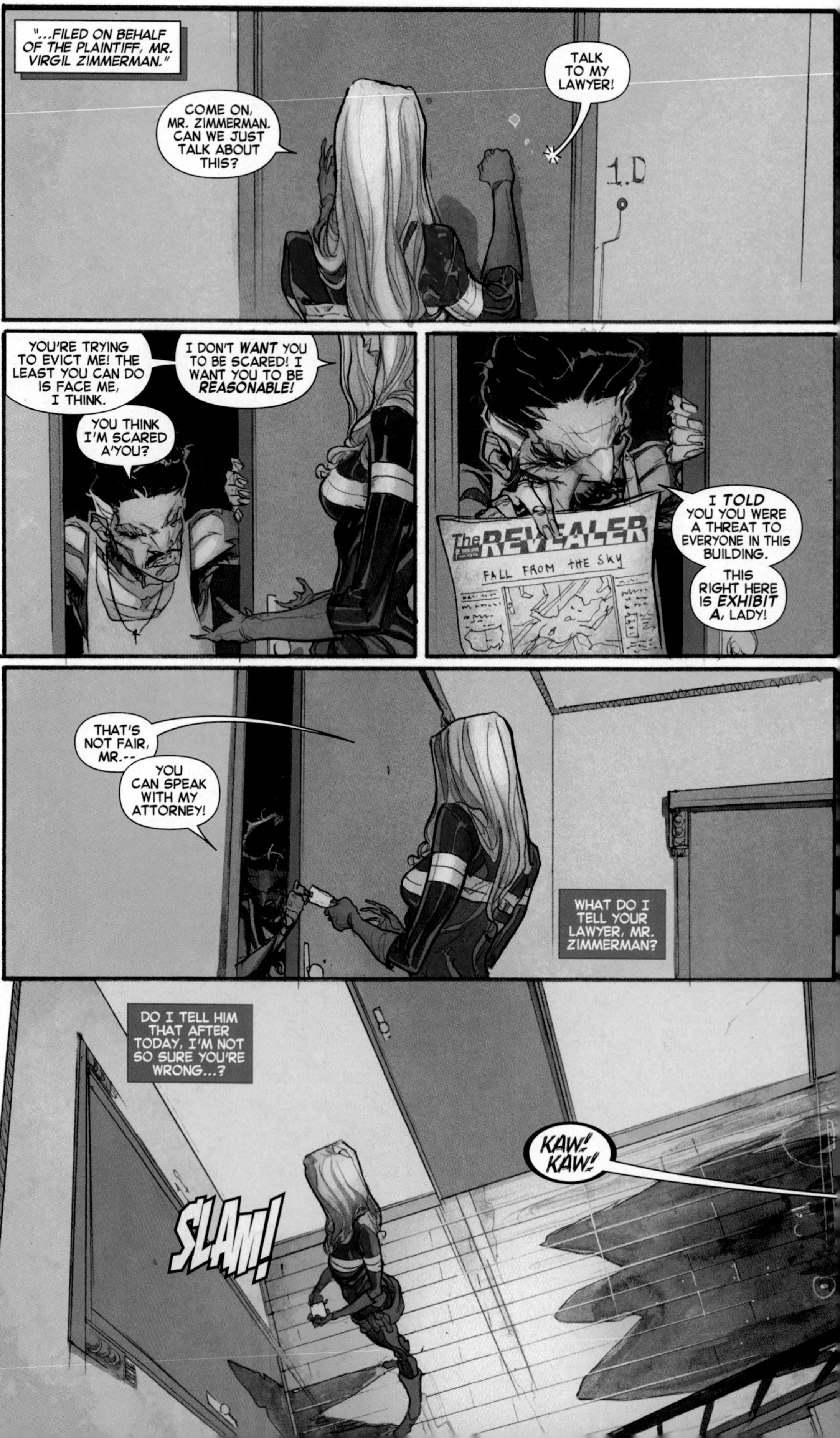
"...FILED ON BEHALF OF THE PLAINTIFF, MR. VIRGIL ZIMMERMAN."
COME ON, MR. ZIMMERMAN. CAN WE JUST TALK ABOUT THIS?
TALK TO MY LAWYER!
1.D
YOU'RE TRYING TO EVICT ME! THE LEAST YOU CAN DO IS FACE ME, I THINK.
YOU THINK I'M SCARED A'YOU?
I DON'T WANT YOU TO BE SCARED! I WANT YOU TO BE REASONABLE!
The REVEALER
FALL FROM THE SKY
I TOLD YOU YOU WERE A THREAT TO EVERYONE IN THIS BUILDING.
THIS RIGHT HERE IS EXHIBIT A, LADY!
THAT'S NOT FAIR, MR.--
YOU CAN SPEAK WITH MY ATTORNEY!
WHAT DO I TELL YOUR LAWYER, MR. ZIMMERMAN?
DO I TELL HIM THAT AFTER TODAY, I'M NOT SO SURE YOU'RE WRONG...?
SLAM!
KAW! KAW!

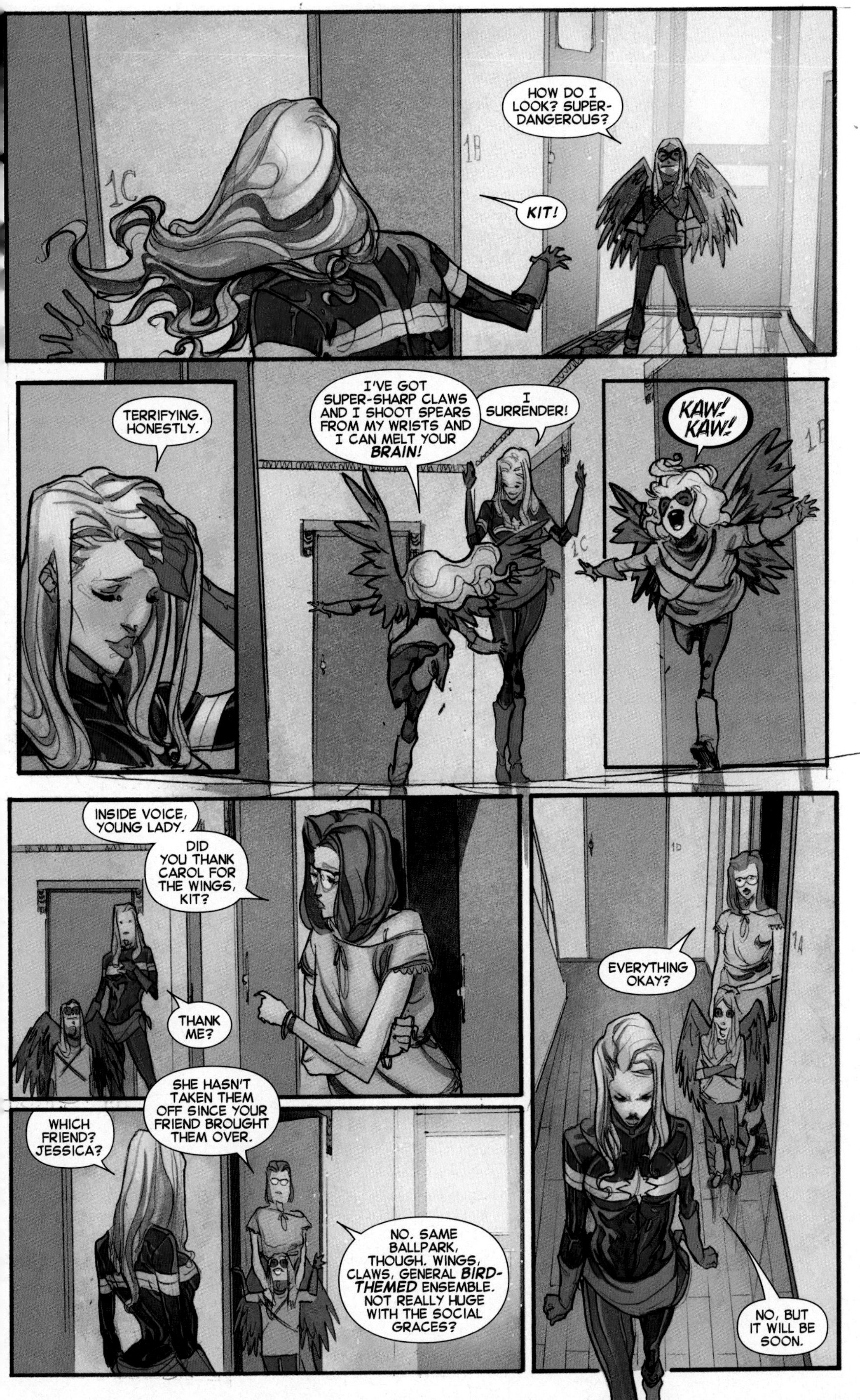

HOW DO I LOOK? SUPER-DANGEROUS?
KIT!
TERRIFYING. HONESTLY.
I'VE GOT SUPER-SHARP CLAWS AND I SHOOT SPEARS FROM MY WRISTS AND I CAN MELT YOUR **BRAIN!**
I SURRENDER!
KAW! KAW!
INSIDE VOICE, YOUNG LADY.
DID YOU THANK CAROL FOR THE WINGS, KIT?
THANK ME?
SHE HASN'T TAKEN THEM OFF SINCE YOUR FRIEND BROUGHT THEM OVER.
WHICH FRIEND? JESSICA?
NO. SAME BALLPARK, THOUGH. WINGS, CLAWS, GENERAL **BIRD-THEMED** ENSEMBLE. NOT REALLY HUGE WITH THE SOCIAL GRACES?
EVERYTHING OKAY?
NO, BUT IT WILL BE SOON.

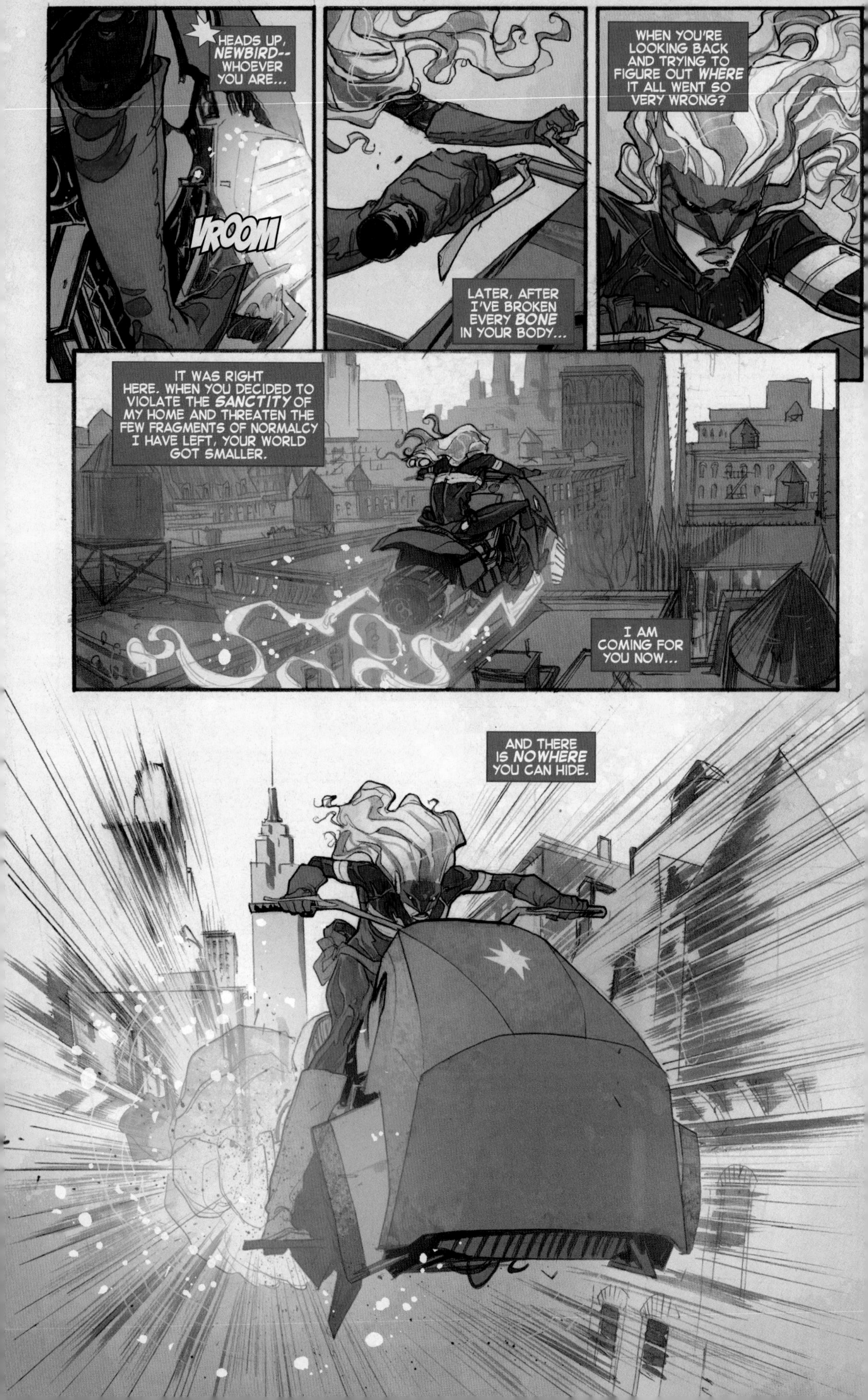

HEADS UP, NEWBIRD-- WHOEVER YOU ARE...
VROOM
WHEN YOU'RE LOOKING BACK AND TRYING TO FIGURE OUT WHERE IT ALL WENT SO VERY WRONG?
LATER, AFTER I'VE BROKEN EVERY BONE IN YOUR BODY...
IT WAS RIGHT HERE. WHEN YOU DECIDED TO VIOLATE THE SANCTITY OF MY HOME AND THREATEN THE FEW FRAGMENTS OF NORMALCY I HAVE LEFT, YOUR WORLD GOT SMALLER.
I AM COMING FOR YOU NOW...
AND THERE IS NOWHERE YOU CAN HIDE.

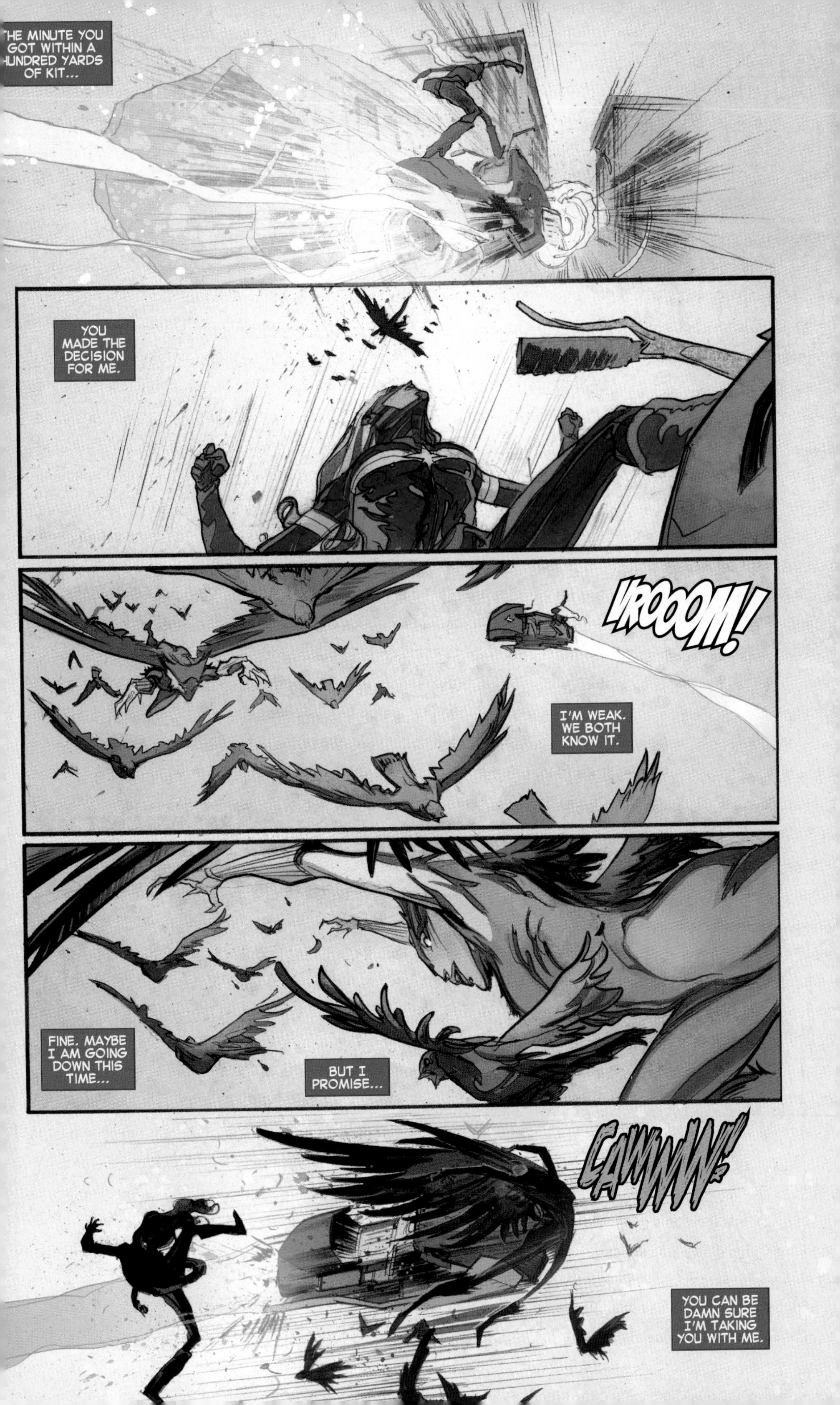
THE MINUTE YOU GOT WITHIN A HUNDRED YARDS OF KIT...
YOU MADE THE DECISION FOR ME.
VROOOM!
I'M WEAK. WE BOTH KNOW IT.
FINE. MAYBE I AM GOING DOWN THIS TIME...
BUT I PROMISE...
CAWWW!
YOU CAN BE DAMN SURE I'M TAKING YOU WITH ME.

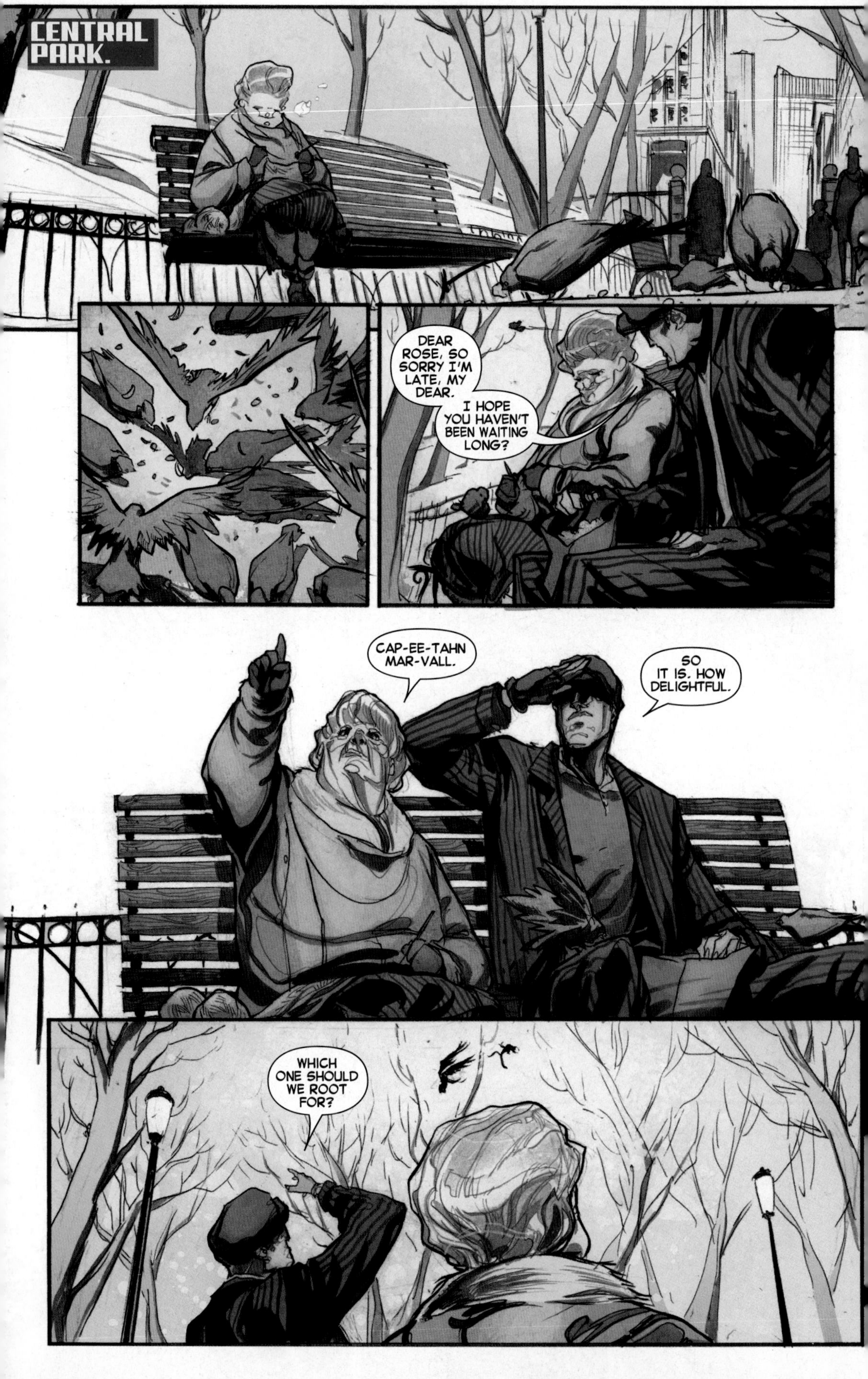
CENTRAL PARK.
DEAR ROSE, SO SORRY I'M LATE, MY DEAR.
I HOPE YOU HAVEN'T BEEN WAITING LONG?
CAP-EE-TAHN MAR-VALL.
SO IT IS. HOW DELIGHTFUL.
WHICH ONE SHOULD WE ROOT FOR?

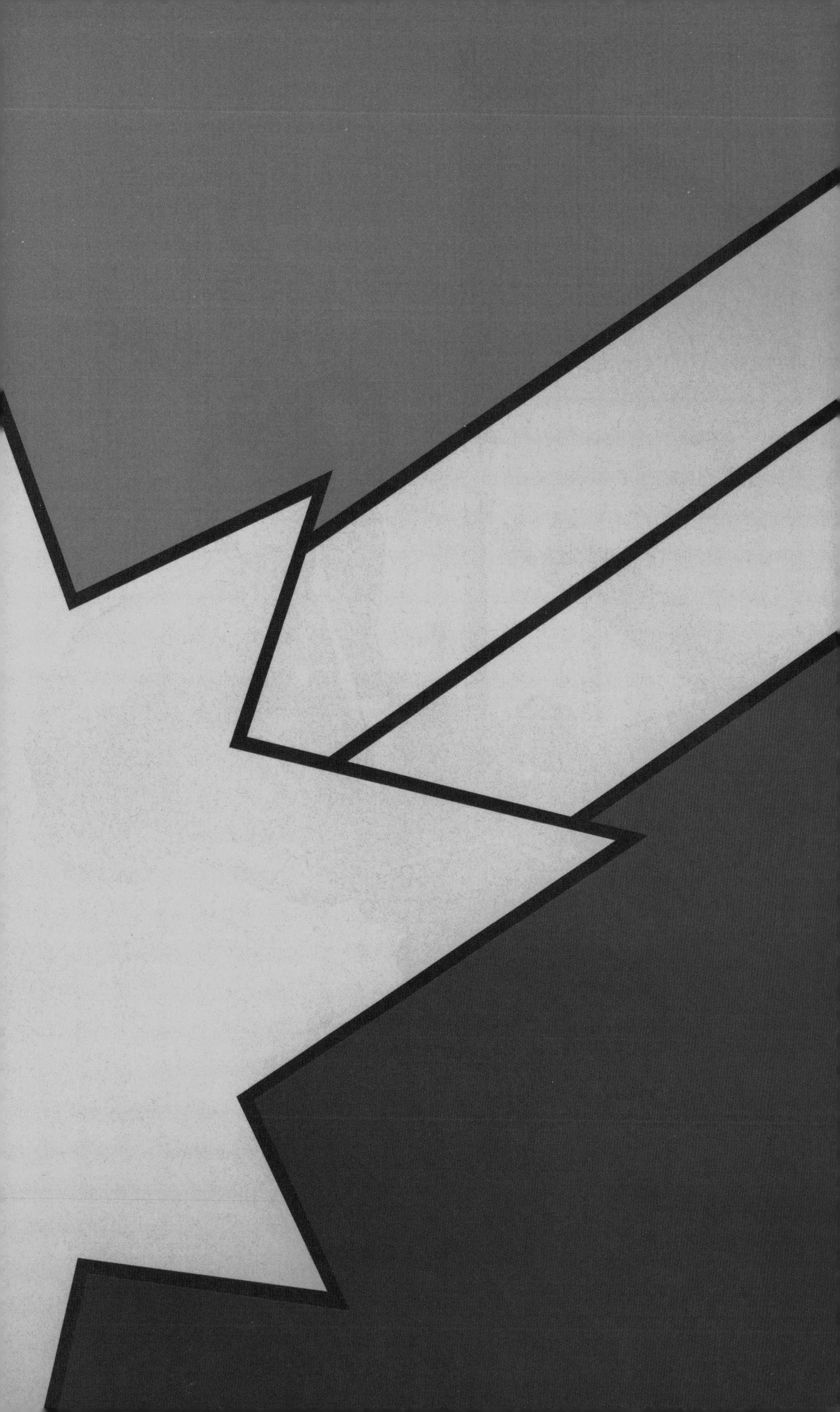

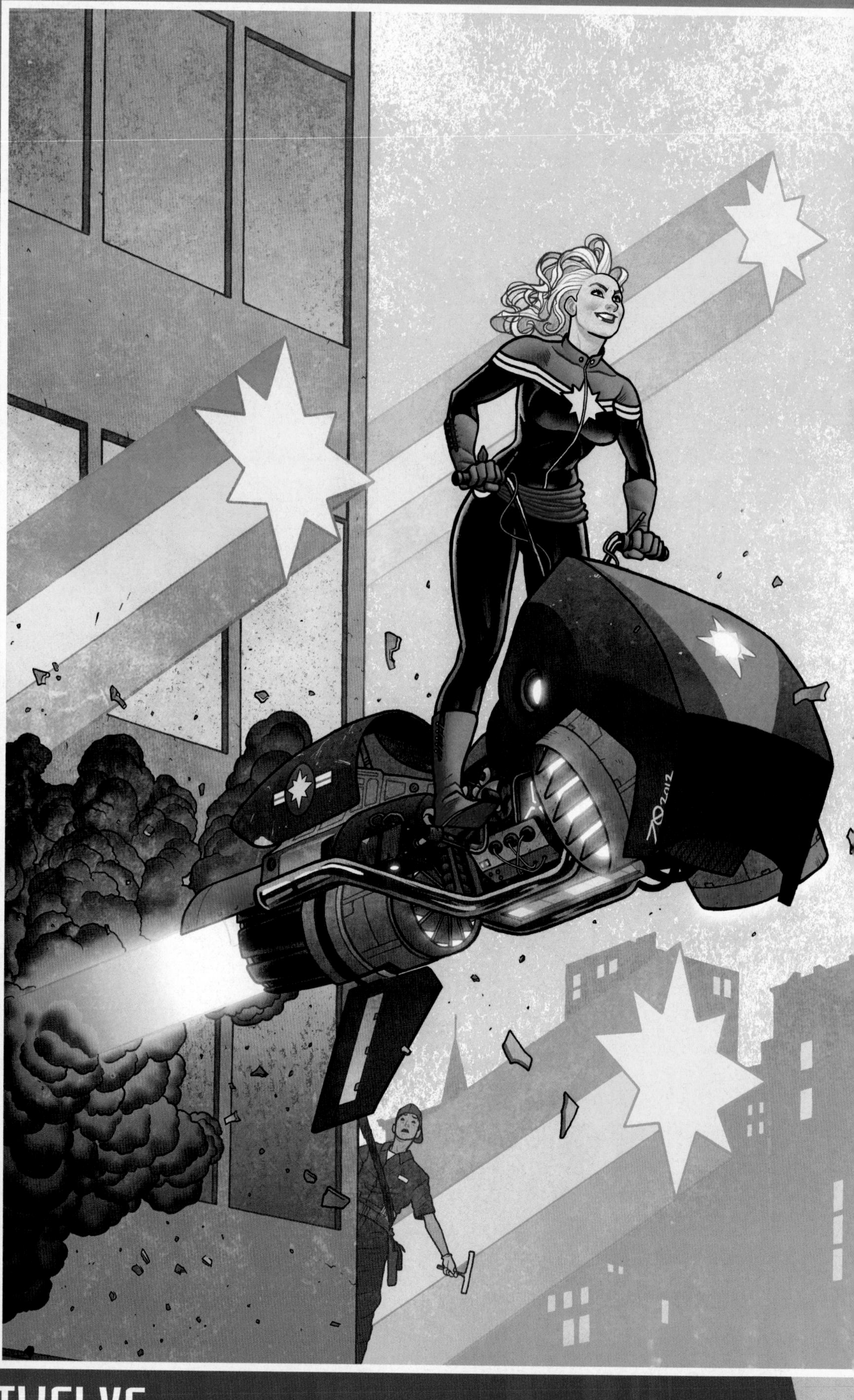

TWELVE

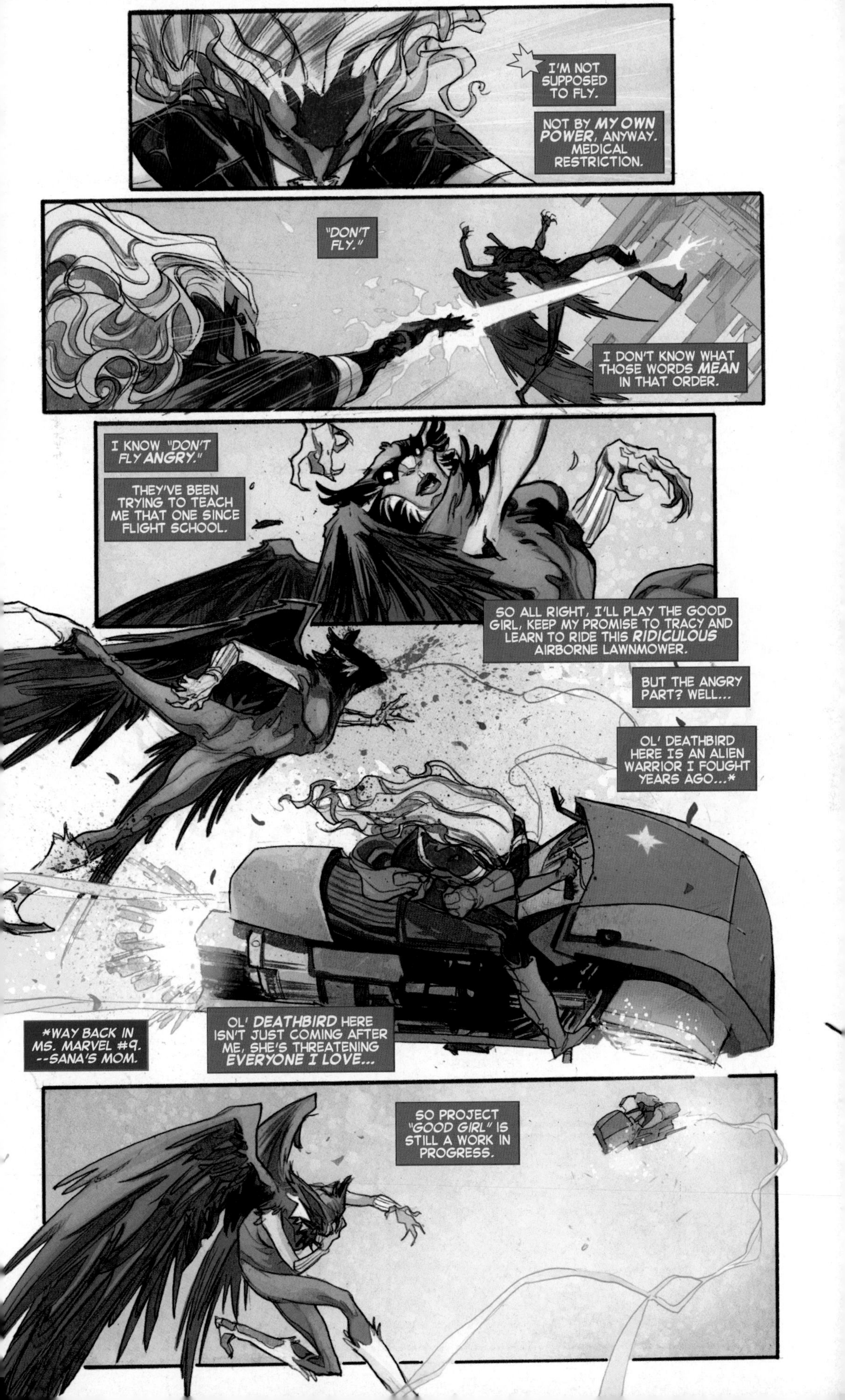

I'M NOT SUPPOSED TO FLY.
NOT BY MY OWN POWER, ANYWAY. MEDICAL RESTRICTION.
"DON'T FLY."
I DON'T KNOW WHAT THOSE WORDS MEAN IN THAT ORDER.
I KNOW "DON'T FLY ANGRY."
THEY'VE BEEN TRYING TO TEACH ME THAT ONE SINCE FLIGHT SCHOOL.
SO ALL RIGHT, I'LL PLAY THE GOOD GIRL, KEEP MY PROMISE TO TRACY AND LEARN TO RIDE THIS RIDICULOUS AIRBORNE LAWNMOWER.
BUT THE ANGRY PART? WELL...
OL' DEATHBIRD HERE IS AN ALIEN WARRIOR I FOUGHT YEARS AGO...*
*WAY BACK IN MS. MARVEL #9. --SANA'S MOM.
OL' DEATHBIRD HERE ISN'T JUST COMING AFTER ME, SHE'S THREATENING EVERYONE I LOVE...
SO PROJECT "GOOD GIRL" IS STILL A WORK IN PROGRESS.

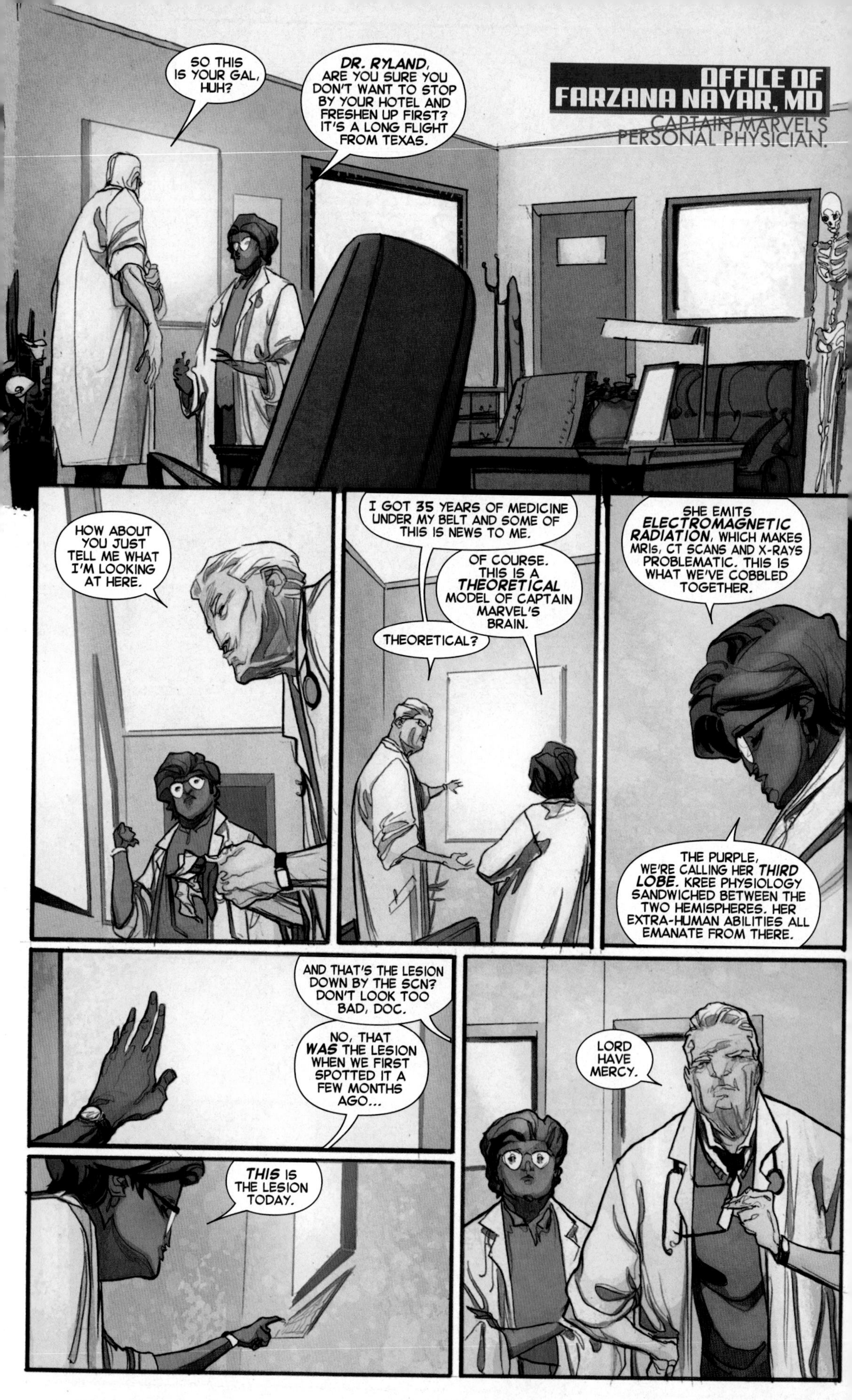
OFFICE OF FARZANA NAYAR, MD
CAPTAIN MARVEL'S PERSONAL PHYSICIAN.
SO THIS IS YOUR GAL, HUH?
DR. RYLAND, ARE YOU SURE YOU DON'T WANT TO STOP BY YOUR HOTEL AND FRESHEN UP FIRST? IT'S A LONG FLIGHT FROM TEXAS.
HOW ABOUT YOU JUST TELL ME WHAT I'M LOOKING AT HERE.
I GOT 35 YEARS OF MEDICINE UNDER MY BELT AND SOME OF THIS IS NEWS TO ME.
OF COURSE. THIS IS A THEORETICAL MODEL OF CAPTAIN MARVEL'S BRAIN.
THEORETICAL?
SHE EMITS ELECTROMAGNETIC RADIATION, WHICH MAKES MRIs, CT SCANS AND X-RAYS PROBLEMATIC. THIS IS WHAT WE'VE COBBLED TOGETHER.
THE PURPLE, WE'RE CALLING HER THIRD LOBE. KREE PHYSIOLOGY SANDWICHED BETWEEN THE TWO HEMISPHERES. HER EXTRA-HUMAN ABILITIES ALL EMANATE FROM THERE.
AND THAT'S THE LESION DOWN BY THE SCN? DON'T LOOK TOO BAD, DOC.
NO, THAT WAS THE LESION WHEN WE FIRST SPOTTED IT A FEW MONTHS AGO...
THIS IS THE LESION TODAY.
LORD HAVE MERCY.

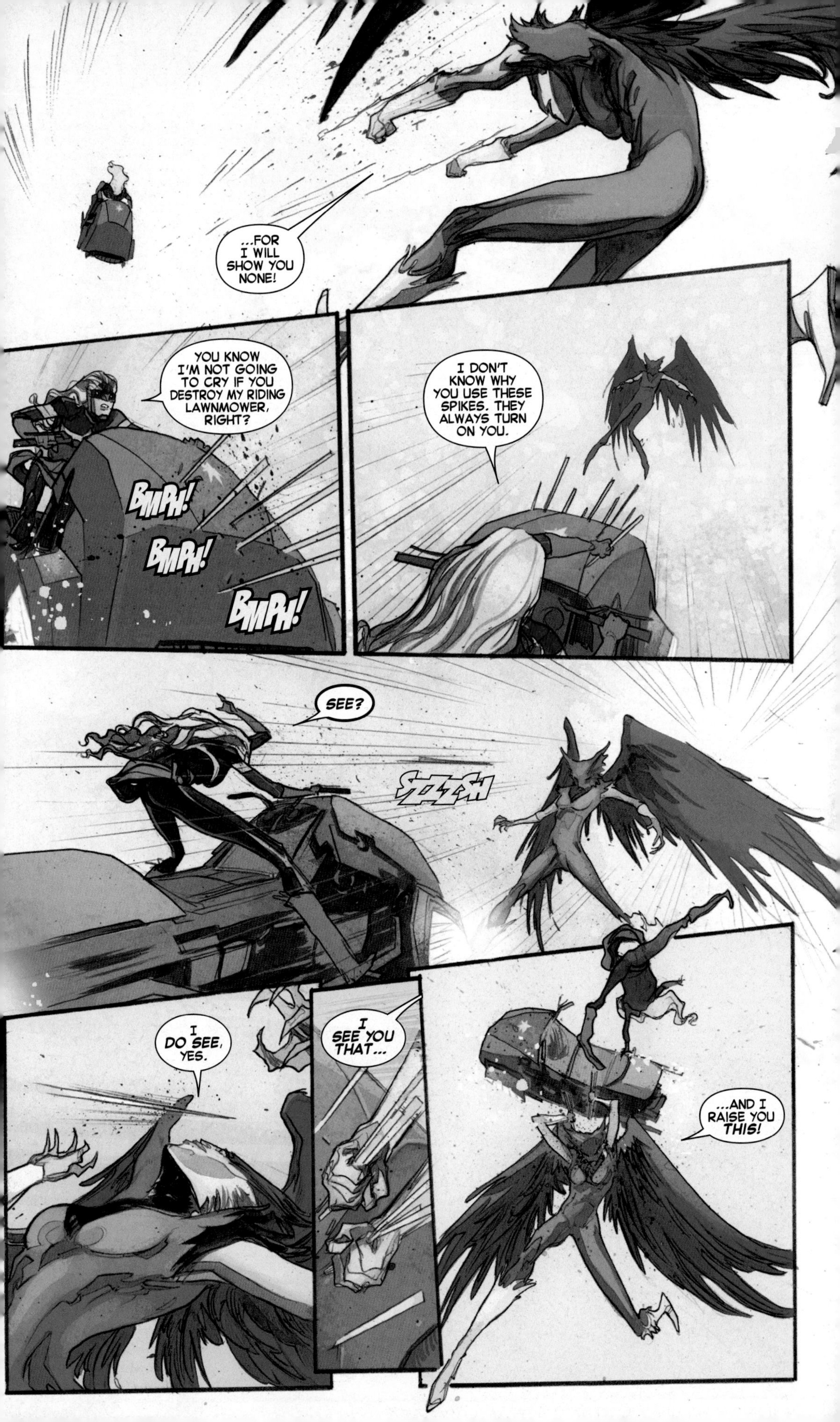
...FOR I WILL SHOW YOU NONE!
YOU KNOW I'M NOT GOING TO CRY IF YOU DESTROY MY RIDING LAWNMOWER, RIGHT?
BMPH!
BMPH!
BMPH!
I DON'T KNOW WHY YOU USE THESE SPIKES. THEY ALWAYS TURN ON YOU.
SEE?
SZZCH
I DO SEE, YES.
I SEE YOU THAT...
...AND I RAISE YOU THIS!

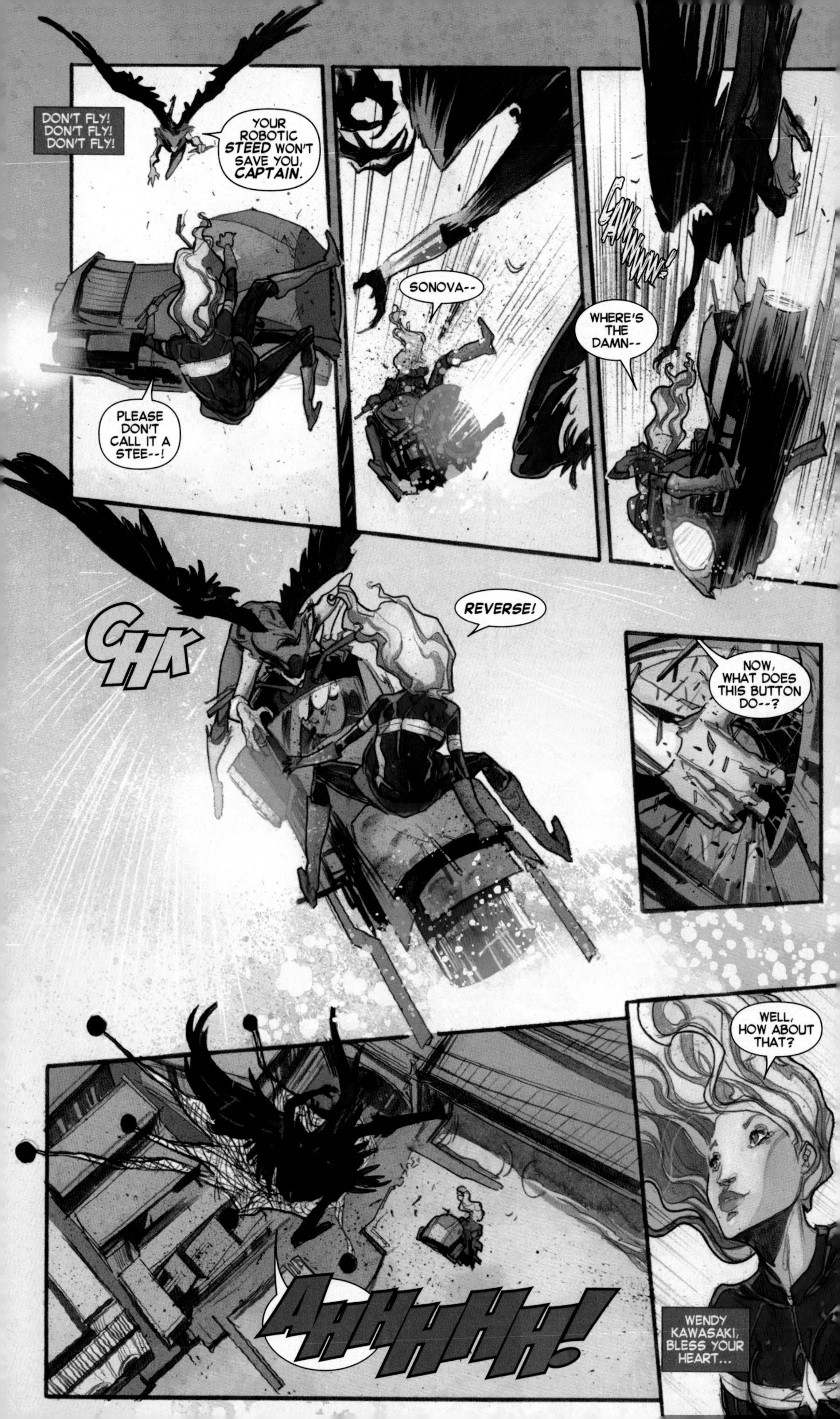

DON'T FLY! DON'T FLY! DON'T FLY!
YOUR ROBOTIC STEED WON'T SAVE YOU, CAPTAIN.
PLEASE DON'T CALL IT A STEE--!
SONOVA--
CAWWWWW!
WHERE'S THE DAMN--
CHK
REVERSE!
NOW, WHAT DOES THIS BUTTON DO--?
AHHHHHH!
WELL, HOW ABOUT THAT?
WENDY KAWASAKI, BLESS YOUR HEART...

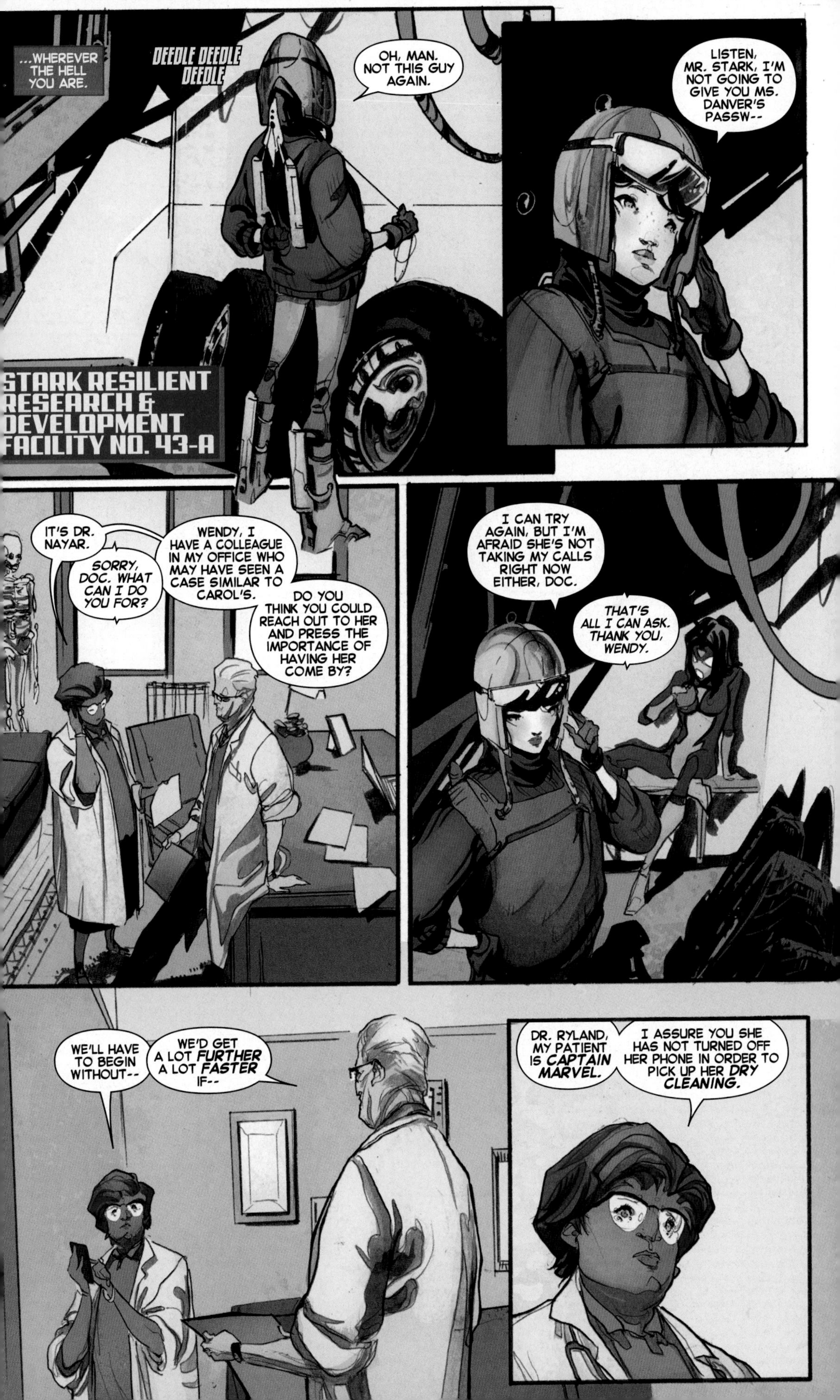
...WHEREVER THE HELL YOU ARE.
DEEDLE DEEDLE DEEDLE
OH, MAN. NOT THIS GUY AGAIN.
STARK RESILIENT RESEARCH & DEVELOPMENT FACILITY NO. 43-A
LISTEN, MR. STARK, I'M NOT GOING TO GIVE YOU MS. DANVER'S PASSW--
IT'S DR. NAYAR.
SORRY, DOC. WHAT CAN I DO YOU FOR?
WENDY, I HAVE A COLLEAGUE IN MY OFFICE WHO MAY HAVE SEEN A CASE SIMILAR TO CAROL'S.
DO YOU THINK YOU COULD REACH OUT TO HER AND PRESS THE IMPORTANCE OF HAVING HER COME BY?
I CAN TRY AGAIN, BUT I'M AFRAID SHE'S NOT TAKING MY CALLS RIGHT NOW EITHER, DOC.
THAT'S ALL I CAN ASK. THANK YOU, WENDY.
WE'LL HAVE TO BEGIN WITHOUT--
WE'D GET A LOT FURTHER A LOT FASTER IF--
DR. RYLAND, MY PATIENT IS CAPTAIN MARVEL.
I ASSURE YOU SHE HAS NOT TURNED OFF HER PHONE IN ORDER TO PICK UP HER DRY CLEANING.

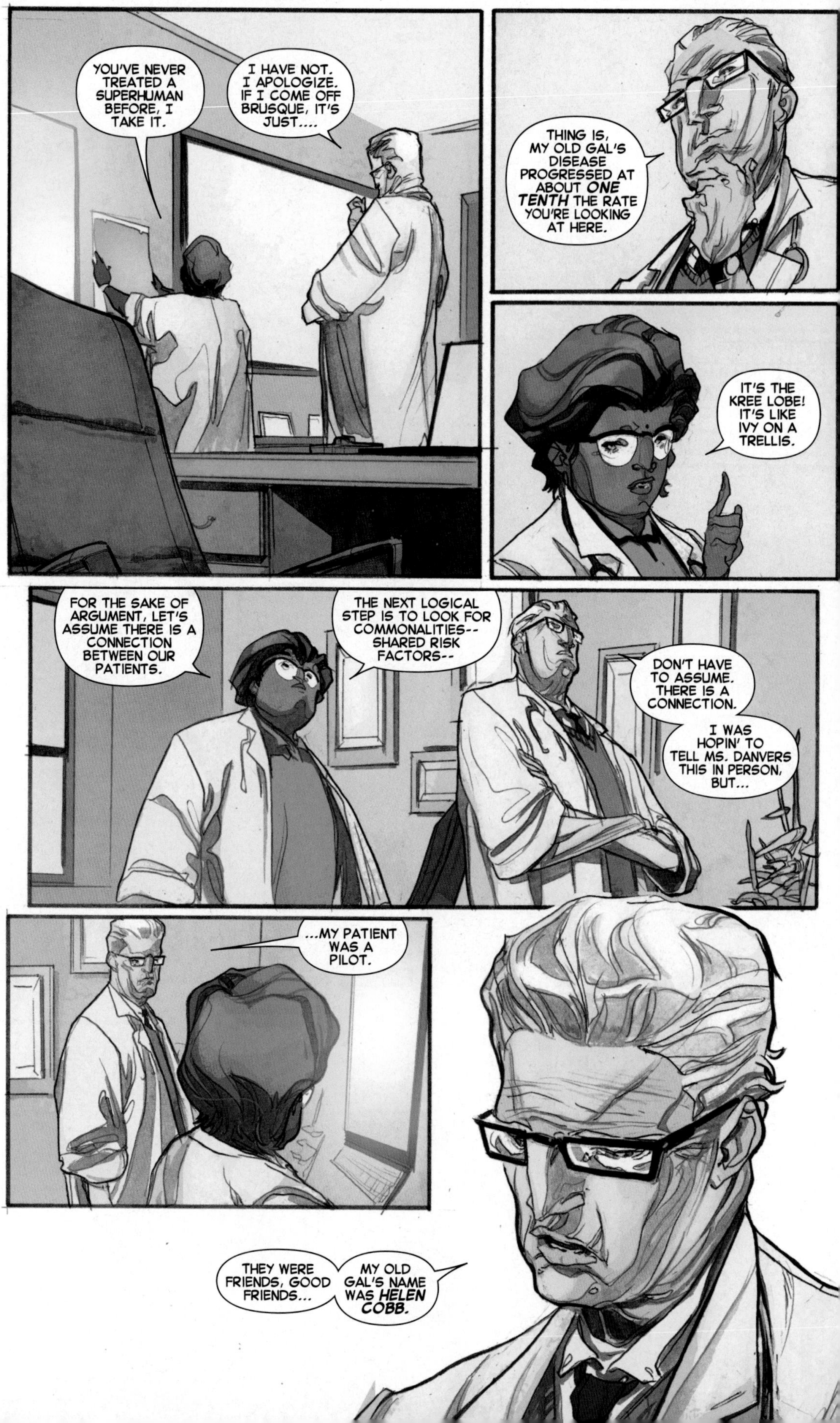

YOU'VE NEVER TREATED A SUPERHUMAN BEFORE, I TAKE IT.
I HAVE NOT. I APOLOGIZE. IF I COME OFF BRUSQUE, IT'S JUST....
THING IS, MY OLD GAL'S DISEASE PROGRESSED AT ABOUT *ONE TENTH* THE RATE YOU'RE LOOKING AT HERE.
IT'S THE KREE LOBE! IT'S LIKE IVY ON A TRELLIS.
FOR THE SAKE OF ARGUMENT, LET'S ASSUME THERE IS A CONNECTION BETWEEN OUR PATIENTS.
THE NEXT LOGICAL STEP IS TO LOOK FOR COMMONALITIES-- SHARED RISK FACTORS--
DON'T HAVE TO ASSUME. THERE IS A CONNECTION.
I WAS HOPIN' TO TELL MS. DANVERS THIS IN PERSON, BUT...
...MY PATIENT WAS A PILOT.
THEY WERE FRIENDS, GOOD FRIENDS...
MY OLD GAL'S NAME WAS ***HELEN COBB.***

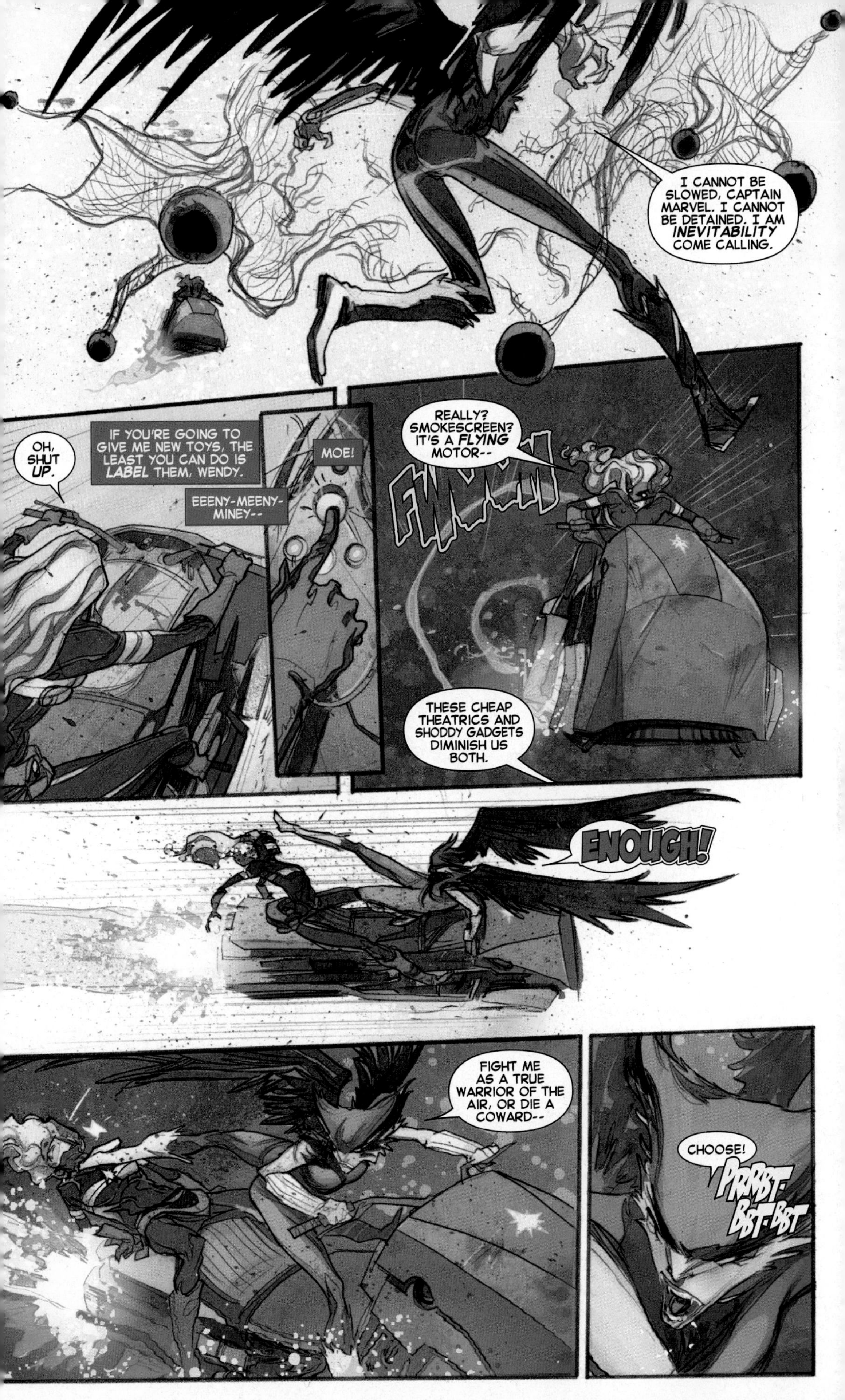
I CANNOT BE SLOWED, CAPTAIN MARVEL. I CANNOT BE DETAINED. I AM INEVITABILITY COME CALLING.
OH, SHUT UP.
IF YOU'RE GOING TO GIVE ME NEW TOYS, THE LEAST YOU CAN DO IS LABEL THEM, WENDY.
EEENY-MEENY-MINEY--
MOE!
REALLY? SMOKESCREEN? IT'S A FLYING MOTOR--
THESE CHEAP THEATRICS AND SHODDY GADGETS DIMINISH US BOTH.
ENOUGH!
FIGHT ME AS A TRUE WARRIOR OF THE AIR, OR DIE A COWARD--
CHOOSE!
PRRBBT-BBT-BBT

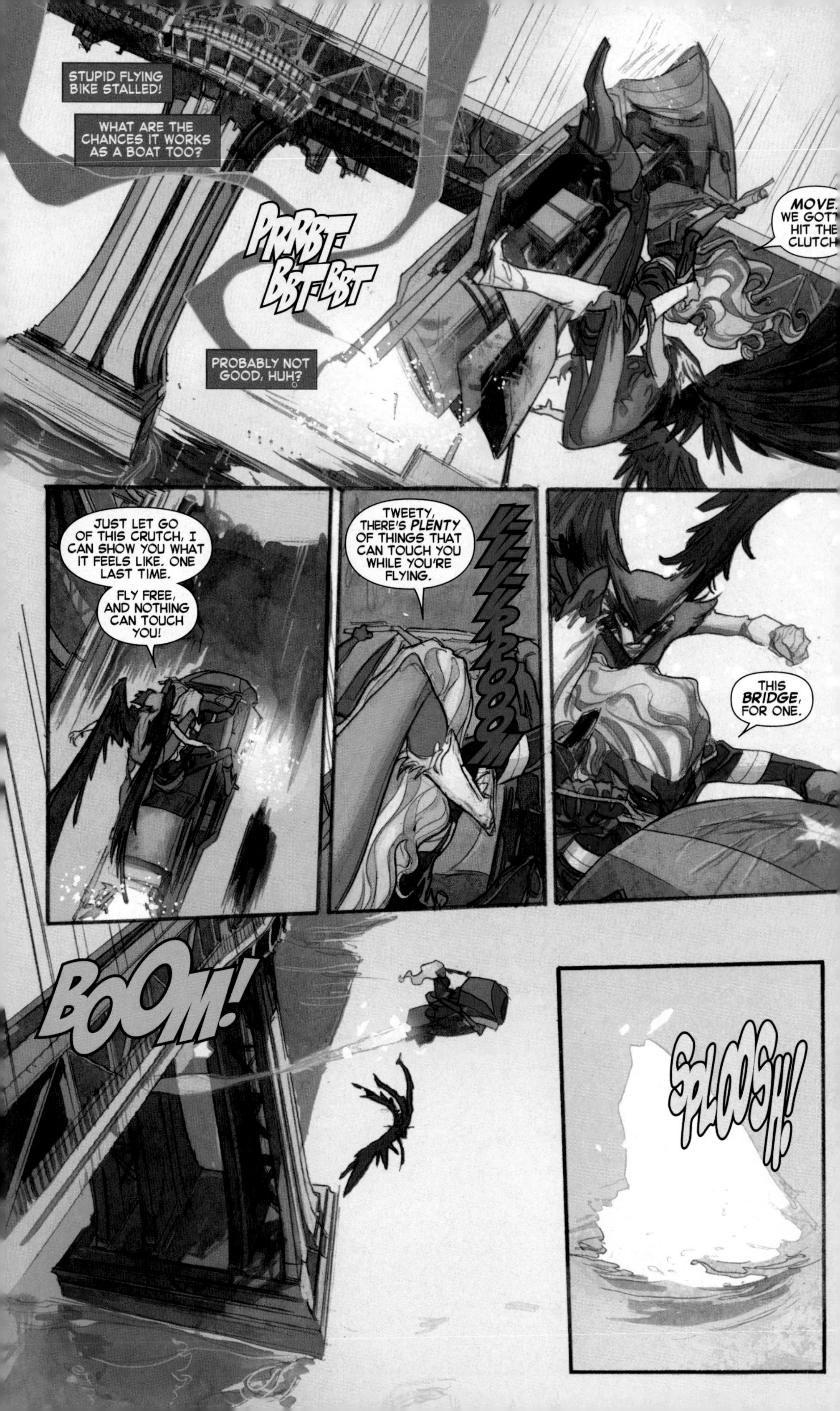

STUPID FLYING BIKE STALLED!
WHAT ARE THE CHANCES IT WORKS AS A BOAT TOO?
PRRRBT-BBT-BBT
PROBABLY NOT GOOD, HUH?
MOVE. WE GOTT HIT THE CLUTCH
JUST LET GO OF THIS CRUTCH, I CAN SHOW YOU WHAT IT FEELS LIKE. ONE LAST TIME.
FLY FREE, AND NOTHING CAN TOUCH YOU!
TWEETY, THERE'S PLENTY OF THINGS THAT CAN TOUCH YOU WHILE YOU'RE FLYING.
THIS BRIDGE, FOR ONE.
BOOM!
SPLOOSH!

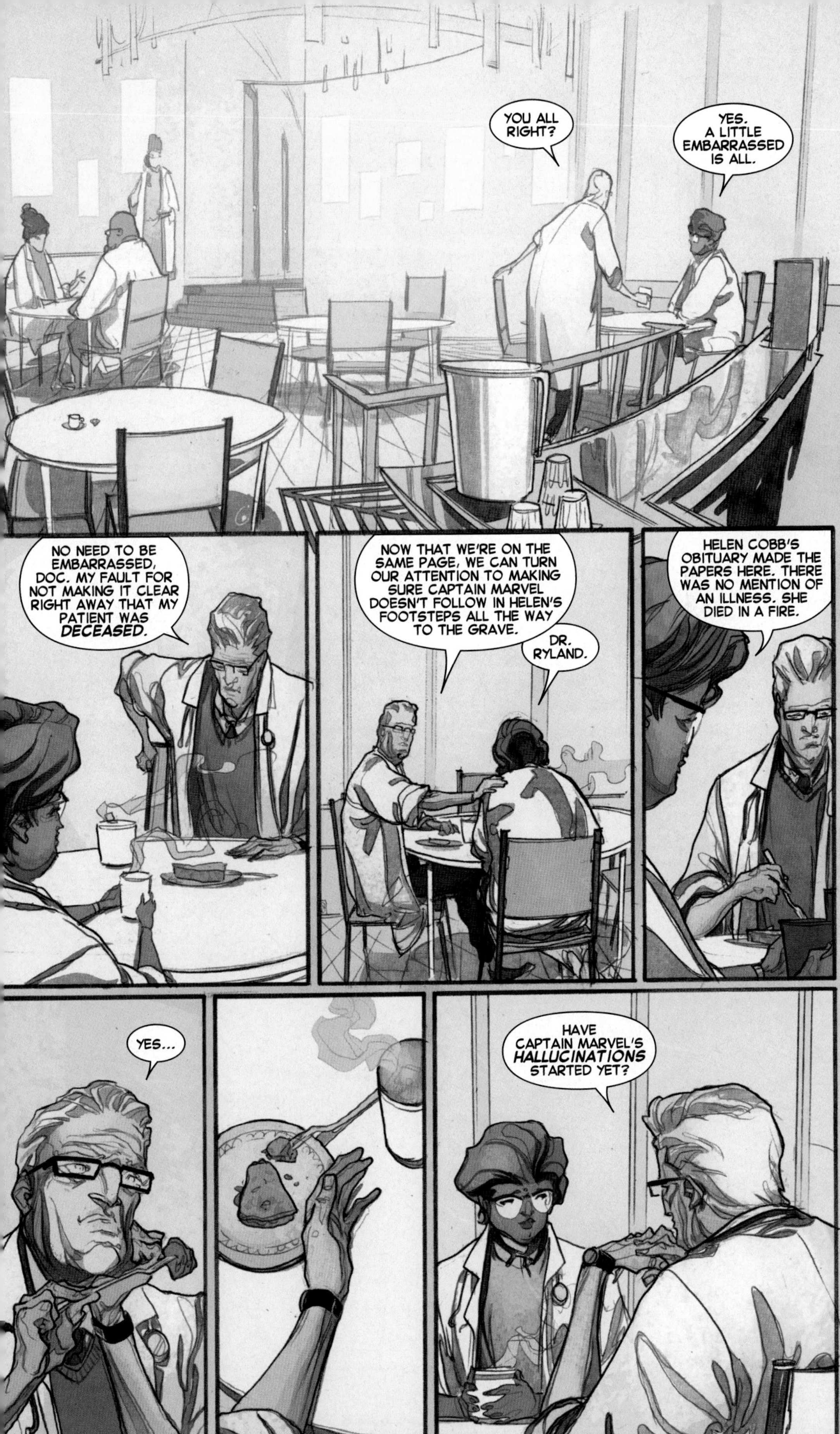

YOU ALL RIGHT?
YES. A LITTLE EMBARRASSED IS ALL.
NO NEED TO BE EMBARRASSED, DOC. MY FAULT FOR NOT MAKING IT CLEAR RIGHT AWAY THAT MY PATIENT WAS *DECEASED*.
NOW THAT WE'RE ON THE SAME PAGE, WE CAN TURN OUR ATTENTION TO MAKING SURE CAPTAIN MARVEL DOESN'T FOLLOW IN HELEN'S FOOTSTEPS ALL THE WAY TO THE GRAVE.
DR. RYLAND.
HELEN COBB'S OBITUARY MADE THE PAPERS HERE. THERE WAS NO MENTION OF AN ILLNESS. SHE DIED IN A FIRE.
YES...
HAVE CAPTAIN MARVEL'S *HALLUCINATIONS* STARTED YET?

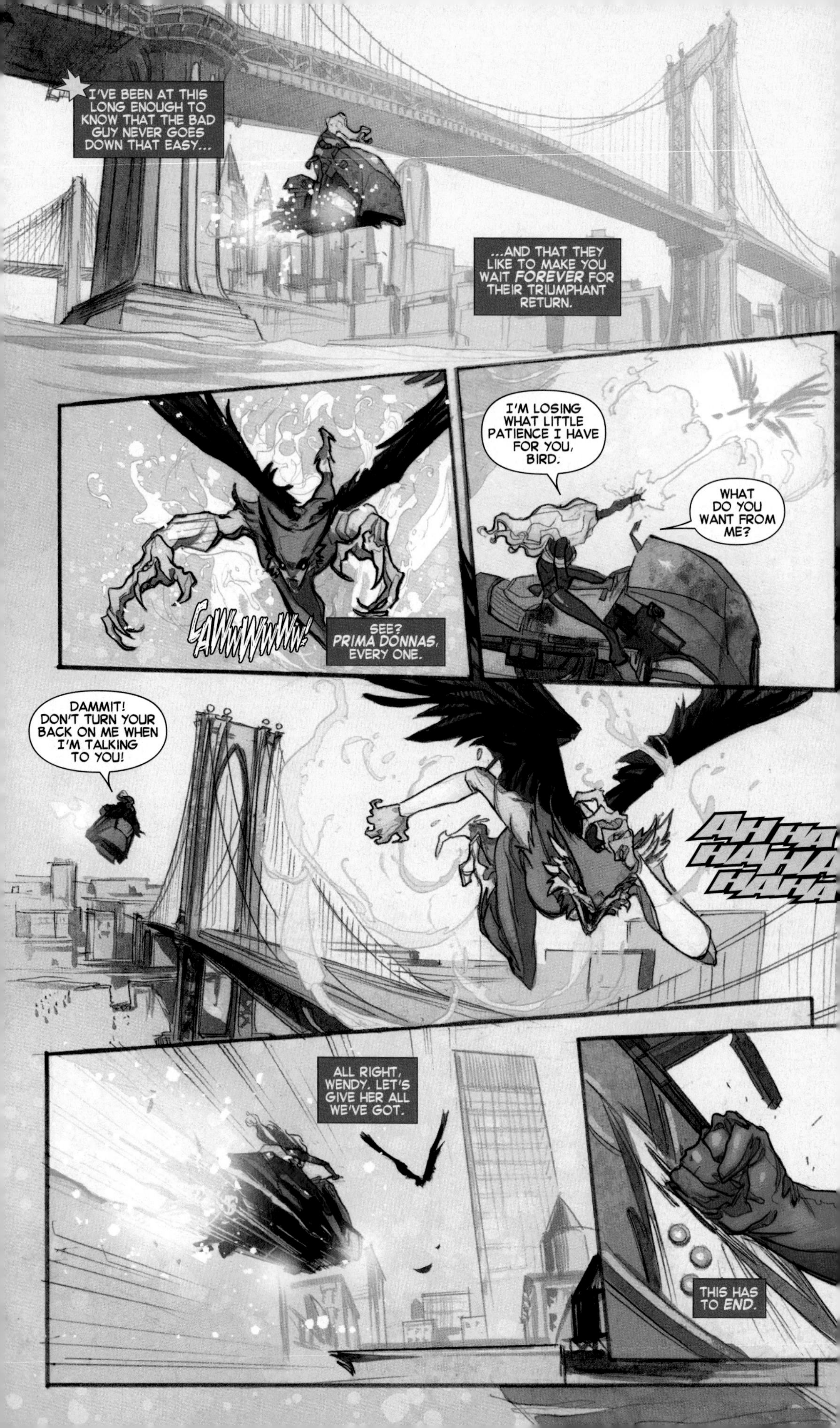
I'VE BEEN AT THIS LONG ENOUGH TO KNOW THAT THE BAD GUY NEVER GOES DOWN THAT EASY...
...AND THAT THEY LIKE TO MAKE YOU WAIT FOREVER FOR THEIR TRIUMPHANT RETURN.
CAWWWWWW!
SEE? PRIMA DONNAS, EVERY ONE.
I'M LOSING WHAT LITTLE PATIENCE I HAVE FOR YOU, BIRD.
WHAT DO YOU WANT FROM ME?
DAMMIT! DON'T TURN YOUR BACK ON ME WHEN I'M TALKING TO YOU!
AH HA HA HA HA HA
ALL RIGHT, WENDY. LET'S GIVE HER ALL WE'VE GOT.
THIS HAS TO END.

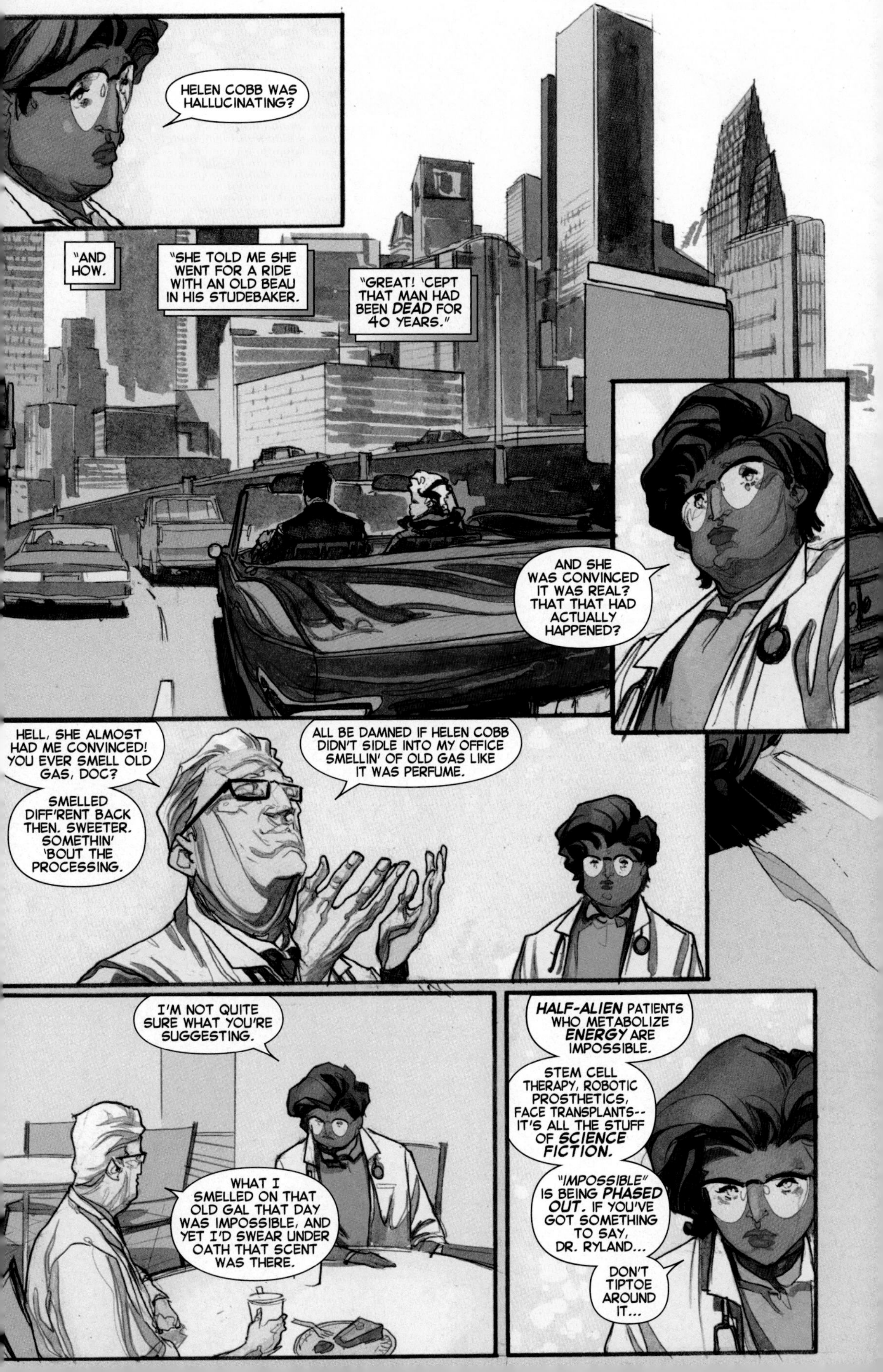
HELEN COBB WAS HALLUCINATING?
"AND HOW.
"SHE TOLD ME SHE WENT FOR A RIDE WITH AN OLD BEAU IN HIS STUDEBAKER.
"GREAT! 'CEPT THAT MAN HAD BEEN DEAD FOR 40 YEARS."
AND SHE WAS CONVINCED IT WAS REAL? THAT THAT HAD ACTUALLY HAPPENED?
HELL, SHE ALMOST HAD ME CONVINCED! YOU EVER SMELL OLD GAS, DOC?
SMELLED DIFF'RENT BACK THEN. SWEETER. SOMETHIN' 'BOUT THE PROCESSING.
ALL BE DAMNED IF HELEN COBB DIDN'T SIDLE INTO MY OFFICE SMELLIN' OF OLD GAS LIKE IT WAS PERFUME.
I'M NOT QUITE SURE WHAT YOU'RE SUGGESTING.
WHAT I SMELLED ON THAT OLD GAL THAT DAY WAS IMPOSSIBLE, AND YET I'D SWEAR UNDER OATH THAT SCENT WAS THERE.
HALF-ALIEN PATIENTS WHO METABOLIZE ENERGY ARE IMPOSSIBLE.
STEM CELL THERAPY, ROBOTIC PROSTHETICS, FACE TRANSPLANTS-- IT'S ALL THE STUFF OF SCIENCE FICTION.
"IMPOSSIBLE" IS BEING PHASED OUT. IF YOU'VE GOT SOMETHING TO SAY, DR. RYLAND...
DON'T TIPTOE AROUND IT...

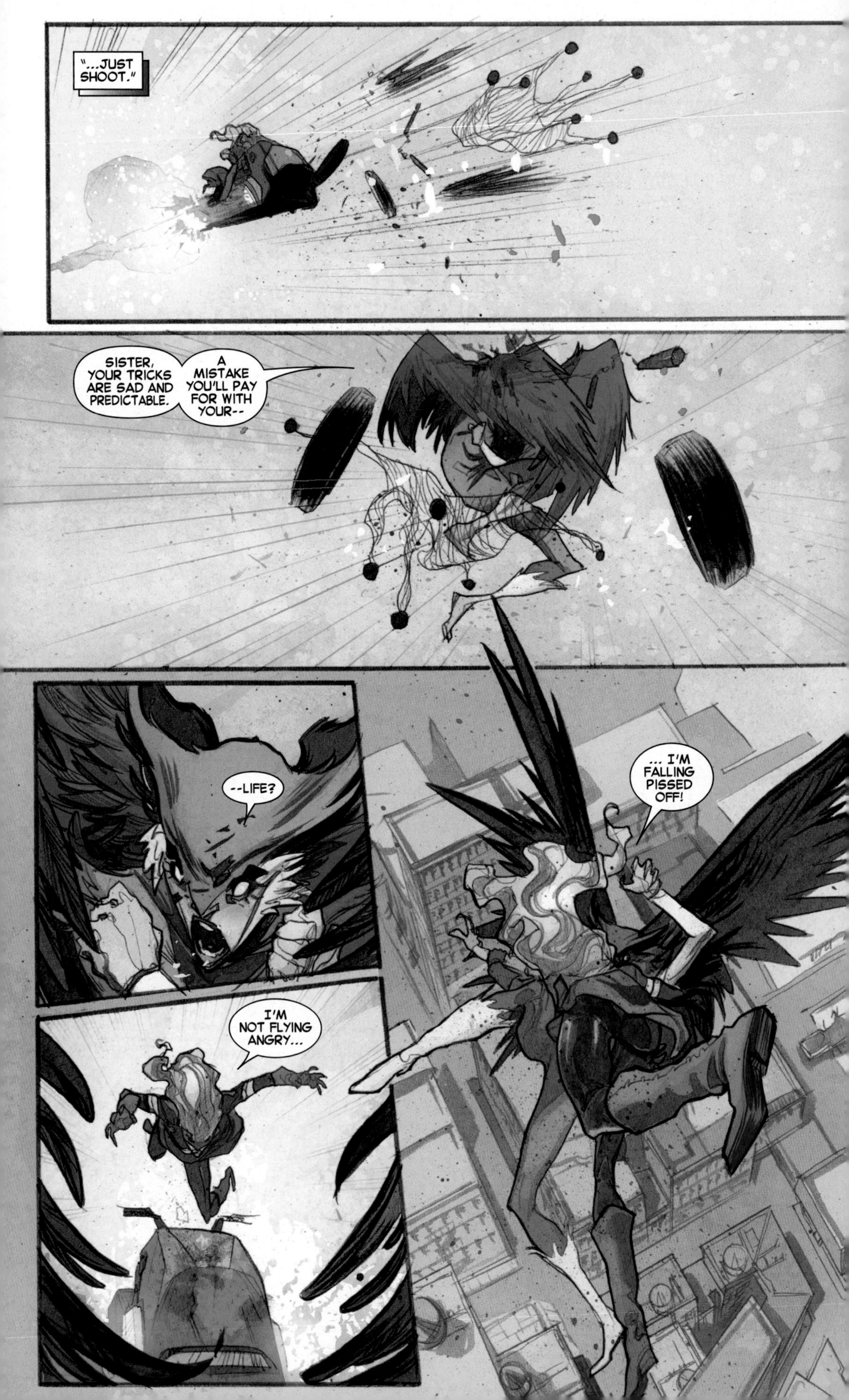
"...JUST SHOOT."
SISTER, YOUR TRICKS ARE SAD AND PREDICTABLE.
A MISTAKE YOU'LL PAY FOR WITH YOUR--
--LIFE?
I'M NOT FLYING ANGRY...
... I'M FALLING PISSED OFF!

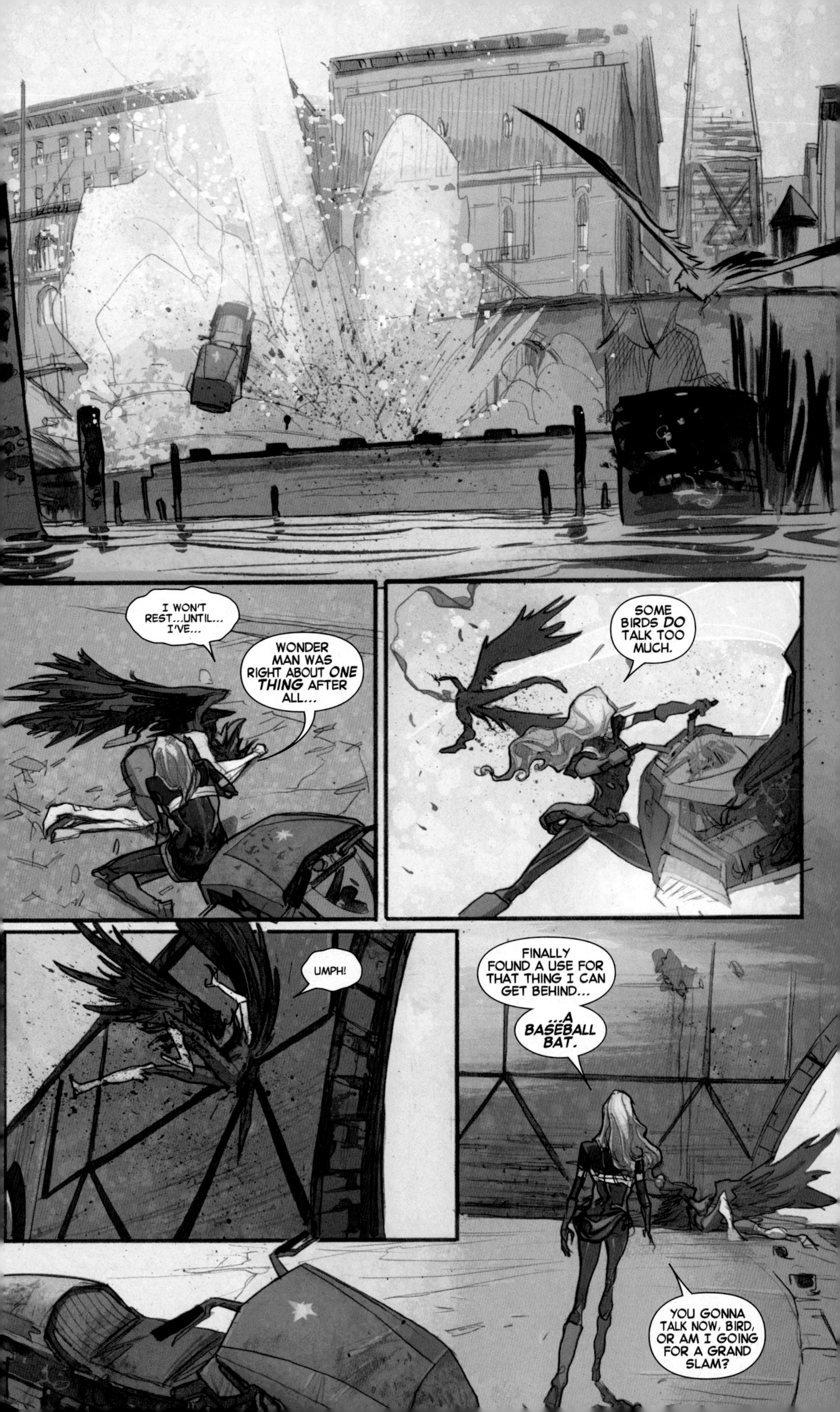
I WON'T REST...UNTIL... I'VE...
WONDER MAN WAS RIGHT ABOUT ONE THING AFTER ALL...
SOME BIRDS DO TALK TOO MUCH.
UMPH!
FINALLY FOUND A USE FOR THAT THING I CAN GET BEHIND...
...A BASEBALL BAT.
YOU GONNA TALK NOW, BIRD, OR AM I GOING FOR A GRAND SLAM?

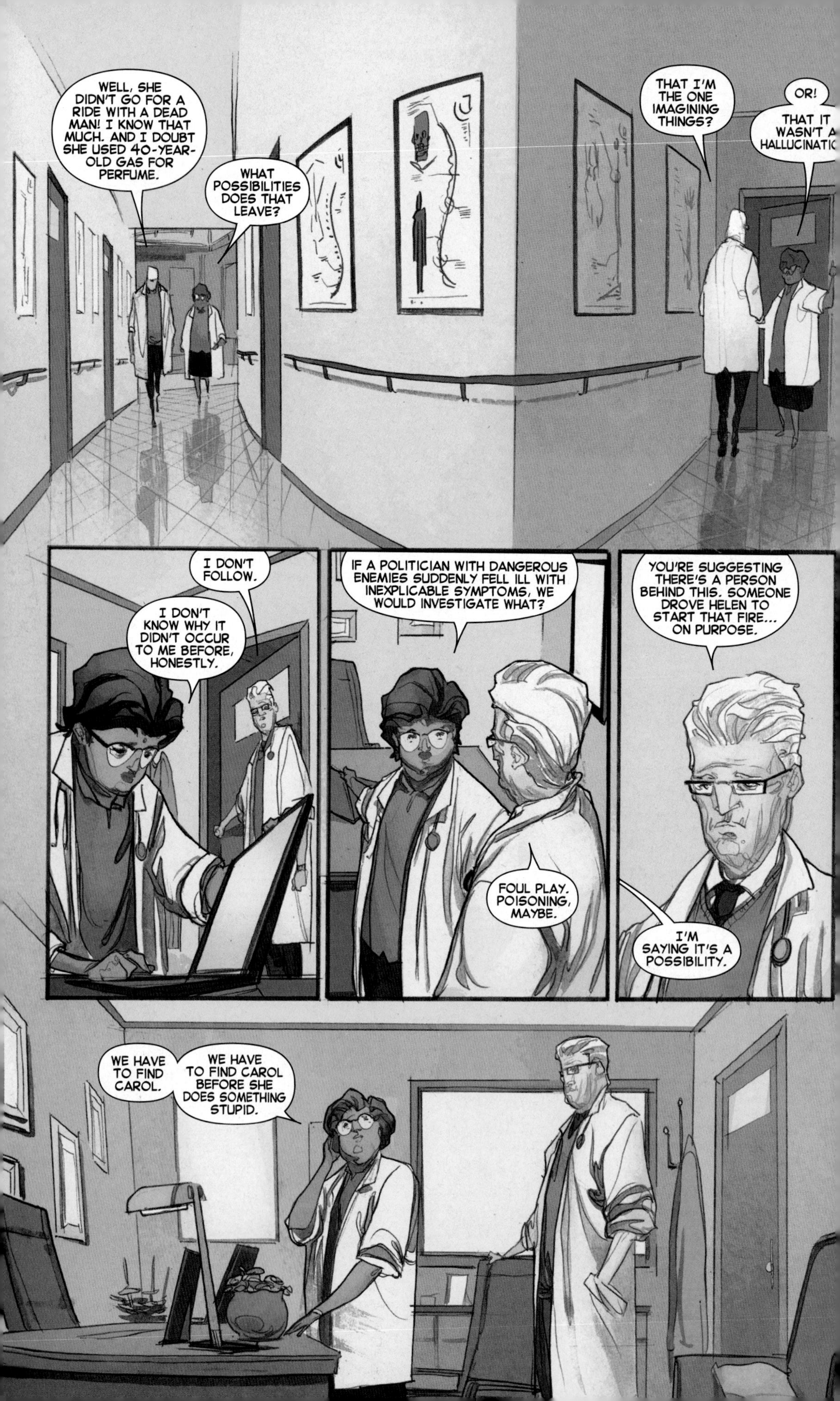
WELL, SHE DIDN'T GO FOR A RIDE WITH A DEAD MAN! I KNOW THAT MUCH. AND I DOUBT SHE USED 40-YEAR-OLD GAS FOR PERFUME.
WHAT POSSIBILITIES DOES THAT LEAVE?
THAT I'M THE ONE IMAGINING THINGS?
OR!
THAT IT WASN'T A HALLUCINATI
I DON'T FOLLOW.
I DON'T KNOW WHY IT DIDN'T OCCUR TO ME BEFORE, HONESTLY.
IF A POLITICIAN WITH DANGEROUS ENEMIES SUDDENLY FELL ILL WITH INEXPLICABLE SYMPTOMS, WE WOULD INVESTIGATE WHAT?
FOUL PLAY. POISONING, MAYBE.
YOU'RE SUGGESTING THERE'S A PERSON BEHIND THIS. SOMEONE DROVE HELEN TO START THAT FIRE... ON PURPOSE.
I'M SAYING IT'S A POSSIBILITY.
WE HAVE TO FIND CAROL.
WE HAVE TO FIND CAROL BEFORE SHE DOES SOMETHING STUPID.

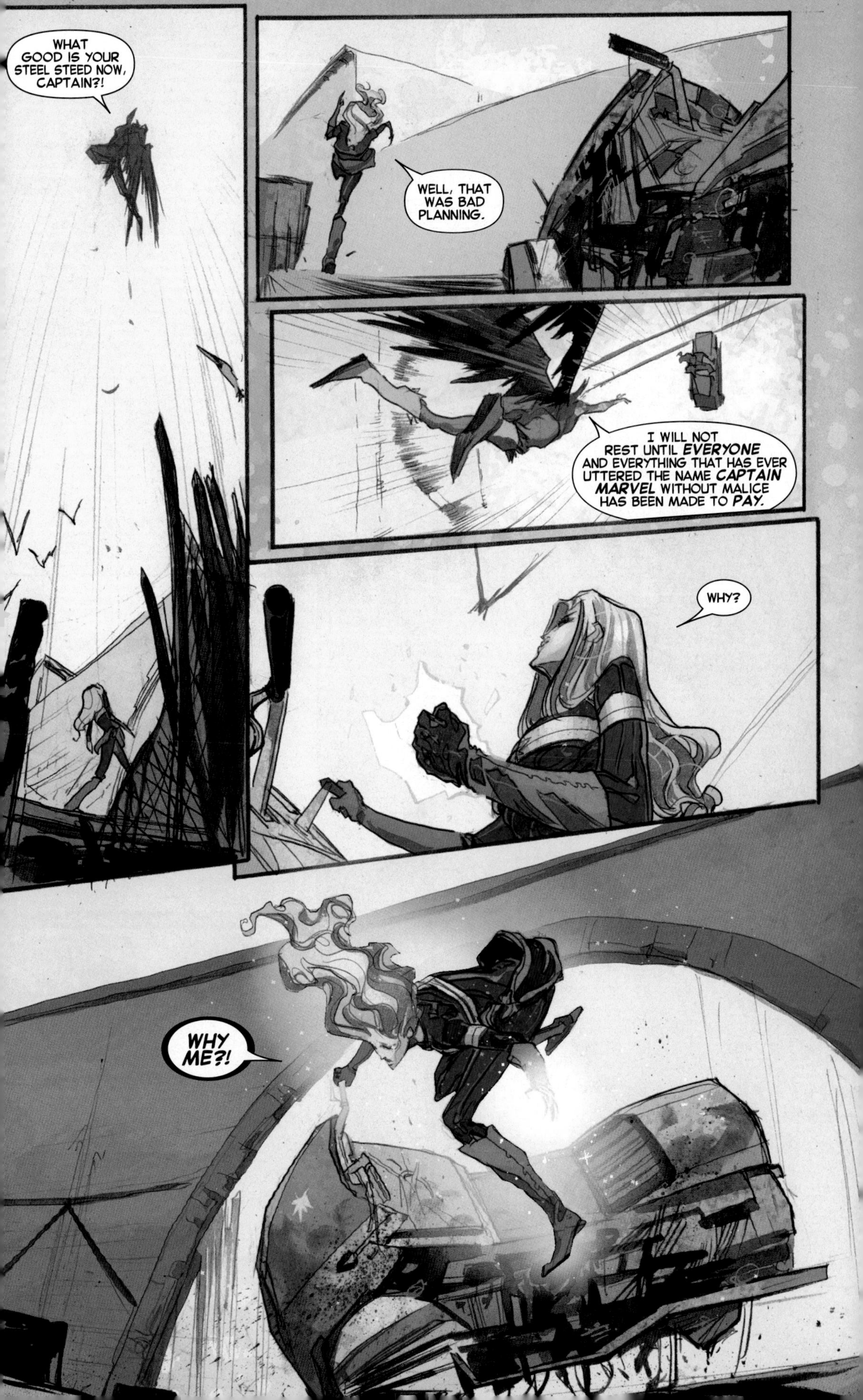

WHAT GOOD IS YOUR STEEL STEED NOW, CAPTAIN?!
WELL, THAT WAS BAD PLANNING.
I WILL NOT REST UNTIL *EVERYONE* AND EVERYTHING THAT HAS EVER UTTERED THE NAME *CAPTAIN MARVEL* WITHOUT MALICE HAS BEEN MADE TO *PAY.*
WHY?
WHY ME?!

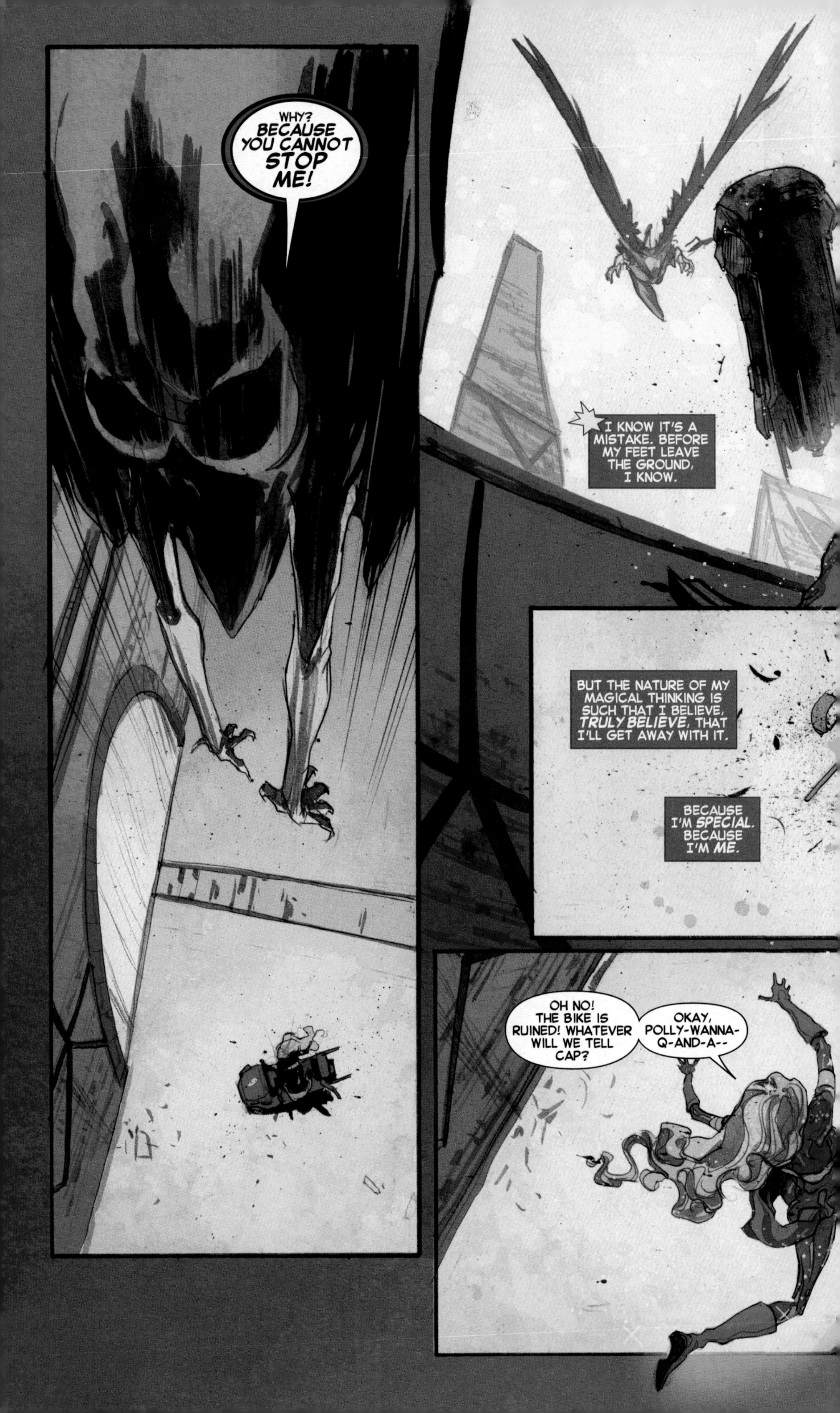
WHY? BECAUSE YOU CANNOT STOP ME!
I KNOW IT'S A MISTAKE. BEFORE MY FEET LEAVE THE GROUND, I KNOW.
BUT THE NATURE OF MY MAGICAL THINKING IS SUCH THAT I BELIEVE, TRULY BELIEVE, THAT I'LL GET AWAY WITH IT.
BECAUSE I'M SPECIAL. BECAUSE I'M ME.
OH NO! THE BIKE IS RUINED! WHATEVER WILL WE TELL CAP?
OKAY, POLLY-WANNA-Q-AND-A--

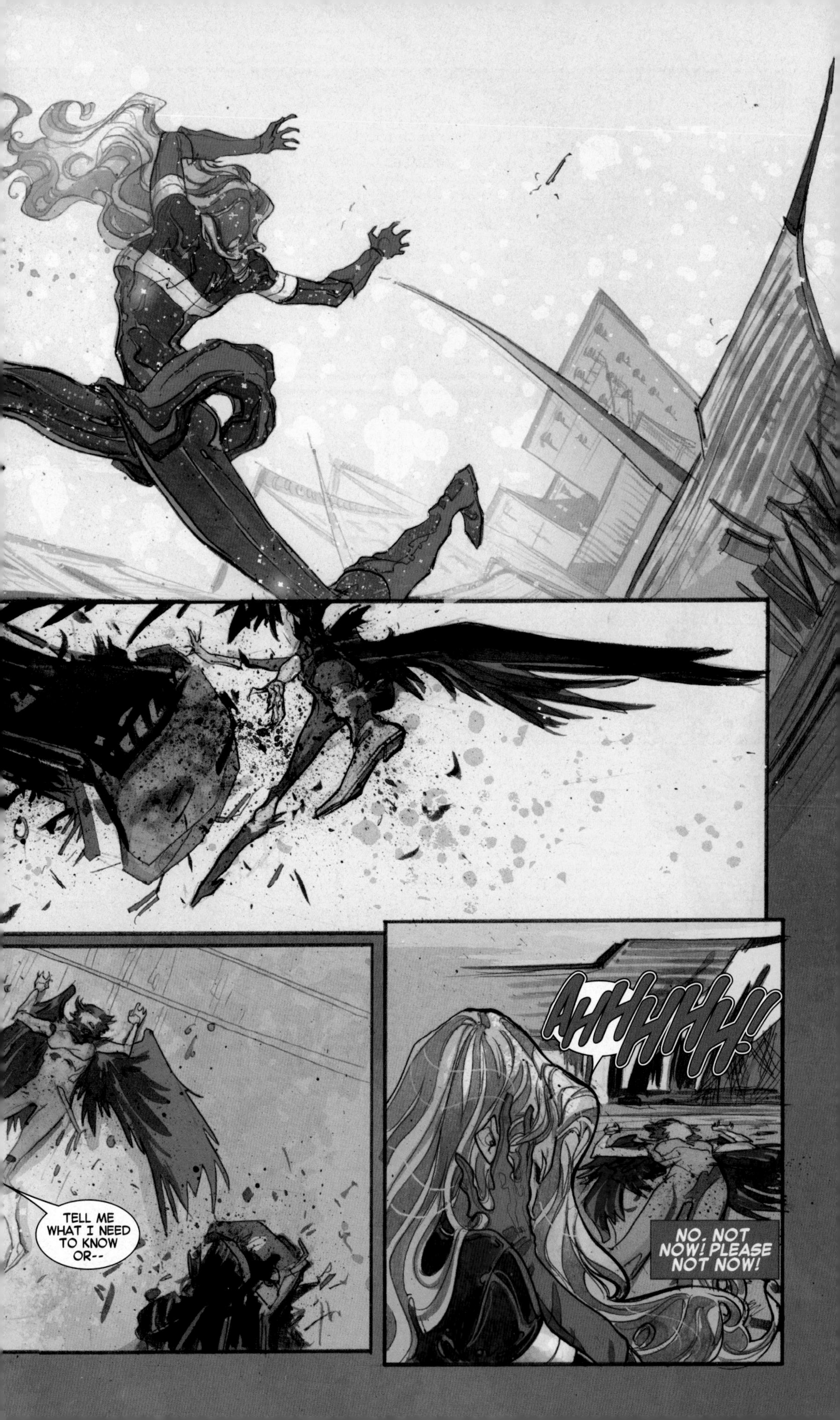
TELL ME WHAT I NEED TO KNOW OR--
AHHHHHH!
NO. NOT NOW! PLEASE NOT NOW!

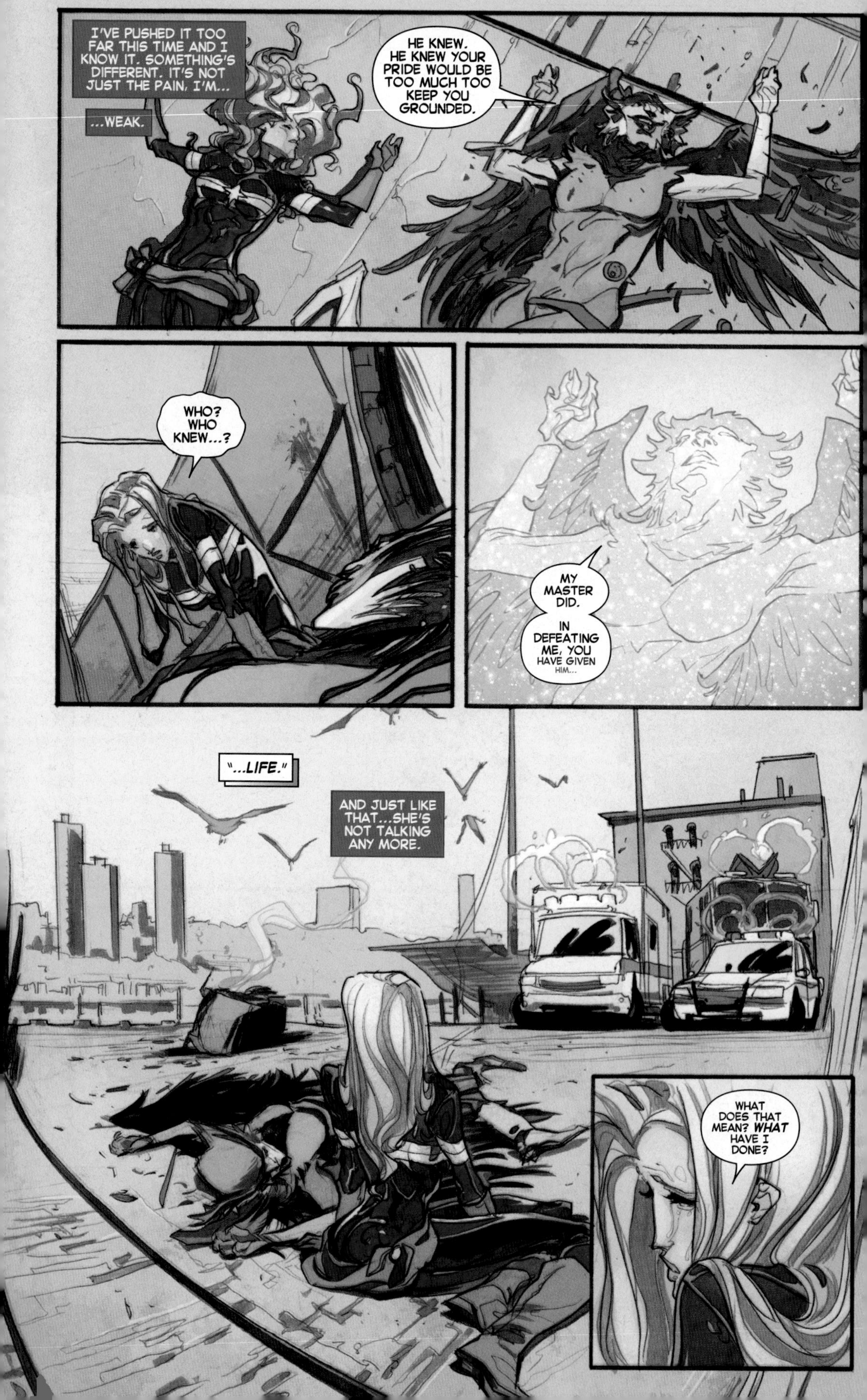

I'VE PUSHED IT TOO FAR THIS TIME AND I KNOW IT. SOMETHING'S DIFFERENT. IT'S NOT JUST THE PAIN, I'M...
...WEAK.
HE KNEW. HE KNEW YOUR PRIDE WOULD BE TOO MUCH TOO KEEP YOU GROUNDED.
WHO? WHO KNEW...?
MY MASTER DID.
IN DEFEATING ME, YOU HAVE GIVEN HIM...
"...LIFE."
AND JUST LIKE THAT...SHE'S NOT TALKING ANY MORE.
WHAT DOES THAT MEAN? WHAT HAVE I DONE?

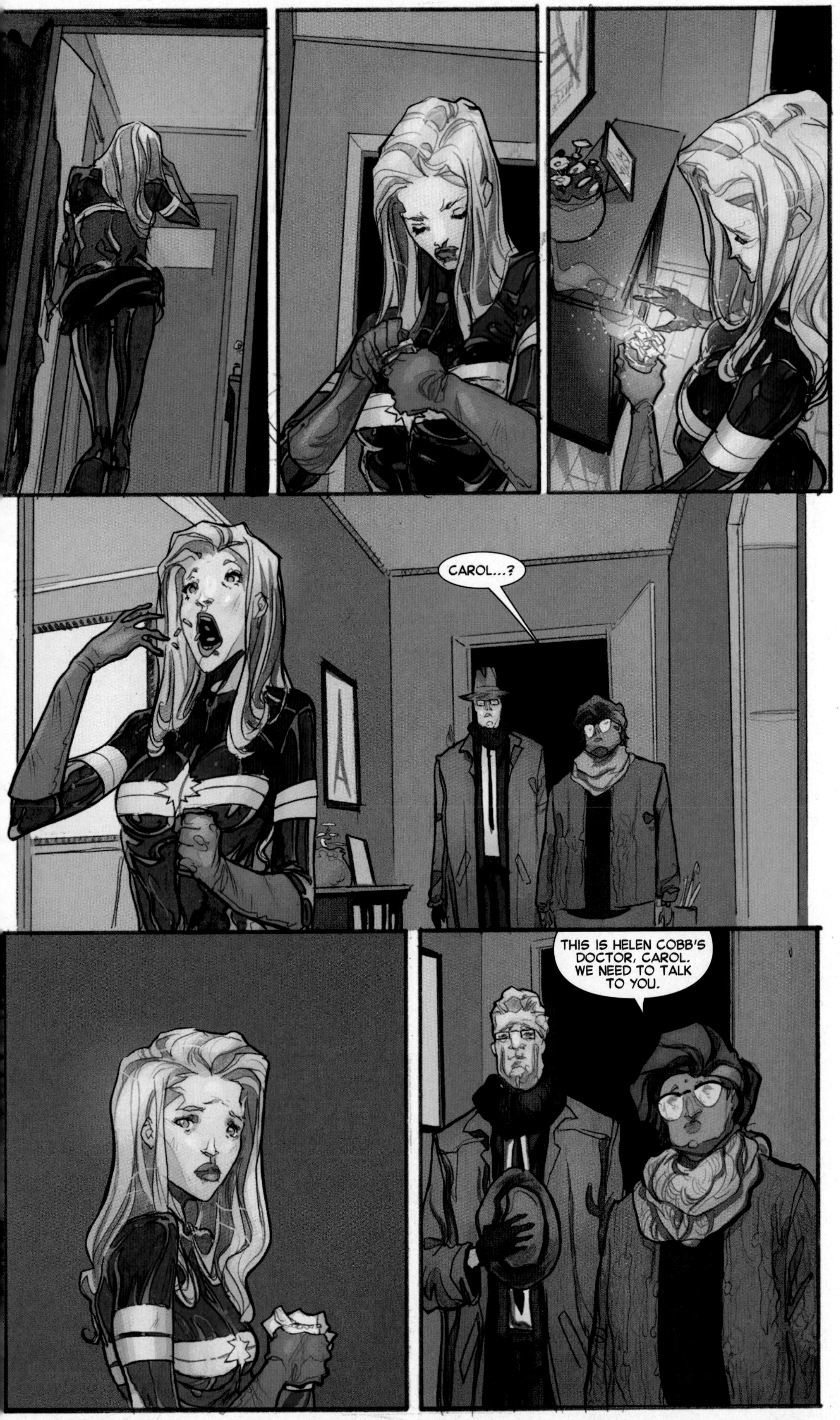
CAROL...?
THIS IS HELEN COBB'S DOCTOR, CAROL. WE NEED TO TALK TO YOU.

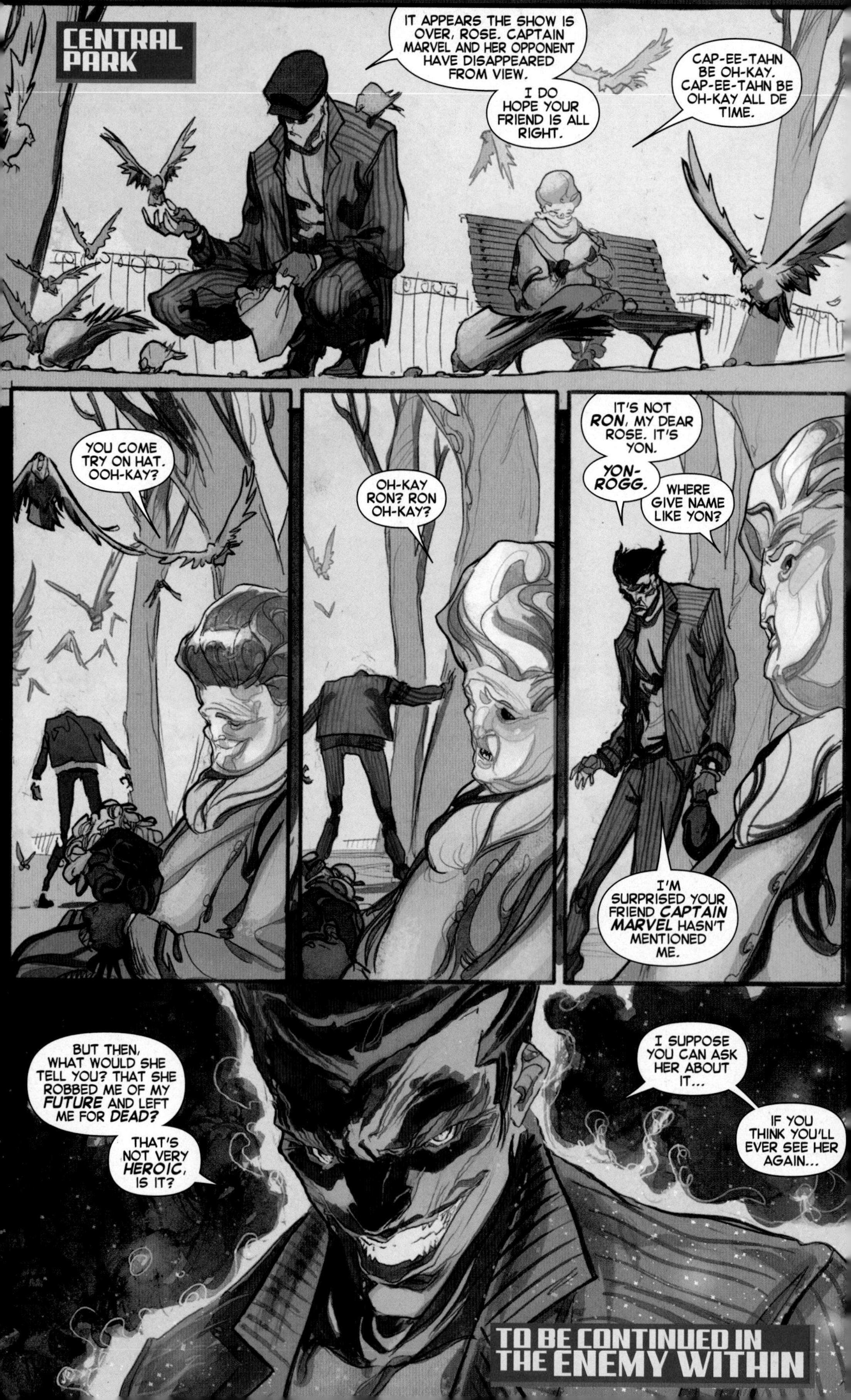
CENTRAL PARK
IT APPEARS THE SHOW IS OVER, ROSE. CAPTAIN MARVEL AND HER OPPONENT HAVE DISAPPEARED FROM VIEW.
I DO HOPE YOUR FRIEND IS ALL RIGHT.
CAP-EE-TAHN BE OH-KAY. CAP-EE-TAHN BE OH-KAY ALL DE TIME.
YOU COME TRY ON HAT. OOH-KAY?
OH-KAY RON? RON OH-KAY?
IT'S NOT RON, MY DEAR ROSE. IT'S YON.
YON-ROGG.
WHERE GIVE NAME LIKE YON?
I'M SURPRISED YOUR FRIEND CAPTAIN MARVEL HASN'T MENTIONED ME.
BUT THEN, WHAT WOULD SHE TELL YOU? THAT SHE ROBBED ME OF MY FUTURE AND LEFT ME FOR DEAD?
THAT'S NOT VERY HEROIC, IS IT?
I SUPPOSE YOU CAN ASK HER ABOUT IT...
IF YOU THINK YOU'LL EVER SEE HER AGAIN...
TO BE CONTINUED IN THE ENEMY WITHIN

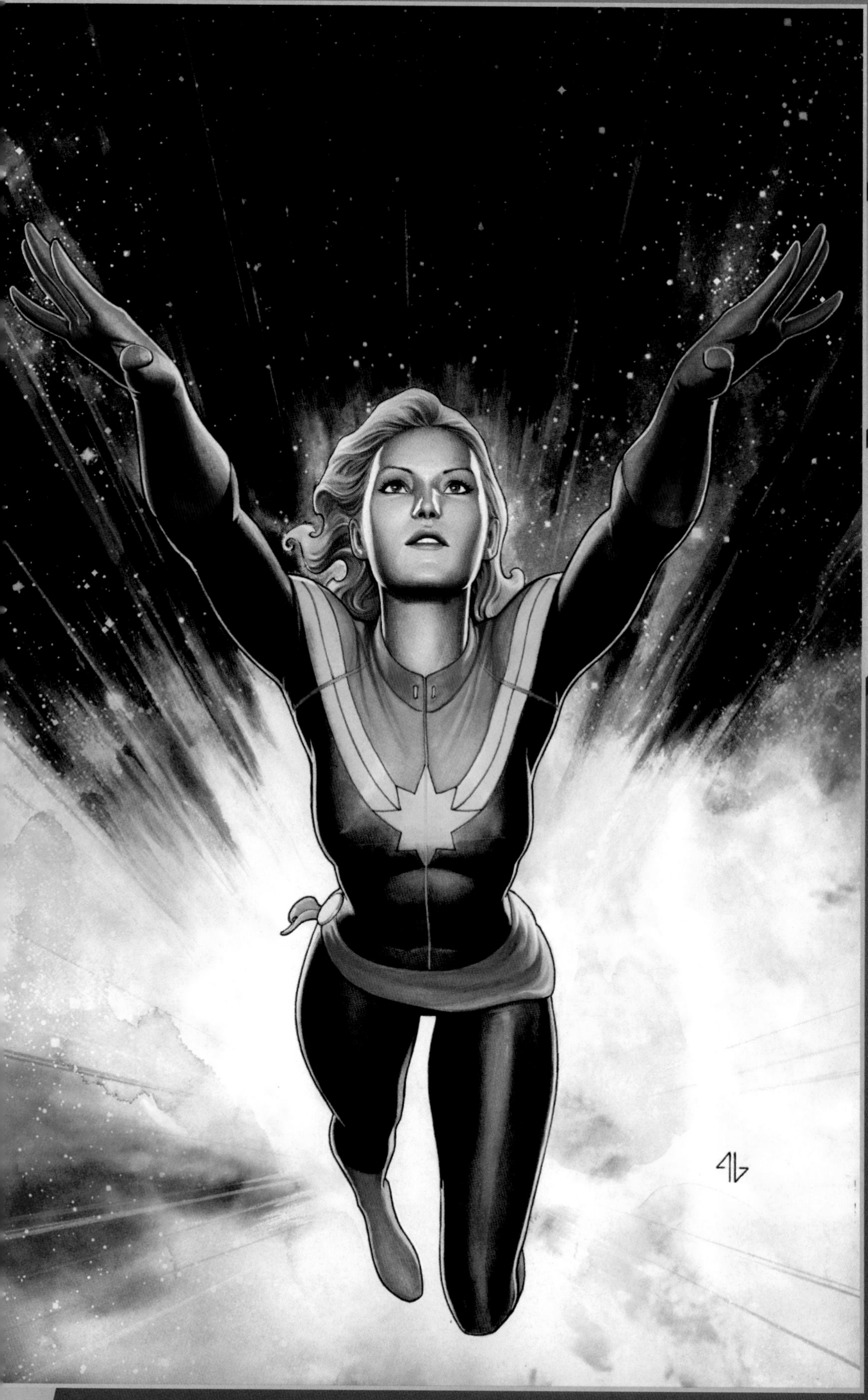

ONE VARIANT BY ADI GRANOV

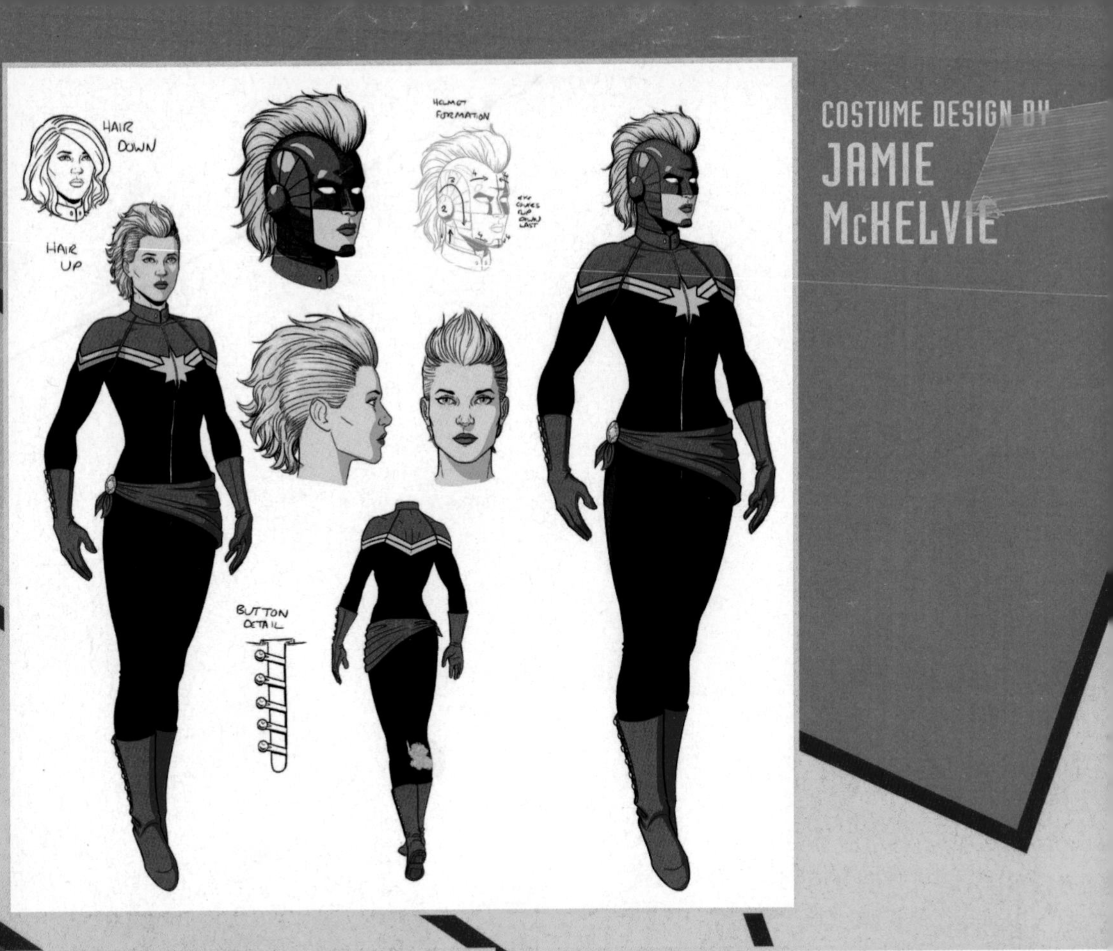
HAIR DOWN
HAIR UP
HELMET FORMATION
BUTTON DETAIL

COSTUME DESIGN BY
JAMIE McKELVIE

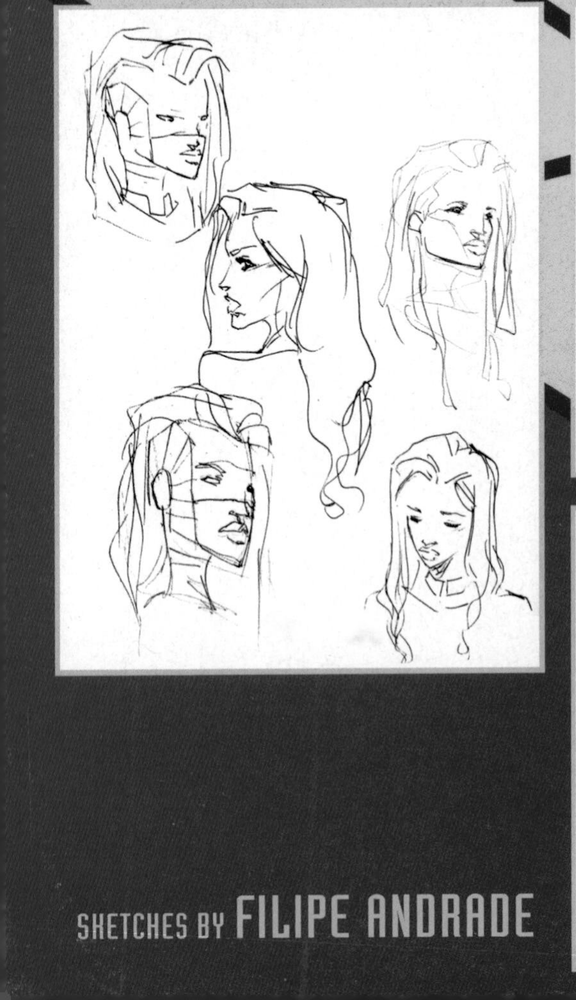

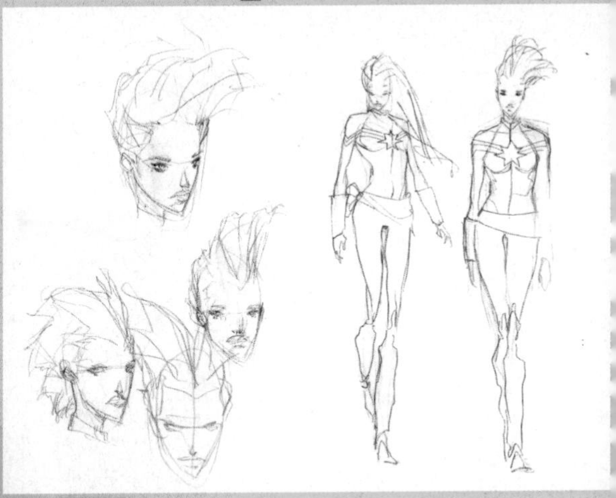

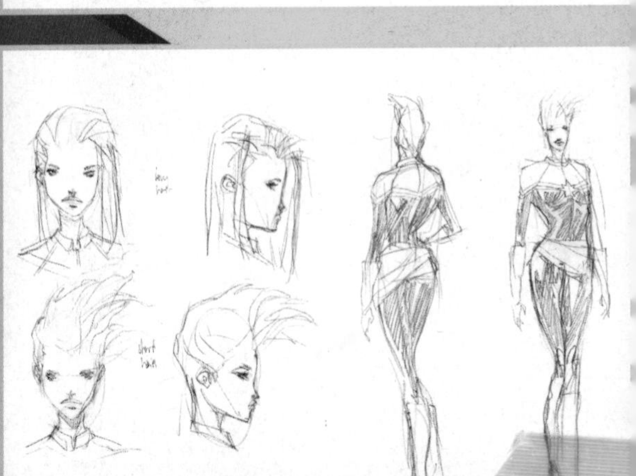

SKETCHES BY FILIPE ANDRADE